BECOMING A TEACHER
FOURTH CANADIAN EDITION

Forrest W. Parkay

Washington State University

Beverly Hardcastle Stanford

Azusa Pacific University

John P. Vaillancourt

Acadia University

Heather C. Stephens

Acadia University

James Robert Harris

Harris Educational Consulting

Pearson Canada
Toronto

This book is dedicated to our students—their spirit continually renews us and inspires confidence in the future of teaching.

Library and Archives Canada Cataloguing in Publication

Becoming a teacher / Forrest W. Parkay . . . [et al.].—4th Canadian ed.

Includes index.
First ed. written by Forrest W. Parkay, Beverly Hardcastle Stanford, and Thomas D. Gougeon.
ISBN 978-0-205-76738-0

1. Teaching—Vocational guidance—Canada.   2. Education—Study and teaching—
Canada.   3. Teachers—Canada—Attitudes.   I. Parkay, Forrest W.   II. Parkay, Forrest W.
Becoming a teacher.

LB1775.4.C3B42 2010   371.10023'71   C2010-905921-2

ISBN 978-0-205-76738-0

Vice-President, Editorial Director: Gary Bennett
Editor-in-Chief: Ky Pruesse
Acquisitions Editor: Joel Gladstone
Marketing Manager: Loula March
Developmental Editor: Megan Burns
Project Manager: Richard di Santo
Production Editor: Lise Dupont
Copy Editor: Sally Glover
Proofreader: Nancy Carroll
Compositor: MPS Limited, a Macmillan Company
Permissions Researcher: Karen Hunter
Art Director: Julia Hall
Interior Designer and Cover Designer: Anthony Leung
Cover image: Veer Inc.

1 2 3 4 5   15 14 13 12 11

Printed and bound in the United States of America.

Managing to Teach (M2T)

This interactive and virtual learning environment will help you develop effective classroom management skills. By watching videos of real classroom scenarios, you can assume the role of decision maker and receive valuable feedback from the program guide on your decisions.

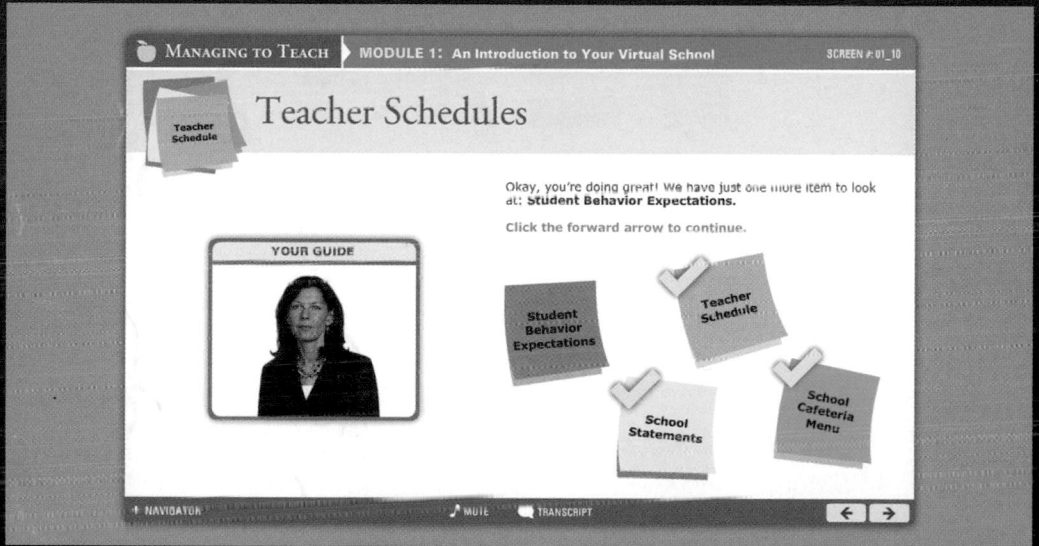

The study and assessment resources that come with your textbook allow you to review content and develop what you need to know, on your own time, and at your own pace.

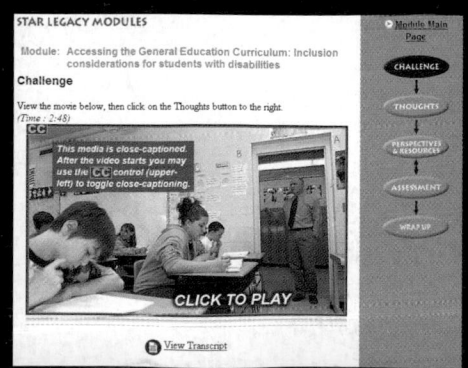

Review, Practice, and Enrichment

You have the opportunity to deepen your understanding of particular concepts and principles of the chapter through exercises, videos, cases, and simulations. Resources include various Canadian education links, access to MySearchLab, and detailed instructions on how to prepare your portfolio.

Pearson eText

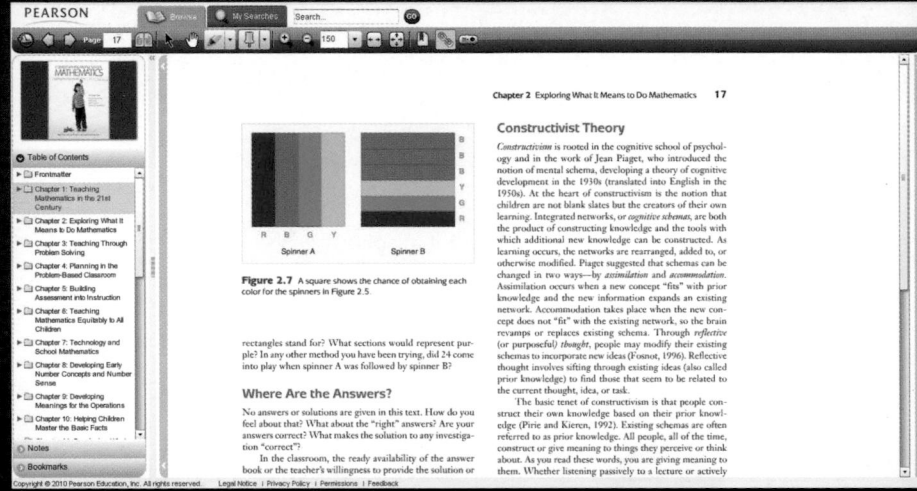

Pearson eText gives students access to the text whenever and wherever they have access to the internet. eText pages look exactly like the printed text, offering powerful functionality for students and instructors.

Users can create notes, highlight text in differnet colours, creat bookmarks, zoom, click hyperlinked words and phrases to view definitions, and choose single-page view.

Pearson eText allows for quick navigation using a table of contents and provides full-text search. The eText may also offer links to associated media files, enabling users to access videos, animations, or other activities as they read the text.

PEARSON myeducationlab™

Improve Your Grade

It's easy to prepare wisely with practice quizzes and tutorials.

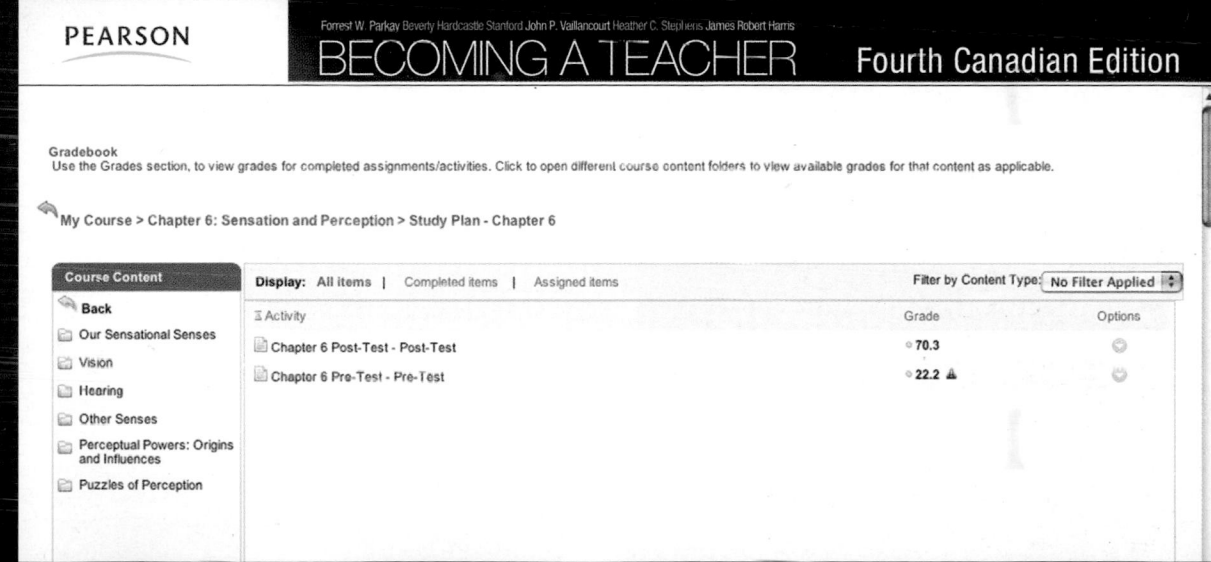

MyEducationLab helps you focus your efforts where they are needed. Know your strengths and weaknesses before your first in-class exam.

Go to **www.myeducationlab.com** and follow the simple registration instructions on the Student Access Code Card provided with the purchase of a new text. Your unique access code is hidden there.

Save Time. Improve Results. www.myeducationlab.com

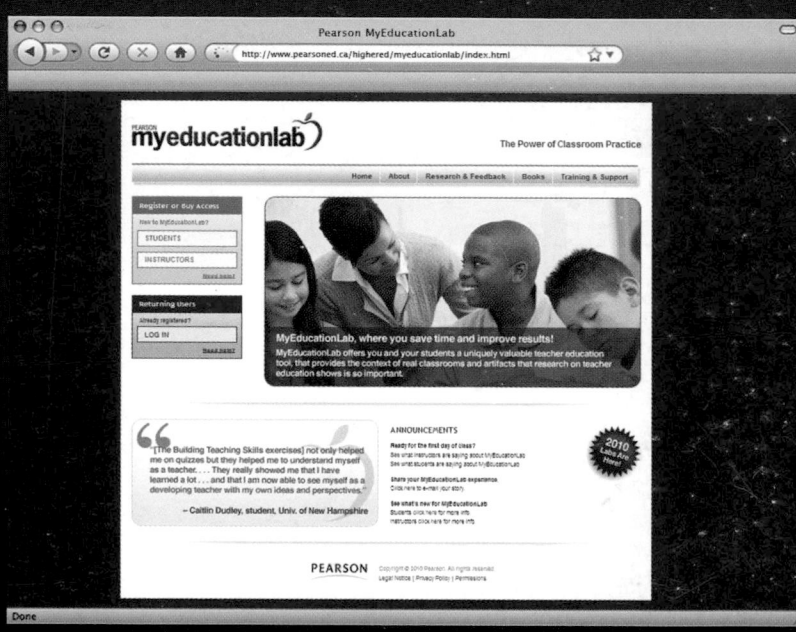

Contents

5   Social and Cultural Realities Confronting Today's Schools   132

Preface

We hope you share our belief that teaching is the world's most important profession. We also hope you recognize the service Pearson Education Canada has provided to preservice Canadian teachers through the publication of this revised guide to the Canadian educational landscape. The demand for a Canadian book of this type was evident for many years. However, until Pearson Canada made the decision to produce this text, instructors at Canadian universities and colleges were faced with a bleak choice: use an American text without any Canadian flavour, use a host of smaller Canadian texts and booklets that touch on selected topics while ignoring many others, or inundate their students with a flood of photocopied handouts. The broad range of topics covered in this fourth Canadian edition of *Becoming a Teacher* helps to overcome these problems. Additionally, the 12 chapters mesh easily with the standard academic term. Canadian examples, historical data, and statistics are included throughout, and, because of its breadth of topics, *Becoming a Teacher* can be customized for use in a variety of courses.

We highlight teacher leadership throughout the book, since today's teachers must assume diverse leadership roles beyond the classroom. For instance, in "Teachers as Educational Leaders" (Chapter 10), readers learn about the exciting new leadership roles that await teachers. In "The Role of Technology in Education" (Chapter 9), which has been extensively updated for this edition, students are given an overview of how educational technologies are influencing schools and the profession of teaching.

Chapters 1 and 2, which make up Part One, focus on the theme of teachers and teaching. After reading these chapters, students will be better able to determine whether teaching is a good career choice for them. Among the topics we address are why people choose to teach, the challenges and realities of teaching, the knowledge and skills needed to become a teacher, and how to establish mentoring relationships.

In Chapters 3 to 5 of Part Two, we consider the foundations of education, which every professional teacher needs to know. These foundational areas include the philosophical, historical, social, cultural, political, financial, and legal dimensions of Canadian education. Philosophical and historical foundations are addressed in "Ideas and Events That Have Shaped Education in Canada" (Chapter 3).

Chapters 6 to 9, which make up Part Three, examine student characteristics and the worlds of the classroom and the school. Here, readers learn about characteristics of students at different stages of development, about students as learners, about the dynamics of classroom life, about the curricula that are taught in schools, and about teaching with technology.

Finally, in Part Four, Chapters 10 to 12, we discuss issues and trends that will impact each student's quest to become an effective teacher—especially the expanding leadership role of teachers, planning for a successful first year of teaching, international education in a changing world, and the teacher's role in shaping the future of education.

Organization of the Book

To allow for comprehensive coverage of critical trends and issues in education, we organized the book into four parts: "Part One: The Teaching Profession," "Part Two: Foundations of Teaching," "Part Three: The Art of Teaching," and "Part Four: Your Teaching Future."

Features and Learning Aids

Included in *Becoming a Teacher* are many features we believe will help to prepare students for rewarding futures as professional teachers. To guide study, "Focus Questions" at the beginning of each chapter reflect the questions addressed in that chapter. Opening scenarios present decision-making or problem-solving situations for students to consider and resolve. These situations are referred to throughout the chapter and give readers an opportunity to apply new learning in specific problem-solving contexts.

The "Where Do You Stand?" feature encourages students to reflect on the realities of teaching and on controversial trends and issues that have aroused public opinion and attracted media attention. "Case to Consider" features include new classroom case studies that present problem-solving and decision-making situations that allow students to apply practical solutions to various challenges.

To inspire preservice teachers, a "Professional Reflection" feature encourages readers to reflect on their beliefs and values and on the issues faced by teachers. This feature is designed to give student teachers practice in the applied reflective inquiry that should characterize every teacher's professional life.

In the "Focus on Research through Experience" boxes, teachers describe dilemmas, and accompanying focus questions help readers who are dealing with such dilemmas. Canadian educators who either work with preservice teachers or mentor beginning teachers were interviewed to determine problem areas that commonly surface during field experiences or the first year of practice.

The "Theory into Practice" feature includes group activities such as role plays that will encourage readers to apply concepts to future practice in a meaningful way. These activities are suitable for large groups. The "Teachers' Voices: Research into Reality" boxes are based on interviews with teachers across the country and illustrate how teachers apply chapter content to actual classroom situations by providing readers with first-hand insights into real-world challenges.

This edition of *Becoming a Teacher* continues to offer the popular end-of-chapter "Professional Portfolio" feature, which will enable preservice teachers to document their growth and accomplishments over time. Each chapter includes guidelines for creating a portfolio entry that readers can use when they begin teaching; in addition, students may wish to use selected portfolio entries during the process of applying for a first teaching position.

As a further study aid, key terms and concepts are boldfaced in the text and listed with page cross-references at the ends of chapters. A glossary at the end of the book helps readers to quickly locate the definitions of key terms and concepts and the text pages on which they appear.

Other end-of-chapter learning aids in this edition include a concise summary and suggested applications and activities, including journal-writing opportunities in "Teacher's Journal" and field experiences in "Observations and Interviews." In "Teacher's Journal," we continue to provide a feature that has proved useful and popular with instructors who encourage active reflection in the form of student journals. These short, optional journal-writing activities are based on the "writing to learn" and "writing across the curriculum" concepts.

New to This Edition

New to the fourth Canadian edition of *Becoming a Teacher* is the "Focus on Research through Experience" feature, highlighting the findings of Canadian educational researchers and describing exciting curricular approaches that take a student-centred approach and directly involve learners.

This edition also incorporates updated references and new material relating to emerging technologies and current research. The text was thoroughly revised to enhance clarity and readability.

At the end of each chapter we have added a section listing relevant material that can be found at www.MyEducationLab.com, including videos and further reading material. MyEducationLab also offers Teacher's Resources, which include both the appendices found in the previous edition of the text and several new "Teacher's Scribe" resources specifically designed to confront issues important to preservice teachers. Examples of these new resources include "Am I boring you?", which addresses how to make lessons more engaging, and "Love and sex in the classroom," which details how to approach potentially inflammatory situations.

With access to MyEducationLab, students also have the opportunity to use the virtual classroom management resource "Managing to Teach." This learning tool is based on a broad conception of classroom management and encompasses the multifaceted dynamics of the student–teacher relationship *and* the organization of the physical classroom space. "Managing to Teach" uses a modular structure and includes:

- Introduction to a virtual school
- Developing constructive expectations
- Preventing and pre-empting problems through prior planning
- Creating positive personal interactions by exhibiting desired modes of behaviour

Supplements

To help students and instructors get the most out of *Becoming a Teacher*, we have provided a number of useful supplements.

Instructor Supplements

The **Instructor's Resource Manual** provides, for each chapter of the text, a "Chapter Overview" and a "Chapter-at-a-Glance" organizer that correlates chapter outlines, learning objectives, and teaching supplements; an "Annotated Lecture Outline" with examples, discussion questions, and student activities; and suggestions for additional readings and media to extend chapter learning. Also included for each chapter is an index to chapter-specific resources that can be found at the MyEducationLab website.

The **Test Item File** includes more than 1000 questions, including multiple-choice and true–false items, essay questions, case studies, and authentic assessments, plus text-page references and answer feedback.

A set of **PowerPoint Presentations** is also provided with this edition. Each chapter is outlined in a series of slides that include key points, figures, and tables.

CourseSmart for Instructors (www.coursesmart .com/instructors) goes beyond traditional expectations to provide instant online access to textbooks and course materials at a lower cost to students. The digital eTextbook allows instructors to search for relevant content in a timely, efficient manner. Whether teachers are evaluating textbooks or creating lecture notes to help students with difficult concepts, CourseSmart can make life a little easier.

Student Supplements

myeducationlab (www.myeducationlab.com) will help students to improve their understanding of the concepts taught in this text. This online tool includes videos of real classroom experiences, sample lesson plans, simulations, case studies, and links to important educational and teaching websites to help students make the transition to teaching.

CourseSmart for Students (www.coursesmart .com/students) provides students with instant online access to textbooks and course materials at an average savings of 50 percent. With the ability to search the text, students will be able to find desired content quickly from any computer. Online tools such as highlighting and note-taking allow students to save time and study efficiently.

Acknowledgments

Many members of the Pearson Canada team provided expert guidance and support during the preparation of this fourth Canadian edition of *Becoming a Teacher*. Megan Burns, our developmental editor, heads the list. From suggestions for revision to feedback on draft manuscripts and skilful coordination of the revision process from beginning to end, Megan's professionalism, patience, keen organizational skills, and good humour are deeply appreciated. The authors also extend a very special thanks to all the other members of the Pearson Canada team for their steadfast support throughout the prepublication period.

We also owe thanks to educators working in schools, teacher professional organizations, and departments of education throughout Canada with whom we consulted during the preparation of *Becoming a Teacher*. Invariably, they were courteous and helpful. A common reaction among them was delight that someone was going to make use of their material. We also wish to thank the *Education Law Reporter*, which generously gave us permission to use material from their excellent journal and website.

We are also very grateful to the authors of the U.S. edition of *Becoming a Teacher* (8th ed.) for the superb foundation they provided for this Canadian edition. We felt a great responsibility to honour the other writers' material. We tried to be consistent in writing style and true to their overall intent—judiciously cutting here, modifying something there, and inserting appropriate Canadian material whenever it was available.

We also wish to thank our reviewers, who provided concise, helpful suggestions during the developmental stages of this book: Derek Allison, University of Western Ontario; Christina Belcher, Redeemer University College; Lorenzo Cherubini, Brock University; Jerry Diakiw, York University; Michael Parr, Nipissing University; Campbell A. Ross, Grande Prairie Regional College; D. T. Rusty Rustemeyer, University of Northern British Columbia; and Jim Wiese, University of the Fraser Valley.

Robert Harris, Heather Stephens, and John Vaillancourt thank the many individuals who provided inspiration and assistance in the preparation of this book. Heather particularly appreciates the contributions made by her graduate students, who continually teach her about the art and craft of teaching. Finally, the support of our partners is acknowledged; the many hours of time spent on the project were made easier by their encouragement and humour.

Robert Harris
Heather Stephens
John Vaillancourt

part one

The Teaching Profession

1

Teaching: Your Chosen Profession

The best part of teaching is being a "learning catalyst." I love it when I can introduce my students to a project or concept and then "take the ball and run with it." My goal is accomplished when they go beyond what I know and I start learning from them.

—Sonya Vanderhoeden-Bracken
Teacher of Senior Mathematics
Laurentian Regional High School
Lachute, Quebec

focus questions

Congratulations on deciding to become a teacher! Teaching is exciting, rewarding, and uplifting. Teachers receive great satisfaction from knowing that they really do make a difference in their students' lives. We hope you share our belief that teaching is the world's most important profession. We also hope your commitment to teaching will become deeper and stronger as you move through your teacher education program.

This book will orient you to the world of teaching and help you to answer your own questions about the career you have chosen. What is teaching really like on a day-to-day basis? What rewards do teachers experience? What are the trends and issues in the profession? What problems can you expect to encounter in the classroom? What will you need to know and to be able to do to become a highly qualified teacher?

We believe that successful teachers know why they want to teach. They examine their motives carefully, and they understand why, at first, they might have been uncertain about choosing teaching as a profession. The first chapter of this book, then, addresses the four focus questions listed above, which will help you decide if teaching is the right profession for you.

The focus questions in each chapter will address your future as a teacher. Answers to these questions will provide you with a realistic view of the world of teachers, students, classrooms, and schools and their surrounding communities. After reading this book, you will have a broad understanding of one of the most exciting, satisfying, and honourable professions the world has ever known. And you will know if teaching is the right profession for you.

Why Do You Want to Teach?

You may want to teach for many reasons. Your desire to teach may be the result of positive experiences with teachers when you were a child. You may see teaching as a way of making a significant contribution to the world and experiencing the joy of helping others grow and develop. Or you may be attracted to teaching because the life of a teacher is exciting, varied, and stimulating.

Desire to Work with Children and Young People

Though the conditions under which teachers work may be challenging, their salaries modest, and members of their communities unsupportive, most teach simply because they care about students.

Effective teachers derive their greatest satisfaction when they are successful in promoting students' learning—when they "make a difference" in students' lives. As a teacher, your day-to-day interactions with students will build strong bonds between you and them. Daily contact will enable you to become familiar with your students' personal and academic needs. Concern for their welfare will help you cope with the difficulties and frustrations of teaching. As the following quotations from highly accomplished individuals illustrate, the teacher's potential to make a difference in students' lives can be profound:

> The dream begins, most of the time, with a teacher who believes in you, who tugs and pushes and leads you on to the next plateau, sometimes poking you with a sharp stick called truth.
>
> —*Dan Rather, national news commentator*

> Compassionate teachers fill a void left by working parents who aren't able to devote enough attention to their children. Teachers don't just teach; they can be vital personalities who help young people to mature, to understand the world and to understand themselves.
>
> —*Charles Platt, science fiction novelist*

> One looks back with appreciation to the brilliant teachers who touched our human feelings. The curriculum is so much necessary raw material, but warmth is the vital element for the growing plant and for the soul of the child.
>
> —*Carl Jung, world-renowned psychoanalyst*

Like most teachers, you may appreciate the unique qualities of youth. You enjoy the liveliness, curiosity, freshness, openness, and trust of young children, or the abilities, wit, spirit, independence, and idealism of adolescents. As one teacher put it, you want to "truly make a difference in the lives of children who [do] not always come 'ready to learn' [and to] be a part of helping students see themselves as literate and able to solve problems" (Ferris 2008, 16).

Teachers also derive significant rewards from meeting the needs of diverse learners. While Canadian students come from increasingly diverse racial and ethnic backgrounds and those with special needs are increasing in number, effective teachers recognize that their classrooms are enriched by the varied backgrounds of students. To enable you to experience the satisfaction of helping all students learn, significant portions of this book are devoted to **student variability** (differences among students in regard to their developmental needs, interests, abilities, and disabilities) and **student diversity** (differences among students in regard to gender, race, ethnicity, culture, and socio-economic status). An appreciation for such diversity will help you to experience the rewards that come from enabling each student to make his or her unique contribution to classroom life.

Like the following two teachers, a likely reason you have been drawn to teaching is the privilege of working with children and youth, regardless of their stages of development or their life circumstances:

> Where else can you regularly get hugged, get smeared with fingerpaints, receive handmade cards, wipe tears, share smiles, wiggle loose teeth, share awful cafeteria food, read silly stories, and know that you are changing the world?

> The rewards are great, when you see a child suddenly grasp a concept or write that poem that he/she thought [he/she] couldn't, these are the moments that let me know that I am in the right profession! (Harris Interactive 2001, 118)

The opportunity to work with young people, whatever their stage of development and whatever their life circumstances, is a key reason people are drawn to teaching and remain in the profession.

A Passion for Teaching

Why do teachers find teaching so satisfying? What does it mean to *love* teaching?

A Passion for the Subject

Teachers who express a love of teaching may mean that they love teaching in their discipline. The opportunity to continually learn more in one's profession and to share that knowledge with students is a definite attraction. In a journal article from *Educational Leadership* (44–46) titled "The Satisfactions of Teaching," Eliot Eisner points out that "teaching provides the occasion to share with others your deep affection for what you teach. When your eyes twinkle with delight at the prospect of introducing students to what you love, you create a sense of contagion and convey your love of what you teach. Your passion for your subject is the sincerest and most powerful invitation you can extend" (March 2006, 45).

A Passion for the Teaching Life

For those teachers who always enjoyed school, it is often the life of a teacher that has appeal—to be in an environment that encourages a high regard for education and for the life of the mind, and to have daily opportunities to see students become excited about learning. Albert Einstein, for example, regretted that he did not devote his career to the teaching life:

> Believe it or not, one of my deepest regrets [is that I didn't teach]. I regret this because I would have liked to have had more contact with children. There has always been something about the innocence and freshness of young children that appeals to me and brings me great enjoyment to be with them. And they are so open to knowledge. I have never really found it difficult to explain basic laws of nature to children. When you reach them at their level, you can read in their eyes their genuine interest and appreciation. (quoted in Bucky 1992, 99)

A Passion for the Teaching–Learning Process

You may be passionate about teaching because you are excited about helping students learn. The prospect of thinking "on your feet" and capitalizing on teachable moments is appealing. Perhaps you have had "expert" teachers who made you realize that "teaching well requires improvisation without constraints" and that "teaching is a custom job" (Eisner 2006, 45).

Philip Jackson describes the unpredictability of teaching in his well-known book *Life in Classrooms*: "[As] typically conducted, teaching is an opportunistic process. . . . Neither teacher nor students can predict with any certainty exactly what will happen next. Plans are forever going awry and unexpected opportunities for the attainment of educational goals are constantly emerging" (Jackson 1990, 166).

"Canada's Top 20 Jobs" reported on an online survey of nearly 8000 Canadians that asked participants to evaluate their jobs based on 11 factors, including salary, corporate culture, creativity, and stress level. The survey revealed, "While corporate executives report the greatest job satisfaction in Canada, a new study shows that teachers—whose average salary is almost $70 000 less than their business counterparts—are the second most content." For teachers, the ability to be creative proved the most rewarding aspect of their profession, and a lack of high salaries the main detriment (*Ottawa Citizen*, 30 March 2007).

A poll of 1000 Ontario teachers released by the Ontario College of Teachers in 2006 revealed that teachers love their jobs, but suffer stress brought on by time constraints, parent complaints, performance reviews, and school politics. Eighty-one percent said they would recommend teaching as a career—a marked jump from the 67 percent who said the same three years before (Toronto Ontario College of Teachers 2006).

Research tells us that teachers may make up to 3000 low-level decisions in a single school day (Jackson 1990). Most decisions are easy and come naturally, but some require critical thinking. Thinking on their feet for teachers becomes easier with experience, as the following example of Ms. Robinson, a Grade 7 English Language Arts teacher, demonstrates:

> I was circulating among the Literature Circle groups in my grade seven English Language Arts class to check on their progress and trouble shoot any problems they were having. At the beginning of class, several groups had individual questions but I asked them to go to their groups to get started and told them I would be around soon to see them. My thinking was that if I stopped to address individual questions, the rest of the class would have to wait to get their directions for the class and things could have gotten out of hand and precious class time would be wasted.
>
> I asked each group to go to their designated places in the room, take out their novels and role sheets, and begin their discussions. I explained that three groups would be evaluated according to a pre-established rubric; I was, however, not going to tell them which groups would be assessed that day. Students had been involved in developing how their participation would be evaluated, including cooperation. My rationale for this was that all groups would be more likely to adhere to the rubric requirements if they knew they would be accountable for their participation and behavior.
>
> The groups quickly settled down and began to engage in discussions of their reading and the role sheets they had prepared for the class. Students in each Literature Circle had previously decided as a group how much reading would be completed for that day's class along with who would assume what role in the day's discussion. This approach appeared to be working well and, overall, the students were taking responsibility for their learning.
>
> One group started complaining about a group member being absent and I helped them to resolve this by encouraging them to problem solve on ways to help the missing student get the work completed.

As I was talking with that group I began to sense something amiss with one of the other groups. The five students in that group appeared to be arguing so I headed over to see if I needed to intervene. Four of the five students in the group seemed upset and were berating the fifth group member. I was able to discern that the problem had stemmed from one student who had not completed the role sheet that the group had agreed upon for homework. The student was offering some weak excuses for his failure to complete the work and voices were becoming loud. All eyes were on the group and on me. I quietly asked the four students who had completed the assignment to share their work and the student who had not would come in at lunch hour and do his work. Although the student started to protest, I did not argue with him, but rather indicated calmly but firmly that this was non-negotiable. On the following day, that student would be expected to share his work with the others at the beginning of class.

Go to www.MyEducationLab.com and access the Managing to Teach resource. Go to Group Work in Module 3 and watch the Group Decision Scenario video. This virtual learning exercise allows you to make decisions and to see how each decision might play out in a Grade 7 classroom where Literature Circle discussions are taking place.

PEARSON
myeducationlab

Influence of Teachers

The journey toward becoming a teacher often begins early in life. While few people are "born teachers," their early life experiences often encourage them to become teachers. With the exception of parents or guardians, the adults who have the greatest influence on children are often their teachers. Perhaps a positive relationship with a teacher was the catalyst for your decision to become one.

Similar to most people who become teachers, you may have been more influenced by your teachers in their roles as fellow human beings, rather than as subject-matter experts. Perhaps you had a teacher similar to Salina Gray, who made the following self-reflective observation during her first year of teaching: "I have evaluated my beliefs as a teacher, asking what education should be, what it means, and what I actually show my students. Do my actions show my values to my students? So, I have become a kinder, more honest Ms. Gray. My students have noticed" (Oakes & Lipton 2007, 490). The inspirational memories you have of teachers from earlier in your life may have led you to the teaching profession.

Desire to Serve

Many choose to teach because they want to serve others; they want the results of their labour to extend beyond themselves and their families. Some decide to select another program or to leave teaching in order to earn more money elsewhere, only to return to teaching, confiding that they found the other program or work lacking in meaning or significance. Being involved in a service profession is their draw to the field.

For many, the decision to serve through teaching was influenced by their experiences as volunteers. During admission interviews, teacher education program applicants often cite their volunteer work in Boy Scouts, Girl Guides, summer camps, church activities, and other child and youth organizations as influential in their decision to enter the profession.

Explore more deeply your reasons for becoming a teacher. The following Professional Reflection feature focuses on several characteristics that may indicate your probable satisfaction with teaching as a career.

Professional Reflection — Assessing Your Reasons for Choosing to Teach

For each of the following characteristics, indicate on a scale from 1 to 5 the extent to which it applies to you.

	Very applicable				Not at all applicable
1. A passion for learning	1	2	3	4	5
2. Success as a student	1	2	3	4	5
3. Good sense of humour	1	2	3	4	5
4. Positive attitudes toward students	1	2	3	4	5
5. Tolerance toward others	1	2	3	4	5
6. Patience	1	2	3	4	5
7. Good verbal and writing skills	1	2	3	4	5
8. Appreciation for the arts	1	2	3	4	5
9. Experiences working with children (camp, church, tutoring, etc.)	1	2	3	4	5
10. Other teachers in family	1	2	3	4	5
11. Encouragement from family to enter teaching	1	2	3	4	5
12. Desire to serve students and the community	1	2	3	4	5

As you read beginning teacher Kelly McCall's story next, notice how she reveals her passion for teaching, desire to work with youth, and the influence of former teachers as reasons for her selection of teaching as her chosen profession.

Practical Benefits of Teaching

Not to be overlooked as attractions to teaching are its practical benefits. Teachers' hours and vacations are widely recognized as benefits. Though the number of hours most teachers devote to their work goes far beyond the number of hours they actually spend at school, their schedules do afford them a measure of flexibility not found in other professions. For example, teachers with school-age children can often be at home during the summer when their children are not in school, and nearly all teachers, regardless of their years of experience, receive the same generous vacation time: holiday breaks and a long summer vacation. For Canadian teachers, the official classroom day usually runs from 8:30 or 9:00 a.m. to 3:30 or 4:00 p.m. Weekends and statutory holidays are not required teaching days, and vacations usually include a Christmas and a spring break of a week or more each, and eight weeks of time off from the classroom during the summer.

Salaries and Benefits

Although intangible rewards represent a significant attraction to teaching, teachers are now demanding that the public acknowledge the value and professional standing of

Teaching: A Calling

Wanting to be a teacher was not something that I had to think about; it was something that I always wanted to do and it seemed to be something that I did naturally. I love to learn and my desire to teach stems from wanting to inspire kids to do great things with what they love. We are all good at something and I feel that I can help students realize this because I believe it.

There is an important connection between confidence and learning. All it took was one teacher to tell me how well I was doing, one teacher to understand how I learned, and one teacher to guide me when I faltered. During my practicum, I felt like a superhero when I helped even a single student through a problem. At the risk of sounding clichéd, I want to be a teacher because I want to provide opportunities and a sense of hope for future generations. Maybe I am looking at the profession from rose-coloured spectacles, but what is wrong with that?

Challenges and Opportunities

With the current focus on differentiation, I am concerned about being able to effectively accommodate every kind of learner. We need to find ways to reach each and every one of the students we encounter; in reality, this can seem like a daunting task. Is it really possible to forge connections with all of our learners when they each bring different emotional, physical, socio-economic, and intellectual needs?

Tools for Learning

I look forward to challenging my future students by providing them with authentic learning opportunities that will help them meet the challenges of the twenty-first century. This includes helping them become competent problem-solvers in the face of the changes they are likely to encounter.

I am becoming more aware of student needs as well as the resources that are available to make learning more accessible and effective. Learning resources can range from a specific strategy that is used to teach a lesson in a classroom to technology such as computer programs to assist in a content area such as literacy or mathematics. These resources can even be used in a more general area such as organization. As teachers we need to be able to make decisions about how we use technology as a tool and to determine the possibilities it affords. However, we need to remember the power of the human connections we make with our students.

I realize that my own positive learning experiences will serve as a foundation for me to tackle and overcome challenges in teaching that may arise in the coming years. One of my passionate beliefs is that disengaged learners can be shown how to love learning. We know our students do not always show up with an enthusiastic approach to learning. However, it starts with hopeful teachers who believe they can transform challenges into opportunities. This is what I want to do for my learners and this is what makes teaching seem like the best job in the world!

Ontario resident Kelly McCall is a beginning teacher who graduated with a Bachelor of Education degree in May 2010 from Acadia University's School of Education in Nova Scotia.

teaching by supporting higher salaries. Though there is still a general consensus that teachers are underpaid, teacher salaries are becoming more competitive with other occupations; in fact, salaries are becoming one of the main draws of the profession.

According to the Canadian Teachers Federation (CTF), in Canada, the basic salary scale and benefit package offered to a newly-hired teacher is established through negotiations between the teachers' association and representatives of the provincial or territorial government. Generally, teacher salary schedules are determined by a combination of years of post-secondary education and years of teaching experience. Additional allowances are paid to teachers whose position will include additional administrative responsibilities.

Depending on the jurisdiction, an entry level salary can range from $36 305 to $58 980 annually, while the maximum salary level can range from $53 545 to $83 158 annually. Teachers with advanced and graduate training can expect salaries that are higher than the maximum level.

Benefit packages can vary from jurisdiction to jurisdiction but will include a combination of the following:

- Dental insurance
- Life insurance
- Maternity leave
- Compassionate leave
- Cumulative sick leave
- Sabbatical and study leave
- Supplementary medical insurance
- Long-term disability insurance
- Retirement gratuities (CTF 2006)

myeducationlab

Go to www.MyEducationLab.com and visit the Teacher's Resource section to view information of interest to Canadian teachers. For example, the URL www.cmec.ca/Pages/Default.aspx takes you to a website that provides important and current information for individuals who are planning to enter the teaching profession in Canada. This includes information on qualifications, finding a teaching position in Canada, teacher qualification by province, salary scales, category placement regulations, and teacher certification regulations. You are encouraged to seek information from the province(s) in which you might be interested in teaching.

Canadian Teacher Supply and Demand

Research from the Nova Scotia Department of Education reflects the teacher supply and demand projections and the predicted trends in the rest of Canada.

In Nova Scotia, there is a slight decline projected in numbers of teachers overall by 7.9 percent from 2005–6 to 2014–15. However, the ratio of number of students per teacher is also expected to decrease due to a projected 15.8 percent decrease in enrolment. Although there is not an aggregated shortage of teachers, some rural regions and other geographical areas across the province may experience difficulty in attracting teachers, especially in certain content areas and specialties. Particularly rural and smaller school boards have reported difficulty finding substitute teachers at the middle school and senior high levels. Overall demand by subject and specialty for 2011–12 and 2014–15 are projected to be highest at the elementary, administration, and resource levels. The market is also likely to be tight in the areas of physical education, fine arts, physics, and family studies, and there may be shortages in technology education and French (Nova Scotia Public Teacher Supply and Demand: 2007 Update Report).

Job Opportunities for Teachers from Diverse Groups

During this first part of the twenty-first century, changing Canadian demographics will be increasingly reflected in the student population. For a society to understand cultural and ethnic diversity, teachers need to reflect that diversity. Clearly, students from diverse racial, ethnic, and cultural backgrounds and students with disabilities benefit from having role models with whom they can easily identify. In addition, teachers from diverse groups and teachers with disabilities may have, in some instances, an enhanced understanding of student diversity and student variability that they can share with other teachers.

Research compiled by the CTF reveals that teachers are underrepresented relative to the under-15 school-aged population for North American Indian, Chinese, and East Indian ethnic origin groups. Aboriginal representation within the Canadian education system is also of equal concern. By province, teacher underrepresentation was highest in Manitoba and Saskatchewan. This is of particular cause for concern given Statistics Canada's recent projection that in 2017, Aboriginal children aged 0 to 14 years in Saskatchewan could account for 37 percent of this age group, while in Manitoba, 31 percent of children 0 to 14 years could be Aboriginal (CTF 2006).

What Challenges Does Teaching Present?

Like all professions, teaching has undesirable or difficult aspects. Frank McCourt, a teacher at four New York City high schools over a 30-year period and a noted author after his retirement from teaching, said a teacher needs to be "a drill sergeant, a rabbi, a disciplinarian, a low-level scholar, a clerk, a referee, a clown, a counselor, and [a] therapist" (Frank McCourt 2005: 19).

As a prospective teacher, you should consider the challenges as well as the satisfactions you are likely to encounter. You can make the most of your teacher education program if you are informed. Awareness of the realities of teaching will enable you to develop your personal philosophy of education, build a repertoire of teaching strategies, strengthen your leadership skills, and acquire a knowledge base of research and theory to guide your actions. In this manner, you can become a true professional—free to enjoy the many satisfactions of teaching and confident of your ability to deal with its challenges.

Classroom Management and Increasing Violence

Not surprisingly, lack of discipline and increased crime and violence among youth are strong concerns for teacher education students. Before teachers can teach, they must manage their classrooms effectively. Even when parents and the school community are supportive and problems are relatively minor, dealing with discipline issues can be a disturbing, emotionally draining aspect of teaching.

Taber, Alberta, in 2004 and Toronto, Ontario, in 2007 were thrust into the national spotlight as a result of fatal school shootings carried out by students. Though acts of violence of this magnitude in schools are rare, the possibility of experiencing such events can cause additional job-related stress for teachers. Students, too, can experience stress regarding their safety at school.

In addition, many schools have high teacher–student ratios, which can make classroom management more difficult. Feeling the pressure of overcrowding and valiantly resisting the realization that they cannot meet the needs of all their students, teachers may try to work faster and longer to give their students the best possible education. All too often, however, teachers learn to put off, overlook, or otherwise attend inadequately to many students each day.

The problem of high teacher–student ratios becomes even more acute when complicated by the high **student-mobility rates** in many schools. In such situations, teachers have trouble not only in meeting students' needs but also in recognizing students and remembering their names! As you will see, developing a leadership plan, a learning environment, and communication skills will help you face the challenges of classroom management.

Of particular concern in recent years is the problem of **cyberbullying**, a digital form of bullying that presents new challenges for schools and communities in general. The 2008 National Issues in Education Poll, commissioned by the Canadian Teachers Federation, revealed that three-quarters of Canadians are aware of the term "cyberbullying." The poll further shows that 34 percent of Canadians surveyed knew of students in their community who had been targeted by cyberbullying in the past year, while one in five was aware of teachers who had been cyberbullied. The poll also shows that almost one in ten knew someone close to them who had been cyberbullied.

According to the CTF policy proposal, cyberbullying is the use of information and communication technologies to bully, embarrass, threaten, or harass another. It also includes the use of these technologies to engage in conduct or behaviour that is derogatory, defamatory, degrading, illegal, or abusive.

Other key findings of the poll that should be of particular concern for educators:

> Nine in 10 Canadians believe that an effective measure to prevent cyberbullying by students is for parents to become more knowledgeable and more responsible in monitoring their child's activities with the Internet and electronic communication devices; 86% believe that an effective measure to prevent cyberbullying by students is to have teachers trained to respond to cyberbullying when it impacts them or their students; 96% believe that school boards should develop and enforce policies that hold their students accountable when they are identified as cyberbullies. About 7 in 10 Canadians think that school boards should hold students accountable when the cyberbullying originates outside the school, such as from the student's home. (CTF 2008)

Social Problems That Impact Students

Many social problems affect the lives and learning of many children and youth. For example, substance abuse, teen pregnancy, homelessness, poverty, family distress, child abuse and neglect, violence and crime, suicide, and health problems such as human immunodeficiency virus (HIV), acquired immune deficiency syndrome (AIDS), and fetal alcohol syndrome all affect students in the classroom. The social problems that place students at risk of school failure are not always easy to detect. Students' low productivity, learning difficulties, and attitude problems demand teacher attention, yet teachers may be unaware of the source of those difficulties. Even when teachers do recognize the source of a problem, they may lack the resources or expertise to offer help. Teachers often feel frustrated by the wasted potential they observe in their students. In addition, when the public calls for schools to curb or correct social problems, that expectation can increase the stress that teachers experience.

Canada's Rural and Urban Challenges

Teacher education programs are being designed to better prepare education students for the challenges they will face in rural and urban schools. Schools in inner-city areas must have teachers who care about children living in poverty and who are willing to make the extra efforts to meet their diverse needs. Many teachers and administrators leave these schools after a year or two because of the immense pressure of the social and educational environment. Beginning teachers need to become familiar with the literature on the literacy levels of children in poverty. In addition, teacher education programs need to emphasize the importance of developing school–family–community partnerships for student success.

Canada's large land mass provides challenges in terms of furnishing equitable educational services to small and isolated communities, especially those in the north. Northern and geographically isolated school boards have difficulty attracting and maintaining staff, and providing appropriate educational experiences is costly. The education systems of these regions must be developed to meet the needs of the students in the context of their communities. The culture of the local communities must be valued and should shape the curriculum. Teachers need to be prepared to meet the special challenges of these regions. In addition, initiatives that encourage young people to become teachers and to remain in their home communities are important.

In recent years, technology has had a positive effect on the ability of rural schools to reach out and communicate with other areas of the country. Continuing technology advances and expansion of online social networks will no doubt assist schools in isolated areas to make important connections.

Diverse Populations

Canada is becoming increasingly diverse in its population, and such diversity enriches the school systems, while providing challenges. Large urban areas, such as Vancouver and Toronto, have significant populations of immigrants from Asia, Africa, and Latin America who have joined the more established populations with European roots, as well as Aboriginal people.

Canadian public schools have a duty to respond to the social and academic needs of immigrant and First Nations students through the enactment of inclusive practices. These include forging strong connections with other social agencies to offer an array of services to support families.

Need for Family and Community Support

Support from parents and the community can make a significant difference in the teacher's effectiveness in the classroom. Increasingly, there has been a realization that school, parents, and community must work together so that children and youth develop to their maximum potential academically, socially, emotionally, and physically. Parents who talk with their children, help with homework, read to them, monitor their television viewing, and attend meetings of the Parent Teacher Organization (PTO) and school open houses can enhance their children's ability to succeed in school (Henry 1996; Moore 1992; Fuligni & Stevenson 1995). Similarly, communities can support schools by providing essential social, vocational, recreational, and health support services to students and their families.

Today's Tech-Savvy Students

Understanding how technology affects students and schools and integrating technology into teaching come easily for some teachers; for other teachers, however, it can be a challenge. Students in your classroom will have grown up in "a techno-drenched atmosphere that has trained them to absorb and process information in fundamentally different ways" (McHugh 2005: 1). For example, students in Grades 3–12 spend an average of 6 hours and 21 minutes each day using some type of media. Because today's students are skilled at multitasking, the figure jumps to about 8½ hours and includes almost 4 hours watching television and 50 minutes of videogame play. Homework, however, receives only 50 minutes of their time (Rideout, Roberts, & Foehr 2005).

For these students, using computers and advanced technology is an everyday part of their lives. How can teachers remain up to date regarding the role that technology plays in their students' lives?

Generally speaking, schools have not kept up with the rapid changes in technology. "For this digital generation, electronic media is increasingly seductive, influential, and pervasive, yet most schools treat the written word as the only means of communication worthy of study" (George Lucas Educational Foundation, February 9, 2008). Today's students have iPods, cell phones, video cameras, laptops, and digital cameras. Websites like Facebook and MySpace are changing the way students communicate, socialize, and network. Sites like YouTube and iTunes bring media to students seamlessly, whether at home, at school, or on the move. Media content comes into schools through cell phones, the Internet, e-mail, text messages, and general entertainment (for example, music, video, and blogs).

To keep up with the media and technology environment today's students inhabit outside school, teachers must integrate technology into their teaching. Moodle, a free virtual learning environment, can be used to manage class-related conversations, homework assignments, and quizzes. Students can be encouraged to keep blogs (short for "web log") using BlogMeister, an online publishing tool developed specifically for classroom use. All school-related activity can be viewed by the teacher in one place and material can be linked from Moodle and BlogMeister using Bloglines.

Effective teachers recognize that technology can be a powerful tool for enhancing students' inquiry, reflection, and problem solving. They also realize that technology cannot be grafted onto existing teaching strategies; it must be integrated within them.

See the following example of how wikis are used in a tenth-grade social studies class:

> Maria Valquez has asked her tenth-grade social studies students to track and report on national election activities. She has organized her four social studies classes into 28 groups of three students each. Each group is assigned an aspect of the election to cover, such as specific political parties, an individual candidate, hot topic issues, media campaign messages, and so on. Maria wants students to be able to share the information they find among the four classes, with the rest of the school, and even with the community. In addition to researching election activities, she hopes that students will strive to find common ground and form a consensus on controversial issues. To facilitate this communication and sharing of information, Maria needs a technology tool that is not controlled by a single group or individual. She needs a tool that allows all students in her social studies classes to have an equal say. She decides to use a wiki.

Coming out of the social web movement, wikis follow the logic that many voices are better than one. A wiki is a website that allows collaborative work by various authors. A wiki website allows anyone or designated members of a group to create, delete, or edit its content. Several free wiki services are available to educators. A simple Google search yields promising results. One example is PBworks, at http://pbworks.com/content/edu+overview. This is one of the most popular wikis and it is free to educators (at the time of publication). According to the authors of the site, "PBwiki lets you quickly set up your own free, hosted, password-protected wiki to edit and share information. It's as easy as a peanut butter sandwich" (PBWiki Inc. 2008). In addition to creating your own wiki, you can see how others have used wiki tools to increase student engagement.

What Is the Work of Teachers?

At first, this question may appear easy to answer. Based on your own experiences as a student, you know that teachers assign learning tasks. Teachers ask questions and evaluate students' responses; they lecture and, on occasion, demonstrate what students are to do. Teachers assign chapters to read in the text and then conduct recitations or give quizzes on that material. They praise some students for right answers or good work, and they prod, chastise, and at times embarrass others in the hope that their work will improve. And, near the end of the term or semester, teachers decide who has passed and who has failed. However, the role of today's teachers includes responsibilities that go beyond actual teaching in the classroom.

Teaching is more than the sum of the behaviours you observed in your own teachers. As you move ahead in your journey toward becoming a teacher, you will discover that teaching involves more than performing certain behaviours in front of a group of students. A significant portion of a teacher's work is mentally based and involves problem solving in response to unforeseen events that emerge in the classroom (Martinez 2006).

Teaching is a creative act in which teachers continually shape and reshape lessons, events, and the experiences of their students. A former teacher and now head of an organization that creates small, personalized public high schools in collaboration with their communities describes the creative dimensions of teaching this way. "The act of being a teacher is the act of . . . using your skills and love for kids to figure out how to create the best environment to help your students [learn]" (Littky 2004, 12).

Although your teachers reflected different personalities and methods, your experiences as a student are similar to the experiences of other students. Our recollections about teachers who had a good or bad influence, were easy or hard on us, and were interesting or dull educators are drawn from a commonly shared set of experiences. The universality of these experiences leads us to conclude that we know "the way teaching is" and what teachers do. However, in a seminal article aptly titled "The Way Teaching Is," noted education researcher Philip Jackson points out that teaching is "fleeting and ephemeral" because of the "fragile quality of the psychological condition that is created by the teacher" (1965, 62).

The following sections examine three dimensions of teaching that illustrate how, on the one hand, teaching involves "enduring puzzlements, persistent dilemmas, complex conundrums, [and] enigmatic paradoxes" (Eisner 2006, 44), while on the other it offers opportunities for "saving lives, rescuing a child from despair, restoring a sense of hope, soothing discomfort" (46). Effective teachers understand that they are role models for students, spontaneous problem-solvers, and reflective thinkers.

Teacher as a Role Model for Students

Clearly, teachers are role models for their students. In the elementary grades, teachers are idolized by their young pupils. At the high school level, teachers have the potential to inspire students' admiration if they model positive attitudes and behaviours. Actually, teachers teach "not only by what [they] say but also by what [they] do"

(Ormrod 2003, 342). Teachers are "active agents whose words and deeds change lives and mold futures, for better or worse. Teachers can and do exert a great deal of power and influence in the lives of their students" (Nieto 2003, 19).

A high school teacher explains why developing positive relationships with students is so important: "[The] relationship between teachers and students is becoming one of the most important aspects of teaching. [In] a world of broken homes and violence, the encouragement of their teachers may be the only thing students can hold onto that makes them feel good about themselves" (Henry et al. 1995, 127).

Teachers also model attitudes toward the subjects they teach and show students through their example that learning is an ongoing, life-enriching process that does not end with diplomas and graduations. The need for teachers to function as role models for students confirms the timeless message of Sir Rabindranath Tagore that is inscribed above the doorway of a public building in India: "A teacher can never truly teach unless he is still learning himself. A lamp can never light another lamp unless it continues to burn its own flame."

On the next page is a letter of advice from a seasoned teacher to a former student who is entering the teaching profession. Reflect on how the teacher highlights important characteristics of "good teaching."

Teacher as a Spontaneous Problem-Solver

In the classroom, teachers must respond to unpredictable events that are rapidly changing, multidimensional, and fragmented. Furthermore, "day in and day out, teachers spend much of their lives 'on stage' before audiences that are not always receptive. . . . Teachers must orchestrate a daunting array of interpersonal interactions and build a cohesive, positive climate for learning" (Gmelch & Parkay 1995, 47).

When teachers are preparing to teach or reflecting on previous teaching, they can afford to be consistently deliberate and rational. Planning for lessons, grading papers, reflecting on the misbehaviour of a student—such activities are usually done alone and lack the immediacy and sense of urgency that characterize **interactive teaching**. While working face-to-face with students, however, you must be able to think on your feet and to respond appropriately to complex, ever-changing situations. You must be flexible and ready to deal with the unexpected. During a discussion, for example, you must operate on at least two levels. On one level, you respond appropriately to students' comments, monitor other students for signs of confusion or comprehension, formulate the next comment or question, and remain alert for signs of misbehaviour. On another level, you ensure that participation is evenly distributed among students, evaluate the content and quality of students' contributions, keep the discussion focused and moving ahead, and emphasize major content areas.

During interactive teaching, the awareness that you are responsible for the forward movement of the group never lets up. Teachers are the only professionals who practise their craft almost exclusively under the direct, continuous gaze of up to 30 or 40 clients. Jackson (1990, 119) sums up the experience: "The immediacy of classroom events is something that anyone who has ever been in charge of a roomful of students can never forget."

Teacher as a Reflective Thinker

Teaching involves a unique mode of being between teacher and student—a mode of being that can be experienced but not fully defined or described. On your journey to become a teacher, you will gradually develop your capacity to listen to students and

"Not the Filling of a Pail"

Warren Dobson
Program support teacher at South Queens Junior High School, South Shore Regional School Board

Dear David:

Congratulations! I hear you are about to graduate and soon will have your first assignment as a new teacher. I am sending you a little gift—nothing much, just some words of wisdom that have inspired me in my teaching. It is this quotation from William Butler Yeats. "Education is not the filling of a pail, but the lighting of a fire."

This captures the essence of good teaching in very few words. If you keep them in mind, you may find that teaching will not become any easier, but will certainly become more interesting and more satisfying.

"Education is not the filling of a pail . . . " means that you are teaching human beings. If you learn to know your students as individuals, you will treat them with more consideration and respect. They have deep feelings. Do not, intentionally, do or say anything to embarrass or humiliate a student in front of his or her peers. If you have to discipline a student, speak to him or her privately if possible. Try to be fair with your students—do not play favourites. When it comes to "teacher's pet," all or none is the best rule.

Another thing is implied in those first few words. It is that learning is not a passive process, but an active one. Students need to be doing something with their new skills or information in order to "make the lesson stick. Think of as many different activities as you can to reinforce new learning.

" . . . Not the filling of a pail . . . " also means that you don't have to teach them everything. You do not have to know it all. You should be knowledgeable in your subject area, yet it is not possible to know everything. Admit it when you don't know an answer—it can lead to a good discussion. You should know where to find the answer, however. Invite an expert to class to answer the question, or get the student who came up with the $64 000 question to e-mail it to an expert.

The last part of the quote touches on the artistry of teaching. This is something beyond expert subject knowledge or command of pedagogical technique. The "lighting of a fire" refers to inspiring a student with a lifelong love of learning. There are no lesson plans for this, but if there were, they might include some of these things:

Believe in yourself. Set goals. Be reflective. Keep a journal. Create a welcoming space where students are free from contempt, indifference, and "putdowns." Do not allow students to "put themselves down" or engage in negative self-talk (e.g., "I'm stupid. I can't. . . ."). Believe in your students. Maintain high expectations. Believe that every student has at least one gift, one thing they can do like no other. Help them to find their gift(s). Create opportunities for them to develop their gift(s).

No doubt, you heard a lot about motivation in your studies. Here is another tidbit of advice:

A teacher who is attempting to teach without inspiring the pupil with a desire to learn is hammering on a cold iron.
—Horace Mann (1796–1859)

I mention this because I believe motivation is not well understood. I may be wrong, but I see it in this way. Most of us have what I call a Personal Relevance Filter (PRF). This operates to screen incoming sensory experience and allows us to separate our experiences into two piles—things that are important to us, and things that are not. This natural process prevents our brains from being overloaded by the sheer abundance of sensory impressions. Your goal, as teacher, is to try to get your lessons placed in the "important" pile. A way to do this is to frame your lessons and activities in a "real world" or authentic context. Another way is to use theatrical techniques, particularly humour or suspense. I am sure you will think of more ways to create personal relevance for your students. Knowing what "makes them tick" is a good place to start.

Best of luck from your former teacher,

Warren Dobson

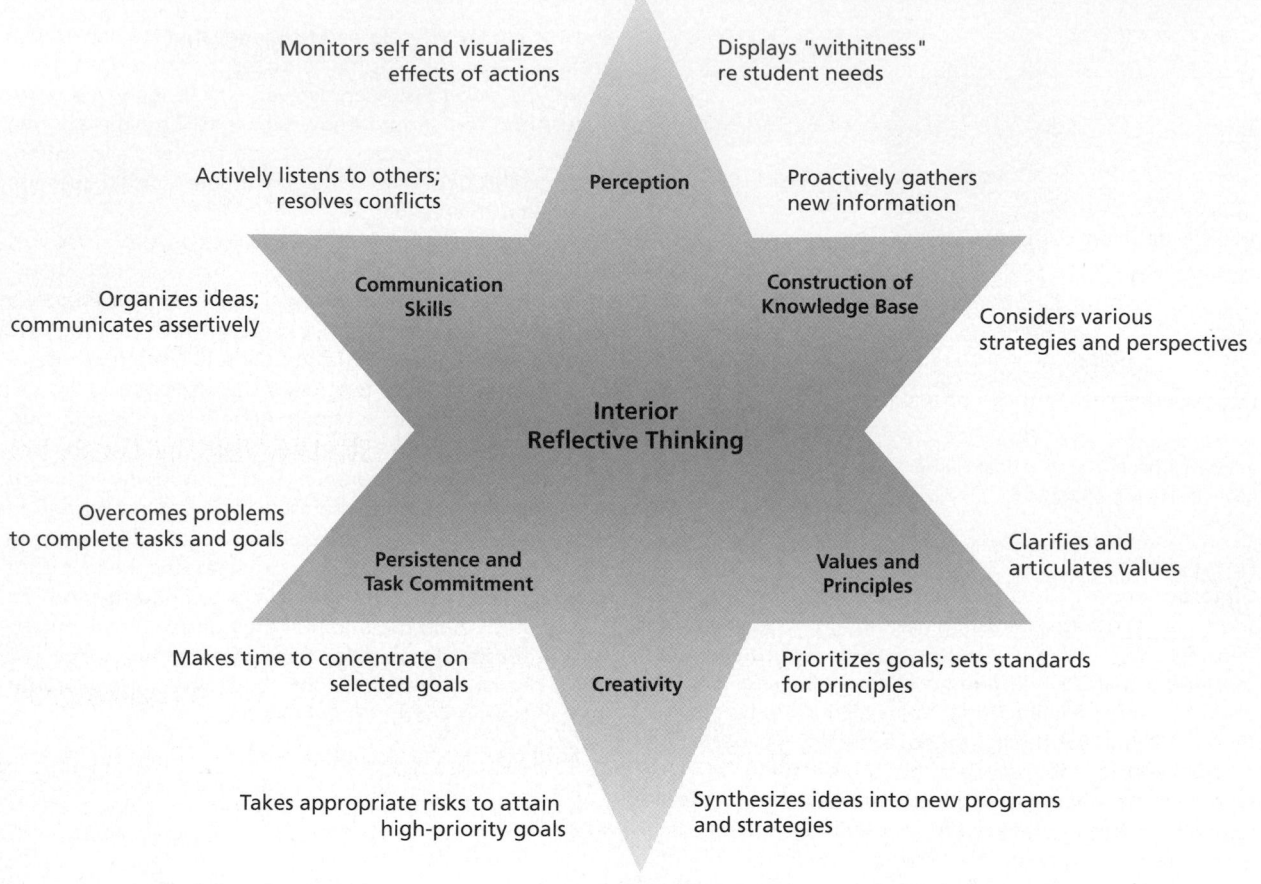

Teacher observes
a class event or
student behaviour

Monitors self and visualizes
effects of actions

Displays "withitness"
re student needs

Actively listens to others;
resolves conflicts

Perception

Proactively gathers
new information

Organizes ideas;
communicates assertively

**Communication
Skills**

**Construction of
Knowledge Base**

Considers various
strategies and perspectives

**Interior
Reflective Thinking**

Overcomes problems
to complete tasks and goals

Clarifies and
articulates values

**Persistence and
Task Commitment**

**Values and
Principles**

Makes time to concentrate on
selected goals

Prioritizes goals; sets standards
for principles

Creativity

Takes appropriate risks to attain
high-priority goals

Synthesizes ideas into new programs
and strategies

**Exterior
Reflective Action**

Figure 1.1

A model of reflective
action in teaching

Source: Judy W. Eby,
*Reflective Planning,
Teaching, and Evaluation:
K–12,* 2nd ed. Upper Saddle
River, NJ: Merrill, 1996,
p. 14. © 1996. Reprinted by
permission of Prentice-Hall,
Inc., Upper Saddle River, NJ.

to convey an authentic sense of concern for their learning. Unfortunately, there is no precise, easy-to-follow formula for demonstrating this. You will have to take into account your personality and special gifts to discover your own best way for showing this concern.

One reason it is difficult to describe teaching is that an important domain of teaching, teachers' thought processes (including professional reflection), cannot be observed directly. Figure 1.1 shows how the unobservable domain of the teacher's "interior reflective thinking" interacts with and is influenced by the observable domain of the teacher's "exterior reflective action." Teachers' thought processes include their theories and beliefs about students and how they learn, their plans for teaching, and the decisions they make while teaching. Thought processes and actions can be constrained by the physical setting of the classroom or by external factors such as the curriculum, the principal, or the community. On the other hand, teachers' thought processes and actions may be influenced by unique opportunities, such as the chance to engage in curriculum reform or school governance. The model also illustrates a further complexity of teaching—namely, that the relationships among teacher behaviour, student behaviour, and student achievement are reciprocal. What teachers do is influenced not only by their thought processes before, during, and after teaching but also by student behaviour and student achievement. This complexity contributes to the uniqueness of the teaching experience.

How Do Accomplished Teachers View Their Work?

Accomplished teachers derive greatest satisfaction when they are effective in promoting students' learning—when they "make a difference" in students' lives. When you recall your most effective teachers, you probably think of particular individuals, not idealizations of the teacher's many roles. What good teachers do can be described in terms of five **modes of teaching**, which are more general and significant than a discussion of roles. You may recognize these modes in your observations of teachers and in the writings of gifted teachers when they reflect on their work. You may even acknowledge these modes of teaching as deeper reasons for becoming a teacher.

A Way of Being

In becoming a teacher, you take on the role and let it become a part of you. Increasingly, the learning of facts can be achieved easily with good books, good television, CD-ROMs, DVDs, and access to the Internet. What cannot be learned in these ways are styles of life and teaching what it means to be, to grow, to become actualized, and to become complete.

Go to www.MyEducationLab.com and access the Managing to Teach resource. Click on the Navigator button at the bottom of the page and go to Module 1, An Introduction to Your Virtual School and then to the Advice link. Click on seasoned teachers Russ and Dave to hear what they have to say about "going beyond," what it means to be prepared, and the need to love teaching.

PEARSON myeducationlab

A Creative Endeavour

Teaching is a creative endeavour in which teachers are continually shaping and reshaping lessons, events, and the experiences of their students. With careful attention to the details of classroom life, effective teachers artistically develop educative relationships with their students; they "read" the myriad events that emerge while teaching and respond appropriately. One high school teacher identified as highly successful by her principal reported: "I have to grab the kids that don't want to do math at all and somehow make them want to do this work. I'm not sure how I do it, but kids just want to do well in my class. For some mysterious reason, and I don't care why, they really want to do well" (Hanson 1995: 13).

A Live Performance

Teaching is a live performance with each class period, each day that involves responding to the unpredictable. Further, teachers are engaged in live dialogues with their classes and individual students. The experience of teaching is thus an intense, attention-demanding endeavour—an interactive one that provides minute-to-minute challenges. Some teachers embrace the live performance aspect of teaching more than others, believing that within it lies true learning.

Knowledge of how to integrate technology into teaching is essential for today's teachers. What steps can you take to remain technologically up to date?

A Form of Empowerment

Power is the dimension of teaching most immediately evident to the new teacher. It is recognized in the first-grader's awed question "Teacher, is this good?" on through the high school senior's query "How much will this paper count?"

Even in the most democratic classrooms, teachers have more influence than students because they are responsible for what happens when students are with them, for establishing the goals, for selecting the methods, for setting the pace, for evaluating the progress, and for deciding whether students should pass or fail. How you use this power is critical. As you know, students at any level can be humiliated by teachers who misuse their power or convey negative expectations to students.

An Opportunity to Serve

To become a teacher is to serve others. Most who come to teaching do so for altruistic reasons. The altruistic dimension of teaching is at the heart of the motivation to teach. The paycheque, the public regard, and the vacations have little holding power compared to the opportunity to serve. Whatever form the altruistic rewards of teaching takes, they ennoble the profession and remind teachers of the significance of their work.

Teaching for Excellence

Many of our country's most talented beginning teachers and most dedicated veteran teachers retain the desire to teach. In part, the desire endures because teachers have been positively influenced by one or more teachers of their own, who enriched, redirected, or significantly changed their lives. The desire also endures because teachers recognize the many joys and rewards the profession offers.

Reflecting on dedicated teachers and their contributions to our lives, we are guided to teaching for the benefit it brings to others. Every year, the Prime Minister's Awards for Teaching Excellence recognize the efforts of outstanding teachers in all disciplines. Go to www.ic.gc.ca/eic/site/pmate-ppmee.nsf/eng/home to view the most recent awards.

SUMMARY

Why Do You Want to Teach?

- An important reason for becoming a teacher is a desire to work with children and young people.

- Other reasons include a passion for teaching based on a love of subject, the teaching life, or the teaching–learning process; the influence of teachers in one's past; and a desire to serve others and society.

- Practical benefits of teaching include on-the-job hours at school, vacations, increasing salaries and benefits, job security, and a feeling of respect in society.

- In contrast to the diversity of student enrolments, the backgrounds of today's teachers are less diverse; thus, teachers from diverse racial and ethnic backgrounds need to be reflected in schools.

What Challenges Does Teaching Present?

- Working conditions for teachers can be difficult and stressful; however, for most teachers, satisfactions outweigh dissatisfactions.

- Though problems in schools vary according to size of community, location, and other factors, teachers in most schools face challenges: classroom management, social problems that impact students, rural and urban populations, diverse ethnicities, need for family and community support, and today's tech-savvy students.

- Maintaining discipline and avoiding school-based violence are major concerns among pre-service teachers.

- Social problems that impact the lives of many children and youth include substance abuse, teen pregnancies, homelessness, poverty, family distress, child abuse, violence and crime, suicide, and health problems such as HIV or AIDS and fetal alcohol syndrome.

What Is the Work of Teachers?

- Teaching is more than the sum of observable behaviours; much of the work of teachers involves responding to unforeseeable events in the classroom.

- With the role of teacher comes the power to influence others by example.

- Students need to be shown that learning is an on-going process.

- Teachers must be spontaneous problem-solvers as they respond to unpredictable events.

- Interactive teaching is characterized by events that are rapid-changing, multi-dimensional, and irregular.

- Teaching involves a unique mode of being between teacher and students—a mode of being that can be experienced but not fully defined or described.

How Do Accomplished Teachers View Their Work?

- Helping students to learn and to make a difference in students' lives provide teachers with their greatest satisfaction.

- The essence of accomplished teaching can be described in terms of modes of teaching illustrating what good teachers do.
- Five modes of teaching are teaching as:
  - A way of being
  - A creative endeavour
  - A live performance
  - A form of empowerment
  - An opportunity to serve

KEY TERMS AND CONCEPTS

benefit packages, 10

modes of teaching, 19

student variability, 4

cyberbullying, 12

student diversity, 4

teacher–student ratios, 11

interactive teaching, 16

student-mobility rates, 12

APPLICATIONS AND ACTIVITIES

Teacher's Journal

1. Consider your reasons for deciding to become a teacher. How do they compare with those described in this chapter?

2. Describe a former teacher who has had a positive influence on your decision to teach. In what ways would you like to become like that teacher?

3. What is your impression of the public's image of teachers in your province, territory, or community today? What factors might be contributing to the kind of attention or lack of attention teachers are receiving?

4. Think about a time when a teacher truly motivated you to learn. What did that teacher do to motivate you? Do you believe other students in the class had the same reaction? Why or why not?

5. Recall and describe specific experiences you had with teachers in elementary school, middle school or junior high school, or high school. Were you ever made uncomfortable because of a teacher's power over you? Were you ever ridiculed or diminished by a teacher? Or have you experienced the opposite—being elevated by a teacher's regard for you?

Theory into Practice

From Individual to Small Group to Whole Class: an Individual Exercise

1. Individual Task: Interview a **beginning teacher** (one with five years or less experience in the profession) and a **seasoned teacher** (one with 10 or more years in the profession) by asking the following guiding questions:

   a. What are the greatest challenges in your daily practice?

   b. What brings you the most satisfaction as a teacher?

c. If you could change one thing about today's education system, what would it be?

d. "If I knew then what I know now . . . ." What is the best single piece of advice you could give to a person who is considering the teaching profession as a career?

In point form, summarize the teachers' responses in a chart such as the following:

Topic Areas	Beginning Teacher	Seasoned Teacher
Biggest challenges		
Greatest satisfaction		
Suggested change in today's education system		
Advice		

2. Small Group Task: In small groups of four to five students, discuss findings by referring to the individual charts. Note similarities and differences between the responses of the beginning and seasoned teachers. As a group, come to an agreement on what you think are the most salient points from your discussion of the results.

Each group will have two pieces of chart paper to complete for presentation of a "poster session." On one piece of chart paper, use the heading "Beginning Teacher" and on the other piece "Seasoned Teacher." Create a chart on each paper that has the same topic areas as in question 1 above

Record your responses and then post the charts on the wall.

3. Whole Class Task: As a class, engage in a "poster session" that invites everyone to tour the room to read the results from the groups.

4. Individual Task: After the "poster session" tour, write a short individual reflective paper on what you learned from the exercise, identifying what surprised you most.

Teacher's Database

1. Make a list of recent portrayals of teachers in movies, television, and other media. Analyze the portrayals in terms of the type of teacher image they present—positive, neutral, or negative. Some classic movies to consider include:

a. *Dangerous Minds*: portrays someone who dares to teach the "unteachables"

b. *Stand and Deliver*: presents the message that teachers should never believe that students are unable to learn

c. *Lean on Me*: features a principal whose goal is to reform a troubled New York high school

d. *Mr. Holland's Opus*: speaks to the impact a teacher can have on the lives of his students

e. *Dead Poets Society*: portrays an unconventional teacher who motivates his students in a conservative private boys' school

2. Clip articles from a major newspaper that relate to one of the focus questions that appear at the beginning of this chapter. Analyze the clippings as sources of information and examples you can use to develop answers to those questions.

3. On the web, use your favourite search engine and search for information by key words on topics such as teacher burnout, accountability, diverse learners, cyberbullying, and teacher–student ratios.

Observations and Interviews

1. Arrange to observe a teacher's class. During your observation, note how the teacher must make decisions on a moment-by-moment basis as discussed in this chapter.

2. Ask your instructor to arrange group interviews between students in your class and students at local elementary, middle, junior, and senior high schools. At each interview session, ask the students what characterizes accomplished and non-accomplished teachers. Also ask the students what advice they would give to beginning teachers.

Professional Portfolio

To help you in your journey toward becoming a teacher, each chapter in this text-book includes suggestions for developing your professional portfolio, a collection of evidence documenting your growth and development while learning to become a teacher. At the end of this course you will be well on your way toward building a portfolio that documents your knowledge, skills, and attitudes for teaching and contains valuable resources for your first teaching position.

For your first portfolio entry, expand on your Teacher's Journal entry number one, which asks you to consider your reasons for becoming a teacher. In your entry (or videotaped version), identify the rewards of teaching. Identify the satisfactions. Also describe the aspects of teaching you will find challenging.

MyEducationLab

PEARSON
myeducationlab

At www.MyEducationLab.com, access the "Resources" menu. Bookmark key links from within the following sections:

- Canadian Boards of Education
- Canadian Teachers' Organizations
- Canadian Teachers' Federation
- Miscellaneous Canadian Education Links
- Provincial Ministries of Education

These websites will be valuable references for Canadian pre- and in-service teachers who are seeking information on teaching and schools in various parts of the country.

Visit the Managing to Teach tab at www.MyEducationLab.com to browse a virtual learning resource for classroom management based on three cornerstones: prior preparation, establishing constructive expectations, and exhibiting desired modes of behaviour. Options available include:

Module 1: An Introduction to Your Virtual School

Module 2: Developing Constructive Expectations for Learning

Module 3: Preventing and Pre-empting Problems through Careful Planning

Module 4: Positive Personal Interactions by Exhibiting Modes of Behaviour

PEARSON
myeducationlab

2

Learning to Teach

The mediocre teacher tells.
The good teacher explains.
The superior teacher demonstrates.
The great teacher inspires.
—William A. Ward

focus
questions

The room was filled with the chatter of a writing workshop. Nat puzzled over two crayons in his hand, one of them blue. "Mrs. Hankins, ain't you had you a blue bicycle when you was a little-girl teacher?" Nat had a way of naming me for what I was: always a teacher—or was it always a little girl? I answered Nat's question, remembering my past blue bicycle and a childhood story about it that I had shared with my students recently.

Perhaps it was one of those "tell-me-about-when-you-were-little" moments that brought writing memoirs to the forefront of my teaching journal. Perhaps it was the need to make some sense of the cacophonous days with my three special students, Nat, Loretta, and Rodney, who had all been damaged in utero by drugs or alcohol. The impetus for these writings is lost to me now, but, as Lucy Calkins (1991, 169) says, writing memoirs "has everything to do with rendering the ordinariness of our lives so that it becomes significant." The past seemed to wrap itself around my present-day questions, and as the number of memoirs grew, my journal became a place for uncovering the significant. . . .

I wrote up a study of Nat, Loretta, and Rodney's journey through kindergarten and presented parts of the study at a conference. After the presentation, I wrote the following reflection in my journal:

So, I keep this journal. It was easier when no one else knew or cared that I wrote. It's a teaching journal. It's a personal journal. It's a research journal. It's both a personal and teaching journal because John Dewey first and Lucy Calkins later taught me to reflect on my day and my life in the same breath. It's both a teaching and research journal because I no longer believe that teaching can be separated from research. (Perhaps it CAN be but it shouldn't be.) The question is . . . I guess . . . can it be both personal and a research journal? That's what people really want me to defend. But how can I tell people what my heart and head do together in my classroom? (journal entry, April)

I wrote at nap time, while waiting for faculty meetings to begin, during the last 10 minutes before turning out the light each night, and on the backs of church bulletins or napkins in restaurants. I had never heard of field notes at the time. I read recently a definition of ethnographic field notes as "the systematic ways of writing what one observes and learns while participating in the daily rounds of the lives of others" (Emerson, Fretz, and Shaw 1995, 18). As the year progressed, I fell into a system of sorts as I recorded the "lives of others." My journal served, then, as the field notes of a teacher. Mine were records of what Emerson et al. (1995) call "headnotes"—mental notes—"hard notes"—direct observations—and "heartnotes"—my feelings and reflections. . . .

When I began seriously listening to my life, my teaching life, I also began to listen to my students' lives at a different level . . . I became more tolerant of those who were different from me. When I began to stop and examine the flashes of memory that jolted me, I became a more patient teacher. I more often saw the students and their parents as people; people walking in and out of pain, in and out of joy, in and out of socially constructed prisons.

In the preceding excerpt from Karen Hale Hankin's (1998) article, "Cacophony to Symphony: Memoirs in Teacher Research," Hale describes how reflective journal writing enabled her to see significant connections between her personal history and her present experiences in the classroom. By purposely examining her "mental notes," "direct observations," and "feelings and reflections," Hankins learned how to "reach and teach" the students with whom she once felt she had little in common. Her ability to reflect upon her experiences in the classroom and her appreciation for the interconnectedness of teaching and research are the hallmarks of a professional teacher. Furthermore, her reflections are reminders that teaching is a complex act—one that requires thoughtfulness, insight into the motivations of others, and good judgment.

What Essential Knowledge and Skills Do You Need to Be a Teacher?

Just as people hold different expectations for schools and for teachers, there are different views of the knowledge and skills teachers need in order to teach well. In addition to being knowledgeable about the subjects they teach, teachers must have the ability to communicate, to inspire trust and confidence, and to motivate students, as well as to understand their students' educational and emotional needs. Teachers must be able to recognize and respond to individual and cultural differences and to employ different teaching methods that will result in higher student achievement. They should be organized, dependable, patient, creative, and able to present their lessons in an interesting manner that leads to the enhancement of student learning. Teachers must also be able to work cooperatively and communicate effectively with other teachers, support staff, parents, and members of the community.

To respond effectively to the complexities of teaching, you must have four kinds of knowledge: knowledge of yourself and your students, knowledge of subject, knowledge of educational theory and research, and knowledge of how to integrate technology into teaching. The following sections examine these four forms of essential knowledge.

Self-Knowledge

Effective teachers understand themselves and are sensitive to students' needs. "They recognize that the child's personality is a fragile work in progress" (Erickson 2008, 225). Naturally, you should understand your students as much as possible. What is the connection, however, between self-knowledge and the ability to promote student learning? If you understand your own needs (and can satisfy those needs), you are in a better position to help students learn. A teacher's self-understanding and self-acceptance help students to know and to accept themselves.

Your self-evaluations as a teacher are influenced by the feelings you may experience while teaching—feelings that may range from great joy and satisfaction to anxiety or loneliness. Anxiety is a common feeling experienced by teachers who are embarking on a new or more complex teaching strategy.

As a teacher, you will likely experience feelings of happiness, excitement, and wonder as a result of the time you spend with students. You may also experience occasional loneliness or isolation because most of your time will be spent with children and youth rather than with adults. Though teachers are in their classrooms most of the day, today's teachers have the opportunity to collaborate with their colleagues, whether it be serving on a school improvement committee, developing new curricula, or mentoring new teachers.

For more on how to engage students, see Teacher's Resource 2.1: The Teacher's Scribe: "Am I boring you?" located at www.MyEducationLab.com.

Knowledge of Students

Without doubt, knowing your students is important. Knowledge of student characteristics such as aptitudes, talents, learning styles, stages of development, and readiness to learn new material is essential. The importance of this knowledge is evident in comments made by an intern at a middle school: "To teach a kid well you have to know a kid well. . . . Teaching middle school takes a special breed of teachers who understand the unique abilities and inabilities . . . [of] those undergoing their own metamorphosis into teenagers" (Henry et al. 1995, 124–125). In Chapter 5 you will learn about the diverse groups of students who comprise today's school population, and in Chapter 6 you will learn about learners' individual needs. In addition, after you become a teacher, you will expand your knowledge of students through further study, observation, and interactions with them.

Dealing with the Unexpected

Teacher education programs do what they can to prepare students for careers in teaching, but in the end, if graduates have not developed good problem-solving skills, their teaching lives will be lacking in success. When dealing with classroom problems, there are some situations in which time for thoughtful consideration exists; in others, the response time can be as short as a few seconds. The examples that follow posed problems for four student teachers during their practicum (field experience) teaching. After reading each problem, give thought to what you might have done if placed in a similar situation.

Problem 1: Bert is one of the few males who elected to become an elementary teacher. His supervising teacher, Mrs. Swenson, is a veteran teacher within a few years of a well-earned retirement. As they enter the classroom after completing recess playground supervision, they notice a mixed group of their Grade 3 students giggling and laughing as they leaf through a book open before them. Approaching the group, Bert and Mrs. Swenson discover that the students are examining a sex manual with some very explicit pictures. Mrs. Swenson turns to Bert and simply says, "Deal with it."

Problem 2: Nadia is teaching a class of Grade 5 students in a small rural school. She notices that one of her male students, who gives the impression of being both sad and fearful, remains in the classroom during recess and spends most of his noon hours in the library, which is supervised by a teacher aide. Careful inquiries of other students convince her that the student is being bullied, but no one will say by whom.

Knowledge of Subject

Teachers are assumed to have extensive knowledge. People who are not teachers expect a teacher to have knowledge far beyond their own. Without doubt, teachers who have extensive knowledge of their subjects are better equipped to help students learn.

However, extensive knowledge of subject matter entails more than being able to recite dates, multiplication tables, or rules of grammar. Accomplished teachers possess what is sometimes called **pedagogical content knowledge**. Such understanding is the joint product of wisdom about teaching, learning, students, and content. It includes knowledge of the most appropriate ways to present the subject matter to students through analogies, metaphors, experiments, demonstrations, and illustrations.

For a debate on the relative merits of content knowledge versus professional knowledge, go to Teacher's Resource 2.2: Where Do You Stand?, located at www.MyEducationLab.com.

PEARSON
myeducationlab

Attempting to be helpful, Nadia and her supervising teacher speak with the student regarding the suspicion, but he denies that that is the case. With her supervising teacher's permission, Nadia contacts the boy's single parent regarding the situation. The parent's response is that her son "has to learn to stick up for himself."

Problem 3: Isaac is teaching mathematics to a class of Grade 9 students. Molly, who is seated at the back of the room, is whispering to her best friend, Carol, who sits directly in front of her. Isaac politely asks her to stop talking. She stops but appears distracted and keeps her head down except for furtive, upward glances towards Isaac. After a short period, Molly is again whispering to her friend. Again, she is asked to cease talking and pay attention. After several repeats of this situation, Isaac walks toward Molly and notices her hiding her cell phone. Molly has apparently been texting and giving Carol regular updates online instead. Given that in-class use of cell phones is explicitly forbidden by school rules, Isaac says confidently, "Molly, you've been texting. Please give me your phone." Molly replies that she was not texting and refuses to hand over her phone.

Problem 4: Amy is an attractive individual who looks younger than her actual age of 23. As part of her field experience assignment, she is teaching Canadian history to a class of academic stream Grade 12 students. One of her students is particularly enthusiastic in his response to her teaching and often lingers after class to discuss various points from her lessons. Two weeks into her practicum, she receives a telephone call from the student asking for advice regarding a project required for another course he is taking. Quite unsuspecting, and rather flattered that a student had asked for her assistance, Amy agrees to help and says she will meet with the student after school the following day. During the meeting the student volunteers that he is "very attracted" to her and asks her out on a date. He also mentions that everyone in the class is aware of his affection for her.

Knowledge of Methods for Applying Educational Theory and Research

Theories about learners and learning will guide your decision making as a teacher. Not only will you know that a certain strategy works, you will also know why it works. Because you realize the importance of theories, you will have a greater range of available options for problem solving than teachers who do not have such a repertoire. Your ultimate goal as a professional is to learn how to apply theoretical knowledge to the practical problems of teaching.

Research on students' learning does not set forth, in cookbook fashion, exactly what you should do to increase it. Instead, it may be helpful to think of educational research as providing you with "rules of thumb" to guide your practice, or, to recall a comment by noted educational psychologist Lee Cronbach (quoted in Eisner 1998, 112), "Educational [research] is to help practitioners use their heads."

Educational researchers are still learning what good teachers know and how they use that knowledge. As a result, many people believe that a **knowledge base** for

What kinds of knowledge and skills do teachers need to do their jobs well?

teaching should consist of not only what educational researchers have learned about teaching but also what teachers themselves know about teaching—often called **teachers' craft knowledge** or practitioner knowledge (Hiebert, Gallimore, & Stigler 2002; Kennedy 1999; Leinhardt 1990). **Teachers' craft knowledge** is developed by teachers in response to specific problems of practice.

Knowledge of How to Integrate Technology into Teaching

As a teacher, you will be expected to know how to integrate technology into your teaching. And throughout your teaching career, you will be expected to be familiar with newly emerging technologies and how they can be used in the classroom.

Using technology to enhance students' learning requires more than knowing how to use the latest hardware and software. Conducting classroom demonstrations augmented with multimedia, using presentation graphics to address students' varied learning styles, and designing lessons that require students to use technology as a tool for inquiry should be second nature for teachers.

Knowledge of how to integrate technology into teaching is essential for today's teachers. Consider taking the following steps to remain technologically up to date. Learn all you can about:

- Software, web courses, virtual learning, and other technology-based learning solutions that are aligned to setting standards, to strengthening basic skills, and to increasing student achievement.
- Digital tools, which are used to broaden and strengthen learning and teaching through authenticity, real-world problem solving, critical thinking, communication, and production for students; and support through online courses, communities of practice, and virtual communication.
- Real-time information that can assist you in making sound instructional decisions.

Reflection and Problem Solving

The preceding discussion of essential knowledge and skills for teaching highlights the fact that teaching is complex and demanding. As you use your knowledge and skills to meet the challenges of teaching, you will be guided by reflection and an orientation toward problem-solving. As Figure 2.1 shows, reflection and problem solving will enable you to determine how to use knowledge of self and students (including cultural differences), knowledge of subject matter, knowledge of educational theory and research, and knowledge of how to integrate technology into teaching to create optimum conditions for student learning. The figure also shows that you can use reflection and problem solving to decide which essential skills to use and how to use them.

Canadian Researcher: Dr. Gregory MacKinnon
University: Acadia University, School of Education
Teaching Specialties: Science and Technology

Technology in Education: Problems, Potentials, Unknown Possibilities

Technology is often defined as "a way of adapting"—a problem-solving process that presumes that humans want to better their lives by using more efficient tools to serve their daily needs. In turn, because improved "life conditions" are central to human existence, technological improvements have become increasingly pervasive throughout society. Everywhere we look we see new technologies that assist in solving both new and old problems. Interestingly, Dr. David Suzuki has often said that as humans we prefer not to reverse technology. In other words, we would rather fix, or adapt, older technologies to respond to new problems than step backward and abandon them entirely.

Technology has an almost insidious way of inserting itself into our lives, a situation that makes it crucial for educators to be critical of, and to teach the critical assessment of, new technologies when they may impact the educational process. To achieve both these goals is a challenging task. Today's students are technologically savvy; they are the "net generation" (Dobbins 2005) that has arisen with the multitude of technologies that have changed the very social fabric of their culture. While communications technologies have arguably had the greatest influence (consider the preponderance of specialized telephones), others, such as portable computers, global positioning systems, and musical storage devices, have also exerted their influence—and newer technologies emerge almost daily. Some researchers are beginning to argue that with the host of co-existing technologies available, students have developed new learning capacities.

Education technology researchers, such as Harvard's Chris Dede, posit that the "millennial" student (Howe & Strauss 2000) represents a distinctly different type of learner—a student who is able to multitask with technologies and to absorb and construct knowledge and understanding in unique ways (Dede 2005). The question for us as educators thus becomes: How do we respond to students with this inherently different set of digital literacies? (Dede, Dieterle, Clarke, Ketelhut & Nelson 2007)

Some argue that present public school curricula represent an abysmal failure to respond to the needs of the net generation. Collins and Halverson (2009) astutely present a challenge to educators that schools should now offer "just-in-case learning," while letting technology foster "just-in-time learning" (48). Much of what we presently teach students has the end purpose of preparing them for the next level of education, whereas what technology potentially affords is the access to, and application of, knowledge of real and current problems. Consider, for instance, the exponential increase in the knowledge available to students through information technologies. It is obvious that computers and satellites have given the nontraditional student access to education as never before. The number of online courses and degree programs available continues to grow as education becomes—unfortunately, some might say—increasingly commodified. Access technologies have moved the classroom from learning "communities of place to communities of interest" (Collins & Halverson 2009: 11). However, beyond simple access issues, the real question becomes: How is the nature of learning changing with technological advancements?

Progress with Second–Order Technology Applications

Jonassen (2000) introduced the concept of using computer technologies as educational mindtools—unique, and sometimes subversive, strategies for using software, strategies that represent a second-order use of technologies (Maddux & Johnson 2006). An example is the electronic encoding of discussion groups (MacKinnon & Aylward 2000). While online discussions are useful synchronous and asynchronous tools, the teacher's assignment of cognitive cuing icons can promote more substantive debate. For instance, consider a model where students participate in an online discussion. The teacher captures the text of the discussion and then assigns graphical icons to individual passages that cue students to consider the quality of their argumentation patterns.

In many cases, while communication technologies may be useful for their intended first-order interactions between students, the nature of this communication within a more complex classroom framework may promote new skills and understandings. Consider a classroom where multiple types of communications are happening between teacher and students via presentation software, e-mail, Internet searches, and webcasting. The potential for unique types of learning is enormous (MacKinnon & Vibert 2002; 2004).

Dede (2005) has conducted extensive research around the use of avatars and virtual worlds in an effort to extend the spectator perspective of students in traditional classrooms to the "player role" by situating them in authentic problem-solving—albeit virtual—worlds. These exercises capitalize on students' desire to learn collaboratively with current technologies. Knowledge building in virtual communities has also been the life work of Canadian researchers Scardemalia and Bereiter (1994; 2003), who have promoted the interaction of diverse and distance learners within the framework of productive constructivist learning.

With the advent of electronic tools, concept mapping has enjoyed a resurgence of use in many Canadian schools. Concept maps (Novak & Gowin 1984) quite simply allow students to articulate, in a graphical manner, their "mind map." While this has many content applications, it has the more important potential of promoting critical thinking and metacognitive learning strategies (MacKinnon 2006).

Teachers are faced with new technology tools of great potential everyday. It is incumbent upon educators to explore such tools as GPS, tablets, probes, handheld devices, etc., in an effort to find unique ways to empower education so that today's children use today's technology to extend both teaching and learning potential.

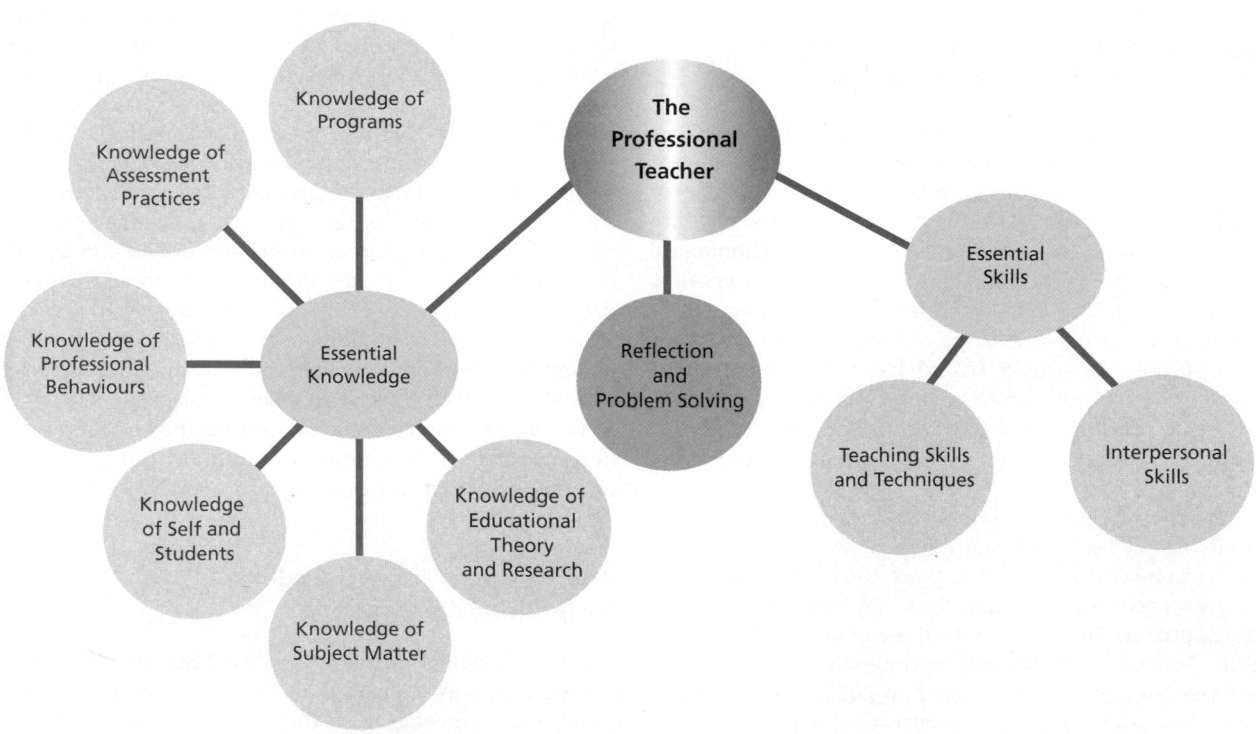

Figure 2.1

Essential knowledge and skills for the professional teacher

What Are Five Ways of Viewing the Teacher Knowledge Base?

Just as people hold different expectations for schools and teachers, there are different views on the knowledge and abilities teachers need in order to teach well. The complexities of teaching make it difficult to describe in exact detail the knowledge base on which teaching as a profession rests. This difficulty results, in part, because there is no universally accepted definition of what good teaching is. Educational researchers are still learning what good teachers know and how they use that knowledge.

A Personal Development View

One view of what teachers need to know and to be able to do places primary emphasis on who the teacher is as a person. According to this view, teachers should be concerned with developing themselves as people so that they may learn to use their insights more effectively. The importance of personal development is described as follows by the authors of On Being a Teacher: "[t]eachers who appear in charge of their own lives, who radiate power, tranquility, and grace in their actions, are going to command attention and respect. People will follow them anywhere. . . . What we are saying is that you have not only the option, but also the imperative, to develop the personal dimensions of your functioning, as well as your professional skills" (Zehm & Kottler 1993, 15).

What this approach requires, then, is that teachers continually develop their powers of observation and reflection so that they can most effectively respond to the needs of students. Teaching becomes an authentic, growth-oriented encounter between teacher and students. An important dimension of this **personal development view** is the teacher's need for self-knowledge, particularly in regard to the self as a learner.

Research-Based Competencies

Since the late 1980s, most provinces, or the school districts within them, have developed their own lists of **research-based competencies** that beginning teachers must demonstrate. These competencies are derived from educational research that has identified what effective teachers do. Typically, many provinces have behavioural indicators for each competency, which trained observers use to determine to what extent teachers actually exhibit target behaviours in the classroom. Teachers are required to demonstrate effective pedagogical behaviours in a number of domains: planning and preparation, effective classroom management, control of student conduct, instructional organization and development, presentation of subject matter, verbal and nonverbal communication, and testing (student preparation, administration, and feedback).

Provincial Standards

In addition to sets of research-based competencies for evaluating practicing teachers, some provinces have developed performance-based standards for what new teachers should know and should be able to do. Known as **outcome-based** or **performance-based teacher education**, the new approach is based on several assumptions:

- Outcomes are demonstrations of learning rather than a list of teaching specializations, college courses completed, or concepts studied.

- Outcomes are performances that reflect the richness and complexity of the teacher's role in today's classrooms—not discrete, single behaviours.
- Demonstrations of learning must occur in authentic settings—that is, settings similar to those within which the teacher will teach.
- Outcomes are culminating demonstrations of what beginning teachers do in real classrooms.

Typically, outcome-based standards are developed with input from teachers, teacher educators, provincial departments of education personnel, and various professional associations. However, outcome-based standards are not without their critics. Sharp criticism of the Atlantic Provinces Education Foundation (APEF) outcomes-based curriculum (see Teacher's Resource 2.3 at www.MyEducationLab.com) is articulated by Dr. David MacKinnon, author of A Wolf in Sheep's Clothing: The Erosion of Democracy in Education (Portelli & Solomon 2001, 136):

> [A]n outcomes-based approach to education provides an inadequate foundation for public education. Behavioral outcomes, by definition, are confined to that which is observable and measurable . . . [P]rojects like the APEF initiative are necessarily incomplete and, perhaps, unwittingly misguided . . . [T]he APEF initiative is a reductionist and anti-democratic exercise at increasing system accountability.

A Job-Analysis Approach

Another view of what teachers need to know and to be able to do is based on the job analyses conducted by some school districts. Typically, a **job analysis** begins with a review of existing job descriptions and then proceeds to interviews with those currently assigned to the job and their supervisors regarding the activities and responsibilities associated with the job. These data are then analyzed to identify the dimensions of the job. Finally, interview questions based on those dimensions are developed and used by district personnel responsible for hiring.

The following excerpt from a study by the Urban Network to Improve Teacher Education (UNITE), an organization comprised of both Canadian and American universities, illustrates the knowledge, skills, and attitudes needed by successful urban teachers.

> Twenty-two teachers and five administrators were involved in focus group interviews conducted during the study. Over half of the 27 participants have been working in the field of education for less than five years, although four have been teaching in their present school for over 15 years. On average, the participants graduated from a faculty of education 11 years ago. The teachers interviewed represented all grade levels, from Kindergarten to senior secondary, and represented a variety of subject areas and roles within a school community (e.g., physical education, visual arts, resource teacher, special education teacher). All but one of the participants received their preservice education in the province of Ontario.

> *Characteristics of a Successful Urban Teacher*

> Eight characteristics were identified in all focus group interviews as being important for teachers to possess in order to be successful in an urban school. These eight characteristics are discussed in order of the degree of emphasis placed on them by the focus group participants.

> *Empathy*—Because most teachers never experience many of the traumas and issues that their students deal with on a daily basis, they strongly believed that teachers in urban schools need to be empathetic. They mentioned the importance of "not placing your morals, judgments and values on the students and parents,"

and "making greater attempts at trying to understand the different cultures and religions."

Respect for the students—Teachers need to respect students and to operate on the belief that all students have the right to learn, and to achieve success. Participants stated that teachers in urban schools should not compromise expectations and that they should "believe that all students have a future."

Flexibility—Teachers in urban schools need to be flexible. Teachers reported that this flexibility was necessary when dealing with such things as curriculum guidelines, programming, evaluation, classroom disruptions, and student behaviour. One teacher stated, "You set up a wonderful day, and then it isn't working, and you have to step back and reassess. It's constant."

Self-care—In order to be a successful teacher in an urban school, participants stressed the need for caring for their personal needs. Since urban schools "really challenge you, you have to make sure you take care of the whole you, emotionally, physically, personally, and manage your stress. You have to find the balance."

Patience—Teachers in urban schools need to be patient. Dealing with the diverse population of students, and all of the other challenges previously mentioned, the need for "infinite patience" was believed to be necessary in order to be successful as a teacher in an urban school.

Sense of humour—Participants in the focus group interviews strongly believed that in order to be a successful teacher in an urban school one must possess a sense of humour. One teacher described this need in connection with self-care, stating, "If you don't have the ability to laugh, you run the risk of becoming emotionally drained."

Collegiality—Another important characteristic for teachers in urban schools is collegiality and peer support. Participants described the need, in urban schools, for staff to work together, to "share their ups and downs," to share their resources, and to be there to support one another.

High energy level—In order to deal with the plethora of daily challenges facing urban school teachers, interview participants stated that these teachers need to have high energy levels. A number of participants extended this characteristic to include a willingness "to make the commitment of time, energy and effort it takes to work in a school like this."

Source: UNITE article reprinted with permission from Patricia J. Rawson Wheeler. Retrieved November 1, 2003 from www.umanitoba.ca/publications/cjeap/issue1/issue6.htm.

Professional Views

While there are differing opinions regarding what teachers should be able to do, it seems evident that becoming a teacher is complex and demanding. Most Canadian school districts have policies that detail the essential skills and responsibilities of the teachers they employ (see Figure 2.2). While details vary from one jurisdiction to another, the following topics are common to most:

- A well-organized learning environment with appropriate learning resources for students. (For suggestions regarding how to make your lessons more interesting, go to www.MyEducationLab.com, Chapter 2 Teacher's Resource: The Teacher's Scribe—"Am I boring you?")
- Interesting and effective teaching skills appropriate to the age and abilities of students
- Effective classroom management and discipline skills

PEARSON
myeducationlab

Directions: As you observe, note the ways that students are motivated intrinsically (from within) and extrinsically (from factors outside themselves).

Intrinsic Motivation	Extrinsic Motivation
What things seem to interest students at this age?	How do teachers show their approval to students?
Which activities and assignments seem to give them a sense of pride?	What phrases do teachers use in their praise?
When do they seem to be confused? Bored? Frustrated?	What types of rewards do teachers give (e.g., grades, points, tangible rewards)?
What topics do they talk about with enthusiasm?	What reward programs do you notice (e.g., points accumulated toward free time)?
In class discussions, when are they most alert and participating most actively?	What warnings do teachers give?
What seems to please, amuse, entertain, or excite them?	What punishments are given to students?
What do they joke about? What do they find humorous?	How do teachers arouse concern in their students?
	How do students motivate other students?
What do they report as being their favourite subjects? Favourite assignments?	What forms of peer pressure do you observe?
What do they report as being their least favourite subjects and assignments?	How do teachers promote enthusiasm for an assignment?
	How do teachers promote class spirit?
How do they respond to personalized lessons (e.g., using their names in exercises)?	How do teachers catch their students' interest in the first few minutes of a lesson?
How do they respond to activity-oriented lessons (e.g., fieldwork, project periods)?	Which type of question draws more answers—recall or open-ended?
How do they respond to assignments calling for presentations to groups outside the classroom (e.g., parents, another class, the chamber of commerce)?	How do teachers involve quiet students in class discussions?
	How do teachers involve inactive students in their work?
How do they respond to being given a choice in assignments?	In what ways do teachers give recognition to students' accomplishments?

Figure 2.2

Guiding questions for observing motivation

- Positive interactions with teachers, other school personnel, parents, and members of the greater school community
- Fair and effective assessment practices
- Strict adherence to local board policies and provincial or territorial curriculum guidelines

For a list of best teaching practices, you might visit the Indianapolis Public Schools' website: www.curriculumresources.ips.k12.in.us. "Sites that Help Classroom Teachers," at www.internet4classrooms.com/teacher.htm, is another excellent resource.

How Are Canadian Teachers Educated and Certified?

Because education is a provincial rather than a federal responsibility, each province is free to elect its preferred method for educating those intent on pursuing careers as professional teachers. The result is a patchwork quilt of Bachelor of Education programs, each with its own specific admission requirements, and each with its own particular curriculum.

Additionally, while the academic body bestows the Bachelor of Education degree on its graduates, each province and territory has a teacher certification body that establishes the requirements that must be met before a teaching licence will be awarded. In some provinces, such as Newfoundland and Labrador and Nova Scotia, the certifying agency is each province's department of education. However, in other jurisdictions, such as British Columbia and Ontario, independent agencies such as the British Columbia College of Teachers and the Ontario College of Teachers are responsible for teacher certification.

In Manitoba, Alberta, and Ontario, teacher associations negotiate their contracts at the regional or local level. In all other provinces and territories, the negotiations are conducted between the teachers' associations and departments of education personnel. Salary scales are quite variable. Canadian teacher salaries are determined by two major factors: years of post-secondary education and years of teaching experience. Depending on the exact combination, and the province or territory in which one is teaching, teacher annual salaries can range from $45 000 to $85 000. Administrators, such as department heads and school principals, receive further allowances in addition to their basic teacher salaries. The highest rates of teacher pay are offered by the Yukon, Nunavut, and the Northwest Territories.

Canadian Schools of Education: A Variety of Models

Concurrent Program

Students enrol in a Bachelor degree and take regular academic courses and education courses at the same time. Most such programs are four years in duration and provide their graduates with the least expensive route to a teaching degree. However, the majority of students in concurrent programs must decide at a very early stage in their lives that teaching is their chosen profession.

Eight-Month Post-Degree Program

This is by far the most common model. Applicants for admission to a school of education first obtain a three- or four-year undergraduate degree that contains the appropriate academic prerequisites as established by the university or department of education. Successful applicants then take a specified number of courses designed to assist them with their teaching practice. As part of their program, they also spend a designated amount of time—usually five to eight weeks—working with associate teachers in the field. Critics of eight-month programs argue that this format does not provide sufficient time for student teachers to learn all of the things necessary for them to be truly effective educators. In addition, provinces with more comprehensive Bachelor of Education programs will sometimes decline to grant teaching licences to those who have graduated from such programs.

Twelve-Month Post-Degree Programs

There are relatively few 12-month Bachelor of Education programs available in Canada. Twelve-month programs have more coursework for students to complete and provide more time for fieldwork in classrooms. They are also more expensive for students, but as they are completed within an extended academic year, graduates can be employed as teachers in September of the year in which they graduate.

Two-Year Post-Degree Programs

At present, only Nova Scotia and Prince Edward Island have two-year post-degree Bachelor of Education programs. Applicants to these programs first obtain a three-year or four-year undergraduate degree, and then complete two academic years of educational studies in combination with 20 or more weeks of field experience. Some colleges and universities also offer two or more of the models described above. Hyperlinks to all of Canada's teacher education programs can be found at www.oise.utoronto.ca/oise.

What Can You Learn from Observing in Classrooms?

Classroom observations are a vital element of many **field experiences**. Students report that these experiences aid them greatly in making a final decision about entering the teaching field. Most become more enthusiastic about teaching and more motivated to learn the needed skills, although a few decide that teaching is not for them. Recognizing the value of observations, many teacher education programs are increasing the amount of field experience required and scheduling such fieldwork earlier in students' programs.

Focused Observations

Observations are more meaningful when they are focused and conducted with clear purpose. Observers may focus on the students, on the teacher, on the interactions between the two, on the structure of the lesson, or on the setting. More specifically, for example, observers may note differences between the ways boys and girls or members of different ethnic groups communicate and behave in the classroom. They may note student interests and ability levels, study student responses to a particular teaching strategy, or analyze the question and response patterns in a class discussion.

Observations may also be guided by sets of questions related to specific areas. For instance, since beginning teachers are frequently frustrated by their lack of success in interesting their students in learning, asking questions specifically related to motivation can make an observation more meaningful and instructive. Similar questions can be generated for other focus areas such as classroom management, student involvement, questioning skills, evaluation, and teacher–student rapport.

Observation Instruments

A wide range of methods can be used to conduct classroom observations, ranging from informal, qualitative descriptions to formal, quantitative checklists. With reform efforts to improve education in Canada has come the development of instruments to facilitate the evaluation of teacher performance, a task now widely required of school administrators. Students preparing to teach can benefit by using these evaluative instruments in their observations.

All teachers, including student teachers, are subject to both formal and informal observations and evaluations. To give you some idea about how you may come to be evaluated for your instructional skills, an actual evaluation of a first-term student teacher's very first formative (preliminary) evaluation is included in Teacher's Resource 2.4 at www.MyEducationLab.com. When reading this report, ask yourself if you might commit any of the errors noted by the associate teacher.

How Can You Gain Practical Experience for Becoming a Teacher?

A primary aim of teacher education programs is to give students opportunities to experience, to the extent possible, the real world of the teacher. Through field experiences and carefully structured experiential activities, preservice teachers are given limited exposure to various aspects of teaching. Observing, tutoring, instructing small groups, analyzing video cases, operating instructional media, performing student teaching, and completing various non-instructional tasks are among the most common experiential activities.

Classroom Experiences

Because of the need to provide opportunities to put theory into practice before student teaching, many teacher education programs enable students to participate in microteaching, teaching simulations, analyses of video cases, field-based practica and clinical experiences, and classroom aide programs.

Microteaching

Introduced in the 1960s, **microteaching** was received enthusiastically and remains a popular practice. The process calls for students to teach brief, single-concept lessons to a small group (5 to 10 students) while concurrently practicing a specific teaching skill, such as positive reinforcement. Often the microteaching is recorded for later study.

As originally developed, microteaching includes the following six steps:

1. Identify a specific teaching skill to learn about and practice.
2. Read about the skill in one of several pamphlets.
3. Observe a master teacher demonstrate the skill in a short movie or on video.
4. Prepare a three- to five-minute lesson to demonstrate the skill.
5. Teach the lesson, which is recorded, to a small group of peers.
6. Critique, along with the instructor and student peers, the recorded lesson.

Simulations

As an element of teacher training, **teaching simulations** provide opportunities for vicarious practice of a wide range of teaching skills. In simulations, students analyze teaching situations that are presented in writing, on audio recordings, in short films, or on video. Typically, students are given background information about a hypothetical school or classroom and the pupils they must prepare to teach. After this orientation, students role-play the student teacher or the teacher who is confronted with the problem situation. Following the simulation, participants discuss the appropriateness of solutions and work to increase their problem-solving skills and their understanding of the teacher's multifaceted role as a decision maker. Additionally, recent technological advances now make computer-based simulations available for use in faculty of education programs.

Video Cases

Teacher education students who view, analyze, and then write about video cases have an additional opportunity to appreciate the ambiguities and complexities of real-life classrooms, to learn that "there are no clear-cut, simple answers to the complex issues teachers face" (Wasserman 1994, 606). Viewing authentic video cases enables students to see how "teaching tradeoffs and dilemmas emerge in the video 'text' as do the strategies teachers use, the frustrations they experience, the brilliant and less-brilliant decisions they make" (Grant, Richard, & Parkay 1996, 5).

Practica

A **practicum** is a short-term field-based experience (usually about two weeks long) that allows teacher education students to spend time observing and assisting in classrooms. Though practica vary in length and purpose, students are often able to begin instructional work with individuals or small groups. For example, a cooperating teacher may allow a practicum student to tutor a small group of students, read a story to the whole class, conduct a spelling lesson, monitor recess, help students with their homework, or teach students a song or game.

Classroom Assistants

Serving as a teacher assistant is another popular means of providing field experience before student teaching. A teacher assistant's role depends primarily on the unique needs of the school and its students. Generally, assistants work under the supervision of a certified teacher and perform duties that support the teacher's instruction. Assisting teachers in classrooms familiarizes teacher education students with class schedules, record-keeping procedures, and students' performance levels, and provides ample opportunity for observation. In exchange, the classroom teacher receives much-needed assistance.

Student Teaching

The most extensive and memorable field experience in teacher preparation programs is the period of student teaching. As The Student Teacher's Handbook points out, student teaching "is the only time in a teaching career that one is an apprentice under the close guidance of an experienced mentor" (Schwebel et al. 1996, 4). Depending on the province, Bachelor of Education students may be required to have as few as five weeks of student teaching or, as in Nova Scotia, as many as 15 weeks before being certified as teachers. The nature of student teaching varies considerably among teacher education programs. Typically, a student is assigned to a cooperating (or master) teacher in the school, and a university supervisor makes periodic visits to observe the student teacher. Some programs even pay student teachers during the student teaching experience.

All schools of education recognize the importance of preparing their students for life as a professional teacher. While the methods by which they do this vary from one school to another, Teacher's Resource 2.5 and Teacher's Resource 2.6 (at www.MyEducationLab.com) present a set of guidelines that students are expected to follow while within a school of education, while conducting field work in an associate school, and later when employed by a provincial or territorial school district.

Student teaching is a time of responsibility. As one student teacher put it, "I don't want to mess up [my students'] education!" It is also an opportunity for growth and a

PEARSON
myeducationlab)

What strategies can you use to make your student teaching experience truly valuable? In what sense will you remain a student teacher throughout your career?

chance to master critical skills. Time is devoted to observing, participating in classroom activities, and actively teaching. The amount of time one actually spends teaching, however, is not as important as one's willingness to reflect carefully on the student teaching experience. Two excellent ways to promote reflection during student teaching are journal writing and maintaining a reflective teaching log.

Student Teacher Journal Writing

Many supervisors require student teachers to keep a journal of their classroom experiences so that they can engage in reflective teaching and can begin the process of criticizing and guiding themselves. The following two entries—the first written by a student teacher in a Grade 4 classroom, the second by a student teacher in a high school English class—illustrate how journal writing can help student teachers develop strategies for dealing with the realities of teaching.

> Today I taught a geography lesson and the kids seemed so bored. I called on individuals to read the social studies text, and then I explained it. Some of them really struggled with the text. Mr. H. said I was spoon-feeding them too much. So tomorrow I am going to put them into groups and let them answer questions together rather than give them the answers. This ought to involve the students in the learning a bit more and enable some of the better readers to help out those who have difficulty, without the whole class watching. I feel bad when I see those glazed looks on their faces. I need to learn how to be more interesting. (Pitton 1998, 120)

> I had good feedback on small groups in their responses to questions on *Of Mice and Men*. They were to find a paragraph that might indicate theme and find two examples of foreshadowing. We found five!

> The short story unit was awful during fourth hour. The kids just didn't respond. I quickly revamped my approach for the next hour. Fifth hour did seem to go better. (Mostly though, I think it was just that I was more prepared, having had

one class to try things out.) I can see how experience really helps. Now that I've tried the story "The Tiger or the Lady," I would use the same material, but I would know HOW to use it more effectively! (Pitton 1998, 143)

Relatively unstructured, open-ended journals, such as the ones from which these entries were selected, provide student teachers with a medium for subjectively exploring the student teaching experience.

Reflective Teaching Logs

To promote the practice of reflecting more analytically, some supervisors ask their student teachers to use a more directed and structured form of journal keeping, the **reflective teaching log**. In this form, a student lists and briefly describes the daily sequence of activities, selects a single episode to expand on, analyzes the reason for selecting it and what was learned from it, and considers the possible future application of that knowledge.

Though student teaching will be the capstone experience of your teacher education program, the experience should be regarded as an initial rather than a terminal learning opportunity—your first chance to engage in reflection and self-evaluation for a prolonged period.

To illustrate a reflective teaching log, a partial entry for one episode follows. The entry shows how a college student can disagree with a supervising teacher's response to a classroom situation.

Log for December 1—Erin Tompkins

Sequence of Events

1. Arrival—end of eighth period

2. Ninth period—helped Sharad study science

3. After-school program—worked on science with Ricki, P.K., and Tom

4. Late bus duty with Ms. Soto

5. Departure

Episode: I was helping Ricki and P.K. fill out a table about the location and function of the different cell parts. P.K. asked me a question and two other students laughed at him. I began to answer his question when Ms. Soto came over to the table where we were working and yelled at P.K. She said, "P.K. I don't need you distracting other students who are trying to get their work done." He started to tell her what he asked me and she said, "I don't care. You can leave the room if you don't knock it off. Just do your work and be quiet or you're out!" She then apologized to me and went back to helping another student.

Analysis: I was very frustrated after this episode. This is the first time I've seen Ms. Soto raise her voice with a student and accuse him of causing problems when he was getting his work done and other students were being disruptive. P.K. had asked me a legitimate question; the other students who laughed at him were the problem. I was frustrated because Ricki and P.K. were working hard and asking me good questions. I was annoyed that P.K. was being reprimanded for asking a question that was relevant to the topic we were working on. I also felt helpless because I wanted to tell Ms. Soto that it wasn't P.K. who was the problem. I didn't feel it was my place to correct her in front of her students and kept quiet. I decided that my saying something would only make things worse because it would encourage P.K. to continue arguing with Ms. Soto and he would be in more trouble. (Posner 2003, 122)

Gaining Experience in Multicultural Settings

Canadian schools will enrol increasing numbers of students from diverse cultural backgrounds during the twenty-first century. As this trend continues, it is vitally important that those entering the teaching profession achieve an understanding of children's differing backgrounds. As a result, many teacher education programs now have courses that deal with equity issues to help prepare student teachers for the diversity that exists in almost every classroom.

As a teacher you can be assured that you will teach students from backgrounds that differ from your own—including students from the more than 100 racial and ethnic groups in Canada, and students who are poor, are gifted, or have disabilities. You will have the challenge of reaching out to all students and teaching them that they are persons of worth and that they can learn. You will also be confronted with the difficult challenge of being sensitive to differences among students, while at the same time treating all equally and fairly. To prepare for these realities of teaching, you should make every effort to gain experiences in multicultural settings.

Supply Teaching

On completion of a teacher education program and prior to securing a full-time teaching assignment, many students choose to gain additional practical experience in classrooms by **supply teaching** or **substitute teaching**. Others, unable to locate full-time positions, decide to supply, knowing that many districts prefer to hire from their pool of supply teachers when full-time positions become available. Supply teachers replace regular teachers who are absent due to illness, family responsibilities, personal reasons, or professional workshops and conferences.

Each day, thousands of supply teachers are employed in schools across Canada. For example, during one school year at the 15 high schools in a large urban district, the total number of absences for 1200 regular teachers equalled 14 229 days. Multiplying this figure by five (the number of classes per day for most high school teachers) yields 71 145 class periods taught by supply teachers in one school year.

Qualifications for supply teachers vary from province to province. An area with a critical need for supply teachers will often relax its requirements to provide classroom coverage. In many districts, it is possible to supply without regular certification if no fully certified teacher can be located. Some districts have less stringent qualifications for short-term, day-to-day supply teachers and more stringent ones for long-term, full-time assignments. In many districts, the application process for supply teachers is the same as that for full-time applicants; in others, the process may be somewhat briefer. Often, supply teachers are not limited to working in their area of certification; however, schools try to avoid making out-of-field assignments. If you decide to supply teach, contact the schools in your area to learn about the qualifications and procedures for hiring supply teachers.

In spite of the significant role supply teachers play in the day-to-day operation of schools, "research tells us that they receive very little support, no specialized training, and are rarely evaluated. . . . In short, the substitute will be expected to show up to each class on time, maintain order, take roll, carry out the lesson, and leave a note for the regular teacher about the classes and events of the day without support, encouragement, or acknowledgement" (St. Michel 1995, 6–7). While working conditions such as these are certainly challenging, supplying can be a rewarding, professionally fulfilling experience. Figure 2.3 presents several advantages and disadvantages of supplying.

Figure 2.3

Advantages and disadvantages of supplying

Source: John F. Snyder, "The Alternative of Substitute Teaching." In *1999 Job Search Handbook for Educators*. Evanston, IL: American Association for Employment in Education, p. 38.

Advantages and Disadvantages of Supply Teaching

Advantages
- Gain experience without all the nightly work and preparation
- Compare and contrast different schools and their environments
- Be better prepared for interviews by meeting administrators and teachers
- Teach and learn a variety of material
- Get to know people—network
- See job postings and hear about possible vacancies
- Gain confidence in your abilities to teach
- Practice classroom management techniques
- Learn about school and district politics—get the "inside scoop"
- Choose which days to work—flexible schedule

Disadvantages
- Pay is not as good as full-time teaching
- No benefits such as medical coverage, retirement plans, or sick days
- Lack of organized representation to improve wages or working conditions
- May receive a cool reception in some schools
- Must adapt quickly to different school philosophies
- Lack of continuity—may be teaching whole language one day; phonetics the next

How Can You Develop Your Teaching Portfolio?

Now that you have begun your journey toward becoming a teacher, you should acquire the habit of assessing your growth in knowledge, skills, and attitudes. Toward this end, you may wish to collect the results of your reflections and self-assessment in a **professional portfolio**. A professional portfolio is a collection of work that documents an individual's accomplishments in an area of professional practice. An artist's portfolio, for example, might consist of a résumé, sketches, paintings, slides and photographs of exhibits, critiques of the artist's work, awards, and other documentation of achievement. Recently, new approaches to teacher evaluation have included a professional portfolio. Teacher education programs at several universities now use portfolios as one means of assessing the competencies of candidates for teacher certification.

Portfolio Contents

What will your portfolio contain? Written materials might include the following: lesson plans and curriculum materials, reflections on your development as a teacher, journal entries, writing assignments given by your instructor, sample tests you have prepared, critiques of textbooks, evaluations of students' work at the level for which you are preparing to teach, sample letters to parents, and a résumé. Non-print materials might include video and audio recordings featuring you in simulated teaching and role-playing activities, audiovisual materials (transparencies, charts, or other teaching

What questions might you ask a mentor teacher that might help you develop as a professional?

aids), photographs of bulletin boards, charts depicting room arrangements for cooperative learning or other instructional strategies, sample grade book, certificates of membership in professional organizations, and awards.

Your portfolio should represent your best work and give you an opportunity to become an advocate of who you are as a teacher. Because a primary purpose of the professional portfolio is to stimulate reflection and dialogue, you may wish to discuss what entries to make in your portfolio with your instructor or other teacher education students. In addition, the following questions from How to Develop a Professional Portfolio: A Manual for Teachers (Campbell, Melenyzer, Nettles, & Wyman 2003, 5) can help you select appropriate portfolio contents:

> Would I be proud to have my future employer and peer group see this? Is this an example of what my future professional work might look like? Does this represent what I stand for as a professional educator? If not, what can I revise or rearrange so that it represents my best efforts?

Using a Portfolio

In addition to providing teacher education programs with a way to assess their effectiveness, portfolios can be used by students for a variety of purposes. A portfolio can be used as:

1. A way to establish a record of quantitative and qualitative performance and growth over time
2. A tool for reflection and goal-setting as well as a way to present evidence of your ability to solve problems and to achieve goals
3. A way to synthesize many separate experiences; in other words, a way to get the "big picture"
4. A vehicle for you to collaborate with professors and advisors in individualizing instruction

5. A vehicle for demonstrating knowledge and skills gained through out-of-class experiences, such as volunteering
6. A way to share control and responsibility for your own learning
7. An alternative assessment measure within the professional education program
8. A potential preparation for national, regional, and state accreditation
9. An interview tool in the professional hiring process
10. An expanded résumé to be used as an introduction during the student teaching experience

How Can You Benefit from Mentoring Relationships?

When asked, "What would have been most helpful in preparing you to be a teacher?" one first-year suburban high school teacher responded with: "I wish I had one [a mentor] here. . . . There are days that go by and I don't think I learn anything about my teaching, and that's too bad. I wish I had someone" (Dollase 1992, 138). In reflecting on how a **mentor** contributed to his professional growth, Forrest Parkay defined **mentoring** as

> an intensive, one-to-one form of teaching in which the wise and experienced mentor inducts the aspiring protégé [one who is mentored] into a particular, usually professional, way of life. . . . [T]he protégé learns from the mentor not only the objective, manifest content of professional knowledge and skills but also a subjective, non-discursive appreciation for how and when to employ these learnings in the arena of professional practice. In short, the mentor helps the protégé to "learn the ropes," to become socialized into the profession. (1988, 196)

An urban middle school intern's description of how his mentor helped him develop effective classroom management techniques exemplifies "learning the ropes": "'You've got to develop your own sense of personal power,' [my mentor] kept saying. 'It's not something I can teach you. I can show you what to do. I can model it. But I don't know, it's just something that's got to come from within you'" (Henry et al. 1995, 114).

Those who have become highly accomplished teachers frequently point out the importance of mentors in their preparation for teaching. A mentor can provide moral support, guidance, and feedback to students at various stages of professional preparation. In addition, a mentor can model for the protégé an analytical approach to solving problems in the classroom.

What Opportunities for Continuing Professional Development Will You Have?

Professional development is a lifelong process; any teacher, at any stage of development, has room for improvement. Many school systems and universities have programs in place for the continuing professional development of teachers. Indeed, teachers are members of a profession that provides them with a "continuous opportunity to grow, learn, and become more expert in their work" (Lieberman 1990, viii).

Self-Assessment for Professional Growth

Self-assessment, or **reflection,** is a necessary first step in pursuing opportunities for professional growth. The simplest level of reflection occurs when, after a particular lesson has been taught, a teacher asks such questions as: How did that lesson go?

What might have been done to improve it? What were the good lesson elements that should be retained when I teach it again? A deeper level of reflection might include such questions as: How has that lesson contributed to my students' overall educational growth? Is society as a whole in any way better off as a consequence of what my students just learned?

Several questions can help you make appropriate choices as a teacher: In which areas am I already competent? In which areas do I need further development? How will I acquire the knowledge and skills I need? How will I apply new knowledge and practice new skills? Answers to such questions will lead you to a variety of sources for professional growth: teacher workshops, teacher centres, professional development schools, the opportunity to supervise and mentor student teachers, and graduate programs. Figure 2.4 illustrates the relationship of these professional development experiences to your teacher education program.

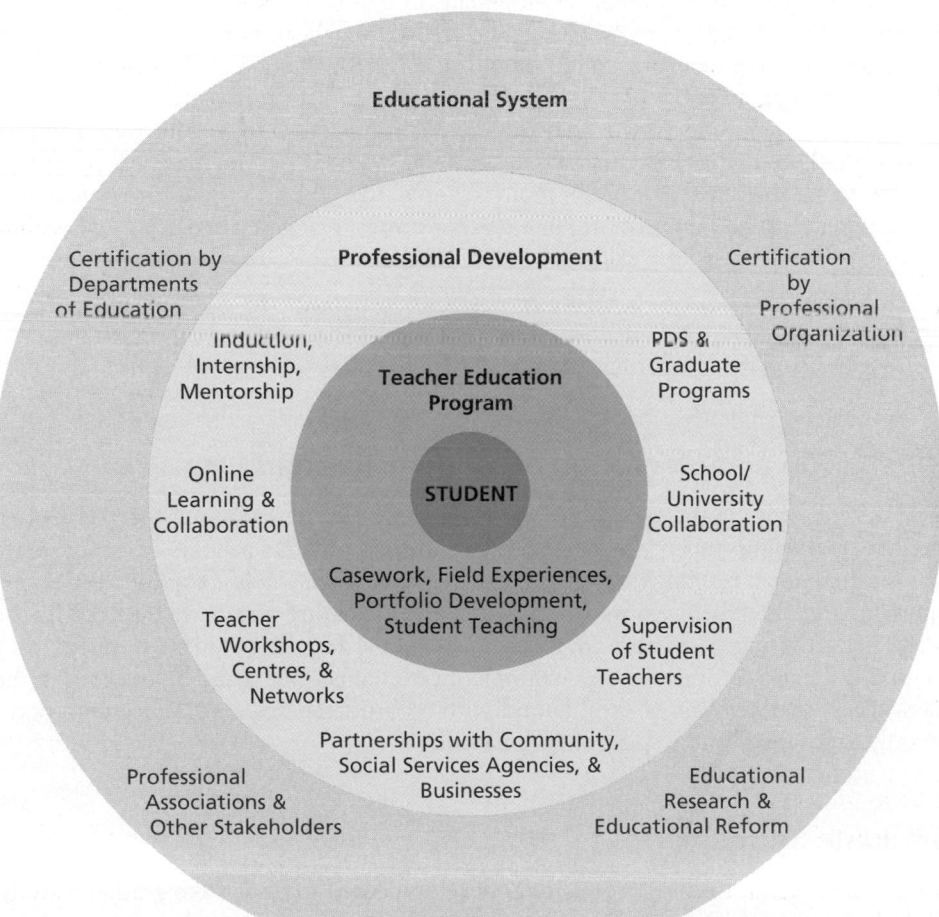

Figure 2.4

Professional development: From teacher education student to practitioner

Teacher Workshops

The quality of **in-service workshops** is uneven, varying with the size of school district budgets and with the imagination and knowledge of the administrators and teachers who arrange them. It is significant that the most effective in-service programs tend to be the ones that teachers request—and often design and conduct.

Some workshops focus on topics that all teachers (regardless of subject or level) can benefit from: classroom management, writing across the curriculum, multicultural education, and strategies for teaching students with learning disabilities in the general education classroom, for example. Other workshops have a sharper focus and are intended for teachers of a subject at a certain level—for example, whole language techniques for middle school students, discovery learning for high school science students, and student-centred approaches to teaching literature in the high school classroom.

Teacher Centres

Teacher centres provide opportunities for teachers to take the lead in the decision making and implementation of staff development programs based on the needs of teachers. Within limits, they provide opportunities for teachers to have a level of control over their own professional development. In contrast to in-service programs, the initiatives undertaken are more clearly directed by teachers. Some centres cooperate with a local or neighbouring college of education and include members of the faculty on their planning committees.

Many teachers find teacher centres stimulating because they offer opportunities for collegial interaction in a quiet, professionally oriented setting. Teachers often find that the busy, hectic pace of life in many schools provides little time for professional dialogue with peers. Furthermore, in a teacher centre, teachers are often more willing to openly discuss areas of weakness in their performance. As one teacher put it:

> At the teacher centre, I can ask for help. I won't be judged. The teachers who have helped me the most have had the same problems. I respect them, and I'm willing to learn from them. They have credibility with me.

Supervision and Mentoring of Student Teachers

After several years in the classroom, teachers may be ready to stretch themselves further by supervising student teachers. Some of the less obvious benefits of doing so are that teachers must rethink what they are doing so that they might explain, and sometimes justify, their behaviours to someone else, learning about themselves in the process. Furthermore, because they become a model for their student teachers, they continually strive to offer the best example. In exchange, they gain an assistant in the classroom—another pair of eyes, an aid with record keeping—and, more than occasionally, fresh ideas and a spirit of enthusiasm.

Graduate Study

A more traditional form of professional development is to undertake graduate study. With the recent reforms, many provinces now require teachers to take some graduate courses to keep their certifications and knowledge up to date. Some teachers take only courses that are of immediate use to them; others use their graduate study to prepare for new teaching or administrative positions; and still others pursue doctoral work in order to teach prospective teachers or others in their discipline at the college level.

Study on the Internet

If you have access to the **internet**, you can find many possibilities for continuing professional development. Teachers use the Internet to exchange ideas and experiences and to acquire additional expertise in teaching or to share their expertise with others. See "Professional Development Opportunities on the Internet" on this book's website. There you'll also find a periodically updated list of professional development opportunities available online for teachers. If you decide to visit any of these links, remember that web addresses change frequently or are taken off the Internet. The web addresses given throughout this book were active at the time of writing. It is estimated that 10 000 websites are added to the Internet every day, so you should regularly do searches using keywords related to education to gather the latest information and resources.

SUMMARY

What Essential Knowledge Do You Need to Be a Teacher?

- Professional teachers reflect upon their classroom experiences.
- Teachers need three kinds of knowledge: knowledge of self and students, knowledge of subject, and knowledge of educational theory and research.
- Teachers' self-knowledge influences their ability to understand students.
- The ambiguities of teaching can cause teachers to experience anxiety.
- Teachers can experience loneliness because they are isolated from adults.
- Teachers must know their students' aptitudes, talents, learning styles, stage of development, and readiness to learn new material.
- Teachers must understand their subjects deeply so that they can modify instructional strategies based on students' perception of content.
- Knowledge of educational theory enables professional teachers to know why certain strategies work.
- Educational research provides teachers with rules of thumb for practice.

What Are Five Ways of Viewing the Teacher Knowledge Base?

- There is no universally accepted definition of "good" teaching.
- The teacher knowledge base (essential knowledge and abilities) can place primary emphasis on personal development, research-based competencies, provincial or territorial standards, job analyses, or the views of professional organizations.
- Many provinces have developed standards for outcome-based or performance-based teacher education. Outcomes are based on what beginning teachers do in real classrooms.

- The job-analysis view of teaching is based on identifying job dimensions—the knowledge, skills, and attitudes teachers need.
- Effective teachers are guided by reflection and a problem-solving orientation.

How Are Canadian Teachers Educated and Certified?

- Provincial departments of education and independent professional organizations both set criteria for the certification of teachers.

What Can You Learn from Observing in Classrooms?

- The opportunity to observe in classrooms helps some students make a final decision about becoming a teacher.
- Many teacher education programs are providing students with more and earlier opportunities to observe in classrooms.
- Distance-learning classrooms, using compressed video, link teacher education programs to schools off-campus.
- Observations can focus on a particular aspect of classroom life or be guided by a set of questions related to a specific area, such as how the teacher motivates students.
- Observation instruments range from informal, qualitative descriptions to formal, quantitative checklists.

How Can You Gain Practical Experience for Becoming a Teacher?

- Teacher education students can gain practical experience through focused classroom observations, microteaching, teaching simulations, analyses of video cases, field-based practica and clinical experiences, and classroom assistant programs.
- In microteaching, students practice specific skills by teaching brief lessons that are later analyzed.
- Computer simulations and virtual reality—as well as written and video- and audio-recorded cases—are being used for teaching simulations.
- Journal writing and reflective teaching logs increase the benefits of the student teaching experience.
- To prepare to teach students from diverse backgrounds, teacher education students should actively seek field experiences in multicultural settings.
- Supply teaching provides additional practical experience after completing a teacher education program.

How Can You Develop Your Teaching Portfolio?

- A portfolio documents professional growth and development over time.
- A portfolio can be organized around specific outcomes or standards.
- Portfolio contents should represent one's best work.
- Professional portfolios can be used in teacher evaluation, self-evaluation, and hiring.

How Can You Benefit from Mentoring Relationships?

- Ask for advice from teachers you admire.
- Mentoring can be a source of professional growth for experienced teachers.
- Mentoring enables the protégé to "learn the ropes."

What Opportunities for Continuing Professional Development Will You Have?

- Self-assessment is necessary to select appropriate professional development experiences.
- Opportunities for professional development include teacher workshops, teacher centres, professional development schools, supervision and mentoring of student teachers, graduate study, and the Internet.

KEY TERMS AND CONCEPTS

field experiences, 40
in-service workshops, 50
internet, 51
job analysis, 36
knowledge base, 31
mentor, 48
mentoring, 48
microteaching, 41
observations, 40
outcome-based teacher education, 35

pedagogical content knowledge, 30
performance-based teacher education, 35
personal development view, 35
practicum, 42
professional portfolio, 46
reflection, 49
reflective teaching log, 44

research-based competencies, 35
self-assessment, 49
substitute teaching, 45
supply teaching, 45
teacher centres, 50
teachers' craft knowledge, 32
teaching simulations, 41

APPLICATIONS AND ACTIVITIES

Teacher's Journal

1. What does self-knowledge mean to you? Why is self-knowledge important in teaching? What steps can you take to achieve greater self-knowledge?

2. As a teacher, you will encounter challenges related to student variability (differences in developmental needs, interests, abilities, and disabilities) and student diversity (differences in gender, race, ethnicity, culture, and socio-economic status). To begin thinking about how you will acquire and use knowledge about your students, write a brief profile of yourself as a student in elementary school, in middle school or junior high school, and in high school.

3. Reflect on your education as a teacher. What are your primary concerns about the preparation you are receiving? What experiences do you think will be most helpful to you as you move toward becoming a teacher? What qualities would you look for in a mentor?

4. On the basis of your field experiences to date and the information in Chapters 1 and 2, ask yourself these questions and respond in your journal: Do I have the aptitude to become a good teacher? Am I willing to acquire the essential knowledge and skills teachers need? Do I really want to become a teacher?

Theory into Practice

1. Most applicants to teacher education programs select either the elementary stream, with a majority stating a preference for teaching at the K–4 grade levels, or the secondary stream, with a majority stating a preference for teaching at the 10–12 grade levels. Applicants with a stated preference for teaching at the other grade levels, which, depending on a district's organizational structure, can be considered either middle school or junior high, are relatively low in number. In a small group, discuss the possible reasons for this situation.

2. One of the best methods for the avoidance of discipline problems is to energetically and effectively deliver a well-constructed and interesting lesson. In some cases, the content of the curriculum is of intrinsic interest to students, and keeping their attention is a relatively simple task. Unfortunately, there is also material within the curriculum of modest or no interest to students, with the consequence that the teacher must work diligently to maintain their attention. All lessons should have some degree of "sparkle" (the things included within a lesson to give it life and interest). Consider the following partial list of possibilities; then see the instructions that follow.

"Sparkle" Possibilities

- Tell or read an interesting anecdote.
- Bring an interesting object (or objects) to class. Explain its/their origin, use, or purpose.
- On occasion, use interesting body language such as facial expressions or gestures.
- Read part or all of an interesting article from a newspaper, etc.
- Use word play of all types.
- Ask truly interesting questions.
- Give interesting examples.
- Present the students with novel information regarding the subject of your lesson.
- Take an instant poll, by secret ballot or a show of hands, on a subject of interest or relevance.
- Present an interesting visual.
- Use a variety of teaching techniques: group work, simulations, and role plays.
- Do whatever you can to inspire in students a "sense of wonder."
- Note: Do not tell a joke unless you have a special talent for doing so.

Task 1: Form a group and add three additional items to the above list.
Task 2: Select two lesson topics for instruction at one (or two) grade levels.
Task 3: Select three ways in which you could bring some sparkle to the first topic, and three additional ways to the second. (For this task you may assume that you have unlimited time and resources.)

Teacher's Database

1. Find out more about the use of technology to enhance teaching and learning. Join one of the Internet teacher discussion groups that deal with the educational use of information technology.

2. Instead of using "outside experts" to deliver professional development workshops to teachers, some school districts and teacher associations have implemented teacher networks in which teachers address problems of mutual concern. For example, the Nova Scotia Teachers Union organizes an annual conference specifically designed to assist new teachers with the problems they encounter. You can visit the Nova Scotia Teachers Union website at www.nstu.ca for more information.

Observations and Interviews

1. Think about areas for focused observations of teaching, such as classroom management, student involvement, questioning techniques, evaluation, or teacher–student rapport. For one or more areas, brainstorm and order in logical sequence a set of questions you could use to guide your next observations. Include a list of questions to ask the teacher you will observe.

2. As a collaborative project with classmates, interview students who have completed student teaching at your university. What tips do they have for developing a positive relationship with a cooperating teacher? For establishing rapport with students? For developing confidence in presenting lessons?

3. Arrange to interview a school administrator about the knowledge, skills, and aptitude he or she thinks teachers must have. Which of the knowledge and skills discussed in this chapter does the administrator mention? Does he or she mention knowledge and skills not discussed?

4. Observe a teacher in the classroom for the purpose of identifying examples that help to answer the following questions: How does the teacher demonstrate or use knowledge of self and students? Knowledge of subject matter? Knowledge of educational theory and research?

5. Observe a classroom in which there is likely to be some teacher–student interaction (for example, questions and answers, discussion, or oral review and feedback). On the basis of the data you collect, what conclusions can you draw about life in this classroom?

Professional Portfolio

1. Create a plan for developing your portfolio. What specific outcomes or standards will you use to organize your portfolio entries? What artifacts will you use to demonstrate your professional growth and development?

2. Evaluate the products of your studies in education so far in your preparation for becoming a teacher. Identify a few examples of your best work to include in your portfolio. Also evaluate your Teacher's Journal, Teacher's Database, and Observations and Interviews for possible inclusion in your portfolio.

MyEducationLab

Watch a video explaining the different types of "Professional Knowledge" in the Video Lab at www.MyEducationLab.com.

Watch a video called "Grade Level Meeting" to learn about teaching at different grade levels in the Video Lab at www.MyEducationLab.com.

To see a geometry teacher explain his favorite software program, watch "Geometer's Sketchpad" in the Video Lab at www.MyEducationLab.com.

For suggestions regarding how to make your lessons more interesting, go to Teacher's Resource 2.1, The Teacher's Scribe: "Am I boring you?" on www.MyEducationLab.com.

For a discussion of whether teachers need more subject-matter knowledge or professional knowledge, go to Teacher's Resource 2.2: "Where do you stand?" on www.MyEducationLab.com.

To read the English Language Arts Outcome Statement by the Atlantic Provinces Education Foundation, go to Teacher's Resource 2.3 on www.MyEducationLab.com.

To see a sample evaluation form for a Term 1 Field Experience, go to Teacher's Resource 2.4 on www.MyEducationLab.com.

For sample guidelines of professional conduct and a teachers' code of ethics, go to Teacher's Resource 2.5 and Teacher's Resource 2.6 on www.MyEducationLab.com.

part two

Foundations of Teaching

3

Educational philosophy is a way not only of looking at ideas, but also of learning how to use ideas in better ways.

—Howard A. Ozmon and Samuel M. Craver
Philosophical Foundations of Education, 6th ed., 1999.

Ideas and Events That Have Shaped Education in Canada

focus questions

1. What determines your educational philosophy?
2. What are the branches of philosophy?
3. What are five modern philosophical orientations to teaching?
4. What psychological orientations have influenced teaching philosophies?
5. How can you develop your educational philosophy?
6. What cultural traditions have led to the development of the Canadian educational landscape?
7. What were teaching and schools like in Canada prior to 1875?
8. What patterns developed in Canadian education from 1875 to 1918?
9. What is the history of schooling for First Nations peoples?
10. What educational advancements took place between the Great Wars (1918–1939)?
11. What are the major characteristics of today's system of education in Canada?
12. How are Canadian schools funded?
13. What are some current trends in Canadian education?
14. What are some alternative types of Canadian schools?

You are having an animated conversation in the teacher's lounge with four colleagues—Manjit, Yuliya, Kim, and Claude—about educational reform and the changes being made throughout Canada's schools. The discussion was sparked by a television special that had aired the night before about new approaches to teaching and assessing students' learning.

"I was really glad to see teachers portrayed in a professional light," you say. "The message seemed to be 'Let's get behind teachers and give them the support and resources they need to implement new ideas and technologies. Effective schools are important to our nation's well-being.'"

"I think it's just a case of schools trying to jump on the bandwagon," Claude says. "All this talk about restructuring schools, developing partnerships with the community, and using technology—they're supposed to be the silver bullets that transform education. These ideas just take time away from what we should be doing, and that's teaching kids how to read, write, and compute. If we don't get back to what really matters, our country is going to fall apart." He paused. "But that's my educational philosophy."

"But times have changed—the world is a different place," Manjit replies. "Look at how the internet has changed things in just a few years. We can't return to the 'good old days.' Students need to learn how to learn. They need to learn how to solve problems we can't even imagine today."

"Just a minute," Yuliya interjects. "I don't think the 'good old days' ever were. That's a nostalgia trap. What kids need is to see how education is the key to understanding themselves and others. If we can't get along as human beings on this planet, we're in trouble. Look at the ethnic cleansing in Kosovo, the killing in Rwanda, Angola, Northern Ireland . . . Sure, we've got the internet and all this technology, but, as a species, we haven't evolved at all."

"Of course we can't return to the past," Kim says, "but we can learn a lot from it. That's one of the main purposes of education—to see how the great ideas can help us improve things. Like I tell my students, there isn't one problem today that Shakespeare didn't have tremendous insight into 400 years ago—racism, poverty, war . . ."

"Well, all I know is that, when I started teaching 30 years ago, we taught the basics," Claude says. "It was as simple as that. We were there to teach, and the kids, believe it or not, were there to learn. Nowadays, we have to solve all of society's problems—eliminate poverty, racism, crime, or whatever."

Claude pauses a moment then turns his attention to you. "What do you think? What's your educational philosophy?"

What do you say?

You may wonder about the value of studying the philosophy and history of Canadian education. Will such knowledge help you to become a better teacher? Yes. Knowledge of the ideas and events that have influenced our schools will help you more effectively evaluate current proposals for change. You will be in a better position to evaluate these changes if you understand how schools developed and how current proposals might relate to previous change efforts. In addition, awareness of ideas and events that have influenced teaching is an important facet of professionalism in education.

The first half of this chapter presents several basic philosophical concepts that will help you answer five important questions teachers should consider in the development of an educational philosophy:

1. What should the purposes of education be?
2. What is the nature of knowledge?
3. What values should students adopt?
4. What knowledge is of most worth?
5. How should learning be evaluated?

We cannot understand schools today without a look at what they were yesterday. The current system of public and private education in Canada is an ongoing reflection of its philosophical and historical foundations and of the aspirations and values brought to this country by its founders and by generations of settlers. Developing an appreciation for the ideas and events that have shaped the school system in Canada is an important part of your education as a professional. For a quick analysis of your own philosophical outlook with regard to education, take the Philosophical Inventory (Teacher's Resource 3.1) at www.MyEducationLab.com.

The second half of the chapter presents brief overviews of how education developed in Canada's major geographical regions. We will discuss the philosophical concepts, social forces, and events that have had the greatest impact on education in our country.

What Determines Your Educational Philosophy?

In simple terms, your **educational philosophy** comprises what you believe about education—the set of principles that guides your professional action (see Figure 3.1). Every teacher, whether he or she recognizes it, has a philosophy of education—a set of beliefs about how human beings learn and grow and what one should learn in order to follow a successful path. Teachers differ, of course, in regard to the amount of effort they devote to the development of their personal philosophy or educational platform. Some feel that philosophical reflections have nothing to contribute to the actual act of teaching. (This belief is itself a philosophy of education.) Other teachers recognize that teaching, because it is concerned with what ought to be, is an essentially philosophical enterprise.

Your behaviour as a teacher is strongly connected to your personal values and your beliefs about teaching and learning, students, knowledge, and what is worth knowing. Regardless of where you stand in regard to these five dimensions of teaching, you should be aware of the need to continually reflect on what you believe and why you believe it.

Beliefs about Teaching and Learning

One of the most important components of your educational philosophy is how you view teaching and learning. In other words, what is a teacher's primary role? Is the teacher a subject-matter expert who can efficiently and effectively impart knowledge to students? Is he or she a helpful adult who establishes caring relationships with students and nurtures their growth in needed areas? Or is the teacher a skilled technician who can manage the learning of many students at once?

Some teachers emphasize individual student experiences and cognitions. Others stress students' behaviour. Learning, according to the first viewpoint, is seen as the changes in thoughts or actions that result from personal experience; that is, learning is largely the result of internal forces within the individual. In contrast, the other view defines learning as the associations between various stimuli and responses. Here, learning results from forces that are external to the individual.

Beliefs about Students

Your beliefs about students will have a great influence on how you teach. Every teacher formulates an image in her or his mind of what students are like—their dispositions, skills, motivation levels, and expectations. What you believe students are like is based on your unique life experiences, particularly your observations of young people and your knowledge of human growth and development.

Negative views of students may promote teacher–student relationships based on fear and coercion rather than on trust and helpfulness. A teacher with extremely positive views may risk not providing students with sufficient structure and direction and not communicating sufficiently high expectations. In the final analysis, the truly

For each pair of statements about the teacher's role, circle the response that most closely reflects where you stand regarding the two perspectives. Remember, there are no correct responses, and neither perspective is better than the other.

Constructivist Perspective		*Transmission Perspective*
"I mainly see my role as a facilitator. I try to provide opportunities and resources for my students to discover or construct concepts for themselves."	*VS.*	"That's all nice, but students really won't learn the subject unless you go over the material in a structured way. It's my job to explain, to show students how to do the work, and to assign specific practice."

Definitely Prefer	Tend to Prefer	Cannot Decide	Tend to Prefer	Definitely Prefer

Constructivist		*Transmission*
"It is a good idea to have all sorts of activities going on in the classroom. Some students might produce a scene from a play they read. Others might create a miniature version of the set. It's hard to get the logistics right, but the successes are so much more important than the failures."	*VS.*	"It's more practical to give the whole class the same assignment, one that has clear directions, and one that can be done in short intervals that match students' attention spans and the daily class schedule."

Definitely Prefer	Tend to Prefer	Cannot Decide	Tend to Prefer	Definitely Prefer

"The most important part of instruction is that it encourage 'sense-making' or thinking among students. Content is secondary."	*VS.*	"The most important part of instruction is the content of the curriculum. That content is the community's judgment about what children need to be able to know and do."

Definitely Prefer	Tend to Prefer	Cannot Decide	Tend to Prefer	Definitely Prefer

"It is critical for students to become interested in doing academic work—interest and effort are more important than the particular subject-matter they are working on."	*VS.*	"While student motivation is certainly useful, it should not drive what students study. It is more important that students learn the history, science, math, and language skills in their textbooks."

Definitely Prefer	Tend to Prefer	Cannot Decide	Tend to Prefer	Definitely Prefer

Figure 3.1

Philosophical assessment

Source: Adapted from Jason L. Ravitz, Henry Jay Becker, and Yan Tien Wong. *Constructivist-Compatible Beliefs and Practices Among U.S. Teachers*. Center for Research on Information Technology and Organizations, University of California, Irvine; and University of Minnesota, July 2000.

professional teacher—the one who has a carefully thought-out educational philosophy—recognizes that, although children differ in their predispositions to learning and growing, they all can learn.

Beliefs about Knowledge

How a teacher views knowledge is directly related to how she or he goes about teaching. If teachers view knowledge as the sum total of small pieces of subject matter or discrete facts, their students will most likely spend a great deal of time learning that information in a straightforward, rote manner.

Other teachers view knowledge more conceptually—that is, as consisting of big ideas that enable us to understand and influence our environment. Such teachers would want students to be able to explain how legislative decisions are made in provincial capitals, how an understanding of the eight parts of speech can empower the writer and vitalize one's writing, and how chemical elements are grouped according to their atomic numbers.

Finally, teachers differ in their beliefs as to whether students' increased understanding of their own experiences is a legitimate form of knowledge. Knowledge of self and one's experiences in the world is not the same as knowledge about a particular subject; yet personal knowledge is essential for a full, satisfying life.

Beliefs about What Is Worth Knowing

Teachers have different ideas about what should be taught. Some believe it is most important that students learn the basic skills of reading, writing, and computation. These teachers believe that such skills are needed in order for students to be successful in their chosen occupations, and it is the school's responsibility to prepare students for the world of work. Other teachers, however, believe that the most worthwhile content is to be found in the classics or the "great books." Through mastering noteworthy ideas in the sciences, in mathematics, in literature, and in history, such teachers believe that students will be well prepared to deal with the future. Still others are most concerned with students learning how to reason, how to communicate effectively, and how to solve problems. Students who master these cognitive processes will have learned how to learn—and this is the most realistic preparation for an unknown future. And, finally, some teachers are deeply concerned with developing the whole child and teaching students to become self-actualizing. Thus the curriculum should be meaningful and contribute to the student's efforts to become a mature, self-possessed individual.

What Are the Branches of Philosophy?

To provide you with further tools to formulate and clarify your educational philosophy, this section presents brief overviews of six areas of philosophy that are of central concern to teachers: metaphysics, epistemology, axiology, ethics, aesthetics, and logic. Each area focuses on some of the questions that have concerned the world's greatest philosophers for centuries: What is the nature of reality? What is the nature of knowledge? Is truth ever attainable? What values should one follow? What is good and what is evil? What is the nature of beauty and excellence? What processes of reasoning will yield consistently valid results?

Metaphysics

Metaphysics is concerned with explaining, as rationally and as comprehensively as possible, the nature of reality (in contrast to how reality appears). What is reality? What is the world made of? These are metaphysical questions. Metaphysics is also concerned with the nature of being and explores questions such as: What does it mean to exist? What is humankind's place in the scheme of things? Metaphysical questions such as these are at the very heart of educational philosophy. As two educational philosophers put it, "Our ultimate preoccupation in educational theory is with the most primary of all philosophic problems: metaphysics, the study of ultimate reality" (Morris & Pai 1994, 28).

Metaphysics has important implications for education because school curricula are based on what we know about reality. And what we know about reality is driven by the kinds of questions we ask about the world. In fact, any position regarding what schools should teach has behind it a particular view of reality—and a particular set of responses to metaphysical questions.

Epistemology

The next major set of philosophical questions that concerns teachers can be classified as **epistemology**. These questions focus on knowledge: What knowledge is true? How does knowing take place? How do we know that we know? How do we decide between opposing views of knowledge? Is truth constant, or does it change from situation to situation? What knowledge is of most worth? How you answer the epistemological questions that confront all teachers will have significant implications for your teaching. First, you will need to determine what is true about the content you will teach; then you must decide on the most appropriate means of conveying this content to students. Even a casual consideration of epistemological questions reveals that there are many ways of knowing about the world, at least five of which are of interest to teachers:

1. *Knowing Based on Authority*—for example, knowledge from the sage, the poet, the expert, the ruler, the textbook, or the teacher
2. *Knowing Based on Divine Revelation*—for example, knowledge in the form of supernatural revelations from the sun god of early peoples, the many gods of the ancient Greeks, or the Judeo/Christian/Moslem god
3. *Knowing Based on Empiricism (Experience)*—for example, knowledge acquired through the senses, the informally-gathered empirical data that direct most of our daily behaviour
4. *Knowing Based on Reason and Logical Analysis*—for example, knowledge inferred from the process of thinking logically
5. *Knowing Based on Intuition*—for example, knowledge arrived at without the use of rational thought

Axiology

The next set of philosophical problems concerns values. Teachers are concerned with values because "school is not a neutral activity. The very idea of schooling expresses a set of values. [We] educate and we are educated for some purpose we consider good. We teach what we think is a valuable set of ideas. How else could we construct education?" (Nelson, Carlson, & Polonsky 2000, 304).

Among the axiological questions teachers must answer are: What values should teachers encourage students to adopt? What values raise us to our highest expression of humanity? What values are held by a truly educated person?

Axiology highlights the idea that the teacher has an interest not only in the quantity of knowledge that students acquire but also in the quality of life that becomes possible because of that knowledge. Extensive knowledge may not benefit the individual if he or she is unable to put that knowledge to good use. This point raises additional questions: How do we define quality of life? What curricular experiences contribute most to quality of life? All teachers must deal with the issues raised by these questions.

Ethics

While axiology addresses the question "What is valuable?", **ethics** focuses on "What is good and evil, right and wrong, just and unjust?"

Knowledge of ethics can help a teacher solve many of the dilemmas that arise in the classroom. Frequently, teachers must take action in situations where they are unable to gather all of the relevant facts and where no single course of action is totally right or wrong. For example, say a student whose previous work was above average plagiarizes a term paper: Should the teacher fail the student for the course if the example of swift, decisive punishment will likely prevent other students from plagiarizing? Or should the teacher, following her hunches about what would be in the student's long-term interest, have the student redo the term paper and risk the possibility that other students might get the mistaken notion that plagiarism has no negative consequences? Another ethical dilemma: Is an elementary mathematics teacher justified in trying to increase achievement for the whole class by separating two disruptive girls and placing one in a mathematics group beneath her level of ability?

Aesthetics

The branch of axiology known as **aesthetics** is concerned with values related to beauty and art. Although we expect that teachers of music, art, drama, literature, and writing regularly have students make judgments about the quality of art, we can easily overlook the role that aesthetics ought to play in all areas of the curriculum.

Aesthetics can also help a teacher increase his or her effectiveness. Teaching, because it may be viewed as a form of artistic expression, can be judged according to artistic standards of beauty and quality. In this regard, the teacher is an artist whose medium of expression is the spontaneous, unrehearsed, and creative encounter between teacher and student.

From an examination of this famous statue by Rodin, what might art teachers want their students to learn about aesthetics? How were aesthetic values reflected in the K–12 curricula you experienced?

Logic

Logic is the area of philosophy that deals with the process of reasoning and identifies rules that will enable the thinker to reach valid conclusions. The two kinds of logical thinking processes that teachers most frequently have students master are deductive and inductive thinking. The deductive approach requires the thinker to move from a general principle or proposition to a specific conclusion that is valid. By contrast, inductive reasoning moves from the specific to the general. Here, the student begins by examining particular examples that eventually lead to the acceptance of a general proposition. Inductive teaching is often referred to as discovery teaching—students discover, or create, their own knowledge of a topic.

Perhaps the best-known teacher to use the inductive approach to teaching was the Greek philosopher Socrates (ca. 470–399 BCE). His method of teaching, known today as the Socratic method, consisted of holding philosophical conversations (dialectics) with his pupils. The legacy of Socrates lives in all teachers who use his questioning strategies to encourage students to think for themselves.

For more information regarding good questioning practice, see Teacher's Resource 3.2, Teacher's Scribe: "Does anyone have a question?" on www.MyEducationLab.com.

What Are Five Modern Philosophical Orientations to Teaching?

Five major philosophical orientations to teaching have been developed in response to the branches of philosophy we have just examined. These orientations, or schools of thought, are perennialism, essentialism, progressivism, existentialism, and social reconstructionism. The following sections present a brief description of each of these orientations, beginning with those that are teacher-centred and ending with those that are student-centred (see Figure 3.2).

Perennialism

Perennialism, as the term implies, views truth as constant, or perennial. The aim of education, according to perennialist thinking, is to ensure that students acquire knowledge of unchanging principles or great ideas. Perennialists believe that the great ideas continue to have the most potential for solving the problems of any era.

Curricula, according to perennialists, should stress students' intellectual growth in the arts and sciences. To become "culturally literate," students should encounter in these areas the best, most significant works ever created. Thus a high school English teacher would require students to read Melville's *Moby Dick* or any of Shakespeare's plays rather than a novel on the current best-seller list.

Similarly, science students would learn about the three laws of motion or the three laws of thermodynamics rather than build a model of the space shuttle.

Perennialist Educational Philosophers

Two of the best known advocates of the perennialist philosophy have been Robert Maynard Hutchins (1899–1977) and, more recently, Mortimer Adler, who together developed an undergraduate curriculum based on study of the great books and discussions of these classics in small seminars. Adler and Hutchins were instrumental in organizing the Great Books of the Western World curriculum. Through focusing study on over 100 enduring classics, from Plato to Einstein, the great books approach aims at the major perennialist goal of teaching students to become independent and critical thinkers. It is a demanding curriculum that focuses on the enduring disciplines of knowledge rather than on current events or student interests.

Figure 3.2

Five philosophical orientations to teaching

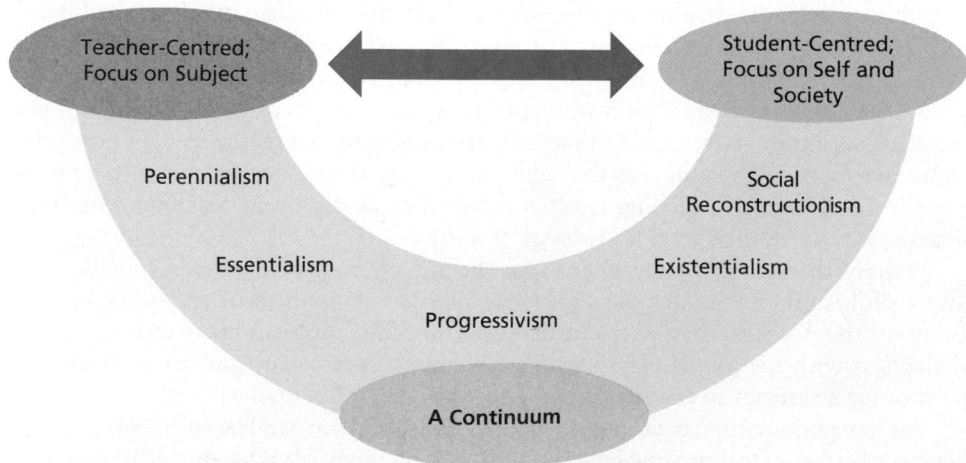

Teacher-Centred; Focus on Subject

Student-Centred; Focus on Self and Society

Perennialism

Social Reconstructionism

Essentialism

Existentialism

Progressivism

A Continuum

Essentialism

Essentialism, which has some similarities to perennialism, is a conservative philosophy of education. It was originally formulated by William C. Bagley (1874–1946), an American professor of education, as a criticism of progressive trends in schools. Essentialists believe that human culture has a core of common knowledge that schools are obligated to transmit to students in a systematic, disciplined manner. Unlike perennialists, who emphasize a set of external truths, essentialists stress what they believe to be the essential knowledge and skills (often termed "the basics") that productive members of our society need to know.

According to essentialist philosophy, schooling should be practical and provide children with sound instruction that prepares them to live life; schools should not try to influence or set social policies. Critics of essentialism, however, charge that such a tradition-bound orientation to schooling will indoctrinate students and rule out the possibility of change. Essentialists respond that, without an essentialist approach, students will be indoctrinated in humanistic and behavioural curricula that run counter to society's accepted standards and need for order.

Progressivism

Progressivism is based on the belief that education should be child-centred rather than teacher- or content-centred. The writing of John Dewey (1859–1952) in the 1920s and 1930s contributed a great deal to the spread of progressive ideas. Briefly, Deweyan progressivism is based on three central assumptions:

1. The content of the curriculum ought to be derived from students' interests rather than from the academic disciplines.
2. Effective teaching takes into account the whole child and his or her interests and needs in relation to cognitive, affective, and psychomotor areas.
3. Learning is essentially active rather than passive.

Progressive Strategies

The progressive philosophy also contends that knowledge that is true in the present may not be true in the future. Hence, the best way to prepare students for an unknown future is to equip them with problem-solving strategies that will enable them to discover meaningful knowledge at various stages of their lives.

Educators with a progressive orientation give students a considerable amount of freedom in determining their school experiences. Contrary to the perceptions of many, though, progressive education does not mean that teachers do not provide structure or that students are free to do whatever they wish. Progressive teachers begin where students are and, through the daily give-and-take of the classroom, lead students to see that the subject to be learned can enhance their lives.

In a progressively oriented classroom, the teacher serves as a guide or resource person whose primary responsibility is to facilitate student learning. The teacher helps students learn what is important to them rather than passing on a set of so-called enduring truths. Students have many opportunities to work cooperatively in groups, often solving problems that the group, not the teacher, has identified as important.

Existentialism

Existential philosophy is unique in that it focuses on the experiences of the individual. Other philosophies are concerned with developing systems of thought for identifying and understanding what is common to all reality, human existence, and values. **Existentialism,** on the other hand, offers the individual a way of thinking about his or her own life, what has meaning for him or her, and what is true for him or her. In general, existentialism emphasizes creative choice, the subjectivity of human experiences, and concrete acts of human existence over any rational scheme for human nature or reality.

Life, according to existential thought, has no meaning, and the universe is indifferent to the situation humankind finds itself in. Moreover, "existentialists [believe] that too many people wrongly emphasize the optimistic, the good, and the beautiful— all of which create a false impression of existence" (Ozmon & Craver 1999, 253). With the freedom we have, however, each individual must commit him- or herself to assign meaning to his or her own life. As Maxine Greene, an eminent philosopher of education whose work is based on existentialism, states, "We have to know about our lives, clarify our situations, if we are to understand the world from our shared standpoints . . ." (1995, 21). The human enterprise that can be most helpful in promoting this personal quest for meaning is the educative process. Teachers, therefore, must allow students freedom of choice and provide them with experiences that will help them find the meaning of their lives. This approach, contrary to the belief of many, does not mean that students may do whatever they please; logic indicates that freedom has rules, and respect for the freedom of others is essential.

Existentialists judge the curriculum according to whether it contributes to the individual's quest for meaning and results in a high level of personal awareness. The ideal curriculum is one that provides students with extensive individual freedom and requires them to ask their own questions, to conduct their own inquiries, and to draw their own conclusions.

Social Reconstructionism

As the name implies, **social reconstructionism** holds that schools should take the lead in changing or reconstructing society. Theodore Brameld (1904–1987), acknowledged as the founder of social reconstructionism, based his philosophy on two fundamental premises about the post–World War II era: (1) We live in a period of great crisis, most evident in the fact that humans now have the capability of destroying civilization overnight, and (2) humankind also has the intellectual, technological, and moral potential to create a world civilization of "abundance, health, and humane capacity" (Brameld 1959, 19). In this time of great need, then, social reconstructionists like Yuliya, whom we met in this chapter's opening scenario, believe that schools should become the primary agent for planning and directing social change. Schools should not only transmit knowledge about the existing social order; they should seek to reconstruct it as well.

Social Reconstructionism and Progressivism

Social reconstructionism has clear ties to progressive educational philosophy. Both provide opportunities for extensive interactions between teacher and students and among students themselves. Furthermore, both place a premium on bringing the community, if not the entire world, into the classroom. Student experiences often include field trips, community-based projects of various sorts, and opportunities to interact with people beyond the four walls of the classroom.

According to Brameld and social reconstructionists such as George Counts, who wrote *Dare the School Build a New Social Order?* (1932), the educative process should provide students with methods for dealing with the significant crises that confront the world: war, economic depression, international terrorism, hunger, inflation, and ever-accelerating technological advances. The logical outcome of such education would be the eventual realization of a worldwide democracy (Brameld 1956). Unless we actively seek to create this kind of world through the intelligent application of present knowledge, we run the risk that the destructive forces of the world will determine the conditions under which humans will live in the future.

Another of the important contributors to the reconstructivist viewpoint is Paulo Freire, founder of the **critical pedagogy** school of educational philosophy. Freire strongly recommended a teaching approach that assists students in questioning and challenging commonly accepted beliefs and practices. He was very concerned with **praxis**—informed action based on specific values—and believed that students would eventually reach a point of revelation where, recognizing their society as oppressive and deeply problematic, they would work toward bringing about positive change. Freire also believed that true education requires a mutually respectful dialogue among individuals and that people work positively with one another. Too much teaching, he argued, was like a form of banking with the educator making deposits in the heads of students.

For more information, go to MyEducationLab, Chapter 3, and view the video "Developing a philosophy of education."

myeducationlab

What Psychological Orientations Have Influenced Teaching Philosophies?

In addition to these five philosophical orientations to teaching, several schools of psychological thought have also formed the basis for teaching philosophies. These psychological theories are comprehensive world views that serve as the basis for the way many teachers approach teaching practice. Psychological orientations to teaching are concerned primarily with understanding the conditions that are associated with effective learning. In other words, what motivates students to learn? What environments are most conducive to learning? Chief among the psychological orientations that have influenced teaching philosophies are humanistic psychology, behaviourism, and constructivism.

Humanistic Psychology

Humanistic psychology emphasizes personal freedom, choice, awareness, and personal responsibility. As the term implies, it also focuses on the achievements, motivations, feelings, actions, and needs of human beings. The goal of education, according to this orientation, is individual self-actualization.

Humanistic psychology is derived from the philosophy of **humanism**, which developed during the European Renaissance and Protestant Reformation and is based on the belief that individuals control their own destinies through the application of their intelligence and learning. People "make themselves." The term "secular humanism" refers to the closely related belief that the conditions of human existence relate to human nature and human actions rather than to predestination or divine intervention.

In the 1950s and 1960s, humanistic psychology became the basis of educational reforms that sought to enhance students' achievement of their full potential through self-actualization (Maslow 1954, 1962; Rogers 1961). According to this psychological orientation, teachers should not force students to learn; instead, they should create a climate of trust and respect that allows students to decide what and how they learn, to question authority, and to take initiative in "making themselves." Teachers should be what noted psychologist Carl Rogers called "facilitators," and the classroom should be a place "in which curiosity and the natural desire to learn can be nourished and enhanced" (1982, 31). Through their non-judgmental understanding of students, humanistic teachers encourage students to learn and grow.

Behaviourism

Behaviourism is based on the principle that desirable human behaviour can be the product of design rather than accident. According to behaviourists, it is an illusion that humans have a free will. Although we may act as if we are free, our behaviour is really determined by forces in the environment that shape our behaviour. "We are what we are and we do what we do, not because of any mysterious power of human volition, but because outside forces over which we lack any semblance of control have us caught in an inflexible web. Whatever else we may be, we are not the captains of our fate or the masters of our soul" (Power 1982, 168).

Founders of Behaviouristic Psychology

John B. Watson (1878–1958) was the principal originator of behaviouristic psychology, and B. F. Skinner (1904–1990) its best-known promoter. Watson first claimed that human behaviour consisted of specific stimuli that resulted in certain responses. In part, he based this new conception of learning on the classic experiment conducted by Russian psychologist Ivan Pavlov (1849–1936). Pavlov had noticed that a dog he was working with would salivate when it was about to be given food. By introducing the sound of a bell when food was offered and repeating this several times, Pavlov discovered that the sound of the bell alone (a conditioned stimulus) would make the dog salivate (a conditioned response). Watson came to believe that all learning conformed to this basic stimulus–response model (now termed classical or type S conditioning).

Skinner went beyond Watson's basic stimulus-response model and developed a more comprehensive view of conditioning known as operant (or type R) conditioning. Operant conditioning is based on the idea that satisfying responses are conditioned, and unsatisfying ones are not. In other words, "The things we call pleasant have an energizing or strengthening effect on our behaviour" (Skinner 1972, 74). Thus the teacher can create learners who exhibit desired behaviours by following four steps:

1. Identify desired behaviours in concrete (observable and measurable) terms.
2. Establish a procedure for recording specific behaviours and counting their frequencies.
3. For each behaviour, identify an appropriate reinforcer.
4. Ensure that students receive the reinforcer as soon as possible after displaying a desired behaviour.

Constructivism

In contrast to behaviourism, **constructivism** focuses on processes of learning rather than on learning behaviour. According to constructivism, students use cognitive processes to construct understanding of the material to be learned—in contrast to the view that they receive information transmitted by the teacher. Constructivist approaches support student-centred rather than teacher-centred curricula and instruction. The student is the key to learning.

Unlike behaviourists who concentrate on directly observable behaviour, constructivists focus on the mental processes and strategies that students use to learn. Our understanding of learning has been extended as a result of advances in **cognitive science**—the study of the mental processes students use in thinking and remembering. By drawing from research in linguistics, psychology, anthropology, neurophysiology, and computer science, cognitive scientists are developing new models for how people think and learn.

Teachers who base classroom activities on constructivism know that learning is an active, meaning-making process, and that learners are not passive recipients of information. In fact, students are continually involved in making sense out of activities around them. Thus the teacher must understand students' understanding and realize that students' learning is influenced by prior knowledge, experience, attitudes, and social interactions.

How Can You Develop Your Educational Philosophy?

As you read the preceding brief descriptions of five educational philosophies and three psychological orientations to teaching, perhaps you felt that no single philosophy fit perfectly with your image of the kind of teacher you want to become. Or there may have been some element of each approach that seemed compatible with your own emerging philosophy of education. In either case, don't feel that you need to identify a single educational philosophy around which you will build your teaching career. In reality, few teachers follow only one philosophical stance. Rather, most have an eclectic position based on strands taken from the various branches of educational philosophy.

The self-knowledge you glean from the philosophical constructs presented in the first half of this chapter will provide a useful framework for studying the six periods in the historical development of schools that follow. For example, you will be able to see

These children are active learners in a real or relevant context, and they are constructing their own meanings through direct experience. How might this lesson be seen as an eclectic blend of progressive, existential, and constructivist ideals?

how philosophical orientations to education waxed and waned during each period—whether it was the perennialism and essentialism that characterized colonial schools, the progressivism of the 1920s and 1930s, the essentialism of the 1950s and 1980s, the humanism and social reconstructionism of the 1960s, or the constructivism of the past two decades.

What Cultural Traditions Have Led to the Development of the Canadian Educational Landscape?

The Canadian educational landscape has roots that can be traced to four cultural traditions. The earliest schools of New France were, quite naturally, modelled after the educational practices common in France. Later, after the fall of Quebec and the rise to governmental supremacy of the British, practices common to English schools were introduced. Later still, after the American Revolution of 1776 and the resultant emigration of the Loyalists to Canada, educational practices based on the American model were given support. And finally, during the period 1760–1840, thousands of Scots immigrated to Canada, bringing with them their strong regard for schools based on democracy and merit. In areas of the country where only one cultural tradition was common, as in New Brunswick, where the Loyalists initially had the field to themselves, development of a coherent education system was accomplished with ease. However, in Nova Scotia, where the Scottish, English, and American traditions were all represented, several systems vied for supremacy, with the consequence that factionalism, tumult, and discord enriched the level of educational discourse.

The French Tradition

During the period 1650–1700, most adult citizens of New France—an area that extended from Cape Breton to the Great Lakes—had received their education in France. In the **French tradition**, the dominant educational philosophy was based on the traditions of the Roman Catholic Church. Elementary **parochial schools**, known as **petites écoles**, were relatively common in most areas of France. While there was a general belief among the upper classes that the children of the lower classes should be educated, their education was to deal with only the most rudimentary facts. Girls and boys attended **separate schools**, with the boys' education tending to be of a better quality. Instruction in the curriculum (catechism, singing, arithmetic, reading, writing, and grammar) was delivered by the parish priests or their assistants.

Funding for the support of the petites écoles was provided by the church and those parents who could afford to make contributions. Teacher colleges, also known as **normal schools**, were starting to appear, and several religious orders, most notably the Jesuits priests and the Ursuline nuns, were becoming involved in the education process. Secondary schools, while not common, did exist and were almost exclusively the responsibility of specific religious orders.

The English Tradition

During the period 1760–1840, the English school system emerged. The **English tradition** reflected the beliefs and attitudes of the upper classes and had two salient characteristics. First, education was primarily a responsibility of the church rather than the state; second, education was a function of class rather than merit. Education for the lower classes was primarily provided by the Church of England, although other organizations did have some modest involvement. While charitable groups sometimes provided schooling for the poor, some children attended **dame-schools** run by widows and housewives, who taught within their own homes and collected small fees from their students' parents. At the other end of the educational spectrum were the "public" schools reserved for the privileged and the wealthy.

There were various religious groups who wanted to improve the quality of education given to the lower classes—most notably the Puritans, who eventually decamped to the American colonies. The group with the most outstanding success, however, was the Society for the Propagation of the Gospel in Foreign Parts (SPG). While its main goal was the teaching of the Bible for the benefit of overseas British settlers, the SPG soon involved itself with the development of schools in Canada and other parts of the British Empire.

The American Tradition

The United States's education system, the **American tradition**, had its primary roots in English culture. The settlers initially tried to develop a system of schooling that paralleled the British two-track system. If students from the lower classes attended school at all, it was at the elementary level for the purpose of studying an essentialist curriculum of reading, writing, and computation and receiving religious instruction. Students from the upper classes had the opportunity to attend Latin grammar schools, where they were given a college-preparatory education that focused on subjects such as Latin and Greek classics. Above all, the American colonial curriculum stressed religious objectives. Generally, no distinction was made between secular and religious life in the colonies. The religious motives that impelled the Puritans to endure the hardships of settling in a new land were reflected in the schools' curricula. The primary objective of elementary schooling was to learn to read so that one might read the Bible and religious catechisms and thereby achieve salvation.

In the period immediately following the American Revolution of 1776, thousands of Loyalists fled to Canada. However, because they had a strong distrust of all things Republican, and because they were staunchly loyal to Britain, the Loyalists tended to reinforce the provincial elites, who were predominantly Anglicans in control of government counsels. In reality, the American influence on early Canadian education was essentially a modified, somewhat more practical, version of the English influence. During the many nineteenth-century battles fought for control of Canadian schools, the Loyalists usually supported the entrenched "family compacts" that favoured the English educational tradition. It was a struggle they were destined to lose.

The Scottish Tradition

At the time of the great Scottish migration (1760–1840), the **Scottish tradition** of education, based on a combination of parish and burgh (town) schools, had several characteristics that led to its easy transference to the New World. The first of these characteristics was of primary importance; it resulted in the Scots having an educational impact that far outweighed their actual numbers as a percentage of the Canadian population. In Scotland, almost every child attended a school, which frequently had students from all ranks of society. The class-based system of education found in England was absent. In addition, both male and female students often attended the same school, and had done so for hundreds of years. The practice of having separate schools for boys and girls, a dominant characteristic of the French educational tradition, was absent. Additionally, many Scottish schools provided education at both the elementary and secondary levels. There was no great divide between the two. Rather than placing a strong emphasis on the classics as the foundation of the curriculum, subjects such as science and art were also taught. In combination with its strong democratic tradition, the characteristics of the Scottish education system would flourish in Canada's frontier environment.

What Were Teaching and Schools Like in Canada Prior to 1875?

Canada can be roughly divided into five geographic regions: Atlantic Canada, Quebec, Ontario, the West, and the North. As each region was settled at a different time by immigrants from a variety of cultural, linguistic, and religious backgrounds, it is not surprising that the school systems that evolved had their own individual characteristics. In the early years, almost all schooling was controlled by religious authorities. However, as Canada's population increased in size, and as economic development became more important to the life of the citizenry, the state began to take a greater interest in educational matters. This increased interest led to the two great educational questions of the eighteenth and nineteenth centuries: Who would control the schools? Who would pay for their maintenance and operation? These questions were largely answered by 1875—but how they were answered differed from one geographic region to another.

Quebec

1608–1760

The earliest Quebec schools were modelled exactly after the petites écoles of the mother country. There were separate schools for girls and boys with instruction usually provided by members of religious orders. However, lay teachers who met the moral and competency requirements of the clergy were present in small numbers. Student attendance (by those who had access to a school) varied, and most students left soon after learning the rudiments of reading, writing, and arithmetic. Financial support for the petites écoles was provided by the church, by the students' parents, and, in some cases, by the king of France. If an educational issue required resolution, an appeal was made to the bishop of Quebec. It was not until after 1760 that any civil laws concerning the schools came into existence.

From its earliest days until 1760, the pattern of education in New France underwent little change. The various religious societies continued to provide a modest degree of schooling to those children who lived in or near urban communities; children in rural areas had very limited access to schools and many received no education of any kind. However, the ecclesiastical school system established by the religious orders formed the basis for the system that would evolve after the start of British rule.

Jean-Baptiste Meilleur, first superintendent of education in Lower Canada (1842–1855)

1760–1875

During the first 30 years of British rule, Protestant immigrants from England, Scotland, Ireland, and other British colonies settled in the urban areas of Quebec. During this period, a few Anglo-Protestant schools were established through the initiative of interested clergy and lay persons. Nothing resembling a coherent school system for either the English-speaking or French-speaking citizens was evident. Education was still an essentially private or church-sponsored enterprise.

The first tentative steps toward the establishment of a centralized school system took place in the last 10 years of the eighteenth century, when citizens of all religious groups recognized that economic and social development required a sound education system. But there were some immediate problems. Should the schools be English or French, Protestant or Roman Catholic? Should the state or the church control the schools? And, most importantly, who should pay for the maintenance and operation of the education system that would be established? It would take an additional 75 years of acrimonious political and social debate before these questions were answered.

By 1875, all the elements of a systematic school system were in place. In actuality, there were two distinct and totally separate school systems: one for Protestants and one for Roman Catholics. While religious groups would continue to operate their schools, it would be the state, via a centralized bureaucracy, that would establish teaching standards, set curriculum, and, through taxation based on local assessment, pay for school maintenance and teacher salaries. The state would also provide grants for the establishment of normal schools for the training of teachers. By the late 1850s, three such schools had been successfully established. While this separate system of schools was a political solution acceptable to both religious groups, it created a divide between them that lasted well into the twentieth century.

Atlantic Canada

Despite their geographical proximity, the school systems that developed in the four Atlantic provinces were the result of significantly different influences. During the formative years of its education system, Nova Scotia had a population that was predominantly Scottish in origin, whereas New Brunswick was composed primarily of Loyalists. Both Prince Edward Island and Newfoundland had populations that were much more varied. The degree of difficulty each province would experience in its drive to establish a comprehensive school system became a function of the cultural traditions within each, and of how these cultural traditions interacted.

Nova Scotia

After the expulsion of the Acadians in 1755, 8000 New England citizens (traditionally referred to as the Planters) moved to Nova Scotia to take over the vacant farm lands. Prior to the Planters' arrival, most of the schools in existence were administered by the Church of England's Society for the Propagation of the Bible (SPG). In an effort to keep the Planters from establishing their own schools, the SPG had the House of Assembly pass *An Act Concerning Schools and Schoolmasters* in 1766. This act, designed to protect the Church of England's monopoly over education, ironically marked the first official recognition that education was actually the responsibility of the state.

In the 10 years following the 1776 American War of Independence, the Loyalists formed a second, larger wave of American immigrants to Nova Scotia. At approximately the same time, an even larger group of Scottish settlers started their migration to the province. The Scots arrived in such numbers that they quickly became the largest, and eventually most influential, faction within the colony.

By 1800, there was recognition that an effective school system was needed for the ever-expanding population. The questions that needed to be answered were somewhat simple in nature: Should the state or the Church of England control the schools? Who

Sir John William Dawson, first superintendent of education in Nova Scotia (1850–1853) and later president of McGill University (1855–1893)

should pay for the maintenance and operation of the education system? The numerical strength of the Scots provided the answers. By 1875, after the usual series of acrimonious debates in the legislature, there was agreement that the state would be responsible for the governance and maintenance of schools, and that financial support would be provided through taxation based on local assessment.

New Brunswick

Prior to 1783, New Brunswick was sparsely settled. There were pockets of Acadians who had fled there as a result of their expulsion from Nova Scotia, and a few New England Planters were also present in small numbers. Therefore, when large numbers of Loyalists arrived in the 1775–1785 period, they quickly became the dominant group within the colony. The school system envisaged by the Loyalists, most of whom were Anglican, was one in which church and state would work together in support of the aristocratic English tradition. Initially, this is what took place. The SPG had the full support of the Executive Council of the legislature, and grammar schools and other institutions of higher learning had their enrolments limited to members of the Anglican Church.

Unfortunately for the Loyalists, settlers from other areas of the world began to arrive in large numbers during the period 1815–1825. In particular, there was a great influx of immigrants from Ireland. Scots, business people from other parts of the British Empire, and settlers from non-Anglican denominations were also becoming increasingly common. After years of confused and rancorous debate among the various factions, the situation began to improve. In 1871, the *Common School Act* made provision for free, non-sectarian schools supported by taxation based on local assessment.

Prince Edward Island

The early history of education in Prince Edward Island is one of unrelenting sectarian strife. Acadians missed by the expulsion formed a small part of the population, but there were also Loyalists, Irish, Roman Catholic and Protestant Scots, and English immigrants. In the early part of the 1800s, a small number of private schools were in existence. In general, they were operated by itinerant schoolmasters who made their services available to the residents of PEI's ethnic communities.

In 1800, there were fewer than 5000 people in the colony; that number had grown to 70 000 by 1855. Roman Catholics comprised approximately 40 percent of the population, whereas various Protestant denominations formed the remainder. It was this approximate balance between the two religious groups that was at the heart of the sectarian warfare and dominated discussion in the provincial legislature. The fundamental issue upon which the two groups could not agree concerned authorization of the Bible for use in PEI public schools. Both groups recognized the need for establishing a comprehensive system of education, but the "Bible Question" hindered progress until the *Public School Act* was passed in 1873. This act established the office of Superintendent of Education; decreed that taxation based on local assessment would support free, non-denomination schools; and created an improved Board of Education for administration of the new system of schooling.

Newfoundland and Labrador

While Prince Edward Island experienced a great deal of sectarian strife during its journey toward a system of publicly funded, non-sectarian schools, the situation in Newfoundland was more protracted and bitter, by several orders of magnitude. The roots of Newfoundland's education system are similar to the roots of other systems in

Canada. The first schools were established and operated by the SPG. Roman Catholics, Methodists, and other Protestant groups established schools in various communities, and private schools also sprang up. However, for reasons deeply locked in Newfoundland's cultural history, the state's battle for free, non-denominational schools was lost. In 1874, the legislature gave its formal approval to funding all of the parochial schools that had been founded. Separate schools for everyone became part of the established educational order. Of all the British North American colonies, Newfoundland was the only one to develop such a unique educational model. It would be 1998 before the system of parochial schools was discontinued.

Labrador, with its harsh climate and very scattered and nomadic Inuit population, also had a church-based system of schooling. In the second half of the 1700s, the Church of the United Brethren (also known as the Moravian Church) took an interest in converting and educating the indigenous Inuit population. The Moravians carried out their work with skill and energy and helped to make their Inuit students literate in their own language. Unlike Newfoundland, where numerous religious groups vied for the souls and minds of the citizens, the Moravians carried out their work without competition from any other church.

The Little Red School House

During the early days of Canadian education, any available room in a church, tavern, or public meeting house was pressed into service as a school. If a community did go to the trouble and expense of building a school, the structure was usually made of five-metre long, rough-cut logs. In very few instances was it painted red. The ceiling was relatively low and a simple fireplace was the only source of heat. Students were required to supply the firewood. During the winter months, those who sat farthest from the fireplace were often uncomfortably cold.

The older students sat on simple benches arranged around three of the walls. In some cases, these benches were accompanied by crude desks. Arranged around the centre of the room were more deskless, backless benches for the younger children. Other than a desk for the teacher, the room was almost completely empty. There were no blackboards, no maps, no reference books, and no teaching aids. Quill pens were common, however, and students would practise their writing skills for as long as two hours each day. In cases where paper was scarce, birch bark was used. Writing slates, which the students would often "erase" by spitting and wiping, became relatively common after 1825.

Textbooks were in very short supply, and the modern concept of a "class set" was unknown. Students would bring to school any textbook they might have been able to buy or borrow. Those who could not supply a textbook shared with students who could. The few textbooks that were available were often of American origin, much to the annoyance of the Loyalist faction.

The teaching strategies were simple. Students were often required to memorize and then recite material assigned to them by the teacher. Instruction of groups within the school was rare. Most often, the teacher dealt with individual students.

The strap was freely used to maintain discipline, and, depending on the seriousness of the offence, a specific number of lashes was administered to the offender. Arriving at school with dirty hands might result in two lashes, and fighting might result in five; swearing or playing cards at school would engender even more.

The teacher was usually an unmarried young woman who, if she married and became pregnant, would be expected to resign her position. The administration of the school was usually in the hands of three male trustees—some of whom might be illiterate.

Ontario

Prior to the arrival of approximately 6000 Loyalists in 1884–1886, Upper Canada (Ontario) had very few settlers. While most of the new Loyalist settlers were farmers, among them were small numbers of well-educated individuals with a high regard for good schooling. These Loyalists wanted their children to have access to American grammar (secondary) schools in addition to the locally supported non-denominational schools. Their educational concerns received support from a second wave of American settlers who, enticed by offers of free land grants, arrived in large numbers during the 20 years preceding the War of 1812. However, while these two groups of American settlers constituted a majority of the population, the government was primarily in the hands of British officials, who believed that the state should control education while leaving its administration to Church of England officials. As most of the population had religious affiliations that were non-Anglican, it is not surprising that a struggle between the English and American traditions developed.

In 1816, the passage of the *Common School Act* suggested that free schools might come into existence with a minimum of difficulty. This act, which permitted any community with sufficient resources to establish a public school, toward which the government would make an annual grant for a teacher's salary, was undermined by the 1820 *Common School Act*, which reduced the government grant. It effectively neutralized the act of 1816 and established a pattern that would last for another 25 years, where acts regarding schools would be passed and later rescinded or rendered irrelevant by later acts. While Upper Canada would not be spared the legislative struggles that had dogged the other Canadian provinces, it did continue to make incremental steps toward a comprehensive education system. By the early 1840s, progress toward a centralized bureaucracy had been made, and provisions for a normal school had been put in place. Local assessment in support of schools was effectively introduced in 1846 and, with the passing of the *School Act* in 1843, members of religious groups were permitted to operate their own schools. Interestingly, the impetus for separate schools came not from Roman Catholics but from adherents of the Church of England and other Protestant groups. Leading the fight to keep schools under church influence was Right Rev. Dr. John Strachan, a staunch supporter of the British monarchy and the Church of England. One of his major objectives, in an effort to avoid what he considered to be the tainted influence of American settlers, was to keep

The District School in Cornwall, Ontario, ca. 1810.

the schools under the control of the Church of England. Opposing him was Egerton Ryerson, an individual who was dismayed at the dismal shape of Upper Canadian schooling. Promoted to the office of Chief Superintendent of Schools in 1846, Ryerson soon persuaded the government to undertake responsibility for education. The result was common schools publicly supported by government grants whenever 20 students could be gathered together. Other advances soon followed, and, by the early 1870s, the major features common to Ontario's present system of schooling had been established.

The West of Canada

The Prairies

Until 1869, Western Canada was under the control of the Hudson Bay Company, which had the fur trade as its exclusive interest. Prior to 1810, most of those living in what would eventually become Manitoba, Saskatchewan, and Alberta were either First Nations peoples or French-speaking Catholic métis. However, in 1811, Thomas Douglas, the fifth Earl of Selkirk, made the first concerted effort to colonize this area. He wanted to provide relief to distressed Scottish farmers while also providing the Hudson Bay Company with a source of food and labour. To this end, he established the agriculturally based Red River Settlement near present-day Winnipeg. Early attempts to provide the settlers with a school were unsuccessful, and it would be almost 40 years before a Presbyterian school was established. In the interim, schools that did exist for the French-speaking population were run by Roman Catholic priests or their French-Canadian lay recruits. By 1820, Roman Catholics had access to three schools, while Protestants had access to none.

Between 1820 and 1870, the population of the Prairies experienced a slow but steady growth and a concurrent increase in the number of schools (see Figure 3.3). In general, the schools that were established during this period were of a sectarian nature. By 1840, the Roman Catholics and Methodists were active in what is presently northern Alberta. By the late 1860s, Saskatchewan also had a small number of Protestant schools. While both Saskatchewan and Alberta recognized separate schools based on religious affiliation, Manitoba followed a separate path.

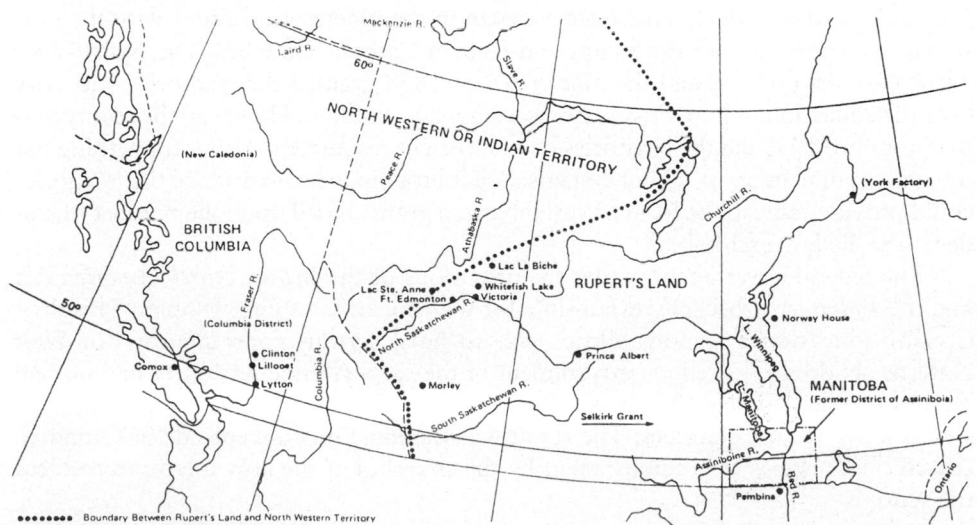

Centres Where Schools Were Established in Western Canada Before 1873

Figure 3.3

Centres where Western schools were established prior to 1873.

Source: G. F. Stanley, *The Birth of Western Canada: The Riel Rebellions.* Reprinted with permission from the University of Toronto Press.

With the completion of the Canadian National Railway in 1885, access to settlement areas in Western Canada became much easier. In the period from 1886 to 1914, over 750 000 immigrants entered Canada from the United States, Sweden, Germany, Norway, Iceland, Hungary, and the Ukraine. Because many of the new immigrants spoke little or no English, attempts to assimilate them were concentrated on their second-generation children, who were expected to have their schooling conducted only in English. Objections to this practice were raised by many of the newcomers—in particular, the Ukrainians who settled in Manitoba, who wished to preserve their language and culture. These objections led in turn to the Rutharian issue, also known as the "Manitoba School Question." In 1897, a compromise that satisfied neither side was reached. Officially termed the Laurier-Greenway Agreement, a uniform, non-denominational school system with English as the formal language of instruction was to be imposed. However, if the parents of 10 students at a school requested that their children be instructed in a language other than English, the school was to make the necessary accommodations. In effect, Manitoba developed Canada's only multilingual education system.

British Columbia

Like the Prairies, British Columbia was initially under the control of the Hudson Bay Company. Prior to 1858, the non-indigenous population was less than 1000. As a result, the first British Columbia school was not established until 1849. Nine years later, the gold rush of 1858 brought about dramatic changes. Thousands of gold seekers from all parts of the world descended on the territory and brought an end to the influence of the Hudson Bay Company. The new arrivals, who were of numerous cultural and ethnic backgrounds, immediately began to agitate for schools that were both non-denominational and free. Unlike other areas of Canada, where protracted battles for control of the schools had been waged by primarily sectarian interests, the conflict in BC was remarkably brief. The *Common School Act* of 1865, supplemented by the common School Ordinance of 1869, decreed that BC schools would be both free and non-sectarian. The state was now firmly in control of the education system.

The Canadian North

Canada's northern educational history began in the nineteenth century with the missionary activities of both Protestant and Roman Catholic churches. The *North-West Territories Act* of 1875 and the *Yukon Act* of 1898 granted the territories authority over the education of non–First Nations school-age children. However, the reality was that not until 1950 did the territories have sufficient resources to support anything but the most rudimentary of school systems. What little financial assistance the territories could provide came in the form of variably sized grants based upon the number of students enrolled in a school.

The federal government, under the provisions of the *British North America Act* and the *Indian Act*, became responsible for the education of First Peoples. This division of educational responsibilities was to have serious consequences for First Nations children. The federal government of the early twentieth century had no real interest in educating First Nations children and simply passed its educational responsibilities over to the churches. The result was the most horrific episode in Canadian educational history: the establishment by the churches of the now infamous residential schools.

Confederation and the *British North America Act* of 1867

As Canada's colonial period came to an end, political figures from all parts of England's remaining North American provinces discussed a confederation that would bind them together as one nation. The *British North America Act* (BNA) of 1867 was the legal instrument used to set out the federal and provincial responsibilities of those provinces that wished to become part of this new country. Under Article 93 of the agreement, education was to be a provincial responsibility. Careful reading of Article 93 clearly indicates that the diverse school systems established in the various geographical areas of the country would not be threatened by the newly established federal government. Indeed, any separate school rights acquired by a minority group prior to 1867 were constitutionally guaranteed by the *BNA Act*. The act also placed Canada in a unique category: Today, it is one of the few developed countries in which there is no national system of education.

What Patterns Developed in Canadian Education from 1875 to 1918?

In 1875, Canada's population was primarily rural. Most schools were relatively small, with most accurately representing the concept of the little red school house. The curriculum was simple and concentrated on the 3 Rs. However, as Canada approached the twentieth century, the number of immigrants increased significantly, while industrialization and urbanization also began to place additional strains on every province's education system. The basic education provided by existing schools was becoming inadequate for the needs of a society that was slowly but certainly changing from a rural focus to an urban one. A result of this evolving demographic was a philosophical debate over the basic goals of education. Was the purpose of schools to help individuals to read the Bible, do simple mathematical calculations, and write simple communications, or was the purpose to provide skilled workers who could meet the demands of commerce and industry?

While the roots of science and technical education can be traced back to the work of educators such as Sir John William Dawson, president of McGill University from 1855 to 1896, by the early twentieth century, science had become a significant component of provincial curricula. Technical education had also made significant inroads, and by 1918, it was available in most urban centres. However, while urban-area schools were successfully making the transition to a more scientifically and technologically based curriculum, rural areas were experiencing serious educational distress. The Federal Census of 1871 indicated that almost 88 percent of Canada's population resided in rural areas, but the Census of 1911 indicated that rural populations had decreased to only 54 percent. Additionally, urban areas paid teachers salaries that were often twice as high as those available in rural communities. This led to most of the best qualified teachers moving to and remaining in urban centres. Rural groups, composed mainly of farmers, began to make demands for a more relevant curriculum, better teachers, and better educational opportunities for their children.

By the early 1900s, the demand for teachers had grown dramatically. An increasing number of women entered the teaching field at this time, beginning a trend often referred to as the "feminization of teaching." Female teachers were given less respect from the community than their male predecessors, though they were still more highly regarded than women who worked in factories or in the domestic sphere. In addition, they were expected to be of high moral character. They were subjected to a level of public scrutiny hard to imagine today.

Attempts by education officials to meet the demands of their rural citizens encountered varying degrees of success. Perhaps the most successful of these efforts was the consolidation of small rural school districts into larger ones, a process which, to some degree, is still taking place as Canada's rural population continues to shrink. Because of their larger student bodies, consolidated schools could provide greater opportunities for curriculum diversity. However, rural education still faced many challenges. The Prairie provinces, for example, had experienced a large influx of settlers from eastern and central Europe. Some of these settlers wanted their children to be at home working the land rather than at school. Others wanted their children educated in their native tongue; but as there were few teachers with the linguistic knowledge to provide such a service, English became the language of instruction.

At the conclusion of World War I in 1918, the Canadian education system was taking on the basic elements of its present form. All provinces had developed centralized educational bureaucracies. Curricular issues around the preparation of students for an industrial, urban-focused life were being discussed and implemented; secondary schools were becoming more prevalent; normal schools for the preparation of teachers were becoming more common; and, while some provinces had separate schools, these schools were publicly funded.

What Is the History of Schooling for First Nations Peoples?

From the beginning, settlers' efforts to indoctrinate First Nations children with European values through education was a shameful exercise, undertaken to exterminate First Nations peoples by assimilation. The settlers and the clerics—first Roman Catholic, and later also Protestant—shared a common belief that the First Nations way of life was inferior in every way to their own.

However, as Barman, McCaskill, and Hebert point out in *Indian Education in Canada, Volume 1: The Legacy* (1986, 2–4), there was much that was admirable about the education provided by First Nations for their children. They taught about the unity of all life, honourable conduct, family responsibilities, individual responsibility, the importance of sharing, self-reliance, and survival skills. Their history was transmitted through stories, myths, and legends.

Unfortunately for First Nations peoples, the colonial clerical and other designated educators were primarily interested in "civilizing" First Nations peoples by converting them to Christianity. Because First Nations languages, culture, and political structures were different and non-Christian, they were deemed barbaric, and thus worthy of eradication. This belief in First Nations inferiority was institutionalized in the Treaty of Utrecht (which transferred Acadia from France to Britain) and was incorporated into the *British North America Act* in 1867.

The *British North America Act*, Section 91:24, placed the responsibility for "Indians and Indian Lands" firmly in the hands of the federal government. The later *Indian Act* of 1876 was enacted by Canada's Parliament to manage that responsibility, with the goal being the complete assimilation of First Nations peoples—following exactly the British example.

The *Indian Act* of 1876 included paternalistic provisions for how the government would manage band membership, education, First Nations estates, and practically every social service. First Nations governments were made subservient to the federal government. Residential schools for First Nations children were first established in the

1840s. Like First Nations day schools, residential schools were created to assimilate First Nations peoples. Children were forcibly taken from their families, locked up, forbidden to speak their own languages, and often subjected to harsh or even criminal acts. The stories of mental, physical, and sexual abuse to which they were subjected are deeply disturbing. In 1907, Dr. Peter Bryce, former medical inspector for the Department of Indian Affairs (DIA), published *The Story of a National Crime: An Appeal for Justice to the Indians of Canada*. On this tract's cover page, Bryce revealed his discovery that a death rate of almost 50 percent was evident among First Nations children enrolled in residential schools, a fact actively suppressed by the Canadian government and the involved churches. Fortunately, the National Indian Brotherhood's (NIB) 1972 call for greater First Nations control of education was eventually heeded.

One example of what the future may hold is Piqqusilirivvik, "a place that has those things important to us," a school so radically different from a conventional educational institution that government officials claim it should not even be called a school. Located in Nunavut, students don't need to show grades to gain entry, tuition and living expenses are paid by the territory, and classrooms are called "learning studios."

While the funding for First Nations schools is provided by the federal government, some control of education, primarily through federal–provincial agreements, is now in the hands of various bands. There are still difficulties, however. High dropout rates are an ongoing problem, and they perpetuate the shortage of First Nation teachers and other professionals. School funding and equipment shortages also continue to exist.

On the positive side, educational challenges faced by First Nations children are now well-recognized, and First Nations leaders are working toward the creation of a fairer and more effective system of schools. Thus the wrongs of the past are unlikely to be repeated. The rest of Canadian society watches with supportive hope as Canada's First Nations attempt the recreation of the first-class education system that was taken from them over the past 350 years.

Note: This section was collaboratively written by one of the authors and Mr. Daniel Paul, a First Nations author and former district chief for the Shubenacadie Mi'kmaq Bands.

What Educational Advancements Took Place between the Great Wars (1918–1939)?

World War I made government officials recognize the need for technical and industrial education. War was becoming more automated and scientific. Soldiers with technical experience were becoming a necessity of modern warfare. As a consequence, through the *Technical Education Act* of 1919, the federal government made funds available to the provinces for the development of technical/vocational schools and programs. While all areas of the country participated to a greater or lesser degree in the establishment of vocational programs, the exact nature of what was developed varied. Some added programs to existing schools, some established schools devoted exclusively to technical and vocational training, and others set up correspondence courses or summer schools.

The problems associated with the decline of rural populations continued throughout this period. Studies of these problems were conducted in provinces such as Ontario, New Brunswick, and Alberta. However, other than through the continued amalgamation of rural school districts into ever larger consolidated ones, little could be done to alleviate the rural school issue.

The period between the wars also saw a dramatic increase in the number of students who went on to post-elementary education. A partial explanation for this may lie with the Great Depression, which started in 1929. Students who might have wanted to enter the labour force could not do so as there were no jobs. However, other factors were likely involved. Schools were becoming more appealing places, and there was a growing recognition that a good education was often the prerequisite for a good job. An additional factor almost certainly relates to the school-leaving age requirements that were beginning to be introduced. For example, in 1922, Ontario had a law that every child must attend school; it also required children to attend until they were 16 years of age.

Curriculum and student discipline were subjects of great concern and much discussion during this period. What should be taught? Should the emphasis be placed on traditional academic courses, such as English and mathematics? Should there be technical and vocational courses? Should some courses be required for all students to take, while others could be electives? Should junior high schools be established, thus changing the model of eight years of elementary education followed by three or four years of secondary school? What types of disciplinary procedures should be established? Opinions on these and related topics varied from province to province. There was little agreement, and definitive answers would not be determined until after 1945.

Other newer ideas and issues also made their appearance during this period. The theories of psychologists such as Edward Lee Thorndike started to receive attention, as did the concepts of progressive education espoused by John Dewey. Universities began to take an interest in teacher education, and, as early as 1923, the University of British Columbia established a school of education for university graduates. Other universities followed this lead, and within the next 50 years, most of the traditional normal schools would cease to exist.

The period from 1918 to 1939 did not result in a great number of truly significant changes to the Canadian education system. The ideas and forces that were to give our present-day system its final characteristics were now in place. The extended period of peace and prosperity that followed World War II would provide the ideal environment for the final evolution of Canada's present system of education.

What Are the Major Characteristics of Today's System of Education in Canada?

At the end of World War II, Canadian education continued its evolution into the system we know today. The trend evident by 1945 would, for the most part, become well established by the end of the twentieth century. While each of the 10 provinces and 4 territories has its own distinctive features, there are many commonalities.

Elementary

Education is compulsory for all children between the ages of 6 and 16, although most provinces and territories have kindergarten (called Primary in some jurisdictions) for students who are five years of age. The length of the elementary program varies from five years in Saskatchewan to eight years in Ontario and Manitoba. Depending on the length of their elementary program, students next proceed to middle school (normally Grades 6 to 8), junior high (Grades 7 to 9), or secondary school (in many areas, Grades 9 to 12).

Secondary

Secondary schools (high schools) offer a variety of courses, both academic and vocational. High school students have compulsory courses in areas such as mathematics, languages, social studies, and the sciences. Elective courses, such as music, drama, and geology, also form part of the high school curriculum. Most schools have programs that prepare students for admission to university or to community college. In Quebec, the model is somewhat different. At the end of Grade 11, students can attend a collège d'enseignement général et professional (**CEGEP**) for either two years of preparatory study toward admission to university or three years of study in a technical/vocational program.

School Year

The lengths of both the **school year** and the school day are set by each province or territory's department of education. The Canadian average is 188 student days, with seven additional professional development days for teachers. However, Alberta, Saskatchewan, and Quebec have set the school year at 200 days. An additional factor in determining what constitutes a school year is the length of the school day. On average, this constitutes 300 minutes of teacher–student contact time per day, but there are variations.

All Alberta students receive 950 hours of instruction per year, while secondary students in Ontario receive 925 hours and elementary students only 850. By way of comparison with other countries, Canada's school year is in the middle. China has 251 days in its school year, Taiwan has 222 days, and the United Sates has 178 days. At 172 days, the school years of Portugal and Ireland are the shortest.

Separate Schools

Canada's publicly funded separate schools reflect the country's religious and linguistic diversity. Alberta, Saskatchewan, Ontario, Quebec, New Brunswick, and Newfoundland all have separate school systems based on religious affiliation or language. While Nova Scotia does not have a separate school system, it does have schools whose students are almost exclusively French Acadians.

How Are Canadian Schools Funded?

It costs approximately $5.5 billion a year to finance Canada's 5.4 million elementary and secondary students, who attend any of the country's 15 500 public and separate schools. Teacher salaries consume an estimated 80 percent of the school budget, while the remainder goes for maintenance, student transportation, school supplies, and new construction. On average, it costs $6500 to $8000 to educate one student for one year.

As Figure 3.4 indicates, Canada's per-student level of educational spending is one of the highest in the world. The actual money required for the operation of schools is raised through taxation at the territorial or provincial and municipal levels.

School Funding Formulas

School funding formulas are used to determine how much money is allocated to the operation of schools within a particular school district. While these formulas vary from one jurisdiction to another, the following constitutes a representative example.

International comparison of direct public spending on education

Source: Organization for Economic Co-operation and Development, Education at a glance: OECD indicators, 2006.

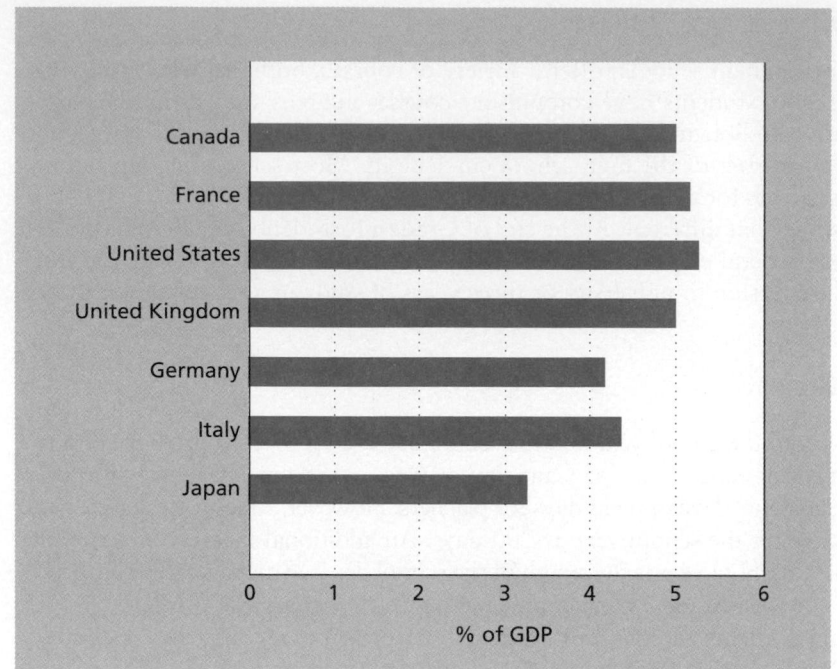

% of GDP

Operating Formula for the Basic Costs of School Operation

- For every student in a school district, the government gives the board a specified amount of money.
- A student is defined as someone who is under 21 years of age and listed on a class register as of September 30. (Some provinces give schools half their funding for students enrolled on September 30, and the remainder for students enrolled as of May 30.)
- Rural school districts receive a special allocation to cover the costs of student transportation.
- Some students are more expensive than others to educate. For example, a student who is deaf or blind might cost as much to educate as 2.2 students without special needs.

Maintenance Formula for the Upkeep and Repair of a School

- Very similar to operating formulas but pertaining to buildings and equipment.
- Boards are given a grant for each instruction area (classroom = 1.0) with adjustments made for laboratories (2.1 classroom units) and gymnasiums (4.5).
- Telephone costs, paper costs, janitorial services, and other similar expenses are covered by this formula.

Capital Funding for Major Repairs or New Construction

- A school board submits to its department of education a proposal for construction of a new school or major repairs to an existing school.
- Department of education officials then review the proposal, compare it to other similar requests, and make a decision to accept or reject each on a case-by-case basis.

Local Funding

- A municipality must pay a specified percentage of its board's operating expenses. Typically, this percentage can range from a low of 1 percent to as much as 20 percent. The municipality can, however, elect to allocate funds above the required percentage should it wish to do so.
- Municipalities raise their required funding through the taxation of local property.

What Are Some Current Trends in Canadian Education?

Several educational trends have developed during recent years. Some have had a very positive impact and reflect the vibrant nature of our collective public and separate school systems. Many of these topics will receive greater attention in later chapters.

Evaluation and Assessment

Most Canadians have a great interest in educational matters and are quick to express their concerns about curriculum issues and issues related to the quality of instruction their children receive. As a direct consequence of the criticism levelled at schools in these areas, there has been an increased emphasis on the evaluation and assessment of the curriculum and the teachers who deliver it. The Council of Ministers of Education, Canada (CMEC), which meets regularly for the discussion of issues of common interest, established the Pan-Canadian Assessment Program (PCAP) as one method for determining the effectiveness of provincial and territorial education programs. PCAP, which came into effect in 2007, initially assesses student performance in mathematics, reading and writing, and science, and will evaluate other subjects if the need arises. Additionally, many school districts have created their own evaluation instruments to determine how well their schools are performing. While PCAP, national teacher conferences, and other groups with an interest in education now share their practices regarding evaluation and assessment, they also deal with other topics. This mutual sharing of ideas has become one of the most valuable trends in Canadian education.

Students with Special Needs

The inclusive school movement has made significant gains in making schools more responsive to the needs of children with learning difficulties or physical disabilities. (Chapter 8 will deal with the complexities related to this topic.) The needs of groups such as children of recent immigrants, members of our First Nations communities, and African-Canadian students are also being addressed. Indeed, many school districts now have departments or officials designated with the responsibility of meeting the needs of minorities.

Ancillary Services

Canadian schools are responding to requests for additional services. Daycare facilities, for example, are now available in some secondary schools, as are programs in anger-management, peer mediation, peer drug-education, and respect for differences. The educational role of schools is becoming increasingly intermixed with providing guidance traditionally thought to be the responsibility of the family.

Technology

The advent of the internet and the need to prepare students for the proliferation of technology have led to increased funding for computers, data projectors, printers, scanners, and other related pieces of hardware and software. Teachers now require increased professional development to deal with new teaching and learning methodologies that rely on technology. Persuading them to give up some of their more traditional teaching strategies is one of the many challenges facing the leaders of today's technology-enriched schools.

Curriculum Development

All departments of education now provide teachers with curriculum guides that contain specific learning outcomes. There is increased emphasis on language development and use, mathematical skills and concepts, thinking skills, and the sciences. Teachers no longer have to develop curricula based on some general guidelines for a particular subject at a specific grade level. The trend is now to provide a very specific curriculum to deliver along with concrete suggestions as to how it might be delivered effectively. On the one hand, this constitutes a reduction in teacher autonomy; on the other, it is a response to the criticisms of those who believe that teachers require more guidance to carry out their classroom responsibilities.

Second Language Acquisition

Canada is a leader in the area of second language instruction. French as a second language is taught in most Canadian school districts, and French immersion (FI) programs are common in many areas. However, the shortage of qualified French immersion teachers is generating concerns. While most FI programs start at some point in the lower elementary grades, the true difficulties arise at the secondary level where subjects such as physics, mathematics, and chemistry need to be taught in French. Finding a qualified English-speaking teacher for these subjects is already very difficult. Finding someone who can teach them in French is more challenging still.

A particular difficulty for many schools, especially those in large urban centres such as Montreal, Toronto, and Vancouver, is the large number of immigrant children who, upon enrolment, speak little or no English. **English as a second language** (ESL) classes are an absolute requirement, but the number of teachers qualified to instruct such classes is still rather limited.

There can be no doubt that Canadian schools are still in an evolutionary process. However, the independence of each province or territory, which makes our education system quite different from those of other countries, provides Canadians with a great advantage. The provinces and territories are uniquely free to experiment with new educational practices without having to seek permission from a centralized federal bureaucracy. If a new practice is successful, the high degree of collaboration among the various Canadian units ensures that it may be instituted in other areas of the country. The cultural divisiveness and sectarian wrangling that characterized much of Canada's educational history has actually been a valuable gift. Rather than having a centralized bureaucracy within which a single bureaucrat might have the authority to stifle a good idea, Canada has 14 independent departments of education. As a consequence, the possibilities for a novel educational practice to receive a valid field test are much higher here than in many other countries.

What Are Some Alternative Types of Canadian Schools?

While the large majority of Canadian students attend government-funded public or separate schools, there are several other options available to parents who are unhappy with the education provided by these schools. While it is not possible to list all of these options, the following examples provide a representative sample.

Independent Schools

Independent schools have existed from the earliest days of Canadian education. Often referred to as private schools (a term not embraced in such schools because of its elitist connotation), these schools charge tuition that can range from as low as $2000 per year to as high as over $50 000 annually. Most are religious in nature, or at least in origin, and often have a boarding school component. Parents who elect to send their children to independent schools do so for a variety of reasons. Some want the religious and/or social values of the home reinforced by the school, some believe the quality of the education delivered is better than in public schools, and others believe that the characteristically small class sizes foster an environment in which their children are more likely to thrive.

In some provinces, such as Quebec and the Western provinces, limited public funding is available under certain conditions. In all other areas, independent schools must provide their own funding. Overall, perhaps 5 to 6 percent of Canadian students attend independent schools.

Montessori Schools

Maria Montessori (1870–1952), an Italian physician who was influenced by Rousseau, believed that children's mental, physical, and spiritual development could be enhanced by providing them with developmentally appropriate educational activities.

At Montessori's school for poor preschool-age children in Rome, teachers created learning environments based on students' levels of development and readiness to learn new material. According to the **Montessori method**, prescribed sets of materials and physical exercises are used to develop students' knowledge and skills, and students are allowed to use or not use the materials as they see fit. The materials arouse students' interest, and the interest motivates them to learn. Through highly individualized instruction, students develop self-discipline and self-confidence. Montessori's ideas spread throughout the world. While most Canadian Montessori schools are located in Ontario and British Columbia, there are a few in other provinces (Webb, Metha, & Jordan 1999). Today, Montessorian materials and activities are a standard part of the early childhood and elementary curricula in public schools throughout Canada.

Home-Schooling

While there are laws requiring that all children be educated, there is no legal requirement that parents send their children to a publicly or privately funded institution. It is perfectly valid for children to be educated at home. Fifteen years ago, there were fewer than 2000 Canadian children who were being home-schooled. The situation has since changed, and there are now over 40 000 children being taught at home by one or both parents. The **home-schooling** movement is growing at such a rate that provincial and territorial departments of education are developing new rules, regulations, and procedures for parents who wish to home-school their children. While there is little formal research that compares the later academic success of home-schooled children with that of children who had a more traditional educational experience, initial indications suggest that home-schooled children do as well on standardized achievement tests as those who attend publicly or privately funded schools. When one home-schooled child was asked what she did not like about the practice, her only complaint was: "We don't get storm days off like the other kids."

Virtual Schools

New **virtual schools** are becoming popular in Canada, especially in British Columbia and Alberta. Virtual schools vary in significant ways from traditional schools. The courses are taken electronically via the internet rather than in person in a regular classroom, and while some courses are scheduled for a particular time, others may be taken at the convenience of the student. In the model that has specifically scheduled class times, all students taking a particular class are expected to be online at the same time. They can take part in discussions, listen to a lecture, and send or receive information. In the model without scheduled online time, the student takes the course as she or he decides. There is no "real-time" discussion, and communication with the instructor is via e-mail or a dedicated mailing list.

SUMMARY

What Determines Your Educational Philosophy?

■ An educational philosophy is a set of beliefs about education—a set of principles to guide professional action.

■ A teacher's educational philosophy is made up of personal beliefs about teaching and learning, students, knowledge, and what is worth knowing.

What Are the Branches of Philosophy?

■ The branches of philosophy and the questions they address are (1) metaphysics (What is the nature of reality?), (2) epistemology (What is the nature of knowledge, and is truth attainable?), (3) axiology (What values should one live by?), (4) ethics (What is good and evil, right and wrong?), (5) aesthetics (What is beautiful?), and (6) logic (What reasoning processes yield valid conclusions?).

What Are Five Modern Philosophical Orientations to Teaching?

■ Progressivism—The aim of education should be based on the needs and interests of students.

■ Perennialism—Students should acquire knowledge of enduring great ideas.

■ Essentialism—Schools should teach students a core of "essential" knowledge and skills in a disciplined and systematic manner.

- Social reconstructionism—In response to the significant social problems of the day, schools should take the lead in creating a new social order.

- Existentialism—In the face of an indifferent universe, students should acquire an education that will enable them to assign meaning to their lives.

What Psychological Orientations Have Influenced Teaching Philosophies?

- Humanism—Children are innately good, and education should focus on individual needs, personal freedom, and self-actualization.

- Behaviourism—By careful control of the educational environment and with appropriate reinforcement techniques, teachers can cause students to exhibit desired behaviours.

- Constructivism—Teachers should "understand students' understanding" and view learning as an active process in which learners construct meaning.

How Can You Develop Your Educational Philosophy?

- Instead of basing their teaching on only one educational philosophy, most teachers develop an eclectic educational philosophy.

- Professional teachers continually strive for a clearer, more comprehensive answer to basic philosophical questions.

What Cultural Traditions Have Led to the Development of the Canadian Education Landscape?

- Early Canadian education was founded on the cultural traditions of France, England, Scotland, and the United States. The primary purpose of each tradition was the promotion of religion.

- The French tradition, in schools known as petites écoles, provided a rudimentary education. Instruction was provided by parish priests or their assistants. Boys and girls attended separate schools.

- The English tradition was primarily controlled by the Church of England, with the quality of the education delivered being a function of class rather than merit. There were "public" schools for the wealthy and various other schools for the poor.

- The American tradition was originally modelled after the British tradition, but the practicalities of frontier life led to its becoming increasingly more practical.

- The Scottish tradition provided elementary and secondary education to students of both genders regardless of their social rank. Unlike other traditions, the curriculum of Scottish schools included subjects such as science and art.

What Were Teaching and Schools Like in Canada Prior to 1875?

- During this formative period of Canada's educational history, the school systems that evolved were a reflection of the cultural traditions of Quebec, Atlantic Canada, Ontario, and the Northwest. In all areas, the struggle for state-supported schools was the cause of rancorous debate.

- In Quebec, during the period between its founding and fall (1608–1760), the school system was modelled after that of France. Later, with the arrival of English, Scottish, and Irish settlers, tentative steps toward a more coherent school system were taken. By 1875, Quebec had two school systems: one for the English and one for the French. The government of Quebec paid for the support of the schools via taxation based on local property assessment.

- In Nova Scotia, Prince Edward Island, and New Brunswick, waves of settlers arrived from England, Scotland, and the United States. The school systems that evolved were state-supported and -operated. However, in Newfoundland and Labrador, the schools eventually came to be supported by the state but operated by various religious denominations.

- In Ontario, where most of the settlers were either Loyalists or Americans who emigrated to that province, state-supported and -operated schools were firmly established by 1850.

- The Northwest was a thinly populated area during this period. However, by 1870, Manitoba and British Columbia had state-supported and -operated schools. Alberta and Saskatchewan would later establish a system of state-supported and -operated separate schools based on religious tradition.

- The *British North America Act* of 1867 established that education was to be a purely provincial responsibility.

What Patterns Developed in Canadian Education from 1875 to 1918?

- In 1875, Canada's population was primarily rural; by 1918, it had become increasingly urban.

- All areas of the country developed centralized educational bureaucracies.

- Secondary schools became common; normal schools for the training of teachers became prevalent.

What Is the History of Schooling for First Nations Peoples?

- First Nations peoples used myths and legends to teach their children about the unity of all life, honourable conduct, individual and family responsibilities, and survival skills.

- Colonial clerical educators initially attempted to assimilate First Nations peoples by converting them to Christianity.

- Residential schools, established in the 1840s, were created to assimilate First Nations peoples into European culture. Children at these schools were forbidden to speak their native language and were often abused.

- Since the 1970s, control of education has been in the hands of various First Nations bands.

What Educational Advancements Took Place between the Great Wars (1918–1939)?

- Vocationally based education became common.

- Larger numbers of students went on to post-elementary education.

- Discussions about curricular and student discipline issues became common.
- The writings of educational psychologists and philosophers began to have an impact on Canadian schools.

What Are the Major Characteristics of Today's System of Education in Canada?

- Education is compulsory for all children.
- Most provinces have an elementary component (Grades 1 to 6), a junior high component (Grades 7 to 9), and a high school program (Grades 10 to 12).
- The average school year in most provinces and territories is 188 days.
- Some jurisdictions have separate schools based upon either religion or language; others do not.

How Are Canadian Schools Funded?

- The costs of operating all of Canada's schools for one year is approximately $50 billion.
- School boards receive their operating, maintenance, and capital funding needs according to funding formulas, which differ from one province or territory to the next.

What Are Some Current Trends in Canadian Education?

- Evaluation and assessment are receiving increased attention.
- The inclusive school movement has led to students with special needs receiving increased attention and funding.
- Many Canadian schools now provide a variety of ancillary services, such as day care and respect-for-differences programs.
- Information technology is now widely available in most schools.
- Curriculum guides with specific recommendations for teachers are available in all school districts.
- French immersion programs are available in all provinces and territories.

What Are Some Alternative Types of Canadian Schools?

- Independent schools, also known as private schools, charge tuition for the educational services they provide. Many of these schools have a religious affiliation. Some provide boarding facilities; others do not.
- Montessori schools, which base their curriculum upon the Montessori method, are most commonly found in Ontario and British Columbia.
- The home-schooling movement is becoming more popular. Departments of education are developing regulations and procedures for parents who wish to teach their children at home.
- Virtual schools are becoming more prevalent. Students "attend" class electronically via the internet.

KEY TERMS AND CONCEPTS

aesthetics, 65
American tradition, 73
axiology, 64
behaviourism, 70
British North America Act
   (BNA Act), 81
CEGEP, 85
cognitive science, 71
constructivism, 70
critical pedagogy, 69
dame-schools, 73
educational
   philosophy, 61

English as a second
   language (ESL), 88
English tradition, 72
epistemology, 64
essentialism, 67
ethics, 64
existentialism, 68
French tradition, 72
home-schooling, 90
humanism, 69
humanistic psychology, 69
independent schools, 89
logic, 65

metaphysics, 63
Montessori method, 89
normal schools, 72
parochial schools, 72
perennialism, 66
petites écoles, 72
praxis, 69
progressivism, 67
school year, 85
Scottish tradition, 73
separate schools, 72
social reconstructionism, 68
virtual schools, 90

APPLICATIONS AND ACTIVITIES

Teacher's Journal

1. Assume you are not an Essentialist but subscribe to one of the other philosophical orientations to teaching. State your position and write a memo to an Essentialist explaining why you think he or she should give up his or her position and instead subscribe to your own.

2. Recall one of your favourite teachers in grades K–12. Which of the educational philosophies or psychological orientations to teaching described in this chapter best captures that teacher's approach to teaching? Write a descriptive sketch of that teacher in action.

3. Based on what you have read in this chapter, identify several broad or long-term trends in the development of Canadian education that continue today. How were those trends reflected in educational policies and practices throughout the past decade? How is this trend evident at different points in the past and now? How might it manifest in the future?

4. Write a personal history of your experience as a student, focusing on the age or grade level of the students you plan to teach. Conclude with an analysis of how you expect your experience as a student will influence your teaching practice.

5. What does the history of textbooks tell us about education in Canada? What values and priorities do textbooks today seem to reflect in comparison to textbooks of the seventeenth, eighteenth, and nineteenth centuries?

6. Investigate Canada's growing home-school movement and answer the following questions as put forward by the Fraser Institute in "Home Schooling: From the extreme to the Mainstream" (P. Basham, J. Merrifield, & C.R. Hepburn) at http://www.fraserinstitute.org/research-news/display.aspx?id=13089.

   ■ How does the government regulate home-schooling?
   ■ What is the history of home-schooling in North America?
   ■ How many children are home-schooled?

- What are the socio-demographic characteristics of home-schooling families?
- How do home-schooled children perform academically?
- What is known about the socialization of home-schooled children?
- What are the public policy implications of this experiment in private education?

Theory into Practice

1. With a partner or partners, as your instructor directs, and with a maximum of five minutes preparation time, prepare a short skit or role play for one of the following situations:

   - School trustees deciding on a dress code for present-day teachers and for students
   - Secondary students deciding on a dress code for themselves and for school dances
   - Why music and physical education or other subjects should or should not be considered to be essential and required school subjects
   - Parents or students describing the characteristics of the perfect elementary or secondary teacher
   - Parents complaining about the high cost of school fees for various supplies or activities
   - Parents or students discussing the practical and philosophical reasons for
     – the requirement that school uniforms be worn
     – why the traditional summer vacation for students and teachers should be abolished
     – why the present school-leaving age of 15 should be raised or lowered, and to what age

2. Just for Fun: Who Are You?

   This is a minor psychological quiz (rated as generally accurate by 75 percent of respondents and totally inaccurate by the remainder). The possible meaning of your responses to the five questions in this activity may be found in Teacher's Resource 3.3 at www.MyEducationLab.com.

   Respond to each of the following questions with a noun and two and preferably three emotive adjectives. Emotive adjectives are words that describe something about the essential nature of a thing or being. For example, if asked to give three emotive adjectives to describe a shark, you might say dangerous, aggressive, and frightening. Three non-emotive adjectives would be descriptors such as sharp-toothed, scaled, or finned.

   Note: You will not be expected to show your responses to either the instructor or to other students—unless you elect to do so.

   1. What is your favourite animal?

   2. What is your second favourite animal?

   3. What is your favourite bird?

   4. What do you see when I ask you to picture something in the natural world that is made of or contains liquid water.

   5. What do you see when I ask you to picture a vessel or object from which you would drink liquid?

   6. What do you see when I ask you to picture a wall?

1. Explore encyclopedias, bibliographies, periodicals, news sources, and online reference works to research in greater detail the contributions of a pioneer in education or a historical development described in Chapter 3.

Observations and Interviews

1. Interview a teacher for the purpose of understanding his or her educational philosophy. Formulate your interview questions in light of the philosophical concepts discussed in this chapter. Discuss your findings with classmates.

2. Administer a philosophical inventory to a group of teachers at a local school. Analyze the results and compare your findings with classmates.

3. Observe the class of a teacher at the level at which you plan to teach. Which of the five philosophies or three psychological orientations to teaching discussed in this chapter most characterizes this teacher?

4. Visit a school and interview the principal about the school's educational philosophy. Ask him or her to comment on what is expected of teachers in regard to achieving the goals contained in the statement of philosophy.

5. Interview veteran teachers and administrators at a local school and ask them to comment on the changes in education they have observed and experienced during their careers. What events do respondents identify as having had the greatest impact on their teaching? Record, videotape, or transcribe respondents' stories to share with classmates.

6. As a collaborative project with classmates, conduct on-site interviews and observations for the purpose of researching the history of a particular school and its culture or way of life. You might collaborate with teachers and students of history or social studies at the school to help you in your investigation.

7. Individually or with a classmate, visit a school and conduct a three- to four-hour school observation. Details describing your expected conduct at such a visit are available from your instructor.

Professional Portfolio

1. Prepare a written (or videotaped) statement in which you describe a key element of your educational philosophy. To organize your thoughts, focus on one of the following dimensions of educational philosophy:

   - Beliefs about teaching and learning
   - Beliefs about students
   - Beliefs about knowledge
   - Beliefs about what is worth knowing
   - Personal beliefs about the six branches of philosophy

   Develop your statement of philosophy throughout the course, covering all dimensions. On completion of your teacher-education program, review your portfolio entry and make any appropriate revisions. Being able to articulate your philosophy of education and your teaching philosophy will be an important part of finding your first job as a teacher.

2. Prepare a video- or audiotaped oral history of the school experiences of older members of the community. Focus on a topic or issue of special interest to you and prepare some questions in advance. For instance, you might be interested in an aspect of curriculum or student relations. Analyze the oral histories in relation to the development of education in Canada and record your analysis.

MyEducationLab

For a quick analysis of your own philosophical outlook with regard to educational matters, take the Philosophic Inventory (Teacher's Resource 3.1) at www.MyEducationLab.com.

For suggestions regarding asking questions, read Teacher's Resource 3.2, Teacher's Scribe: "Does anyone have a question?" at www.MyEducationLab.com.

Watch the video "Developing a philosophy of education," in the Video Lab at www.MyEducationLab.com.

4

Canadian School Governance and Law

The drastic reduction in the number of units of local government for education has been one of the most dramatic of all changes in Canada's pattern of government. And yet, it has occurred and is continuing with relatively little public concern or debate.

—Canadian Teachers' Federation, as quoted in *Provincial Initiatives to Restructure Canadian School Governance in the 1990s* (Fleming, 1997)

focus questions

1. Who is involved in Canadian school governance?
2. What is the historical basis for the governance of Canadian schools?
3. What is the role of the federal government in Canadian education?
4. What is the role of provincial governments in Canadian education?
5. Who do school boards serve, and what is the difference between governance and administration?
6. Why do you need a professional code of ethics?
7. What are your legal rights as a teacher?
8. What are your legal responsibilities as a teacher?

On entering the staff room during your preparation period, you can tell immediately that the four teachers in the room are having a heated discussion.

"I don't see how you can say that teachers have much control over the schools," says Kim, a language arts teacher at the school for three years. "It's all so political. The provincial department of education and the school boards—it's the politicians who really control the schools. We have minimal input into the design of the standardized tests our kids take. The scores of those tests seem to be the only thing people use to judge the schools' effectiveness. When the test scores are released, the politicians talk about making the education system more accountable, but they're just exploiting the schools so they can get elected."

"If you want to know who really controls the schools," you hear Serge, a mathematics teacher, contend, "it's big business. The politicians are actually their pawns. Big business is concerned with international competition, so they exert tremendous pressure on the politicians who, in turn, lean on the teachers. And then . . ."

"Just a minute," says Frank, raising his hand to silence Serge. Frank is one of the school's senior teachers and participates in several curriculum development teams. "Maybe that's the way things were in the past, but it's changing. I'm not saying that politics or big business don't have influence, but teachers have a lot of influence over what we teach and how. Look at our various curriculum committees and all the school-based program decisions our staff has made during the past two years— teaching teams, outcomes-based curricula, integrated teaching approaches, and textbook and technology purchases."

"You're right, teaching really is changing," Sharmila, a science teacher and multimedia coordinator, agrees. She motions for you to join the discussion. Feeling a bit uncomfortable about the intensity of the talk but anxious to fit in with your new colleagues, you do. "When I first started teaching 10 years ago," Sharmila continues, "I never thought I'd see as many changes as I've seen in the past few years."

"Things are still top-down," counters Kim. "The premier, the minister of education, the department of education, the school board, the superintendent, the principal—they all tell us what to do."

"Well, as Frank says, look at all the decisions our school-based committees have made," Sharmila responds. "Plus, just think about the professional development opportunities. We have a variety of ways to remain current in our practices. Some of us take university course and others do workshops and attend conferences. There are more opportunities available now than when I started teaching. The union takes part in collective bargaining on our behalf—that means we get to have a say in our salary, benefits, and working conditions."

"Exactly," says Frank. "Our last contract gave us a 4 percent increase in pay."

"Well, I don't quite share your optimism about how teachers have all this influence," says Kim. "Look at every provincial election—the politicians always try to exploit education. They talk about all the changes they'd make—higher standards, more accountability for teachers, more input for parents, and so on. Politicians use education to build their political careers, and teachers are the ones who have to implement their utopian ideas."

"I agree to some extent," says Sharmila. "Politicians will always use education for their own ends, but that's just rhetoric. What's really happening, bit by bit, is that teachers are becoming much more influential."

"Let's just ask this new teacher here," says Frank as he smiles and nods in your direction. "Don't you think teachers have a lot of influence over how schools are run? During the rest of your career, you'll be involved in school governance, won't you?"

Frank, Sharmila, Serge, and Kim look at you, awaiting your response. What do you say?

Who Is Involved in Canadian School Governance?

Understanding how power is shared in the governance of schools and being aware of the rights and responsibilities of today's educators are important and somewhat confusing matters for beginning teachers. While teachers have much to gain from being involved in curriculum development, policy issues can be complex as a result of the

Table 4.1

Influential Forces on the Governance of Canadian Schools

Groups	Concerns
Parents	Controlling local schools so that quality education programs are available to their children
Students	Observing policies related to freedom of expression, dress, behaviour, curricular offerings, and extracurricular activities
Teachers	Playing a role in decision-making, improving working conditions, terms of employment, other professional issues, and managing student behaviour
Administrators	Providing leadership so that various interest groups, including teachers, participate in the shared governance of schools and the development of quality education programs
Taxpayers	Proving that tax dollars are spent on quality education programs
Politicians	Implementing public school programs, guidelines, and legislative mandates related to the operation of schools; ever mindful of public expectations
Minorities	Ensuring availability of equal educational opportunity for all
Educational theorists and researchers	Using theoretical and research-based insights as the bases for improving schools at all levels
Businesses and corporations	Receiving graduates who have the knowledge, skills, attitudes, and values to help an organization realize its goals

different levels of jurisdiction involved in policy-making, including provincial departments of education, local school boards, teachers unions, local parent councils, and individual schools.

Today, a number of forces influence the governance of Canadian schools. Each of these groups has specific concerns and affects the shaping of school policies (see Table 4.1).

The following sections examine the governance of Canadian schools and the degree to which they are influenced by various political forces.

What Is the Historical Basis for the Governance of Canadian Schools?

The defining moment in the governance of Canadian schools was the confederation of Canada in 1867 with the passage of the *British North America Act*, later renamed the *Constitution Act, 1982*. The *British North America Act* established the nation and laid out a framework for public institutions. Section 93 of the act granted authority for education to the provinces in the following terms:

> In and for each Province, the Legislature may exclusively make laws in relation to Education, subject, and according to the following Provisions:

> (1) Nothing in any law shall prejudicially affect any Right or Privilege with respect to Denominational Schools which any Class of Persons have by Law in the Province at the Union:

Under Section 4 of the *Constitution Act, 1871*, all constitutional power in extra-provincial territories (the Northwest Territories, Nunavut, and Yukon) was vested in the Parliament of Canada. However, most of this power has been delegated to the territorial legislatures. All three territories have departments of education that resemble their legislative counterparts, and they perform similar functions (Bezeau 2007).

Apart from the limitations of the Constitution with respect to denominational and minority language education rights, the provinces have the authority to enact legislation dealing with education and have assumed full legal responsibility for it. The systems that have been implemented are partly centralized and partly decentralized. Centralized functions were placed under the administration of provincial departments of education, while decentralized functions became the responsibility of locally appointed or elected school boards.

What Is the Role of the Federal Government in Canadian Education?

The granting of authority over education to the provinces meant there would be no national or federal education office to direct or coordinate educational activities. This influenced the shape and direction of school governance in Canada today.

In the absence of a federal ministry of education, most relevant education programs at the elementary and secondary school levels come under the purview of the Secretary of State. The Secretary of State is involved in funding, but not delivering, such federal interest programs as official languages, Canadian studies, and multiculturalism (Bezeau 2007).

The federal government still plays an important role in education in Canada, however. At the national level, a number of federal departments interact with provincial education ministries.

- Statistics Canada provides data and analysis about all aspects of education.
- Human Resources Development Canada (HRDC) conducts surveys, provides services and information, and does research in the areas of literacy, lifelong learning, and school–work transition.
- Industry Canada (IC) offers services, technological initiatives, and links to Canadian schools and teachers through SchoolNet.
- The Social Sciences and Humanities Research Council (SSHRC) and the Canadian Institute for Health Research (CIHR) fund educational research.

There are also several important national organizations that provide coordination and exchange of information; these include the Canadian Education Association (CEA); the Association of Canadian Community Colleges (ACCC); and the Association of Universities and Colleges of Canada (AUCC). (Canadian Education Research Information System [CERIS], n.d.).

In 1967, the **Council of Ministers of Education, Canada** (CMEC) was formed to act as the national voice of education in Canada. The CMEC provides a forum for provincial and territorial ministers to meet and discuss matters of mutual interest. This organization is also the body that represents provincial and territorial interests in working with national education organizations, the federal government, foreign governments, and international organizations (www.cmec.ca, n.d.).

The federal government has responsibilities relating to the elementary and secondary education of registered First Nations children attending First Nations–administered or federal schools on reserves, or provincially administered schools off reserves, and provides financial assistance to these students at the post-secondary level. In working to develop more responsive, inclusive, and culturally affirming First Nations education, some provincial school divisions and band schools have combined efforts through co-governance or co-management. There have been joint initiatives and increased sharing of responsibility, with First Nations and Métis peoples actively participating in decision-making in the field of education. For example, the 2003 Saskatchewan document *Building Partnerships: First Nations and Métis Peoples and the Provincial Education System* outlined a policy framework for Saskatchewan's pre-kindergarten to Grade 12 education system that encourages more collaborative working relationships between the provincial government and First Nations and Métis communities.

The nature and extent of federal involvement in education has been debated for decades. Federal involvement in elementary and secondary education in Canada ranks among the lowest of the industrialized world. Canada is one of the few countries without a federal office, department, or ministry of education. Although there have been calls for more federal input, strong opposition from many groups and provinces exists (Bezeau 2007).

Current education trends at the national level include greater cooperation among organizations and provinces in matters of curriculum and general policy, sharing of information, and efforts to link research, policy, and practice (CERIS n.d.).

What Is the Role of the Provincial Government in Canadian Education?

Provincial legislatures pass statutes that provide for educational management and funding. Most provinces have one primary statute, called an **education act** or public schools act. Other statutes that relate directly to education include such matters as the creation of the ministry or **department of education**, private schools, teacher organizations, collective bargaining by teachers, and pension funds.

In most provinces, education at the elementary and secondary levels is the formal responsibility of a **minister of education**, who has authority over the department of education and its staff. A **deputy minister of education**, an appointed civil servant, reports directly to the minister and manages the department on a day-to-day basis (Bezeau 2007).

Although there are similarities among Canada's 10 provinces and 3 territories, each is affected by the diversity of its own regional culture, history, and geography. Provincial departments of education use legislation on education and related regulations to exercise jurisdiction in the following areas (Fleming, 1997):

- Curriculum content
- School funding
- Professional training and accreditation of teachers
- Student testing and assessment procedures
- School structures
- Development and publishing of curriculum guides
- Constitutions of school boards
- Choice and approval of authorized materials
- Selection and arrangements for the purchase of textbooks
- Determination of school district boundaries
- Development of criteria to open and close schools

In most provinces, the public education system begins with primary or kindergarten (sometimes preceded by pre-K or pre-P programs), followed by elementary school for five to eight years. Education is compulsory from ages 5, 6 or 7 to age 16. Secondary schools usually then continue to Grade 12. Many provinces include a junior high or middle school between the elementary and secondary levels; these usually run from two to four years.

In addition to public schools, publicly funded separate schools (Catholic schools and a small number of separate Protestant schools) exist in Quebec, Ontario, Manitoba, Alberta, and Saskatchewan. Changes continue to take place in the structures of these institutions.

Most provinces have minority-language schools; these are francophone in most cases and anglophone in Quebec. New Brunswick and Ontario have extensive French-language school programs. French immersion programs are available in most provinces (CERIS n.d.).

Local School Districts

Local school districts vary greatly in regard to demographics, such as numbers of school-age children; educational, occupational, and income levels of parents; operating budgets; numbers of teachers; economic resources; and numbers of school buildings.

At the local level, public education comes under the jurisdiction of **school boards**. These boards are known in some provinces as school districts, as school divisions, and, in New Brunswick, as district education councils. The powers and duties of school boards are defined in provincial or territorial statutes, and school board members are generally elected to office in public elections (www.cmec.ca/pages/canadawide. aspx#03, n.d.).

The statutes that define school boards and prescribe how they are created, dissolved, funded, and elected are of considerable importance. The powers of school boards are spelled out in detail and are the only powers the boards can wield. All provinces have a system of grants to school boards administered by the Department of Education. These grants supplement money raised from local property taxes in some provinces and provide virtually all of the funding for boards in others. Provincial grants are often accompanied by prescribed accounting and budgeting procedures and expenditure controls (Bezeau 2007).

Restructuring of School Districts

Since the early 1990s, many Canadian provinces have been involved in areas of school reform and have examined issues of educational governance. Efficiency, accountability, financial equity, parental and community involvement, and educational improvement are all reasons cited for governance restructuring (Saskatchewan School Trustees Association 1997).

The **Canadian School Boards Association** identifies recent trends in school governance across Canada, including reductions in the number of school boards, a redefinition of roles and responsibilities, and an increased emphasis on student outcomes and responsibilities. This has resulted in changes in the roles and responsibilities of school boards, ministries and departments of education, parents, teachers, and administrators. There has been a move away from locally elected school board powers toward centralization at the provincial level. There has also been greater parent–community involvement through avenues such as mandated **school advisory councils**, delegations, petitions, study groups, and focus groups. Generally, provincial governments have taken greater control over financing, curriculum development, and academic outcomes while encouraging parent and community members to become more involved in school-level decision-making through school councils (Pansegrau 1997).

Many provinces have reduced their number of school boards and enlarged their size. During the 1990s, the number of school boards in Canada fell from 815 to 397 (CEA, 2007).

A common characteristic of the restructuring initiatives across Canada was a top-down model of implementation that saw governments develop the models and processes used in the reorganization efforts. Generally, there was little response from the public to the restructuring effort, although it was seen as a significant issue to those most directly affected—namely, school board members, administrators, and others working within the provincial systems.

School Boards

Canadian provinces have the authority to enact laws governing their education systems. Local school board power is expressly granted by statute. In most communities, school board members are chosen in general elections; this affords all citizens the opportunity to select their representatives or run for office. In most provinces, school board elections are held in conjunction with, and resemble, municipal elections (Bezeau 2007).

School boards are corporations, and, as such, are legal entities that can enter into contracts, sue, and be sued. School boards benefit from limited liability. Taxpayers and board members acting in good faith are not liable for the obligations of the board (Bezeau 2007).

Many school board meetings are open to the public; in fact, many communities even provide radio and television coverage. Open meetings allow parents and interested citizens the opportunity to express their concerns and to get more information about problems in the district.

Canada's largest school boards have greater enrolment than the total population of the three territories. The Toronto District School Board is responsible for educating more than 260 000 students in 565 schools; Peel District School Board, one of the largest and fastest-growing boards in Canada, swells by 4000 students per year (Toronto District School Board 2009). Large boards are sometimes divided into families of schools with sub-district offices.

The Canadian School Boards Association (CSBA) contends that in most communities, school boards rarely make front page news, but they do make a difference.

The CSBA outlines the following common functions of school boards:

- Hiring the district superintendent, who in turn hires school district staff on behalf of the board
- Serving as a check to provincial powers
- Ensuring that provincial education legislation and regulations are implemented at the local level
- Managing and controlling school property
- Setting annual budgets, hiring administrators and teachers
- Making policy
- Operating schools
- Developing district education plans

Superintendent of Schools

School board organization varies, but most boards have a chief executive officer, its highest-ranking employee, who reports directly to the board. In most Canadian provinces, this person is the superintendent of schools, or **superintendent**. Though school boards operate very differently, the superintendent is invariably the key figure in determining a district's educational policy. The superintendent is the chief administrator of the school district, the person charged with the responsibility of seeing that schools operate in accordance with provincial guidelines as well as policies set by the local school board. Though the school board delegates broad powers to the superintendent, his or her policies require board approval.

How the superintendent and his or her board work together appears to be related to the size of the school district, with superintendents and school boards in larger districts more likely to conflict. In large districts, the board's own divisiveness makes it less likely that it might successfully oppose the superintendent (Wirt & Kirst 1997).

Superintendents must have the ability to respond appropriately to the many external political forces that demand attention, and conflict is inevitable. It is a demanding position; effective superintendents demonstrate that they are able to play three roles simultaneously: politician, manager, and teacher (Hurwitz 1999).

Focus on Research
through Experience

Features of School System Governance

The roles and responsibilities of school boards, superintendents (or equivalent terms assigned to a school board's chief executive officer), senior staff (directors or assistant superintendents), and school principals are typically outlined in legislation. In Canada, this legislation comes from provincial or territorial governing bodies, most of which are called legislatures. Essentially, school boards engage in school governance. This means they develop legal policies and procedures that determine how the schools under their jurisdiction will function. Distinct from this are the day-to-day behaviours of administrators, executives and managers employed by a school board who put board policies and procedures into place. Within the framework provided by legislation, school boards and their superintendents must develop professional working relationships that balance roles that are very distinct yet tempered by collaborative flexibility. While this relationship can be described simply as one of board governance and superintendent administration, in practice, the relationship is highly complex, is dynamic, is sometimes fluid, and, from time to time, is confusing.

Essential to effective school systems are a shared vision, a common mission, effective communication, and earned trust. Careful attention to the development of mutual beliefs and goals—anchored in concern for student achievement—sets forth the groundwork for strategic success. In flourishing school organizations, team work exists at all levels: board chair and board; board and superintendent; chair and superintendent; superintendent and directors; senior administrators and principals; principal and school staff.

Successful governance and competent administration are contingently interdependent. This means that, although those responsible for governance and those responsible for administration carry out different roles, their initiatives, actions, and decisions continually engage with each other. Consequently, it is essential that those involved in governance and in senior administration take into account the agendas of individual board members, the experience (both shared and divergent) of the board and senior staff, the evolving political environment, and situational factors applicable to the communities served.

Board members are elected or appointed by specific geographic or cultural communities. With such representation comes the expectation that the individual member will be involved in the local school community and will ensure that the needs of that community or constituency are supported at the board table. At the same time, however, individual board members have no formally described authority, and once elected, they represent all students receiving educational services under the board's jurisdiction. Balancing these aspects of the role is facilitated when the board maintains both a focus on planning strategically and a focus on policy development. With this in mind, board members can be involved in school-based activities without straying into the realm of day-to-day administration.

For principals and school staff, having a local board member who is interested and involved can increase community support and ensure that the strengths and needs of the school are understood at the board table. On the other hand, overly zealous involvement of an elected board member can inadvertently—and, in certain circumstances, intentionally—interfere with the effective administration of a school. Such a situation can undermine a principal's effectiveness, and if this occurs, the lines separating administration and governance become blurred. Subsequently, if the school and its community become negatively affected, concerns can develop at the senior administrative level. In almost every situation, accurate and clear communication between the school and the local board member will result in the development and maintenance of a positive relationship. When constructive rapport is the norm, effective support for the school benefits everyone involved. To enhance the likelihood of positive relationships among all components of the school system, it is essential that the superintendent ensure that principals and staff understand their responsibilities. The board chair is responsible for the communication and establishment of clear roles by the members of the board.

The reality for teachers is that, on a day-to-day basis, there may be little or no information provided concerning the actions of the school board and superintendent. However, teachers, in collaboration with school principals, can be proactive in ensuring that school board members are aware of, and invited to, events and celebrations that showcase student learning. With the support of the principal and superintendent, appropriate involvement of board members is invaluable in ensuring that policies and procedures are both responsive to the needs of students and teachers, and supportive of educational opportunities for the entire school community.

—Nancy Pynch-Worthylake

Nancy Pynch-Worthylake is the Superintendent of Schools for the South Shore Regional School Board in Nova Scotia. She has been an education administrator for more than 20 years. Her primary area of research and post-secondary instruction is leadership development.

The Role of Parents

Parents may not be involved legally in the governance of schools, but they play an important role in education. One characteristic of successful schools is that they have developed close working relationships with parents. Additionally, children whose parents or guardians support and encourage school activities have a definite advantage in school.

Through participation on school advisory councils, parents make important contributions to school efforts. Groups such as parent–teacher associations (PTA), parent–teacher organizations (PTO), or parent–teacher advisory councils (PTCA) provide an opportunity for parents to communicate with teachers on matters of interest and importance to them.

Through these groups, parents can become involved in the life of the school in a variety of ways—from making recommendations regarding school policies to providing much-needed volunteer services and initiating school-improvement activities such as fund-raising drives.

Many parents influence the character of education through involvement in the growing number of private schools in Canada. In addition, many parents are activists in promoting school choice and the home-schooling movement.

An example of a national parent organization that has influenced programs in public schools is **Canadian Parents for French** (CPF), a nationwide voluntary organization with its head office in Ottawa. Established in 1977, the CPF promotes the teaching of French in Canadian schools. It is primarily anglophone and is devoted to the teaching of French as a second language. CPF has a research and publishing program that provides information to parents interested in French instruction, particularly French immersion. It lobbies at the federal, provincial, and school board levels (Bezeau 2007).

School-Based Management

One of the most frequently used approaches to restructuring schools is **school-based management** (SBM). Most SBM programs have three components:

1. Power and decisions formerly made by the superintendent and school board are delegated to teachers, principals, parents, community members, and students at local schools. At SBM schools, teachers can become directly involved in making decisions about curricula, textbooks, standards for student behaviour, staff development, promotion and retention policies, teacher evaluation, school budgets, and the selection of teachers and administrators.
2. At each school, a decision-making body known as a board, cabinet, site-based team, or council—made up of teachers, the principal, and parents—implements the SBM plan.
3. SBM programs operate with the whole-hearted endorsement of the superintendent.

School Choice

In recent years, the **school choice** or "school of choice" issue in Canadian education has emerged in parts of the country. School boards across Canada are responding to public pressure for education choice. The Prince George School District in British Columbia, Edmonton Public Schools in Alberta, and the province of Manitoba have all developed comprehensive school-choice policies. Technology provides Canadian educators with the opportunity to offer choice not tied to a physical structure; virtual schools and distance education courses are becoming more common (Wagner 1998).

The debate continues about whether school choice programs can promote equity and excellence. Advocates of school choice believe that giving parents more options will force public schools to adjust to free-market pressures—low-performing schools would be forced to improve or shut down. Moreover, they contend that parents whose children must now attend inferior, and sometimes dangerous, inner city schools would be able to send their children elsewhere.

On the other hand, opponents believe that school choice could have disastrous consequences for public schools and lead to students being sorted by race, income, and religion. School choice, they argue, could subsidize the wealthy by siphoning money away from public schools and further widen the gap between rich and poor districts. Opponents also contend that research does not indicate that school choice improves education (Smith & Meier 1995) or promotes educational equity:

Since poor parents lack the supplemental resources that rich people have for helping their children, it is foolish to argue that [school choice] would help to equalize educational opportunities. (For example, rich parents can afford the extra costs for transportation, clothing, and educational supplies when they send their children to a distant, private school; poor parents cannot). (Berliner & Biddle 1995, 175)

Wagner (1998) cautions policy-makers to examine the following questions in relation to the issue of school choice:

- Can choice increase opportunities for all children to learn successfully?
- Can choice increase parental involvement and support for students and schools?
- Can choice increase the overall accountability of the public education system?
- Can choice inform successful practice?

Corporate–Education Partnerships

To develop additional sources of funding for equity and excellence, many local school districts have established partnerships with the private sector. These partnerships are sometimes referred to as P3s—**public–private partnerships**. Businesses may contribute funds or materials needed by a school, sponsor sports teams, award scholarships, provide cash grants for pilot projects and teacher development, and even construct school buildings.

There are differing opinions about the trend toward corporate partnerships in Canadian schools. Those who are concerned fear that it will result in some schools obtaining better programs and facilities than others and that profit-driven companies will have too much influence on education. However, supporters of the initiative claim that it can provide schools with much-needed funding and expertise (Weinberg 2000).

 **Professional Reflection** School Board Budgeting Simulation

In the following simulation, consider a rural school board faced with budget cuts. As you read through the exercise, reflect on the chapter issues surrounding the topic of school governance.

School Board Budgeting Simulation

A rural school board is faced with the following situation:

1. The board is in the third year of a "period of restraint" and is faced with an overall 3 percent reduction in the operating budget.
2. Local taxpayers are unlikely to vote for further increases in their basic tax rate.
3. The previous two years of restraint, each of which reduced revenues by 3 percent, have done away with any "fat" in the system. The board is running a barebones operation with large class sizes and overworked teachers and administrators, and has had to postpone many needed renovations to schools and equipment.
4. While teachers' salaries have been frozen, the costs of fuel, electricity, paper, and other supplies have continued to increase at an average annual rate of 4 percent. An early retirement package for teachers has been vetoed by the teachers' union. Unless the board can find some method for reducing costs even further, it will have to start cutting programs.

(continued...)

Here are the basic facts with which the board must deal:

1. The number of students in the district is 9000. The average class size is in the 30 to 40 range (even at the elementary level), with some classes at the secondary level in the low 40s.

2. The number of teachers in the school district is 350; of this number, 10 are probationary teachers who can be released without difficulty at an annual savings of $40 000 each. Teachers with "permanent contracts" can be released in reverse order of seniority. All of the probationary teachers, and almost all of those with limited seniority, are the "bright lights" in the system. The release of these teachers will leave the system with an aging, tired staff, most with no time or energy for extracurricular activities. In addition, many of the most recently hired educators teach science, math, and information technology at the secondary level. If they leave, there is no one to replace them and, while someone will have to take on their courses, the quality of instruction is certain to suffer. Release of any non-term teacher will save approximately $50 000.

3. The total budget last year was $31.2 million.

4. The total budget this year is $30 million.

5. Salaries and benefits are $24 million.

6. Transportation, fuel, maintenance, administration, paper, telephone, and other services consume $6 million a year, but all the reductions possible in these areas have already been made. Further cuts would mean the heat would be turned off, the few remaining secretaries would be laid off, and the teaching staff would perform janitorial work in addition to their teaching duties.

The options for the school board in reducing expenses by $1.2 million include:

1. Reducing the number of teachers, thereby making class sizes even larger.

2. Reducing the number of programs offered to students. Programs that cannot be cut are "core" items such as math, English, French, social studies, and science. Anything else is "up for grabs."

3. Possibilities for cuts (with the saving potential for each area in parentheses) include:

   ■ Music, which will engender tremendous public outcry from parents and probably result in school board members not being re-elected. ($400 000)

   ■ Family Studies and Technology Education, which are the only courses keeping some of the students in school. ($400 000)

   ■ Guidance counselling services (already severely cut), which will have serious consequences for students with emotional problems, for those needing help with career choices and university applications, and for those with various types of special needs. ($250 000)

   ■ Drama courses at the secondary level. ($75 000)

   ■ Cafeteria services of one kind or another at all schools, which could result in various nutritional problems for students. ($50 000)

   ■ Bus service, a necessity in this rural area ($1 million)

   ■ Secondary physical education teachers (already removed from elementary schools). ($250 000)

   ■ Resource teachers who deal with the 10 to 20 percent of students with learning problems; most schools have only one. ($200 000)

   ■ Trained librarians (already replaced by library technicians at the elementary level) at the secondary level. ($150 000)

   ■ Information technology teachers at all levels, which would place students at a tremendous disadvantage compared with other areas of the province. ($400 000)

(continued...)

- Art programs at the elementary level, already scaled back, could be cut entirely. ($150 000)
- Speech pathologist, who has a caseload of 100 students. ($50 000)
- Psychometrician, who coordinates all aspects of special education and administers specialized tests for students with special needs. ($60 000)
- Vice-principals, many of whom now teach half-time. ($150 000)
- Central office personnel have already been reduced to an accountant, a supervisor of personnel, a supervisor of operations, the superintendent, and a couple of receptionists. Cutting a supervisor will save $80 000 and leave the system in disarray.

(Next year you have to find another $1.2 million—but that's another story.)

Instructions for Individual to Large Group Role Play

Individual Activity:

1. Put yourself in the role of an elected school board member. Each board member has been asked to individually review the budget problems as they have been outlined and to make a list of cuts from each of the areas listed. Consider all social, economic, political, and educational aspects. Reflect on the advantages and disadvantages associated with making cuts in each of the areas listed. Make a list of the cuts you eventually decide to make, giving the rationale that underlies each decision.

Small Group Activity:

2. Present your list to a "school board meeting." In groups of six to eight, role-play a meeting where you share your individual lists. During the "meeting" you must, as a "board," reach a consensus.

Large Group Activity:

3. Each "school board" group should present its list to the whole class and compare and contrast their decisions with the other groups. Vote on a final list of cuts that will be released to the "public."
4. The final part of this exercise will involve the role-play of a large town meeting, where people have an opportunity to react to the final list of cuts. Twelve people will act as the "school board"; these board members must defend the choices that have been made against the criticism of the citizens. The rest of the class will assume different perspectives and will express their reaction to the cuts. Suggestions for the different perspectives include:

- elementary, middle, and secondary teachers and administrators
- parents of special needs students
- parents of gifted students
- parents of students involved in athletics, drama, music, and other extracurricular activities
- taxpayers with school-age children
- taxpayers with no school-age children
- business representatives

Ethical and Legal Questions

Closely related to issues of school governance are ethical and legal considerations. In this section of the chapter, we examine significant ethical and legal issues that affect the rights and responsibilities of teachers, administrators, students, and parents.

What are the goals of school restructuring? In school-based management, who participates in the governance and management of schools? How is school-based management different from the school board model of local governance?

Teachers must act in accordance with a wide range of federal and provincial legislations and court decisions. As a teacher, you may need to deal with such legal issues as the teacher's responsibility for accidents, freedom of speech, and student rights. Without knowledge of the legal dimensions of such issues, you will be ill-equipped to protect your rights and the rights of your students.

Why Do You Need a Professional Code of Ethics?

The actions of professional teachers are determined not only by what is legally required of them, but also by what they know they *ought* to do. They do what is legally right, and they do the right thing. A specific set of values guides them. A deep and lasting commitment to professional practice characterizes their work. They have adopted a high standard of professional ethics and they model behaviours that are in accordance with that code of ethics.

At present, the teaching profession does not have a uniform **code of ethics** similar to the Hippocratic oath that all doctors are legally required to take when they begin practice. However, many provincial teachers' associations have developed codes of ethics for educators.

Ethical Teaching Attitudes and Practices

Teaching is an ethical enterprise—that is, a teacher has an obligation to act ethically, to follow what he or she knows to be the most appropriate professional action. The best interests of students, not the teacher, provide the rule of thumb for determining what is ethical. Behaving ethically is more than a matter of following the rules or not breaking the law—it means acting in a way that promotes the learning and growth of students and helps them realize their potential.

Ontario teacher and curriculum supervisor Lori Bryden has the following to say about ethics in teaching in that province:

In Ontario, the importance of a common vision for the teaching profession was recognized by the 1998 establishment of the Ontario College of Teachers as a self-regulatory body to define the values, professional knowledge and skills inherent in the teaching profession. The primary role of the Ontario College of Teachers was to form the Foundations of Professional Practice for the teaching profession, including the Standards of Practice for the Teaching Profession, The Professional Learning Framework for the Teaching Profession as well as the Ethical Standards.

Together, the Standards of Practice and the Ethical Standards of Practice provide the foundation for pre-service and in-service teacher education. These principles of practice are based on the premise that personal and professional growth is a developmental process.

The Ethical Standards provide a vision of professional practice. They outline all of the principles of ethical behaviour for the teaching profession. They clearly describe the professional beliefs and values that guide the decision-making and professional actions of teachers in their professional roles and relationships.

The four Ethical Standards—Care, Respect, Trust and Integrity—establish the core ethics of teaching. The Ethical Standard of *care* requires teachers to express their commitment to students' well-being and learning through positive influence, professional judgment and empathy in practice. The Ethical Standard of *respect* requires teachers to model respect for spiritual and cultural values, social justice, confidentiality, freedom, democracy and the environment. The Ethical Standard of *trust* embodies fairness, openness and honesty. The Ethical Standard of *integrity* asks teachers to exercise integrity in their professional commitments and responsibilities.

The Ethical Standards believe that at the heart of a strong and effective teaching profession is a commitment to students and their learning. I consider a professional code of ethics to be fundamental in forming a common vision and in guiding my daily decisions. Teachers are in a position of trust and responsibility with students, parents and the larger community. It is absolutely crucial that they have ethical guidelines to follow.

Unethical acts break the trust and respect upon which good student–teacher relationships are based. An example of unethical conduct would be publicly discussing students' problems and actions. Other examples include using grades as a form of punishment, expressing rage in the classroom, or intentionally tricking students on tests. You can no doubt think of other examples from your own experience as a student.

Provincial Codes of Ethics for Teachers

The following websites provide information on specific provincial codes of ethics for teachers. Review these codes of ethics before you read "Case to Consider." Think about whether there are specific links between the codes and the problems posed in the case study *Open for Debate*. (For a complete listing of teachers' associations across Canada, visit www.ctf-fce.ca/MembersLink/Default.aspx?cats=MO.

Alberta Teachers' Association
www.teachers.ab.ca/About%20the%20ATA/MissionandObjects/Pages/Mission%20Statement.aspx

BC Teachers' Federation
http://bctf.ca/ProfessionalResponsibility.aspx?id=4292

Open for Debate

What kinds of ethical issues might confront a student teacher?

Shoshonna Hegman is enjoying a successful student teaching block in the North Hills Consolidated High School. Thanks to her strong background in drama and English language arts, Shoshonna is being considered for a high school position next year when the Grade 11 teacher retires. She sets high standards for her students, and engages her classes in challenging and active learning activities. It is obvious that Shoshonna spends a great deal of time on lesson planning and that she is willing to go the extra mile by becoming involved in the extracurricular life of the school. This term, she not only helped to direct the school musical, she also helped her associate teacher, Ms. Carmen, to coach the debate club—an established group that always attracts proud, capable students.

Debating is a well-respected, prestigious activity at the school, and every year the team spends hours practising and honing their skills. Shoshonna, a debater in university, is a keen competitor and stayed after school several evenings each week to help prepare the team. Parents and the school administration have complimented Shoshonna on the team's strong showing at the district level this term. In fact, for the first time in North Hill's history, the team earned the district title. After winning the regional championship last weekend, the team is preparing to head to the provincials this Friday at noon. The whole school is behind the team and its coaches, and Shoshonna is excited to be part of this history-making trip. If the team wins at the provincial level, the team and the coaches will have a shot at a national title.

At lunchtime on Thursday, Shoshonna receives a phone call from the school that hosted last weekend's regional competition; she takes the call in the main office since her associate teacher is off on a professional development day. The debate coach from

Manitoba Teachers' Society
www.mbteach.org/inside-mts/professionalcode.html

New Brunswick Teachers' Association
www.nbta.ca/resources/code_of_ethics/Code_of_Professional_Conduct.pdf

Nova Scotia Teachers' Union
www.nstu.ca/app?service=direct/1/Foundation/$NewsLetterTree.Tree.treeNodeValue
.direct&sp=SC82&sp=F&sp=AFoundation%2F%24NewsLetterTree.Tree
.treeView&sp=2

Nunavut Teachers Association
www.ntanu.ca/assets/files/NTA%20resources/Code%20of%20Ethics.pdf

Yukon Teachers' Association
www.yta.yk.ca/documents/pdfs/yta_code_of_ethics.pdf

that school is calling to let Shoshonna and Ms. Carmen know that North Hills's star debater has been accused of using a racial slur against one of the opposing team members over lunch during the regional competition. The coach, Mr. Mallory, is extremely upset and wants North Hills to cooperate in investigating whether the allegation levelled against their debater is true. Further, he suggests that the individual in question should not be allowed to represent North Hills until a thorough investigation has been carried out. Shoshonna promises to look into the matter and assures the coach she will do so promptly.

Shoshonna leaves the office dumbfounded; she cannot believe that the student against whom the accusations were made could be guilty. The young man is an honours student involved in many extracurricular activities, and is the student council vice-president. His father's business sponsors the team, and his parents plan to drive team members to the provincials this weekend.

There are less than 24 hours before the team is scheduled to leave, and a pep rally is planned for the end of the day to wish the team luck in their pursuit of the provincial title. Shoshonna leaves the main office in turmoil.

Questions

1. There are many problems inherent in this case for a student teacher. Put yourself in Shoshonna's situation and identify as many issues as you can that would impact her and influence her response to the complaint she received.

2. Is there more than one ethical issue involved in the case?

3. What is the most prudent action for Shoshonna to take?

4. Is there anything wrong with Shoshonna choosing to do nothing until after the provincial competition?

Ethical Dilemmas in the Classroom and School

Teachers routinely encounter **ethical dilemmas** in the classroom. They often have to take action in situations in which all the facts are not known or for which no single course of action can be called right or wrong. At these times, it can be quite difficult to decide what an ethical response might be. Dealing satisfactorily with ethical dilemmas in teaching often requires the ability to see beyond short-range consequences to consider long-range effects.

Consider, for example, the following three questions based on actual case studies. On the basis of the information given, how would you respond to each situation?

1. Should the sponsor of the high school literary magazine refuse to print a well-written story by a budding writer if the piece appears to satirize a teacher and a student?
2. Is an English teacher justified in trying to increase achievement for an entire class by separating two disruptive students and placing one in a reading group beneath his reading level?

3. Should a chemistry teacher punish a student (on the basis of circumstantial, inconclusive evidence) for a laboratory explosion if decisive, swift punishment will likely prevent the recurrence of a similar event and thereby ensure the safety of all students?

As a student teacher, it is important that you begin your student teaching assignment with knowledge of the legal aspects of teaching and a clear idea of your rights and responsibilities.

What Are Your Legal Rights as a Teacher?

The necessary balance between rights and responsibilities is perhaps more critical to teaching than to any other profession. While schools have limited power over teachers, teachers' rights to **due process** cannot be violated. Teachers, like all citizens, are protected from arbitrary treatment by those in authority. A principal who disagrees with a teacher's methods cannot suddenly fire that teacher. A school board cannot ask a teacher to resign merely by claiming that the teacher's political activities outside of school are "disruptive" of the education process. A teacher cannot be dismissed for "poor" performance without ample documentation and without being given sufficient time to meet clearly stated performance evaluation criteria.

Because board of education policies and regulations vary, you should carefully read any available teacher handbook or school policy handbook in your province (see Figure 4.1).

Most provinces have **collective bargaining** laws that require them to negotiate contracts with teacher organizations. An important part of most collective bargaining agreements is the right of a teacher to file a **grievance**—a formal complaint against his or her employer. A teacher may not be dismissed for filing a grievance, and he or she is entitled to have the grievance heard by a neutral third party. Often, the teachers' union or professional association that negotiated the collective bargaining agreement will provide free legal counsel to a teacher who has filed a grievance.

What Are Your Legal Responsibilities as a Teacher?

Teachers are legally responsible for the safety and well-being of students assigned to them. Although it is not expected that a teacher be able to completely control the behaviour of young, energetic students, he or she can be held liable for any injury to a student if it is shown that the teacher's negligence contributed to the injury.

Since it is the duty of teachers and school administrators to maintain a safe and orderly learning environment, it is important for you to have an understanding of the legal and regulatory frameworks that govern schools. These frameworks confer duties and place constraints on the exercise of power within the context of a school.

Legal Frameworks

The legal authority of schools in Canada is derived from the following areas of law:

- Federal and provincial statutes
- Common law
- Constitutional law

Additionally, federal statutes such as the *Youth Criminal Justice Act* (April 2003) contain provisions relevant to school discipline.

Federal and Provincial Law

In Canadian provinces, the various school acts impose the obligation on teachers and principals to maintain order and discipline in schools. For example, in Alberta, Section 15 of the *School Act* (1988) requires that a principal must "maintain order and discipline in the school and on the school grounds and during activities sponsored or approved by the board."

Although provincial laws have the most direct application to public education in Canada, there are federal statutes that influence responses to cases of serious student misconduct. One of most important of these is the *Youth Criminal Justice Act* (2003), a federal criminal statute applying to persons aged 12 to 17. Certain actions committed by students may not only violate school rules but may also be considered criminal offences. These may include theft, assault, and possession of prohibited items such as weapons and drugs (Brien 2002).

Common Law

The interpretation of provincial and federal laws is the responsibility of the courts and judges, whose decisions are recorded and published for use in successive cases. This creates a body of jurisprudence known as common law. A key legal principle derived from common law has provided the foundation of teachers' disciplinary authority over their students for centuries. This principle holds that teachers stand *in loco parentis* ("in the place of parents") with respect to their students, and may thus exercise discipline consistent with that of a parent. The teacher–student relationship established under common law can be assumed to regulate teachers' disciplinary authority over students except where expressly altered by statute or policy.

Constitutional Law

With the proclamation of the *Canadian Charter of Rights and Freedoms* in 1982, Canadian courts gained expanded authority to review provincial and federal legislation for consistency with constitutional principles. Since public schools are created under provincial statutory authority, the actions of school-based personnel exercising authority are subject to Charter scrutiny. Educators must ensure that decisions made regarding disciplinary matters are taken according to constitutional principles and respect students' Charter rights (Brien 2002).

The Influences of the *Canadian Charter of Rights and Freedoms*

In the school setting, various Charter protections affect different types of rights, including the following (McCoubrey & Sitch 2001, 15):

- Students' freedom of expression or mobility in the classroom
- Discipline and criminal issues that relate to protection against unreasonable detentions, searches, and procedural fairness issues
- Discrimination and accommodation issues, religious practice, and student conduct

School and School District Policies

School employees are also subject to policies established by schools and school boards according to their statutory authority. This means they are legally bound by policies set out by their school boards, superintendents, and school principals. District policies may, for example, regulate the procedures to be followed before suspending a student. These policies may be more restrictive than the statutory provisions (Brien 2002).

Legal Role and Status of Teachers

MacKay and Sutherland (2006) provide a clear framework from which to examine the legal roles and responsibilities of educators. Two of these major roles, "teachers as parents" and "teachers as state agents," are featured in the following sections:

Teachers as Parents: Negligence, Liability, Corporal Punishment

Negligence in the school setting is of importance to teachers who may worry about under what circumstances they can be sued. Negligence cases follow a three-step analysis:

1. What was the **duty of care** owed to the injured person?
   - Teachers must take reasonable steps to minimize the risk of injury.
   - Teachers are entrusted with large numbers of students and their duties of care extend inside and outside the classroom.
   - Teachers must take care to ensure that students are not exposed to any unnecessary risk of harm.

2. What is the **standard of care** required by the person?
   - Standard of care may vary depending on circumstance.
   - Courts attempt to establish what a "reasonable person" would do in similar circumstances; the question is one of good judgment.
   - Courts have determined that a teacher's standard of care is that of a "careful parent."
   - Some factors that are considered in determining appropriate conduct in a particular situation: age of student(s), nature of activity, amount of instruction given to student(s), school policies, foreseeable risk of danger, previous accidents in similar circumstances.

3. Was this standard of care breached?
   - The law expects teachers to act reasonably to minimize the occurrence of accidents.
   - Courts must consider whether students contributed to their own misfortune.
   - What damages, if any, were suffered by the injured person?
   - The plaintiff must have suffered some ascertainable damage as recognized by law.

Negligence in School Settings: Tort Liability

A tort is a civil wrong done by one person to another. According to **tort liability** law, an individual who is negligent and at fault in the exercise of his or her legal duty may be required to pay monetary damages to the injured party. Teachers are held to a higher standard than ordinary citizens and certain teachers (physical education and chemistry teachers, for example) are held to an even higher standard because of the increased risk of injury involved in the classes they teach.

A Grade 8 science teacher in Louisiana left her class for a few moments to go to the school office to pick up some forms. While she was gone, her students continued to do some laboratory work that involved the use of alcohol-burning devices. Unfortunately, one girl was injured when she tried to relight a defective burner. Could the teacher be held liable for the girl's injuries?

This event actually occurred in 1974 *(Station v. Travelers Insurance Co.)*. The court that heard the case determined that the teacher had failed to provide adequate supervision while the students were exposed to dangerous conditions. Considerable care is required, the court observed, when students handle inherently dangerous

Should the teacher supervising this activity have any concerns about tort liability? How might this teacher reduce the risk of liability?

objects, and the need for this care is magnified when students are exposed to dangers they don't appreciate.

Specific Areas of Responsibility

The Classroom

- Teachers have a duty to supervise students in their classrooms.
- Reasons for absence, its duration, the type of accident, and the nature of the class are factors that are considered in determining negligence.

Playgrounds and Outside

- Injuries outside schools are examined to determine if an adequate system of supervision was in place and if teachers sufficiently performed their tasks.
- Playground equipment should be monitored for safety (loose boards, nails, broken glass, etc.).

Before and after School

- It is advisable for schools to establish clear hours of supervision before and after school hours and to communicate this information to parents.
- In the area of after-school supervision, teachers have the responsibility to abide by parents' instructions and to be mindful of special circumstances such as early dismissal or emergencies and inclement weather.

Special Classrooms and Labs

- Classrooms in which there are increased dangers, such as special equipment, dangerous tools, open flames, or chemicals, require a greater degree of supervision by school personnel, proper protection and adequate instruction, and precise warnings to students.
- Specialist teachers in industrial arts shops, science labs, gymnasiums, and home economics classes are held to a higher standard of care than regular classroom teachers.

Emergencies

- Teachers who take students on field trips or are in charge of high-risk activities such as physical education classes may be directly confronted with emergency situations.

- Teachers are expected to take reasonable measures to cope with emergency situations.
- Basic first aid, life-saving techniques such as CPR, and proper training in emergency procedures are recommended for such teachers.
- Children who have severe anaphylactic reactions due to allergies from foods (peanuts or peanut butter, for example) or bee stings, or who suffer from diabetes, seizures, or other serious medical conditions need special protection and monitoring. Teachers should make every effort to obtain medical information from parents at the beginning of the school year. A plan for management should be devised with the parents; this may include the storing and administration of medication such as epinephrine.

Off School Property—Field Trips

- Protecting against legal liability is a must for field trips. Proper risk management can reduce the possibility of a lawsuit resulting from accidents.
- Teachers should be aware of the need for waivers and parental permission forms, proper insurance, and safe practices. For more information concerning Field Trips, see Teacher's Resource 4.1 at www.MyEducationLab.com.

Liability for Corporal Punishment in Schools

Corporal punishment refers to the intentional use of physical force for an alleged offence or misbehaviour.

- Touching without consent is a technical assault; in real terms, legal action is likely only when the touching results in some physical or emotional damage to the victim.
- Corporal punishment (the use of the strap, for example) in schools has been largely abolished by school board policies.
- Criminal Code protections that allow teachers to use force as a means of correction remain in Section 43:

Every schoolteacher, parent or person standing in the place of a parent is justified in using force by way of correction toward a pupil or child, as the case may be, who is under his care, if the force does not exceed what is reasonable under the circumstances. (Department of Justice Canada. Retrieved March 10, 2010, from http://laws.justice.gc.ca/eng/C-46/page-2.html#anchorbo-ga:s_3_1-gb:s_25)

- In spite of Section 43, it is not recommended practice for teachers to resort to physical violence as a means of correction (MacKay & Sutherland 2006).

As an employer, the school board is generally held liable for the acts of its employees. If teachers are negligent, a ruling of **liability** is usually found against the relevant school board under what is known as **vicarious liability**.

To protect students from harm and themselves from litigation, teachers should be vigilant about potentially harmful or dangerous situations. They are, for example, encouraged to be vigilant about seeking permission from a school administrator or the school board for trips off school property and should also ensure that they have adequate personal insurance coverage if they are transporting students in their own vehicles.

Teachers as Educational State Agents

Most provincial education acts define teachers as **state agents**. Sections of the *Canadian Charter of Rights and Freedoms* directly affect how teachers, as state agents, deal with and relate to students. The following sections of Charter rights apply to education:

Section 2: Fundamental Freedoms
Section 8: The Right to Be Secure
Section 9: The Right Not to Be Arbitrarily Detained
Section 12: The Right Not to Be Subjected to Cruel or Unusual Punishment
Section 15: Equality before the Law

The full Charter can be accessed at http://laws.justice.gc.ca/en/charter.

Reporting Child Abuse

Virtually every school board in Canada has policies, regulations, and guidelines for protecting students from abuse (see the MyEducationLab.com exploration at the end of this chapter for an example). Teachers, who are *required* by law to report any suspected **child abuse**, are in a position to monitor and prevent physical, emotional, and sexual abuse and the neglect and exploitation of children. Teachers' professional journals and information from local, provincial, and federal child welfare agencies encourage teachers to be more observant of children's appearance and behaviour in order to detect symptoms of abuse. Such sources often provide lists of physical and behavioural indicators of potential child abuse, similar to that shown in Table 4.2. Many communities, through their police departments or other public and private agencies, provide programs to educate children about their rights in child-abuse situations and about how to ask for help.

Table 4.2

Physical and Behavioural Indicators of Child Abuse and Neglect

Signs of Physical Abuse

Physical Indicators

- Unexplained bruises and welts on the face, throat, upper arms, buttocks, thighs, or lower back in unusual patterns or shapes that suggest the use of an instrument (belt buckle, electrical cord) on an infant in various stages of healing and that regularly appear after an absence, the weekend, or a vacation.
- Unexplained burns or cigarette burns, especially found on the palms, the soles of feet, abdomen, buttocks; immersion burns producing "stocking" or "glove" demarcations on hands and feet; doughnut-shaped burns on buttocks or genital area.
- Rope burns.
- Infected burns indicating delay in treatment; burns in the shape of common household utensils or appliances.

Behavioral Indicators

- Behavioral extremes (withdrawal, aggression, regression, depression).
- Inappropriate or excessive fear of parent or caretaker.
- Antisocial behavior such as substance abuse, truancy, running away, fear of going home.
- Unbelievable or inconsistent explanation for injuries.
- Lies unusually still while surveying surroundings (for infants).
- Unusual shyness; wariness of physical contact.

Signs of Sexual Abuse

Physical Indicators

- Torn, stained, or bloody underclothes.
- Frequent, unexplained sore throats; yeast or urinary infections.
- Somatic complaints, including pain and irritation of the genitals.
- Sexually transmitted diseases.
- Bruises or bleeding from external genitalia, vagina, or anal region.
- Pregnancy.

Table 4.2 *(continued)*

Behavioral Indicators

- The victim's disclosure of sexual abuse.
- Regressive behaviors (thumb sucking, bed-wetting, fear of the dark).
- Promiscuity or seductive behaviors.
- Disturbed sleep patterns (recurring nightmares).
- Unusual and age-inappropriate interest in sexual matters.
- Avoidance of undressing or wearing extra layers of clothes.
- Sudden decline in school performance; truancy.
- Difficulty in walking or sitting.

Signs of Emotional Abuse

Physical Indicators

- Eating disorders, including obesity or anorexia.
- Speech disorders (stuttering, stammering).
- Developmental delays in the acquisition of speech or motor skills.
- Weight or height substantially below norm.
- Flat or bald spots on head (infants).
- Nervous disorders (rashes, hives, facial tics, stomachaches).

Behavioral Indicators

- Habit disorders (biting, rocking, head banging).
- Cruel behavior; seeming to get pleasure from hurting children, adults, or animals; seeming to get pleasure from being mistreated.
- Age-inappropriate behaviors (bed-wetting, wetting, soiling).
- Behavioral extremes: overly compliant–demanding; withdrawn–aggressive; listless–excitable.

Signs of Neglect

Physical Indicators

- Poor hygiene, including lice, scabies, severe or untreated diaper rash, bedsores, body odor.
- Squinting.
- Unsuitable clothing; missing key articles of clothing (underwear, socks, shoes); overdressed or underdressed for climate conditions.
- Untreated injury or illness.
- Lack of immunizations.
- Indicators of prolonged exposure to elements (excessive sunburn, insect bites, colds).
- Height and weight significantly below age level.

Behavioral Indicators

- Unusual school attendance.
- Chronic absenteeism.
- Chronic hunger, tiredness, or lethargy.
- Begging or collecting leftovers.
- Assuming adult responsibilities.
- Reporting no caretaker at home.

Source: Adapted from Childabuse.com (2008). Anchorage AK: Arctic Originals, Inc. Retrieved from http://childabuse.com/help.htm

Physical and Behavioural Indicators of Child Abuse and Neglect

If you are concerned for a student's well-being, the indicators listed below may help guide your thought process. It's possible that many of these symptoms or signs could be the result of things other than abuse or neglect. Generally, though, these indicators suggest that a child's safety may be at risk and, at the very least, the situation should be assessed by a professional.

In dealing with suspected abuse cases, schools usually have a specific process involving the principal and a counsellor as well as the reporting teacher. Because a child's physical welfare may be further endangered if abuse is reported, caution and sensitivity are required. Teachers are in a unique position to help abused student, both because they have daily contact with them and because children learn to trust them.

Four Cases: You Be the Judge!

The following four cases illustrate some of the principles discussed in this chapter. Judge the cases and then read the decisions of the courts provided after each case description.

Legal Cases

Plumb Case

The plaintiff, a 15-year-old from British Columbia, was injured when struck by a ball thrown during a game of catch. The plaintiff had forgotten his glove that day and was not participating in the game. Instead, he was lying on the grass to one side of the game. He was injured by a wild throw, which was missed by the intended catcher, bounced once on the grass, and struck the plaintiff. The supervising teacher had seen the game but did not believe it posed any special risks. The school board and the child who had thrown the ball were named as defendants.

Guiding Question: Were the school board and the child who threw the ball liable in this case? Was the supervising teacher negligent?

Cropp Case

In this Saskatchewan case, the 14-year-old plaintiff was wearing cowboy boots with 5 cm heels when he slipped, fell, and injured himself on a temporary walkway on school grounds. He was required to take two classes in adjacent buildings and was moving between buildings one morning when the accident happened. This walkway was made of coarse crushed rock held in place by board sidewalls supported by stakes.

Guiding Question: Was the school negligent in this case?

Simard Case

In a Quebec case, an eight-year-old child was injured in a fall while climbing down from closing a classroom window. The teacher had asked her to close the window, which required that she step onto a chair, then onto a radiator, and then onto a small table on the windowsill in order to reach. After closing the window, the child fell, striking the chair.

Guiding Question: Was the teacher liable in this incident?

Road Pizza Case

In *Strong v. Moon*, the mother of an elementary school child suffered minor, though painful, injuries in an automobile accident that occurred just after she had dropped her daughter off at school. While the mother was lying on the road awaiting an ambulance, a school bus passed by, carrying children to the same school. Some children recognized the accident victim and later described the scene to her daughter, referring to the mother as "road pizza." Although the mother quickly recovered, the daughter suffered continuing psychological disturbances and was eventually forced to repeat her year. The plaintiff child and her mother sued the driver who had caused the mother's injuries for the suffering of the child.

Guiding Question: Was the driver liable in this case?

Judicial Decisions

The following verdicts on the cases just described illustrate a range of decisions. The first involves a failure or alleged failure of supervision, and the second and third concern only occupiers' liability. The fourth case has elements of both, but was decided on the basis of supervision. The final case, although not a school case strictly speaking, has important implications for teachers.

Plumb Decision

The judge found no negligence on the part of any defendants. The level of supervision was adequate and the game of catch was not inherently dangerous. There had been no recklessness or intent to injure. The injury resulted from a purely accidental misthrow, which could not have been anticipated. A careful and prudent parent would reasonably allow teenaged children to play catch.

Cropp Decision

The school board was found to be negligent in failing to provide a safe walkway. The vice-chairman of the board admitted during the cross-examination that he believed the walkway to be unstable and below the standard of safety that a school board should provide for its students. The student was not found to be contributorily negligent.

Simard Decision

The teacher was found to be negligent and fully responsible in asking the child to close the window. She had not acted as diligently as a conscientious parent. Because of the age of the child and the request of the teacher that the child close the window, the Quebec Superior Court found neither voluntary assumption of risk nor contributory negligence on the part of the child.

Road Pizza Decision

In the *Strong v. Moon* case, school officials had done everything they could to console and help the child and were not named as defendants. The driver responsible for the mother's injuries was not liable on grounds of excessive remoteness. The court held that the child's problems were not reasonably foreseeable by the offending driver. This case poses an obvious question for teachers: Can they prevent the type of behaviour that caused the child's distress? If so, how?

Source: © Lawrence M. Bezeau 2007.

SUMMARY

Who Is Involved in Canadian School Governance?

- Parents, students, teachers, administrators, taxpayers, politicians, minorities, educational theorists and researchers, and businesses and corporations are among the groups that exert influence on school policies in Canada.

- Schools reflect the society they serve and are thus influenced by out-of-school factors such as the mass media, demographic shifts, international events, and social issues.

What Is the Historical Basis for the Governance of Canadian Schools?

- The *British North America Act* of 1867 established the nation of Canada and laid out the framework for public institutions such as schools.

- Section 93 of the *British North America Act* granted authority for education to the provinces.

- Provinces have the authority to enact legislation dealing with education and have full legal responsibility for education.

What Is the Role of the Federal Government in Canadian Education?

- There is no national or federal education office to direct or coordinate educational activities in the Canadian provinces and territories; most relevant programs fall under the Secretary of State.

- At the national level, a number of federal departments and national organizations intersect with education.

What Is the Role of the Provincial Government in Canadian Education?

- Canadian systems of education begin at the provincial level with the passing of statutes that create the education system and provide for its management and funding.

- Most Canadian provinces have an education act or public school act and an elected minister of education who is responsible for education at the elementary and secondary levels, and an appointed deputy minister who manages the day-to-day operations of the department.

Local School Districts and School Boards

- At the local level, public education comes under the jurisdiction of school boards, and school boards exist as a result of provincial legislation.

- Local school districts, which vary greatly in size, setting, organizational structure, demographics, and wealth, are responsible for the management and operation of schools.

- Among the functions of school boards are the implementation of provincial education legislation and regulations at the local level, the operation of schools, the setting of policy, the determination of annual budgets, and the hiring of administrators and teachers.

- The superintendent, the chief administrator of a local district, has a complex array of responsibilities and must work cooperatively with the school board and others in an environment that is often politically turbulent.

- The key to successful governance and administration in a school board is clear communication and an understanding of the roles of the board and of the superintendent and senior staff.

- Provinces fund school boards through a system of grants that, in some provinces, supplement money raised from local property taxes, and in others provide virtually all of the funding.

- Local school boards, whose members are usually elected, set educational policies for a district; however, many people believe that boards should be more responsive to individual school needs.

- As part of restructuring in Canada, the number of school boards in most provinces has been reduced in recent years.

Why Do You Need a Professional Code of Ethics?

- Teaching requires ethical behaviour, and many provincial teachers' associations have developed codes of ethics to guide their members.

- A professional code of ethics guides teachers' actions and enables them to build relationships with students based on trust and respect.

- A code of ethics helps teachers see beyond the short-range consequences of their actions to long-range outcomes, and helps them respond appropriately to ethical dilemmas in the classroom.

What Are Your Legal Rights as a Teacher?

- The right to due process protects teachers from arbitrary treatment by school districts and education officials regarding certification, nondiscrimination, contracts, tenure, dismissal, and academic freedom.

- Most provinces have collective bargaining laws that require the negotiation of contracts with teacher organizations and allow for teachers to file grievances or formals complaint against employers.

What Are Your Legal Responsibilities as a Teacher?

- Teachers are responsible for meeting the terms of their teaching contracts, including providing for their students' safety and well-being.

- Student teachers should be aware of their potential liability and should clarify their rights and responsibilities prior to beginning student teaching.

- Legal authority of schools in Canada is derived from federal and provincial statute law, common law, and constitutional law.

- Legal roles and responsibilities of teachers include teacher as parent and teacher as educational state agent.

- The *Canadian Charter of Rights and Freedoms* directly affects how teachers deal with, and relate to, students.

- Among the legal responsibilities that concern teachers are: avoiding tort liability (specifically negligence), recognizing the physical and behavioural indicators of child abuse and reporting suspected instances, and observing copyright laws as they apply to photocopies, video recordings, computer software, and materials published on the internet.

Recommended Sources

Canadian Charter of Rights and Freedoms. (1982). Department of Justice Canada. Available at http://laws.justice.gc.ca/en/Charter.

Freeman, M. (1993). "Whither children: protection, participation and autonomy?" *Manitoba Law Journal* (22), 307.

Proudfoot, A. and Hutchings, L. (1998). *Teacher beware: a legal primer for the classroom teacher.* Calgary: Detselig Enterprises Ltd.

Sussel, T. (1995). *Canada's legal revolution: public education, the Charter and human rights.* Toronto: Emond Montgomery Ltd.

Best, C. "Best guide to Canadian legal research." Available at www.legalresearch.org.

Watkinson, A. (1999). *Education, students' rights and the Charter.* Saskatoon: Purich Publishing Ltd.

KEY TERMS AND CONCEPTS

British North America Act, 101
Canadian Parents for French, 108
Canadian School Boards Association, 104
child abuse, 121
code of ethics, 112
collective bargaining, 116
Constitution Act, 1982, 101
corporal punishment, 120
Council of Ministers of Education, Canada, 102

department of education, 103
deputy minister of education, 103
due process, 116
duty of care, 118
education act, 103
ethical dilemmas, 115
grievance, 116
liability, 120
minister of education, 103
negligence, 118

public–private partnerships, 109
school advisory councils, 104
school-based management, 108
school boards, 104
school choice, 108
standard of care, 118
state agents, 120
superintendent, 106
tort liability, 118
vicarious liability, 120
Youth Criminal Justice Act, 117

APPLICATIONS AND ACTIVITIES

Teacher's Journal

1. Read the code of ethics for teachers in your province. (Refer to the Ethical Teaching Attitudes and Practices section of this chapter.) Record in your journal examples of situations you have observed or experienced in which you feel a teacher may have violated the principles. Conclude your analysis of these cases with a personal statement about your goals for ethical conduct.

2. What is your position regarding corporal punishment? Are there circumstances under which its use is justified? (Refer to the Liability for Corporal Punishment in Schools section of this chapter.)

3. Based on your own experiences, describe an ethical dilemma that you have confronted. Then answer each of the following questions: What actions did you take in response to the dilemma? Would you respond any differently today? Why? In general, what steps should a person take to ensure that his or her response to an ethical dilemma is the "best" course of action? (Refer to the Ethical and Legal Questions section of this chapter.)

4. In a Canadian province, a grade 12 student who had been suspended for almost a full school year for assaulting a fellow student and causing him serious injury in the hallway at lunchtime returned to school the following September. He was passing all his courses, but had borderline results in English, a subject required for

graduation. Then, near the end of the school year, he wrote a short story for an English assignment that counted heavily toward the term mark. The story was filled with guns and violence and depicted fellow students getting shot. It was also well written. The teacher gave a mark of 25 percent for "expression" and 0 percent for "content" on the assignment and insisted that the student re-write the violent scenes—or risk failing the course and not graduating. How should teachers respond to student work, including essays, creative writing, videos, and art, that has violent content? (Refer to the Teachers as Educational State Agents section of this chapter.)

Theory into Practice

1. Review the case in this chapter titled "Open to Debate." Let's say Shoshonna calls her associate teacher that night and they decide to wait until Monday to follow up on the complaint. The North Hills team wins the provincials, and the complaint turns out to be true. A meeting takes place the week after the provincial win. Assign the following roles: Shoshonna, the associate teacher, the administrators from both schools, the coach from the other school, the student who was harassed, the North Hills star debater, the parents of both students involved, and the Race Relations, Cross-Cultural Understanding, and Human Rights Policy (RCH) Officer from the school board. Role play what might transpire during the meeting. What ethical issues arise?

2. Most school districts have an RCH in place. Locate such a policy for the school district in which you will be teaching and review its intent, recommendations, and guiding principles. What value is there for student teachers to be familiar with such a policy? Would such a policy inform how Shoshonna should handle the incident with the star debater?

3. As a class, develop a plan for how the case should have been handled.

Teacher's Database

1. Conduct an internet search on one or more of the topics listed below or on another topic from Chapter 4. Narrow your search to issues and information relating to school law and the legal rights and responsibilities of school districts and schools, teachers and administrators, and students and parents. Include a search of news sources, such as the *Canadian Journal of Educational Administration and Policy* on the web, for summaries of recent court rulings pertaining to education and school law.

   Topics to search from Chapter 4:
   - School uniforms
   - Free speech
   - Search and seizure
   - Collective bargaining
   - Corporal punishment
   - Professional ethics

2. Use the internet to gather information about the structure of education and school funding in your province. How many school boards are in your province? Which

is the largest? What are enrolment figures, trends, and projections for your province? What are the figures for household income and the poverty rate? Begin your data search at Statistics Canada and the provincial department of education.

Observations and Interviews

1. During an observation of a teacher's day, identify an ethical dilemma that the teacher confronts. Describe the dilemma and the teacher's response in a journal entry.

2. Visit a private school. Find out how teachers and other staff members are hired and how the school is organized and governed. How does the management and operation of this school differ from public schools?

3. Interview a school superintendent and ask him or her to comment on the role of the school board in that school district.

4. Interview a teacher and ask how the department of education affects the teacher's work. Would the teacher like to see the government more or less involved in education? Report your findings to the rest of the class.

5. Attend a meeting of a local school board and observe the communication and decision-making process at that meeting.

Professional Portfolio

Survey a group of students, teachers, or parents regarding a legal issue in education. Among the issues and questions you might address are the following:

- Under what circumstances should restrictions be placed on what teachers teach and how they teach it?
- Should parents be allowed to provide home-schooling for their children?
- Are parents justified in filing educational malpractice suits if their children fail to achieve in school?
- Under what circumstances should restrictions be placed on students' freedom of expression?
- Should schools have the right to implement dress codes? Guidelines for students' hairstyles? School uniforms?
- Should corporal punishment be banned? If not, under what circumstances should it be used?
- To combat drug abuse, should schools implement mandatory drug testing of students? Of teachers?
- Should students have access to their educational records? Should their parents or guardians?
- As part of an HIV prevention program, should condoms be distributed to high school students? Should parental approval be required for participation?

1. The report summarizing the results of your survey should include demographic information such as gender, age, whether they have children in school, level of education, and so on. When you analyze the results, look for differences related to these variables.

2. In your portfolio, write a personal reflection that presents your position on the issues of curriculum choice, home-schooling, educational malpractice, freedom of expression, dress codes, corporal punishment, mandatory drug testing, access to student records, and the role of the school in encouraging safe sex practices.

MyEducationLab

PEARSON
myeducationlab

For a province-by-province list of Canadian Boards of Education, go to the Resources tab at www.MyEducationLab.com. To compare the policies of different boards across the country, follow the links to see what they may have in common.

To read sample school statements, including a philosophy statement, a guiding principles statement, mission and vision statements, and a principal's cover letter, go to Module 1 in the Managing to Teach tab at www.MyEducationLab.com.

Read "A Checklist for Teachers Taking Students on Field Trips" in Teacher's Resource 4.1 on www.MyEducationLab.com.

5

**Social and Cultural
Realities Confronting
Today's Schools**

*The educational system is part of
the common life and cannot escape
suffering the consequences that
flow from the conditions prevailing
outside the school building.*
—John Dewey "Introduction,"
The Use of Resources in Education

focus questions

1. What are the aims of education today?

2. How can schools be described?

3. What are schools like as social institutions?

4. How is cultural diversity represented in Canadian schools?

5. What is multicultural education?

6. How is gender a dimension of multicultural education?

7. What characteristics distinguish successful schools?

8. What social problems affect schools and place students at risk?

9. What are schools doing to address social problems?

Jeff Banks, a history teacher at Lakeside High School, enters the faculty lunchroom and sees a group of his colleagues at their usual table in the corner. Lakeside, located in a low- to medium-income area of a fairly large city in central Canada, has an enrolment of almost 1400 students. About 70 percent of the student body self-identify as Anglo-European Canadians, with the remaining 30 percent from various ethnic and cultural groups. After English, Italian and several East Indian languages are the most common mother tongues. Lakeside has a reputation for being a "good" school—for the most part, students are respectful of their teachers and many parents are involved in school activities in spite of their heavy work schedules. The consensus among teachers is that most parents recognize that education is key if their children are to "better themselves." Jeff approaches the table and finds his friends discussing a recent tragic shooting at a Canadian high school in which an unhappy student brought a gun to school and shot a fellow student.

"It's so scary," Sue says to the group. "Who knows, something like that could happen right here at Lakeside. We have no idea what kids have to deal with today."

"Yeah, we have no idea who might snap," Bret chimes in. "With a lot of school shootings lately, the perpetrator is a kid that no one would have expected. Quiet, polite, good student . . . You just never know."

"In some cases, that's true," says Jeff, putting his lunch tray down and settling between Sue and Bret. "But a lot of times there are signs. A lot of these kids are loners and outcasts. They're into violent video games, cults, drugs guns—you name it."

"What I want to know," Sue says, "is how we can prevent something like that from happening here. Since the Colorado shootings, there have been bomb scares, threats, and guns confiscated at dozens of schools around the country."

"Well, I don't think metal detectors, more police presence, and stiffer penalties for kids who bring guns to school are necessarily the answer," says Bret. "The question is, why are kids doing it in the first place?"

"Right! And how can we prevent it?" Jeff asks.

"If we're going to change things," says Sue, "we've got to figure out how to identify and help kids who feel so desperate that they turn to violence."

"Well, that's all well and good," adds Nancy with a sigh. "But I don't see where all of this is going to lead. Our responsibility as teachers is to educate our kids. We're not psychiatrists or social workers. We can't change society. Besides, we've got youth agencies, centres for families in crisis, and all kinds of social service agencies."

What is the role of schools? Are teachers responsible for addressing social problems such as violence? What would you say to a teacher who expresses similar views to Nancy's?

The discussion among Jeff and his colleagues highlights the belief of much of the public that schools—and teachers—have a duty to address the problems of modern society. Those who agree with Nancy's opinion tend to believe that teachers are responsible for curriculum material only. Others, however, believe that teachers have an obligation to help manage domestic social problems. Underlying both positions are conflicting views on the aims of education.

What Are the Aims of Education Today?

In Canada, there is consensus that the purpose of schools is to educate. Unlike other institutions in society, schools have been developed exclusively to carry out one very important purpose. That we are not necessarily of the same mind about what the **aims of education** should be, however, is illustrated by our disagreement about what it means to be an educated person. Is a person with a college degree educated? Is a person who has overcome extreme hardships in life with dignity and grace educated?

Debate about the aims of education is not new. Fourth-century BCE philosopher Aristotle expressed the dilemma this way: "The existing practice [of education] is perplexing; no one knows on what principle we should proceed—should the useful in life, or should virtue, or should the higher knowledge, be the aim of our training; all three opinions have been entertained" (1941, 1306). Definitive answers to Aristotle's questions have not been realized; instead, each generation has developed its own idea of what the aims of education should be.

Education for Prosocial Values

Although there is widespread debate about what schools should teach in terms of academic content, there is agreement that **prosocial values** such as honesty, fairness, civility, and respect for the law should be imparted. The well-being of any society requires support of such values; they enable people from diverse backgrounds to live together peacefully. Parents, politicians, business people, and others might include respect for others, industry, perseverance, compassion, civility, and politeness in the list. Strong support for prosocial values reflects societal beliefs that schools should play a key role in promoting the democratic ideal of equality for all.

Education for Socialization

Schools are places where young people are socialized—where they learn to participate intelligently and constructively in Canadian society. In schools, more than in any other institution in our society, persons from various ethnic, racial, religious, and cultural backgrounds learn about Canadian values and customs. Schools also facilitate the learning of English or French for people from diverse backgrounds, teach the nature of the Canadian parliamentary system, and instruct in the basic workings of our economic institutions.

Of the various aims of schools, achievement is the most universally agreed upon. For most people, the primary purpose of schools is to impart to students the academic knowledge and skills that will prepare them either for additional schooling or for the world of work. Regardless of political ideology, religious beliefs, and cultural values, people want schools to teach academic content.

Education for Personal Growth and Societal Improvement

Society places great value on the dignity and worth of the individual. Accordingly, one aim of schools is to enable young people to become all that they are capable of. Unlike socialization or achievement, an emphasis on personal growth puts the individual first and society second. According to this view, the desired outcomes of education go beyond achievement to include the development of a positive self-concept and interpersonal skills, or what psychologist Daniel Goleman has termed "**emotional intelligence**." According to Goleman (1997; 1998), schools should emphasize five dimensions of emotional intelligence: self-awareness, the handling of emotions, motivation, empathy, and social skills. Emotional intelligence is essential for achievement in school, job success, marital happiness, and physical health; it enables students to live independently and to seek out the "good" life according to their own values, needs, and wants. The knowledge and skills students acquire at schools are seen as facilitating the achievement of personal growth and self-actualization. To determine your own emotional intelligence, you might take the test at www.psychtests.com/tests/iq/emotional_iq_r2_access.html.

Urie Bronfenbrenner, one of the world's leading developmental psychologists, advanced the **bioecological systems theory**, which has significantly influenced how psychologists and others approach the study of children. This theory suggests that children have five major ecologies (environments) within which they interact (socialize) that mould and shape their development (Bronfenbrenner 1979). An excellent description of this theory can be found at http://pt3.nl.edu/boemmelbriscoewebquest.pdf.

Schools also provide students with the knowledge and skills to improve their quality of life and to adapt to rapid social change. Naturally, a wide range of opinions exists about how society might be improved. Some teachers, like Jeff, Sue, and Bret in this chapter's opening scenario, believe that one purpose of schooling is to address social problems such as violence, whereas others, like their friend Nancy, believe schools should teach academic content and not try to change society. However, as James Banks (1999, 4) suggests, "Education within a pluralistic society should affirm and help students understand their home and community cultures. [To] create and maintain a civic community that works for the common good, education in a democratic society should help students acquire the knowledge, attitudes, and skills needed to participate in civic action to make society more equitable and just."

How Can Schools Be Described?

Many models have been proposed for describing the distinguishing characteristics of schools. Schools can be categorized according to the focus of their curricula; for example, high schools might be college preparatory, vocational, or general. Another view is based on organizational structure; for example, elementary (K–5), middle school (6–8), or high school (9–12).

Other models view schools metaphorically; that is, what is a school like? Some schools, for example, have been compared to factories, where students enter as raw material, move through the curriculum in a systematic way, and exit as finished products. Terrence Deal and Kent Peterson (1999, 21) suggest that exemplary schools "become like tribes or clans, with deep ties among people and with values and traditions that give meaning to everyday life." Other views see schools as similar to banks, gardens, prisons, mental hospitals, homes, churches, families, or teams. In the school-as-family metaphor, for example, the effective school is an inclusive, anti-oppressive, caring community of adults who attend to the academic, emotional, social, and physical needs of the children and youth entrusted to their care.

Schools and Social Class

In spite of a consensus that schools should promote social improvement and equal opportunity, some individuals believe that schools "reproduce" the existing society by presenting different curricula and educational experiences to students from different socio-economic classes. Students at a school in an affluent suburb, for example, may study chemistry in a well-equipped lab and take a field trip to a high-tech firm to see the latest application of chemical research, while students attending a school in another school district may learn chemistry from out-of-date texts, with no adequate lab in which to conduct experiments and limited opportunities for field trips due to limited funding. Schools, in effect, preserve the stratification within society and maintain the differences between the "haves" and the "have-nots." As Joel Spring puts it: "[t]he affluent members of . . . society can protect the educational advantages and, consequently, economic advantages of their children by living in affluent school districts or by using private [independent] schools. Their children will attend the elite institutions of higher education, and their privileged educational background will make it easy for them to follow in the footsteps of their parents' financial success" (Spring 1999, 290–91).

What Are Schools Like as Social Institutions?

Schools are social institutions. An **institution** is an organization established by society to maintain and improve its way of life. Schools are the institutions our society has established for the purpose of educating the young. During the past 200 years, Canadian schools have developed complex structures, policies, and curricula to accomplish this mission (see Figure 5.1).

The School as a Reflection of Society

As you might expect, schools mirror the national, provincial or territorial, and surrounding local culture and other special interests. Independent and parochial schools, for example, are often maintained by groups that see the school as a means of perpetuating their preferred way of life. Nevertheless, as Mary Henry (1993, 29) points out, "Schools are . . . not simply puppets of the dominant mainstream society. They have their own unique concerns and their own 'poetry' of people and events. Whether public or private, all schools are not the same."

Rural, Suburban, and Urban Schools

Schools also reflect their location. Schools in rural, urban, and suburban settings have significantly different cultures. Rural schools are often the focal point for community life and reflect values and beliefs that tend to be more conservative than those associated with urban and suburban schools. While the small size of a rural school may contribute to the development of a family-like culture, its size may also make it difficult to provide students with an array of curricular experiences equal to that found at larger schools in more populated areas. In contrast, large suburban or urban schools may provide students with more varied learning experiences, but these schools may lack the cohesiveness and community focus of rural schools.

For an interesting look at the variety of resources and programs offered in Canadian school districts, visit www.educationcanada.com. In addition to school district information, including employment opportunities, there are links to individual public and independent schools.

Schools and Community Environments

The effects of a school's local environment are considerable. Urban schools, especially those in less affluent districts, may reflect the social problems of the surrounding area. Middle-class families who can afford to move away from such urban areas or place their children

In what ways do schools reflect their communities and the wider Canadian society? What influence might the community have on this school? On the students who attend it? On the teachers?

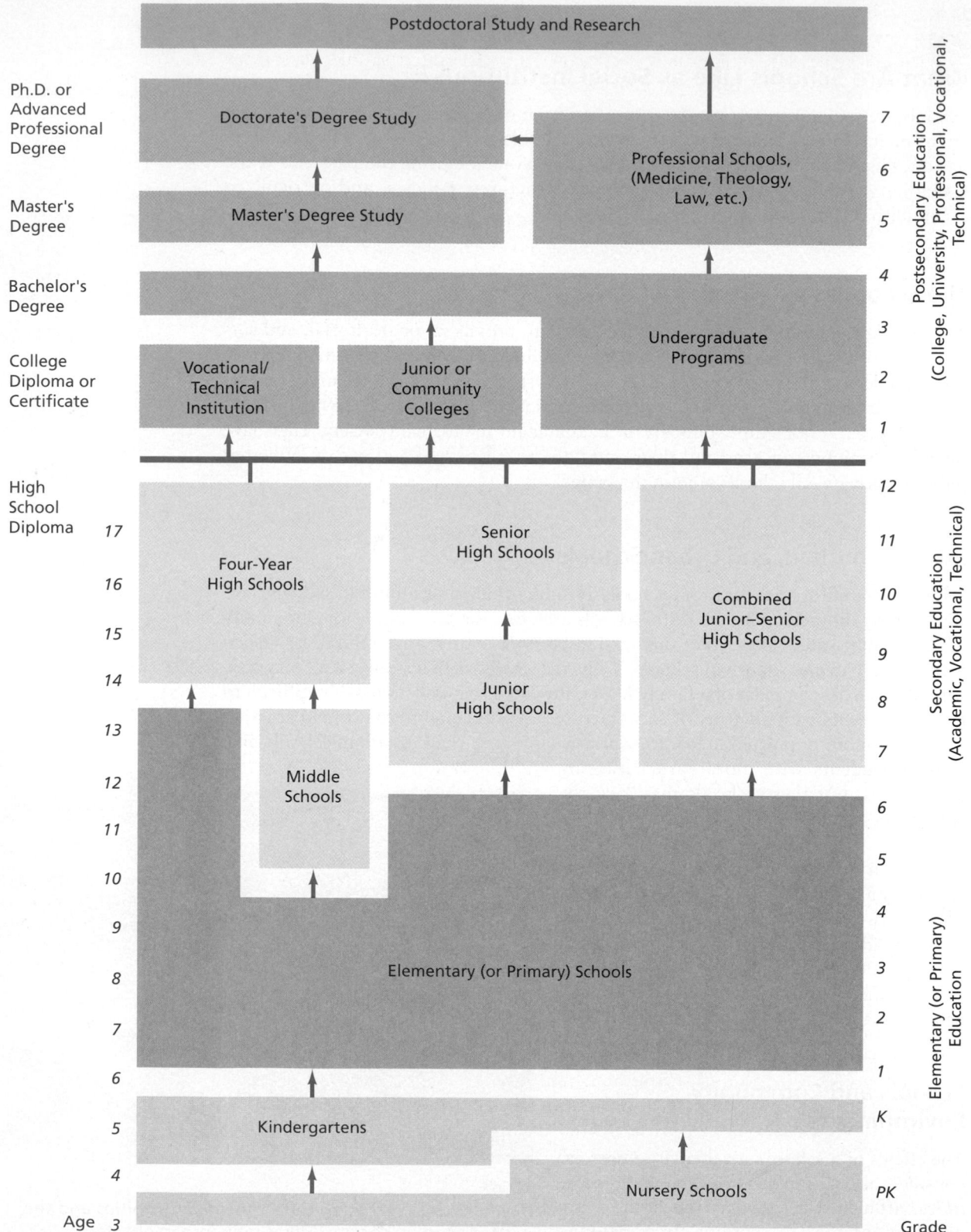

Figure 5.1 The institutional structure of education in Canada

in independent schools often do so. As a result, students in some urban school districts are increasingly from low-income backgrounds.

Though some communities may impact their schools in undesirable ways, many teachers at low-income area schools find their work stimulating and rewarding.

The Culture of the School

Although in general schools share a few universal characteristics, each school is unique. Each has a culture of its own—a network of beliefs, values and traditions, and ways of thinking and behaving that distinguishes it from other schools.

Much like a community, a school has a distinctive culture—a collective way of life. Terms that have been used to describe **school culture** include *climate*, *ethos*, *atmosphere*, and *character*. Some schools may be characterized as community-like places with a shared sense of purpose and commitment to providing the best education possible for all students. Other schools lack a unified sense of purpose or direction. Still others are characterized by internal conflict and divisiveness and may even reflect what Deal and Peterson (1999) term a "toxic" school culture that students, teachers, administrators, and parents feel does not sufficiently meet their needs.

The Physical Environment

The physical environment of a school both reflects and helps to create the school's overall culture. Displays of student art, trophy cabinets, bulletin boards with a section for "Student of the Week" and newspaper clippings highlighting school activities or accomplishments all play a part in the creation of a school's culture. "Whether school buildings are squeezed between other buildings or located on sprawling campuses, their fenced-in area or other physical separation distinguishes them from the community-at-large" (Ballantine 1997, 210).

Formal Practices of Schools

The formal practices of Canadian schools are evident to past and present students. With few exceptions, students attend school from 5 or 6 years of age through 16, at the least, and usually to age 18. Classes run Monday through Friday, September through June, for 12 or 13 years. For the most part, students are assigned to a grade level on the basis of age rather than ability or interest. Assignment to individual classes or teachers at a given grade level, however, may be made on the basis of ability or interest.

Teachers and students are grouped in several ways at the elementary-school level but follow one dominant pattern in junior and senior high school. In elementary schools, the **self-contained classroom** is the most traditional arrangement. In this type of classroom, one teacher teaches all or nearly all subjects to a group of about 25 children, with the teacher and students remaining in the same classroom for the entire day. Art, music, physical education, and computer skills are often taught in other parts of the school, so students may leave the classroom for scheduled periods. Individual students may also attend special classes for remedial or advanced instruction or speech therapy.

In **open-space schools**, students are free to move among various activities and learning centres. Instead of self-contained classrooms, open-space schools have large instructional areas with movable walls and furniture that can be rearranged easily.

Grouping for instruction is much more fluid and varied. Students do much of their work independently, with a number of teachers providing individual guidance as needed.

In middle schools and junior and senior high schools, students frequently study four or five academic subjects taught by teachers who specialize in them. In this organizational arrangement, called **departmentalization**, students move from classroom to classroom for their lessons. High school teachers often share their classrooms with other teachers and use their rooms only during scheduled class periods.

The Culture of the Classroom

Just as schools develop their unique cultures, each classroom develops its own culture or way of life. The culture of a classroom is determined in large measure by the manner in which teachers and students participate in common activities. An additional factor is the diversity of cultural, ethnic, and linguistic groups represented within some classrooms. In Canada's larger urban areas, it is not uncommon for an individual school to have students from as many as 50 different cultural, ethnic, or linguistic groups. In addition, the environment of the classroom and the inhabitants of that environment—students and teachers—are constantly interacting. Each aspect of the classroom affects all others (Woolfolk 1998, 440). Indeed, as any teacher can attest, the addition or removal of as few as one or two students from a class can positively or negatively affect the classroom's culture.

The quality of teacher–student interactions is influenced by the physical characteristics of the setting (classroom, use of space, materials, resources, etc.) and the social dimensions of the group (norms, rules, expectations, cohesiveness, distribution of power and influence). These elements interact to shape **classroom culture**. Teachers who appreciate the importance of the salient elements of classroom culture are more likely to create environments that they and their students find satisfying and rewarding.

How Is Cultural Diversity Represented in Canadian Schools?

The percentage of ethnic minorities in Canadian schools has been growing steadily since the end of World War II. According to Statistics Canada's report on the census of 2006, 18.4 percent of Canada's population was born in other countries, the highest percentage of any country except Australia. Statistics Canada also reports that over 90 percent of new citizens settle in large urban areas, with Montreal, Toronto, and Vancouver accounting for approximately 75 percent of the total. Table 5.1 provides a list of the most common ethnic origins of immigrants.

Clearly, the increasing **diversity** of Canadian society has extensive implications for schools. There is, for example, an increased demand for English as a second language (ESL) programs and teachers. All but a few school districts face a critical shortage of minority teachers. As well, there is an imperative to develop curricula and strategies that address the needs and backgrounds of all students—regardless of their social class, gender, sexual orientation, or ethnic, racial, or cultural identity.

Table 5.1

Population by Selected Ethnic Origins, Canada

Canadian	10 066 290	N.A. Indian	1 253 615	Filipino	436 190
English	6 570 015	Dutch	1 055 965	Métis	409 065
French	4 941 210	Polish	984 565	Swedish	339 765
Scottish	4 719 850	East Indian	962 665	Hungarian	315 510
Irish	4 354 155	Norwegian	422 515	American	316 350
German	3 179 425	Portuguese	410 850	Greek	242 685
Italian	1 346 510	Welsh	440 985	Spanish	325 730
Chinese	1 253 610	Jewish	315 120	Jamaican	231 110
Ukrainian	1 209 085	Russian	500 600	Vietnamese	180 125

Source: Statistics Canada 2007. Retrieved November 17, 2009 from www12.statcan.ca/english/census06/data/highlights/ethnic/pages/Page.cfm?Lang=E&Geo=PR&Code=01&Data=Count&Table=2&StartRec=1&Sort=3&Display=All&CSDFilter=5000. With the permission of the Minister of Public Works and Services.

The Meaning of Culture

Culture is *the way of life* common to a group of people. It consists of the values, attitudes, and beliefs that influence their traditions and behaviour. It is also a way of interacting with and looking at the world. Although at one time it was believed that Canada was a "melting pot" in which ethnic cultures would melt into one, ethnic and cultural differences have remained very much a part of life in Canada. A "salad-bowl" analogy more accurately captures the multicultural diversity of Canadian society. That is, the distinguishing characteristics of cultures tend be preserved and valued rather than blended into a single monoculture. An **ethnic group** is made up of individuals within a larger culture who share a self-defined racial or cultural identity and a set of beliefs, attitudes, and values. Members of an ethnic group distinguish themselves from others in the society both physically and socially. The composition of ethnic groups can change over time, and there is often as much variability within groups as between them. The biological concept of **race** suggests that there are natural physical variations among humans that are hereditary, reflected in body shape and skin coloration, and identifiable by terms such as Negroid, Caucasoid, and Mongoloid. While most individuals have a personal concept of what constitutes race, this issue is complicated and goes far beyond the scope of this text.

Dimensions of Culture

Within Canada, we find cultural groups that differ according to other distinguishing factors, such as religion, politics, economics, and geographic region. The regional culture of Newfoundland, for example, is quite different from that of Alberta. Similarly, British Columbians are culturally different from *les québécois*. However, everyone in Canada shares some common dimensions of culture. James Banks, an authority on multicultural education, has termed this shared culture the "national macro-culture" (Banks 1999). In addition to belonging to the national macro-culture, people in Canada are often members of specific ethnic groups.

Students in today's classrooms have diverse cultural identities. As a teacher, what steps will you take to integrate all students into the classroom?

Cultural Identity

Besides membership in the macro-culture, every Canadian individual participates in an array of subcultures, each with its own customs and beliefs. Collectively, these subcultures determine an individual's **cultural identity**, an overall sense of who one is. Elements that shape a person's cultural identity include age, racial background, language, religion, gender, sexual orientation, and income level. These elements can have varied influence on an individual. For example, cultural identity for some people is most strongly determined by their occupations; for others, by their ethnicity; and for others still, by their religious beliefs.

Remember that your future students will have their own complex cultural identities, which are no less valid than your own. For some, these identities foster a sense of "disconnection" from the attitudes, expectations, and values conveyed by the school. At present, the educational curriculum in Canada has a strong Eurocentric focus. Ratna Ghosh (2004) argues such a biased approach is unfair to culturally diverse students, especially new immigrants, as they do not understand the cultural context and often even the language in which they are taught. As well, minority students may feel they are being treated unfairly if they believe they are required to be "representatives" of their culture. Teachers should not require such students to teach the rest of their classmates about their cultures, as singling them out from their Euro-Canadian peers constitutes an insensitive practice.

As a teacher, you will be challenged to understand the subtle differences in cultural identities among your students and to create a learning environment that enables all students to feel comfortable in school and "connected to" their school experiences.

Figure 5.2

Four types of bilingual education programs

Four Types of Bilingual Education Programs

Immersion programs: Students learn English and other subjects in classrooms where only English is spoken. Aides who speak the first language of students are sometimes available, or students may also listen to equivalent audiotaped lessons in their first language.

Transition programs: Students receive reading lessons in their first language and lessons in English as a Second Language (ESL). Once they sufficiently master English, students are placed in classrooms where English is spoken and their first language is discontinued.

Pull-out programs: On a regular basis, students are separated from English-speaking students so that they may receive lessons in English or reading lessons in their first language. These are sometimes called sheltered English programs.

Maintenance programs: To maintain the student's native language and culture, instruction in English and instruction in the native language are provided from Kindergarten through Grade 12. Students become literate.

Language and Culture

Culture is embedded in language, a fact that has sometimes resulted in conflict between the English- and French-speaking groups in our society. While Canadians generally support the preservation of ethnic cultures, most believe that new immigrants should learn one of the two official languages in order to function effectively within Canadian society. ESL programs vary from one jurisdiction to another (see Figure 5.2). Interestingly, Statistics Canada reported in its 2001 Longitudinal Survey of Children and Youth that, over time, children with immigrant parents "caught up to, and sometimes surpassed, the academic performance of their classmates with Canadian-born parents."

Advice for Monolingual Teachers

Teachers must meet the needs of language-minority students. These needs are best met by teachers who speak their native language as well as English. However, this is often not possible, and monolingual teachers, particularly those in large urban areas, can expect to find increasing numbers of ESL students in their classrooms.

The Concept of Multiculturalism

Multiculturalism is a set of beliefs based on seeing the world from different cultural frames of reference and on recognizing and valuing the rich array of cultures within a nation and within the global community. For teachers, multiculturalism affirms the need to create schools in which differences related to race, ethnicity, gender, disability, and social class are acknowledged, and all students are viewed as enriching the teaching–learning process. Furthermore, a central purpose of teaching, according to the multiculturalist view, is to prepare students to live in a culturally pluralistic world—a world that "contrasts sharply with cultural assimilation, or 'melting pot' images, where ethnic minorities are expected to give up their traditions and blend in or be absorbed by the mainstream society or predominant culture" (Bennett 1999, 11).

Stereotyping and Racism

Although teachers should expand their knowledge of and appreciation for the diverse cultural backgrounds of their students, they should also guard against forming stereotypes or overgeneralizations about those cultures. **Stereotyping** is the process of attributing behavioural characteristics to all members of a group. In some cases, stereotypes are formed on the basis of limited experiences with, and information about, the group being stereotyped, and the validity of these stereotypes is often not questioned.

Within any cultural group that shares a broad cultural heritage, however, considerable diversity exists. For example, two Asian-Canadian children who live in the same community and attend the same school may appear alike to their teachers but in reality are very different. One may come from a home where Mandarin is spoken and Chinese holidays are observed; the other may be Vietnamese, speak no language but English, and observe only Canada's official holidays.

To help immigrant students adjust to Canadian culture, Qiu Liang offers the following advice based on his school experiences as a Chinese immigrant (Igoa 1995, 99–100):

> They [teachers] should be more patient [with an immigrant child] because it is very difficult for a person to be in a new country and learn a new language. Have patience.

> If the teacher feels there is no hope in an immigrant child, then the child will think, "Well, if the teacher who's helping me thinks that I can't go anywhere, then I might as well give up myself."

Similarly, Dung Yoong offers recommendations based on her educational experiences as a Vietnamese immigrant (Igoa 1995, 103):

> Try to get them to talk to you. Not just everyday conversation, but what they feel inside. Try to get them to get that out, because it's hard for kids. They don't trust—I had a hard time trusting and I was really insecure because of that.

> [P]utting an immigrant child who doesn't speak English into a classroom, a regular classroom with Canadian students, is not very good. It scares [them] because it is so different. [Teachers] should start [them] slowly and have special classes where the child could adapt and learn a little bit about Canadian society and customs.

As a teacher, you will not be able to eliminate stereotypic thinking in society. However, you have an obligation to all your students to see that your curriculum and instruction are free of any forms of stereotyping or racism. Providing equal educational opportunity to all students means that teachers and schools promote the full development of students as individuals, without regard for race, ethnicity, gender, sexual orientation, socio-economic status, abilities, or disabilities. More specifically, educators fulfill this important mission by continually evaluating the appropriateness of the curricular and instructional experiences they provide. The following Professional Reflection will help you examine, and possibly reassess, your cultural attitudes and determine whether you have stereotypes about other cultural groups.

In a Teacher's Journal entry, describe your cultural identity. Who are you? What beliefs, customs, and attitudes are part of your culture? Which of these are most important to your cultural identity?

Next, think of the ethnic and cultural groups in Canada with which you are unfamiliar. When you become a teacher, some of your students may be from these groups. What are some stereotypes about these groups that you tend to believe? How might these stereotypes influence your teaching and teaching effectiveness? How will you test or change your beliefs as part of the process of becoming a teacher?

What Is Multicultural Education?

Multicultural education, sometimes referred to as **inter-cultural education**, is committed to the goal of providing all students—regardless of socio-economic status, gender, sexual orientation or ethnic, racial, or cultural background—with equal opportunities to learn in school. Multicultural education is based on the notion that students do not learn in a vacuum—their culture predisposes them to learn in certain ways. Multicultural education also recognizes that current school practices have provided, and continue to provide, some students with greater opportunities for learning than students who belong to other groups.

Dimensions of Multicultural Education

According to James A. Banks, "[M]ulticultural education is a complex and multidimensional concept" (Banks 1999, 13). More specifically, Banks suggests that multicultural education may be conceptualized as consisting of five dimensions: (1) content integration, (2) knowledge construction, (3) prejudice reduction, (4) an equity pedagogy, and (5) an empowering school culture. As you progress through your teacher education program and eventually begin to prepare curriculum materials and instructional strategies for your multicultural classroom, remember that integrating content from a variety of cultural groups is just one dimension of multicultural education. Multicultural education is not "something that is done at a certain time slot in the school day where children eat with chopsticks or listen to Peruvian music . . . [it is] something that is infused throughout the school culture and practiced daily" (Henry 1996, 108).

Multicultural education promotes students' positive self-identity in their heritage, acceptance of people from diverse backgrounds, and critical self-assessment. In addition, it can prompt students, perhaps with guidance from teachers, to take action against prejudice and discrimination within their school. Indeed, as Joel Spring says, "[m]ulticultural education should create a spirit of tolerance and activism in students. An understanding of other cultures and of differing cultural frames of reference will . . . spark students to actively work for social justice" (Spring 1998, 163). For example, students might reduce the marginalization of minority-group students in their school by inviting them to participate in extracurricular and after-school activities.

Multicultural Curricula

As a teacher, you will teach students who, historically, have not received full educational opportunity—students from the many racial and ethnic minority groups in Canada, students from low-income families or communities, students with exceptional abilities or disabilities, students who are gay or lesbian, and students who are male or female. You will face the challenge of reaching out to all students and teaching them that they are persons of worth who can learn.

In developing a multicultural curriculum, you should be sensitive to how your instructional materials and strategies can be made more inclusive so that they reflect cultural "voices" that were previously silent or marginalized in discussions about what should be taught in schools and how it should be taught. "Non-dominant groups representing diversity in the school whose voices traditionally have not been heard include those defined by race, language, gender, sexual orientation, alternative family structures, social class, disability, bilingualism, and those with alien or refugee status" (Henry 1996, 108). Effective teachers attend to these previously unheard voices not as an act of tokenism but with a genuine desire to make the curriculum more inclusive and to "create space for alternative voices, not just on the periphery but in the center" (Singer 1994, 286).

Multicultural Instructional Materials and Strategies

To create classrooms that are truly multicultural, teachers must select instructional materials that are sensitive, accurately portray the contributions of ethnic groups, and reflect diverse points of view. Teachers must also recognize that "[s]ome of the books and other materials on ethnic groups published each year are insensitive, inaccurate, and written from mainstream and insensitive perspectives and points of view" (Banks 1997, 124). Some guidelines for selecting multicultural instructional materials are as follows:

- Books and other materials should accurately portray the perspectives, attitudes, and feelings of ethnic groups.
- Fictional works should have strong ethnic characters.
- Books should describe settings and experiences with which all students can identify and yet should accurately reflect ethnic cultures and lifestyles.
- The protagonists in books with ethnic themes should have ethnic characteristics but should face conflicts and problems universal to all cultures and groups.
- The illustrations in books should be accurate, ethnically sensitive, and technically good.
- Ethnic materials should not contain racist concepts, clichés, phrases, or words.
- Factual materials should be historically accurate.
- Resources and textbooks should discuss major events and documents related to ethnic history. (Banks 1997, 125–26)

Yvonne Wilson, an Aboriginal elementary teacher, points out that a teacher's willingness to learn about other cultures is very important to students and their parents:

People in the community know if you are trying to understand their culture. Students also see it. Becoming involved—going to a powwow or participating in other cultural events—shows people that here is a teacher who is trying to learn about our culture.

Participating wholeheartedly in cross-cultural experiences will help you to grow as a teacher.

How Is Gender a Dimension of Multicultural Education?

Although it may be evident that gender affects students' learning in many ways, it may not be as clear that gender is an important dimension of multicultural education. However, "culturally democratic classrooms also consider gender differences" (Oakes & Lipton 2007, 277). For example, the following comments by a first-year high school science teacher stress the importance of gender differences in the classroom.

> I have high expectations for all of my students, not just the boys. If I challenge a boy to figure out the answer to a scientifically engaging problem for himself, and then go and give the answer to a girl, I send an unconscious message that I do not think my female student can figure it out by herself. I encourage the girls' active participation when it is easy for them to be drowned out by the louder and more aggressive boys. I encourage girls to ask questions and help them use scientific methodology to find answers. I challenge them to think about why there are more men who do science than women. (Oakes & Lipton 2007, 278)

Gender Differences

Cultural differences between males and females are partially shaped by society's traditional expectations of them. Through **sex role stereotyping**, families, media, schools, and other powerful social forces condition boys and girls to act in certain ways regardless of abilities or interests. As mentioned previously, one of the aims of schools is to socialize students to participate in society. One dimension of the **sex role socialization** process sometimes conveys to students certain expectations about the way boys and girls are "supposed" to act. We used to suggest that girls are supposed to play with dolls, and boys with trucks. It was also believed that girls are supposed to be passive, whereas boys should be active. Girls are supposed to express their feelings and emotions when in pain; boys should repress their feelings and deny pain. In attempts to understand how males and females develop and interact with the world, various gender theories have been advanced. Each has its supporters and critics, which suggests that no single theory has the complete answer. Among the more popular gender theories are two from the field of psychology: social learning theory, which suggests that children learn gender passively, and cognitive development theory, which suggests that children learn gender actively. Synopses of these and other gender theories can be found at www.cla.purdue.edu/academic/engl/theory/genderandsex.

Students may be socialized into particular gender-specific roles as a result of the curriculum materials they use at school. By portraying males in more dominant, assertive ways, and portraying females in ways that suggest they are passive and helpless, textbooks can subtly reinforce expectations about the way girls and boys "should" behave. Over the past few decades, though, publishers of curriculum materials have become more vigilant about avoiding these stereotypes.

However, some gender differences in academic skills do appear to exist. In 2002, the Council of Ministers of Education, Canada (CMEC), as part of its School Achievement Indicators Program (SAIP), released the following data regarding the writing skills of Canadian 13- and 16-year-old students. These results indicate a gender gap in the relative writing skills of boys and girls. The assessment was administered to approximately 24 000 students in all provinces and territories except Nunavut. Performance was reported on a five-point scale, with one being the lowest and five the highest.

Some major findings of the SAIP test are:

1. More than 80 percent of 13-year-olds reached level two and above. According to the test designers, level two is the level that most 13-year-olds should reach. Over 40 percent reached level three and above.
2. Over 60 percent of 16-year-olds reached level three or above. Level three is the level most 16-year-olds should reach, according to test designers.
3. Significantly more girls in both age groups performed at higher levels than boys. This gender gap is consistent with current trends in Language Arts assessment as confirmed in the Programme for International Student Assessment (PISA) 2000 reading assessment.
4. Among francophones, students in Quebec outperformed francophone students in minority-language settings for both age groups.

In recent years, the academic gender-gap between male and female students has become so serious that some are now advocating separate schools for boys. For a good overview of this problem in Canadian schools you might review William A. Draves' article *Why Boys Under-Perform in School*, located on the LERN website at www.williamdraves.com/works/boys.htm.

Gender-Fair Classrooms and Curricula

Although research and debate about the bias boys and girls encounter in school will no doubt continue, it is clear that teachers must encourage girls and boys to develop to the full extent of their abilities and must provide an education free from **gender bias**—subtle favouritism or discrimination on the basis of gender. In her article "The Quality Teacher" (1993, 6), Kimberley Burstall reports the results of a survey she administered to a gender-balanced group of 300 Nova Scotia students from Grades 5, 8, and 11. The survey asked the students to select, from an extensive list of options, the three characteristics they considered most important for a "good teacher." In first place, with a score of 200, was "Treats boys and girls equally." Because it is through language that gender fairness is most easily observed, it is important for teachers to be very careful in their selection of words when interacting with students. To check your own sensitivity to gender-fair language, we suggest you complete the Gender-Neutral Questionnaire located on www.MyEducationLab.com.

Following is a list of basic guidelines for creating a **gender-fair classroom**. Adherence to these guidelines will help teachers "address the inequities institutionalized in the organizational structure of schools, the curriculum selected to be taught, the learning strategies employed, and their ongoing instructional and informal interactions with students" (Stanford 1992, 88).

- Become aware of differences in interactions with girls and boys.
- Promote boys' achievement in reading and writing and girls' achievement in mathematics and science.
- Reduce young children's self-imposed sexism.
- Teach about sexism and sex-role stereotyping.
- Foster an atmosphere of collaboration between girls and boys.

PEARSON
myeducationlab

Sexual Orientation

In addition to gender bias, some students experience discrimination on the basis of their sexual orientation. A study of 8000 Canadian and American college students found that "80–85 percent of both sexes could be classified as exclusively heterosexual" (Ellis, Robb, & Burke 2005, 569–81) with the remainder identifying on a spectrum from exclusively gay to exclusively lesbian. These findings are probably an accurate reflection of the situation in Canadian schools.

To help all students realize their full potential, teachers should acknowledge the special needs of gay, lesbian, and bisexual students, for "there is an invisible gay and lesbian minority in every school, and the needs of these students are often unknown and unmet" (Besner & Spungin 1995, xi). While many Canadian schools have been slow or reluctant to meet the needs of gay, lesbian, and bisexual students, one notable exception is Victoria Park Collegiate Institute (Grades 9–12) in Toronto. This forward-looking school has an Anti-Homophobic Alliance (AHA) club for teachers and students of all sexual orientations—including those who are strictly heterosexual. Victoria Park has recognized that teachers and other school personnel can provide much-needed support to students with differing gender identities. It creates an inclusive environment that encourages students to respect differences and to see the contributions that persons from all groups have made, and can make, to society.

For examples of problems teachers have faced regarding gender-related issues, see Teacher's Resource 5.2: The Teacher's Scribe, "Love and sex in the classroom" located at www.MyEducationLab.com.

Gender-orientation symbols

PEARSON
myeducationlab

What Characteristics Distinguish Successful Schools?

At this point in your professional education, you may, because of the diverse nature of today's school populations, be uncertain of your ability to develop a positive classroom climate. However, many schools in all settings and with all kinds of students are highly successful, including inner-city and isolated rural schools and schools that serve pupils of all socio-economic, racial, and ethnic backgrounds. What are the characteristics of these schools? Do they have commonalities that account for their success?

Measures of Success

First, we must define what we mean by a **successful school**. One measure of success, naturally, is that students at these schools achieve at a high level and complete requirements for graduation. Whether reflected in scores on standardized tests or other documentation of academic gains, students at these schools are learning. They are achieving literacy in reading, writing, and computer skills. They are learning to solve problems and to think creatively and analytically, and, most importantly, they are learning to learn.

Additionally, successful schools are those that are improving, rather than deteriorating. School improvement is a slow process, and schools that are improving in achievement and student morale can be considered successful.

Research on School Effectiveness

During the 1980s and early 1990s, much research was conducted to identify the characteristics of successful (or effective) schools. These characteristics were defined in different ways in several research projects. The following list, which is a synthesis of these findings, presents the five most commonly mentioned characteristics.

- *Strong leadership*—Successful schools have strong leaders—individuals who value education and see themselves as educational leaders, not just as managers or bureaucrats. They monitor the performance of everyone at the school—teachers, staff, students, and themselves. These leaders have a vision of the school as an effective learning environment, and they take decisive steps to bring that about.
- *High expectations*—Teachers at successful schools have high expectations of students. These teachers believe that all students, rich or poor, can learn, and they communicate this through realistic, yet high, expectations.
- *Emphasis on basic skills*—Teachers at successful schools emphasize student achievement in the basic skills of reading, writing, and mathematics.
- *Orderly school environment*—The environments of successful schools are orderly, safe, and conducive to learning. Discipline problems are at a minimum, and teachers are able to devote greater amounts of time to teaching.
- *Frequent, systematic evaluation of student learning*—The learning of students in successful schools is monitored closely. When difficulties are noticed, appropriate remediation is provided quickly.

In short, the cultures of effective schools encourage teachers to grow and develop in the practice of their profession. As the Secondary Schools in Canada: The National Report of the Exemplary Schools Project states (Gaskell 1995, 278):

> School success is a complex and constantly evolving concept; different communities place emphasis on different elements. Success is a fragile quality that always involves a balance among different demands and pressures. It needs to be constantly reevaluated as conditions change. Successful schools are consciously trying to improve themselves by continuing inquiry and deliberative change.

What Social Problems Affect Schools and Place Students at Risk?

A complex and varied array of social issues impact schools. These problems often detract from the ability of schools to educate students according to the seven aims discussed at the beginning of this chapter: educational goals, prosocial values, socialization, achievement, personal growth, social change, and equal opportunity. Furthermore, schools are often charged with the difficult (if not impossible) task of providing a frontline defence against such problems.

One of the most vocal advocates of the role of schools in solving social problems was George S. Counts. In his 1932 book *Dare the School Build a New Social Order?*, he said, "If schools are to be really effective, they must become centers for the building, and not merely the contemplation, of our civilization" (p. 12). Many people, however, believe that schools should not try to build a new social order, and should be concerned only with the academic and social development of students. Nevertheless, the debate over the role of schools in regard to social problems will continue to be vigorous. For some time, schools have served to combat social problems by offering an array of health, education, and social service programs. Schools provide breakfasts, nutritional counselling, diagnostic services related to health and family planning, after-school child care, job placement, sex and drug education, and other services. In the following sections, we examine several societal problems that directly influence schools, teachers, and students.

Identifying Students at Risk

An increasing number of young people live under conditions of extreme stress, chronic poverty, crime, and lack of adult guidance. As James Garbarino (1999, 12) points out: "In almost every community . . . growing numbers of kids live in a socially toxic environment." Frustrated, lonely, and feeling powerless, many youths escape into music with violent or obscene lyrics, violent video games, cults, movies, and television programs that celebrate gratuitous violence and sex, and cruising shopping malls or "hanging out" on the street. Others turn to crime, gang violence, promiscuous sex, or substance abuse. Not surprisingly, these activities place many young people at risk of dropping out of school. **Students at risk** of dropping out tend to get low grades, perform below their grade level academically, are older than the average student at their level because of previous retention, and have behaviour problems at school. It is estimated that the following percentages of 14-year-olds are likely to exhibit one or more at-risk behaviours (substance abuse, sexual behaviour, violence, depression, or school failure) and to experience serious negative outcomes as a result: 10 percent at very high risk, 25 percent at high risk, 25 percent at moderate risk, 20 percent at low risk, and 20 percent at no risk (Dryfoos 1998).

Unfortunately, 19 percent of Canadian students fail to complete a high school education. As the Statistics Canada paper *In and Out of High School* indicates, in 2002, approximately 44 percent of students who discontinued their studies did so for reasons related to school climate. Among other things, they "felt that discipline at their schools was not handled fairly, that students were not respected, and that their school was not a friendly place" (Statistics Canada 2002a, 18).

Family Stress

The stress placed on families in a complex society is extensive and not easily handled. For some families, such stress can be overwhelming. The structure of families experiencing the effects of financial problems, substance abuse, or violence, for example, can easily begin to crumble. Health challenges in which a family member has developed cancer or another serious disease can also lead to significantly increased levels of stress.

Stress within the family can have a significant negative effect on students and their ability to focus on learning while at school. Such stress is often associated with health and emotional problems, failure to achieve, behavioural problems at school, and dropping out.

With the rise in the divorce rate and women's increased presence into the workforce over the past few decades, family constellations have changed dramatically. No longer is a working father, a mother who stays at home, and two or three children the only kind of family in Canada. The number of single-parent families, step-parent families, blended families, and extended families has increased dramatically. In 2005, the **Pan-Canadian Education Indicators Program (PCEIP)**, a joint venture of Statistics Canada and the Council of Ministers of Education, Canada, reported that 25 percent of children in single-parent homes live below the poverty line. An earlier report based on data from the 1996 Statistics Canada Longitudinal Survey of Canadian Children and Youth (LSCCY) indicated that children from single-parent homes were more likely to suffer from conduct disorders and to have academic difficulties. Just as there is diversity in the composition of today's families, so, too, is there diversity in the styles with which children are raised. Because of the large number of single-parent homes, an alarming number of **latchkey children** are unsupervised during much of the day. To meet the needs of these children, some schools now offer before- and after-school programs (Statistics Canada 2001c).

Substance Abuse

One of the most pressing social problems confronting today's schools is the abuse of illegal drugs, tobacco, and alcohol. The use of drugs among young people varies from community to community and from year to year, but overall, the incidence is disturbingly high. Mind-altering substances used by young people include the glue, white correction fluid, and felt marker, as well as marijuana, amphetamines, and cocaine. The abuse of drugs not only poses the risks of addiction and overdose, it is also related to problems such as HIV and AIDS, teenage pregnancy, depression, suicide, automobile accidents, criminal activity, and dropping out. For an alarming number of young people, drugs provide a means of coping with life's problems.

Violence and Crime

While Canada experienced a decline in serious violent crime during the 1990s, crime rates among Canada's 2 million adolescents have remained relatively constant in recent years. However, Canadian concern about school crime and safety has led to increased security measures within schools. It is now commonly required that all visitors to a school sign in, for most school-access doors to be locked at all times, and for all school grounds to be supervised whenever students are using them. Because of several shooting incidents at both Canadian schools and schools in other countries, the installation of metal detectors has also been given careful consideration. Additional measures include **Child Abuse Registry** and **criminal record** checks for anyone working with or supervising students. Many schools have also developed crisis management plans to cope with violent incidents on campus and regularly review their ability to provide students, faculty, and staff with a safe environment for learning. The "School Safety Checklist" below presents a starting point for evaluating school safety.

School Safety Checklist

Give your school a thorough crime prevention inspection. Use this checklist (National School Safety Center, 2007) as a guideline to determine your school's strengths and weaknesses.

1. Is there a policy for dealing with violence and vandalism in your school? (The reporting policy must be realistic and strictly adhered to.)
2. Is there an incident reporting system?
3. Is the incident reporting system available to all staff?
4. Is there statistical information available as to the scope of the problems at your school and in the community?
5. Have the school, school board, and administrators taken steps or anticipated any problems through dialogue?

6. Does security fit into the organization of the school? (Security must be designed to fit the needs of the administration and must be available on-site.)
7. Are the teachers and administrators aware of laws that pertain to them? To their rights? To students' rights? Are they aware of their responsibility to enforce and respect rules, regulations, policies, and laws?
8. Is there a working relationship with your local law enforcement agency?
9. Are students and parents aware of expectations and school discipline codes?
10. Are there any actual or contingency action plans in place to deal with student disruptions and vandalism?
11. Is there a policy for dealing with restitution or prosecution of perpetrators of violence and vandalism?
12. Is there in-service training available for teachers and staff in the areas of violence, vandalism, and required reporting procedures?
13. Is there a policy for consistent monitoring and evaluation of incident reports?
14. Is the staff trained in standard crime prevention behaviour?

Now that you have completed the checklist, consider the following excerpt that describes a program called "Peaceful Schools International." As explained below by V. Lois Ross, principal of Meadows School in Brandon, Manitoba, the mandate of this program is to foster a safe and peaceful school environment.

Peaceful Schools International

Increased incidents of aggression and bullying among young people has school authorities and parents alike worried about the long-term effects of such behaviour on individual students, as well as the climate of schools. How does violence—of all levels—affect the educational environments of schools and their communities?

Imagine a school of about 350 students from Kindergarten to Grade 6 which is nestled on the outskirts of a mid sized city. Many of the educators and the

Increased incidence of aggression and bullying among young people has school authorities and parents worried about the long-term effects of such behaviour on individual students, as well as on the climate of schools. How does violence—of all levels—affect the educational environments of schools and their communities?

principal have long-standing experience at this school. Historically, this student body has been described as a rural and urban mixture from relatively stable, white, middle class families.

Now, imagine this same school which, over a period of three years, has been transformed to include nearly 500 students from Kindergarten to Grade 8. A number of educators have transferred into this school to teach at the new levels, and a new principal has been assigned. Due to the opening of a large pork processing facility in the city, several families have moved into a high-density apartment residence located in the area, and as a result the student body now reflects much more diversity and transience. The school is now operating over capacity and space has become an issue.

Although the situation described above reflects challenges, it also poses opportunities for the staff, students and parent body to collaborate and implement a number of positive initiatives to foster the development of a healthy K to 8 learning community; one that attempts to negate the traumas of misbehaviour including bullying* and other social concerns. One such initiative included the application for, and adoption of, Peaceful Schools International. The appeal of this program comes from its mandate to support schools in their quest to establish and maintain a peaceful, caring and safe atmosphere. Acceptance into this organization is based on an application process which includes, for example, documentation of collaborative decision-making, multi-disciplinary approaches and overall commitment from all stakeholders at the school. Participants are challenged to generate creative, grassroots ideas, so instead of a "canned program," each school develops approaches which are uniquely tailored to its own setting.

Poetry, songs, drama, class challenges, community service and art are all being utilized, to date, to energize our focus of a safe, respectful, caring, peaceful K to 8 learning community. Both staff and students are now strongly engaged in this focus. Just imagine the possibilities now!

Source: Reprinted by permission of V. Lois Ross.

*For more information on this important topic, visit www.canadiancrc.com/Bullying.htm.

Teen Pregnancy

Each year, thousands of Canadian women (1 in every 20) between the ages of 15 and 19 will become pregnant, and about 85 percent of these pregnancies are unintended. Indeed, most teachers of adolescents today may expect to have at least some students who are, or have been, pregnant. Teenage pregnancy can be a serious problem, since many teen mothers drop out of school, forfeiting their high school diplomas and limiting their access to decent, higher-paying job opportunities. As a consequence, they and their children often tend to remain at the bottom of the economic ladder. However, with the increasing numbers of Canadian high schools now making daycare facilities available, some of the problems arising from teen pregnancies are being addressed.

Suicide among Children and Youths

The increase in individual and multiple suicides is alarming: In any given year, approximately 500 Canadian youths and adolescents will take their own lives. Among teenagers, it is the third leading cause of death. Additionally, it is estimated that there are 8 to 25 attempted suicides for one completion. According to the Canadian Institute of Child Health, approximately 12 percent of male youth and 21 percent of female youth have seriously considered committing suicide (Canadian Institute of Child Health 2000).

Although female students are almost two times more likely than male students to seriously consider suicide, about six times as many male students as females follow through. Lesbian and gay youth are two to three times more likely to attempt suicide than their heterosexual peers, and they account for up to 30 percent of all completed suicides among youth (Besner & Spungin 1995).

What Are Schools Doing to Address Social Problems?

Responding to the needs of at-risk students will be a crucial challenge for schools, families, and communities during the twenty-first century. Since most children attend school, it is logical that this pre-existing system be used for reaching large numbers of at-risk children and their families. During the past decade, many school districts have taken innovative steps to address social problems that impact students' lives.

Though programs that address social problems are costly, the public believes that schools should be used for the delivery of health and social services. However, there is some disagreement about the extent to which school facilities should be used for anything but meeting students' educational needs. There is a widespread belief that the primary goal of schools should be the education of children, and that schools should not be expected to solve all of society's ills.

Intervention Programs

Under pressure to find solutions to increasing social problems among children and adolescents, educators have developed an array of intervention programs. In general, the aim of these programs is to address the behavioural, social, and academic adjustment of at-risk children and adolescents so they can receive maximum benefit from their school experiences.

In the following sections, we briefly review two comprehensive strategies that have proven effective in addressing academic, social, and behavioural problems: peer counselling and school-based interprofessional case management. This chapter presents additional information about recent, innovative steps for the *prevention* of the effects of social problems on students. See Teacher's Resource 5.1 on www.MyEducationLab.com for a list of resources on the social problems encountered by children and youth.

PEARSON
myeducationlab

Peer Counselling

Some schools have initiated student-to-student **peer counselling** programs—usually monitored by a counsellor or another specially trained adult. In peer counselling programs, students can address issues such as low academic achievement, interpersonal problems at home and at school, substance abuse, and career planning. Evidence indicates that both peer counsellors and students experience increased self-esteem and greater ability to deal with problems.

When peer counselling is combined with cross-age tutoring, younger students can learn about drugs, alcohol, premarital pregnancy, delinquency, dropping out, HIV and AIDS, suicide, and other relevant issues. Groups are often comprised of college-age students meeting with high schoolers, or high school students meeting with junior high or middle school students. In these preventative programs, older students

Teachers are increasingly asked to provide students with special needs assistance that goes beyond the purely academic. How far do you think classroom teachers should be expected to go in responding to this request?

sometimes perform dramatic role plays that portray students confronting problems and model strategies for handling the situations presented.

Alternative Schools and Curricula

To meet the needs of at-risk students, many school districts have developed alternative schools and curricula. Usually, an **alternative school** is a small, highly individualized school separate from the regular school; in other cases, the alternative school is organized as a **school-within-a-school**. Alternative school programs usually provide remedial instruction, some vocational training, and individualized counselling. Since they generally offer much smaller class sizes than conventional schools, alternative school teachers can monitor students' progress more closely and, when problems arise, respond more quickly and with greater understanding of student needs.

To reach students who are not successful at regular schools, alternative schools offer a program of individualized instruction, small class sizes, and various enrichment programs delivered in what school staff describe as a supportive, non-coercive, non-traditional setting. Most students are expected to return to their regular schools after a minimum of four weeks.

Many highly effective conventional-school teachers develop alternative curricula to meet the unique learning needs of students at risk. Many teachers, for example, link students' learning to business, civic, cultural, and political segments of their communities. The rationale is that connecting at-risk students to the world beyond their schools will enable them to see the relevance of education.

SUMMARY

What Are the Aims of Education Today?

- Though debate about the aims of education continues, there is general agreement that schools have a responsibility to address problems confronting Canadian society.

- Agreement exists regarding six additional broad educational aims—education for prosocial values, socialization, achievement, personal growth, social change, and equal opportunity.

How Can Schools Be Described?

■ Schools can be categorized according to the focus of their curricula and according to their organizational structures.

■ Metaphors for schools have suggested that schools are like families, tribes or clans, banks, gardens, prisons, and so on, with the school-as-family metaphor often describing schools that are successful.

■ Some people believe that schools reproduce the existing social class structure—that they maintain the differences between the "haves" and "have-nots."

What Are Schools Like as Social Institutions?

■ As social institutions that contribute to the maintenance and improvement of society, schools mirror Canadian values and the surrounding local culture.

■ Schools develop their own unique cultures, and the community environment that surrounds a school can impact it positively or negatively.

■ Elements of a school's physical environment, such as self-contained classrooms, open-space arrangements, and departmentalization, contribute to a school's character and culture. Similarly, each classroom develops its own culture, which is influenced by the physical setting and the social dimensions of the group.

How Is Cultural Diversity Represented in Canadian Schools?

■ The percentage of ethnic *minorities* in Canadian schools has been growing steadily since the end of World War II. According to the 2006 Census, almost 20 percent of Canada's population was born in other countries, the highest percentage of any country except Australia. Statistics Canada reports that over 90 percent of new citizens settle in large urban areas, with Montreal, Toronto, and Vancouver accounting for approximately three-quarters of the total.

■ Culture is defined as the way of life common to a group of people, including beliefs, attitudes, habits, values, and practices.

■ Dimensions of cultural identity include beliefs, attitudes, and values; racial identity; language; religion; gender; ethnicity; income level; and occupation.

■ *Ethnicity* refers to a commonly shared racial or cultural identity and a set of beliefs, values, and attitudes. The concept of race is used to distinguish among people on the basis of biological traits and characteristics. A minority group is a group of people who share certain characteristics and are fewer in number than the majority of a population.

■ Stereotyping is the process of attributing certain behavioural characteristics to all members of a group, often on the basis of limited experiences with, and information about, the group being stereotyped. Individual racism is the prejudicial belief that one's own ethnic or racial group is superior to others, and institutional racism refers to laws, customs, and practices that lead to racial inequalities.

What Is Multicultural Education?

■ Five dimensions of multicultural education have been suggested: content integration, knowledge construction, prejudice reduction, an equity pedagogy, and an empowering school culture.

- A multicultural curriculum addresses the needs and backgrounds of all students—regardless of their cultural identity—and expands students' appreciation for diversity. Effective multicultural materials and instructional strategies include the contributions of ethnic groups that reflect diverse points of view, including "voices" that previously may have been silenced or marginalized in society.

How Is Gender a Dimension of Multicultural Education?

- Gender includes ways of knowing and modes of conduct, thought, and expression specific to sex.
- Both boys and girls experience inequities in the classroom; teachers, however, can provide an education free of *gender bias* by creating gender-fair classrooms and curricula.
- Teachers should acknowledge the special needs of students who are gay, lesbian, or bisexual, and provide them with safe, supportive learning environments.

What Characteristics Distinguish Successful Schools?

- Three aspects of successful schools have been suggested: (1) their students manifest a high level of learning; (2) their results surpass those for comparable schools; (3) they are improving rather than getting deteriorating.
- Research has identified seven characteristics of effective schools: strong leadership, high expectations, emphasis on basic skills, an orderly school environment, frequent and systematic evaluation of student learning, sense of purpose, and collegiality and a sense of community.
- Research indicates that successfully restructured schools emphasize student learning, authentic pedagogy, building organizational capacity, and external support.

What Social Problems Affect Schools and Place Students at Risk?

- Among the many social problems that impact a school's ability to educate students are poverty, family stress, substance abuse, violence and crime, teen pregnancy, HIV and AIDS, and suicide.
- Children at risk, regardless of ethnic and racial background or socio-economic level, tend to get low grades, to underachieve, to be older than other students at the same grade level, and to have behaviour problems at school.

What Are Schools Doing to Address Social Problems?

- Schools have developed intervention and prevention programs to address social problems. Two effective intervention programs are peer counselling and school-based interprofessional case management.
- Many school districts have developed alternative schools or schools-within-a-school that provide highly individualized instructional and support services for students who have not been successful in regular schools. Highly effective teachers modify their techniques and develop alternative curricula to meet the needs of students at risk.

aims of education, 134
alternative school, 156
bioecological systems
    theory, 135
Child Abuse Registry, 152
classroom culture, 140
criminal record, 152
cultural identity, 142
culture, 141
departmentalization, 140
diversity, 140
emotional intelligence, 135

ethnic group, 141
gender bias, 148
gender-fair classroom, 148
institution, 137
inter-cultural education 145
latchkey children, 152
multicultural education, 145
multiculturalism, 143
open-space schools, 139
Pan-Canadian Education
    Indicators Program
    (PCEIP), 151

peer counselling, 155
prosocial values, 135
race, 141
school culture, 139
school-within-a-school, 156
self-contained
    classroom, 139
sex role socialization, 147
sex role stereotyping, 147
stereotyping, 144
students at risk, 151
successful school, 149

APPLICATIONS AND ACTIVITIES

Teacher's Journal

1. Collect and summarize several newspaper and magazine articles that contain references to public expectations of education and schools. To what extent do the articles address the four aims discussed in this chapter? To what extent do they identify social problems that schools are expected to address?

2. Identify and then defend your choice of school improvements that you consider most important for increasing the quality of education in Canada. What aims of education do your choices reflect?

3. Reflect on your experiences with the impact of social problems on teaching and learning at the elementary, middle, or high school levels. Select one of the social issues or problems discussed in this chapter and describe its influence on you or your peers.

4. Reflecting on your experience in schools, describe any steps your teachers or other personnel took to create an empowering school culture and social climate.

5. During your school years, did you ever experience discrimination as a member of a "different" group? Write about one outstanding incident that you feel affected your performance as a student.

6. As a teacher, what activities and materials might you use in a specific learning context to reduce the prejudices of students toward groups different from theirs?

7. Describe an example of sex-role stereotyping or gender bias that you experienced or observed in a school setting and how you felt about it.

Theory into Practice

1. In a small group, discuss the following topic, record your results, and be prepared to share them with the class.

    If it is the role of the school to produce responsible, self-directed graduates, should the almost universal practice of having students request permission to leave the classroom be discontinued? As long as there are reasonable guidelines to govern such a practice, would students receive any benefit from having this freedom? Would the overall culture of the classroom be changed?

2. In a small group, read the paragraph below and the instructions that follow.

The culture of a classroom can be directly affected by the physical ambience of the room and the items within it. Bare walls, external noise from traffic or other sources, poor lighting, crowded seating, and a miscellany of other items can have affect student learning. Which of the following would you see as reasonable components for inclusion in your elementary school classroom? Your secondary school classroom?

Give each item in the list a rating according to the scale below. (Note: Be prepared to share your five most highly rated items with the class.)

1: Of little or no value to a classroom's climate
2: Of some value to a classroom's climate
3: Of significant value to a classroom's climate

List of Possible Classroom Components

(___) Stereo system for quiet music during student seat work
(___) One or more mirrors for student (or teacher) use
(___) Box of tissues for use by all
(___) Bulletin board with displays changing weekly
(___) Hanging plants or aquaria for various living creatures
(___) Area with a few comfortable chairs for student use on some established basis
(___) Several computers with internet connections
(___) Staplers, hole-punches, paper clips, and other related items for use by all
(___) Display board for thoughts, news, or question-of-the-day items
(___) Small podium for student use when making presentations in front of the class
(___) Reading or educational games area for students who complete in-class assignments before others
(___) Suggestion box for students to leave comments or suggestions regarding one of your lessons
(___) For multi-cultural classrooms, items that reflect the cultural backgrounds of your students

What other items could be added to this list?

3. In a small group, discuss the following topic, record your results, and be prepared to share them with the class.

At the secondary level, it is not uncommon for impressionable young students to develop a "crush" on a young teacher who is single. There are two immediate problems with this situation. First, members of the class usually know before the teacher what is taking place and are watching the situation with interest. Second, the teacher must deal with the student's affection while maintaining the respect of the interested onlookers. How should a teacher, and in particular a teacher in training, handle such a delicate situation? Who else should be involved? What support should be available to a teacher in this situation?

Teacher's Database

1. Join or start an interactive online discussion on one or more of the following topics discussed in this chapter. You might join a newsgroup already in progress or request discussion partners via e-mail or from one of the message board opportunities offered at many of the sites you have already explored. You might also establish a communication link among your classmates or with students in other schools who are taking a similar course.

teen pregnancies	effective schools
at-risk students	family stress
gender equity	English as a second language (ESL)
cultural diversity	multicultural education
substance abuse	latchkey children
crime and violence in schools	youth suicide
school improvement	school-based clinics
children in poverty	alternative schools

2. Formulate a research question concerning demographic aspects of students and their families, and go online to gather current national and provincial statistics on topics related to your question. Your question might relate to one or more of the above topics.

3. Develop a collaborative project with classmates to investigate and report on issues in at-risk intervention, or drug-abuse or violence prevention. Begin by exploring websites of the Children, Youth and Families Education and Research Network (CYFERNet), and Children, Youth, and Families at Risk (CYFAR). Both sites have extensive resources, and services for at-risk children, youth, and their families.

Observations and Interviews

1. Visit a school in your community recognized as successful or effective. What evidence do you find of the characteristics of successful schools (or successfully restructured schools) discussed in this chapter? Are there other characteristics you would add to the list, based on your observations?

2. Reflect on your experiences relating to social problems at the elementary, middle, or high school levels. Then gather statistics and information about how a local school or school district is responding to the social problems discussed in this chapter.

3. Obtain at least one statement of philosophy, or mission statement, from a school with which you are familiar. Analyze the statement(s), identifying and highlighting portions that refer to the major aims of education discussed in this chapter (educational goals, prosocial values, socialization, achievement, cultural and ethnic groups, personal growth, social change, and equal educational opportunity).

4. If possible, visit a school that has an enrolment of students whose cultural or socio-economic backgrounds differ from your own. What feelings and questions emerge as a result of your observations? How might your feelings affect your teaching effectiveness? How might you go about finding answers any questions that arose?

5. Interview a teacher at the school identified in the previous exercise. What special satisfactions does he or she experience from teaching at the school? What significant problems relating to diversity does he or she encounter, and how are they dealt with?

Professional Portfolio

1. Analyze a school as a social institution. How is the school organized in terms of roles and status? How does the school's organization and functioning reflect the wider society or the community in which it is located? What characteristics of the school and its people relate to the urban, rural, or suburban nature of the school environment?

2. Develop a case study of a school's culture. Visit a local school, or base your study on a school you have attended. Organize your case in terms of the following categories of information:

   - *Environment*—How would you describe the school facility or physical plant and its material and human resources? How is space organized? What is the climate of the school?
   - *Formal Practices*—What grades are included at the school? How is the school year organized? How is time structured? How are students and teachers grouped for instruction?
   - *Traditions*—What events, activities, and products seem important to students, teachers, and administrators? What symbols, slogans, and ceremonies identify membership in the school? How do community members view and relate to the school?

   Draw conclusions from your case study: What aspects of the school culture seem to support learning and academic achievement? On the basis of your study, draft a position statement on the kind of culture you would like to create or promote in your classroom.

3. Prepare an annotated directory of local resources for teaching students about diversity, for implementing multicultural curricula, and for promoting harmony or equity among diverse groups. For each entry, include an annotation—a brief description of the resource materials and their availability.

   Resources for your personalized directory should be available locally through your university library, the public library, community agencies, and so on. Among the types of resources you might include are the following:

   - Films, video and audio recordings, books, and journal articles
   - Simulation games designed to improve participants' attitudes toward diversity
   - Motivational guest speakers from the community
   - Ethnic museums and cultural centres
   - Community groups and agencies dedicated to promoting understanding among diverse groups
   - Training and workshops in the area of diversity

To view videos dealing with multicultural education, go to the Video Lab at www.MyEducationLab.com.

Watch a video explaining the different types of "Professional Knowledge" in the Video Lab at www.MyEducationLab.com.

To read a list of books for meeting the needs of students considered at risk, go to Teacher's Resource 5.1 on www.MyEducationLab.com.

To see examples of problems that teachers have faced regarding gender-related issues, go to Teacher's Resource 5.2 on MyEducationLab.

6

I was . . . . fortunate that I chose
theoretical physics, because it is all in
the mind. So my disability has not
been a serious handicap.
—Stephen W. Hawking
In A Brief History of Time:
From the Big Bang to Black Holes

Addressing Learners'
Individual Needs

focus questions

1. How do the needs of students change as they develop?
2. How do students vary in intelligence?
3. How do students vary in ability and disability?
4. What are special education, mainstreaming, and inclusion?
5. How can you teach all learners in your inclusive classroom?

It's late Friday afternoon at the end of the fourth week of school, and you've just finished arranging your classroom for the cooperative learning groups you're starting on Monday. Leaning back in the chair, you survey the room and imagine how things will go next week. Your outlook is positive, with one possible exception—11-year-old Rick. Since the first day of school, he's been very disruptive. His teacher last year described him as "loud, aggressive, and obnoxious."

Since the start of the school year, Rick has been belligerent and noncompliant. For the most part, he does what he wants. As far as you know, he has no close friends; he teases the other kids constantly and occasionally gets into fights.

Rick's parents divorced when he was in Grade 2. His father was given custody of Rick and his younger sister. Two years later, Rick's father married a woman with three children of her own. You've heard that Rick's two new half-brothers, 13 and 15, are "out of control," and the family has been receiving counselling at a local mental health clinic.

Rick's school records indicate that other teachers have had trouble with him in the past. Academically, he's below his classmates in all subjects except physical education and art. Comments from two of his previous teachers suggest Rick is a talented artist. Last year, he was diagnosed with mild learning and behaviour disorders.

Mr. Macdonald, the school guidance counsellor, and Ms. Tamashiro, the school's special educator, have been working with you on developing an individualized educational program (IEP) for Rick. In fact, before school on Monday, you're meeting with Ms. Tamashiro to discuss how to involve Rick in the cooperative learning groups. You're anxious to get her suggestions, and you're confidant that, with her help and Mr. Macdonald's, you can meet Rick's learning needs. (Please see Teacher's Resource 6.3 for a sample IEP form.)

Teachers must understand and appreciate students' unique learning and developmental needs. They must be willing to learn about students' abilities and disabilities and to explore the special issues and concerns of students at three broad developmental levels—childhood, early adolescence, and late adolescence. It is important to learn about the intellectual and psychological growth of students at the age level you plan to teach. In addition, understanding how students' interests, questions, and problems will change throughout their school years will better equip you to serve them in the present. In this chapter, we examine how students' needs change as they develop and how their needs reflect various intelligences, abilities, and disabilities.

How Do the Needs of Students Change as They Develop?

Development refers to the predictable changes that all human beings undergo as they progress through the life span from conception to death. It is important to acknowledge that students develop at different rates. Within a given classroom, for example, some students will be larger and physically more mature than others; some will be socially more sophisticated; and some will be able to think at a higher level of abstraction.

As humans progress through different **stages of development**, they mature and learn to perform the tasks that are a necessary part of daily living. There are several different types of human development. For example, as children develop physically, their bodies undergo numerous changes. As they develop cognitively, their mental capabilities expand to allow the use of language and other symbol systems to solve problems. As they develop socially, they learn to interact effectively with other people—as individuals and in groups. And as they develop morally, their actions come to reflect a greater appreciation of principles such as equity, justice, fairness, and altruism.

Because no two students progress through the stages of cognitive, social, and moral development in quite the same way, teachers need perspectives on the three types of development that are flexible, dynamic, and, above all, useful. By becoming familiar with models of cognitive, social, and moral development, teachers at all levels can better serve their students. Three such models are Piaget's theory of **cognitive development**, Erikson's stages of **psychosocial development**, and Kohlberg's stages of **moral reasoning**.

Piaget's Model of Cognitive Development

Jean Piaget (1896–1980), noted Swiss biologist and epistemologist, made extensive observational studies of children. He concluded that children reason differently from adults and have different perceptions of the world. Piaget surmised that children learn through actively interacting with their environments, much as scientists do, and proposed that a child's thinking progresses through a sequence of four cognitive stages. According to Piaget's theory of cognitive development, the rate of progress through the four stages varies from individual to individual.

During the school years, students move through the **preoperational stage**, the **concrete operations stage**, and the **formal operations stage**; yet because of individual interaction with the total environment, each student's perceptions and learning will be unique. According to Piaget:

> The principal goal of education is to create [learners] who are capable of doing new things, not simply repeating what other generations have done—[learners] who are creative, inventive, and discoverers. [We] need pupils who are active, who learn early to find out by themselves, partly by their own spontaneous activity and partly through material we set up for them; who learn early to tell what is verifiable and what is simply the first idea to come to them. (Quoted in Ripple and Rockcastle 1964, 5)

Erikson's Model of Psychosocial Development

Erik Erikson's model of psychosocial development delineates eight stages, from infancy to old age (see Table 6.1). For each stage, a **psychosocial crisis** is central in the individual's emotional and social growth. Erikson expresses these crises in polar terms; for instance, in the first stage (infancy), the psychosocial crisis is trust versus mistrust. Erikson explains that the major psychosocial task for the infant is to develop a sense of trust in the world but not to give up totally a sense of distrust. In the tension between the poles of trust and mistrust, a greater pull toward the more positive pole is considered healthy and is accompanied by a virtue. In this case, if trust prevails, the virtue is hope. Shortly before his death in 1994 at the age of 91, Erikson postulated a ninth stage in the human life cycle, *gerotranscendence,* during which some people mentally transcend the reality of their deteriorating bodies and faculties. In the final chapter of an extended version of Erikson's *The Life Cycle Completed,* first published in 1982, his wife and lifelong colleague, Joan M. Erikson (1901–1997), described the challenge of the ninth stage:

> Despair, which haunts the eighth stage, is a close companion in the ninth, because it is almost impossible to know what emergencies and losses of physical ability are imminent. As independence and control are challenged, self-esteem and confidence weaken. Hope and trust, which once provided firm support, are no longer the sturdy props of former days. To face down despair with faith and appropriate humility is perhaps the wisest course. (Erikson 1997, 105–6)

When we examine the issues and concerns of students in childhood and early and late adolescence later in this chapter, we will return to Erikson's model of psychosocial development. For further information on this significant and useful theory, we recommend that you read Erikson's first book, *Childhood and Society* (1963).

Kohlberg's Model of Moral Development

According to Lawrence Kohlberg (1927–1987), the reasoning process people use to decide what is right and wrong evolves through three levels of development. Within each level, Kohlberg has identified two stages. Table 6.2 shows that, at Level I (the preconventional level), the individual decides what is right on the basis of personal needs and rules developed by others. At Level II (the conventional level), moral

Table 6.1

Erikson's Eight Stages of Psychosocial Development

Stage	Approximate Age	Psychosocial "Crisis"	Description	"Basic Strength" (Positive Result if Crisis Is Adequately Resolved)
1. Infancy	Birth to 18 months	Trust versus basic mistrust	Infant needs to be nurtured and loved; if not, he or she becomes insecure and mistrustful.	Drive and hope
2. Early childhood	18 months to 3 years	Autonomy versus shame	Child focuses on developing physical skills—toilet training, walking, talking, feeding self; inadequate resolution of crisis leads to feelings of shame and doubt.	Self-control, courage, and will
3. Play age	3 to 6 years	Initiative versus guilt	Child learns to develop skills through play and cooperation; inadequate resolution of crisis leads to sense of guilt and fearfulness.	Purpose and direction
4. School age	6 to 12 years	Industry versus inferiority	Child acquires new skills, knowledge; develops sense of achievement; inadequate resolution of crisis leaves child feeling inadequate and inferior.	Competence and method
5. Adolescence	12 to 20 years	Identity versus role confusion, identity diffusion	Adolescent focuses on clarifying identity, developing social relationships with peers and others, and grappling with moral issues; inadequate resolution of crisis leads to self-doubt and self-consciousness.	Fidelity and devotion
6. Young adulthood	20 to 35 years	Intimacy versus isolation	Young adult seeks companionship and love through relationships with friends and becoming intimate with a "significant other"; inadequate resolution of crisis leads to feelings of isolation and distance from others.	Love and affiliation
7. Middle adulthood	35 to 65	Generativity versus self-absorption or stagnation	Adult focuses on family relationships, parenting, and creative and meaningful work; inadequate resolution of crisis leads to feelings of stagnation and alienation.	Care and production
8. Late adulthood	65 to death	Integrity versus despair	Adult focuses on meaning and purpose in one's life, lifetime accomplishments and contributions, acceptance of oneself and fulfillment; inadequate resolution of crisis leads to feelings of failure, disdain for world, and fear of death.	Wisdom and acceptance

Table 6.2

Kohlberg's Theory of Moral Reasoning

I. Preconventional Level of Moral Reasoning

Child is responsive to cultural rules and labels of good or bad and right or wrong, but interprets these in terms of consequences of action (punishment, reward, exchanges of favours).

Stage 1: Punishment-and-obedience orientation
Physical consequences of action determine its goodness or badness.
Avoidance of punishment and deference to power are valued.

Stage 2: The instrumental-relativist orientation
Right action consists of that which satisfies one's own needs and occasionally the needs of others.
Reciprocity is a matter of "You scratch my back and I'll scratch yours."

II. Conventional Level of Moral Reasoning

Maintaining the expectations of the individual's family, group, or nation is perceived as valuable, regardless of consequences.

Stage 3: The interpersonal concordance or "good boy–nice girl" orientation
Good behaviour is that which pleases or helps others and is ap-proved by them.

Stage 4: The "law and order" orientation
Orientation toward fixed rules and the maintenance of social order. Right behaviour consists of doing one's duty and showing respect for authority.

III. Postconventional, Autonomous, or Principled Level of Moral Reasoning

Effort to define moral principles that have validity and application apart from the authority of groups.

Stage 5: The social-contract, legalistic orientation
Right action defined in terms of rights and standards that have been agreed upon by the whole society.

Stage 6: The universal-ethical-principle orientation
Right is defined by conscience in accord with self-chosen ethical principles appealing to logic and universality.

Source: Adapted from Lawrence Kohlberg, "The Cognitive-Developmental Approach to Moral Education." In *Curriculum Planning: A Contemporary Approach*, 7th ed., Forrest W. Parkay and Glen Hass (eds.). Boston: Allyn and Bacon, 2000, p.137. The original version appeared in *Journal of Philosophy, 70*(18), 1973, pp. 631–32.

---

decisions reflect a desire for the approval of others and a willingness to conform to the expectations of family, community, and country. At Level III (the postconventional level), the individual has developed values and principles that are based on rational, personal choices that can be separated from conventional beliefs.

Kohlberg suggests that "over 50 percent of late adolescents and adults are capable of full formal reasoning [i.e., they can use their intelligence to reason abstractly, form hypotheses, and test these hypotheses against reality], but only 10 percent of these adults display principled (Stages 5 and 6) moral reasoning" (2000, 138–39). In addition, Kohlberg purports that maturity of moral judgment is not highly related to IQ or verbal intelligence.

Some individuals have criticized Kohlberg's model as being too systematic and sequential, limited because it focuses on moral reasoning rather than on actual behaviour, or biased because it tends to look at moral development from a male perspective (Bracey 1993). Carol Gilligan suggests that male moral reasoning tends to address the rights of the individual, whereas female moral reasoning addresses the individual's responsibility to others. In her book *In a Different Voice: Psychological Theory and Women's Development* (1993), Gilligan refers to women's principal moral voice as the "ethics of care," which emphasizes care of others over the male-oriented "ethics of justice." Thus, when confronted with a moral dilemma, females tend to suggest solutions based more on altruism and self-sacrifice than on rights and rules (Gilligan 1993).

The question remains: Can moral reasoning be taught? Can teachers help students develop so that they live according to principles of equity, justice, care, and empathy? Kohlberg (2000, 144) suggests that the following three conditions can help children internalize moral principles:

1. Exposure to the next higher stage of reasoning
2. Exposure to situations posing problems and contradictions for the child's current moral structure, leading to dissatisfaction with his [her] current level
3. An atmosphere of interchange and dialogue combining the first two conditions, in which conflicting moral views are compared in an open manner

One approach to teaching values and moral reasoning is known as **character education,** a movement that stresses the development of students' "good character." *Character Education,* a 2001 report by the Calgary Board of Education illustrates the need for character education to make a "comeback" in our society (Jeary 2001). This report, which draws heavily on the work of Piaget, Kohlberg, Kohn, and other primarily American theorists, strongly suggests that a movement grounded chiefly in the United States has now taken root in Canada. Books and resources for Canadian teachers who wish to introduce character education into their classrooms are becoming more readily available, and most provincial departments of education are giving varying degrees of attention to the topic. Even service organizations are becoming involved. The Lions Club of Canada now offers its Lions-Quest life skills program to students and teachers. "Lions-Quest programs teach youth to accept responsibility, communicate effectively, set goals, make healthy decisions, and resist pressure to use alcohol and drugs. Lions clubs, districts and multiple districts support Lions-Quest through funding, coordination of teacher training, and in other ways." Figure 6.1 illustrates 12 strategies teachers can use to create moral classroom communities.

Maslow's Model of Hierarchy of Needs

Students' developmental levels also vary according to how well their biological and psychological needs have been satisfied. Psychologist Abraham Maslow (1908–1970) formulated a model of a **hierarchy of needs** (see Figure 6.2) that suggests that people are motivated by basic needs for survival and safety first. When these basic needs have been met sufficiently, people naturally seek to satisfy higher needs, the highest of which is self-actualization—the desire to use one's talents, abilities, and potential to the fullest. Students whose needs for safety have been fairly well satisfied will discover strong needs for friendship, affection, and love, for example. If efforts to satisfy the various needs are thwarted, the result can be maladjustment and interruption or delay in the individual's full and healthy development.

The hierarchy of needs model has particular relevance for teachers, because students differ markedly in terms of where they are on the hierarchy. Many families lack the resources to adequately provide for children's basic needs. Children from families that are concerned with day-to-day survival may not receive the support that could help them succeed in school. They come to school tired and hungry and may have trouble paying attention in class. Others may be well fed and clothed but feel unsafe, alien, or unloved; they may seek to protect themselves by withdrawing emotionally from activities around them.

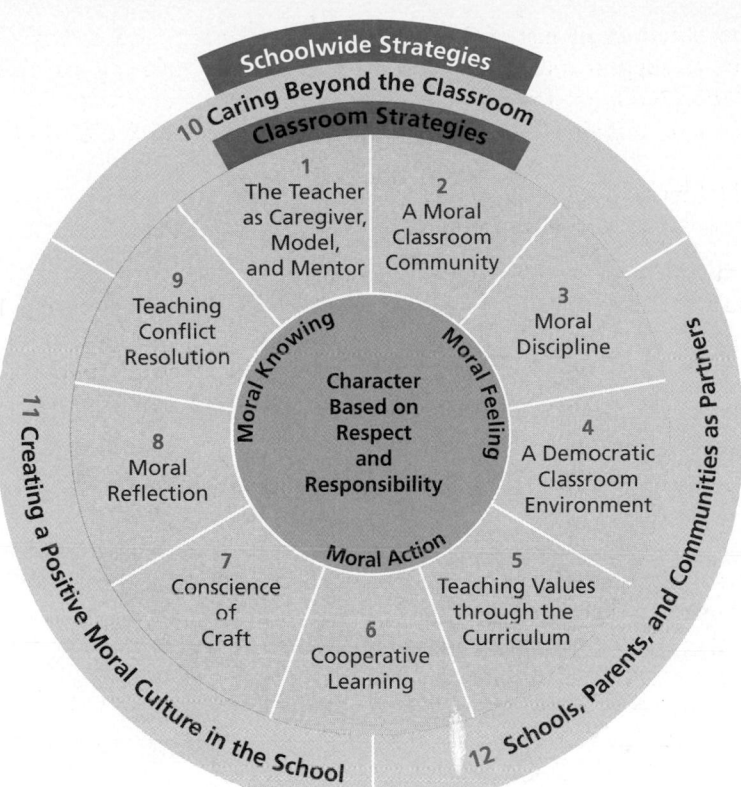

Figure 6.1

A comprehensive approach to values and character education

1. *Act as caregiver, model, and mentor,* treating students with love and respect, setting a good example, supporting positive social behaviour, and correcting hurtful actions through one-on-one guidance and whole-class discussion.

2. *Create a moral community,* helping students know one another as persons, respect and care about one another, and feel valued membership in, and responsibility to, the group.

3. *Practice moral discipline,* using the creation and enforcement of rules as opportunities to foster moral reasoning, voluntary compliance with rules, and a respect for others.

4. *Create a democratic classroom environment,* involving students in decision making and the responsibility for making the classroom a good place to be and learn.

5. *Teach values through the curriculum,* using the ethically rich content of academic subjects (such as literature, history, and science) as vehicles for teaching values and examining moral questions.

6. *Use cooperative learning* to develop students' appreciation of others, perspective taking, and the ability to work with others toward common goals.

7. *Develop the "conscience of craft"* by fostering students' appreciation of learning, capacity for hard work, commitment to excellence, and sense of work as affecting the lives of others.

8. *Encourage moral reflection* through reading, research, essay writing, journal keeping, discussion, and debate.

9. *Teach conflict resolution,* so that students acquire the essential moral skills of solving conflicts fairly and without force.

10. *Foster caring beyond the classroom,* using positive role models to inspire altruistic behaviour and providing opportunities at every grade level to perform school and community service.

11. *Create a positive moral culture in the school,* developing a schoolwide ethos that supports and amplifies the values taught in classrooms.

12. *Recruit parents and the community as partners in character education,* letting parents know that the school considers them their child's first and most important moral teacher.

Figure 6.2

Maslow's hierarchy of needs

Note: The four lower-level needs are called Deficiency Needs because the motivation to satisfy them decreases when they are met. On the other hand, when Being (Growth) Needs are met, motivation to fulfill them increases.

Source: Compiled from Abraham H. Maslow, *Toward a Psychology of Being,* 3rd ed. New York, New York: John Wiley & Sons, 1999; and *Motivation and Personality,* 3rd ed. Addison-Wesley Publishing Company, 1987.

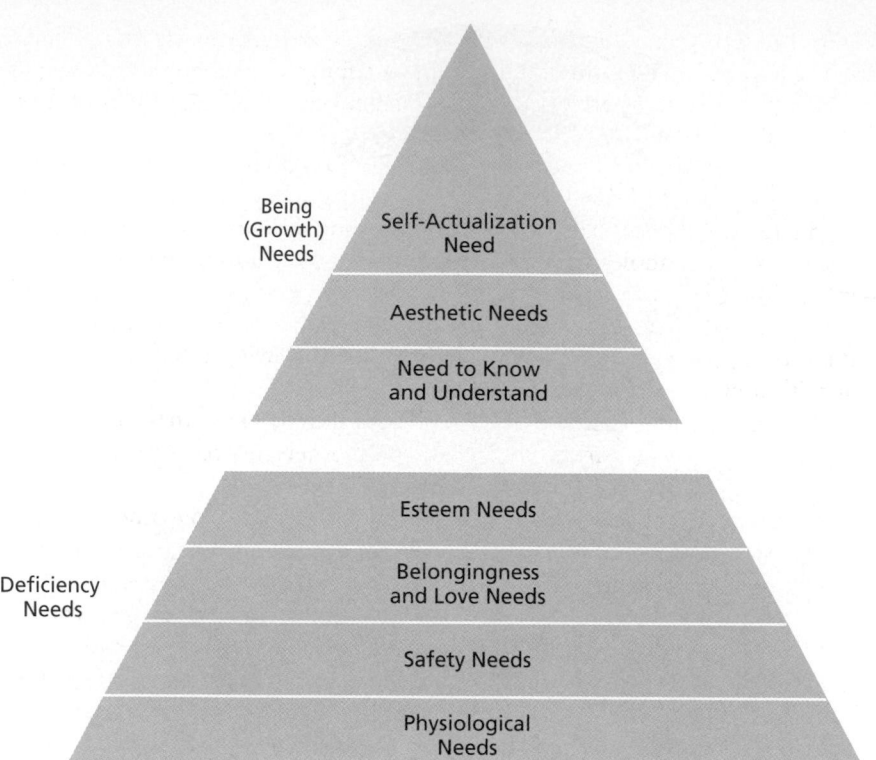

Developmental Stresses and Tasks of Childhood

During Erikson's school-age stage, children strive for a sense of industry and struggle against feelings of inferiority. If successful, they gain the virtue of competence, believing in their abilities to do things. If children find evidence that they are inferior to others, if they experience failure when they try new tasks, and if they struggle without ever gaining a sense of mastery, then they feel incompetent.

Children gain the sense of industry needed at this age by playing seriously, mastering new skills, producing results, and being workers. When they first go to school, they are oriented toward accomplishing new things (some kindergartners expect to learn to read on their first day of school and are disappointed when they don't). For young children, the idea of work is attractive; it means that they are doing something grown-up.

Is childhood a time of carefree play or a period of stress? Certainly, the answer depends on the life circumstances and personality of the individual child. In a study of stressful events in the lives of more than 1700 children in Grades 2 to 9 in six countries, Karou Yamamoto and his associates found that the most stressful events "threaten[ed] one's sense of security and occasion[ed] personal denigration and embarrassment" (Yamamoto et al. 1996, 139). Other studies have shown that serious stress is experienced by latchkey children, who are left on their own or in each other's care for part or all of the day.

Developmental Stresses and Tasks of Adolescence

Many psychologists believe that adolescence contains two distinct stages: an early period from the ages of 10 to 12 through the ages of 14 to 16, and a late period from approximately 15 to 16 years old through 19. Although continuity exists in each individual's life, the psychosocial issues of adolescence—coping with change and seeking identity—vary in form and importance as individuals progress through the transition from childhood to adulthood.

In Erikson's eight-state model, identity versus role diffusion is the psychosocial crisis for the adolescent years. Although the quest for identity is a key psychosocial issue for both early and late adolescence, many believe that Erikson's identity-versus-role diffusion stage fits best for early adolescence. During this time, young adolescents, using their new thinking abilities, begin integrating a clearer sense of personal identity. Erikson's role diffusion refers to the variety of roles that adolescents have available to them.

According to Erikson's theory, when adolescents identify with a peer group, with a school, or with a cause, their sense of fidelity—the "virtue" of this stage—is clear and strong. At this stage, adolescents are loyal and committed, sometimes to people or ideas that may dismay or alarm their parents, and sometimes to high ideals and dreams.

In late adolescence, the quest for identity shifts from relying on others to self-reliance. Young people continue to work on strengthening their sense of identity in this period, but as they do so, they draw less on the reactions of their peers and more on their own regard for what matters. Although late adolescents possess an array of interests, talents, and goals in life, they share a desire to achieve independence. More like adults than children, late adolescents are anxious to use newly acquired strengths, skills, and knowledge to achieve their own purposes, whether through marriage, parenthood, full-time employment, education beyond high school, a career, or military service.

The vulnerability of today's adolescents is evident in the results of a survey of 1 million students based on 40 "developmental assets" (positive relationships, opportunities, skills, and values) adolescents need in order to become healthy, mature adults: "[O]n average, youth have less than half of the 40 assets they need to grow up healthy, caring, and responsible . . . . [T]his statistic remains relatively consistent among urban, rural, and suburban communities" (Search Institute, 2002). Moreover, "a solid

What needs must be met for these students for healthy development? What stresses do they face? What developmental tasks must they accomplish? What needs, stresses, and developmental tasks will affect them as adolescents? Why is information about development important to teachers?

majority of American adults—two thirds—spontaneously describe adolescents in starkly negative terms: *wild, rude, irresponsible*. Half give those descriptions even to younger children" (Scales 2001, 64). The list of alarming concerns in adolescence includes academic failure and retention, accidents, assaultive behaviour, criminal activity, cultism, depression, discipline problems, dropping out, drug abuse, eating disorders, homicide, incest, prostitution, running away, school absenteeism, suicide, teenage pregnancy, vandalism, and the contraction of sexually transmitted diseases. While there is little data to support a contention that an exactly similar situation exists in Canada, Canadian students do face an alarming number of risks.

What can teachers do to help children and adolescents develop to their full potential? To help prevent the problems that place them at risk, an energetic, creative, and multifaceted approach is necessary. Figure 6.3 presents several strategies for assisting students in developing competence, positive self-concepts, and high esteem, and for intervening to prevent or address problems that place them at risk.

How Do Students Vary in Intelligence?

In addition to developmental differences, students differ in terms of their intellectual capacity. Unfortunately, test scores, and sometimes intelligence quotient (IQ) scores, are treated as accurate measurements of students' intellectual ability because of their convenience and long-time use. What is **intelligence** and how has it been redefined to account for the many ways it can be expressed? Though many definitions have been

Figure 6.3

What teachers can do to help children and adolescents develop

1. **Provide opportunities and encouragement for students to develop competence.**

   - Provide a learning environment in which students can risk making mistakes.
   - Assign work that students can perform successfully and still be challenged.
   - Have realistic but high expectations for students.
   - Express belief in students a bility to succeed.
   - Encourage industry by letting students work on goals or projects of their choosing.
   - Provide opportunities for students to take special responsibility.
   - Assign older students to work with younger ones.
   - Reward industry and competence.

2. **Promote the development of positive self-concept and high self-esteem.**

   - Give praise more than criticism.
   - Take students and their work seriously.
   - Respect students' dignity.
   - Plan individual and group activities that boost morale.
   - Provide opportunities for students to interact and work cooperatively.
   - Teach and model acceptance of human diversity and individuality.
   - Develop systems for the recognition and reward of individual and group achievement.
   - Support students' efforts to achieve and appropriately express independence.

3. **Intervene to prevent or address problems that place students at risk.**

   - Provide a safe and structured learning environment where students feel secure.
   - Practice effective leadership and classroom management.
   - Provide opportunities to discuss preferences, values, morals, goals, and consequences.
   - Teach and model critical thinking, decision making, and problem solving.
   - Teach and model prosocial attitudes and behaviours and conflict resolution strategies.
   - Provide information on subjects of special concern to students and parents.
   - Cultivate family involvement.
   - Collaborate, consult, network, and refer on behalf of students.

proposed, the term has yet to be completely explained. One view is that intelligence is the ability to learn. As David Wechsler, the developer of the most widely used intelligence scales for children and adults, said: "Intelligence, operationally defined, is the aggregate or global capacity to act purposefully, to think rationally, and to deal effectively with the environment" (Wechsler 1958, 7). Other proposed definitions of intelligence include the following:

- Goal-directed adaptive behaviour
- Ability to solve novel problems
- Ability to acquire and think with new conceptual systems
- Problem-solving ability
- Planning and other metacognitive skills
- Memory access speed
- What people think intelligence is
- What IQ tests measure
- The ability to learn from bad teaching (Woolfolk 1998, 109)

Intelligence Testing

The intelligence tests now in use can be traced to the 1905 Metrical Scale of Intelligence designed by French psychologists Alfred Binet and Theodore Simon, who were part of a Paris-based commission that wanted a way to identify children who would need special help with their learning. Binet revised the scale in 1908, which was adapted for American children in 1916 by Lewis Terman, a psychologist at Stanford University. Terman's test was, in turn, further adapted, especially by the U.S. Army, which transformed it into a paper-and-pencil test that could be administered to large groups. The use of such intelligence tests has continued throughout the years. Approximately 67 percent of the population have an IQ between 85 and 115—the range of normal intelligence. "Gifted" individuals have an IQ of 130 or more, while those at the genius level have an IQ of 140 or better.

Individual intelligence tests are presently valued by psychologists and those in the field of special education because they can be helpful in diagnosing a student's strengths and weaknesses. However, group intelligence tests given for the purpose of classifying students into like-score groups have received an increasing amount of criticism and have been greatly reduced in scope. Most Canadian school districts have policies similar to this example from the Ottawa-Carlton District School Board (2000).

Commercial standardized tests in the schools of the Ottawa-Carleton district should be used sparingly, as one method of providing information concerning student strengths and weaknesses and as one of the bases for program adjustment or improvement. Commercial standardized tests should be considered in conjunction with additional data derived from the following methods:

1. Classroom observation, teacher-made tests and assignments, and student portfolios
2. Conferences with parents
3. Locally developed (district) testing
4. Results and recommendations by Special Education/Student Services staff based on individual assessment(s)

The most significant and dramatic criticism of group IQ tests has been that test items and tasks are culturally biased, drawn mostly from white middle-class experience. Thus the tests are more assessments of how informed students are about features in a specific class or culture than of intelligence in general. A number of psychometricians continue to design culture-free intelligence tests.

Multiple Intelligences

Many theorists believe that intelligence is a basic ability that enables one to perform mental operations in the following areas: logical reasoning, spatial reasoning, number ability, and verbal meaning. However, "the weight of the evidence at the present time is that intelligence is multidimensional, and that the full range of these dimensions is not completely captured by any single general ability" (Sternberg 1996, 11; 2002, 447–448). Howard Gardner, for example, believes that humans possess at least eight separate forms of intelligence: "[e]ach intelligence reflects the potential to solve problems or to fashion products that are valued in one or more cultural settings. [Each] features its own distinctive form of mental representation" (Gardner 1999, 71–72). Drawing on the theories of others and research findings on savants, prodigies, and other exceptional individuals, Gardner originally suggested in *Frames of Mind* (1983) that humans have seven intelligences: logical-mathematical, linguistic, musical, spatial, bodily-kinesthetic, interpersonal, and intrapersonal. In the mid-1990s, he identified an eighth intelligence, that of the naturalist, and in his most recent book, *The Disciplined Mind*, he suggests that "it is possible that human beings also exhibit a ninth, existential intelligence—the proclivity to pose (and ponder) questions about life, death, and ultimate realities" (Gardner 1999, 72). According to Gardner, every person possesses the eight intelligences (see Figure 6.4), yet each person has his or her particular blend of them.

Gardner's theory of **multiple intelligences** is valuable for teachers. As Robert Slavin suggests, "Teachers must avoid thinking about children as smart or not smart because there are many ways to be smart (Slavin 2000, 130). Some students are talented in terms of their interpersonal relations and exhibit natural leadership abilities. Others seem to have a high degree of what Peter Salovey and David Sluyter (1997) term *emotional intelligence*—awareness of and ability to manage their feelings. Differences in musical, athletic, and mechanical abilities can be recognized by even the minimally informed observer. Because these intelligences are not tested or highlighted, they may go unnoticed and possibly wasted.

However, keep in mind Gardner's "reflections" 12 years after the publication of *Frames of Mind* (Gardner 1995, 206):

> MI [multiple intelligence] theory is in no way an educational prescription. [E]ducators are in the best position to determine the uses to which MI theory should be put . . . .

For more information regarding multiple intelligence theory, and to take a test to determine your own set of intelligences, please visit www.edu-cyberpg.com/IEC/iecMI.html.

Learning Styles

Students vary greatly in regard to **learning styles**, the approaches to learning that work best for them. These differences, also known as *learning style preferences* or *cognitive styles* (Woolfolk 1998), lead students to interact with their environments in differing ways. Some, for example, might prefer a highly structured approach to learning, while others might have a preference for a learning environment that is less structured and

Figure 6.4

The eight intelligences

Source: Project SUMIT (Schools Using Multiple Intelligence Theory), "Theory of Multiple Intelligences."

The Eight Intelligences

Linguistic intelligence allows individuals to communicate and make sense of the world through language. Poets exemplify this intelligence in its mature form. Students who enjoy playing with rhymes, who pun, who always have a story to tell, who quickly acquire other languages—including sign language— all exhibit linguistic intelligence.

Musical intelligence allows people to create, communicate, and understand meanings made out of sound. While composers and instrumentalists clearly exhibit this intelligence, so do the students who seem particularly attracted by the birds singing outside the classroom window or who constantly tap out intricate rhythms on the desk with their pencils.

Logical-mathematical intelligence enables individuals to use and appreciate abstract relations. Scientists, mathematicians, and philosophers all rely on this intelligence. So do the students who "live" baseball statistics or who carefully analyze the components of problems—either personal or school-related—before systematically testing solutions.

Spatial intelligence makes it possible for people to perceive visual or spatial information, to transform this information, and to recreate visual images from memory. Well-developed spatial capacities are needed for the work of architects, sculptors, and engineers. The students who turn first to the graphs, charts, and pictures in their textbooks, who like to "web" their ideas before writing a paper, and who fill the blank space around their notes with intricate patterns are using their spatial intelligence.

Bodily-kinesthetic intelligence allows individuals to use all or part of the body to create products or solve problems. Athletes, surgeons, dancers, choreographers, and craftspeople all use bodily-kinesthetic intelligence. The capacity is also evident in students who relish gym class and school dances, who prefer to carry out class projects by making models rather than writing reports, and who toss crumpled paper with frequency and accuracy into wastebaskets across the room.

Interpersonal intelligence enables individuals to recognize and make distinctions about others' feelings and intentions. Teachers, parents, politicians, psychologists, and salespeople rely on interpersonal intelligence. Students exhibit this intelligence when they thrive on small-group work, when they notice and react to the moods of their friends and classmates, and when they tactfully convince the teacher of their need for extra time to complete the homework assignment.

Intrapersonal intelligence helps individuals to distinguish among their own feelings, to build accurate mental models of themselves, and to draw on these models to make decisions about their lives. Although it is difficult to assess who has this capacity and to what degree, evidence can be sought in students' uses of their other intelligences—how well they seem to be capitalizing on their strengths, how cognizant they are of their weaknesses, and how thoughful they are about the decisions and choices they make.

Naturalist intelligence allows people to distinguish among, classify, and use features of the environment. Farmers, gardeners, botanists, geologists, florists, and archaeologists all exhibit this intelligence, as do students who can name and describe the features of every make of car around them.

less predictable. The variety of student learning styles strongly suggests that teachers develop a broad range of instructional methodologies as a fundamental part of their educational practice. It is equally important for teachers to recognize their own preferred learning styles and, that if they are not careful, they will have a strong tendency to teach in a manner that reflects how they themselves would prefer to be taught. To learn more about your learning style, take the online assessment located at *Carter's Multiple Pathways to Learning* located in Chapter 6 of MyEducationLab.

Students' learning styles are determined by a combination of hereditary and environmental influences. Some quickly learn things they hear; others learn faster when they see material in writing. Some need a lot of structure; others learn best when they can be independent and follow their desires. Some learn best in formal settings; others excel in informal, relaxed environments. Some need almost total silence to concentrate; others learn well in noisy, active environments. Some are intuitive learners; some prefer to follow logical, sequential steps.

There is no one "correct" view of learning styles to guide teachers in their daily decision making. Culture-based differences in learning styles are subtle, variable, and difficult to describe, and learning styles change as the individual matures. Moreover, critics maintain that there is little evidence to support the validity of dozens of conceptual models for learning styles and accompanying assessment instruments. Nevertheless, you should be aware of the concept of learning styles and realize that any given classroom activity may be more effective for some students than for others. Knowledge of your own and your students' learning styles will help you individualize instruction and motivate your students.

Professional Reflection   **Identify Your Learning Style Preferences**

Describe your preferred learning environment. Where, when, and how do you learn best? Does certain lighting, food, or music seem to enhance your learning? Think about how you acquire new information—do you prefer being analytical and abstract or commonsensical and concrete? Do you prefer thinking about things or doing things? Do you like to learn alone, in a small group, or in a large group? When given an assignment, do you like a lot of structure and details, or do you prefer more unstructured or open-ended assignments?

How Do Students Vary in Ability and Disability?

Students also differ according to their special needs and talents. Some enter the world with exceptional abilities or disabilities; others encounter life experiences that change their capabilities significantly; and still others struggle with conditions that medical scientists have yet to understand. Where possible, all children and youth with exceptionalities are given a public education in provincial and territorial schools.

Exceptional Learners

Children "who require special education and related services if they are to realize their full human potential" (Hallahan & Kauffman 2000, 7) are referred to as **exceptional learners**. They are taught by special education teachers and by regular teachers into whose classrooms they have been integrated or *included*. Among the many exceptional children that teachers may encounter in the classroom are students who have physical, mental, or emotional disabilities and students who are gifted or talented.

Special-needs students are often referred to synonymously as *handicapped* or *disabled*. (However, it is important for teachers to understand the following distinction between a disability and a handicap:

> A disability . . . results from a loss of physical functioning (e.g., loss of sight, hearing, or mobility) or from difficulty in learning and social adjustment that significantly interferes with normal growth and development. A handicap is a limitation imposed on the individual by environmental demands and is related to the individual's ability to adapt or adjust to those demands. (Hardman, Drew, & Egan 1999, 3)

For example, Stephen W. Hawking, the gifted physicist who provides the epigraph for this chapter, has amyotrophic lateral sclerosis (also known as Lou Gehrig's disease), which requires him to use a wheelchair for mobility and a speech synthesizer to communicate. If Hawking had to enter a building accessible only by stairs, or if a computer virus infected his speech synthesizer program, his disability would become a handicap.

Teachers should know that current language use emphasizes the concept of "people first." In other words, a disabling condition should not be used as an adjective to describe a person. Thus, one should say "a child with a visual impairment"—not "blind child" or even "visually impaired child."

Teachers should also realize that the definitions for disabilities are generalized, open to change, and significantly influenced by the current cultural perception of normality. During the past half century, the definition of mental retardation has gone through several evolutions to reflect shifting views of people with cognitive disabilities.

Cautions about labelling should also apply to gifted and talented students. Unfortunately, people commonly have a negative view of gifted and talented youngsters. Like many ethnic groups, gifted students are "different" and thus have been the target of many myths and stereotypes. However, a landmark study of 1528 gifted males and females begun by Lewis Terman (Terman, Baldwin, & Bronson 1925; Terman & Oden 1947; 1959) in 1926, which continued until 2010, "exploded the myth that high-IQ individuals [are] brainy but physically and socially inept. In fact, Terman found that children with outstanding IQs were larger, stronger, and better coordinated than other children and became better adjusted and more emotionally stable adults" (Slavin 2000, 428).

Students with Disabilities

In December 2001, the Ontario Human Rights Commission (OHRC) stated that "there is a lack of reliable, current information on children with disabilities in Canada" (www.ohrc.on.ca/en/resources/discussion_consultation/Education?page=Education-IV_.html). Additionally, determining what to consider a disability is an exceptionally difficult problem. The following data must therefore be regarded as approximations of the **students with disabilities** situation in Canada.

1. The Canadian Council on Social Development (CCSD), using information gathered since 1994 by the National Longitudinal Survey of Children and Youth in Canada, estimates that 13 percent of children aged 11 or younger have a chronic or activity limitation—excluding allergies, emotional problems, and learning disabilities. If children with allergies are added in, the figure rises to 23 percent, and if those with emotional problems and learning disabilities are also included, the number rises to over 30 percent. To order the publication, see *Children and Youth with Special Needs* (November 2001) online at www.ccsd.ca (Hanvey 2001).

2. A more recent study by Statistics Canada, released on May 31, 2007, determined that the majority of children with disabilities attend schools without special education classes. Approximately 55 percent of those surveyed attended regular classes in a regular school setting, whereas 25 percent attended a combination of regular and special education classes, 7 percent had special education classes only within a mainstream school, 6 percent did not attend a regular school, 3 percent were not in school, and 1 percent were home-schooled.

3. Research from the National Population Health Survey found that 14.6 percent of children aged six to eleven had a disability related to limited physical activity, emotional problems, or learning disabilities (Statistics Canada 2001a).

4. The Roehr Institute, in *Count Us In: A Demographic Overview of Childhood and Disability in Canada* (2000), states that between 5 and 20 percent of Canadian families have children with disabilities. In 15 percent of cases, the disability is moderate to severe.

5. The OHRC reports that, in the fall of 2000, approximately 260 000 (12.5 percent of the entire student population) were having special education programs and services delivered to them. Results from other provinces and territories are comparable.

6. A reasonable estimate regarding the number of students with a special need that requires some form of intervention by educators would be 10 to 15 percent. Table 6.3 gives a brief definitional overview of the various types of disabilities students may experience.

Since the term **learning disability (LD)** was first introduced in the early 1960s, there has been no universally accepted definition. However, the following statement, adopted by the Learning Disabilities Association of Canada on January 30, 2002, provides an excellent overview of how broadly defined this specialized area has become.

Table 6.3

Types of Disability

1. Specific learning disabilities (LD)—Learning is significantly hindered by difficulty in listening, speaking, reading, writing, reasoning, or computing

2. Speech or language impairments—Significant difficulty in communicating with others as a result of speech or language disorders

3. Mental retardation—Significant limitations in cognitive ability

4. Serious emotional disturbance (SED)—Social and/or emotional maladjustment that significantly reduces the ability to learn

5. Hearing impairments—Permanent or fluctuating mild to profound hearing loss in one or both ears

6. Orthopedic impairments—Physically disabling conditions that affect locomotion or motor functions

7. Other health impairments—Limited strength, vitality, or alertness caused by chronic or acute health problems

8. Visual impairments—Vision loss that significantly inhibits learning

9. Multiple disabilities—Two or more interrelated disabilities

10. Deaf-blindness—Vision and hearing disability that severely limits communication

11. Autism and other—Significantly impaired communication, learning, and reciprocal social interactions

"Learning Disabilities" refer to a number of disorders which may affect the acquisition, organization, retention, understanding or use of verbal or nonverbal information. These disorders affect learning in individuals who otherwise demonstrate at least average abilities essential for thinking and/or reasoning. As such, learning disabilities are distinct from global intellectual deficiency.

Learning disabilities result from impairments in one or more processes related to perceiving, thinking, remembering or learning. These include, but are not limited to: language processing; phonological processing; visual spatial processing; processing speed; memory and attention; and executive functions (e.g., planning and decision-making).

Learning disabilities range in severity and may interfere with the acquisition and use of one or more of the following:

- Oral language (e.g., listening, speaking, understanding)
- Reading (e.g., decoding, phonetic knowledge, word recognition, comprehension)
- Written language (e.g., spelling and written expression); and
- Mathematics (e.g., computation, problem solving)

Learning disabilities may also involve difficulties with organizational skills, social perception, social interaction and perspective taking.

Learning disabilities are lifelong. The way in which they are expressed may vary over an individual's lifetime, depending on the interaction between the demands of the environment and the individual's strengths and needs. Learning disabilities are suggested by unexpected academic under-achievement or achievement which is maintained only by unusually high levels of effort and support.

Learning disabilities are due to genetic and/or neurobiological factors or injury that alters brain functioning in a manner which affects one or more processes related to learning. These disorders are not due primarily to hearing and/or vision problems, socio-economic factors, cultural or linguistic differences, lack of motivation or ineffective teaching, although these factors may further complicate the challenges faced by individuals with learning disabilities. Learning disabilities may co-exist with various conditions including attentional, behavioural and emotional disorders, sensory impairments or other medical conditions.

For success, individuals with learning disabilities require early identification and timely specialized assessments and interventions involving home, school, community and workplace settings. The interventions need to be appropriate for each individual's learning disability subtype and, at a minimum, include the provision of: specific skill instruction; accommodations; compensatory strategies; and self-advocacy skills.

Source: Official Definition of Learning Disabilities. (2002, January). Reprinted by permission of the Learning Disabilities Association of Canada. Retrieved August 16, 2007 from www.ldac-taac.ca/Defined/defined_new-e.asp.

Imagine you are concerned about two of your new students—Mary and Beomjoon. Mary has an adequate vocabulary and doesn't hesitate to express herself, but her achievement in reading and mathematics doesn't add up to what you believe she can do. Often, when you give the class instructions, Mary seems to get confused about what to do. In working with her one-on-one, you've noticed that she often reverses letters and numbers the way much younger children do—she sees a *b* for a *d* or a *6* for a *9*. Mary may have a learning disability, causing problems in taking in, organizing, remembering, and expressing information. Like Mary, students with learning disabilities often show a significant difference between their estimated intelligence and their actual achievement in the classroom.

Beomjoon presents you with a different set of challenges. He is obviously bright, but he frequently seems to be "out of sync" with classroom activities. He gets frustrated when he has to wait for his turn. He sometimes blurts out answers before you've even asked a question. He can't seem to stop wiggling his toes and tapping his pencil, and he often comes to school without his backpack and homework. Beomjoon may have **attention deficit hyperactivity disorder (ADHD)**, one of the most commonly diagnosed disabilities among children. Students with ADHD have difficulty remaining still so they can concentrate. Students with an **attention deficit disorder (ADD)** have difficulty focusing their attention long enough to learn well.

Treatment for students with ADD or ADHD includes behaviour modification and medication. Since the early 1980s, Ritalin has become the most commonly prescribed drug for ADD and ADHD, and thousands of Canadian children are currently prescribed Ritalin to increase their impulse control and attention span.

By being alert for students who exhibit several of the following characteristics, teachers can help in the early identification of learning disabilities so that these students can receive the instructional adaptations or special education services they need.

- Significant discrepancy between potential and academic achievement
- Tendency toward distraction or an inability to pay attention for as long as peers do
- Hyperactive behaviour, exhibited through excessive movement
- Inattentiveness during lectures or class discussions
- Impulsiveness
- Poor motor coordination and spatial relation skills
- Inability to solve problems
- Poor motivation and little active involvement in learning tasks
- Over-reliance on teacher and peers for class assignments
- Evidence of poor language and/or cognitive development
- Immature social skills
- Disorganized approach to learning
- Substantial delays in academic achievement (Smith 1998, 139)

Students Who Are Gifted and Talented

You are concerned about the poor performance of Paul, a student in your eighth-period high school class. Paul is undeniably bright. When he was 10, he had an IQ of 145 on the Stanford-Binet Intelligence Scale. Last year, when he was 16, he scored 142. Paul's father is a physician and his mother is a professor. Both parents clearly value learning and are willing to give Paul any needed encouragement and help.

Throughout elementary school, Paul had an outstanding record. His teachers reported that he was brilliant and very meticulous in completing his assignments. He entered high school amid expectations by his parents and teachers that he would continue his exceptional performance. Throughout his first two years of high school, Paul never seemed to live up to his promise. Now, halfway through his junior year, Paul is failing English and geometry. He seems to be well adjusted to the social side of school. He has a lot of friends and says he likes school. Paul explains his steadily declining grades by claiming an aversion to studying.

Paul may be gifted. **Gifted and talented** students—those who have demonstrated a high level of attainment in intellectual ability, academic achievement, creativity, or visual and performing arts—are evenly distributed across all ethnic and cultural groups and socio-economic classes. Although you might think it is easy to meet the needs of gifted and talented students, you will find that this is not always the case. "Students with special gifts or talents often challenge the system of school, and they can be verbally caustic. Their superior abilities and unusual or advanced interests demand teachers who are highly intelligent, creative, and motivated" (Hallahan & Kauffman 2000, 497). The ability of such students to challenge the system is reflected in a recent U.S. Department of Education study that found that gifted and talented elementary schoolchildren master 35 to 50 percent of the grade curriculum in five basic subject areas *before* starting the school year. The situation in Canada is likely similar.

Giftedness can take many forms. Joseph S. Renzulli (1998, 310), director of the National Research Center on the Gifted and Talented at the University of Connecticut, for example, suggests two kinds of giftedness: "schoolhouse giftedness [which] might also be called test-taking or lesson-learning giftedness" and "creative-productive giftedness." The trend of the past few decades has been to broaden our view of what characterizes giftedness.

Drawing from the work of Renzulli and his colleagues, Woolfolk defines *giftedness* "as a combination of three basic characteristics: above-average general ability, a high level of creativity, and a high level of task commitment or motivation to achieve in certain areas. Truly gifted children are not the students who simply learn quickly with little effort. The work of gifted students is original, extremely advanced for their age, and potentially of lasting importance" (Woolfolk 1998, 126). Depending on the criteria, estimates of the number of gifted and talented students range from 3 to 5 percent of the total population.

Strategies for educating students who are gifted and talented begin with effective teachers. Educational psychologist Anita Woolfolk suggests that "[T]eaching methods for gifted students should encourage abstract thinking (formal-operational thought), creativity, and independence, not just the learning of greater quantities of facts. In working with gifted and talented students, a teacher must be imaginative, flexible, and unthreatened by the capabilities of these students. The teacher must ask, What does this child need most? What is she or he ready to learn? Who can help me to challenge them?" (Woolfolk 1998, 129).

Research indicates that effective teachers of gifted and talented children share many of the characteristics of their students (Davis & Rimm 1998; Piirto 1999). In

Gifted and talented students benefit from accelerated and enriched learning experiences. What are some forms of acceleration and enrichment that you will offer your students?

fact, Feldhusen (1997) suggests that teachers of gifted students should be gifted themselves and should possess the following traits:

- Be highly intelligent
- Have cultural and intellectual interests
- Strive for excellence and high achievement
- Be enthusiastic about talent
- Relate well to talented people
- Have broad general knowledge

Teachers might draw from a range of innovative approaches for meeting the educational needs of gifted students.

- *Acceleration*—Accelerated programs for intellectually precocious students have proven successful. For example, an analysis of 314 studies of the academic, psychological, and social effects of acceleration practices at the elementary and secondary levels found "generally positive academic effects for most forms of acceleration" and no negative effects on socialization or psychological adjustment (Rogers 1991, 8–12). In addition, the analysis identified the following options as the most beneficial at different grade levels:

  - *Elementary school*—early entrance, grade-skipping, non-graded classes, and curriculum compacting (modifying the curriculum to present it at a faster pace)
  - *Junior high school*—grade-skipping, grade telescoping (shortening the amount of time to complete a grade level), concurrent enrolment in a high school or college, subject acceleration, and curriculum compacting
  - *Senior high school*—concurrent enrolment, subject acceleration, advanced placement (AP) classes, mentorships, credit by examination, and early admission to college

- *Self-directed or independent study*—For some time, self-directed or independent study has been recognized as an appropriate way for teachers to maintain the interest of gifted students. Gifted students usually have the academic backgrounds and motivation to do well without constant supervision and the threat or reward of grades.
- *Individual education programs*—Because all Canadian provinces and territories have some version of individual education programs (IEPs) for special education students, IEPs have been promoted as an appropriate means of educating gifted students. Most IEPs for gifted students involve various enrichment experiences, self-directed study, and special, concentrated instruction given to individuals or small groups in pull-out programs.

What Are Special Education, Mainstreaming, and Inclusion?

Prior to the twentieth century, children with disabilities were usually segregated from regular classrooms and taught by teachers in provincially or privately operated schools. Today, an array of programs and services in both general and special education classrooms is aimed at developing the potential of exceptional students. Three critical concepts to promote their growth, talents, and productivity are special education, mainstreaming, and inclusion.

Special education refers to "specially designed instruction that meets the unusual needs of an exceptional student" (Hallahan & Kauffman 2000, 12). Teachers trained in special education become familiar with special materials, techniques, and equipment and facilities for students with disabilities. For example, children with visual impairment may require reading materials in large print or Braille; students with hearing impairment may require hearing aids or instruction in sign language; those with physical disabilities may need special equipment; children with emotional disturbances may need small and highly structured classes; and students with special gifts or talents may require access to working professionals. "Related services—special transportation, psychological assessment, physical and occupational therapy, medical treatment, and counselling—may be necessary if special education is to be effective" (Hallahan & Kauffman 1997, 14).

Special Education Laws

Prior to 1980, the needs of students with disabilities were primarily met through self-contained special education classes within regular schools. However, over the past 25 years, this situation changed dramatically. The self-contained special education class has disappeared from most school districts and a more inclusive educational philosophy, based on an increased concern for human rights, has taken hold. Students who would previously have been placed in segregated classrooms are now integrated into regular classrooms. All provinces and territories now have laws, regulations, or policies that support this practice. While the exact nature of how inclusion is accomplished varies from one jurisdiction to another, as does the degree to which the various laws, policies, and regulations are enforced, the advocates of children with special needs have achieved a remarkable degree of success. Of particular assistance to these advocates has been the *Canadian Charter of Rights and Freedoms*. Because only Quebec and Saskatchewan have human rights codes that guarantee every citizen the right to an education, the Charter has been increasingly used to support the rights of students with special needs, as illustrated in the ruling in Figure 6.5.

Landmark Special Education Decision

Figure 6.5

Landmark special education decision

Eaton v. Brant county board of Education (February 15, 1995) Toronto, O.J. No. 315/No. C19214 (Ont. CA)

In a decision long fought for by advocates for the disabled and dreaded by school authorities, The Ontario Court of Appeal held that the Canadian Charter of Rights and Freedoms did indeed create a presumption, and a very strong presumption, in favour of the integration of handicapped persons into the mainstream of the community, and particularly the integration of disabled students into the regular classroom. The Court held that to rebut this presumption, school authorities would bear the onus of proving not only that integration in the regular school was not appropriate in a given circumstance, but also that placement in a segregated setting would be the only appropriate alternative. Further, the Court rewrote the legislative scheme for special education in Ontario, a scheme that sought to provide disabled students with procedural fairness in seeking a reasonable educational program. It held that the legislation must ensure that when a parent, acting on behalf of the disabled student, refuses to consent to a segregated educational placement for the student, school authorities must comply with the wishes of the parent "unless alternatives are proven inadequate."

Source: Reprinted from *Education Law Reporter: Elementary and Secondary Schools*, (6) p. 49.

Individualized education plan—A student with a disability of sufficient severity is given a written **individualized educational program** or individualized program plan that meets the child's needs and specifies educational goals, methods for achieving those goals, and the number and quality of special educational services to be provided. The IEP is regularly reviewed by five parties: (1) a parent or guardian, (2) the child, (3) a teacher, (4) a professional who has recently evaluated the child, and (5) others, usually the principal or a special-education resource person from the school district. When appropriate, IEPs sometimes have related agreements to ensure that students with disabilities receive any necessary services such as special transportation arrangements or other supportive services as may be required. (See Teacher's Resource 6.1 and Teacher's Resource 6.2 at www.MyEducationLab.com.)

Confidentiality of records—Protocols ensure that records on a child are kept confidential. In some provinces, parental permission is required before any official examines a child's records. Moreover, parents can amend a child's records if they feel information in them is misleading, inaccurate, or violates the child's rights.

Due process—Parents have the right to disagree with an IEP or an evaluation of their child's abilities. If a disagreement arises, in most boards it is settled through an impartial hearing where due process is followed. At the hearing, parents may be represented by a lawyer, may give evidence, and may cross-examine the school personnel involved. If the parents or guardians of a child disagree with the outcome, they may appeal the decision to the provincial department of education. If still dissatisfied, the case may then be taken to the civil court.

Canadian educators recognize that children with disabilities should be educated in the **least restrictive environment**. In other words, a student must be placed within a general education classroom whenever such inclusion is feasible and appropriate and the child would receive educational benefit. Figure 6.6 shows the educational service options for students with disabilities, from the most inclusive to the most restrictive.

Meeting the Challenge of Inclusion

To help teachers satisfy the requirements of the new inclusive paradigm, school districts across Canada have developed in-service programs designed to acquaint classroom teachers with the unique needs of students with disabilities. In addition, colleges and universities with preservice programs for educators have added courses on teaching students with special educational needs.

The new guidelines require that schools make a significant effort to include *all* children in the classroom. However, *it is not clear how far schools must go to meet this requirement.* For example, should children with severe disabilities be included in general education classrooms if they are unable to complete the academic work? Recent court cases have ruled that such students must be included if there is a potential benefit for the child, if the class would stimulate the child's language development, or if other students could act as appropriate role models for the child. School districts, departments of education, and the Canadian judicial system are presently in an extended process of determining the answers to these and other concerns.

To meet the challenges of inclusion, teachers must have knowledge of various disabilities and the teaching methods and materials appropriate for each. Since teachers with negative attitudes toward students with special needs can convey these feelings to all students in a class and thereby reduce the effectiveness of inclusion (Lewis & Doorlag 1999), general education teachers must maintain positive attitudes toward students with special needs. An accepting, supportive climate can significantly enhance the self-confidence of students with disabilities.

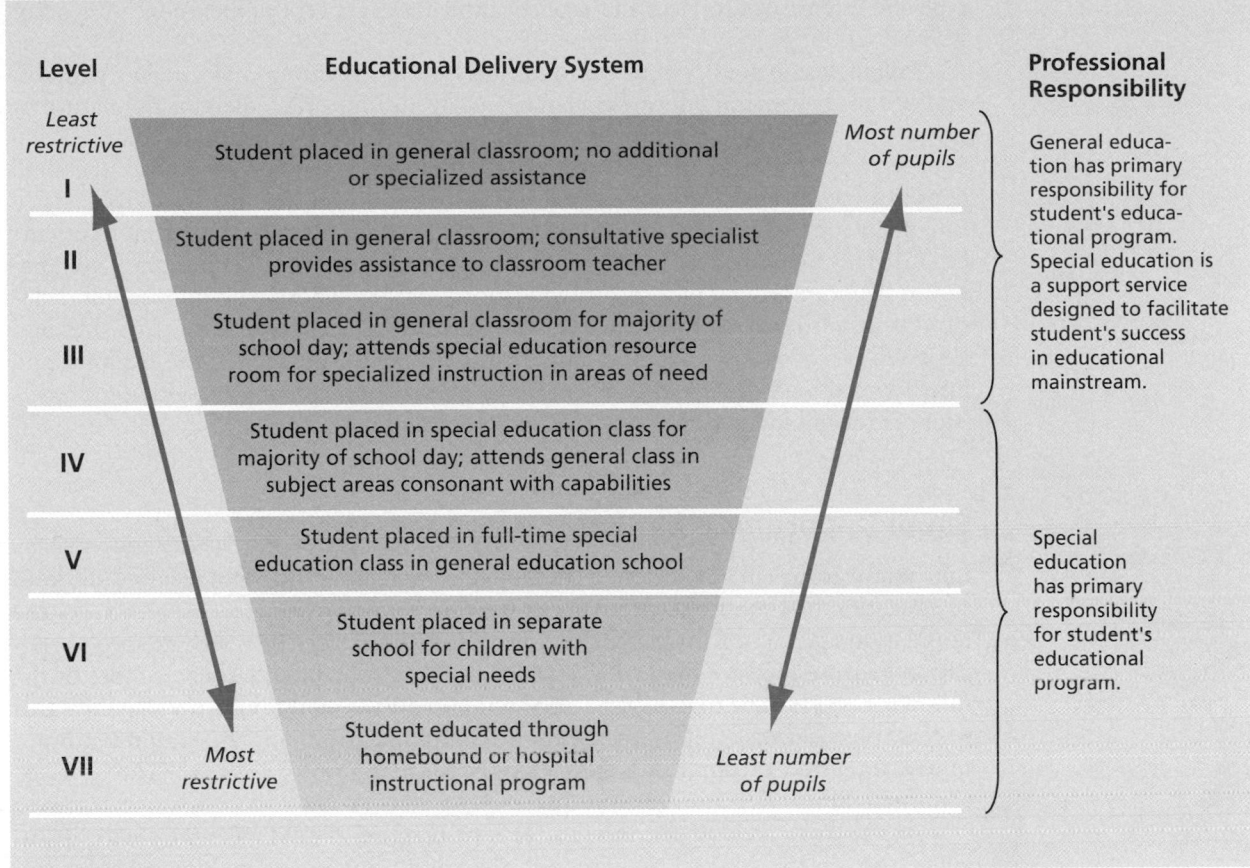

Level	Educational Delivery System		Professional Responsibility
Least restrictive I	Student placed in general classroom; no additional or specialized assistance	*Most number of pupils*	General education has primary responsibility for student's educational program. Special education is a support service designed to facilitate student's success in educational mainstream.
II	Student placed in general classroom; consultative specialist provides assistance to classroom teacher		
III	Student placed in general classroom for majority of school day; attends special education resource room for specialized instruction in areas of need		
IV	Student placed in special education class for majority of school day; attends general class in subject areas consonant with capabilities		Special education has primary responsibility for student's educational program.
V	Student placed in full-time special education class in general education school		
VI	Student placed in separate school for children with special needs		
VII	*Most restrictive* Student educated through homebound or hospital instructional program	*Least number of pupils*	

Figure 6.6

Educational service options for students with disabilities

Source: Michael L. Hardman, Clifford J. Drew, and M. Winston Egan, *Human Exceptionality: Society, School and Family,* 7th ed. Boston: Allyn and Bacon, 2002, p. 29. Copyright © 1999 by Allyn and Bacon. Reprinted by permission.

In addition, Hallahan and Kauffman (2000, 20–22) suggest that all teachers should be prepared to participate in the education of exceptional learners. Teachers should be willing to do the following:

1. Make maximum effort to accommodate individual students' needs.
2. Evaluate academic abilities and disabilities.
3. Refer [students] for evaluation [as appropriate].
4. Participate in eligibility conferences [for special education].
5. Participate in writing individualized education programs.
6. Communicate with parents or guardians.
7. Participate in due process hearings and negotiations.
8. Collaborate with other professionals in identifying and making maximum use of exceptional students' abilities.

The Debate over Inclusion

While **mainstreaming** refers to the provision of a least restrictive environment, **inclusion** goes beyond mainstreaming to integrate all students with disabilities into general education classes with the active support of special educators and other specialists, as well as **assistive technology** and adaptive software. Advocates of inclusion believe that "if students cannot meet traditional academic expectations, then those expectations should be changed. They reject the mainstreaming assumption that settings dictate the type and intensity of services and propose instead the concept of inclusion" (Friend & Bursuck 2002, 4).

Full inclusion goes even further and calls for "the integration of students with disabilities in the general education classrooms at all times regardless of the nature or severity of the disability" (Friend & Bursuck 1999, 4). According to the full-inclusion approach, if a child needs support services, these are brought *to the child*; the child does not have to participate in a pull-out program to receive support. Advocates of full inclusion maintain that pull-out programs stigmatize participating students because they are separated from general-education classmates and discourage collaboration between general and special education teachers. Those who oppose full inclusion contend that classroom teachers, who may be burdened with large class sizes and assigned to schools with inadequate support services, often lack the training and instructional materials to meet the needs of all exceptional students. However, while support for full inclusion varies, the trend toward it continues.

Equal Opportunity for Exceptional Learners

Like many groups in our society, exceptional learners have often not received the kind of education that most effectively meets their needs. Approximately 10 percent of the population aged 3 to 21 is classified as exceptional; that is, "they require special education because they are markedly different from most children in one or more of the following ways: They may have . . . learning disabilities, emotional or behavioral disorders, physical disabilities, disorders of communication, autism, traumatic brain injury, impaired hearing, impaired sight, or special gifts or talents" (Hallahan & Kauffman 2000, 7).

Just as there are no easy answers for how teachers should meet the needs of students from diverse cultural backgrounds, there is no single strategy for teachers to follow to ensure that all exceptional students receive an appropriate education. The key, however, lies in not losing sight of the fact that *"the most important characteristics of exceptional children are their abilities"* (Hallahan & Kauffman 2000, 6).

To build on students' strengths, classroom teachers must work cooperatively with special education teachers, and students in special education programs must not be isolated from their peers. In addition, teachers must understand how some people might be perceived as "different" and presumed to be "handicapped" because of their appearance or physical condition. Evidence suggests, for example, that people who are short, obese, or unattractive are often victims of discrimination, as are people with conditions such as AIDS, cancer, multiple sclerosis, or epilepsy. Significantly, many individuals with clinically diagnosable and classifiable impairments do not self-identify as *handicapped*. The term itself means permanently unable to be treated equally.

Officially labelling students has become a necessity with the passage of the laws that provide education and related services for exceptional students. Classification labels help determine which students qualify for the special services, educational programs, and individualized instruction afforded by law, and they bring to educators' attention many exceptional children and youth whose educational needs could be overlooked, neglected, or inadequately served otherwise. Detrimental aspects include the fact that classification systems are imperfect and have arbitrary cut-off points that sometimes lead to injustices. Labels can evoke negative expectations, which can cause teachers to avoid or underteach exceptional students and cause their peers to isolate or reject them, thereby creating a stigma—sometimes a permanent one. The most serious detriment, however, is that students so labelled are taught to feel inadequate, inferior, and limited in terms of their options for growth.

How Can You Teach All Learners in Your Inclusive Classroom?

Teachers have a responsibility to address all students' developmental, individual, and exceptional learning needs. Although addressing the range of student differences in the inclusive classroom is challenging, it can also be very rewarding. While it is beyond the scope of this book to present in-depth instructional strategies to address students' diverse learning needs, attention to three key areas will enable you to create a truly inclusive classroom: collaborative consultation, partnerships with parents, and assistive technology for special learners. However, it is important to remember whether teaching students with or without special needs that it is critical that the facts and ideas you convey be presented in a clear and understandable manner. For additional information on this topic, go to www.MyEducationLab.com and read Teacher's Resource 6.1, The Teacher's Scribe: "Let me be clear."

myeducationlab

The Challenge of "Gentle Teaching"

Historically, schools have dealt with student misbehaviour with a series of punishments, which, while some such as strapping and caning have since been abandoned, still rely heavily on various punitive actions. Almost every Canadian school or school district now has a disciplinary policy that outlines the procedures (and consequences) for dealing with such relatively minor things such as student tardiness or absenteeism and insubordination, and more serious offences such as bullying, selling drugs to other students, and bringing weapons to school. All such policies have, as their ultimate punishment, expulsion; that is to say, as a final resort, students are told to behave or be gone.

In general, teachers have given various levels of support to discipline policies based primarily on this "stop it or we'll hurt you" philosophy. However, in the United States during the 1970s, recognition developed that the sometimes harsh methods of behaviour modification then in use needed to be evaluated. The concepts and practices of the philosophical stance that resulted are now known as **gentle teaching**. Based directly on Maslow's *hierarchy of needs* (see Figure 6.2), "deficiency needs" such as student physiological, safety and belongingness requirements must be addressed by educators. Additionally, the applied practices of gentle teaching are of particular importance to students with any type of physiological need—such as blindness, deafness, or paralysis—or cognitive needs brought about by autism, fetal alcohol spectrum disorder, or clinically weak mental processing. Students with these or other special needs are often likely to exhibit aggression or other antisocial behaviours, but, rather than using punishment as a corrective measure, gentle teaching recommends a focus on teaching students what they need to learn in order to behave well.

There are significant differences between the standard model for controlling student behaviour and the practices followed by adherents of gentle teaching. For a better understanding of these differences, please refer to Teacher's Resource 6.4 at www.MyEducationLab.com. For each of the identified behaviours and their corrective techniques, ask yourself how you might react if faced with the student actions given as examples.

myeducationlab

Collaborative Consultation with Other Professionals

Another approach to meeting the needs of all students is **collaborative consultation**, in which a classroom teacher meets with one or more other professionals (a special

Year of the Four Boys

Jessica,* a very talented teacher with seven years of teaching experience, refers to one of her Grade 9 teaching assignments as the Year of the Four Boys. Her school's principal decided that, rather than assign four male students with various physical and mental difficulties to separate classes, she would place all four in the same section. She did, however, restrict the class's size to 24, with 20 of the students categorized as "good."

Boy #1: Quadriplegic as the result of a recent accident, average intelligence, angry, very unhappy, and possibly somewhat embarrassed about his condition. Comes with a full-time personal educational assistant, a large reclining wheelchair, and a laptop computer, which he is just beginning to learn to use.

Comment: No recommendations received as to how to assist this recently paralyzed student.

Boy #2: Brain damaged as the result of oxygen deprivation at birth, smartest student in the class, marvelous sense of humour, spastic body movements. Any loud or unexpected noise causes him to spasm uncontrollably, which can jolt him out of his seat and onto the floor—to the great amusement of his classmates.

Comment: Feeder school recommended keeping all loud or unexpected classroom noises to a minimum.

Boy #3: Suffers from fetal alcohol syndrome (FAS). Has both short-term and long-term memory problems. Work is far below grade level. Often acts out in an inappropriate manner, which causes other students to laugh at him—not with him. Socially promoted for peer group reasons.

Comment: Feeder school recommended giving him all the extra help possible.

educator, a school psychologist, or a resource teacher, for example) to focus on the learning needs of one or more students. A first-year teacher describes how collaborative consultation enabled her to meet the needs of a special student:

> I taught a child with Down's Syndrome [Notice that she did not use the phraseology "Down's Syndrome child"] who was very frustrated. I convened a meeting that included school district experts, his parents, and a resource teacher, suggesting a change in educational strategy. All agreed to pilot the plan, and things have worked more smoothly ever since. It was a very rewarding experience. (Sallie Mae Corporation 1995, 11)

Collaborative consultation is based on reciprocity (Hallahan & Kauffman 2003), and participants assume equal responsibility for meeting students' needs. Friend and Bursuck (2002) make the following suggestions for working with a consultant:

1. Do your homework. Working with a consultant should be an intervention you seek only after you have attempted to identify and resolve the problem by analyzing the

Boy #4: Clinically dead for several minutes before being rescued from the bottom of a lake during a recent summer. Serious short-term memory problems. Formerly an energetic and interested student, his behaviour is now less enthused.

Comment: Parents asked his teachers to do everything possible to help him "get back to his normal self."

Jessica's bachelor of education program included only a single three credit-hour course on how to deal with students with special needs, and none of that course's content offered any specific suggestions for how to deal with the difficulties experienced by the four boys. However, by the end of the school year, she felt she had learned more about how to effectively deal with students with special needs than any number of courses could have taught her.

*Jessica teaches in Western Canada.

Questions

1. What do you think of the principal's decision to place all four boys in the same class section with 20 "good" students? Why do you think she undertook this action?

2. Do you think the action of the school principal represents good inclusive practice?

3. If you were Jessica, what would be some of the basic elements of the action plan you would construct for dealing with the four boys' situations?

4. Boy #2's situation appears to be the easiest to deal with. List three specific things you, or your school, could immediately put into place to spare him, as much as possible, the spasmodic effects of loud or unexpected noises.

5. What other questions are raised regarding Jessica's and the four boys' situations?

situation yourself, talking about it with parents, presenting it at a grade-level meeting, and so on.

2. Demonstrate your concern with documentation. At your initial meeting with a consultant, bring samples of student work, notes recounting specific incidents in the classroom, records of correspondence with parents, and other concrete information.

3. Participate actively. If you clearly describe the problem, contribute specific information about your expectations for how the situation should change, offer your ideas on how best to intervene to resolve the problem, implement the selected strategy carefully, and provide your perception of the effectiveness of the strategy, you will find consultation very helpful.

4. Carry out the consultant's suggestions carefully and systematically.

5. Contact the consultant if problems occur. (Friend & Bursuck 2002, 95–96)

To enhance the educational experiences of students with disabilities, general education teachers are often assisted by special educators and other support professionals.

The following professionals are among those who consult and/or collaborate with general education teachers:

- *Consulting teacher*—A special educator who provides technical assistance, such as arranging the physical setting, helping to plan for instruction, or developing approaches for assessing students' learning
- *Resource-room teacher*—A special educator who provides instruction in a resource room for students with disabilities
- *School psychologist*—Consults with the general education teacher and arranges for the administration of appropriate psychological, educational, and behavioural assessment instruments; may observe a student's behaviour in the classroom
- *Speech and language specialist*—Assesses students' communication abilities and works with general education teachers to develop educational programs for students with speech and/or language disorders
- *Physical therapist*—Provides physical therapy for students with physical disabilities
- *Occupational therapist*—Instructs students with disabilities to prepare them for everyday living and work-related activities

Working with Parents

In addition to working with education professionals to meet the learning needs of all students, effective teachers develop good relationships with parents. Parents of exceptional children can be a source of valuable information about the characteristics, abilities, and needs of their children; they can be helpful in securing necessary services; and they can assist you by reviewing skills at home and praising their children for their learning. Some school districts, such as the Toronto District School Board, require that teachers contact all of their students' parents or guardians on a regular basis. While this adds one more task to each teacher's workload, boards that have such policies obviously recognize the importance having a strong relationship with students' homes.

Assistive Technology for Special Learners

The ability of teachers to create inclusive classrooms has increased dramatically as a result of many technological advances that now make it easier for exceptional students to learn and communicate. For example, computer-based word processing software and math tutorials can greatly assist students with learning disabilities in acquiring literacy and computer skills. Students with hearing impairments can communicate with other students using telecommunications equipment, and students with physical disabilities can operate computers through voice commands or with a single switch or key. Among the recent developments in assistive technology are the following:

1. Talking word processor
2. Speech synthesizer
3. Touch-sensitive computer screens
4. Computer screen image enlarger
5. Teletypewriter (TTY) (connects to telephone and types a spoken message to another TTY)
6. Customized computer keyboards
7. Ultrasonic head controls for computers

Braille and hearing horns were among the first assistive technologies. How might educators use various types of technology to assist the learning of students with special needs?

8. Voice-recognition software
9. Television closed captioning
10. Kurzweil reading machine (scans print and reads it aloud)

In addition, assistive technology includes devices to enhance the mobility and everyday activities of people with disabilities (wheelchairs, lifts, adaptive driving controls, scooters, laser canes, and feeders, for example).

Modern technology-related special education resources and curriculum materials are available on the internet. The website of the National Center to Improve Practice in Special Education through Technology, Media, and Materials (www.2.edc.org/NCIP) maintains discussion forums for teachers of students with disabilities. Clearly, the dazzling revolution in electronics will continue to yield new devices to enhance the learning of all students.

SUMMARY

How Do Students' Needs Change as They Develop?

- People move through different stages of cognitive, psychosocial, and moral development throughout their life spans.

- Piaget maintains that children, who reason differently from adults, pass through four stages of cognitive development as they mature. Effective teachers are aware of the characteristics of school-age children's thinking during three of these stages: the preoperational stage, the concrete operations stage, and the formal operations stage.

- According to Erikson's model of psychosocial development, people pass through eight stages of emotional and social development throughout their lives. Each stage is characterized by a "crisis" with a positive and negative pole. Healthy development depends upon a satisfactory, positive resolution of each crisis.

- Kohlberg believes that moral development, the reasoning people use to decide between right and wrong, evolves through three levels. Evidence suggests that males may base their moral reasoning on rights and rules, and females on altruism and self-sacrifice. Many teachers and schools emphasize character education to "teach" moral reasoning and values.

- Maslow suggests that human growth and development depends on how well the individual's biological and psychological needs have been met. According to his hierarchy of needs model, people must satisfy their survival and safety needs before addressing "higher" needs such as self-actualization.

- Teachers must be aware of the developmental stresses and tasks students encounter during childhood and early and late adolescence.

How Do Students Vary in Intelligence?

- There are conflicting definitions of *intelligence*; they range from "what IQ tests measure" to "goal-directed adaptive behaviour." Some theorists believe intelligence is a single, basic ability, though recent research suggests that there are many forms of intelligence.

- According to Howard Gardner's theory of multiple intelligences, there are at least eight human intelligences.

- Students differ in their learning styles—the patterns of behaviour they prefer to use while learning. Although there is conflict about the concept of learning styles, effective teachers are aware of differences among students regarding their preferences for learning activities.

How Do Students Vary in Ability and Disability?

- Some students are "exceptional" because they have abilities or disabilities that distinguish them from other students. Students with physical, cognitive, or emotional disabilities and students who are gifted and talented have unique learning needs.

- There is a lack of agreement regarding the definition of *learning disability*. Teachers can identify students with learning disabilities by noting difficulties students have acquiring and processing new information. Learning disabilities are the most prevalent disability among students, with attention deficit hyperactivity disorder (ADHD) and attention deficit disorder (ADD) the most common.

- There are many forms of giftedness. Among the approaches used to meet the learning needs of gifted students are acceleration, self-directed or independent study, individual education programs, special or magnet schools, and weekend and summer programs.

What Are Special Education, Mainstreaming, and Inclusion?

- Special education involves a variety of educational services to meet the needs of exceptional students. Provincial and territorial laws, regulations, and policies support models such as the least restrictive environment, individualized educational programs, confidentiality of records, and due process.

- *Mainstreaming* is the process of integrating students with disabilities into regular classrooms.

- *Inclusion* integrates all students with disabilities into regular classrooms, with the support of special education services as necessary. *Full inclusion* is the integration of students with disabilities in general education classrooms at all times regardless of the severity of the disability.

How Can You Teach All Learners in Your Inclusive Classroom?

- Though challenging, teachers have a responsibility to create inclusive classrooms that address the developmental, individual, and exceptional learning needs of all students.

- Through collaborative consultation—an arrangement whereby the regular classroom teacher collaborates with other education professionals—teachers can meet the needs of exceptional students. Collaborative consultation is based on reciprocity, and all participants assume responsibility for meeting students' needs.

- By developing effective relationships with parents of exceptional students, teachers acquire valuable information and support.

- An array of assistive technologies and resources is available to help exceptional students learn and communicate in inclusive classrooms.

KEY TERMS AND CONCEPTS

assistive technology, 187
attention deficit disorder (ADD), 182
attention deficit hyperactivity disorder (ADHD), 182
Canadian Charter of Rights and Freedoms, 185
character education, 170
cognitive development, 166
collaborative consultation, 189
concrete operations stage, 167

exceptional learners, 178
formal operations stage, 167
full inclusion, 188
gentle teaching, 189
gifted and talented, 182
hierarchy of needs, 170
inclusion, 187
individualized educational program (IEP), 186
intelligence, 174
learning disability (LD), 180
learning styles, 176

least restrictive environment, 186
mainstreaming, 187
moral reasoning, 166
multiple intelligences, 176
preoperational stage, 167
psychosocial crisis, 167
psychosocial development, 166
special education, 184
stages of development, 166
students with disabilities, 179

APPLICATIONS AND ACTIVITIES

Teacher's Journal

1. Through a series of vignettes, relate Erikson's stages of psychosocial development to your own experiences as a child and as an adolescent. How did sources of stress, psychosocial crises, and your resolution of them affect your learning in school?

2. Do you know your IQ or recall participating in an IQ test? How do you regard yourself in terms of intelligence, and how did you come by your beliefs about your intelligence? Do you think these beliefs influenced your motivation, choices, and achievement as a student? Do you think they influenced your school or class

placements? Do you think they influenced the way your teachers and peers responded to you? What criteria would you now use to evaluate the fairness of IQ testing and the appropriateness of the use of IQ scores?

3. Recount an experience you had with an exceptional student or one that involved a person with disabilities. What did you learn from this experience or from your reflection on it that could help you as a teacher?

Theory into Practice

1. If an individual is described as *handicapped*, *disabled*, or *challenged*, is the meaning of these three descriptors the same in each instance? Write a definition for each italicized word. Which of the three descriptors would be the most appropriate? Why?

2. In your everyday speech, indicate which of the following patterns you would typically use. Select one from each of the three examples and, in a small group, discuss your choices. Are the choices you made important? Be prepared to justify your position to the class.

   a. a child with Down's syndrome

   b. a Down's syndrome child

   a. a mentally retarded person

   b. a person with mental retardation

   a. a physically challenged person

   b. a person with physical challenges

   c. neither a) nor b)

3. Sensitivity training specialists are fond of activities that sensitize individuals to people with mental or physical limitations. Review the types of disability listed in Table 6.3, select any three of the disabilities, and, in a small group, develop one sensitization activity you could conduct with a class for each of the selections you made.

Teacher's Database

1. Investigate sources of information on students with disabilities or exceptional learners, including SchoolNet (www.schoolnet.com) or the following website, which has links to numerous sites that deal with special education topics: www.statcan.gc.ca/kits-trousses/edu05_000-eng.htm.

2. "Observe" children online by locating chat rooms for children and youth. As an adult, you may not be allowed to participate, but in many cases you will be invited to visit (called "lurking" in internet jargon). What educational interests, needs, and concerns do students share with one another? How might visiting students' sites online be viewed as an extension of your field experiences as an education student or as a student teacher? What teacher observation techniques and protocols could you use in this situation? What are some ethical concerns about

this practice? How might any new knowledge of students gained in this way help to make you a more effective teacher?

Observations and Interviews

1. Observe in a classroom that has exceptional students. What steps does the teacher take to meet the needs of these students? Interview the teacher to determine what he or she sees as the challenges and rewards of teaching exceptional students.

2. Observe and interview a student in the age group you wish to teach to conduct a brief case study that focuses on common developmental tasks for that age group and the areas of individual differences highlighted in this chapter. Prepare a written portrait of the student.

3. Visit a school at the level you plan to teach. Interview the counsellor, asking questions about the problems that bring students to the counsellor most often. If possible, shadow him or her for a day.

4. Attend an extracurricular event such as a high school basketball game or Little League soccer game. Observe the students on the field as well as any students watching the players. Notice the differences among the students in terms of their physical appearance, clothing and hairstyles, athletic abilities, social skills, and evidence of personal interests and confidence. Share your observations in class.

Professional Portfolio

For the grade level and content area you are preparing to teach, identify learning activities that address each of the eight multiple intelligences as identified by Gardner. For example, you might plan activities such as the following. For one activity in each category, list the preparations you would need to make and the materials you would need to gather, and add this information to your portfolio.

Logical-Mathematical
- Design an experiment on . . .
- Describe the rules for a new board game called . . .

Linguistic
- Write a short story about . . .
- Write a biographical sketch of . . .

Musical
- Write song lyrics for . . .
- Locate music that sounds like . . .

Spatial
- Draw, paint, or sculpt a . . .
- Create an advertisement for . . .

Bodily–Kinesthetic
- Do a dance that shows . . .
- Role play a person who is . . .

Intrapersonal
- Assess your ability to . . .
- Describe how you feel about . . .

Interpersonal
- Show one or more of your classmates how to . . .
- In a small group, construct a . . .

Naturalist
- Identify the trees found in . . .
- Classify the rocks found in . . .

MyEducationLab

myeducationlab

For suggestions on how to make your lessons more interesting, go to Teacher's Resource 6.1: The Teacher's Scribe: "Let me be clear" on www.MyEducationLab.com.

To review Nova Scotia's policy regarding individualized education plans, go to Teacher's Resource 6.2 on www.MyEducationLab.com.

To read a sample individualized education plan, go to Teacher's Resource 6.3 on www.MyEducationLab.com.

To learn more about how to help students with disabilities, go to Teacher's Resource 6.4: Gentle Teaching, on www.MyEducationLab.com.

7

Creating a Community of Learners

As a teacher I role model the qualities that I seek to nurture in my students—an open, curious mind and a willingness to explore new ideas. My job is to provide a framework that supports them in building experience of a new environment and provide a foundation for taking new risks. I use the comfort of working with their peers in small groups to move them into a new frame of reference.

—Shirley R. Turner
Secondary level teacher at Vancouver Technical School in British Columbia

Recipient of a Prime Minister's Award for Excellence in Teaching in October 2009

focus questions

1. What determines the culture of the classroom?
2. How can you create a positive learning environment?
3. What are the keys to successful classroom management?
4. What teaching methods do effective teachers use?
5. What are some characteristics of effective teaching?

What do Canadian public school classrooms look like? That depends on many variables, including, but not limited to, the following:

- School level (elementary, middle/junior or senior high)
- Age of school (built in the past 10 years, built in the past 30 years, or built more than 30 years ago
- Location (rural, suburban, urban)
- Size (small, medium, large) and configuration (K–12, P–6, 7–9, 10–12, etc.)
- School leadership
- Socio-economic background of students
- Content area
- Class size
- Class composition
- Individual teacher experience and philosophy

Let's look inside a kindergarten classroom in a typical Canadian school . . .

Kindergarten teacher Ms. Patronis explains that the first year of school is usually a challenging one for children, and the beginning of the year is mostly spent developing routines and behaviours that are conducive to a positive learning environment. Some of the daily instructional time is spent in large group activities, whereas other parts of the day involve smaller group or individual work.

As we enter the kindergarten classroom, the students are involved in charting their plans for the morning. The classroom is set up in learning stations comprising physical areas designed for various content area learning experiences. There are specific mathematics, geography, science, language arts, and multimedia learning centres, along with areas for art and storytelling.

A voice comes over the public address system instructing the students to stand, then sit, to listen to a few announcements read by the school's principal. Immediately afterward, Ms. Patronis starts to sing, "It's time, it's time, it's time for Morning Meeting now" and the students join in the song.

The teacher has explained to us that one of the most important times in her classroom is referred to as Morning Meeting, which occurs immediately after "O Canada" has been sung and the announcements read, and sets the tone for the day. It is during this time that many concepts are presented that involve literacy and math, the calendar, and the oral sharing of news. By the end of September, students are aware of the behaviour expectations during this important instructional time.

As we view Morning Meeting in action, it is obvious that it creates an accepting environment where students share, have fun, and laugh. Morning Meeting is broken into greetings, sharing, group activity, news, and announcements.

We watch as students greet each other by name; which today they sing to one another. Next, two students share information about an event in their lives. One student tells the group he is feeling sad today because his grandmother is in the hospital, which means he can't go to her house after school. Several students offer empathy and share stories about how special their grandparents are and what they do when they visit them. Another student shares the news that her cat's kittens have opened their eyes, and the other students react excitedly, telling tales about their own pets. The group activity for the meeting comprises students' miming the action of flying kites to mark the first day of March; they have been learning about March winds. For news and announcements, two students read aloud a list of items Ms. Patronis has printed on a flipchart. The flipchart explains that the students are due to attend a puppet show in the gymnasium that afternoon, and the class reviews what being a good audience looks like. It is obvious that the students understand the importance of listening and of clapping for performers to demonstrate their enjoyment. Morning Meeting concludes with a review of the morning's schedule and which learning stations the students have chosen to work at that morning.

As the meeting ends, the students seem focused and ready to work, and they move into the various learning stations with a minimum of teacher direction. It is obvious that the time has included an emphasis on social, emotional, and intellectual learning.

The opening vignette highlights the importance of organizing the classroom to create a positive learning environment—a cohesive community of learners. For teacher education students, the transition between the study of teaching and actual teaching can be a challenge. You will make that transition smoothly, however, if you understand that to create a cohesive community of learners, "teachers must (1) earn the respect and affection of students; (2) be consistent and, therefore, credible and dependable; (3) assume responsibility for seeing that their students learn; and (4) value and enjoy learning and expect students to do so, too" (Good & Brophy 2008, 77).

What Determines the Culture of the Classroom?

As you learned in Chapter 5, one definition of culture is the way of life common to a group of people. In much the same way, each classroom develops its own culture. The culture of a classroom is determined by the manner in which teachers and students participate in common activities.

Classroom activities are influenced by several factors. As a teacher, you will make countless decisions that will shape the physical and social milieus of your classroom. From seating arrangements to classroom rules and procedures and the content of the curriculum, you will have a strong influence on the culture that emerges. You will have many methodological choices to make—when to shift from one activity to another, when to use discussion rather than lecture, and whether to make one requirement more imperative than another, for example.

Go to www.MyEducationLab.com and select the Managing to Teach tab. Open Module 1: An Introduction to Your Virtual School to consider a broad definition of classroom management that includes the teacher–student relationship and the physical classroom space. Listen to the guide talk about the various dimensions of classroom management and the decision-making that teachers engage in as they build their classroom communities.

myeducationlab

Classroom Climate

One dimension of classroom culture is **classroom climate**—the atmosphere or quality of life in a classroom. The climate of your classroom will be decided by how you interact with your students and "by the manner and degree to which you exercise authority, show warmth and support, encourage competitiveness or cooperation, and allow for independent judgment and choice" (Borich 2007, 167).

Classroom climates are complex and multidimensional; their character is determined by a wide array of variables, many of which are beyond the teacher's control. Nevertheless, our observations of high-performing teachers have confirmed that they take specific steps to create classroom climates that incorporate the following eight characteristics:

1. A productive, task-oriented focus
2. Group cohesiveness
3. Open, warm relationships between teacher and students
4. Cooperative, respectful interactions among students
5. Low levels of tension, anxiety, and conflict
6. Humour
7. High expectations
8. Frequent opportunities for student input regarding classroom activities

The degree to which these dimensions are present within your classroom will be influenced by your style of communication with students. As the following case illustrates, creating a classroom climate characterized by these eight dimensions is not easy. The moment-to-moment decisions teachers make about how to respond to events can enhance or reduce group cohesiveness and students' motivation to learn.

Dari feels uncomfortable as she makes the seemingly endless trip from her desk to the drinking fountain at the back of the room. If she had a choice, she wouldn't make the trip at all. She is well aware that her classmates resent her being allowed to get a drink whenever she wants to, whereas they have to wait until recess or lunch. They know that the medicine she takes every morning makes her thirsty, but they still tease her about being "Teacher's Pet."

"Why can't the others get drinks when they want to?" she wonders. "It wouldn't be any big deal. Besides, Ms. Patterson is always drinking her coffee. She carries that stupid coffee mug around so much that it looks as if it's attached to her body."

"Hey, Ms. Patterson, can I get a drink?" Craig calls out. "It's a really hot day, and I'm thirsty'."

"Of course not, Craig. You know my rule about that." Ms. Patterson is obviously annoyed at his question.

Craig persists. "It's not fair. You can drink your coffee whenever you want to."

"I never said life is fair," Ms. Patterson replies. "I'm the teacher, so I have certain privileges. I need to have something to drink because I do most of the talking and my mouth gets dry. Besides, my job is to make sure that you children learn, and I can't do that if you're running to the drinking fountain all the time. It won't kill you to wait until recess to get a drink."

"But we could use a water bottle," Huong suggests.

"No. that won't work. A couple of years ago, I let my students bring water bottles to school, and they used them to squirt one another all the time. When are you people going to learn that no means no?"

"But you let Dari go to the fountain whenever she wants to," Shelby points out.

"Dari has medical problems," Ms. Patterson responds. "Anyway, I know that she'll only get a drink if she really, really needs one. Right, Dari?"

Dari nods self-consciously and then tries to make herself smaller by scrunching low in her seat.

"Yeah, she's special, all right," Guy scoffs. "She's Teacher's Pet." (Ormrod & McGuire 2007, 111)

How would you describe this classroom climate using the eight dimensions? Should Ms. Patterson allow her students to get a drink during class? Is it fair that she drinks coffee in front of her students? Could Ms. Patterson help Dari feel more socially connected to her classmates?

Although teachers influence the classroom climate by the way they treat students, they also shape it by their instructional decisions. David Johnson and Roger Johnson, two researchers in the area of classroom communication and dynamics, delineate three types of interactions promoted by instructional decisions: cooperative or positive interdependence, competitive or negative interdependence, and individualistic or no interdependence (Johnson and Johnson 1999). To illustrate, Johnson and Johnson

What words might describe the interaction between this teacher and student? What do you think the teacher is saying?

suggest that a group project to measure classroom furniture would promote cooperative interdependence, a race to be the first student to measure the furniture would call for competitive interdependence, and having a student measure the furniture independently would be an example of no interdependence. Johnson and Johnson believe that teachers should use strategies that foster all three forms of interaction, depending on their instructional goals, but that ideally the emphasis should be on furthering cooperative interdependence.

Classroom Dynamics

Interactions between teachers and students are the very core of teaching. The quality of these interactions reveals to students how the teacher feels about them. Teachers who empathize with students, genuinely respect them, and expect them to learn are more likely to develop a classroom climate free of management problems. In classrooms with positive group dynamics, teachers and students work toward a common goal—learning. In classrooms with negative interactions, the energy of teachers and students may be channelled into conflict rather than into learning.

There is no precise formula to guarantee success in the classroom; however, a classroom climate characterized by the following four qualities results in greater student motivation to learn and more positive teacher–student and student–student interactions:

1. Learning activities are well organized, progress smoothly, and are free from distractions or interruptions.
2. The teacher is caring, patient, and supportive, and never ridicules or criticizes students for their efforts to learn.
3. The curriculum is challenging but not so difficult that students become frustrated and decide not to learn.
4. Learning activities are authentic and, to the degree possible, relevant to students' interests and experiences.

Communication Skills

Successful teachers possess effective communication skills. They express themselves verbally and nonverbally in a manner that is clear, concise, and interesting. They "are able to communicate clearly and directly to their students without wandering, speaking above students' levels of comprehension, or using speech patterns that impair their presentation's clarity" (Borich 2007, 10). In addition, they are good listeners. Their students feel that not only are they heard, they are understood.

Effective teachers relish the interactive, spontaneous dimensions of classroom discourse. They respond appropriately to events that could sabotage the plans of less effective teachers—a student's misbehaviour, announcements on the PA system, interruptions by other teachers or parents, arguments between students, or the mood of the class at a given time.

Interactions Among Students

In addition to engaging in positive, success-oriented interactions with their students, effective teachers foster positive, cooperative interactions among them. As a result, students feel supported by their peers and free to devote their attention to learning. The climate of such a classroom is "mature" and "self-renewing" (Schmuck & Schmuck 2001). Typically, the classroom climate has evolved through four stages of group development (see Figure 7.1).

During stage 1, students are on their best behaviour. Teachers can use this honeymoon period to their advantage. They can discuss classroom rules and procedures, outline learning goals, and clarify expectations. During stage 2, teachers can encourage student participation and communication while discouraging the formation of cliques.

Groups that have reached stage 2 then move into stage 3, which may last for the remainder of the school year. In stage 3, the group sets clear goals, shares tasks, and agrees on deadlines. A fully evolved group reaches stage 4. In this stage, group members accept responsibility for the quality of life in the group and continuously strive to improve it.

How Can You Create a Positive Learning Environment?

A positive classroom climate and positive classroom dynamics are prerequisites for a good learning environment. Creating and maintaining a positive learning environment is a multidimensional challenge. While no single set of strategies will ensure success in all situations, educational researchers have identified teacher behaviours that tend to be associated with high levels of student learning. Effective teachers know how to use these behaviours and for what purposes they are best suited. The following sections address three important dimensions of positive learning environments: the caring classroom, the physical classroom environment, and classroom

Figure 7.1

Characteristics of Groups at Four Stages of Development

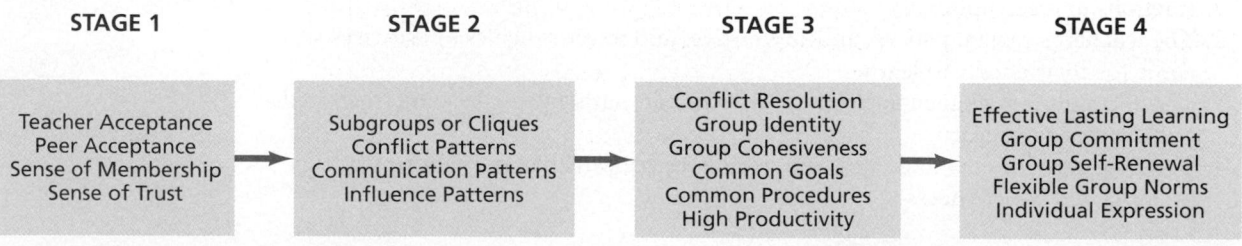

STAGE 1	STAGE 2	STAGE 3	STAGE 4
Teacher Acceptance Peer Acceptance Sense of Membership Sense of Trust	Subgroups or Cliques Conflict Patterns Communication Patterns Influence Patterns	Conflict Resolution Group Identity Group Cohesiveness Common Goals Common Procedures High Productivity	Effective Lasting Learning Group Commitment Group Self-Renewal Flexible Group Norms Individual Expression

organization, including procedures for grouping students for instruction and for managing time.

The Caring Classroom

At this point in your preparation to become a teacher, you may feel uncertain of your ability to create a positive classroom climate and to orchestrate the complex dynamics of the classroom so that you and your students become a cohesive, productive, and mutually supportive group. In your quest to achieve these aims, it will help to remember that an authentic spirit of caring is at the heart of an effective learning environment. "*[C]aring pedagogy* can . . . create or restore self confidence needed for participating in the positive learning opportunities in the classroom. It can also help form the moral foundation of responsible citizenship, productive community membership and leadership, and lifelong engagement in learning" (italics added) (Paul & Colucci 2000, 45).

How can you establish a **caring classroom**? First, you can demonstrate caring through your efforts to help all students learn to their fullest potential. You can learn as much as you can about your students' abilities and what motivates them to do their best. You should actually become a student of your students; as one Grade 10 student states, an effective teacher "[gets] to know all students well" (Harris Interactive 2001). You can also support student learning by encouraging and conveying appropriate—neither too high nor too low—expectations.

In addition, teachers should recognize that how they speak and listen to students determines the extent to which students believe they are cared about. In a synthesis of research on classroom environments that enhance students' learning, Herbert Walberg and Rebecca Greenberg (1997, 46) found that "students learn more when their classes are satisfying, challenging, and friendly and they have a voice in decision making. [When] classes are unfriendly, cliquish, and fragmented, they leave students feeling rejected and therefore impede learning." Table 7.1, based on Walberg and Greenberg's work, presents 15 dimensions of classroom life and how each influences students' learning at the junior and senior high levels.

While students learn best in caring classrooms, Nel Noddings has suggested they must also learn to care for others. Toward this end, she recommends reorganizing the school curriculum around "themes of care" and suggests that "all students should be engaged in a general education that guides them in caring for self, intimate others, global others, plants, animals, the environment, objects and instruments, and ideas" (2002, 99). In addition, Noddings asserts that "relations of care and trust should improve (or at least not hurt) achievement, [and] they also might contribute to greater safety, stronger social ties, better citizenship, and greater satisfaction for both teachers and students" (2007, 83).

The Physical Environment of the Classroom

When you become a teacher, the physical environment you work in will probably be similar to that of schools you attended. However, we encourage you, with the help of your students, to make your surroundings as safe, pleasant, and convenient as possible. Fresh air, plants, clean walls, displays of students' work, a comfortable reading or resource area, and a few prints or posters can enhance the quality of teacher–student relationships. Seating arrangements and the placement of other

Table 7.1

Fifteen Dimensions of the Classroom Environment

Dimension	Percent Positive Influence on Learning	Description
Satisfaction	100 (17)	Students enjoy classroom work and find it satisfying.
Challenge	87 (16)	Students find the work difficult and challenging.
Cohesiveness	86 (17)	Students know one another well and are helpful and friendly toward one another.
Physical Environment	85 (15)	Adequate books, equipment, space, and lighting are available.
Democracy	85 (14)	Students share equally in making decisions that affect the entire class.
Goal Direction	73 (15)	Learning goals are clear.
Competition	67 (9)	Competition among students is minimized.
Formality	65 (17)	Class is informal, with few rules to guide behaviour.
Speed	54 (14)	Students have sufficient time to finish their work.
Diversity	31 (14)	Students' interests differ and are provided for.
Apathy	14 (15)	Students don't care about what the class does.
Favouritism	10 (13)	All students do not enjoy the same privileges; the teacher has favourites.
Cliquishness	8 (13)	Certain students work only with close friends and refuse to interact with others.
Disorganization	6 (17)	Activities are disorganized and confusing, rather than well organized and efficient.
Friction	0 (17)	Tension and quarrelling among students characterize the classroom.

Note: Percent indicates the percentage of research studies that reported a positive influence on learning for that dimension; numbers in parentheses indicate number of research studies that investigated that dimension.

Source: Adapted from Herbert J. Walberg and Rebecca C. Greenberg, "Using the Learning Environment Inventory," *Educational Leadership*, May 1997, p. 47.

This kindergarten class exhibits some of the characteristics of a caring classroom climate.

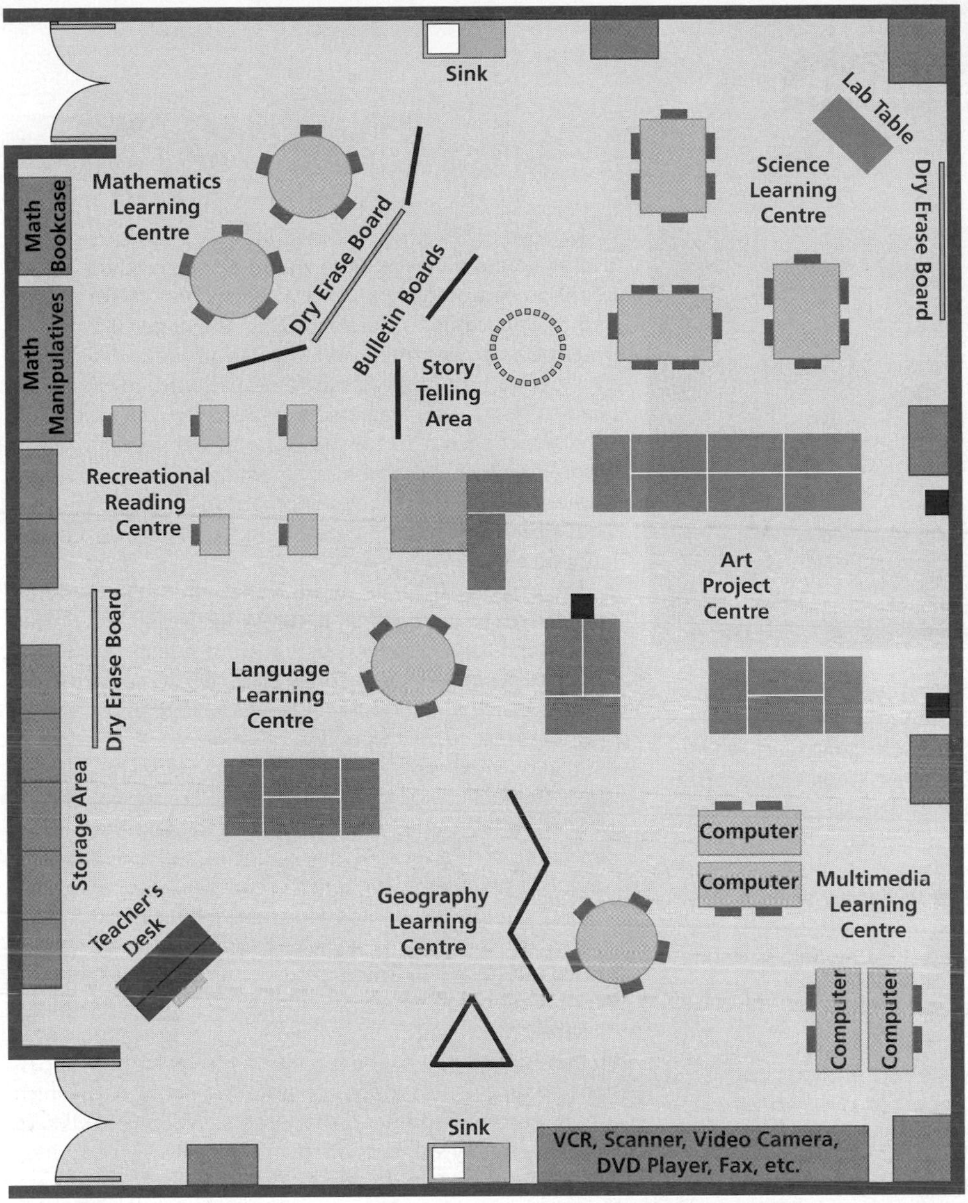

Figure 7.2

Learning centres in an elementary classroom

The labels visible in the figure include: Sink, Lab Table, Dry Erase Board, Science Learning Centre, Math Bookcase, Mathematics Learning Centre, Math Manipulatives, Bulletin Boards, Story Telling Area, Recreational Reading Centre, Dry Erase Board, Storage Area, Language Learning Centre, Art Project Centre, Computer, Computer, Multimedia Learning Centre, Teacher's Desk, Geography Learning Centre, Computer, Computer, Sink, VCR, Scanner, Video Camera, DVD Player, Fax, etc.

classroom furniture also do much to shape the classroom environment. Although seating by rows may be appropriate for whole-group instruction or examinations, other arrangements may be more beneficial for different activities. For example, you can enhance small-group activities by moving desks into small clusters in different parts of the room. Figure 7.2 shows the arrangement of a classroom at an exemplary elementary school. The room is designed to encourage students to learn through discovery at various learning centres.

However you design your classroom, take care to ensure that seating arrangements do not reduce the opportunity of some students to learn. For example, students in some classrooms receive more attention if they are seated in the "action zone"—the middle front-row seats and seats on the middle aisle. Teachers often stand near this area and unknowingly give students seated there more opportunities to speak.

Some teachers create opportunities to break down the walls of the traditional classroom and move the learning experience outside of the school. Consider teacher Shirley R. Turner, recipient of a 2009 Prime Minister's Award for Excellence in Teaching, who considers the great outdoors her classroom:

As teachers, our real challenge is to show our passion for learning and share it in a meaningful way with our students.—Shirley R. Turner

On an unfamiliar trail above the tree line, the summit came into view. We had only one short, steep leg of the path ahead of us to reach the viewpoint below Black Tusk, but, for some of the students, fatigue had overtaken the will to reach the top. I watched intently as two of my groups' strongest hikers dropped to the back together; they seemed to be moving as one force.

"C'mon," said one of these two young women, "We can make it together."

That day every student reached the summit. The student's words still resonate years later. For me this is the ultimate reward: seeing my students demonstrate their understanding that learning is a group effort.

I was attracted to British Columbia because of its outstanding natural beauty. During my work at an inner city school in Vancouver I slowly came to realize that many of my students, while surrounded by immense natural wilderness, had never actually experienced the wealth of learning experiences afforded by their own backyard. Although I am a seasoned recreational hiker in my personal life, having climbed Mount Kilimanjaro and kayaked BC's pristine waterways, this was the first time that I played with the idea, dare I say the need, for moving my classroom to the great outdoors.

My love of teaching is rooted in revealing new perspectives to young minds and the charm of watching the subsequent process of integration. I share my passion for physics and its application all around us in the hope of inspiring potential scientists to play creatively with new ideas. However, before I could share the wilderness with my students, I had to find a valid framework within which to work. This vehicle turned out to be the Duke of Edinburgh Awards Program, which incorporates community service, physical recreation, and life-skill development in a forum that provides a basis for working together in a consultative and collaborative way.

The process of communicating that which I know to be valid, while remaining open to new information, has been a cornerstone to my teaching over the last twenty years. As a teacher I role model the qualities that I seek to nurture in my students—an open, curious mind and a willingness to explore new ideas. My job is to provide a framework that supports them in building experience of a new environment and provide a foundation for taking new risks. I use the comfort of working with their peers in small groups to move them into a new frame of reference. Planning their expeditions together, we build from a single night in the backwoods to more challenging multiple day backpacking in alpine meadows.

As with the best of my classroom practices, this has turned out to be a learning experience for all of us, providing us with multiple opportunities to build understanding.

Rarely has the social construction of knowledge had a greater direct impact. There continue to be endless discussions about the best food and dickering about with which groups each will cook and share tents. Wherever it is safe practice, I let my students discover the best way to address their difficulties. I hold them accountable for their success. The wilderness dictates some of its own rules, and I supplement these minimally in an attempt to enhance the experience. One of the challenges for the students in this approach to learning is for students to shed their digital devices for the sole comfort of each other's company for a few days. Collectively the participants digest their new environment, support each other as they adapt themselves to new standards, and return home with a new appreciation of themselves and their urban lives.

In reaching out beyond themselves and their achievements as individuals to support each other in their collective quest for the success, students show each other their potential for greatness. In the classroom we share our understanding of our subject's perspective and create experiences to explore its facets.

As teachers, our real challenge is to show our passion for learning and share it in a meaningful way with our students. We need to fully engage our students in education while connecting with them in a way which is authentic and true to ourselves as teachers. Like the leaders from the hiking group, we need to be prepared to walk alongside them, be attentive to their process, willing to share our experience and, above all, patient enough to follow their steps with joy in our shared achievement. At the end of the day we can celebrate our achievements together as we contemplate a new panorama richer in possibilities for being shared with the whole group and more poignant with opportunity.

Shirley R. Turner is a secondary level teacher at Vancouver Technical School in British Columbia. As a recipient of a Prime Minister's Award for Excellence in Teaching in October 2009, Ms. Turner was recognized as a champion of science for students of all ability levels and for her work in developing outdoor adventures and community service. More information on Shirley Turner is available at www.ic.gc.ca/eic/site/pmate-ppmee.nsf/eng/wz01539.html.

Classroom Organization

A characteristic of positive learning environments is **classroom organization**—the way teachers and students are grouped for instruction, the way learning tasks are structured, and the way other resources are used. The following sections focus on these aspects of classroom organization.

Grouping Students by Ability

Two common approaches for grouping students on the basis of shared characteristics are between-class ability grouping, often called tracking, and within-class ability grouping. Students who attend schools where **between-class ability grouping** is practised are assigned to classes on the basis of ability or achievement. This system is not common in Canadian schools. Another form of between-class ability grouping, especially at the high school level, is based on students' goals after graduation. For example, many high schools offer honours classes or French immersion programs.

Research suggests that, for the most part, between-class ability grouping does not contribute to greater achievement (Good & Brophy 2008). Although supporters nevertheless claim that teachers are better able to meet the needs of students in homogeneous groupings, most Canadian schools employ heterogeneous grouping that includes students of varying abilities, including those who are gifted and other have special needs.

Within-class ability grouping is often used for instruction in reading and mathematics within a class, where a teacher instructs students in homogeneous, small groups. Within-class grouping is used widely in elementary classrooms. Perhaps you can recall learning to read in a small group with a name such as the Sparrows, the Robins, or the Blue Jays. Like tracking, within-class ability grouping can heighten preexisting differences in achievement between groups of students, especially if teachers give high-achieving groups more attention. Once students are grouped, they tend not to be regrouped, even when differences in achievement are reduced.

At best, evidence to support student groupings is mixed. Whether students are grouped on the basis of ability, curricular interests, or disabling conditions, there is a danger that some group labels can evoke negative expectations, causing teachers to underteach certain students and prompting their peers to isolate or reject them. The most serious consequence, of course, is that students so labelled are taught to feel inadequate, inferior, and limited in their options for growth.

Grouping Students for Cooperative Learning

Cooperative learning is an approach to teaching in which students work in small groups or teams, sharing work and helping one another complete assignments. Student-team-learning, for example, is a cooperative approach teachers use to increase the basic skills achievement of at-risk students. In cooperative learning arrangements, students are motivated to learn in small groups through rewards that are made available to the group as a whole as well as to individual members. Cooperative learning includes the following key elements:

- Small groups (four to six students) work together on learning activities.
- Assignments require that students help one another while working on a group project.
- In competitive arrangements, groups may compete against one another.
- Group members contribute to group goals according to their talents, interests, and abilities.

In addition, cooperative learning is an instructional method that can strengthen students' interpersonal skills. When students from different racial, ethnic, and cultural backgrounds and mainstreamed special-needs students all contribute to a common group goal, friendships increase and group members tend to view one another as more equal in status and worth.

Cooperative learning also enables students to learn a variety of roles and responsibilities. Erik Korporaal, a first-year teacher of Grades 4 and 5, explains his experience:

> I began by having my students work on simpler, shorter activities in teams of two. For instance, the small groups worked on math problems that they were already familiar with. I did this so that they could focus on working together rather than struggling to understand the problem. Gradually, I increased the difficulty of the tasks as well as the size of the groups. I reinforced positive behaviour and pointed out the types of interactions that led to successful groups. Over time students began to realize the sorts of interactions (e.g., effective communication, listening, delegation of responsibilities, and attention to each member's contributions) that needed to occur in order for their group to succeed. (Oaks & Lipton 2007, 193)

Delivering Instruction

The delivery of instruction is a key element in creating positive learning environments. What the teacher does and what students do have a powerful influence on learning and on the quality of classroom life. A common activity format in elementary schools consists of students doing seatwork on their own or listening to their teachers and participating in whole-class recitations. In addition, students participate in reading groups, games, and discussions; take tests; check work; view films; give reports; help clean up the classroom; and go on field trips.

A teacher must answer the question, "What activity will enable me to accomplish my instructional goals?" Teachers must realize that learning activities should meet students' goals; that is, the activities must be meaningful and authentic for students. **Authentic learning tasks** enable students to see the connections between classroom learning and the world beyond the classroom—both now and in the future.

To understand how authentic learning tasks can motivate students to learn, reflect on your own school experiences. Do you recall memorizing facts only because they would appear on a test? Did you ever wonder why a teacher asked you to complete a learning task? Did you ever feel that a teacher asked you to do busywork?

What kinds of learning tasks motivated you the most? How often were you involved in authentic learning activities such as the following?

- Giving oral reports based on research you conducted
- Writing an editorial for the school or local newspaper
- Representing the pro or con side in a debate
- Conducting an experiment and then writing the results
- Creating a model to illustrate a process, such as photosynthesis, a solar eclipse, or combustion in a gasoline engine
- Completing an art project and then participating in an art exhibit for the community
- Tutoring younger children in reading, mathematics, or science
- Developing a website to document an in-class project
- Creating an infomercial using video-editing software and then getting reactions from other classes in your school
- Developing a science WebQuest and then posting it for evaluation

A comprehensive nationwide study of successfully restructured schools reported that "authentic pedagogy" helps students to (1) "construct knowledge" through the use of higher-order thinking, (2) acquire "deep knowledge" (relatively complex understandings of subject matter), (3) engage in "substantive conversations" with teachers and peers, and (4) make connections between substantive knowledge and the world beyond the classroom (Newmann et al., 1996; Newmann & Wehlage, 1995).

Structuring the Use of Time

How teachers use time affects student learning. **Allocated time** is the time teachers allocate for instruction in various areas of the curriculum. Teachers vary widely in their use of time. Educational researchers Tom Good and Jere Brophy report, for example, that "some students [may receive] as much as four times more instructional time in a given subject than other students in the same grade" (Good & Brophy 2003, 29).

Researchers have shown that **time on task**—the amount of time students are actively engaged in learning activities—is directly related to learning. As anyone who has ever daydreamed while appearing to pay attention can confirm, time on task is difficult to measure. In response to this difficulty, researchers have introduced the concept of **academic learning time**—the amount of time a student spends working on academic tasks with a high level of success (80 percent or higher) Not surprisingly, learning time, like allocated time, varies greatly from classroom to classroom.

An additional concept that is proving useful in understanding teachers' use of time in the classroom is known as **opportunity to learn** (**OTL**). OTL is based on the premise that teachers should use time to provide all students with challenging content through appropriate instruction.

Some provincial departments of education have set specific minimum daily guidelines regarding how time should be used in classrooms. For example, the 2007 Nova Scotia Education Department document "Opportunity to Learn: Quantity of Instructional Time" outlines the provincial policy on the quantity of time that should be dedicated to specific programs, including guidelines on the use of instructional time. The entire document can be found at www.ednet.ns.ca/index.php?t=sub_pages&cat=741.

To increase the time available for active learning, many high schools have implemented block or semester scheduling arrangements. **Block scheduling** uses longer blocks of time for each class period, with fewer periods each day. Longer blocks of time allow more in-depth coverage of subject matter and lead to deeper understanding and higher-level applications. Block scheduling also gives teachers more time to present complex concepts and gives students more time to practice applying those concepts to authentic problems.

What Are the Keys to Successful Classroom Management?

For most new teachers, **classroom management** is a primary concern. How can you prevent discipline problems from arising and keep students productively engaged in learning activities? Effective classroom management cannot be reduced to a cookbook recipe. However, you can take definite steps to create an effective learning environment in your classroom.

Sound classroom management techniques are based on the guidelines for creating an effective learning environment presented earlier in the chapter: (1) creating a caring classroom, (2) organizing the physical classroom environment, (3) grouping students for instruction, (4) providing authentic learning tasks, and (5) structuring the use of time to maximize students' learning. Positive leadership and preventive planning are thus central to effective classroom management.

In addition, you should remember that classroom management refers to how teachers structure their learning environments to prevent or minimize behavioural problems. Discipline refers to the methods teachers use after students misbehave. Classroom management is prevention-oriented, while discipline is control-oriented. The goal of classroom management is to structure the classroom environment to maximize student attention and minimize disruptive behaviour.

Go to www.MyEducationLab.com and select the Managing to Teach tab. Click on the Navigator button in the lower left corner of the page and access Module 3 "Preventing and Preempting Problems Through Careful Planning" and go through the exercises embedded in Group Work.

The following strategies will help you create a well-managed classroom environment:

- Arrange classroom furniture so that you can easily monitor students' behaviour for signs of inattention, boredom, and misbehaviour from any point in the room.
- Arrange classroom furniture so that students can move from place to place without disturbing their classmates.
- Keep interesting instructional materials (for example, a replica of a human skeleton, a model of the solar system, or a large collection of insects) out of sight until you need to use them.
- Separate friends who tend to misbehave and get off-task when they are seated near one another, or separate students who dislike one another and are more likely to misbehave if they are seated too closely.
- Assign chronically misbehaving students to seats close to your desk.

The Democratic Classroom

Teachers who allow students to participate in making decisions about the physical classroom environment, classroom rules and procedures, modifications to the curriculum, and options for learning activities have fewer discipline problems. Students in **democratic classrooms** have more power and more responsibility than students in conventional classrooms. If students are to live in a democracy, they must learn to manage freedom responsibly; teachers model democracy by giving their students some choices and some control over classroom activities.

William Glasser, well-known psychiatrist and author of *Quality School* (1998a), *The Quality School Teacher* (1998b), *Choice Theory* (1998c), and (with Karen Dotson) *Choice Theory in the Classroom* (1998), recommends that teachers develop "quality" classrooms based on democratic principles. According to Glasser, many teachers struggle with classroom management because their actions are guided by stimulus-response theory. They try to coerce students through reward or punishment, or what many teachers term logical consequences. Instead, Glasser believes that teachers should establish "quality" environments in the classroom by following choice theory. Choice theory recognizes that human beings make choices that enable them to create "quality worlds" that satisfy four needs: the need to belong, the need for power, the need for freedom, and the need for fun.

From a choice theory perspective, misbehaviour in the classroom arises when students' learning experiences do not enable them to create quality worlds for themselves. Therefore, teachers "must give up bossing and turn to 'leading'" (Glasser 1997, 600). We follow leaders, Glasser says, because we believe they are concerned about our welfare. To persuade students to do quality schoolwork, teachers must establish warm, noncoercive relationships with students; teach students meaningful skills rather than ask them to memorize information; enable them to experience satisfaction and excitement by working in small teams; and move from teacher evaluation to student self-evaluation.

Creating a democratic classroom community is not easy, but the benefits can be significant—as the following comments from Janene Ashford, a first-year teacher of Grade 6, illustrate:

> As the year progressed, my students and I began to realize a democratic classroom community. It was an incredible and sometimes difficult evolution from a teacher-centered and controlled environment to a community created and strengthened by students. "Guess what the teacher wants" (under the guise of democracy) evolved into "What should we do?" under guidelines I determined, and then into "I can't/don't need to do it myself, what do you guys think we should do?" Over the next couple of months, my students and I developed and maintained a wonderfully strong community. (Oakes & Lipton 2007, 284)

Preventive Planning

Establishing Rules and Procedures

Successful classroom managers have carefully planned rules and procedures, which they teach early in the year using clear explanations, examples, and practice (Emmer & Evertson 2009; Evertson & Emmer 2009; Good & Brophy 2008). Your classroom rules should be clear, concise, reasonable, and few in number. For example, five general rules for elementary-age students might include: (1) be polite and helpful; (2) respect other people's property; (3) listen quietly while others are speaking; (4) do not hit, shove, or hurt others; and (5) obey all school rules (Evertson & Emmer 2009). Rules for the secondary level might stipulate the following: (1) bring all needed materials to class, (2) be in your seat and ready to work when the bell rings, (3) respect and be polite to everyone, (4) respect other people's property, (5) listen and stay seated while someone else is speaking, and (6) obey all school rules (Emmer & Evertson 2009).

It is important to enforce classroom rules consistently and fairly. "Consistency is a key reason why some rules are effective while others are not. Rules that are not enforced or not applied consistently over time result in a loss of prestige and respect for the person who has created the rules and has the responsibility for enforcing them" (Borich 2007, 174).

Procedures—the routines your students follow as they participate in learning activities—are also essential for smooth classroom functioning and minimizing opportunities for misbehaviour. How will homework be collected? How will supplies be distributed? How will housekeeping chores be completed? How will attendance be taken? How do students obtain permission to leave the classroom? Part of developing classroom rules and procedures is to decide what to do when students do not follow them. Students must be made aware of the consequences for failing to follow rules. For example, consequences for infractions can range from an expression of teacher disapproval to penalties such as loss of privileges, detention after school, disciplinary conference with a parent or guardian, or temporary separation from the group.

Organizing and Planning for Instruction

Organizing instructional time, materials, and activities so that classes run smoothly enables teachers to keep students engaged in learning, thereby reducing the need for discipline. Time spent planning authentic learning activities that are appropriate for students' needs, interests, and abilities provide the opportunity to enjoy the professional satisfaction that comes from having a well-managed classroom.

The following examples illustrate how one Grade 8 teacher began the school year by carefully organizing and planning for instruction. The teacher across the hall, however, was not as well organized; as a consequence, she is more likely to experience misbehaviour in her classroom as the year progresses.

> Donnell Alexander is waiting at the door for her eighth graders with prepared handouts as students come in the room. She distributes them and says, "Take your seats quickly, please. You'll find your name on the desk. The bell is going to ring in less than a minute and everyone needs to be at his or her desk and quiet when it does. Please read the handout while you're waiting." She is standing at the front of the room, surveying the class as the bell rings. When it stops, she begins, "Good morning, everyone."
>
> Vicki Williams, who also teaches eighth-graders across the hall from Donnell, is organizing her handouts as the students come in the room. Some take their seats while others mill around, talking in small groups. As the bell rings, she looks up and says over the hum of the students. "Everyone take your seats, please. We'll begin in a couple minutes," and she turns back to finish organizing her materials. (Eggen & Kauchak 2007, 380)

Go to www.MyEducationLab.com and select the Managing to Teach tab. Click on the Navigator button in the lower left corner of the page and access Module 3 "Preventing and Preempting Problems Through Careful Planning" and listen to the advice from Dale, Bruce, and Jane. Think about what they have to say about the importance of prior preparation and organization.

PEARSON
myeducationlab)

Effective Responses to Student Behaviour

When student misbehaviour does occur, effective teachers draw from a repertoire of problem-solving strategies. These strategies are based on their experience and common sense, their knowledge of students and the teaching–learning process, and their knowledge of human psychology. There are many structured approaches to classroom management; some are based on psychological theories of human motivation and behaviour, while others reflect various philosophical views regarding the purposes of education. None of these approaches, however, is appropriate for all situations or for all teachers or for all students, and the usefulness of a given method depends, in part, on the teacher's individual personality, leadership style, and ability to analyze the complex dynamics of classroom life. In addition, what works should not be the only criterion for evaluating structured or "packaged" approaches to discipline; what students are taught about their self-worth, acting responsibly, and solving problems is also important (Curwin & Mendler 1988; 1989).

Severity of Misbehaviour

Your response to student misbehaviour will depend, in part, on whether an infraction is mild, moderate, or severe and whether it is occurring for the first time or is part of a pattern of chronic misbehaviours. For example, a student who throws a wad of paper at another student might receive a warning for the first infraction, while another student who repeatedly throws objects might receive an after-school detention. Definitions of the severity of misbehaviour vary from school to school and from province to province.

Constructive Assertiveness

The effectiveness of your responses to students' misbehaviour depends on your ability to use constructive assertiveness (Emmer & Evertson 2009; Evertson & Emmer 2009). Constructive assertiveness "lies on a continuum of social response between aggressive, overbearing pushiness and timid, ineffectual, or submissive responses that allow some students to trample on the teacher's and other students' rights. Assertiveness skills allow you to communicate to students that you are serious about teaching and about maintaining a classroom in which everyone's rights are respected" (Emmer & Evertson 2009; Evertson & Emmer 2009). Communication based on constructive assertiveness is not hostile, sarcastic, defensive, or vindictive; it is clear, firm, and concise. Constructive assertiveness includes three basic elements:

- A direct, clear statement of the problem
- Body language that is unambiguous (for example, direct eye contact with students, erect posture, and facial expressions that are congruent with the content and tone of corrective statements)
- Firm, unwavering insistence on correct behaviour

Lee Cantor developed an approach to discipline based on teacher assertiveness. The approach calls on teachers to establish firm, clear guidelines for student behaviour and to follow through with consequences. Cantor (1989, 58) remarks on how he arrived at the ideas behind assertive discipline: "I found that, above all, the master teachers were assertive; that is, they taught students how to behave. They established clear rules for the classroom, they communicated those rules to the students, and they taught students how to follow them." **Assertive discipline** requires teachers to do the following:

1. Make clear that they will not tolerate anyone preventing them from teaching, stopping learning, or doing anything else that is not in the best interest of the class, the individual, or the teacher.
2. Instruct students clearly and in specific terms about what behaviours are desired and what behaviours are not tolerated.
3. Plan positive and negative consequences for predetermined acceptable or unacceptable behaviours.
4. Plan positive reinforcement for compliance. Reinforcement includes verbal acknowledgment, notes, free time for talking, and, of course, tokens that can be exchanged for appropriate rewards.
5. Plan a sequence of steps to punish noncompliance. These range from writing a youngster's name on the board to sending the student to the principal's office. (MacNaughton & Johns 1991, 53)

Research on the effectiveness of assertive discipline is mixed. "Substantial evidence indicates that giving rewards for good behaviour can actually diminish students' intrinsic motivation to learn or to conform to the social norms of the classroom" (Oakes & Lipton 2007, 258). In the following, Javier Espindola, a first-year kindergarten teacher, explains why he eventually decided not to use assertive discipline:

> When my students were sitting quietly and listening to me or when they were on task writing in their journals, I would give them a sticker or happy face to motivate them to continue that behaviour. When I saw them talking with peers and not working, I would put their names on the board or give them a sad face.

> At first, these strategies worked. Over time, however, I noticed negative effects. Students . . . began to refuse to follow classroom directions, work productively, and respect and listen to their peers and me if they did not receive any rewards.

> The first step in removing Assertive Discipline from my classroom was discussing it with my students. I told them that they were no longer going to receive happy faces, stars, stickers, and candies when they were behaving and performing well or consequences such as check marks, sad faces, or names on the board when they were behaving inappropriately. I removed from the chalkboard the chart where I posted check marks when students misbehave and stars when they behave well . . .

> I no longer feel the need to have complete control of my students. I have implemented group activities that encourage my students to interact, share experiences, and work with their peers . . . everyone is capable of improving his or her academic and social skills in a comfortable environment. (Oakes & Lipton 2007, 260)

Go to www.MyEducationLab.com and select the Managing to Teach tab. Click on the Navigator button in the lower left corner of the page and access Module 4 "Positive Personal Interactions by Exhibiting Modes of Behaviour" and check out the classroom scenarios on curiosity, teacher judgment, and defiance.

Teacher Problem Solving

When a teacher's efforts to get a student to stop misbehaving are unsuccessful, a problem-solving conference with the student is warranted. A problem-solving conference may give the teacher additional understanding of the situation, thus paving the way for a solution. A conference can also help the teacher and student understand one another's perceptions and begin to build a more positive relationship.

The goal of a problem-solving conference is for the student to accept responsibility for his or her behaviour and make a commitment to change it. While there is no "right way" to conduct a problem-solving conference, Glasser's **"choice theory"** lends itself to a conferencing procedure that is flexible and appropriate for most situations.

Students will usually make good choices (such as behaving in an acceptable manner) if they experience success and know that teachers care about them. The following steps are designed to help misbehaving students see that the choices they make may not lead to the results they want.

1. Have the misbehaving student evaluate and take responsibility for his or her actions. Often, a good first step is for the teacher to ask, "What are you doing?" and then, "Is it helping you?"
2. Have the student make a plan for a more acceptable way of behaving. If necessary, the student and the teacher brainstorm solutions. Agreement is reached on how the student will behave in the future and the consequences for failure to follow through.
3. Require the student to make a commitment to follow the plan.

4. Don't accept excuses for failure to follow the plan.
5. Don't use punishment or react to a misbehaving student in a punitive manner. Instead, point out to the student that there are logical consequences for failure to follow the plan.
6. Don't give up on the student. If necessary, remind the student of his or her commitment to desirable behaviour. Periodically ask how things are going.

Focus on Research
through Experience

Facilitating Effective Whole Class Discussion

Teacher: Alexis Juurlink, Grade 8 Healthy Living

Action Research is a framework that guides the energies of teachers toward an understanding of why, when, and how students become better learners. This form of inquiry can provide a rich opportunity for reflection on practice and it can contribute to ongoing professional development.

One such project was carried out by teacher Alexis Juurlink in her Grade 8 Healthy Living class. It started with baseline data collection that identified a problem with some students' disruptive behaviour, including speaking out and moving around the room at inappropriate times, negatively affecting whole-class discussions. Teacher-directed whole-class discussions are an important part of the Healthy Living class for clarifying instructions for assignments, reviewing curriculum material, and providing students with opportunities to share their thoughts. This prompted Alexis to ask, "What are some instructional strategies for decreasing students' disruptive behaviour during whole-class discussions with middle school students?"

A review of current literature was undertaken to examine strategies and methods that Alexis could implement with her class to facilitate more effective whole-class discussions. The literature emphasized the potential value of explicit teaching of social skills, student self-monitoring, and positive reinforcement of behaviour using a school wide initiative called Positive Effective Behaviour Supports (PEBS).

Alexis crafted three solution strategies that included:

- social skills lessons on attentive listening using role play and discussion
- increasing positive reinforcement through PEBS hi-notes and verbal praise
- student self-monitoring of attentive listening during whole-class discussions

It was determined that during solution-skills implementation, data would be collected using:

- student self-monitoring of appropriate behaviour (focus areas included raising hands to speak, listening quietly, focusing on speaker)
- teacher observation journal
- tally of disruptive student behaviour by an educational assistant

Alexis concluded that it was unclear which of the solution strategies had the greatest impact on student behaviour and notes that variables such as a new seating arrangement and schedule changes may have influenced the results. However, the data seemed to indicate a decrease in disruptive behaviour following implementation. She plans to disseminate her action research with other teachers in her middle school, particularly those who had indicated similar problems during whole-class discussions.

Alexis Juurlink is a classroom teacher and part-time program support teacher in a small rural school in the Chignecto Central School Board in Nova Scotia.

Developing Your Own Approach to Classroom Management

No approach to classroom management is effective with all students at all times. How you respond to misbehaviour in your classroom will depend on your personality, value system, and beliefs about children, and will range along a continuum from the "minimum power" of giving students nonverbal cues to the "maximum power" of physical intervention.

Classroom management expert Charles Wolfgang asserts that teachers usually present one of three "faces" (or attitudes) to students who misbehave:

1. The relationship-listening "face" involves the use of minimum power. This reflects a view that the student has the capabilities to change his or her own behaviour, and that if the student is misbehaving, it is because of inner emotional turmoil, flooded behaviour, or feelings of inner inadequacy.
2. The confronting-contracting "face" is one of "I am the adult. I know misbehaviour when I see it and will confront the student to stop this behaviour. I will grant the student the power to decide how he or she will change, and encourage and contract with the student to live up a mutual agreement for behavioural change."
3. The rules and consequences "face" is one that communicates an attitude of "This is the rule and behaviour that I want and I will set out assertively to get this action." (Wolfgang 2001, 4–5)

In your journey toward becoming a professional teacher, you will develop a repertoire of strategies for classroom management; then, when you encounter a discipline problem in the classroom, you can analyze the situation and respond with an effective strategy. The ability to do so will give you confidence, as illustrated by these comments made to the authors by a beginning teacher:

> I went into the classroom with some confidence and left with lots of confidence. I felt good about what was going on. I established a comfortable rapport with the kids and was more relaxed. Each week I grew more confident. When you first go in you are not sure how you'll do. When you know you are doing OK, your confidence improves.

myeducationlab

Go to www.MyEducationLab.com and select the Managing to Teach tab. Click on the Navigator button in the lower left corner of the page and access Module 4 "Positive Personal Interaction by Exhibiting Modes of Behaviour." Take the Classroom Management Style Profile and reflect on the results.

What Teaching Methods Do Effective Teachers Use?

Beliefs about teaching and learning, students, knowledge, and what is worth knowing influence the instructional methods a teacher uses. In addition, variables such as the teacher's style, learners' characteristics, the culture of the school and surrounding community, and the resources available influence the methods you use. A model of teaching provides rules of thumb to follow to create a particular kind of learning environment. As the authors of *Models of Teaching* point out, "[m]odels of teaching are really models of learning. As we help students acquire information, ideas, skills, values, ways of thinking, and means of expressing themselves, we are also teaching them how to learn" (Joyce, Weil, & Calhoun 2008, 7). Table 7.2 presents brief descriptions of four widely used models of teaching.

Effective teachers use a repertoire of teaching models and assessment strategies, depending on their situations and the goals and objectives they wish to attain. Your teaching strategies in the classroom will most likely be eclectic—that is, a combination of several models and assessment techniques. As you gain classroom experience and acquire new skills and understanding, your personal model of teaching will evolve, enabling you to respond appropriately to a wider range of teaching situations.

Table 7.2

Four Instructional Models

	Goals and Rationale	Methods
Cooperative Learning	Students can be motivated to learn by working cooperatively in small groups if rewards are made available to the group as a whole and to individual members of the group.	■ Small groups (four to six students) work together on learning activities. ■ Assignments require that students help one another while working on a group project. ■ In competitive arrangements, groups may compete against one another. ■ Group members contribute to group goals according to their talents, interests, and abilities.
Theory into Practice	Teachers make decisions in three primary areas: content to be taught, how students will learn, and the behaviours the teacher will use in the classroom. The effectiveness of teaching is related to the quality of decisions the teacher makes in these areas.	The teacher follows seven steps in the classroom: ■ Orients students to material to be learned ■ Tells students what they will learn and why it is important ■ Presents new material that consists of knowledge, skills, or processes students are to learn ■ Models what students are expected to do ■ Checks for student understanding ■ Gives students opportunity for practice under the teacher's guidance ■ Makes assignments that give students opportunity to practise what they have learned on their own
Behaviour Modification	Teachers can shape student learning by using various forms of enforcement. Human behaviour is learned, and behaviours that are positively reinforced (rewarded) tend to increase and those that are not reinforced tend to decrease.	■ Teacher begins by presenting stimulus in the form of new material. ■ The behaviour of students is observed by the teacher. ■ Appropriate behaviours are reinforced by the teacher as quickly as possible.
Nondirective Teaching	Learning can be facilitated if teachers focus on personal development of students and create opportunities for students to increase their self-understanding and self-concepts. The key to effective teaching is the teacher's ability to understand students and to involve them in a teaching–learning partnership.	■ Teacher acts as a facilitator of learning. ■ Teacher creates learning environments that support personal growth and development. ■ Teacher acts in the role of a counsellor who helps students to understand themselves, clarify their goals, and accept responsibility for their behaviour.

Methods Based on Learning New Behaviours

Many teachers use instructional methods that have emerged from our greater understanding of how people acquire or change their behaviours. **Direct instruction,** for example, is a systematic instructional method that focuses on the transmission of knowledge and skills from the teacher (and the curriculum) to the student. Direct instruction is organized on the basis of observable learning behaviours and the actual products of learning. Generally, direct instruction is most appropriate for step-by-step knowledge acquisition and basic skill development, but is not appropriate for teaching less structured, higher-order skills such as writing, the analysis of social issues, and problem solving.

Extensive research was conducted in the 1970s and 1980s on the effectiveness of direct instruction (Gagné 1974; 1977; Good & Grouws 1979; Rosenshine 1988; Rosenshine & Stevens 1986). The following eight steps are a synthesis of research on direct instruction and may be used with students ranging in age from elementary to senior high school.

1. Orient students to the lesson by telling them what they will learn.
2. Review previously learned skills and concepts related to the new material.
3. Present new material, using examples and demonstrations.
4. Assess students' understanding by asking questions; correct misunderstandings.
5. Allow students to practise new skills or apply new information.
6. Provide feedback and corrections as students practice.
7. Include newly learned material in homework.
8. Review material periodically.

A direct instruction method called **mastery learning** is based on two assumptions about learning: (1) virtually all students can learn material if given enough time and taught appropriately, and (2) students learn best when they participate in a structured, systematic program of learning that enables them to progress in small, sequenced steps (Carroll 1963; Bloom 1981). Mastery learning includes the following:

1. Set objectives and standards for mastery.
2. Teach content directly to students.
3. Provide corrective feedback to students on their learning.
4. Provide additional time and help in correcting errors.
5. Follow a cycle of teaching, testing, reteaching, and retesting.

In mastery learning, students take diagnostic tests and are then guided to complete corrective exercises or activities to improve their learning. These may take the form of programmed instruction, workbooks, computer drill and practice, or educational games. After the corrective lessons, students are given another test and are more likely to achieve mastery.

Methods Based on Child Development

As you learned in Chapter 6, children move through stages of cognitive, psychosocial, and moral development. Effective instruction includes methods that are developmentally appropriate, meet students' diverse learning needs, and recognize the importance of learning that occurs in social contexts. For example, one way that students reach higher levels of development is to observe and then imitate their parents, teachers, and peers, who act as models. "Modeling provides students with specific demonstrations of working with the content. . . . The teacher explicitly demonstrates how the students can be successful in the lesson" (Dell'Olio & Donk 2007, 79).

Effective teachers use **modelling** by thinking out loud and following three basic steps: (1) demonstrating to students the thinking involved in a task, (2) making students aware of the thinking involved, and (3) focusing students on applying the thinking. In this way, teachers can help students become aware of their learning processes and enhance their ability to learn. "For example, as a teacher demonstrates cutting out a construction paper square to serve as a math manipulative during the next lesson, she might 'think out loud' in class, saying, 'I am cutting this square very carefully because we will be using it today to create fractional shapes. I need the sides of my square to be very neat. My smaller, fraction pieces should be accurate in size'" (Dell'Olio & Donk 2007, 80).

These students are building on prior knowledge and using inquiry to acquire new knowledge. What kinds of learning activities require students to use their cognitive abilities in this way?

Since the mid-1980s, several educational researchers have examined how learners construct understanding of new material. "Constructivist views of learning, therefore, focus on how learners make sense of new information—how they construct meaning based on what they already know" (Parkay, Anctil, & Hass 2006, 168). Teachers with this view focus on students' thinking about the material being learned and, through carefully orchestrated cues, prompts, and questions, help students arrive at a deeper understanding of the material. The common elements of **constructivist teaching** include the following:

- The teacher elicits students' prior knowledge of the material and uses this as the starting point for instruction.
- The teacher not only presents material to students but also responds to students' efforts to learn the material. While teaching, the teacher must learn about students' learning.
- Students not only absorb information but also actively use that information to construct meaning.
- The teacher creates a social milieu within the classroom, a community of learners that allows students to reflect and talk with one another as they construct meaning and solve problems.

Constructivist teachers provide students with support, or **scaffolding**, as they learn new material. By observing the child and listening carefully to what he or she says, the teacher provides encouragement, suggestions, or other assistance to guide the student's learning efforts. The teacher varies the amount of support given on the basis of the student's understanding—if the student understands little, the teacher gives more support; conversely, the teacher gives progressively less support as the student's understanding becomes more evident. Overall, the teacher provides just enough scaffolding to enable the student to "discover" the material on his or her own.

The concept of scaffolding is based on the work of L. S. Vygotsky, a well-known Soviet psychologist. Vygotsky (1978; 1986) coined the term zone of proximal development to refer to the point at which students need assistance to continue learning. The effective teacher is sensitive to the student's *zone of proximal development* and ensures that instruction neither exceeds the student's current level of understanding nor underestimates the student's ability.

Methods Based on the Thinking Process

Some instructional methods are derived from the mental processes involved in learning, thinking, remembering, problem solving, and creativity. **Information processing,** for example, is a branch of cognitive science concerned with how people use their long- and short-term memory to access information and solve problems. The computer is often used as an analogy for information processing views of learning:

> Like the computer, the human mind takes in information, performs operations on it to change its form and content, stores the information, retrieves it when needed, and generates responses to it. Thus, processing involves gathering and representing information, or encoding; holding information, or storage; and getting at the information when needed, or retrieval. The whole system is guided by control processes that determine how and when information will flow through the system. (Woolfolk 2007, 250)

Although several systematic approaches to instruction are based on information processing—teaching students how to memorize, how to think inductively or deductively, how to acquire concepts, or how to use the scientific method, for example—they all focus on how people acquire and use information (see Table 7.3). Psychologists have identified three types of memory stores used in information processing:

1. Sensory memory—information stored briefly until it can be processed by the information-processing system; sensory memory retains information for about one second for vision and two to four seconds for hearing (Leahey & Harris 2001; Pashler & Carrier 1996).
2. Working memory—holds information while a person processes it; working memory is the conscious part of our information-processing system.
3. Long-term memory—a permanent store of information; working memory is limited to about seven items of information for a few seconds; however, long-term memory is vast and may remain for a lifetime (Schunk 2004).

In **inquiry learning** and **discovery learning**, students are given opportunities to inquire into subjects so that they "discover" knowledge for themselves. When teachers ask students to go beyond information in a text to make inferences, draw conclusions, or form generalizations, and when teachers do not answer students' questions, preferring instead to have students develop their own answers, they are using methods based on inquiry and discovery learning. These methods are best suited for teaching concepts, relationships, and theoretical abstractions, and for having students formulate and test hypotheses. The following example shows how inquiry and discovery learning in a Grade 1 classroom fostered a high level of student involvement and thinking.

> The children are gathered around a table on which a candle and jar have been placed. The teacher, Jackie Wiseman, lights the candle and, after it has burned brightly for a minute or two, covers it carefully with the jar. The candle grows dim, flickers, and goes out. Then she produces another candle and a larger jar, and the exercise is repeated. The candle goes out, but more slowly. Jackie produces two more candles and jars of different sizes, and the children light the candles, place the jars over them, and the flames slowly go out. "Now we're going to develop some ideas about what has just happened," she says. "I want you to ask me questions about those candles and jars and what you just observed." (Joyce, Weil, & Calhoun 2004, 3)

Methods Based on Peer-Mediated Instruction

Student peer groups can be a deterrent to academic performance (Sternberg, Dornbusch, & Brown 1996), but they can also motivate students to excel. Because school learning occurs in a social setting, **peer-mediated instruction** provides teachers with

Table 7.3

Applying an Understanding of Memory Stores in Your Classroom

Sensory Memory

1. To keep students from losing a sensory memory trace, give them a chance to attend to one stimulus before presenting a second one.

   - **Elementary:** A second-grade teacher asks one question at a time and gets an answer before asking a second question.
   - **Middle school:** A pre-algebra teacher displays two problems on the overhead and waits until students have copied them before she starts talking.
   - **High school:** In a geography lesson, a teacher places a map on the overhead and says, "I'll give you a minute to examine the geography of the countries on this map in the front of the room. Then we'll go on."

Working Memory

2. To avoid overloading students' working memories, conduct lessons with questioning.

   - **Elementary:** A first-grade teacher gives students directions for seatwork by presenting them slowly and one at a time. He asks different students to repeat the directions before he has them begin.
   - **Middle school:** A teacher in a woodworking class begins by saying, "The hardness and density of wood from the same kind of tree vary, depending on the amount of rainfall the tree has received and how fast it grows." Then, she waits a moment, holds up two pieces of wood, and says, "Look at these wood pieces. What do you notice about the rings on them?"
   - **High school:** An Algebra II teacher walks students through the solution to problems by having a different student describe each succeeding step to the solution.

3. Provide frequent practice to develop automaticity, and present information in both verbal and visual forms.

   - **Elementary:** A first-grade teacher has his students practice their writing by composing two sentences each day about an event of the previous evening.
   - **Middle school:** To capitalize on the dual-processing capability of working memory, an eighth-grade history teacher prepares a flowchart of the events that led up to the Revolutionary War. As she questions the students about the topic, she refers to the flowchart for each important point and encourages students to use the chart to organize their note taking.
   - **High school:** As a physics teacher discusses the relationship between force and acceleration, he demonstrates by pulling a cart along the desktop with a constant force so the students can see that the cart accelerates.

Long-Term Memory

4. To develop schemas, encourage students to explore relationships between ideas, and between new ideas and prior understanding.

   - **Elementary:** During story time, a second-grade teacher asks students to explain how the events in a story contribute to the conclusion.
   - **Middle school:** In developing the rules for solving equations by substitution, an algebra teacher asks, "How does this process compare to what we did when we solved equations by addition? What do we do differently? Why?"
   - **High school:** To help his students understand cause-and-effect relationships in their study of ancient Greece, a world history teacher asks questions such as: "Why was shipping so important in ancient Greece?" "Why was Troy's location so important, and how does its location relate to the location of today's big cities?" and "Why did Greek city-states exist (instead of larger nation-states)?"

options for increasing students' learning. Cooperative learning, described earlier in the chapter, is an example of peer-mediated instruction. Another example is **group investigation**, in which the teacher's role is to create an environment that allows students to determine what they will study and how. Students are presented with a situation to which they "react and discover basic conflicts among their attitudes, ideas, and modes of perception. On the basis of this information, they identify the problem to be investigated, analyze the roles required to solve it, organize themselves to take these roles, act, report, and evaluate these results" (Thelen 1960, 82).

The teacher's role in group investigation is multifaceted; he or she is an organizer, guide, resource person, counsellor, and evaluator. The method is very effective in increasing student achievement (Sharan & Sharan 1989/90, 17–21), positive attitudes toward learning, and the cohesiveness of the classroom group. The model also allows students to inquire into problems that interest them and enables each student to make a meaningful, authentic contribution to the group's effort based on his or her experiences, interests, knowledge, and skills.

Other common forms of peer-mediated instruction include peer tutoring and cross-age tutoring. In **peer-tutoring** arrangements, students are tutored by other pupils in the same class or the same grade. **Cross-age tutoring** involves, for example, Grade 6 students tutoring Grade 2 students in reading. Research clearly shows that, with proper orientation and training, cross-age tutoring can greatly benefit both "teacher" and learner (Henriques 1997; Schneider & Barone 1997; Utay & Utay 1997; Zukowski 1997). Pilot programs pairing students at risk of dropping out of school with younger children and with special-needs students have proved especially successful.

What Are Some Characteristics of Effective Teaching?

The outcomes of effective teaching are relatively easy to enumerate: (1) Students acquire an understanding of the subject at hand; (2) they can apply what they have learned to new situations; and (3) they have a desire to continue learning. However, if we wish to identify the characteristics of effective teaching, we find ourselves confronted with a more difficult task.

What do effective teachers do when they teach? How do they communicate with students? How do they manage classroom activities? What models of teaching do they use? As the previous discussions of classroom cultures, learning environments, classroom management, and teaching methods suggest, answers to questions such as these are not easy to formulate. However, one broad, helpful view of the characteristics that underlie all effective teaching is the "Framework for Teaching," developed as part of the Praxis Series: Professional Assessments for Beginning Teachers. According to the Praxis framework, teachers must be proficient in four domains: planning and preparation, structuring classroom environment, instruction, and professional responsibilities. Teachers must be effective in these domains while taking into account individual, developmental, and cultural differences among students and differences among subjects.

Go to www.MyEducationLab.com and select the Managing to Teach tab. Click on the Navigator button in the lower left corner of the page and access Module 4 "Positive Personal Interaction by Exhibiting Modes of Behaviour." Choose the Effective Teaching Approaches page and go through the exercise. Then view the video of a physical education teacher demonstrating the cornerstones of effective classroom management. Reflect on how this class reflects many of the principles and practices outlined in Chapter 7.

PEARSON
myeducationlab

SUMMARY

What Determines the Culture of the Classroom?

- From seating arrangements to classroom rules and procedures to the content and relevance of the curriculum, teachers make many decisions that influence the culture of the classroom.

- Classroom climate refers to the atmosphere or quality of life in a classroom. The climates established by high-performing teachers are characterized by a productive, task-oriented focus; group cohesiveness; open, warm relationships between teacher and students; cooperative, respectful interactions among students; low levels of tension, anxiety, and conflict; humour; high expectations; and frequent opportunities for student input regarding classroom activities.

How Can You Create a Positive Learning Environment?

- An important element of a positive learning environment is a caring classroom climate. Teachers show care for students by providing support, structure, and appropriate expectations.

- The physical environment of a classroom—seating arrangements and the placement of other classroom furniture, for example—can make a positive contribution to students' learning.

- Classroom organization (how students are grouped for instruction and how time is used) is an important element of the effective learning environment. Among the patterns for organizing classrooms are grouping students by ability, grouping students for cooperative learning, using activity formats based on authentic learning tasks, and using time to maximize students' learning.

What Are the Keys to Successful Classroom Management?

- The key to successful classroom management is preventing problems before they occur. Teachers who prevent problems foster effective, harmonious interpersonal interactions, understand how their leadership style influences students, and facilitate the development of a cohesive and supportive classroom group.

- Teachers who establish a democratic classroom climate, which allows students to participate in making decisions, rules and procedures, curriculum materials, and learning activities, have fewer discipline problems.

- When management problems occur, effective teachers use a repertoire of problem-solving skills based on experience, common sense, and understanding of the teaching–learning process. Regardless of the management strategy used, effective teachers base their response to problems on three elements of "constructive assertiveness": a clear statement of the problem or concern, unambiguous body language, and a firm, unwavering insistence on appropriate behaviour.

What Teaching Methods Do Effective Teachers Use?

- Although it is difficult to identify all the skills teachers need, research indicates that effective teachers use a repertoire of models of teaching based on students' learning behaviours, child development, the thinking process, and peer mediation.

- Direct instruction and mastery learning are based on the view that learning is the acquisition of new behaviours.

- Modelling, constructivism, and scaffolding are based primarily on an understanding of how students construct meaning as they learn new material.

- Information processing, inquiry learning, and discovery learning are based on our understanding of the cognitive processes involved in learning.

- Peer-mediated instruction, which views learning as taking place in social situations, includes cooperative learning, group investigation, and peer- and cross-age tutoring.

What are Some Characteristics of Effective Teaching?

- Effective teaching focuses on outcomes—the results of teaching.
- "Framework for Teaching" is a broad view of the characteristics underlying effective teaching. The four domains include:

  1. Planning and preparation
  2. The classroom environment
  3. Instruction
  4. Professional responsibilities

KEY TERMS AND CONCEPTS

academic learning time, 213
allocated time, 213
assertive discipline, 217
authentic learning tasks, 212
between-class ability
    grouping, 211
block scheduling, 213
caring classroom, 207
choice theory, 218
classroom climate, 203
classroom management, 214

classroom organization, 211
constructivist teaching, 223
cooperative learning, 212
cross-age tutoring, 226
democratic classrooms, 214
direct instruction, 221
discovery learning, 224
group investigation, 226
information processing, 224
inquiry learning, 224
mastery learning, 222

modelling, 222
opportunity to learn
    (OTL), 213
peer-mediated
    instruction, 224
peer-tutoring, 226
scaffolding, 223
time on task, 213
within-class ability
    grouping, 211

APPLICATIONS AND ACTIVITIES

Teacher's Journal

1. Recall the teachers and classmates you had during your school career. Select one class and analyze its group processes in terms of the stages of group development discussed in this chapter. What stage of development was reached by the group near the end of the school year? What conditions facilitated or impeded the development of this group?

2. Describe the "ideal" physical classroom environment for you. How would the seating arrangement facilitate the attainment of your instructional goals and objectives? How would you involve students in arranging the classroom?

3. Describe your leadership style as it relates to classroom management. In which aspects of leadership and classroom management do you feel most and least confident? What might you do, or what skills might you acquire, to strengthen your effectiveness in areas you feel you lack confidence? Develop your ideas into a statement of professional goals.

Theory into Practice

Safe School Initiatives

1. In groups of four to six, research a safe school initiative designed to encourage school-wide positive behaviour. Two examples are Positive Effective Behaviour Support (PEBS) and the League of Peaceful Schools.

   Find a description of a Canadian school board that has implemented PEBS at www.cbv.ns.ca/pebs.

   Find a description of the League of Peaceful Schools at www.leagueofpeacefulschools.ednet.ns.ca.

2. As a group, choose one safe school initiative that seems to hold promise. Present an overview of the initiative to the class, including a rationale for its adoption and its obvious benefits to a school. Each group must be prepared to defend its choice.

3. During group presentations, the rest of the class will be encouraged to find any potential difficulties and challenges faced by a school planning to implement the initiative. After each presentation, the group will field questions from the rest of the class regarding their choice of safe school initiative.

4. After all the groups have presented their choices, the class will act as a school staff and vote on the adoption of one plan.

5. Each class member will write a short paper on how this initiative would look in his or her classroom.

Teacher's Database

1. Visit the websites of three or more of the following research publications. These journals focus on educational research, learning theories, student and teacher attitudes and behaviours, and the effectiveness of teaching methods. Some journals especially emphasize the implications of educational psychology theory and research for policy-making and application to teaching practice. Note the kinds of studies and research topics each selected journal reports. How might articles in these journals help you as an education major? As a classroom teacher? As a teaching professional?

   Cognition and Instruction
   Contemporary Educational Psychology
   Educational Psychologist
   Educational Psychology Review
   Educational Researcher
   Journal of Educational Psychology
   Review of Research in Education

Journal of Teaching and Teacher Education
Social Psychology of Education
Review of Educational Research

Observations and Interviews

1. Observe several teachers at the level for which you are preparing to teach and try to identify the teaching methods they are using as part of their instructional repertoires.

2. Interview a classroom teacher about the assessment of students' learning. How do the assessment methods used by this teacher relate to his or her goals and objectives? To what extent does the teacher use authentic assessments?

Professional Portfolio

1. Prepare a poster depicting a classroom arrangement appropriate for the subject area and grade level for which you are preparing to teach. The poster should indicate the seating arrangement and location of other classroom furniture. In addition, make a list of classroom rules that will be posted in the room. You may wish to organize the rules according to the following categories.

   - Rules related to academic work
   - Rules related to classroom conduct
   - Rules that must be communicated on your first teaching day
   - Rules that can be communicated later

2. Prepare a flow chart depicting routine activities for a typical day. This chart could include procedures for the following:

   - Handling attendance, tardy slips, and excuses
   - Distributing materials
   - Turning in homework
   - Doing seatwork or various in-class assignments
   - Forming small groups for cooperative learning activities
   - Returning materials and supplies at the end of class

MyEducationLab

Visit the Managing to Teach tab at www.MyEducationLab.com to browse a virtual learning resource for classroom management based on three cornerstones: prior preparation, establishing constructive expectations, and exhibiting desired modes of behaviour.

8

Developing and
Implementing the
Curriculum

An educator is entrusted with the
most serious work that confronts
humankind: the development of
curricula that enable new generations
to contribute to the growth of human
beings and society.
—William H. Schubert
*Curriculum: Perspective, Paradigm, and
Possibility*

focus
questions

1. What is taught in schools?
2. How is a school curriculum developed?
3. What are some current content-area trends?

As a beginning teacher, you are attending your school's open house held one evening during the early fall. From 7:30 to 9:00 p.m., teachers stay in their classrooms and visit with parents as they drop by. Several parents have already visited your classroom and heard you explain your curriculum. Judging by their comments and questions, you think they appear pleased with what their children are learning.

Shortly before 9:00 p.m., the parents of one of your students enter the room. After greeting them, you start to outline the goals and objectives of your curriculum. They listen attentively; the father even jots down a few notes on the cover of the open house program he was given at the orientation session in the auditorium.

"My curriculum is organized around an integrated, thematic approach," you explain. "Each theme addresses a key concept—how animals have influenced the lives of human beings on earth, for example. As kids explore each theme, they learn relevant skills from areas such as language, reading, mathematics, science, art, and music."

To illustrate the thematic approach, you direct the parents' attention to a nearby bulletin board display titled "How Do Animals Influence Our Lives?" The display features children's drawings clustered into categories such as "companionship," "transportation," "food," "work," and "recreation."

After a brief pause, you continue. "Overall, one of the main goals of my curriculum is for students to go beyond the basics. I want them to know how to use the material they learn and how to solve problems. The curriculum should be a unified whole, rather than separate, disconnected parts."

At this point, your student's mother says, "I'm not sure I agree. The purpose of the curriculum should be to learn the basics. We want our child to do well on the provincial test of basic skills. If the curriculum is organized around themes, how can we be sure the kids master the basics?"

"Right," her husband agrees. "If kids don't do well on the test, they're less likely to continue their education. To focus on anything other than the basics is to emphasize needless frills. That may sound harsh, but that's the way I feel."

How do you justify your curriculum to these parents?

Think back to your experiences as a student at the elementary, middle, junior, and secondary schools you attended. What did you learn? Certainly, the curriculum you experienced included reading, comprehension, writing, spelling, geography, and history. In addition to these topics, though, did you learn something about cooperation, competition, stress, physical fitness, video games, computers, popularity, and the opposite sex? Or did you learn to love chemistry and to hate English grammar?

What Is Taught in Schools?

The countless things you learned in school make up the curriculum that you experienced. Curriculum theorists and researchers have suggested several definitions for **curriculum**, with no one universal meaning. Here are some definitions in current use.

1. A course of study, derived from the Latin *currere*, meaning "to run a course"
2. Course content, the information or knowledge students are expected to learn
3. Planned learning experiences
4. Intended learning outcomes, the results of instruction as distinguished from the means (activities, materials, etc.) of instruction
5. All the experiences students have while at school

None of the meanings in the list is in any sense the "right" definition. The way we define curriculum depends on our purposes and our situation. If, for example, we were advising a high school student on the courses he or she needed to take in order to prepare for college, our operational definition of curriculum would most likely be "a course of study." However, if we were interviewing Grade 6 students for their views on the K–6 elementary school they attended, we would probably want to view curriculum as "all the experiences students have while at school." Let us posit an additional definition of curriculum: Curriculum refers to the experiences, both planned and unplanned, that enhance (and sometimes impede) the education and growth of students.

Kinds of Curricula

Elliot Eisner, a noted educational researcher, said that "schools teach much more—and much less—than they intend to teach. Although much of what is taught is explicit and public, a great deal is not" (2002, 87). For this reason, we need to look at the four curricula that all students experience. The more we understand these curricula and how they influence students, the better we will be able to develop effective educational programs.

Explicit Curriculum

The explicit, or overt, curriculum refers to what a school intends to teach students. This curriculum is made up of several components: (1) the goals, aims, and learning objectives the school has for all students, (2) the actual courses that make up each student's course of study, and (3) the specific knowledge, skills, and attitudes that teachers want students to acquire. If we ask a principal to describe the education program at his or her school, our inquiry would be in reference to the explicit curriculum. Similarly, if we ask a teacher to describe what he or she wishes to accomplish with a particular class, we would be given a description of the explicit curriculum.

In short, the **explicit curriculum** represents the publicly announced expectations the school has for its students. These expectations range from learning how to read, write, and compute to learning to appreciate music, art, and cultures other than one's own. In most instances, the explicit curriculum takes the form of written plans or guides for the education of students. Examples of such written documents are course descriptions, curriculum guides that set forth the goals and learning objectives for a school or district, texts and other commercially prepared learning materials, and teachers' lesson plans. Through the instructional program of a school, then, these curricular materials are brought to life.

Hidden Curriculum

The hidden, or implicit, curriculum refers to the behaviours, attitudes, and knowledge the culture of the school unintentionally teaches students (Parkay et al. 2006). What students learn via the **hidden curriculum** can be positive or negative, depending on their day-to-day experiences at school. For example, from teachers who are knowledgeable, well organized, and personable, students are likely to develop positive habits and abilities—cooperating with others, taking responsibility, planning ahead, and forgoing immediate gratification to attain long-range goals. On the other hand, from teachers who are ill prepared, apathetic, or aloof, students are likely to acquire habits and attitudes that are negative and that discourage personal growth and development—a dislike for learning, the ability to deceive or defy adult authority figures, or a tendency to procrastinate.

In the following examples, four students describe the hidden curricula they experienced in school. In examples 1 and 2 (excerpts from letters students wrote their teachers), the hidden curricula "taught" students to be more confident in their ability to learn. In examples 3 and 4, the hidden curricula undermined the students' confidence and desire to learn.

Example 1

I was in your Grade 10 English class. I sure felt safe to take a risk in your class. I actually tried hard, knowing I might fail, but felt safe enough to do so. (Paul, Christensen, & Falk 2000, 23)

Example 2

I was in your Grade 9 class and you praised me for my creative writing. Until that time, I had never thought of myself as a very creative person but your faith in me spurred me on to choose English as my major at the university. (Paul et al. 2000, 23)

Example 3

The teacher just put [material] on the board and if you don't know how, the teacher get angry. I try to get help but when I come after school, they gotta go somewhere and can't help you . . . like when I ask somebody to help me, just because some other kid won't need help, then they think others won't either; some kids are smarter. (Wilson & Corbett 2001, 38)

Example 4

I was in your 11th grade biology class. I loved science and biology until I took your class. You gave me a great disdain for the subject. Your teaching methods bored the class to tears. We read each chapter out loud at the beginning of the week and spent the rest of the week working quietly on the questions at the end of the chapter along with the endless dittos you passed out. We never discussed anything and you never taught us anything. We were graded on how well we could come up with the answers you thought were right and heaven forbid if we did not head our paper using the "correct" format. I think the only thing I learned in your class was conformity. (Colucci 2000, 38)

As a result of hidden curricula, students learn more than their teachers imagine. In your role as a teacher, you will not be aware of all that students are learning through the hidden curriculum of your classroom. However, you can increase the likelihood that what it teaches will be positive. By allowing students to help determine the content of the explicit curriculum, by inviting them to help establish classroom rules, and by providing them with challenges appropriate for their stage of development, teachers can ensure that the outcomes of the hidden curriculum are more positive than negative.

Null Curriculum

Discussing a curriculum that cannot be observed directly is like talking about dark matter or black holes—unseen phenomena in the universe whose existence must be inferred because their incredible denseness and gravitational fields do not allow light to escape. In much the same way, we can consider the curricula we do not find in schools; it may be as important as what we do find. Eisner labelled the intellectual processes and content that schools do not teach "the **null curriculum**—the options students are not afforded, the perspectives they may never know about, much less be able to use, the concepts and skills that are not a part of their intellectual repertoire" (2002, 106–7).

For example, the kind of thinking that schools foster among students is largely based on manipulations of words and numbers. Thinking that is imaginative, subjective, and poetic in nature is stressed only incidentally. Students are seldom taught anthropology, sociology, psychology, law, economics, filmmaking, or architecture.

Eisner contends that "certain subject matters have been traditionally taught in schools not because of a careful analysis of the range of other alternatives that could be offered but rather because they have traditionally been taught. We teach what we teach largely out of habit, and in the process neglect areas of study that could prove to be exceedingly useful to students" (2002, 103).

Extracurricular/Cocurricular Programs

The curriculum includes school-sponsored activities—music, drama, special interest clubs, sports, and student council, to name a few—that students may pursue in addition to their studies in academic areas. When such activities are perceived as additions to the academic curriculum, they are termed extracurricular. When these activities are seen as having important educational goals—and not merely as extras added to the academic curriculum—they are termed cocurricular. To reflect the fact that these two labels are commonly used for the same activities, we use the term extracurricular/cocurricular activities.

Though **extracurricular/cocurricular programs** are most extensive at the secondary level, many elementary, middle, and junior high schools also provide students with a broad assortment of extracurricular/cocurricular activities. For those who choose to participate, such activities provide an opportunity to use social and academic skills in many different contexts.

Research shows that the larger a school is, the less likely it is that a student will take part in extracurricular/cocurricular activities. At the same time, those who do participate tend to have a higher self-concept than those who do not (Coladarci & Cobb 1996). The actual effects of extracurricular/cocurricular activities on students' development, however, are not entirely clear. Although it is known that students who participate in extracurricular/cocurricular activities tend to receive higher grades than nonparticipants and are more frequently identified as gifted (Jordan & Nettles 1999; Modi, Konstantopoulos, & Hedges 1998; Gerber 1996), it is not known whether participation influences achievement, or whether achievement influences participation. However, research has shown that participation has a positive influence on the decision to remain in school (Mahoney & Cairns 1997), educational aspirations (Modi et al. 1998), and the occupation one aspires to and eventually attains (Holland & Andre 1987; Brown, Kohrs, & Lanzarro 1991). Furthermore, students tend to identify extracurricular/cocurricular activities as a positive influence on their school careers.

It is also clear that students who might benefit the most from participating in extracurricular/cocurricular activities—those below the norm in academic achievement and students at risk—tend not to participate. In addition, students from low socio-economic backgrounds participate less often (National Center for Education Statistics 2008).

Curriculum Content

There is considerable disagreement as to the purpose of schools and where the emphasis of curriculum should be placed. Many Canadians believe that the "basics" of reading, writing, and mathematics plus the development of good work habits should be at the heart of the curriculum. However, there are some who feel that school curricula should also emphasize social and life skills. Many schools have introduced curricula aimed at combating such social problems as violence and racism, including antibullying programs.

When considering what students need to know and to be able to do, curriculum developers should evaluate the role of the public school and determine a balance between core curriculum academics and social issues.

The following comments by two parents typify the concern many people have about what is included in school curricula:

Education is becoming more about social issues as opposed to reading, writing, and arithmetic. Some of it's fine, but I think schools need to stay with the basics. . . . You can't get by in the business world on social issues if you can't add and subtract.

They all talk all the time about this "whole child educational process." . . . It's not your business to make a "whole child." Your business is to teach these students how to read, how to write, and give them the basic skills to balance their checkbook. It's not to make new Emersons out of them. (Johnson & Immerwahr 1994, 13)

How Is a School Curriculum Developed?

Although there is no easy-to-follow set of procedures for developing curricula, Ralph Tyler provided four fundamental questions that must be answered in developing any plan of instruction. These four questions, known as the **Tyler rationale**, are as follows (Tyler 1949, 1):

1. What educational purposes should the school seek to attain?
2. What educational experiences can be provided that are likely to attain these purposes?
3. How can these educational experiences be effectively organized?
4. How can we determine whether these purposes are being attained?

Some educators believe the Tyler rationale underestimates the complexities of curriculum development because it advocates a straightforward, step-by-step process that is difficult to follow in the "real" classroom. Nevertheless, Tyler's classic work has been used by a great number of school systems to bring some degree of order and focus to the curriculum development process.

The Focus of Curriculum Planning

In discussing curriculum development, it is helpful to clarify the focus of curriculum planning. The target of curriculum planning may be at the macro or the micro level. At the macro level, decisions about the content of the curriculum apply to large groups of students. The national goals for education and provincial-level curriculum guidelines are examples of macro-level curricular decisions. At the micro level, curriculum decisions are made that apply to groups of students in a particular school or classroom. To some extent, all teachers are micro-level curriculum developers—that is, they make numerous decisions about the curricular experiences they provide in their classrooms.

Another dimension of curriculum planning is time orientation—does the planning focus on the present or the future? In addition to national goals and provincial-level curriculum guidelines, semester-long or monthly plans or unit plans are examples of future-oriented curriculum planning. Present-oriented curriculum planning usually occurs at the classroom level and is influenced by the unique needs of specific groups of students. Daily or weekly curriculum decisions and lesson plans are examples of present-oriented curriculum planning.

Student-Centred versus Subject-Centred Curricula

A key concern in curriculum development is whether greater emphasis should be given to the requirements of the subject area or to the needs of students. It is helpful to imagine where a school curriculum might be placed on the following continuum.

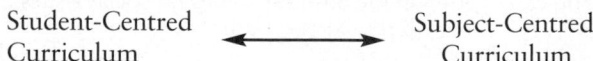

Student-Centred   ⟷   Subject-Centred
Curriculum   Curriculum

Although no course is entirely subject- or student-centred, curricula vary considerably in the degree to which they emphasize one or the other. A **subject-centred curriculum** places primary emphasis on the logical order of the discipline students are to study. The teacher of such a curriculum is a subject-matter expert and is primarily concerned with helping students understand the facts, laws, and principles of the discipline. Subject-centred curricula are more typical of high school education.

Some teachers develop curricula that reflect greater concern for students and their needs. Though teachers of a **student-centred curriculum** also teach content, they emphasize the growth and development of students. This emphasis is generally more typical of elementary school curricula.

The Integrated Curriculum

Used most frequently with elementary-age students, an **integrated curriculum** draws from several different subject areas and focuses on a theme or concept rather than on a single subject. Early childhood education expert Suzanne Krogh (2000, 340) suggests that an integrated approach based on thematic "webs" is a more "natural" way for children to learn:

> [Children] do not naturally learn through isolating specific subjects. These have been determined by adult definition. Children's natural learning is more likely to take place across a theme of interest: building a fort, exploring a sandbox, interacting with the first snow of winter. Teachers can create a good deal of their curriculum by building webs made up of these themes of interest. Done with knowledge and care, a web can be created that incorporates most, or even all, of the required and desired curriculum.

Who Plans the Curriculum?

Various agencies and people outside the school are involved in curriculum planning. Textbook publishers, for example, influence what is taught because many teachers use textbooks as curriculum guides. The Council of Ministers of Education, Canada (CMEC) and the Canadian School Boards Association contribute to curriculum planning by setting national education goals, and individual provincial departments of education develop both broad aims for school curricula and specific minimum competencies for students.

Within a given school, the curriculum planning team and classroom teachers plan the curriculum that students actually experience. As a teacher, you will draw from a reservoir of curriculum plans prepared by others, thus playing a vital role in the curriculum-planning process. Whenever you make decisions about what material to include in your teaching, how to sequence content, and how much time to spend teaching certain material, you are planning the curriculum.

What Influences Curricular Decisions?

From the earliest colonial schools to schools of the twenty-first century, curricula have been broadly influenced by a variety of religious, political, and utilitarian agendas. Figure 8.1 illustrates the influence of community pressures, court decisions, students' life situations, testing results, teachers' professional organizations, research results, and other factors. The inner circles of the figure represent factors that have a more direct influence on curriculum development (such as students' needs and school district policies). The outer circle represents factors that are more removed from the school setting or have less obvious effects on the curriculum. Individual schools respond to these influences differently, which further affects their curricula. Let us examine some of these influences in greater detail.

From the Classroom to the World

A Look into the Learning for a Cause Student Press Initiative

Classrooms Without Walls

What you choose to do in your classroom can remain in your classroom and end up in the recycle bin or it can become part of the real struggle to improve our lives and the lives of others.

—Michael Ernest Sweet

When I began teaching the only thing I had in my classroom were walls: the very thing I could have done without. In 2002 I left studies in law to become a teacher because I wanted to make a genuine difference in the lives of people. However, when I first stepped into a classroom as a teacher, I realized that this would not be as easy as I thought. I knew right away that if all I did was what was asked of me, I would not only fall short of making a real difference, I would also become disillusioned and burn out.

The very first time I returned a creative writing assignment to my students I sat and watched in amazement the scene that unfolded. They were anxious to get their papers but not to see my comments or to continue to perfect their work. No, they were anxious to get their numerical grades, to compare them to their peers and then toss the papers into the recycle bin and get the whole thing out of their lives. With all the papers neatly resting in the bin the students returned to their desks and patiently awaited my next assignment. They were not bad students; in fact, they were great kids. This, for them, was the business of school.

I knew there had to be more. I knew this could not be my life as a teacher. It was then that I became obsessed with the question "What could school be?" I knew what it was—a pantheon of busywork—but what could it

become? I set out on a journey; it would take five years and a lot of dedication but, in the end, I would come to realize that teaching really is the best career on earth.

As a published writer, I knew there was something fundamentally wrong with children throwing away their creative work. I knew there was something wrong with students only writing one draft, not sharing their ideas and not having an audience. I also knew, as a writer, that what we all want is for someone to read our work and tell us what is good about it. This process can open the floodgates of our imagination and allow us to move forward and excel as writers. It is this authentic appreciation that was missing for my students.

Using print-on-demand technology and companies like our official partner Lulu.com (which were just emerging) and creating assignments relevant to the curriculum, real classroom anthologies of writing concerned with social issues would be produced. I would clear the path for students to receive authentic appreciation for their imaginative creations by getting their work out into the world. Furthermore, I would begin to teach my students that using their passion and imagination might possibly contribute to the resolution of many of our world's most pressing problems. I would show my students that they could learn and make a difference in the world outside our classroom. It would be a defining moment in my teaching career—the moment I decided to make my lessons concern actual world issues—to make my teaching take on a greater purpose and to tear down my classroom walls.

The result was the founding of Learning for a Cause (LFC) in 2004 at Lester B. Pearson High School in Montreal; in the years since its inception, LFC has published five full-length anthologies of student writing. The books' themes include war, violence, racism, prejudice, environment and poverty and they have received endorsements from Emmy-award-winning actor Martin Sheen and celebrated environmentalist David Suzuki to world-renowned philosopher Maxine Greene and legendary artists Alex Colville and Robert Bateman. LFC books and students have been featured on CTV and CBC as well as NPR and Vermont Public Radio time and again. They have received review in the *Globe and Mail*, the *Montreal Gazette* and *Canadian Teacher Magazine*. Learning for a Cause won a Quebec Entrepreneurial Award in 2006 and again in 2009. *Down to Earth*, a collection of poetry in response to global warming, recently placed in two categories at the World Indie Book Awards. This is just some of the recognition our student press has been afforded.

I don't share these accolades to impress, but rather to demonstrate that what goes on in a classroom really can connect to, and impact positively on, the world outside—humanity at large. What you choose to do in your classroom can remain in your classroom and end up in the recycle bin or it can become part of the real struggle to improve our lives and the lives of others. What goes on in your classroom can be trapped there as busywork or it can be showcased to the world as a part of a dialogue on creating a better tomorrow. Using student imagination to envision how things "could be" rather than always asking children to regurgitate what "merely is" can make all the difference in your teaching practice. It did for me.

While engaged in writing for authentic audiences, my students still learn the prescribed curriculum—and a lot more. They write in various forms, communicate their learning, edit and proofread and collaborate; they even reach across disciplines and forge connections among issues, peoples and countries. But what is truly different is that they do it with purpose; they work on real issues in the real world. My students are writing their own story and helping to change minds, awaken ideas and create a better tomorrow—one book at a time; they are Learning for a Cause.

Michael Ernest Sweet is the founder of the Learning for a Cause student press initiative in Montreal. In 2008 he was appointed to the Canadian Commission for UNESCO in recognition of his contributions to public education. A 2009 recipient of the Prime Minister's Award for Teaching Excellence and an inductee of the National Teachers Hall of Fame, Michael divides his time between Montreal and New York City.

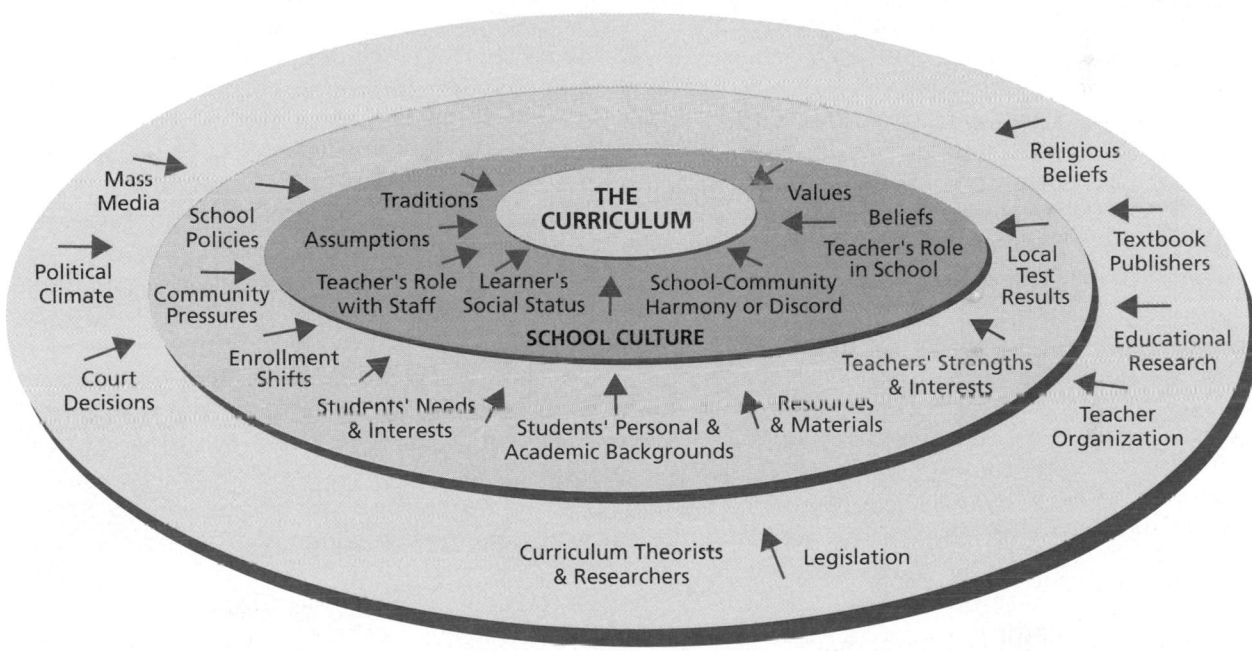

Figure 8.1

Influences on the school curriculum

Social Issues and Changing Values

Values that affect curriculum planning include prevailing educational theories and teachers' educational philosophies. In addition, curriculum planners respond to social issues and changing values in the wider society. As a result, current social concerns find their way into textbooks, teaching aids, and lesson plans. Curriculum changes are often made in the hope that changing what students learn will help solve social problems or achieve local, province-wide, or national goals.

As Canada's population has grown more culturally diverse, changes in curricula have been made to reflect divergent interests and values. This divergence has led to

The Challenge: Meeting the Needs of Learners

Recent teacher education graduate Natanya Chavez is beginning her first year at Rosemount School, a P–5 elementary school located in a diverse Canadian neighbourhood. Her recent practice teaching placement in a Grade 5 class in the small, rural Oak Creek Elementary School was positive and rewarding. The associate teacher with whom she worked encouraged her to try a variety of teaching approaches, including workshops for reading and writing, problem-based learning in mathematics, and WebQuests in social studies. Natanya benefitted from her associate teacher's 12 years of experience and appreciated the team teaching model employed by her mentor. Parents volunteered on a daily basis and there was a strong sense of community within the classroom. The modern school had enjoyed strong community support and was the meeting place for many community groups, activities and events. The students' families worked in a variety of sectors including business, retail, manufacturing, and agricultural industry, along with health, education, government, and community service. Many of the students had attended the school from primary grade and were well versed in its expected behaviours. Natanya appreciated the students' respect for staff, self, and others.

Natanya's new school is a one-level brick and cinder-block building that has essentially remained unchanged since its construction in 1963. There is little emphasis on technology in the school and Natanya inherits a bare classroom with worn and dated resources.

Students come from several racially and culturally diverse communities with low- to middle-class socio-economic backgrounds. There is little industry in the area and many parents of students in the school receive social assistance. Families are transient in the communities served by the school and students regularly move in and out of Rosemount Elementary during the school year.

Natanya accepts her first teaching position with enthusiasm and is eager to employ the various theories she learned at university and the curriculum approaches she tested during her practice teaching.

The week before school commences, Natanya is given her Grade 2 class list and learns that there are 29 students in her class: 19 boys and 10 girls. Eight students have been diagnosed with learning disabilities and have individual program plans, four require curriculum adaptations, six have literacy support plans, and one has a part-time educational assistant for severe behavioural problems.

Although she feels a bit overwhelmed and ill-prepared to handle such a large and diverse class, she has a sincere desire to be a caring and effective educator. Natanya

controversies over curriculum content and to conflicting calls for reform. Additional controversies have arisen over calls for the elimination of all activities or symbols that have their origins in organized religion, including even secularized or commercialized ones such as Halloween and the Easter bunny. Curriculum changes to promote greater social integration or equity among racial or ethnic groups may draw complaints of decides to go ahead with the curricular approaches that worked well during her practice teaching. In terms of her literacy curriculum, Natanya plans to use reading and writing workshops, although she finds that there are limited resources and few texts to draw from. She makes a disappointing trip to the school library, where she discovers that there are few appropriate materials. Undaunted, Natanya decides that she will hold a book fair in mid-September so that her students can make some purchases; she also intends to send home a note with her students asking that parents consider donating new or "gently used" books to add to the classroom library. Further, Natanya plans to take her students to the local library on a field trip so that they can each get a library card and borrow books throughout the year.

Natanya assumes her students will respond positively to the workshop approach she begins during the first week of school. It is not long before she discovers that the students are not able to follow the routines and structure that worked for her previously. The students are simply not able to work independently and they require many warnings to remain on task during workshop time.

On the first day of school, Natanya requested that each student bring in a bag suitable for taking books back and forth from class to home. At the end of the second week of school, over half of her students still do not have a book bag. It is obvious that the books that are being sent home daily with the children are largely being returned unread and the required reading forms are not being signed by parents. When she asks how many students will be buying a book at the book fair, only two students raise their hands. When she tries to organize a field trip to the local library, Natanya cannot find enough parent volunteers to help with transportation and supervision.

Natanya realizes that there is limited parental and community support for the school and the students. She also observes that many of the children come to school without lunches, and that most of her students take part in the daily breakfast program. Personal hygiene is an issue with several students and it is obvious that they do not get enough sleep—they are often cranky or listless.

Natanya goes home tired every evening and begins to feel discouraged; in fact, she is starting to wonder how she will even make it through the year. When she shares her frustration with some of her friends, they tell her that teachers should not be expected to take on roles other than that of classroom instructor. Her sister tells her that she is a teacher, not a social worker. She says that Natanya needs to focus on teaching the curriculum and not worry about other things that are beyond her control. However, Natanya is determined to do something to make a difference in the lives of her students so that they can experience academic success.

irrelevancy or reverse discrimination. Traditionalists may object to curriculum changes that reflect feminist views.

As you can imagine, consensus on many curriculum reform issues is never achieved. However, because of their public accountability, schools must consider how to respond to such issues. In the end, the creative and evaluative tasks of choosing and developing curriculum materials are a source of both empowerment and frustration for teachers. Budget constraints, social and legal issues, and provincial and local curriculum mandates often determine curriculum choices.

The Canadian Teachers' Federation believes that education must be provided on an equitable basis to all students through elementary and secondary school programs that do the following:

- Develop the intellectual, aesthetic, physical, emotional, and ethical capacities of each student.
- Prepare students to become responsible and productive members of society.
- Provide opportunities for students to learn about Canadian history, literature, culture, government, and heritage.
- Enable students to learn about the global community, and about Canada's place within it.

The Canadian School Boards Association issued a statement of national educational goals in 1992. The statement stressed the importance of equal access to quality programs for all school-age children and suggested that school choice should take the form of a range of public school programs designed to address diverse learning needs and interests.

Textbook Publishing

Like curriculum planners, textbook authors and publishers are influenced by trends in education and by social issues. In response to criticism, for example, publishers now tend to avoid bias in terms of gender, religion, class, race, and culture. However, because the goal of business is profit, publishers are most responsive to market trends and customer preferences. They are often reluctant to risk losing sales by including subjects that are controversial or that may be offensive to their bigger customers. They may also modify textbooks to appeal to decision makers in populous provinces, such as Ontario and British Columbia, where province-wide adoptions are possible.

Educators have criticized textbooks for inoffensiveness to the point of blandness, for artificially lowering reading levels (called "dumbing down"), and for using pedagogically questionable gimmicks to hold students' attention. "The quality problem [with textbooks also] encompasses [f]actors such as poor writing, poor content 'coverage,' and failure to engage students in the skills needed to create the knowledge contained in a particular area of study" (Sowell 1996, 158). Although the publishing industry continually responds to such criticisms, you would be wise to follow systematic guidelines in evaluating and selecting textbooks and other curriculum materials.

The Core Curriculum

The school reform movement of the 1980s led to provinces reviewing their curricula, and the result was that many departments of education increased the number of required courses for graduation, or the **core curriculum**. For example, in Saskatchewan, credit requirements were increased in 1987 to 24 from 21. The current Saskatchewan core curriculum principles (shown in the following excerpt) include the teaching of basic skills and an expanded range of new knowledge and abilities.

> The two major components of core curriculum are the Required Areas of Study and the Common Essential Learnings. Seven Required Areas of Study form the framework for the curriculum. Six categories of Common Essential Learnings are to be incorporated in an appropriate manner into all courses of study offered in Saskatchewan schools. . . .

To meet community and student needs at the local level, provision is made within the core curriculum to offer Locally Determined Options. In recognition of the diverse needs of students, provision is made through the Adaptive Dimension for teachers to adapt instruction.

Required Areas of Study within the Core Curriculum

- Language arts
- Mathematics
- Science
- Social studies
- Health education
- Arts education
- Physical education

Each required area has unique knowledge, skills, and values that are essential for all students at the elementary, Middle, and Secondary Levels. The Required Areas of Study, therefore, are included throughout the school program from the Elementary to Secondary Levels. (Saskatchewan Government Policy Document of Core Curriculum. retrieved August 22, 2010, from www.sasked.gov.sk.ca/docs/policy/corecurr_pta/intro.html)

Performance-Based Education

A recent approach to reforming curricula to ensure that all students learn and perform at high levels is known as **performance-based** or **outcome-based education**. The performance-based approach focuses on assessing students' mastery of a set of rigorous learning goals or outcomes. Opponents to performance-based education have expressed concern about the content of the outcomes, who determines them, and how they will be assessed.

The Canadian Curriculum Scene: Web Resources

Most Canadian provinces and territories have similar approaches to their programs of studies. The following regional, provincial, and territorial curriculum websites provide information about core curricula for individual provinces and territories.

Council of Atlantic Ministers of Education and Training
http://camet-camef.ca

Western Canadian Protocol for Collaboration in Basic Education, Kindergarten to Grade 12
www.edu.gov.mb.ca/k12/cur/process.html

Alberta Ministry of Education
www.education.gov.ab.ca/k_12/curriculum/DevelImp.asp

British Columbia Department of Education
www.bced.gov.bc.ca/irp/welcome.php

Manitoba Curriculum Development Process
www.edu.gov.mb.ca/k12/cur/process.html

New Brunswick Department of Education
www.gnb.ca/0000/anglophone-e.asp#cd

Newfoundland and Labrador Department of Education
www.ed.gov.nl.ca/edu/k12/curriculum/guides/index.html

Northwest Territories Teachers' Association
www.nwtta.nt.ca/links-curriculum.html

Nova Scotia Department of Education
www.ednet.ns.ca/index.php?sid=236589593&t=sub_pages&cat=73

Ontario Ministry of Education
www.edu.gov.on.ca/eng/curriculum

Prince Edward Island Department of Education and Early Childhood Development
www.gov.pe.ca/eecd/index.php3?number=1025899&lang=E

Québec Ministere de l'Education Curriculum Publications
www.mels.gouv.qc.ca/GR-PUB/m_englis.htm

Saskatchewan Department of Education Curriculum and Instruction Branch
www.sasked.gov.sk.ca/branches/curr/index.shtml

Yukon Educational Student Network
www.yesnet.yk.ca/staffroom/index.html

Future Direction of Canadian Education: A National Influence

In September 1993, the CMEC endorsed the Victoria Declaration, which outlined a plan for future directions in Canadian education. The declaration put forth the following beliefs held in common by all education ministers.

> We believe that education is a lifelong learning process. We also believe that the future of our society depends on informed and educated citizens who, while fulfilling their own goals of personal and professional development, contribute to the social, economic, and cultural development of their community and country as a whole. Beyond our borders, Canadian education should reflect the priorities of Canadians while contributing to strengthening Canada's place internationally.

> In February 1995, the Council of Ministers of Education, Canada adopted the Pan-Canadian Protocol for Collaboration on School curriculum. The protocol acknowledges that education is a provincial and territorial responsibility, while recognizing that interjurisdictional cooperation can contribute to improving the quality of education in the country. In keeping with the protocol, participating jurisdictions believe that sharing human and financial resources can increase the quality and efficiency of the curriculum development processes in Canada. (Council of Ministers of Education, Canada 1995)

What Are Some Current Subject-Area Trends?

The final section of this chapter examines briefly some of the current trends and issues regarding curricula in elementary, middle, junior high, and high schools. When developing outcomes, provincial departments of education make use of recommended curriculum guidelines from professional associations.

Literacy

The importance of attaining a minimum level of literacy cannot be underestimated; the language arts are the tools through which students learn in nearly all other areas of a curriculum. Most students who are deficient in reading and writing skills are at a significant disadvantage when it comes to seeking employment or additional education.

The teaching of reading at all levels should focus on acquiring basic comprehension skills and learning to appreciate literature in its various forms: novels, essays, poetry, short stories, and so on. Reading teachers, however, are currently far from united as to how these aims should be realized. Does instruction in phonics enhance reading comprehension? Is a whole-language approach to the teaching of reading superior to teaching isolated decoding and comprehension skills? Should children be taught the alphabet before learning to read? Although media coverage frequently dichotomizes the teaching of reading between the phonics approach and the whole-language approach, Cheeks, Flippo, and Lindsey (1997, 130) contend that "this polarization is more political than representative of the real issues. Those who advocate for whole language do not believe that phonics is not important. Instead, they argue about how it should be presented to students."

The following comments by a Grade 1 teacher reflect the position of many teachers regarding the "reading wars": "I don't think there is one best method of teaching reading or one best program. What I have done over my twenty-seven years is pick what I think works and incorporate it" (Smolkin 1999, 1A). The eclectic approach to teaching reading is also advocated by the International Reading Association, which states that "there is no single method or single combination of methods that can successfully teach all children to read. Therefore, teachers must be familiar with a wide range of methods for teaching reading and a strong knowledge of the children in their care so they can create the appropriate balance of methods needed for each child" (International Reading Association 1999). As part of a trend to de-escalate the reading wars, then, many schools that emphasized a whole-language approach during the 1990s began to shift to a balanced approach at the start of the new decade.

Advocates of the **whole-language approach** believe that reading is part of general language development, not an isolated skill students learn apart from listening, speaking, and writing. Teachers in whole-language classrooms seldom use textbooks; instead, young students write stories and learn to read from their writing, and older students read literature that is closely related to their everyday experiences.

During the past two decades, several new approaches have been incorporated into language arts curricula. Many English teachers have reduced the amount of time spent on grammar, electing instead to teach it as needed within the context of a writing program. English teachers also have generally broadened their view of literature to include more contemporary writing and the work of minority or ethnic writers. Teaching in the English classroom now frequently incorporates such techniques as creative writing, drama, journal writing, guided fantasy exercises, and group discussions. In addition, many teachers use computers to explore new ways to teach reading and writing skills.

After three years of collaborative development, the International Reading Association and the National Council of Teachers of English in the United States released voluntary national standards for English-language arts in 1996. These standards continue to stimulate discussion and debate about the goals of language arts instruction.

Based on their review of literacy research, Cheeks, Flippo, and Lindsey (1997, 83–84) recommend that teachers do the following to develop children's language abilities:

1. Allow many opportunities for social imaginative play and other verbal peer interaction, which enhance language and cognitive development.
2. Develop learning activities that integrate listening, speaking, reading, and writing (oral and written language).
3. Use art, music, and drama activities to further develop language opportunities.
4. Read many books and stories to children every day.
5. Choose books and stories that you believe will be of high interest to children and will further stimulate their interest in reading books.
6. Give children opportunities to respond to the books and stories you read.
7. Reread favourite stories as often as children request them.

8. Give children opportunities to retell and/or act out stories in their own words after listening to you read them.

9. Give children many opportunities to make their own books. Children can dictate stories as the teacher writes the stories down in the children's own words. Children also can write their own books using scribble writing, pictures, and invented spellings to tell their stories in their own words.

10. Give children many opportunities to share with others the stories they write.

11. Accept "less than perfect" readings, retellings, writing, and other literacy attempts for all children.

12. Provide classroom activities and an environment that enhances the idea that literacy is part of communication and that meaning is essential for communication to take place.

The Canadian Council of Teachers of English Language Arts (CCTLA) and its provincial affiliates have not published national standards, but they are associated with the National Council of Teachers of English (NCTE) and the International Reading Association (IRA) and follow many of the standards established by these organizations. There appears to be consistency in English language arts curriculum documents throughout the country. The Western Canadian Protocol for Collaboration in Basic Education (British Columbia, Alberta, Saskatchewan, Manitoba, Nunavut, and Yukon) accepted a Common Curriculum Framework for English Language Arts in 1998. The Council of Ministers of Education and Training (Nova Scotia, New Brunswick, Prince Edward Island, and Newfoundland and Labrador) and the ministries of Quebec and Ontario all recognize the importance of language and communications skills in society, and they embrace the concept that literacy has moved beyond print by encompassing media and other ways of representing language.

myeducationlab

Go to www.MyEducationLab.com and choose the Resources tab from the top menu. Go to Curriculum Resources to access the Language Arts and Literacy Arts Zone, which provides you with a variety of activities and case studies for early elementary, elementary, middle, and secondary levels.

Suggestions:

- Elementary: "Literature Circles Open the World of Literature"
- Middle school: "Book Discussion Groups"
- Secondary: "Authentic Reading and Writing Assignments for High School Students"

Mathematics

Although there is no pan-Canadian framework in mathematics curricula, most provinces follow a similar approach to this content area. The current teaching approaches in mathematics embrace a constructivist, learner-centred focus with the learning goal of mathematical literacy. New math curricula across Canada emphasize problem solving and inquiry. For example, the Common Curriculum Framework for K–12 Mathematics (Western Canadian Protocol for Collaboration in Basic Education 2000) incorporates the following seven interrelated mathematical processes:

- Communication
- Connections
- Estimation and mental mathematics
- Problem solving
- Reasoning
- Technology
- Visualization

Action Research in a Junior High Reading and Writing Workshop

Teacher: Lisa Wilson, Grade 8 English Language Arts

Action Research is a framework that guides the energies of teachers toward a better understanding of why, when, and how students become better learners. This form of inquiry can provide a rich opportunity for reflection on practice and can contribute to ongoing professional development. One such project was carried out by Canadian teacher Lisa Wilson with her Grade 8 English language arts classes. It started with baseline data collection that identified 12 students who experienced difficulties in self-selecting books, staying focused on texts, and writing quality journal reflections. This prompted Lisa to ask, "What strategies might help my struggling and striving readers to experience more success in workshop activities?"

A review of current literature was undertaken to examine strategies and methods that Lisa could implement in her silent reading and writing workshops to foster improvement in student performance and enhance the workshop experience. The literature review helped Lisa understand that the problems her students were experiencing were common, and aided her in developing strategies. The literature emphasized the importance of providing class time for reading, underlined the value of informal reading conferences and observation of student behaviour, and the need for individual instruction. Further, student accountability may be encouraged through reading logs, reflection journals, and projects.

Lisa wanted to see her students improve and experience success in:

- choosing an appropriate book (interest and reading level)
- using the big xix reading strategies (making connections, questioning, inferring, visualizing, determining importance and synthesizing)
- comprehension skills
- thinking deeply about what has been read

It was determined that students could demonstrate this by providing a well-written journal reflection and being able to discuss their reading during informal reading conferences. One of the key strategies Lisa used was involving the students directly in co-constructing criteria for journal reflections, including format, content, and matters of correctness. She developed formal instruments to collect data; specifically, informal reading conference forms and observational checklists.

During the implementation of the strategies, Lisa collected data from student reflection journals, informal teacher–student conferences, and observational checklists. The data seemed to suggest that:

- students benefitted from co-constructing criteria for quality journal reflections
- the quality of writing improved and the quantity increased
- students were inclined to start reading right away when the teacher began the class by reading silently herself
- allowing in-class time for students to read was valuable

Lisa Wilson is a Grade 8 English language arts teacher at Amherst Junior High School in Amherst, Nova Scotia. She is also the literacy mentor in her school. She plans to disseminate the results of her research with her colleagues and fellow literacy mentors in her school district.

The curriculum development process in Canada has tended to draw on such sources as the National Council of Teachers of Mathematics (NCTM) Curriculum and Evaluation Standards for Mathematics. This American organization has widespread membership in Canada. Since it began working on the Standards 2000 project, a set of pre-K–12 standards released in April 2000, the NCTM has made it clear that basic mathematical skills for the new century should consist of more than computation skills. Standards 2000 emphasizes five mathematical content standards (number and operation; patterns, functions, and algebra; geometry and spatial sense; measurement; and data analysis, statistics, and probability) that students should study with increasing breadth and depth as they move through the grades. In addition, Standards 2000 emphasizes five mathematical processes through which students should acquire and use their mathematical knowledge: problem solving, reasoning and proof, communication, connections, and representation.

What is needed is **problem-centred learning**, in which students work in small groups on problems that have many or open-ended solutions. Rather than memorizing facts, working on sets of problems in textbooks, and competing against their classmates, students discover concepts, solve problems similar to those they will encounter in life, and learn to cooperate in small groups.

PEARSON
myeducationlab)

In the Resources tab on www.MyEducationLab.com, go to Curriculum Resources and access the Math Zone. Here you will find a variety of activities and resources for teaching math at early elementary, elementary, middle, and secondary levels.

Science and Technology

Current science curriculum approaches underline the need for students to acquire scientific knowledge, skills, and processes through an inquiry, discovery, or problem-centred method. The teacher's primary role is to guide students in their search for knowledge rather than to act solely as a source of information or right answers.

The first joint development project initiated by the CMEC's 1995 common frameworks for curricula was in the content area of science learning outcomes. This common set of guidelines laid out a framework for scientific literacy in Canada and outlines learning outcomes, which include attitudes, knowledge, and skills for students.

Four foundation statements of science learning guide the development of science curricula across Canada:

- Foundation 1: Science, technology, society, and the environment
- Foundation 2: Skills

How might these students be meeting science curriculum aims of the Council of Ministers of Education, Canada?

- Foundation 3: Knowledge
- Foundation 4: Attitudes

This framework emphasizes a constructivist approach to science learning and encourages learner-centred techniques. The framework is intended to be used as a guide rather than a prescription for science curriculum development and the selection of learning resources.

In the Resources tab on www.MyEducationLab.com, go to Curriculum Resources and access the Science Zone. Here you will find a variety of activities and resources for teaching science at early elementary, elementary, middle, and secondary levels.

Social Studies

Goals for social studies lack the precision found in other subject areas. Consider, for example, Charles Beard's comment in 1938 that social studies aim at the "creation of rich and many-sided personalities, equipped with practical knowledge and inspired by ideals so that they can make their way and fulfill their mission in a changing society which is part of a world complex" (1938, 179). Consider also the following 10 "strands" from the National Council for the Social Studies' (1994) Expectations of Excellence: Curriculum Standards for Social Studies:

1. Culture and cultural diversity
2. Humans' views of themselves over time
3. People, places, and environments
4. Individual development and identity
5. Interactions among individuals, groups, and institutions
6. How structures of power, authority, and governance are changed
7. The production, distribution, and consumption of goods and services
8. Relationships among science, technology, and society
9. Global interdependence
10. Citizenship in a democratic society

The Western Canadian Protocol for Collaboration in Basic Education (2000, 6) has adopted the following formal definition for social studies:

Social studies is the study of people in relation to each other and their world. It is an interdisciplinary subject that draws upon history, geography, economics, law, political science, and other disciplines. Social studies focuses on people's relationships with their social, physical, spiritual, cultural, economic, political, and technological environments. Social studies helps students become active and responsible citizens within their communities, locally, nationally, and globally, in a complex and changing world.

Canada does not have national guidelines or standards in the social studies curriculum area but common themes can be recognized in the various provinces and territories. The Atlantic Provinces Education Foundation (APEF) (1999, 12) identifies the following six strands to categorize social studies content, along with general outcomes for each:

1. Citizenship, power, and governance. Students need to understand the rights and responsibilities of citizenship and the origins, functions, and sources of power, authority, and governance.
2. Individuals, societies, and economic decisions. Students need to make responsible economic decisions, both as individuals and as members of society.

3. People, place, and environment. Students need to understand how people, places, and the environment interact.
4. Culture and diversity. Students need to understand culture, diversity, and world-view, and to recognize similarities and differences among personal, cultural, racial, and ethnic perspectives.
5. Interdependence. Students need to understand that relationships among individuals, societies, and the environment—locally, nationally, and globally—are interdependent, and the relationships have implications for a sustainable future.
6. Time, continuity, and change. Students need to understand the past and how it affects the present and the future.

Social studies curricula have been expanded in recent years to keep pace with societal trends; specifically, courses or units in African-Canadian and Aboriginal studies and women's history have been developed to give voice to minorities whose stories were previously ignored. Efforts will continue in this area to address such issues as racial, ethnic, cultural, gender, and socio-economic biases and to promote multiculturalism, diversity, and anti-discrimination in society.

Social studies curricula have also experienced a rapid expansion of information related to the proliferation of the internet. This development underlines the need to develop media literate students who can critically interpret and analyze information.

In the Resources tab on www.MyEducationLab.com, go to Curriculum Resources and access the Social Studies Zone. Here you will find a variety of activities and resources for teaching social studies at early elementary, elementary, middle, and secondary levels.

Second-Language Instruction

The majority of Canadian students take school courses in English or French, Canada's two official languages. The federal government funds French and English instruction as second languages. Publicly-funded schooling in either language is guaranteed "where numbers warrant" and is decided on a case-by-case basis. In Quebec, only a child whose parent was educated in English can attend an English-language public school (UN Reporting Category: Education, Leisure, and Cultural Activities). Canada has been in the forefront of the French immersion movement.

Many jobs in Canada require French language skills. In its 2003 Action Plan for Official Languages, the federal government identified education as one of its priorities in the promotion of linguistic duality in Canada. The action plan sets out objectives that aim to improve the quality of existing second-language instruction and increase participation in second-language programs. In core French, the second language is taught in periods that vary in length from school to school. Provinces may recommend a basic core French structure, and school boards may also influence the program. The aims of core French are as follows:

■ Basic communication skills
■ Language knowledge
■ An appreciation of French culture in Canada and beyond (Turnbull 2000)

Core French concentrates on speaking, reading, listening, and writing in French. The trend in core French instruction is teaching through themes designed to interest students by considering learners' life experiences, intellectual development, and interests. Core French now aims to expose students to more spoken French and allow them to use their skills to communicate in real-life situations. At the start of a core French program, curricula emphasize listening and speaking. Later, emphasis on reading and writing increases. Core French also features learning about Francophone culture, with an emphasis on French-speaking Canada.

French immersion subjects such as math, science, and music are taught in French. The language is the medium and not the object of instruction. The goal of immersion is for learners to achieve a level of fluency to function well in a French-speaking community, work in a French-speaking organization, or pursue post-secondary education in French. The Canadian Association of Immersion Teachers (CAIT) works to promote and improve immersion programs in Canada.

The Canadian Association of Second Language Teachers (CASLT) promotes the advancement of second-language opportunities. There are no national standards for second-language teaching in Canada, but CASLT (2003) issued the following statement of beliefs to act as a guide:

- We believe that being able to communicate in a second language contributes to the full development of the human potential.
- We believe that every individual is capable of learning a second language according to his or her needs, interests, and abilities.
- We believe that the opportunity to learn a second language is a fundamental human right.
- We believe that second language learning is an essential component of a formal education.

The Arts

More than any other area, the arts have held an insecure position in school curricula. When faced with budgetary cutbacks or pressure to raise scores on basic skills tests, a cost-conscious public has often considered the elimination of music and art. The arts as a means of expression are especially important in the context of current educational reform. "Hard" evidence on the importance of the arts has appeared in media, academic journals, and various national reports. "Arts Education: Basic to Learning," a report by the Northwest Regional Educational Laboratory, points out the following:

- In 1995 College Board testing, students who studied the arts for at least four years score 59 points higher on the verbal portion of the SAT, and 44 points higher on math, than students with no experience or coursework in the arts.
- According to a 1997 report from the Department of Education, "Children naturally sing, dance, draw, and role-play in an effort to understand the world around them and communicate their thoughts about it. A growing body of evidence demonstrates that when their caretakers engage them in these activities early in life on a regular basis, they are helping to wire the children's brains for successful learning."
- In studies at [the] University of California at Irvine, IQ scores go up among college students who listen to classical recordings immediately before testing—a phenomenon nicknamed the "Mozart Effect."
- Arts education programs are related to safer and more orderly school environments.
- Schools with strong arts programs report better attendance, increased graduation rates, improved multicultural understanding, greater community support, invigorated faculty, and the development of higher-order thinking skills, creativity, and problem-solving ability among students.

- The arts serve students with special needs, including those who are in danger of falling through the cracks of the educational system, and allow success "for people who have been defined as failures." (Northwest Regional Educational Laboratory 1999, 5)

Typically, elementary art and music are limited to one period a week, with instruction given either by regular teachers or by special teachers who travel from school to school. In addition, most elementary students have occasional opportunities to use crayons, watercolour paints, clay, and other art materials as they learn in other subject areas. And, from time to time, many children have the opportunity to participate in dance, puppetry, role play, pantomime, and crafts.

At the middle and junior high levels, instruction in art and music is more structured, as well as more voluntary. Students may choose from band, chorus, arts, and crafts. At the high school level, art and music are usually offered as electives.

Physical Education

The ultimate aim of physical education is to promote physical activities that develop a desire in the individual to maintain physical fitness throughout life. At one time, physical education programs consisted largely of highly competitive team sports. Many children, less aggressive and competitive than their peers, did not do well in such programs and experienced a lowered sense of self-esteem. Gradually, instructors began to offer activities designed to meet the needs and abilities of all students, not just the athletically talented. In addition to traditional team sports such as football, baseball, and basketball, and individual sports such as swimming and wrestling, many students in Grades K–12 may now participate in a broad array of physical activities, including aerobics, archery, badminton, dodge ball, folk and square dancing, gymnastics, handball, hockey, table tennis, golf, racquetball, shuffleboard, skating, volleyball, soccer, and yoga.

The Canadian Association for Health, Physical Education, Recreation and Dance (CAHPERD) is an advocacy group that lobbies for health and fitness programs in schools and communities. Although there are no pan-Canadian standards in the area of physical education curricula, most provinces endorse the Quality Daily Education program standards of daily activity for 30 to 60 minutes that emphasizes enjoyment, health, personal fulfillment, and success (CAHPERD 2006).

In May 2006, Active Healthy Kids Canada (AHKC) released its "Report Card on Physical Activity" to draw attention to the serious problem of physical inactivity among Canadian youth.

School-to-Work Transitions

Many high schools form partnerships with the private sector and develop school-to-work programs to address current and future needs in industry. In many provinces, **school-to-work programs** and **cooperative education programs** offer students the opportunity to develop employment skills and explore career options. For example, the objectives of cooperative education programs in New Brunswick are as follows:

- To provide students with an opportunity to gain knowledge and work experience in a career area of their choice.
- To assist students in developing and expanding employment skills.
- To foster positive student expectations and attitudes toward self, others, school, and work.

- To develop awareness of better accessibility to students in various occupations.
- To encourage cooperation between the business community and the educational system.
- To provide employers with a talent pool of trained and prepared potential employees.

The program allows students to participate in a regular school program while at the same time developing employment skills through participation in 40–55 hours of in-school instruction and 125–195 hours of nonpaid work experience.

In Nova Scotia, the School-to-Work Transition program is offered in Grades 11 and 12 and features an in-school component and a work-experience component. The objective of the program is to facilitate transitions from school to work by providing skills that might increase high school students' likelihood of becoming employed in desirable jobs. It is also designed to help students make better educational and occupational choices and to gain realistic expectations about future occupations.

Implemented in the fall of 2002, the new Ontario high school program reflects a belief in the importance of out-of-class, career-related experiences for students. It requires all school boards to offer cooperative education, work experience, and school-to-work transition programs. In addition, students are required to participate in 40 hours of community involvement that will give them additional experience outside the classroom.

Curricula will likely continue to focus on opportunities that take students outside the traditional walls of the classroom to develop knowledge, confidence, and skills that will help them succeed in the workplace.

SUMMARY

What Is Taught in Schools?

- There are many different definitions for the term "curriculum." A general definition is that curriculum refers to the experiences, both planned and unplanned, that either enhance or impede the education and growth of students.

- There are four curricula that all students experience. In addition to learning what teachers intend to teach (the explicit curriculum), students learn from the hidden curriculum, the null curriculum, and extracurricular/cocurricular programs.

- From school policies to national politics, many factors influence what is taught (and not taught) in schools.

How Is a School Curriculum Developed?

- Curricula are based on the needs and interests of students and reflect a variety of professional, commercial, local, provincial, national, and international pressures.

- Teachers must be prepared to assume important roles in the curriculum development process, especially in developing student-centred and integrated curricula.

What Are Some Current Subject-Area Trends?

- Alternative curricula for literacy, multiculturalism, character education, art, problem-centred learning, thinking skills, computer literacy, and career education are examples of curriculum trends today.

- Curriculum trends also involve, for example, redefining foreign language study and sex or health education, developing school-to-work programs, providing for active and authentic learning, determining what students will need to know and be able to do in the twenty-first century, and establishing standards in content areas.

KEY TERMS AND CONCEPTS

cooperative education programs, 254
core curriculum, 244
core French, 252
curriculum, 234
explicit curriculum, 235
extracurricular/cocurricular programs, 237
hidden curriculum, 235
integrated curriculum, 239

null curriculum, 236
outcome-based education, 245
performance-based education, 245
problem-centred learning, 250
school-to-work programs, 254

student-centred curriculum, 239
subject-centred curriculum, 238
Tyler rationale, 238
whole-language approach, 247

APPLICATIONS AND ACTIVITIES

Teacher's Journal

1. List in order of importance the five factors that you believe have the greatest impact on the curriculum. Then list the five factors that you believe ideally should have the greatest influence. What differences do you notice between your actual and ideal lists? What might be done to reduce the differences between the two lists?

2. Reflect on the 12 000 or so hours that you have spent as a student in K–12 classrooms. What did the hidden curriculum in the classes teach you about yourself?

3. What religious and political emphases affected your learning in elementary school or high school? Which experiences do you view as having been positive? Which do you view as having been negative?

4. In your opinion, how should teachers and schools respond to censorship issues in curricula and complaints about the content of instructional materials?

5. What is your opinion of the current emphasis on preparing students for the world of work as the chief aim of education? What influences have created this emphasis? What curriculum goals might be sacrificed through a focus on turning out good employees?

Theory into Practice

Case Study: Group Work Response Questions

Consider the chapter case study. Divide the class into groups and have each group prepare a response to one of the following questions:

1. How much should teachers be expected to do about socio-economic and other challenges from outside the classroom?

2. What are the key social justice issues facing today's teachers?

3. Can teachers be expected to teach curricula that address social justice issues?

4. What are some of the ways that teachers can support struggling students and their families so that they might experience more success in school?

5. Can all students be expected to achieve the same learning outcomes?

6. Is Natanya naive and overly optimistic about the extent to which she can help her Grade 2 students?

7. As a first year teacher, how can Natanya realistically work to meet the social and academic needs of her students?

8. Is it possible or advisable for Natanya to employ the same teaching approaches, to teach the same curriculum, and to have the same expectations for students in Rosemount and Oak Creek elementary schools?

9. Given the same first year teaching assignment as Natanya, how would you approach the needs of your students?

Class Debate:

Develop an argument for the affirmative and negative sides of the following debate resolution:

Be it resolved that teachers are not responsible for the nonacademic needs of their students.

Large Group Challenge:

After reading Chapter 8, your class will assume the role of a school staff that has been given the assignment of working together on an interdisciplinary project with the overarching theme of "If You Love This Planet: Making a Difference Locally and Globally."

Directions:

1. Individually, go to "Interdisciplinary Learning in Your Classroom" at www.thirteen.org/edonline/concept2class/interdisciplinary/index.html.

   ■ Concept to Classroom is an extensive website that presents a series of workshops, including the one above on interdisciplinary learning that includes an introduction by interdisciplinary learning expert Heidi Hayes Jacobs. Go through the workshop lessons to develop an understanding of interdisciplinary learning.

2. As a class, meet and take on the roles of staff members in a school.

   ■ The choice of school level will depend on the composition of your education class. For example, if the class is made up of students specializing in elementary, junior high or middle school, and senior high school levels, then assume you are working in a kindergarten to Grade 12 school. If all of the students in your class are specializing at the junior high or middle school and senior high levels, then assume that you are working in a Grade 7–12 school.

   ■ Each student in the class will choose a grade level and a content area in which to become an "expert" (for example, Grade 1 math, Grade 7 science, Grade 11 English language arts [ELA]). In the end, if possible, all content areas taught in your provincial schools should be represented.

3. Individually, visit the appropriate provincial department of education website for the content area and grade level you have chosen. Explore the information provided to develop an understanding of the various curriculum outcomes set out by the department.

   ■ For example, ELA content specialists might find that the main strands of focus in the ELA curriculum are reading and viewing, speaking and listening, and writing and representing. You may also find that there are general and specific outcomes for each of these strands at various grade levels.

4. It's time to meet again as a "staff"; everyone now has a basic understanding of the outcomes that need to be met by students in the school at various grade levels and content areas. The staff must explore how students can meet the curriculum outcomes while making a difference locally and globally in the health of the planet.

5. Ultimately, the staff must arrive at a direction and focus for this project, and decide how the interdisciplinary theme will be dealt with at each grade level and in each content area.

   ■ Possible topics within the theme might include alternative transportation, recycling, reduction of greenhouse emissions, protection of species and ecosystems, and alternate energy sources.

6. The culminating product of this challenge will be a staff presentation on how this interdisciplinary project will look at each grade level and in each content area. Decisions regarding what format the presentation will take and who will be presenting the plan will have to be made by the "staff."

   Remember that this task will require brainstorming, cooperation, and consensus building!

Teacher's Database

1. Survey the internet to begin locating and bookmarking websites, schools, networks, and teacher discussion groups that you could use to help develop a subject-area curriculum for your students.

2. Find the professional curriculum standards for your subject area(s) online and compare them to the curriculum standards for that subject area in the province where you plan to teach. For example, you might download the National Council for Teachers of Mathematics (NCTM) standards and then compare them with the mathematics curriculum in the province where you plan to teach.

Observations and Interviews

1. Spend a half-day at a school observing the level you plan to teach and record your impressions regarding the types of curricula. If possible, chat briefly with administrators, teachers, and students about your impressions. Include observations of students outside the classroom during the school day.

2. As a collaborative project, conduct an informal survey on what people think are the four most important subjects to be taught at the elementary, middle, junior, and senior high levels. Compare your data with the information in this chapter.

3. With classmates, as an experiment, practise the process of curriculum development described in this chapter. Assign some members of the group to observe and report on their observations in relation to the concepts presented.

Professional Portfolio

Compare and contrast two or more textbooks or curriculum guides that are currently used to teach a unit in a subject area at a grade level you are preparing to teach. Assess the strengths and weaknesses of the unit in each textbook or curriculum guide. Would you use the materials in your classroom? How would you improve them? What other curriculum materials would you incorporate? How would you integrate educational technology? How would you adapt the curriculum for the unit for individual students according to their needs and characteristics?

MyEducationLab

At www.MyEducationLab.com, choose the Resources tab from the top menu. A number of links to various content areas provide activities, resources, case studies, lesson planning tools, video clips, and simulations.

To access a list of selected subject-area references for curriculum planning, go to Teacher's Resource 8.1 on www.MyEducationLab.com.

PEARSON
myeducationlab)

9

The Role of Technology in Education

[E]ffectively integrating new technology into educational practice is not just a matter of learning how to use the technology. It is also a process of reflecting on how technology-enhanced practices challenge assumptions about what and how to teach and how students can learn more effectively in today's world.

—Martha Stone Wiske, Kristi Rennebohm Franz, and Lisa Breit

Teaching for Understanding with Technology, 2005, p. 3

focus
questions

1. How is technology transforming teaching and learning?
2. What technologies are available for teaching?
3. How do Canadian teachers use computers and the internet?
4. What are the effects of computer technology on learning?
5. Should technology be at the forefront of efforts to improve schools?
6. What advantages are derived from the implementation of technological innovations by educators in remote communities?

It is mid-February, and today you are introducing your class of 24 Grade 3 students to a unit on basic geometric shapes. Your province's curriculum guidelines specify that students "will develop an understanding of geometric concepts and relationships as the basis for geometric modelling and reasoning to solve problems involving one-, two-, and three-dimensional figures." In addition, students will "recognize basic properties of, and similarities and differences between, simple geometric figures (e.g., number of sides, corners)" and they will be able to "predict and describe the results of putting together and taking apart two- and three-dimensional geometric figures."

Last year, you taught the unit for the first time. You have a firm grasp of geometric concepts, and your students really enjoyed the unit. However, only 50 percent of the students met all of the geometric outcomes assessed on tests of math and reading skills at the end of the year.

Your approach to teaching the unit this year will be very different. Your district's school received funding in September to improve student achievement through effective use of technology. Since the beginning of this school year, you have attended once-a-month workshops on using The Geometer's Sketchpad in the classroom. During the workshops you learned about the "teaching for understanding" framework presented in *Teaching for Understanding with Technology* (Wiske, Rennebohm Franz, & Breit 2005). You learned how to organize your curriculum around generative topics that focus on fascinating "big ideas" that go beyond memorizing information and practicing routine skills.

The Geometer's Sketchpad is a software program that enables students to construct geometric shapes and then explore their geometric properties by dragging the objects with the mouse. Students can examine an entire set of similar cases in a matter of seconds, leading them through a process of discovery to understand basic geometric concepts. Using the sketchpad, students first visualize and analyze a problem and then make conjectures before attempting a proof.

You have divided your students into six cooperative learning groups, each with a computer. Today, students will work on two collaborative explorations. First, for the "balance" activity, students will use mathematical reasoning to determine the relative weights of different shapes and explore the use and effectiveness of various problem-solving strategies. This sketchpad activity contains a collection of five different shapes: a star, a square, a circle, a triangle, and a diamond. The weight of these shapes can be compared using the provided balance scale. Students will drag one or more shapes onto the balance and it will tilt in the direction of the heavier shape(s). Next, for the "making a kaleidoscope" activity, students will create their own sketchpad kaleidoscopes. In the process, they will learn about rotation and reflection of geometric shapes.

You are working on the computer at the multimedia cart near your desk. A projector plugging into the computer shows the image on the screen at the front of the room.

"Okay, class, click on the link that says 'balance activity.' You're going to like this. It's amazing what you can do with this . . ."

Technology has transformed teaching and learning. Each day, students communicate with others around the world via the internet. Students search the web for information about whales, the Amazon rainforest, or the planet Mars. They go to chat rooms for children where they can "talk" to others in other countries or participate in global networking projects.

In the very late 70s and early 1980s, a few teachers began teaching with "computers" as the object of study. Later in the decade, teachers started using computers as a method of delivering information to students. Today, however, while some teachers use computers for highly structured drill-and-practice exercises, most educators regard information and communications technology (ICT) as supports for inquiry and discovery.

How Is Technology Transforming Teaching and Learning?

Educational technology has transformed teaching and learning at many of our nation's schools. Various provincial ministries of education have specific curriculum components related to ICT, with expected achievements defined for each grade level. Examples of the requirements include

- Nova Scotia's "Vision for the Integration of Information Technologies in the Nova Scotia Public School System"
- Manitoba's "Technology as a Foundation Skill Area: A Journey Toward Information Technology Literacy"
- Alberta's "ICT Complete Program of Studies"

Technology enables students to experience events or study phenomena that they cannot witness firsthand. By integrating technology into various learning tasks and across subject areas, teachers can provide students with learning experiences that would have been impossible a few years ago. Most important, careful and purposeful use of educational technology changes the roles of teachers and students and enhances students' higher-order learning and problem-solving skills. As you read the following vignette, consider how the use of educational technology affects the roles of teachers and students.

There's no shortage of vivid description in stories from Linda Mitchell's third-grade language arts students; she thinks that happy circumstance may have something to do with giving her students a number of ways to come to the writing, including through technology.

Before Tamlyn and Quinn did their descriptive writing, they created storyboards about the action they wanted to represent in an assignment on "expanding the moment"—making the story more intense by describing a fleeting instant in great detail. From their storyboard, they each created a computer animation of the action. Frame by frame, the animation in turn sparked their imaginations and helped them create word pictures. "It gives you ideas about what you see," says Quinn. HyperStudio and Kid Pix were among the computer programs they used.

"What the animation does is it assists the children in visualizing the action," explains Mitchell, who teaches language arts enrichment classes. "The animation is a way of them developing the picture so they relate that to the writing, to what they hear, what they see, what they feel. Technology gives you one more way of teaching something."

In the library, first-graders are following the progress of Miss Junie 2, an endangered sea turtle they adopted (for 85 cents each) from the Caribbean Conservation Corporation (CCC). Miss Junie 2 started her trip in Tortuguero, Costa Rica, and students regularly click onto the CCC site to check her movements as tracked by satellite and then write about her travels and ocean life in journals. Teacher Erin Okata integrated social studies, language arts, science, math, fine arts, and technology into the project as a way to help students develop an awareness of ocean life and to meet specific curriculum standards. (George Lucas Educational Foundation 2004)

The vignette demonstrates students and teachers using computer technology in a variety of ways. Classroom teachers use computers to present information to students and to encourage them to expand their understanding of cultural diversity. Further, technology encourages the development of research, writing, and communication skills. In the Queen Charlotte School District, students with visual impairment are provided with tools to assist them in the learning process. For adult learners living in remote locations, technology enables them access to formal learning opportunities not present in their own communities. Although these examples are strikingly different, they are similar in that teachers are using computers as a tool to achieve educational goals and to create particular kinds of learning environments.

Technology and the Challenge to Schools

The internet, and related telecommunications technologies have the potential to transform teaching and learning. However, an issue for education in the twenty-first century is to ensure that committed teachers, administrators, policy-makers, parents, and the general public assist students in realizing the full impact technology can have on their learning. As the following passage suggests, the future of schools may depend on educators' response to this challenge.

> The doubling of technological power through the 1990s morphed us into a high-speed, high-tech society. As a result, we are all experiencing accelerated change at a pace never before experienced in human history. Most of us involved in education are simply unprepared for this, and, consequently, we have not been able to respond to it as quickly as the world outside of education has. We must quickly catch up or face the unenviable prospect of becoming irrelevant. (McCain & Jukes 2001, 58–59)

Additionally (and significantly), educators must develop new assessment techniques to evaluate students' learning through the use of advanced telecommunications such as the internet. The number of correct responses on homework, quizzes, and examinations will no longer suffice to measure educational outcomes.

When you think about your future as a teacher who will be expected to use technology to enhance student learning, you may find that future at once exciting and intimidating, enticing and threatening. You may ask, "Will I be ready to meet the challenge of integrating technologies into my teaching?" In a very real sense, people like you will be expected develop new ways of using technology in the classrooms of tomorrow.

"One Bite at a Time!"

One Canadian principal of a technology-enriched elementary school, Cheryl Scotland-Moxon, describes how her school staff has embraced technology:

> I have had the opportunity, in my capacity as principal, to experience first-hand all the trials, tribulations, and triumphs information technology creates in a new school. A saying frequently used at our school is, "You must eat the elephant one bite at a time." In other words, we had to realize that professional development opportunities were scarce, and no amount of complaining about being ill-trained to use the technology was going to make it easier on us.
>
> We realized that everyone had a different comfort zone with using and integrating technology in their teaching. Given the demands of the curriculum, it was not very long before everyone clearly understood that technology is not curriculum. Rather, technology is a wonderful tool with endless possibilities to support the curriculum.
>
> The challenge for teachers is learning from others, having opportunities to share and observe, first-hand, examples of quality technology integration in the curriculum, and time to become "tech-savvy." This takes time, personal motivation on behalf of the teacher to learn, support from the school administrator, support from the School Board, and from colleagues. It also means that we keep in balance our work in technology integration with all the other demands of the classroom. Remember, one bite at a time!
>
> *Source*: Reprinted with permission from Cheryl Scotland-Moxon.

The Professional Reflection feature on the next page is designed to help you begin the process of planning for your future role.

Following is a list of educational technologies and instructional strategies that are changing teaching and learning. For each, indicate with an X whether you are "proficient," "somewhat proficient," or "not proficient" with that technology or strategy. Then indicate whether you are "highly committed," "somewhat committed," "opposed," or "neutral" toward using that technology or strategy in your teaching. Space is provided for you to add technologies and strategies not on the list.

After responding to the items, reflect on those to which you are "highly committed" to integrating into your teaching. What steps will you take from this point on to ensure that those technologies and strategies will, in fact, be part of your teaching practice in the future?

Technology or Instructional Strategy	Proficiency Level			Commitment to Using			
	Proficient	Somewhat proficient	Not proficient	Highly committed	Somewhat committed	Opposed	Neutral
1. Student networking via computer							
2. Video teleconferencing							
3. Interactive multimedia/ hypermedia							
4. Web page authoring							
5. CD-ROMs/ DVD							
6. Computer assisted instruction (CAI)							
7. Word processing							
8. Desktop publishing							
9. Presentation graphics							
10. Spreadsheets/graphing							
11. Databases							
12. email							
13. Attaching files to email							
14. Newsgroups							
15. Electronic gradebook							
16. Information retrieval on the web							
17. Networking with a file server							
18. Scanners							
19. Faxes							
20. Digital cameras							
21. Video cameras							
22. Other _____							
23. Other _____							

The Education Technology Advisory Council (ETAC, 2010, available at www.doe.mass.edu/boe/sac/edtech/STaR.doc) provides the Massachusetts School Technology and Readiness (STaR) chart, a comprehensive approach towards improving teaching and learning using technology; its design assumes continuous appraisal of the efficacy of technology's contribution to teaching and learning.

What Technologies Are Available for Teaching?

To enhance their classroom instruction, today's teachers can draw from a dazzling array of technological devices. In the early 1980s, the technology available to teachers who wished to use more than the chalkboard was limited to an overhead projector, a 16-mm movie projector, a tape recorder, and, in a few forward-looking school districts, television sets and VCRs. Today, "new interactive, multimedia, hyperlinked, networked technologies offer a myriad possibilities . . . beyond what is possible with traditional materials such as books, paper, and chalkboards" (Wiske, Rennebohm Franz, & Breit 2005). Teachers and students can use ever-more-powerful desktop and laptop computers with built-in modems, faxes, and **CD-ROM** players; videodisc players; camcorders; optical scanners; speech and music synthesizers; laser printers; digital cameras; and LCD projection panels. In addition, they can use sophisticated software for web browsing, e-mail, word processing, digital publishing, presentation graphics, spreadsheets, databases and multimedia applications, and e-books.

Although the array of currently available technology for the classroom is impressive, Ted McCain and Ian Jukes, authors of *Windows on the Future: Education in the Age of Technology* (2001, 44), predict even more incredible technologies in the future. "Electronics have increased in power more than 1 000 000 times since the development of ENIRC [electronic numerical integrator and calculator, an early computer introduced in 1946], but the greatest changes still lie ahead. Fasten your seat belts!" This chapter's Case to Consider feature focuses the on technologies a high school student might use in the year 2020.

While the term *educational technology* is usually assumed to mean computers in the classroom, many different forms of technology have influenced education. If we broadly define **educational technology** as inventions that enable teachers to reach their goals more effectively, it is clear that, for some time, teachers have been integrating into their classrooms many forms of educational technology, from the humble chalkboard and the overhead projector to televisions and DVD players.

For example, excellent educational television programs are aired by the Canadian Broadcasting Corporation (CBC), by the Public Broadcasting Service (PBS), and by some cable and commercial networks. With the increased availability of video equipment, many schools see students producing their own television documentaries, news programs, oral histories, and dramas. Teachers use closed-circuit television systems to prepare instructional materials for students in the district. In increasing numbers, school districts have **distance learning networks** that use two-way, interactive telecommunications to offer staff development opportunities to teachers, to provide enrichment instruction to students in remote areas, and, in the case of students who live great distances from the nearest school, to offer curriculum to students at home.

E-Learning and Virtual Schools

Canada is a country with wide expanses where small populations are sometimes scattered over great distances. Consequently, there is a growing number of high schools in the nation that are using **e-learning**, or online education, to supplement the school curriculum. **Virtual schools**, in which instruction takes place over the internet rather than in a traditional classroom, have become increasingly prevalent.

With many hundreds of students now taking multicast video classes in subjects such as pure math, science, physics, Aboriginal studies, and career exploration, distance learning courses have become so popular that, in some cases, administrators have had to limit enrolment.

With the spread of virtual schools, some educators, policy-makers, and researchers have expressed concern about exaggerated claims for online learning. In addition, they are worried about what is lost when students do not meet face-to-face with their classmates and teachers. The trend toward e-learning and virtual schools will no doubt continue. Meanwhile, several questions must be addressed to ensure that virtual students have quality online learning experiences:

- While online learning may be appropriate for high school students, should it be made available to elementary and middle school students? At what stage or age should learners be considered "too young" for e-learning?
- Should online courses be aligned with provincial curricular standards?
- Who should provide for students' technological needs when they take an online course? Who should cover the costs?
- How can we ensure that online teachers are trained effectively to teach via the internet?
- Should parental approval be required before a child enrols in an online course?
- Should students receive the same credit for an online course as they would for an interactive, face-to-face class?
- How can school officials ensure the quality of online courses, especially those offered by teachers in other provinces or countries?

Computer Technology in the Classroom

Schools are discovering the power of technology to enhance the teaching–learning process. An example of corporations supporting the use of technology in education is the Hewlett-Packard (HP) Technology for Teaching grant program that aims to improve learning in the classroom through innovative uses of technology. Other goals of the program include encouraging student leadership in the digital workforce and creating interest in careers in math, science, and technology. In 2005, HP (Canada) Co. provided eight Canadian schools with a total of $336 000 in wireless technology, cash, and professional development through the HP Technology for Teaching grant program. Recipients of the grants included Harbour View High School in Saint John, New Brunswick, where the funding aided the science team's focus on the teaching of motion within the Grade 9/10 science curriculum and in-car and off-road vehicle safety in the Grade 11/12 physics curriculum. At Mackay Center School in Montreal, teachers used the HP Tablet PC in combination with SmartBoard interactive whiteboard technology to present curricula in a more visual way, aiming to improve the skills of children with language disabilities (HP News 2005).

Although personal computers may not have transformed all schools so that all students have learning experiences like those described above, information communication

Technology in the Life of a Student: 2020

Eddy's day starts when his internet earring starts playing his favourite music at 6:30 a.m. He wakes up and looks over at his schedule for the day on his wall screen. He notices that he has early lunch, so once he's up he packs a snack for the morning. After getting ready, Eddy grabs his learning tablet and opens a bus alert with an exact GPS location. His bus is running 15 minutes late, so he relaxes a little. He tells his virtual mentor to identify his daily learning packet that he has received from school, which contains all of his work projects, meetings, and notes for the day. They are read to Eddy via a voice in his earring.

Eddy has team deliverables due to be presented in his first class period. He will review the presentation with his team through his two-way video tablet on the way to school. He compares his schedule to his teacher's schedule and picks a time he can log in for a remote one-on-one meeting. His calendar is automatically updated with the new appointment and a message is sent to all the team members, including the teacher. Eddy's virtual mentor checks the bus online and announces that it is just turning down his street.

After boarding the bus, Eddy's clothes are scanned for his student number and the school is immediately notified that he has made the bus and will be conferencing in en route. He arrives to school 15 minutes late, but has been in constant communication with his team, going over last minute details for the presentation, so they're good to go. He queues his music to play and listens to his favourite song as he walks across campus. He arrives and joins his project team as they review details about the Persian Gulf War that are relevant to Eddy's schoolmates in Egypt. Reviewing a vision of the history

technology has had a significant impact on education. Like the dawn of the television era in the 1950s, the widespread availability of personal computers and handheld devices has been heralded as a technological innovation that will change the teaching–learning process.

Computers and Instruction

Since the early 1980s, the use of computers to enhance instruction has grown steadily. Two of the more common approaches are **computer-assisted instruction (CAI)** (sometimes called computer-*aided* instruction) and computer-managed instruction (CMI). Computer-assisted instruction relies on computer programs that provide students with highly structured drill-and-practice exercises or tutorials. Research has shown CAI to be effective with at-risk students and students with disabilities because it accommodates their special needs and instruction is appropriately paced (Bitter & Pierson 2005; Bowerman 2005; Jones 1994; Norris 1994; Wiske, Rennebohm Franz, & Breit 2005.). Moreover, CAI can provide students with a positive, supportive environment for learning; students can avoid embarrassment since their inevitable mistakes while of the discussion, he watches as personalized information puts the discussion into context for him. A set of questions are automatically configured for his review and a green light blinks on his tablet, indicating it's his turn to engage.

An alert appears on the tablet just before the end of the period, reminding Eddy to meet his science team outside. In class today, Eddy is completing his personalized learning project. This project was designed especially for Eddy's learning style and allows him to use an observation-based instructional process. While outside, Eddy works on the effects of light on plants, using his virtual biosphere to experiment. He collects real-time data from various laboratories throughout the world, helping him manage his unique ecosystem.

Eddy heads to the cafeteria, where he picks up his pre-ordered lunch and debits his student account. After lunch, he has three other projects to check in on and then a free period. During his spare, Eddy signs in to a Chinese course being offered by a school in Beijing and begins talking to his classmates via embedded cameras and a virtual interface. (Adapted from Hinrichs 2002, 6–7)

Questions

1. How realistic is this scenario for a typical day in the life of a high school student in the year 2020?
2. Technology obviously plays a significant role in Eddy's life. How do you think it shapes the work of Eddy's teachers?
3. Based on this scenario, how will the work life of teachers change between now and the year 2020?

learning are not exposed to peers. Figure 9.1 presents several additional student-centred and technology-centred advantages of CAI.

Computer-managed instruction (CMI) relies on programs that evaluate and diagnose students' needs and then, based on that assessment, guide them through the next steps in their learning. CMI records students' progress for teachers to monitor. CAI and CMI can result in reduced teacher–student interactions if the teacher interprets his or her role as primarily that of record keeper or manager. On the other hand, CAI and CMI can also enhance teacher–student interactions: "Technology can aid greatly in making time spent in routine administrative tasks effective and efficient, and this undoubtedly can lead to more minutes available for meaningful contact with an educator's clients, the young learners" (Bitter & Pierson 2005, 304).

An increasingly popular approach to computer-based instruction is **computer-enhanced instruction (CEI)**. Unlike CAI and CMI, computer-enhanced instruction (CEI) is less structured and more inquiry-oriented. The following example illustrates how CEI was used in a Grade 9 mathematics class to examine a topic of interest to most students: sports data.

Figure 9.1

Advantages of
computer-assisted
instruction (CAI)

**Advantages of
computer-assisted
instruction**

Student-Centred Advantages

Students' self-tasking and self-pacing of their learning
Opportunities for individualized instruction
Low-risk learning context for learners who are less able
Multisensory modes of communication (voice, sound, text, graphic, art, animation)
Motivating, high-interest content
Enabling learning context for students with disabilities
Opportunities to learn for students with limited English proficiency
Likelihood of higher achievement (remediation or enrichment)

**COMPUTER-
ASSISTED
INSTRUCTION**

Technology-Centred Advantages

Efficiency and effectiveness
Savings in teachers instru ctional time
Systematic response to users and high rates of reinforcement
Skill training in formal logic and technical skills
Consistent, reliable instruction independent of teacher, day/time, or place
Automatic record–keeping and performance–monitoring capabilities
Access to expanded knowledge base and global information resources
Enabling context for customizing or creating curricula, instructional materials, software

Students begin by researching recent news stories about sports, noting how statistics are used. The teacher then guides the class through a model inquiry about athletes' academic and athletic performance in major universities. Students make observations and pose questions about the data and note how the data are used in news articles and various sports-related policies. As they learn to evaluate claims based on statistics, students develop questions about a sports issue that interests them.

Students then apply mathematics to analyze their topic. They learn to use linear equations, correlation and regression analysis, and a variety of visual representations (plots, tables, charts, and graphs) as they apply statistical methods to the analysis of sports issues. They use graphing calculators and spreadsheets to evaluate sports writers' inferences and predictions, as well as to explore different ways of presenting, analyzing, and displaying sports data. Students use word processors, digital images, and *PowerPoint* to record, reflect on, and present their understandings of statistics in sports.

As students delve into the data, they realize that statistics can be accurate or inaccurate, informative, misconstrued, or unclear, depending on how data are processed and represented. They learn how to determine whether claims based on data seem reasonable and are supported by contextual information. (Wiske, Rennebohm Franz, & Breit 2005, 37)

Unlike in CAI or CMI, in CEI teachers play a critical role in facilitating interactions between computer and student. Teachers must do more than seat students in front of a computer—they must guide students through learning activities that enable them to use technology to arrive at a deeper understanding of the topic at hand.

Some schools are using another inquiry-oriented approach to enhancing instruction with computers—the **microcomputer-based laboratory (MBL)**, sometimes called

CBL (computer-based laboratory). Through probes and sensors attached to computers, microcomputer-based laboratories enable students to measure and graph data such as light, sound, temperature, voltage, skin resistance, magnetic field, and heat flow. Students can gather data in the school laboratory or use a battery-operated interface to gather data in the field. For example, Concord Consortium (located at www.concord.org) is a nonprofit research and development organization dedicated to "digital equity" (equal learning opportunities for all students) and to finding new ways to use technology in teaching. It developed MBL curriculum materials that enable students to learn about rainforests using a sensor to gather local data for such variables as humidity, light, dissolved oxygen in rivers and streams, and acid rain. Students then compare local data with those obtained in an actual rainforest. It is clear from this scenario that, as with any meaningful set of instructional objectives and outcomes, teachers engaged in using information communication technology must also engage in a great deal of preparation.

The "Magic" of Media

Some of the most exciting forms of media magic involve CD-ROMs, videodiscs, and interactive multimedia. Recent advances in computer technology make it possible for students to be much more active in shaping their learning experiences. On a 10-cm CD-ROM, they can access the equivalent of 270 000 pages of text (about 900 books at 300 pages each), or, on a 30-cm **videodisc**, they can access the equivalent of about 54 000 photographic slides. Computer-supported **interactive multimedia** allow students to integrate information from e-books and from huge text, audio, video libraries, as well as a range of readily available hardware and software.

Hypermedia systems consisting of a computer, a CD-ROM drive, a videodisc player, a video monitor, and speakers now allow students to control and present sound, video images, text, and graphics with an almost limitless array of possibilities. Students who use such hypermedia systems, the most familiar of which is the internet, can follow their curiosity, browse through enormous amounts of information, and develop creative solutions for multidimensional, real-life problems. Online databases in many fields are changing the way students conduct library research as more computerized reference works—such as directories, dictionaries, and encyclopedias— become available.

The term *hypermedia* refers to documents composed of text, audio, and visual information stored in a computer and accessed by the user in a nonlinear fashion. "Hypermedia environments let the user access information in any order he or she wishes. This access simulates the natural, nonlinear ways in which humans learn, and allows for individual construction of knowledge" (Bitter & Pierson 2005, 270). A hypermedia system is an effective learning tool because it allows students to actively construct their own learning experiences based on their interests, preferences, and learning style.

Computer Simulations

For students, computer simulations can be engaging and very motivational. Simulations model complex, multidimensional events in the real world, and can range from a lemonade stand planned and run by elementary school students, who vicariously practice basic arithmetic and problem-solving skills, to a mock trial in which law students can participate via videodisc and computer. Simulations can allow students to visit the great museums of the world, explore the bottom of the Pacific Ocean, or experience what it was like to be a pioneer travelling west by wagon. Further, as learners work

highlights

How Can Word Prediction Software Enhance the Writing Skills of Students with Disabilities?

"What should I write?" "What words will best express what I want to say?" Although most people find these questions at least somewhat difficult to answer, students with disabilities may confront unique challenges when they write. Some students with learning disabilities may not be able to retain ideas in their memories long enough to express them in writing; others may have difficulty spelling; and students with motor disabilities may be challenged when forming letters with a pen or pencil or making repetitive keystrokes on a word processor.

Students with disabilities that affect their ability to write can be assisted by word prediction software that reduces the number of keystrokes needed to type. When writing with word prediction software, a student types the first letter of a word, and then a numbered list of words beginning with that letter appears on the screen. If the desired word is on the list, the student enters the number and the word is typed automatically. For example, assume a student wants to write the word "tonight" to complete the sentence "I will watch television tonight." First, she enters a "t" and a list of common "t" words appears. Since the word "tonight" is not on this

list, she types an "o" and another screen appears. Since "tonight" is on this list, she types a number "3" and the word is entered automatically. Thus, the seven keystrokes needed to write "tonight" were reduced to three.

The following list describes additional features of various word prediction software programs:

- Synthesized speech output
- Prediction methods—Some programs predict on the basis of spelling only, while others consider the words that have come before in the sentence. For example, only nouns are listed after the word "a" or "an."
- List updating—After "learning" a student's vocabulary, some word prediction programs tailor word prediction lists to the student's usage. Some programs update automatically, while others allow the user to decide when to update.
- Prediction window customization
- Keyboard sensitivity adjustment—Keyboard sensitivity can be adjusted to prevent repetition if keys are not quickly released.

their way through a simulation, opportunities are presented for them to make decisions at critical points, enter their decisions into the computer, and then receive feedback on the consequences of those decisions.

Home–School Communication Systems

Computer-based **home–school communication systems** such as the Phone Master Notification System are helping busy teachers and parents exchange information. Interfacing a computer program with its computer-based student records can enable teachers to use EdGear's "Talking Gradebook" software to communicate students' progress to parents. Or, by using a touchtone phone and entering a teacher's room number, students and parents can access homework assignments, test scores, and current grades. Increasingly, schools are using sophisticated home–school communication systems to strengthen their educational programs. Some communication systems even include a "tip line" that uses voice-disguising software to provide students with a safe, anonymous way to provide tips to help reduce school violence. Schools are also using home–school communication systems to disseminate the following kinds of information:

- Absence and tardy parent notification
- Bus schedules

- Club information
- Congratulatory calls
- Invitations to school events
- Lunch menus
- Parent Teacher Association or Parent Teacher Organization information
- Reminders to vote on bond issues
- School cancellations, early dismissals
- Teacher reminders for assignments or activities

The Internet

Observers estimate that the amount of information in the world doubles every 900 days (Bitter & Pierson 2005); the **Internet**, comprising thousands of interconnected computers around the globe, and the **World Wide Web (the web)**—the most popular "entrance" to the internet—make available to teachers and students much of this information. As Table 9.1 illustrates, the size of the web has increased exponentially since 1995. In addition, newsgroups and chat rooms on the internet enable teachers and students to communicate with people around the world.

Newsgroups

Through **newsgroups**, students can create electronic bulletin boards and discuss topics of mutual interest with students at other schools, in the same community, or around the world. Messages are "posted" on the bulletin board for others to read at their convenience. When students "surf" into a newsgroup, they can find messages arranged by subject and author, with responses listed beneath the original message.

Chat Rooms

Students can also participate in "live" discussions held in a **chat room**. Chat rooms use internet relay chat technology and allow users to participate in live, online, typed discussions. In some chat rooms, students can talk to online experts in a wide array of fields and receive immediate responses to their questions.

KIDLINK, a well-known chat room for children aged 10 to 15, is carefully monitored and open only to registered users. The goal of KIDLINK is to promote global dialogue among young people, and students must answer four questions when they register: (1) "Who am I?" (2) "What do I want to be when I grow up?" (3) "How do I want the world to be better when I grow up?" and (4) "What can I do now to make this happen?" Teacher-leaders of KIDLINK organize and monitor numerous projects; for example, the "Draw a Story for Me" project for kindergarten and Grade 1 students around the world has the following objectives.

Students will

1. Communicate with other kids by means of artwork
2. Learn some easy English words and sentences
3. Learn some computer skills:

   - Drawing with a graphics software
   - Using a scanner to import their drawings in the computer
   - Uploading their pictures in KidSpace
   - Sending their pictures as attachments by email to the project moderator
   - Learn some habits and customs of other people
   - Enjoy new friends all over the world. (KIDLINK 2002)

Videoconferencing

Videoconferences can be held over the internet if users have video cameras connected to their computers and C-U SeeMe, PictureTel, or similar software installed. As with any educational technology, care must be taken that **videoconferencing** is more than a high-tech way for teachers to lecture to passive students at other locations. "Video-conferencing best supports meaningful learning by helping diverse learners to collaborate and converse with each other in order to solve problems and construct meaning" (Jonassen, Peck, & Wilson 1999, 82).

How Do Canadian Teachers Use Computers and the Internet?

As this chapter illustrates, an array of technologies is available for teacher use in the classroom. However, to what extent and how are teachers actually using new technologies?

Preparing Lessons

The internet has been termed "the world's largest library," and, as such, it can be a remarkable resource for planning lessons. According to Teaching, Learning, and Computing, a 1998–1999 research project of the Center for Research on Information Technology and Organizations (CRITO) at the University of California at Irvine, 28 percent of teachers with internet access from home used the internet weekly or more to gather information and resources for their teaching, and 40 percent of such teachers did so occasionally. Among teachers who had access to the internet at school as well as at home, 46 percent reported weekly or more frequent use. We can safely assume that teacher use of the internet to gather resources for planning lessons has grown exponentially since then.

Examples of resources that provide extensive websites and web-based student learning activities that support the Ontario Provincial Curriculum include

- Link to Learning Ontario Curriculum: www.linktolearning.com
- Ontario Curriculum Unit Planner: www.ocup.org
- Cyberlinks from the Toronto District School Board: www.tdsb.on.ca/_site/ ViewItem.asp?siteid=205&menuid=1244&pageid=912

Communicating with Other Educators

In addition to being widely used by teachers to prepare lessons and gather resources, the internet also has the potential for enhancing communication with other educators, according to the TLC survey. "By far the most important variable in predicting teachers' internet use is the teacher's level of classroom connectivity" (Becker 1999, 29). For example, a comparison of e-mail use between teachers who had internet access at both home and school with teachers who had access only at home revealed that teachers with classroom access were *three times as likely* to e-mail teachers at other schools. Not surprisingly, if teachers don't have ready access to the internet during their daily professional lives, their use of e-mail is less frequent.

Posting Information and Student Work on the Web

In addition to using e-mail to communicate with other educators, teachers post information, professional opinions, or student work on the web. As with the use of e-mail, the likelihood of teachers posting information online is strongly related to connectivity in the classroom. As classroom access to the internet becomes more common, teachers' use of it to communicate with other educators and to post materials will also increase.

Facilitating Students' Learning via Computers and Cyberspace

In previous sections of this chapter, we saw several instances of how teachers use computers and the internet to enhance students' learning (see Figure 9.2). In the following example, a science teacher comments on the benefits of having students search for information on the internet:

> I think [the internet] provides more opportunities for the kids than relying primarily on a textbook. I think that the Web allows them to go out and see things that the book just can't show them. If they want, they can go out and see excellent schematics of the human cell. They can go out and see excellent photographs of cells. They can spend all day looking underneath a microscope and never see a cell as nice as they can find online because they put the best ones out there. (Wallace 2004, 462)

Increasingly, teachers are encouraging students to use the internet to communicate with others, to collaborate on projects with classes at other schools, and to publish.

The following firsthand account from Vivian Rose, a teacher in Newfoundland, illustrates the potential of technology to foster and develop skills of critical thinking.

> The use of technology to foster and develop skills of critical thinking is an area of great potential in education. Last year, my gifted students in Canadian History 1201 embarked on a new journey using the YouthLinks. This program is designed for teachers and students to engage in discussions through forums and debates on issues important to them. At any time, a student or teacher could enter their own critical issue and engage others in collaborative research that can be shared in the classroom, around the country or across the globe.

> My students researched the social, economic, historical, and geographical aspects of their local communities. As well, they participated in collaborative writing and editing, became familiar with Web protocols, were vocal in online discussion forums with Canadian and international students. This initiative helped to foster in my students an attitude of constructive action on issues of global importance and local relevance. As well, they developed critical thinking, research, and writing skills, and a comfort and familiarity with using and publishing in electronic media. Personally, it provided me with useful resources and a variety of teaching strategies to employ well beyond YouthLinks. It is a fabulous way to engage teachers in collegial discussion of important international issues. We were fascinated with the program. Our online discussions and debates were so well received that we got selected to represent our province at the National YouthLinks Summit in Kingston, Ontario. Now that was an awesome Canadian history learning experience!

> (Historica website's YouthLinks: www.histori.ca/default.do?page=.index)

Figure 9.2

National Education
Technology Standards
(NETS) for teachers,
2008

Source: © International
Society for Technology in
Education. Retrieved
August 25, 2008, from
www.iste.org/Content/
NavigationMenu/NETS/
ForTeachers/2008Standards/
NETS_for_Teachers_2008
.htm.

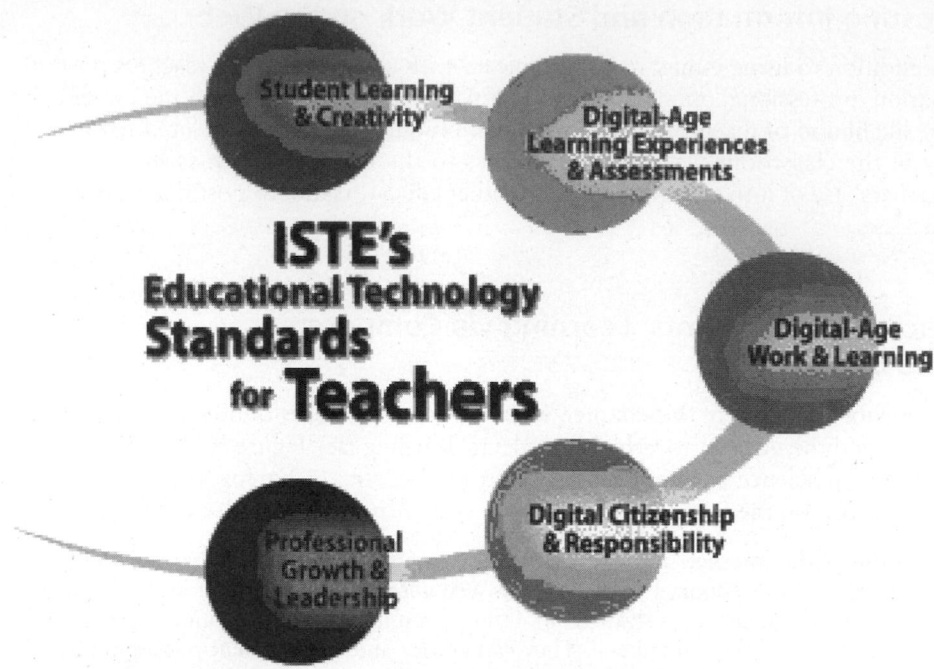

1. **Facilitate and Inspire Student Learning and Creativity**

   Teachers use their knowledge of subject matter, teaching and learning, and technology to
   facilitate experiences that advance student learning, creativity, and innovation in both
   face-to-face and virtual environments. Teachers:

   a. promote, support, and model creative and innovative thinking and inventiveness.
   b. engage students in exploring real-world issues and solving authentic problems using
      digital tools and resources.
   c. promote student reflection using collaborative tools to reveal and clarify students'
      conceptual understanding and thinking, planning, and creative processes.
   d. model collaborative knowledge construction by engaging in learning with students,
      colleagues, and others in face-to-face and virtual environments.

2. **Design and Develop Digital-Age Learning Experiences and Assessments**

   Teachers design, develop, and evaluate authentic learning experiences and assessment
   incorporating contemporary tools and resources to maximize content learning in context
   and to develop the knowledge, skills, and attitudes identified in the NETS•S. Teachers:

   a. design or adapt relevant learning experiences that incorporate digital tools and
      resources to promote student learning and creativity.

   b. develop technology-enriched learning environments that enable all students to
      pursue their individual curiosities and become active participants in setting their own
      educational goals, managing their own learning, and assessing their own progress.

   c. customize and personalize learning activities to address students' diverse learning
      styles, working strategies, and abilities using digital tools and resources.

   d. provide students with multiple and varied formative and summative assessment
      aligned with content and technology standards and use resulting data to inform
      learning and teaching.

Figure 9.2

(Continued)

3. **Model Digital-Age Work and Learning**

Teachers exhibit knowledge, skills, and work processes representative of an innovative professional in a global and digital society. Teachers:

    a.   demonstrate fluency in technology systems and the transfer of current knowledge to new technologies and situations.

    b.   collaborate with students, peers, parents, and community members using digital tools and resources to support student success and innovation.

    c.   communicate relevant information and ideas effectively to students, parents, and peers using a variety of digital-age media and formats.

    d.   model and facilitate effective use of current and emerging digital tools to locate, analyze, evaluate, and use information resources to support research and learning.

4. **Promote and Model Digital Citizenship and Responsibility**

Teachers understand local and global societal issues and responsibilities in an evolving digital culture and exhibit legal and ethical behavior in their professional practices. Teachers:

    a.   advocate, model, and teach safe, legal, and ethical use of digital information and technology, including respect for copyright, intellectual property, and the appropriate documentation of sources.

    b.   address the diverse needs of all learners by using learner-centered strategies providing equitable access to appropriate digital tools and resources.

    c.   promote and model digital etiquette and responsible social interactions related to the use of technology and information.

    d.   develop and model cultural understanding and global awareness by engaging with colleagues and students of other cultures using digital-age communication and collaboration tools.

5. **Engage in Professional Growth and Leadership**

Teachers continuously improve their professional practice, model lifelong learning, and exhibit leadership in their school and professional community by promoting and demonstrating the effective use of digital tools and resources. Teachers:

    a.   participate in local and global learning communities to explore creative applications of technology to improve student learning.

    b.   exhibit leadership by demonstrating a vision of technology infusion, participating in shared decision making and community building, and developing the leadership and technology skills of others.

    c.   evaluate and reflect on current research and professional practice on a regular basis to make effective use of existing and emerging digital tools and resources in support of student learning.

    d.   contribute to the effectiveness, vitality, and self-renewal of the teaching profession and of their school and community.

The Steady Growth of Information Communication Technology and Its Applications to Teaching and Learning

Many teachers who began teaching in 1975 were aware of the existence of huge machines—often located on military installations and in university basements and controlled by a few, select geniuses—that used punch cards to process certain types of computation at fairly high speeds. Such teachers had never seen a desktop computer. But by the early 1980s, they were witness to banks of computers in some schools—schools that perhaps had a particularly forward-thinking staff member who assiduously built and maintained a computer lab through scrounging together dollars and ancillary pieces of hardware. Almost certainly, teachers who taught during the 35-year period between 1975 and 2010 would have ended their careers taking for granted such things as computerized scheduling and class-by-class attendance tracking, laptops, data projectors, and smart boards. Most of those teachers would marvel at how they had ever gotten through the day without access to the personal computing power that would have been unimaginable in their first years in the classroom. The impact of technological change seems vast and impressive; nevertheless, it remains difficult to accurately appraise the effects of information communication technology on teaching and learning.

Apple Classrooms of Tomorrow (ACOT) Project

One of the most informative research studies is based on the Apple Classrooms of Tomorrow (ACOT) project launched in seven K–12 classrooms in 1986. Participating students and teachers each received two computers—one for school and one for home. Eight years later, study results indicated that all ACOT students performed as well as they were expected without computers, and some performed better. More important, perhaps, "the ACOT students routinely and without prompting employed inquiry, collaboration, and technological and problem-solving skills" (Mehlinger 1996, 405). Also, 90 percent of ACOT students went on to college after graduating from high school, compared with only 15 percent of non-ACOT students. Furthermore, the behavior of ACOT teachers also changed—they worked "more as mentors and less as presenters of information" (Mehlinger 1996, 404).

An additional positive finding of the ACOT study was how teachers gradually began to use the computers in new ways in the classroom. "When [ACOT] teachers were able to move past that pervasive teacher-centered view of education, students and teachers, as communities of learners, were able to benefit from the range of individual areas of expertise represented by the entire group" (Bitter & Pierson 2005, 95). Teachers rearranged their classrooms to enable students to work collaboratively on projects, and they frequently made arrangements for students who wished to stay after school to work on multimedia projects. Frequently, "students and teachers collaborated together, with the students often in the role of expert or resource person" (Schwartz & Beichner 1999, 33–34).

Information Communication Technology: A Boon for Education or Not?

A powerful way to determine if certain educational practices actually influence students' learning is to conduct *meta-analyses*— that is, to "take the findings from single studies and calculate a way to compare them with each other. The goal is to synthesize the findings statistically and determine what the studies reveal when examined all together" (Kirkpatrick & Cuban 1998, 5). One such meta-analysis reviewed the results of 133 research studies on educational technology from 1990 through 1994. The results of that study follow (Mehlinger 1996, 405):

- Educational technology has a significant positive impact on achievement in all subject areas, across all levels of school, and in regular classrooms as well as those for special-needs students.
- Educational technology has positive effects on student attitudes.
- The degree of effectiveness is influenced by the student population, the instructional design, the teacher's role, how students are grouped, and the levels of student access to technology.

- Technology makes instruction more student-centered, encourages cooperative learning, and stimulates increased teacher–student interaction.
- Positive changes in the learning environment evolve over time and do not occur quickly.

Another meta-analysis conducted by Heather Kirkpatrick and Larry Cuban (1998) at Stanford University also addressed the complications and difficulties involved in determining the effects of computers on learning, particularly when much of the research in that area is methodologically flawed. Research studies, they pointed out, "are of little use unless they elaborate the children's ages, the subject, the software used, the kinds of outcomes that were sought, and how the study was done" (p.1). With these limitations in mind, the following is a brief summary of Kirkpatrick and Cuban's findings:

- Seven of the single studies of elementary and secondary students yielded positive findings related to achievement and attitude change, while seven studies yielded negative or mixed findings.
- Ten of the single studies on the effectiveness of computers to teach in core areas such as mathematics, reading, science, and social studies yielded results ranging from very positive to "cautiously negative."
- Ten meta-analyses found higher levels of student achievement in computer-using classrooms.
- Five meta-analyses found that student attitudes improved and students learned more in less time in computer-using classrooms.

On the basis of their meta-analysis of the research—much of it considered methodologically flawed due to a lack of scientific controls—Kirkpatrick and Cuban concluded that "we are unable to ascertain whether computers in classrooms have in fact been or will be the boon they have promised to be" (1998, 31).

The ambiguities of research on computer-based instruction aside, it is clear that educational technology *can* have positive effects on learning and teaching, and indications are that technology will influence all aspects of education even more in the twenty-first century. Thus, the question to be asked about the effectiveness of educational technology is not, "Is it effective?" Instead, we should ask: 1) "How and under what circumstances does educational technology enhance students' learning?" and 2) "What are the roles and responsibilities of teachers in ensuring that technology is used to benefit the experiences of learners?" As funds are made available to purchase hardware and software, to train teachers, and to provide technical support, the benefits of classroom media "magic" will become even more widespread.

Should Technology Be at the Forefront of Efforts to Improve Schools?

Are schools falling prey to a tremendous computer-oriented "hype" encouraged by technology corporations, big business, and ambitious superintendents who want their districts to be ahead in the race for the latest technology, or by politicians promoting the latest "quick fix" for education? Will information computer technology help schools develop the kind of students and citizens the nation needs? Is there a "fit" between the undeniable power of computers and the educational goals we seek? Are there more cost-effective ways to achieve these educational goals? These are among the difficult questions that must be addressed as the role of technology in education is debated (see this chapter's Where Do you Stand? feature).

Can computers help to improve schools?

The Opposition: Computers Will Not Improve Education

Among the first to question the role of technology in the classroom was Clifford Stoll, one of the pioneers of the internet and author of *Silicon Snake Oil: Second Thoughts on the Information Highway* (1996). In *High-Tech Heretic: Why Computers Don't Belong in the Classroom and Other Reflections by a Computer Contrarian*, Stoll (1999, xiv) wrote, "I believe that a good school needs no computers. And a bad school won't be much improved by even the fastest Internet links. That a good teacher can handle her subject without any multimedia support. . . . That it's unnecessary—and misleading—to push children's work onto the Internet. That students, justifiably, recognize computer assignments primarily as entertainment, rather than education." Similarly, David Shenk concludes his book *Data Smog: Surviving the Information Glut* (1998, 220), with eight "Principles of Technorealism" endorsed by selected leading experts on technology; principle number five states:

> The art of teaching cannot be replicated by computers, the Net, or by "distance learning." These tools can, of course, augment an already high quality educational experience. But to rely on them as any sort of panacea would be a costly mistake.

Similarly, other critics have cautioned the public against pushing schools into the computer revolution. A sampling of their comments follows:

> Too often, what computers actually connect children to are trivial games, inappropriate adult material, and aggressive advertising. They can also isolate children, emotionally and physically, from direct experience of the natural world. The "distance" education they promote is the opposite of what all children, and especially children at risk, need most—close relationships with caring adults. (Alliance for Childhood 2000, 4)

> So far, the most that can be said about computer-based instruction is that vast sums have been lavished on a technology whose educational potential has yet to be proven. We can only guess the long-term effects of computer use on young children's development. (Armstrong & Casement 2000, xii)

> Policymakers, administrators, and parents have, essentially, demanded that teachers use the Internet. That demand has not been accompanied by serious efforts to understand what it takes for teachers to be able to use the Internet effectively in teaching. In fact, when schools respond to the mantra "Train the teachers," they almost always neglect to answer the question, "To do what?" (Wallace 2004, 482)

Perhaps the strongest argument that computers will not improve education is the fact that computers can distract educators from what should be their focus: students, their learning, and their lives. Computers can depersonalize education, distancing students from one another and from their teachers. Computers are not sensitive to students' needs, nor do they notice when a student's work habits, communication, demeanor, grooming, or dress change abruptly, possibly signalling trouble. Computers don't know when a student is discouraged, sad, lonely, fearful, or "stuck" in his or her learning. They are poor substitutes for true companions—they do not laugh, commiserate, or share warmly with their users. Clearly, they cannot provide the human dimension that is needed greatly in today's schools.

The Advocates: Computers Will Improve Education

Despite media stories and articles critical of the call for more computers in schools, enthusiasm for technology in education remains strong. For example, in a U.S.-based, Media Control Interface–conducted poll in 1998, almost 60 percent of the public answered "a great amount" when asked, "How much do you think computers have helped improve student learning?" (Trotter 1998, 6). Following are a few representative comments that rebut arguments against computers in schools.

> The answer to the poor use of computers or incomplete research about their effect on educational outcomes is not to ignore the machines or banish them from the classroom. . . . The challenge for 21st-century educators is to find balanced, sensible, and pedagogically sound ways of using these remarkable new tools. (Gordon 2003, 4–5)

> It has become fashionable to say that computers in education are a bust. [However,] the new media can positively change the role of the teacher and student, shifting education from broadcast to interactive learning. When done effectively, [the] results are dramatic. (Tapscott 1999)

There are real dangers in looking to technology to be the savior of education. But it won't survive without the technology. (Jane David, Apple consultant, quoted in Oppenheimer 1997)

As long as educators remember that computers are not an end in themselves but a tool for enhancing the educational experiences of students, computers have great potential to improve education. To avoid using computers, whatever the reason, is to limit learning possibilities. Movies, videos, and television, once viewed as threats to education, have become generally accepted in classrooms. Further development of today's educational technology will do the same.

A Note of Caution

Clearly, educational technology *does* have positive effects on learning and teaching, and indications are that technology will influence all aspects of education even more in the future. However, just as every teaching–learning outcome has an overt or declared curriculum, so does every social setting—including the school—have a covert or hidden curriculum (see Chapter 8). Wise teachers and administrators monitor the hidden curriculum carefully because it is a powerful force that helps shape school climate, and it can exert a strong effect on how students feel about their school, their learning, and themselves. Briefly stated, the "hidden curriculum" embraces the social nuances of the classroom, the school, and the total school-community culture.

Information communication technology, through potent mediums such as the many social networking opportunities available online, can create opportunities that are pursued for harmful purposes such as the invasion privacy or cyberbullying. Furthermore, since cell phones can be used to upload images to the internet in a matter of seconds, teachers must be vigilant with regard to students' use of personal technology in the classroom.

In addition, the privacy of teachers and administrators is at risk in the twenty-first century as never before. For example, during the spring of 2010, a school principal in Nova Scotia was removed temporarily from his position after the school board viewed a school security video of him grabbing a student. Later, the images of the altercation were posted without authorization on a popular internet video sharing site and "went viral" as hundreds of thousands of people viewed the fracas.

As you contemplate a teaching career, how do you view the use of personal technologies such as cell phones, video sharing sites, and social networking sites in the contexts of student communication, teacher use, and privacy issues?

Canadian Curriculum Websites

Canadian curricula is the responsibility of individual provinces and territories. For a thorough analysis of the role of educational technology in various curricula across

Technology Is Here to Stay

Joanne Richardson-Landry
Junior High French Teacher, Berwick School
Consultant with the Annapolis Valley Regional School Board, Berwick, Nova Scotia

When teachers hear the words "technology integration," many automatically begin retracing their lesson plans for hints of internet use or the presentation of a project via PowerPoint. The average teacher starts fretting that s/he has not used the new portable LCD projector yet and promises her/himself that it will be put to use during the "next unit." For the busy teacher, allowing students to use technology for research and using PowerPoint and iMovies to present projects has become the norm and is "do-able." Creating WebQuests, PowerPoint presentations and web pages for classroom blogs to make teaching "more exciting" is not as "do-able," and, therefore, does not take place as often as most would like. The question is, how do we integrate technology so that it is meaningful and effective rather than integrating it because "it's a part of our world"? How does technology fit into our postmodern classrooms, or is the postmodern classroom largely about technology?

The internet opens up to us a world of varied perspectives and beliefs on virtually every topic imaginable. One can now find out both sides of an issue simultaneously from a variety of sources; therefore, technology has helped move our society into the postmodern era. On the other hand, it can be felt that, although postmodernism focuses on looking at something with more than one lens, there is a pressure that one "better be looking at it" with the help of technology.

Today's learners seem to have been born with a sense of knowing how to work each new piece of technology as it comes along. This causes educators to panic, because many of us will always be on the outside looking in. Many education systems try to "cure" this by pouring in millions of dollars in technology to make sure all schools are wired. Education departments seem to be more concerned with making sure everyone is "wired" versus everyone knowing what to do with those wires. In a postmodern society, technology is a cornerstone, yet its use in the classroom must be meaningful and effective. Can we say, as educators, that we are using technology in our classrooms in a meaningful way?

So how does technology fit into our postmodern world? As stated before, it is the cornerstone of the postmodern era. It allows us to be exposed to countless viewpoints and ideas within a matter of seconds. It gives us choices on how to obtain, store, and present information. It allows our world to become that much smaller but, at the same time, does nothing to close the gap between the "haves" and "have-nots." Does it make a difference in the educational lives of students whether or not their parents own a car? Probably not. Will it make a difference if their parents can afford neither a computer nor access to the internet? One must also realize that technology is also a well controlled market and is dictated by corporate moguls such as Bill Gates. We need to be mindful that, although technology opens up endless possibilities to us, it also dictates our way of life, what we buy and how we see ourselves.

Technology is here to stay, whether we like it or not. Therefore, it is important that educators are given time and money to explore the capabilities and links between their classroom and technology. There is wonderful technology to be used in our classrooms such as WebQuests, podcasts, blogs and online research, but it takes time for teachers to manipulate these and use them in meaningful ways. "Technology integration" is a popular phrase these days, yet it is important that one integrates it with a purpose and not for the sake of integrating. This is a huge challenge for curriculum developers. Curriculum creators also need to build technology into new textbooks and teacher's guides. Although more and more of this is being done, it is often illustrated as an aside or an added-on activity within the text. This is where technology mentors and consultants play a vital role in educating teachers in finding ways of integrating technology.

It is also important that curriculum developers not become "slaves" to technology in which everything focuses on the "almighty machine." Because our lives are saturated with technology, it is all the more important to focus upon other personal traits that are vital to the healthy functioning of our society, such as cooperation, moral judgment, and empathy. It is the curriculum developer and teacher's ultimate challenge to find a balance between the two.

Canada, refer to the following regional, provincial, and territorial curriculum sites:

Council of Atlantic Ministers of Education and Technology (CAMET)
www.camet-camef.ca/default.asp?mn=1.19.22

Western Canadian Protocol for Collaboration in Basic Education Common Curriculum Framework
www.edu.gov.mb.ca/k12/cur/ela/wcpelak-9.pdf

Government of Alberta Education
http://education.alberta.ca/resources/backtoschool/curriculum.aspx

BC Ministry of Education Curriculum
www.bced.gov.bc.ca/irp

Manitoba Education and Literacy
www.edu.gov.mb.ca

New Brunswick Department of Education
www.gnb.ca/0000/anglophone-e.asp#1

Newfoundland and Labrador Department of Education
www.ed.gov.nl.ca/edu/

Northwest Territories Education, Culture and Employment
www.ece.gov.nt.ca

Nova Scotia Department of Education
www.ednet.ns.ca

Ontario Ministry of Education Curriculum and Policy
www.edu.gov.on.ca/eng/document/curricul/curricul.html

Prince Edward Island Department of Education and Early Childhood Development
www.gov.pe.ca/eecd/ProgramAndServices.php

Quebec Ministère de l'Education: Curriculum Publications
www.meq.gouv.qc.ca/GR-PUB/menu-curricu-a.htm

Saskatchewan Department of Education: Programs and Services
www.education.gov.sk.ca/programs-services

Government of Yukon Education
www.gov.yk.ca/services/edu.html

Broadband Internet Access for All Schools

Internet access is a vital part of a school's capacity to benefit from the vast resources found in cyberspace. Through the internet, teachers and students can draw from the world's best libraries, museums, and cultural resources.

Although schools are acquiring more computer hardware, most cannot afford to hire sufficient support staff. About 30 percent of schools employ a full-time coordinator of technology, close to 40 percent employ a part-time coordinator, and nearly 30 percent have no on-site technical support personnel (Furger 1999). As a result, most schools rely on central district personnel or computer-savvy teachers for support.

What are the potential repercussions for schools that cannot afford to keep investing in technology?

Access to Technology for All Students

Significant strides have been made toward reducing the **digital divide** between poor and affluent schools. While schools have reduced the number of students per computer,

Technology-Mediated Teaching and Learning Enhance Education

Advances in technology have redefined the information landscape on a global scale. Schools have been, and will always be, social spaces where youth learn to make sense of the world through the interpretation of information across disciplines and the expression of their understanding using accessible methods and tools. The printed page has been both the receptacle and conduit for information for the past number of centuries, but the cost, mobility, and pervasiveness of information technologies has changed, and will continue to change, our relationship to information management. Students will still require a "backpack" for school, but the shape, size, and function of the twenty-first-century backpack will change, and possibly reside in a person's pocket.

Alan Kay, personal computing pioneer, suggested in a 1980s press conference that "Technology is anything that wasn' t around when you were born" (http://en.wikiquote.org/wiki/Alan_Kay). As media methods and techniques emerge, so do the dominant technologies present in schools: film strips, records, tapes, lab equipment, overhead projectors, calculators, computer labs, and laptop carts. Recent developments in technology have seen the popularization of "smart surfaces" or interactive whiteboards that allow teachers to display web-based materials on a projected surface without the need for a keyboard or pointing device. Throughout the emergence of technology for teaching and learning in schools, there has been one

persistent trend—the movement from technology in labs or on shared carts to classroom-based technologies accessible at all times by both teacher and student. Technology has become increasingly integrated across disciplines throughout the school day and is less of an "event." As Alan Kay suggests, the idea of multi-modal, rapid access to information may seem like a "technology" to an older generation, but is regarded as common a utility as running water or electricity by younger generations.

Whereas teachers in Canadian schools primarily use information technologies and the internet to support and enrich instruction in school classrooms, increasing numbers of educators are leveraging personal learning environments (PLEs) and social media tools for both teaching and for their own professional development. In the mid 1990s, web-based content management tools were only accessible to educational institutions with budgets healthy enough to support enterprise expenditures. The growth and sophistication of open source software communities in the past 15 years has yielded countless freely available software platforms to educators offering robust, yet intuitive, content management, assessment, and communication tools. Moodle, a popular open source virtual learning environment (VLE), reports nearly 50 000 sites in over 200 countries (http://moodle.org/stats)—nearly 1000 of which are located in Canada.

Adoption of technology-mediated teaching and learning methods does not come without hazards. School leaders and administrators must consider both short- and long-term infrastructure costs when planning for technology investments. Hardware required for application platforms and internet access can have shorter-than-expected life spans and should be implemented with the understanding that ongoing maintenance costs will be required. Some hardware and software vendors offer lease options that bundle service, maintenance, and upgrades into agreements and can often be a better financial option than direct infrastructure investment. Although open source software is offered "free of cost" to users, the cost of maintaining access and service levels rests with technicians based in school districts. In rural and remote districts, such staff are infrequently on site to address issues and troubleshoot problems. Lack of supports and insufficient opportunity for teacher professional development with new methods and technologies can dramatically limit the effectiveness and utility of educational technologies.

Longitudinal research ("Elements of Quality Online Education: Engaging Communities" www.sloanconsortium.org/volume6.asp) from the Sloan Consortium reports that effective implementation of technology that mediates teaching and learning improves effectiveness of instruction in a number of domains such as movement of instructional focus toward higher order learning objectives, improved student access to learning resources and opportunities, and improved student and instructor satisfaction with the learning process. Such research, combined with the growth in dedicated distributed learning schools in school districts across Canada, indicates that students, parents, and teachers value expenditures on technology-mediated learning.

School districts based in northern locales in Canada are adopting technology-mediated learning as both a means to provide compelling learning opportunities to home-schooled student populations and as a means for offering a full complement of high school courses in small, rural schools. For example, British Columbia's School District 22 utilizes both synchronous and asynchronous technologies to provide instruction for Physics 12 and Chemistry 12 classes over three locations. Teachers in "face-to-face" classes broadcast and archive instruction using a provincially licensed web-conference tool to students in rural locations—offering a level of access and support to rural, remote students not possible a decade ago. Adoption and integration of such technologies at provincial, district, and classroom levels will continue to diversify and enrich teaching and learning opportunities for students.

—Grant Potter

Grant Potter is the e-Learning Coordinator at the Centre for Teaching, Learning, and Technology with the University of Northern British Columbia (www.unbc.ca/ctlt/services.html). Grant has been pursing research and development of educational technologies for over 10 years through his work in secondary and post-secondary education in rural, remote areas of the Canadian Arctic, China, and northern British Columbia. Grant coordinates UNBC faculty development regarding effective implementation of educational technologies for teaching and learning. (Used by permission of the author.)

there is evidence of a "digital divide" if computer use at school and at home is compared to family income and minority-group status. However, schools can help equalize the disparity in computer use among children from various income categories

Quality Educational Software and Websites

For students and teachers to benefit from digital technology, high-quality software and websites must be readily available. When computers began to be used extensively in education in the 1980s, inadequacy of software was a common criticism.

Too often, educational software has promoted glitz, glamour, and graphics instead of serious learning. And too often, the internet has promoted the "surfing culture" in which users click their way across an ocean of information and often feel overwhelmed by the vastness of it all, never dipping below the surface (Bennett & Gelernter 2001).

Negative appraisals of educational software aside, the quality of software available to schools has improved. Steadily, new, more powerful hypermedia learning software programs are appearing that present students with problems to solve that are interesting, multifaceted, and embedded in real-world contexts.

High-Quality, Continuous Training in Technology for Teachers

Using technology to enhance students' learning requires more than investing in the latest hardware or software and connectivity to the internet. E-mailing students, parents, and peers; conducting classroom demonstrations augmented with multimedia; using presentation graphics to address students' varied learning styles; and designing lessons that require students to use the internet as a resource for inquiry are practices that should be second nature for teachers. Just as new technological skills are needed in the workplace, a high degree of technological literacy is needed in the classroom. Thus acquiring proficiency in the ever-evolving array of technologies should be an important part of professional development for new and veteran teachers. However, teachers frequently complain of a lack of training in how to use technology to reach their curriculum goals.

In the absence of high-quality, continuous training in how to integrate technology into teaching, some students will continue to make observations such as the following quotes from two high school students included in a 2002 report entitled "The Digital Disconnect: The Widening Gap Between Internet-Savvy Students and Their Schools":

"Our teachers usually . . . don't really know what to do with [the Internet]."

"I never really got an assignment that specifically said you have to use the Internet." (Levin & Arafeh 2002, 16)

Fortunately, as we enter the second decade of the twenty-first century, teachers and others who have an interest in education are becoming more sophisticated in understanding the strengths and limitations of information communication technology as a tool to promote learning. They know that, like another educational tool—the book—the computer *can* be a powerful, almost unlimited medium for instruction and learning if they carefully reflect on *how* it will further the attainment of their goals and aspirations for their students.

SUMMARY

How Is Technology Transforming Teaching and Learning?

- Technology is a tool teachers can use to achieve educational goals and to create particular kinds of learning environments.

- Technology can provide students with a structured, efficient, instructional delivery system, and it can spark their interest in open-ended, inquiry-oriented learning.

- In many schools and classrooms, technology has already transformed teaching and learning; however, teachers, administrators, policy-makers, and parents must realize that advanced telecommunications will require new approaches to teaching and to assessing students' learning.

What Technologies Are Available for Teaching?

- Through technologies such as two-way interactive telecommunications, CD-ROM players, interactive multimedia, computer simulations, e-books, and hypermedia, teachers are creating learning environments that allow students to become more active in shaping their learning experiences.

- If *educational technology* is broadly defined as inventions that enable teachers to reach their goals more effectively, then it is clear that, for some time, all teachers have been using various forms of educational "technology."

- Three common uses of computers in instruction are computer-assisted instruction (CAI), computer-managed instruction (CMI), and computer-enhanced instruction (CEI).

- Some schools have microcomputer-based laboratories (MBLs) that students use to gather and analyze various kinds of data.

- Newsgroups, chat rooms, and videoconferencing on the internet enable teachers and students to communicate with people around the world.

How Do Canadian Teachers Use Computers and the Internet?

- Teachers frequently use the internet to gather information and resources for teaching.

- Teachers who have classroom access to the internet are more likely than those without classroom access to communicate via e-mail and to post information and student work on the web.

- After word processing and using CD-ROM references, performing "research" on the Internet is the most common teacher-directed use of computers by students.

The Steady Growth of Information Communication Technology and Its Applications to Teaching and Learning

- Although how and to what extent computers and other technologies are being used in schools is not known, research indicates that technology has a positive impact on students' achievement and attitudes.

- Single research studies and meta-analyses of large numbers of single studies indicate that the effects of computers on students' learning are varied—some report learning gains, some don't, and others report "mixed" outcomes.

- In spite of the ambiguities of research on computer-based instruction, it is clear that technology *can* have positive effects on learning.

- Enrichment and diversification of teaching and learning opportunities will continue to evolve as information communication technologies become more affordable, more familiar, and easier to use.

Should Technology Be at the Forefront of Efforts to Improve Schools?

- Some critics feel strongly that computers do not aid education and are a drain on scarce capital funds, while several polls have indicated a great deal of support among the general public for computers in the classroom.

- Four challenges must be met so that all students can attend "high-end technology schools": (1) providing broadband internet access for all schools, (2) providing access to technology for all students, (3) obtaining quality educational software, and (4) providing high-quality, continuous training in technology for teachers.

KEY TERMS AND CONCEPTS

CD-ROM, 266
chat room, 273
computer-assisted
   instruction (CAI), 268
computer-enhanced
   instruction (CEI), 269
computer-managed
   instruction
   (CMI), 269

distance learning
   networks, 266
digital divide, 283
e-learning, 267
educational technology, 266
home–school
   communication
   systems, 272
hypermedia, 271

interactive multimedia, 271
Internet, 273
microcomputer-based
   laboratory (MBL), 270
newsgroups, 273
videoconferencing, 274
videodisc, 271
virtual schools, 267
World Wide Web, 273

APPLICATIONS AND ACTIVITIES

Teacher's Journal

1. In your opinion, what are the most important benefits of technology for education, and what are its most important drawbacks?

2. What impact has television had on your life? What steps might teachers take to increase the educational benefits of television in society? Does television have a future in the twenty-first century?

3. A concern voiced by some is that the use of computers in education will lead to a depersonalization of the teacher–learner relationship. How valid is this concern?

4. Write two scenarios: one forecasting how technology will change the teaching profession during the next two decades, and another forecasting the next four decades.

Theory into Practice

In Chapter 8, your class was assigned the task of working together on an interdisciplinary project with the overarching theme of "If You Love This Planet: Making a Difference Locally and Globally." The culminating task of this challenge involved a "staff" presentation on how this interdisciplinary project would look at each grade level and in each content area.

The Theory into Practice assignment for this chapter will also involve the theme of "If You Love This Planet: Making a Difference Locally and Globally" and the constructivist inquiry-based approach known as WebQuests.

1. Individually, go to http://kathyschrock.net/slideshows/webquests/frame0001.htm, which features a PowerPoint slide show by Kathy Schrock on the topic of WebQuests. Familiarize yourself with the concept by going through the slide show, which defines the term WebQuest and describes the critical attributes that must be included in all WebQuests.

2. On your own, visit www.bestwebquests.com.

   ■ Read the article "What WebQuests Are (Really)" by Tom March at www.bestwebquests.com/what_webquests_are.asp.

   ■ Read "Criteria for Assessing Best WebQuests" at www.bestwebquests.com/bwq/matrix.asp.

   ■ Review samples of WebQuests from the grade level and content area in which you worked for the Theory into Practice segment from Chapter 8.

3. Using the grade level and content area groups you worked in from the Chapter 8 exercise, begin to plan for the development of a WebQuest that would explore the theme of making a difference locally and globally in the health of the planet. This WebQuest should include all content areas of the grade level and the necessary attributes of WebQuests.

4. Assign tasks to all of the grade level groups and develop a WebQuest that matches the criteria for assessing best WebQuests and that meets provincial curriculum outcomes.

5. The culminating task of this assignment will be a "staff" presentation of each grade level's WebQuest. These WebQuests will be posted to a common space so that the entire class has access to them.

Teacher's Database

1. With classmates, join or start an online discussion on one or more of the following topics or on another topic from Chapter 9.

   - Computer simulations
   - Educational software
   - Computer-assisted instruction (CAI)
   - Educational technology
   - Computer-managed instruction (CMI)
   - Hypermedia
   - Computer-enhanced instruction (CEI)
   - Interactive multimedia

2. Find out more about educational newsgroups and distance learning networks. How might you use newsgroups or distance learning networks in your preparation as a teacher? How might you and your students use these forms of educational technology? What knowledge and skills do you need to start or join an educational newsgroup or distance learning network? Using the internet, develop a list of resources for both.

Observations and Interviews

1. Survey a local school district to determine the educational technologies used by teachers. How and how often are these technologies used for instruction? What is the availability of computers and software for student use?

2. Find an online chat room frequented by teachers and enter (or initiate) a discussion on educational technology. What are the teachers' views of integrating technology into the classroom? What technologies, software, and instructional activities have they found most effective?

3. Review the brief section in this chapter entitled "A Note of Caution." Do you agree that information communication technology in schools requires a cautious approach? Ask a number of teachers you know how they feel about social networking sites. Do they use such sites themselves? Do they think limits should be placed on social networking sites in schools? Do teachers believe that such sites contribute to cyberbullying?

Professional Portfolio

Prepare a catalogue of interactive multimedia resources and materials that you will use as a teacher. For each entry, include an annotation that briefly describes the resource materials, how you will use them, and where they may be obtained. As with the selection of any curriculum materials, try to find evidence of effectiveness, such as results of field tests, published reviews of educational software, awards, or testimonials from educators. View and report on at least one program you have included in your personal catalogue. Explain in your report how you will integrate this multimedia resource into your curriculum.

MyEducationLab

PEARSON
myeducationlab

To browse a virtual learning resource for classroom management based on the three cornerstones of prior preparation, on establishing constructive expectations, and on exhibiting desired modes of behaviour, go to the "Managing to Teach" tab at www.MyEducationLab.com. Options available include:

- Module 1: An Introduction to Your Virtual School
- Module 2: Developing Constructive Expectations for Learning
- Module 3: Preventing and Pre-empting Problems through Careful Planning
- Module 4: Positive Personal Interactions by Exhibiting Modes of Behaviour

part four
Your Teaching Future

10

Teachers as
Educational Leaders

*Leadership is first and foremost
about making effective decisions. If
the leader makes good decisions,
everything else will fall into place.
The leader must ensure that the
organization objectively evaluates
what is known and makes his or her
decision on the basis of research,
facts and rationality.*

—A classroom teacher
From William G. Cunningham and
Paula A. Cordeiro,
*Educational Leadership: A Bridge to
Improved Practice*, 2nd Edition
Pearson Education Inc., 2003, p. 2

focus questions

1. To What Extent Is Teaching a Full Profession?
2. What Is Professionalism in Teaching?
3. To What Professional Organizations Do Teachers Belong?
4. What New Leadership Roles for Teachers Are Emerging?
5. How Do Teachers Contribute to Educational Research?
6. How Are Teachers Providing Leadership for School Development and Curriculum Improvement?

It is November of your fifth year of teaching, and you are attending a "task force" meeting of the steering committee for a province-wide teacher network that had been launched that September. The department of education divided the province into 12 regions, and you have been elected by your peers to be the network leader for your region. The network was formed on the premise that teachers should have opportunities to participate in, and lead, professional development activities of their own choosing, such as curriculum workshops, leadership institutes, internships, and conferences.

This two-day meeting at the department of education will begin the process of designing a series of two-week summer institutes for teachers. The institutes will be invitational, and institute "fellows" will be selected by the steering committee after an extensive application and interview process. One institute will be held in each region throughout the province, and teachers will receive a $750 stipend plus expenses for attending. To disseminate the knowledge and skills they acquire and to further develop their leadership abilities, the institute fellows will design and deliver staff development programs at their home schools.

The committee chair, a leader from a school in the province's largest city, has just laid out the group's task for the next two days. "By the end of the day tomorrow, we need to have identified which institutes will be offered in each region. Also, we need to have a game plan for how each of you will facilitate the development of the summer institute in your region."

"Well, the way I see it," says the teacher next to you," the institutes should accomplish at least two major purposes. First, they should provide teachers with ways to increase their effectiveness in the classroom by acquiring new strategies and materials. Second, and just as important, the institutes should give teachers opportunities to play key leadership roles in school improvement efforts around the province."

"That's right," says another teacher. "Teachers should recognize that the institutes give them a voice and meaningful opportunities to function as professionals."

"What I like about the institutes," the teacher across the table from you adds, "is that they give teachers a chance to break out of the role of passively receiving in-service training. It's no different for teachers than it is for students—we learn best by actively shaping our learning environment and constructing meaning."

As you and several members of the group nod in agreement, you reflect on what you've just heard. What does it really mean to be a professional? What are the characteristics of a profession, and to what extent does teaching reflect those characteristics? What new leadership roles for teachers are emerging? What leadership roles will you play in educational improvement?

Educational improvement continually and dramatically changes what it means to be a teacher. Provincially sponsored teacher networks, the professionalization of teaching, shared decision making, peer review, and mentor teacher programs are just a few of the strategies that provide unprecedented opportunities for teachers to assume new leadership roles beyond the classroom.

We have referred to teaching as a **profession** throughout this book; however, if we compare teaching with other professions—law and medicine, for example—we find some significant differences. As a result of these differences, current opinion is divided as to whether teaching actually is a full profession.

To What Extent Is Teaching a Full Profession?

We use the terms *professional* and *profession* quite frequently, usually without thinking about their meanings. Professionals "possess a high degree of specialized *theoretical knowledge*, along with methods and techniques for applying this knowledge in their day-to-day work . . . [and they] are united by a high degree of in-group solidarity, stemming from their common training and common adherence to certain doctrines and methods" (Abrahamsson 1971, 11–12).

Several sociologists and educators who have studied teaching have identified additional characteristics of occupations that are highly professionalized, summarized in Figure 10.1. Reflect on each characteristic and decide whether it applies to teaching. Then continue reading about the extent to which teaching satisfies each of these commonly agreed-upon characteristics of full professions. Do our perceptions agree with yours?

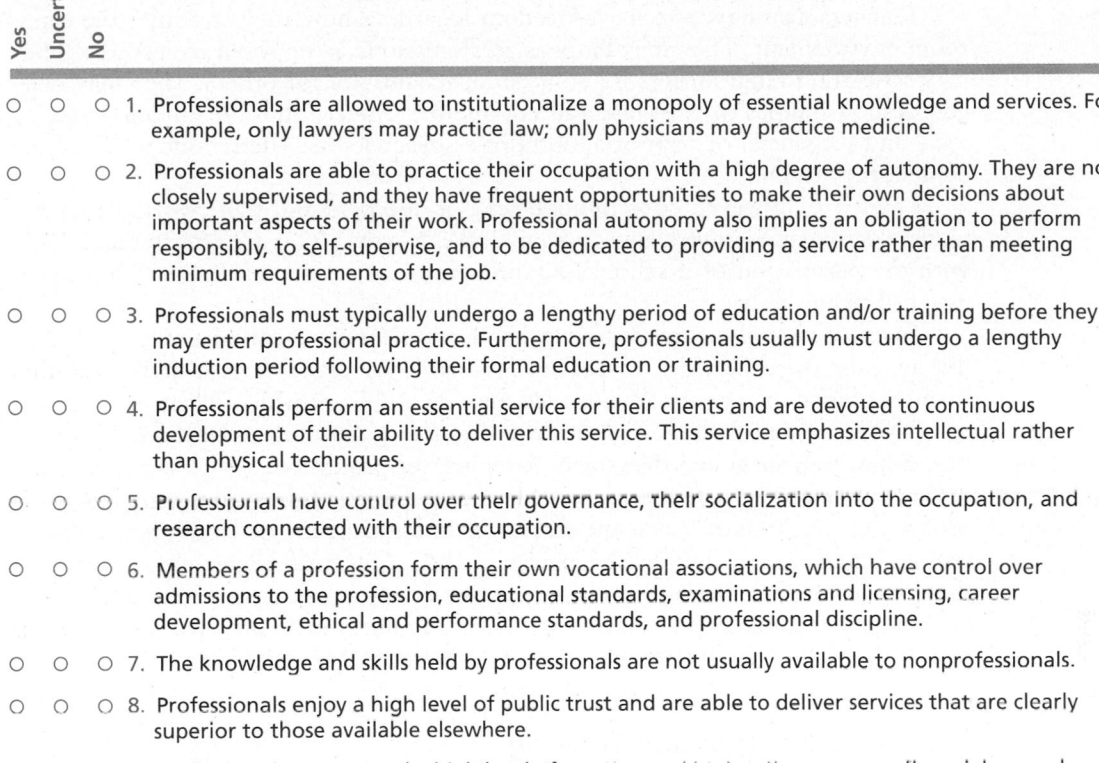

○ ○ ○ 1. Professionals are allowed to institutionalize a monopoly of essential knowledge and services. For example, only lawyers may practice law; only physicians may practice medicine.

○ ○ ○ 2. Professionals are able to practice their occupation with a high degree of autonomy. They are not closely supervised, and they have frequent opportunities to make their own decisions about important aspects of their work. Professional autonomy also implies an obligation to perform responsibly, to self-supervise, and to be dedicated to providing a service rather than meeting minimum requirements of the job.

○ ○ ○ 3. Professionals must typically undergo a lengthy period of education and/or training before they may enter professional practice. Furthermore, professionals usually must undergo a lengthy induction period following their formal education or training.

○ ○ ○ 4. Professionals perform an essential service for their clients and are devoted to continuous development of their ability to deliver this service. This service emphasizes intellectual rather than physical techniques.

○ ○ ○ 5. Professionals have control over their governance, their socialization into the occupation, and research connected with their occupation.

○ ○ ○ 6. Members of a profession form their own vocational associations, which have control over admissions to the profession, educational standards, examinations and licensing, career development, ethical and performance standards, and professional discipline.

○ ○ ○ 7. The knowledge and skills held by professionals are not usually available to nonprofessionals.

○ ○ ○ 8. Professionals enjoy a high level of public trust and are able to deliver services that are clearly superior to those available elsewhere.

○ ○ ○ 9. Professionals are granted a high level of prestige and higher-than-average financial rewards.

Figure 10.1

Does teaching meet the criteria for a profession?

Institutional Monopoly of Services

On one hand, teachers have a monopoly of services. As a rule, only those who are certified members of the profession may teach in public schools. On the other hand, the varied requirements for certification and for teaching in private schools weaken this monopoly. In addition, any claim teachers might have as exclusive providers of a service is further eroded by the practice of provincial education systems approving temporary, or emergency, certification measures to deal with temporary teacher shortages—a move that establishes teaching as the only profession that allows noncertified individuals to practise the profession.

Perhaps the most significant argument against teachers claiming to be the exclusive providers of a service, however, is the fact that a great deal of teaching occurs in informal, nonschool settings and is done by people who are not teachers. Every day, thousands of people teach various kinds of how-to-do-it skills: how to water-ski, how to make dogs more obedient, how to make pasta from scratch, how to tune a car's engine, and how to meditate, for example.

Teacher Autonomy

In one sense, teachers have considerable autonomy. They usually work behind a closed classroom door, and only seldom is their work observed by another adult. In fact, one of the norms among teachers is that the classroom is a castle of sorts, and teacher privacy a closely guarded right. Although the performance of new teachers may be observed and evaluated on a regular basis by supervisors, veteran teachers are observed much less frequently, and they usually enjoy a high degree of autonomy.

Teachers also have extensive freedom regarding how they structure the classroom environment. They may emphasize discussions as opposed to lectures. They may set certain requirements for some students and not for others. They may delegate responsibilities to one class and not another. And, within the guidelines set by local and provincial or territorial authorities, teachers may determine much of the content they teach.

There are, however, constraints placed on teachers and their work. Teachers, unlike doctors and lawyers, must accept all the "clients" who are sent to them. Only with the permission of a school's administrator can a teacher "reject" a student assigned to him or her.

Teachers must also agree to teach what department of education and local officials dictate. Moreover, the work of teachers is subject to a higher level of public scrutiny than that found in other professions. Because the public provides "clients" (students) and pays for schools, it has a significant say regarding the work of teachers. Nevertheless, it has been suggested that some "levelling" of professions will occur in Canada during the early twenty-first century: "More of the work of the traditional high-status professions, particularly medicine, will occur in bureaucratic or large organizational settings under the watchful eye of managers. [While] doctors are accepting more and more regulation, the school teachers . . . will slowly break out of long-established bureaucratic hierarchies and share more of the autonomy previously enjoyed by members of the high-status professions" (Grant & Murray 1999, 231–32).

Years of Education and Training

As sociologist Amitai Etzioni (1969) points out in his classic discussion of the "semi-professions," the training of teachers is less lengthy than that required for other professionals—lawyers and physicians, for example. The initial professional component of teacher education programs is the shortest of all the professions. However, as we learned in Chapter 2, Canadian colleges and universities offer a variety of teacher-education models, with Alberta's being one of the shortest and Nova Scotia's being one of the longest. Additionally, many institutions now offer education degrees at the master's and doctoral levels. If the number of longer bachelor of education graduate-level teacher education programs continues to grow, the professional status of teaching will definitely be enhanced.

In most professions, new members must undergo a prescribed induction period. Physicians, for example, must serve an internship or residency before beginning practice, and most lawyers begin as clerks in law firms. In contrast, teachers do not usually go through a formal induction period before assuming full responsibility for their work. Practice teaching comes closest to serving as an induction period, but it is often relatively short, informal, and lacking in uniformity.

Provision of Essential Service

Although it is generally acknowledged that teachers provide a service that is vital to the well-being of individuals and groups, the public does need to be reminded of this fact from time to time. This importance was driven home on a large scale during the early1980s and 1990s when several reports called for school improvement because:

> Every moment in the lives of teachers and pupils brings critical decisions of motivation, reinforcement, reward, ego enhancement and goal direction. Proper

professional decisions enhance learning and life; improper decisions send the learner towards incremental death in openness to experience and in ability to learn and contribute. Doctors and lawyers probably have neither more nor less to do with life, death, and freedom than do teachers. (Howsam et al. 1976, 15)

Degree of Self-Governance

The limited freedom of teachers to self-govern has detracted from the overall status of the profession. In many provinces and territories, licensing guidelines are set by government officials who may or may not be educators, and at the local level, decision-making power usually resides with local boards of education, largely made up of people who have never taught. As a result, teachers have had little or no say over what they teach, when they teach, whom they teach, and, in extreme instances, *how* they teach.

However, recent efforts to professionalize teaching are creating new roles for teachers and expanded opportunities to govern important aspects of their work. In some educational jurisdictions, teachers have a louder voice in decisions related to curriculum development, staffing, budget, and the day-to-day operation of schools. In other areas, such as Ontario, Atlantic Canada, and parts of Western Canada, teachers are expected to teach to essential learning outcomes. And in some of these regions, there are externally designed examinations set by departments of education that must be administered to students by teachers. The result is a possible net decline in the degree of teacher autonomy.

Professional Associations

Teachers, like other professionals, have formed a number of vocational associations that are vitally concerned with issues such as admission to the profession, educational standards, examinations and licensing, career development, ethical and performance standards, and professional discipline. It is clear, though, that provincial and territorial teacher organizations have not progressed as far as other professions have in gaining control of these areas.

Professional Knowledge and Skills

Professionals are granted a certain status because they possess knowledge and skills not normally held by the general public. Within the profession of teaching, however, the requirements for membership are less precise. In spite of the ongoing efforts of educational researchers, there is less than unanimous agreement on the knowledge and skills considered necessary to teach. This lack of agreement is reflected in the diversity of teachers' education programs offered at colleges and universities.

Level of Public Trust

The level of trust the public extends to teachers as professionals varies greatly. On one hand, the public appears to have great confidence in the work of teachers. Because of its faith in the teaching profession, the public bestows teachers with considerable power over their children. For the most part, parents willingly allow their children to be moulded and influenced by teachers, and this willingness must be based on a high degree of trust. In addition, most parents expect their children to obey and respect teachers. However, the burgeoning number of parents who are electing to send their children to Canada's independent (private) schools is a certain indication that many are not satisfied with the level of education offered by public schools.

Though all professions have some members who might be described as unprofessional, teaching is especially vulnerable to such charges. The sheer size of the teaching force makes it difficult to maintain consistently high professional standards. Moreover, teaching is subject to a level of public scrutiny and control that other, more established professions traditionally have not tolerated. However, the era of widespread public trust may be coming to a close for these other professions—mushrooming malpractice suits against doctors, for example, may be a sign that here, too, public confidence has significantly eroded.

Prestige, Benefits, and Pay

As mentioned in Chapter 1, teachers are viewed as having higher social status than most of the population; however, this higher status is based on level of education attained rather than wealth. Thus teachers have not received salaries in keeping with other professions requiring approximately the same amount of schooling. However, because of the grid system according to which teachers are paid, they can reach their maximum salary levels at a fairly early stage in their careers. This differs from other professions where maximum income levels are reached at a much later point.

What Is Professionalism in Teaching?

The current goal among teachers, teacher educators, policy-makers, and the general public is to make teaching a full profession. Toward this end, teachers are willing to take risks and learn new roles as they press for greater self-governance, better working conditions, and increased financial rewards. In addition, teachers are acquiring the analytical skills needed to understand and provide leadership for the complex processes of educational reform. The following sections look at the three key dimensions of professionalism in teaching presented in Figure 10.2: professional behaviour, lifelong learning, and involvement in the profession.

Professional Behaviour

Professional teachers are guided by a specific set of values. They have made a deep and lasting commitment to professional practice. They have also adopted a high standard of professional ethics and exhibit model behaviours that are in accord with that code of ethics. The professional teacher engages in serious, reflective thought about how to teach more effectively by continually examining experiences that improve practice.

Reflection-in-Action

Donald Schön (1983, 1987, and 1991) describes this professional behaviour as **reflection-in-action** and identifies how a teacher might use it to solve a problem in the classroom:

> An artful teacher sees a child's difficulty in learning to read not as a defect in the child but as a defect "of his [or her] own instruction." And because the child's

Professionalism in Teaching

Reflection-in-Action

Problem Solving

Values

Professional Behaviour

Lifelong Learning

Professionalism in Teaching

Self-Assessment

Risk Taking

Involvement in the Profession

Commitment

Mentoring

Ethics

New Roles and Responsibilities

Figure 10.2

Professionalism in teaching

difficulties may be unique, the teacher cannot assume that his [or her] repertoire of explanations will suffice, even though they are "at the tongue's end." The teacher must be ready to invent new methods and must "endeavor to develop in himself [or herself] the ability of discovering them." (1983, 66)

The highest level of reflection, **critical reflective practice**, is the ability of a teacher to go beyond asking such questions as "How could I have made my lesson more interesting? More effective?" to the greater questions of "What is the higher purpose of my teaching and how can I achieve it?" In other words, "How does my teaching positively influence students in their lives beyond the classroom?" For a sample lesson designed by a teacher concerned with providing her students with beyond-the-classroom skills, go to Teacher's Resource 10.1, The Teacher's Scribe: "It's time to start complaining." at www.MyEducationLab.com.

The professional teacher described by Schön makes careful, sensitive observations of classroom events, reflects on the meaning of those observations, and then decides to act in a certain way. Steven Lacy, an exemplary elementary teacher, describes the reflective decision-making process this way:

> Our effectiveness as teachers is not reflected in the materials and structures of our pedagogy as much as it is in the countless decisions we make every day, decisions that are made in an instant. [D]o I help him with that problem or let him struggle? Do I pursue her question or stick with the lesson? Does this behaviour need to be punished or ignored? Does this composition need to be criticized or praised? (Levey 1996, 2–3)

Becoming a Mentor

As a result of their position in relation to young people, teachers may find opportunities to become mentors to some of their students. Accepting this responsibility

What characteristics distinguish teaching as a profession? What characteristics might distinguish these teachers as professionals?

is another example of professional behaviour. The role of **mentor** is unique in several ways. First, mentorship develops naturally and is not an automatic part of teaching, nor can it be "assigned." True mentorships grow organically from teaching relationships and cannot be artificially promoted. Second, the role of mentor is a *comprehensive* one: Mentors express broad interest in their pupils. Third, the role of mentor is *mutually* recognized by student and teacher: Both realize that their relationship has a special "depth." Fourth, the role of mentor is significant and has the potential to change the quality and direction of students' lives. And finally, the opportunity to work with a mentor is free—a situation Gehrke (1988) terms the mentor's "gift of care."

The longer you teach, the more you will encounter opportunities for mentorships to develop, discovering that you can mentor less experienced teachers and student teachers as well as students. The rewards that come from the unique role of mentor can be immensely satisfying.

Lifelong Learning

The professional teacher is dedicated to continuous learning—both about the teaching–learning process and about the subject taught. No longer is it sufficient for career teachers to obtain only a bachelor's degree and a teaching certificate. Teachers are lifelong members of learning communities.

Several provinces have mandated continuing education for teachers as a condition for maintaining their teaching certificates. For example, in Nova Scotia the requirement is 100 hours of professional development within a five-year period (Nova Scotia Department of Education 2001). The content of curricula and the methods and materials used to teach evolve so rapidly that teachers must be involved in continuous learning to maintain their professional effectiveness. In addition, teachers should practise what they preach. A teacher who is not continuously learning raises serious questions for students: "If it's not important for our teachers to learn, why should we?" The attitude toward learning modelled by teachers may be as important as the content they teach.

Many opportunities are available for teachers to gain new knowledge and skills. Nearly every school district makes provisions for in-service training or staff development. Topics can range from classroom-focused issues, such as authentic assessment, using the internet, classroom management, integrated curricula, or learning styles, to school-wide management issues, such as restructuring, shared governance, or school–community partnerships.

Learning to Become a Leader

For professional teachers, an important goal of lifelong learning is to acquire leadership skills. Successful educational reform in the twenty-first century will require teacher participation in leadership. In fact, it is quite possible that "schools of the [21st] century will be run by teams of teachers who [have] the tools, incentives, and leadership they need to accomplish their jobs" (Gerstner et al. 1994, 169).

Involvement in the Profession

Today's teachers recognize that they have the most important role in the educational enterprise and that they have not always been given the power necessary to improve the profession. Therefore, they are taking advantage of the opportunity to examine the decisions that, as professionals, they have the right to make.

Across the country, professional teachers are deeply involved with their colleagues, with professional organizations, with teacher educators, with legislators, with policy-makers, and with others in a push to make teaching more fully a profession. Through their accomplishments, they are demonstrating that they are truly professionals. During the past 25 years, for example, teachers have become more involved in teacher education programs, teacher certification, and professional governance. And, through the efforts of teacher organizations, teachers have also made gains in improving working conditions, salaries, and benefits.

To What Professional Organizations Do Teachers Belong?

The expanding leadership role of teachers has been supported through the activities of both national and provincial and territorial teacher organizations. These organizations, and the hardworking teachers who run them, support a variety of initiatives to improve teaching and schools. Through their lobbying activities, teacher associations acquaint legislators, policy-makers, and politicians with critical issues in the teaching profession. Many associations have staffs of teachers, researchers, and consultants who produce professional publications, hold conferences, prepare grant proposals, engage in school improvement activities, and promote a positive image of teaching to the public.

The Canadian Teachers' Federation

The following is a slightly amended description of the **Canadian Teachers' Federation** mandate.

> As the national bilingual umbrella organization for teachers in this country, the Canadian Teachers' Federation has 14 provincial and territorial Member organizations representing 240 000 teachers across Canada. It is a powerful voice for the profession and provides much needed support to its Member organizations and teachers at a time when many governments have moved ahead with very regressive education agendas. The CTF's major areas of concern include: defending public education; promoting the teaching profession; providing support to

Member organizations and teachers across Canada; addressing societal issues that affect the health and well-being of children and youth in Canada and abroad; and providing assistance and support to teacher colleagues in developing countries. For over 80 years it has advanced the cause of children, defended the rights of teachers, and promoted a strong public education system. (www.ctf-fce.ca/AboutUS/Default.aspx?id=625900)

The CTF intervenes whenever the interests of teachers and students are at stake. It lobbies federal departments whose work affects education, children, and youth; conducts campaigns to keep commercial interests out of schools; and fights to keep education out of international trade agreements. It also helps teachers in the collective bargaining process. When member organizations head into negotiations, it provides information from across the country on teacher salaries, pensions, and the full spectrum of benefits. The CTF conducts research on education issues such as workload, demographics, testing, and funding; helps its member organizations provide stronger representation for teachers; and supports teachers and member organizations by holding seminars and conferences on educational issues. It conducts research on an array of topics through its Economic Service Notes and Economic Service Bulletins, which are sent to member organizations throughout the year. The CTF has assisted and will continue to assist all teacher organizations across Canada in difficult times. The strength and unity of 240 000 Canadian teachers present a formidable force for any government to reckon with. Learn more about the CTF at www.ctf-fce.ca.

Teacher Unions and Other Professional Organizations

Teacher unions exist in all provinces and territories, although in some jurisdictions the name used is federation rather than union. While most provinces have a single union that represents all teachers, there are some exceptions. New Brunswick has two affiliated teacher unions with membership determined by language usage (English or French), and Quebec has a similar structure with membership determined by religion. Ontario's structure is the most complex, as there are five separate affiliated unions with membership variously determined by such factors as language, gender, religion, and grade-level of instruction. British Columbia has a College of Teachers with compulsory membership and a teachers' federation with voluntary membership. Regardless of the actual structure of a provincial or territorial teachers' union, membership is compulsory. Dues, often in the $500-per-year range, are automatically deducted at source, and the unions negotiate salaries and benefits on behalf of their members. In most jurisdictions, the negotiations are conducted with the provincial or territorial government.

Teacher unions face an interesting dilemma. While they prefer to be viewed as equivalent to professional organizations, such as the provincial bar associations for lawyers or the colleges of physicians for medical practitioners, teacher federations often act more as trade unions than as purely professional associations. They can, and do, organize strikes, and they can, and do, discipline any of their members who fail to cooperate. The reality is that most are both unions and professional associations. By participating in the "Simulation Activity—Union Negotiations" located in Teacher's Resource 10.2 at www.MyEducationLab.com, you can gain some insight into the processes through which teacher unions and governments settle contracts.

In addition to provincial teacher unions and the nationally based Canadian Teachers' Federation, teachers' professional interests are represented by numerous other international, national, and provincial organizations. Several of these are concerned with improving the quality of education at all levels and in all subject areas. **Phi Delta Kappa (PDK)**, for example, is an international professional and honourary fraternity of educators concerned with enhancing quality education through research and leadership activities. Founded in 1906, Phi Delta Kappa now has branches in most Canadian provinces. Members, who are graduate students, teachers, and administrators, belong to one of more than 668 chapters. To be initiated into Phi Delta Kappa, one must have demonstrated high academic achievement, have completed at least 15 semester hours of graduate work in education, and have made a commitment to a career of educational service. Phi Delta Kappa members receive *Phi Delta Kappan,* a journal of education published 10 times a year.

As you will see in Teacher's Resource 10.3 at www.MyEducationLab.com, many professional associations exist for teachers of specific subject areas, such as mathematics, English, social studies, music, and physical education, as well as for teachers of specific student populations, such as exceptional learners, young children, and students with limited English proficiency. A more general site you might visit is Strictly Canadian Sites (www.fvsd.ab.ca/weblinks/strictly_canadian_sites.htm), which contains links to numerous websites of interest to Canadian teachers.

myeducationlab

What New Leadership Roles for Teachers Are Emerging?

Teachers' roles are changing in fundamental and positive ways. Greater autonomy and an expanded role in educational policy-making have led to "unprecedented opportunities for today's teachers to extend their leadership roles beyond the classroom" (Gmelch & Parkay 1995, 48). To prepare for the future, today's teachers will need to develop leadership skills to a degree not needed in the past.

Teacher Involvement in Teacher Education, Certification, and Staff Development

Teacher input into key decisions about teacher preparation, certification, and staff development are important to the teaching profession. Through their involvement with professional certification standards boards (see Chapter 2), and scores of local, provincial, and national education committees, teachers are influencing the character of pre- and in-service education. They serve on curriculum committees, offer workshops and in-service sessions, and act as mentors for teachers new to the profession. Many also teach courses within schools of education on a seconded or part-time basis, for there is a growing belief that such individuals can bring the true flavour of public-school teaching to the university classroom. Teachers are becoming leaders within their profession. As the titles of the following books suggest, the term **teacher–leader** has become part of the vocabulary of educational improvement.

- *Best Practices for Teacher Leadership: What Award-Winning Teachers Do for Their Professional Learning Communities* (Stone & Cuper 2006).
- *Connecting Teacher Leadership and School Improvement* (Murphy 2005).
- *Teacher Leadership* (Lieberman & Miller 2004).
- *Sustaining Teacher Leadership: Beyond the Boundaries of an Enabling School Culture* (Gonzales 2004).
- *Praxis of School Administration and Teacher Leadership* (Armstrong 2004).

- *Improving School through Teacher Leadership* (Harris & Muijs 2004).
- *Teacher Leadership and Behaviour Management* (Rogers 2002).
- *Reframing the Path to School Leadership: A Guide for Teachers and Principals* (Bolman & Deal 2002).
- *Developing Teacher Leaders: How Teacher Leadership Enhances School Success* (Crowther et al. 2002).
- *The Call to Teacher Leadership* (Zepeda, Mayers, & Benson 2002).
- *Leadership Strategies for Teachers* (Merideth 2000).
- *Teacher Leadership in Mathematics and Science: Casebook and Facilitator's Guide* (Miller, Moon, Elko, & Spencer 2000).

"In their new leadership roles, teachers are being called upon to form new partnerships with business and industry; institutions of higher education; social service agencies; professional associations; and local, and provincial governmental agencies. In this new role, teachers will be the key to promoting widespread improvement of our educational system" (Gmelch & Parkay 1995, 50–51). A brief look at the professional activities of Sandra MacQuinn, a teacher–leader who worked with a colleague on a major restructuring effort at a large urban high school, illustrates the wide-ranging roles of a teacher–leader. In addition to teaching, here are just a few of MacQuinn's leadership activities while serving as liaison and on-site coordinator of a school–university partnership.

- Writing grant proposals for teacher-developed projects
- Helping other teachers write grant proposals
- Developing protocol procedures to be followed during "lock-downs"
- Facilitating the development of an integrated school-to-work curriculum
- Preparing newsletters to keep faculty up-to-date on restructuring
- Organizing and facilitating staff development training
- Developing connections with area businesses and arranging "job shadowing" sites for students
- Working with a community college to create an alternative school for Rogers High school students
- Scheduling substitute teachers to provide Rogers teachers with release time to work on restructuring
- Making presentations on the school's restructuring at provincial and regional conferences
- Meeting with the principal, assistant principals, professors, and others to develop short- and long-range plans for implementing site-based management; chairing meetings of the site-based council, the restructuring steering committee, and other restructuring-related committees

In many schools, teachers might have one or more of the following roles: coordinator of special education services, lead teacher of a project, coordinator of the media centre responsible for school-wide implementation of technology, coordinator of the school's whole-language program, or such other temporary roles as the school may determine.

Dimensions of Teacher Leadership Beyond the Classroom

Figure 10.3 illustrates 10 dimensions of teacher leadership beyond the classroom. The many teachers the authors have assisted on school restructuring projects during the past few years have used these skills to reach an array of educational goals. Clearly,

Figure 10.3

Ten dimensions of teacher leadership beyond the classroom

Team-Building

Project Management

Grant Writing/ Seeking External Funding

Designing and Delivering Staff Development

Networking and Partnership Building

Teacher Leadership

Change Facilitation

Researching

Program/ School Evaluation

Public Relations

Mentoring New Teachers

Visioning

these teachers have modelled what Rallis (1990, 193) terms "an elevated conception of teaching."

At schools around the country, teachers and principals are using a "collaborative, emergent" approach to leadership; that is, the person who provides leadership for a particular school wide project or activity may or may not be the principal or a member of the administrative team (Parkay, Schindler, & Oaks, 1997). Such schools are characterized by a "higher level of professional community" (Newmann & Wehlage 1995). They are similar to the schools Wohlstetter (1995, 24) identified as having successfully implemented site-based management (SBM): "[They] had principals who played a key role in dispersing power. [T]he principals were often described as facilitators and managers of change." This collaborative style of leadership represents a distinct change from the traditional model, whereby school principals simply instruct teachers to implement changes decided upon by themselves or by the school district.

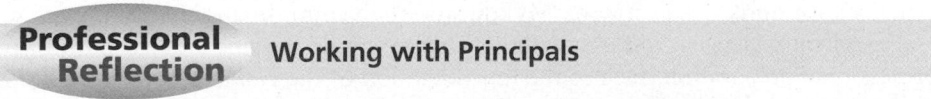

Professional Reflection   **Working with Principals**

The new calls to leadership for teachers suggest that teachers' essential knowledge and skills may not differ much from those traditionally required for educational administrators. Performance requirements (domains) have been established by all provinces and territories for principal teachers. Which of the following domains also apply to teacher–leaders? To what extent are the knowledge and skills required of teacher–leaders and of principals becoming similar?

I. **Functional Domains**
   1. Leadership
   2. Information Collection
   3. Problem Analysis
   4. Judgment
   5. Organizational Oversight
   6. Implementation
   7. Delegation

II. **Programmatic Domains**
   8. Instructional Program
   9. Curriculum Design
  10. Student Guidance and Development
  11. Staff Development
  12. Measurement and Evaluation
  13. Resource Allocation

III. **Interpersonal Domains**
  14. Motivating Others
  15. Sensitivity
  16. Oral Expression
  17. Written Expression

IV. **Contextual Domains**
  18. Philosophical and Cultural Values
  19. Legal and Regulatory Applications
  20. Policy and Political Influences
  21. Public and Media Relationships

How Do Teachers Contribute to Educational Research?

Today's teachers play an increasingly important role in educational research. By applying research to solve practical, classroom-based problems, teachers validate the accuracy and usefulness of educational research and help researchers identify additional areas to investigate. As consumers of educational research, teachers improve their teaching, contribute to educational advancements, and enhance the professional status of teaching.

In addition, increasing numbers of teachers are becoming competent researchers in their own right and are making important contributions to our understanding of teaching and learning. Prior to the mid-1980s, teachers were the missing "voice" in educational research. However, as teachers and staff developers Holly and McLoughlin (1989, 309) noted nearly two decades ago, "We've moved from research on teachers to research with teachers and lately to research by teachers." Since their observation, we have seen the emergence of the **teacher–researcher**, the professional teacher who conducts classroom research to improve his or her practice.

Sources of Educational Research

myeducationlab

Research findings are reported in numerous educational research journals (see Teacher's Resource 10.3 on www.MyEducationLab.com). In addition, there are several excellent reviews of research with which you should become familiar during your professional preparation, such as the fourth edition of the *Handbook of Research on Teaching* (published by the American Educational Research Association (Richardson 2001). Its more than 1200 pages synthesize research in several areas, including studies on teaching at various grade levels and in various subject areas. Other comprehensive, authoritative reviews of research you might wish to consult include the following:

- *Handbook of Research on Improving Student Achievement*, 3rd ed. (Educational Research Service, 2004).
- *Handbook of Research on Multicultural Education*, 2nd ed. (Jossey-Bass, 2004).

- *Handbook of Research and Policy in Art Education* (Lawrence Erlbaum, 2004).
- *Handbook of Research on Teaching the English Language Arts*, 2nd ed. (Lawrence Erlbaum, 2003), sponsored by the International Reading Association and the National Council of Teachers of English.
- *International Handbook of Curriculum Research* (Lawrence Erlbaum, 2003).
- *Handbook of Early Literacy Research* (Guilford Press, 2003).
- *Handbook of International Research in Mathematics Education* (Lawrence Erlbaum, 2002).
- *Handbook of Research in Middle Level Education* (Information Age Publishing, 2001).

The U.S. federal government did Canadian educational researchers a great service when it created the **Educational Resources Information Center (ERIC)**. ERIC is an information system made up of 16 **ERIC clearinghouses** and several adjunct clearinghouses—all coordinated by the central ERIC agency in Washington, D.C. The ERIC system, now available in most Canadian college and university libraries, contains descriptions of exemplary programs, the results of research and development efforts, and related information that can be used by teachers, administrators, and the public to improve education. Each clearinghouse specializes in one area of education and searches out relevant documents or journal articles that are screened according to ERIC selection criteria, abstracted, and indexed.

Organizations such as the Canadian Teachers' Federation, the Canadian Council for the Advancement of Education, the Canadian Education Association, and many others (see Teacher's Resource 10.3 at MyEducationLab.com), are devoted to high-quality, fundamental research at every level of education, with most of the research conducted by scholars at the host university. Among the areas focused on are the processes of teaching and learning, school organization and improvement, the content of education, and factors that contribute to (or detract from) excellence in education.

myeducationlab

Conducting Classroom Action Research

Four decades ago, Robert Schaefer (1967, 5) posed the following questions in *The School as the Center of Inquiry*:

> Why should our schools not be staffed, gradually if you will, by scholar-teachers in command of the conceptual tools and methods of inquiry requisite to investigating the learning process as it operates in their own classroom? Why should our schools not nurture the continuing wisdom and power of such scholar-teachers?

Schaefer's vision for teaching has become a reality. Today, thousands of teachers are involved in **action research** to improve their work. Using their classrooms as "laboratories," these teacher–researchers are systematically studying the outcomes of their teaching through the application of various research methods. In addition, they are disseminating the results of their research at professional conferences and through various publications.

Simply put, action research is the classroom-based study by teachers, individually or collaboratively, of how to improve instruction. As in the *reflection-in-action* approach described earlier in the chapter, action research begins with a teacher-identified question, issue, or problem: "How can I more effectively motivate a group of students? How do students experience the climate in my classroom? What factors limit parental participation in our school? How can our department (or teacher team) become more collegial? How does computer use in the foreign language classroom affect students' oral

David's Story

"David"—who wishes to remain anonymous—was teaching Grades 9 through 11 in an Atlantic Canada high school when one of his students asked for help in making better grades. The student appeared to be bright and alert, and claimed to study on a regular basis, but only occasionally did she make marks above the B level. Thinking a solution to the student's difficulties would be relatively simple, David agreed to help, not realizing that he was setting out on an educational journey that would last for the next five years.

He first approached his school counsellor and requested information on how students might improve their study skills. The one relevant document made available by the counsellor contained little in the way of suggestions, so David sought assistance in other areas. What he discovered amazed and discouraged him: Nowhere within his school district, at either the middle school or high school levels, was anyone teaching students how to study. Teachers were telling students that they must study, but none of them told students how to do so effectively. At that point, he realized that if anything was to be done, he would have to do it himself.

David decided to start with some action research regarding his own students and their personal study habits. He constructed a questionnaire that students completed anonymously after being told the tabulated results would be shared with them (see Teacher's Resource 10.4 on www.MyEducationLab.com). After discussing the data with his students, David set out to find a variety of study skill techniques appropriate to the various learning styles common to all classrooms. He began reading everything he could find that related in any way to the quest he was on when he made a disheartening discovery in a psychology text: The best study skill a person can have is a good reading rate. He went back to his classes, gave them a simple page of material to read, timed them, and then calculated their collective reading speeds. With a few exceptions, their reading rates were all of a very low level. He decided he must teach his students how to read quickly and efficiently if his goal of improving their study skills was to be reached.

myeducationlab

In his search for information on speedy but effective reading skills, he went to school counsellors, reading specialists, special educators, conferences of the International Reading Association, and numerous workshops. He quickly learned that no one in his school district was doing anything to improve student reading skills at the secondary level, nor did anyone appear to know how such improvement might be accomplished. Obviously, special attention was given to students with truly serious reading difficulties, but once these students learned to read at a minimally functional level, support was discontinued.

It took five years of reading, discussions with colleagues, and reflection before David was ready to test what he had learned. He chose his Grade 9 English class for the first trial because no one would regard teaching students at this level how to study and how to read as being outside the approved curriculum. The students were first presented with a variety pack of study techniques and taught the situations in which each might be most useful. Then, after a careful introduction in which students were informed that they were not required to participate (all did), and that not all of them would necessarily benefit from the process they were to undergo, the reading lessons began: 15 minutes daily over a two-week period. The improvements in student reading rates can be seen in Table 10.1.

Table 10.1

Reading Rate Statistics in Words per Minute (WPM)

Student #	Start Speed	Final Speed	Student #	Start Speed	Final Speed
1	230	310	14	160	455
2	200	225	15	165	475
3	330	500	16	150	315
4	175	290	17	180	270
5	250	410	18	215	330
6	230	490	19	150	210
7	195	370	20	125	180
8	310	505	21	190	260
9	190	460	22	230	350
10	230	520	23	170	210
11	220	375	24	240	380
12	360	780	25	310	540
13	350	610			
				WPM=220	WPM=390

Note: These results were acquired by measuring students' comfortable reading rates both before and after the reading rate improvement activities. All results are rounded to the nearest five.

As David's students progressed through the grades, colleagues started to notice that his "graduates" tended to be among their more academically able. His success was garnering interest. Parents started to request that their children be placed in his classes. He received invitations to present at local and provincial conferences. A local university brought David in to share his ideas with pre-service teachers. Individual adults with heavy job-related reading requirements came to him for help. David's action research, which led to his becoming an educational leader, forcefully demonstrates the positive effect that a dedicated, professional teacher can have.

Questions

1. Why do you think a good reading rate is regarded as the most important study skill?

2. Why do you think "David" wishes to remain anonymous?

3. If "David" had two Grade 9 English classes, rather than only the one with whom he tried out his new methodologies, do you believe that he would have been ethically required to give both classes the opportunity to improve their study and reading skills?

4. What generalizations can you make with regard to the data contained in Table 10.1?

5. What is your personal definition of leadership? Do "David's" actions satisfy your definition?

communication?" Identification of the question to be investigated via action research is a critical step, as the staff development coordinator at an urban elementary school points out:

> As a member of the school leadership team responsible for staff development, I helped guide the process of designing and carrying out the [action research] projects. One of the major challenges in conducting action research projects for this particular group of teachers was the first step: defining the question or problem to be studied. The delicate part of the facilitator's role for this part of action research is to guide teachers toward questions that accurately represent their real concerns and to help them articulate questions in ways that clarify the important elements. If action research is to be useful and engaging, then questions must focus on significant issues related to the success of students within the classroom. (Mills 2000, 130)

Action research is also "a natural part of teaching. [T]o be a teacher means to observe students and study classroom interactions, to explore a variety of effective ways of teaching and learning, and to build conceptual frameworks that can guide one's work. This is a personal, as well as a professional quest, a journey toward making sense out of and finding satisfaction in one's teaching. It is the work of teacher–researchers" (Burnaford, Fischer & Hobson 1996, 33).

Action research can be used to study almost any dimension of teaching and learning. At the beginning of the action research cycle, Mills (2000, 41) suggests developing an "action plan" consisting of these steps:

- Write an area-of-focus statement.
- Define the variables.
- Develop research questions.
- Describe the intervention or innovation.
- Describe the membership of the action research group.
- Describe negotiations that need to be undertaken.
- Develop a timeline.
- Develop a statement of resources.
- Develop data collection ideas.

Figure 10.4 presents a "taxonomy" of data collection techniques for action research.

Not surprisingly, becoming a teacher–researcher is hard work, given the daily demands of teaching itself. However, more schools are redefining the teacher's role to include action research. These schools realize that action research can provide data on the effectiveness of educational programs, enhance student learning, and energize teachers for professional growth. Four teachers, all members of an action research team, comment on its benefits:

> By far the most rewarding part of working on an action research team was the opportunity to learn and grow with a small group of teacher colleagues. This experience of mutual commitment provided a wonderful staff development experience; by working with these colleagues consistently throughout the year, we were able to explore new ideas and take risks in the classroom with a type of "safety net" in place. For that reason alone, as well as our desire to explore the new questions and challenges raised by our research, we will continue to conduct action research into the effectiveness of our teaching and grading practices. (Mills 2000, 97)

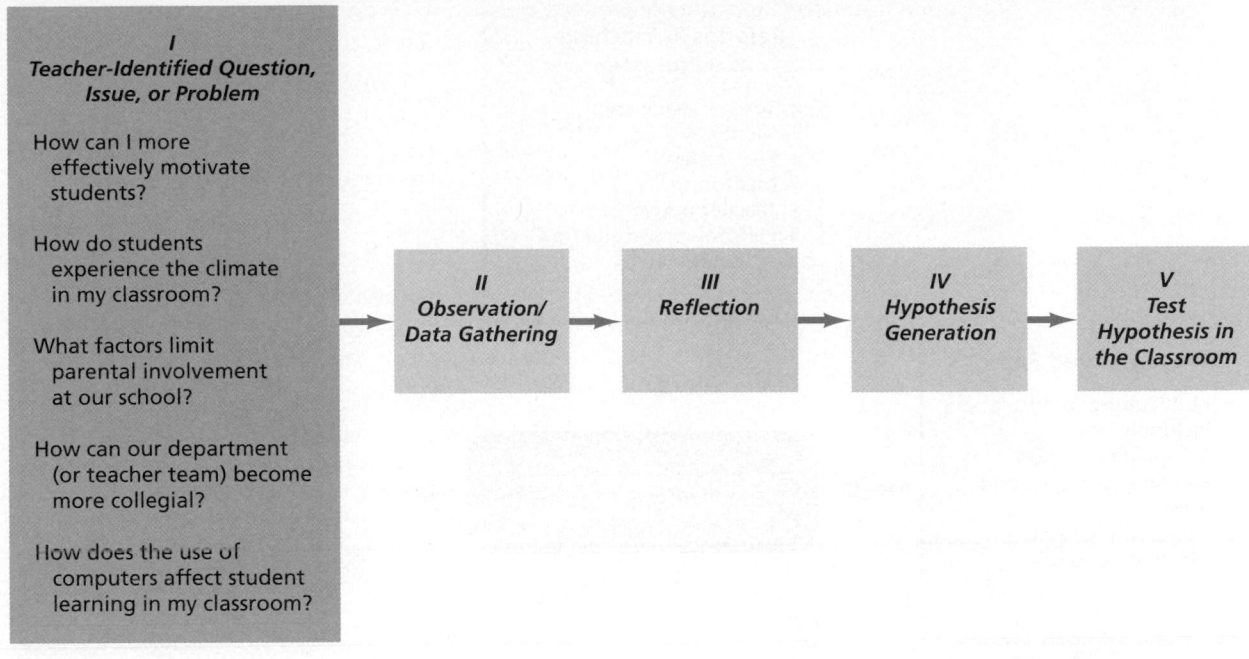

Figure 10.4

A classroom-focused action research cycle

How Are Teachers Providing Leadership for School Development and Curriculum Improvement?

Today's teachers welcome opportunities to provide leadership for school development and curriculum improvement. Although teachers may have played a limited role in school governance in the past, there are currently many opportunities to become educational leaders beyond the classroom. Figure 10.5 presents five clusters of educational improvement concepts, each of which will provide teachers with opportunities to shape policies during the twenty-first century.

The key to successful school development and curriculum improvement is teacher leadership and collaboration. The following strategies are among the many ways in which teachers can demonstrate leadership.

- Participate in professional teacher organizations
- Take part in school decisions
- Define what students need to know and be able to do
- Share ideas with colleagues
- Be a mentor to new teachers
- Improve facilities and technology
- Work with parents
- Create partnerships with the community
- Create partnerships with businesses and organizations
- Create partnerships with colleges and universities to prepare future teachers
- Become a leader in the community
- Lead efforts to make teachers more visible; communicate positive information

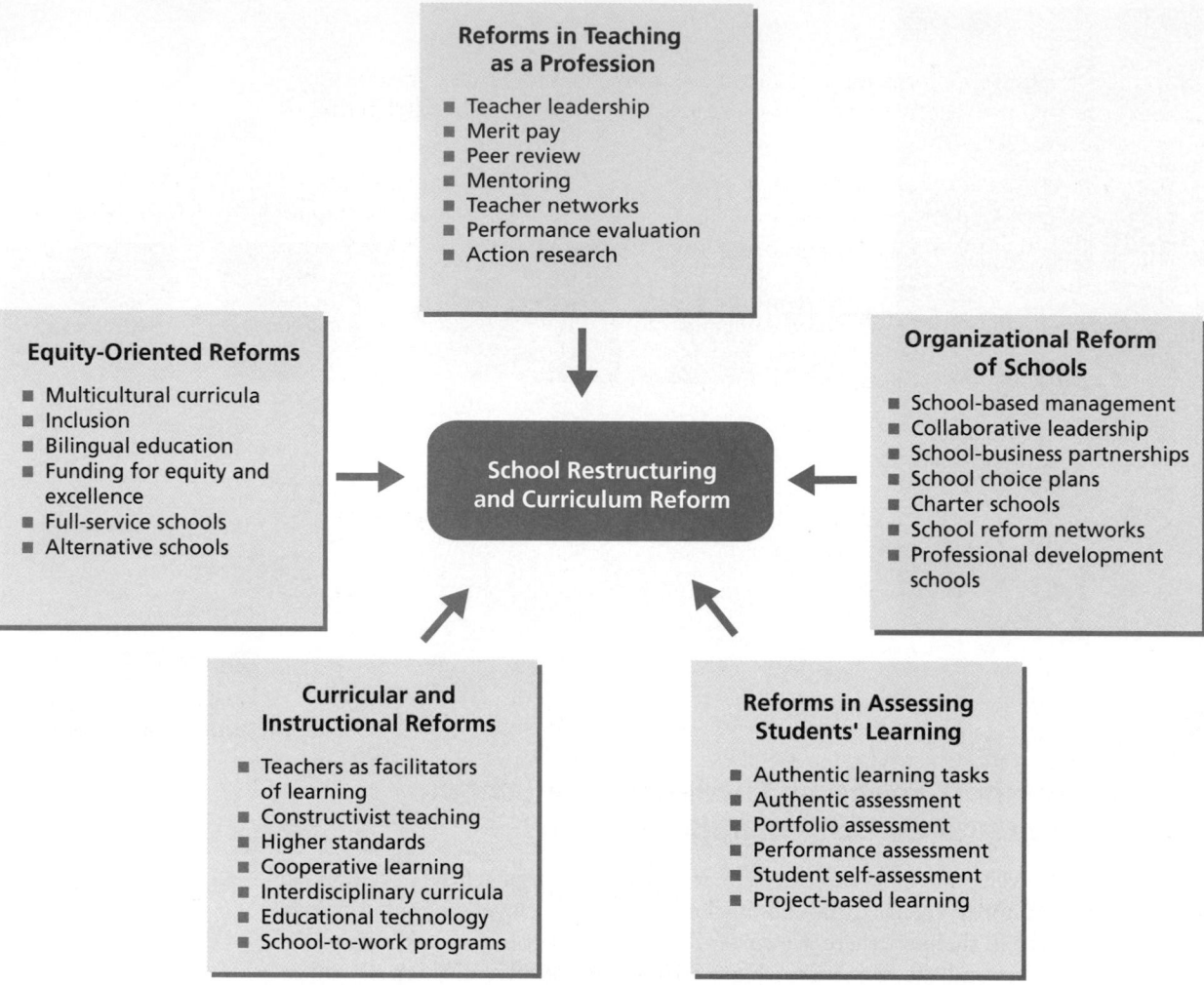

Reforms in Teaching as a Profession

- Teacher leadership
- Merit pay
- Peer review
- Mentoring
- Teacher networks
- Performance evaluation
- Action research

Equity-Oriented Reforms

- Multicultural curricula
- Inclusion
- Bilingual education
- Funding for equity and excellence
- Full-service schools
- Alternative schools

Organizational Reform of Schools

- School-based management
- Collaborative leadership
- School-business partnerships
- School choice plans
- Charter schools
- School reform networks
- Professional development schools

School Restructuring and Curriculum Reform

Curricular and Instructional Reforms

- Teachers as facilitators of learning
- Constructivist teaching
- Higher standards
- Cooperative learning
- Interdisciplinary curricula
- Educational technology
- School-to-work programs

Reforms in Assessing Students' Learning

- Authentic learning tasks
- Authentic assessment
- Portfolio assessment
- Performance assessment
- Student self-assessment
- Project-based learning

Figure 10.5

Opportunities for teacher leadership in school improvement

SUMMARY

To What Extent Is Teaching a Full Profession?

- Teachers are assuming new leadership roles beyond the classroom as education systems become more decentralized and approaches to school leadership become more collaborative and participatory.

- For an occupation to be considered a profession, it must satisfy several criteria. Of the following nine criteria for a profession, teaching meets some more fully than others: (1) institutional monopoly of services, (2) teacher autonomy, (3) years of education and training, (4) provision of essential service, (5) degree of self-governance, (6) professional associations, (7) professional knowledge and skills, (8) level of public trust, and (9) prestige, benefits, and pay.

- Although teaching does not currently satisfy all criteria for a profession, the collaborative efforts of individuals and groups such as the Canadian Teachers' Federation are very active in this area.

What Is Professionalism in Teaching?

- The most potent force for enhancing the professional status of teaching is for teachers to see that their actions are professional and to commit to lifelong learning and active involvement.

- Professional behaviour as a teacher is characterized by reflection-in-action (the ability to observe sensitively in classrooms, to reflect on those observations, and to then act accordingly) and a willingness to serve as a mentor to those entering the profession.

- As lifelong learners, professional teachers actively seek opportunities for growth— from participating in training provided by a school district to arranging "in-service" activities and acquiring new leadership skills.

To What Professional Organizations Do Teachers Belong?

- Teachers help shape education as a profession through their leadership roles in local, provincial, and national teacher organizations.

- Teachers are members of professional associations for specific subject areas and student populations.

What New Leadership Roles for Teachers Are Emerging?

- Through their involvement with local, provincial, national, and international teacher organizations, teachers participate in making key decisions about teacher preparation, certification, and staff development.

- In their new role as teacher–leaders, many teachers are playing a key role beyond the classroom as they form partnerships that focus on the improvement of Canadian schools.

- Teachers who work collaboratively with principals on school improvement use 10 dimensions of teacher leadership beyond the classroom: team-building, project management, designing and delivering staff development, researching, public relations, visioning, program and school evaluation, facilitating change, networking and partnership building, and grant writing and seeking external funding.

How Do Teachers Contribute to Educational Research?

- Teachers validate the accuracy and usefulness of educational research and identify additional areas to examine when they put "research into practice."

- In the role of teacher–researcher, many teachers conduct action research and systematically study the outcomes of their teaching. Teachers use a five-step action research cycle to study their classrooms and improve their teaching: problem identification, planning, organization, evaluation, and action.

How Are Teachers Providing Leadership for School Development and Curriculum Improvement?

- Five "clusters" of educational improvement areas provide teachers with many opportunities to provide leadership for school improvement: reforms in teaching as a profession, equity-oriented reforms, organizational improvement of schools, improvements in assessing students' learning, and curricular and instructional improvements.

KEY TERMS AND CONCEPTS

action research, 307
Canadian Teachers'
    Federation (CTF), 301
critical reflective
    practice, 299

Educational Resources
    Information Center
    (ERIC), 307
ERIC clearinghouses, 307
mentor, 300

Phi Delta Kappa (PDK), 303
profession, 294
reflection-in-action, 298
teacher–leader, 303
teacher–researcher, 306

APPLICATIONS AND ACTIVITIES

Teacher's Journal

1. In your opinion, what accounts for public trust or lack of trust in the teaching profession? What might be the best way to increase trust?

2. Visit the Canadian Teachers' Federation website and review several of the most recently published articles. What topics appear to be receiving the most attention?

3. Do you plan to join a teacher's association after you graduate? What are your reasons? What advantages and disadvantages of joining are most relevant to you?

Theory into Practice

1. Individuals who have career positions that fall under the heading of "essential services" are forbidden by law to participate in a strike. It is believed that the loss of their services could result in widespread harm to the social fabric. Briefly consider which of the following careers should be deemed essential services and formulate a reason, or reasons, in support of your position. In a small group, discuss your ideas with others.

   - Court judges
   - Garbage collectors
   - Grocery clerks
   - Nurses
   - Physicians
   - Police officers
   - Postal workers
   - Power-line workers
   - Snow plow drivers
   - Soldiers
   - Teachers
   - University professors

2. Class discussion: Read the following material, which deals with the powerful influence of teacher unions. Be prepared to support a position regarding whether the arguments in favour of teacher unions are stronger than those that argue teacher unions have a negative effect on the education system. If possible, use examples from your own experiences to support your position if called upon by your professor.

A. Arguments in favour of teacher unions:

- They "protect against efforts to dismantle public education and lobby for increased funding to strengthen schools." (Noll 1999, 355)
- They bring about specific changes that increase students' opportunities to learn. For example, they lobby for smaller class sizes, for assistance for students with special needs, and for increased professional development for teachers.
- They have developed codes of professional conduct for their members, award grants to teachers who have provided proposals for interesting curricular initiatives, and provide both legal and other professional assistance as a member's circumstances may require.
- The wide range of books, videos, and services provided by all teachers' unions are directed toward assisting teachers in their work and improving education.

B. Arguments against teacher unions:

- Their successes in increasing salaries have come at the cost of improvements to education. They have increased the costs of public education, while doing little to improve the final outcomes for students.
- They hurt schools through their insistence that all teachers be paid according to the same scale. In teaching-shortage areas such as math and science, where pay in fields outside the classroom is higher, the only way to meet the demand for teachers is to pay more. Union resistance to doing so shows more caring about teachers than about the education of children and youth.
- They resist merit pay for teachers, layoffs on any other basis than seniority, and teacher dismissal other than for the most serious of offences.
- Teachers are professionals working with human services and should not be permitted to strike under any circumstance.

3. Go to Teacher's Resource 10.4 on www.MyEducationLab.com and carefully examine the data included in "David's" questionnaire. In a small group setting, examine these questions:

- If you were a secondary school student, how would you have responded to the questions asked?
- What generalizations regarding the study practices of secondary students may be drawn from the data?
- Are there any related questions that might have been interesting to see included in the questionnaire?

Teacher's Database

1. With classmates, join or start an online discussion on one or more of the following topics or another topic from this chapter.

- Action research
- Educational reform
- Grant writing
- Mentoring
- School improvement
- Teacher leadership
- Teacher strikes
- Teacher unions
- Teacher–principal collaboration

2. Using your favourite search engine, gather information and resources about school networking and teacher networking. How might online networking contribute to your preparation as a teacher? How might you and your students use networking in connection with your curriculum? What knowledge and skills do you need to participate in a school-based networking project?

Observations and Interviews

1. Survey adults who are not involved in education to get their views on teaching as a profession. What images of teachers and teaching emerge? How do you account for these views?

2. Interview teachers about their involvement in professional associations and the teachers' union. What benefits do teachers obtain from their involvement?

3. Find out if teacher strikes are legal in your province or territory. What risks do striking teachers face? How are disputes between teachers and school districts settled?

4. Collaborate with classmates to study a school that is involved in restructuring and participants' roles in the change process. Compare teachers' activities with the new leadership roles for teachers discussed in this chapter. Are any of the teachers involved in action research in the classroom? How does teacher research contribute to restructuring efforts?

5. Visit a school that has developed a partnership with one or more community agencies, schools of higher education, businesses, parent groups, or neighbourhood associations. Arrange to observe a planning meeting between the school and the community representatives. Write a narrative account of the meeting followed by an evaluation of the effectiveness of this partnership.

Professional Portfolio

Focusing on the grade level and subject area for which you are preparing to teach, consult several of the sources of educational research listed in this chapter, and prepare a set of research findings to guide your teaching. For each entry, include a bibliographic citation and an annotation that briefly describes the research and the results of that research.

For information on the creation of a lesson plan, go to the "Lesson Plan Builder" under the Careers tab at www.MyEducationLab.com.

For information regarding the construction of a personal portfolio, go to "Preparing a Portfolio" under the Careers tab on www.MyEducationLab.com.

For suggestions regarding how to make your lessons more interesting go to Teacher's Resource 10.1, The Teacher's Scribe: "It's time to start complaining" on www.MyEducationLab.com.

To gain some understanding about the complexity of union negotiations, go to Teacher's Resource 10.2 on www.MyEducationLab.com and read the simulation activity.

For a list of Canadian professional organizations for teachers, go to Teacher's Resource 10.3 on www.MyEducationLab.com

11

Your First Teaching Position

Being a good teacher means . . . thinking about teaching, in a long-term, systemic way. By asking the right questions, by continuously critiquing and improving your practice, and by continuing to examine the work you do in your classroom and how it connects with the larger world, you can achieve your Ívision and become the teacher you hope to be.

—Kelley Dawson Salas, Rita Tenorio, Stephanie Walters, and Dale Weiss *The New Teacher Book: Finding Purpose, Balance, and Hope During Your First Years in the Classroom*, 2004, p. 8.

focus questions

1. How will you become certified or licensed to teach?
2. Will you have difficulty finding a teaching job?
3. How will you find your first teaching job?
4. What can you expect as a beginning teacher?
5. How can you become a part of your learning community?
6. How can you participate in teacher collaboration?
7. How important is prior preparation (planning for teaching) to becoming an exceptionally effective teacher?
8. How will your performance as a teacher be evaluated?

Your spring student-teaching seminar has just ended, and you and three other students are seated in the student lounge enjoying coffee and talking about finding a job.

"What was the interview like?" you ask one of your classmates upon learning that he had interviewed yesterday for a position at an urban school.

"Yeah, tell us," another student adds. "I'm really anxious about interviewing. I don't know what to expect. There are so many things they could ask."

"Well, I was interviewed by the principal and two people from the district office—I think they were in personnel. At first, they asked questions like the ones we used in our seminar role plays. 'Why do you want to teach? What are your weaknesses? Use five adjectives to describe yourself.'"

"What else?" you ask, anxious to complete a mental image of the interview process so you'll be ready for your first interview next week.

"They asked me to describe a student teaching lesson that went well," he answers. "After I did that, one of them asked 'How could the lesson have been better—either for the entire class or for a certain student?' That one took some thinking."

As your friend reconstructs his response, you imagine how you would answer the same question.

Moments later, he says, "Then they asked a question that really surprised me— 'What would you do if your principal told you to discontinue a classroom activity because it was too noisy and left a mess for the custodians to clean up? But the activity really involved the kids, and they learned a lot.'"

He pauses for a sip of coffee and then continues. "Another one was, 'Give us an example of a principle that guides your teaching.'"

Impressed with the district's ability to pose challenging questions, you again imagine how you would respond.

A few minutes later, another student asks, "What about portfolios? Did they spend much time looking at yours?"

"Yeah, they really did!" your friend exclaims. "With my application materials, I included a portfolio on DVD that has a video segment of my student teaching, plus I gave them the URL for my website. They were pretty impressed. It was obvious that they had looked at just about everything in the portfolio. They asked all kinds of questions. Half the questions were about how to make a digital portfolio. But they also really wanted to see things that were related to how much my students learned while I was student teaching."

With the mention of portfolios, you feel thankful you took the time to create an electronic one that you can take to your first job interview the following week. However, you wonder what else you should do to prepare for the interview and what steps you could follow to increase your chances of finding the best possible teaching position.

First Steps Toward Becoming a Teacher

On completion of your teacher education program, you will still have several important steps to take before securing your first teaching position. Preparing well for these steps will go a long way in helping you begin teaching with confidence.

It is natural that you feel both excited and a bit fearful when thinking about your first job. While taking the courses required in your teacher education program, you probably feel secure in your role as a student: You know what is expected of you. As a teacher, however, you will assume an entirely new role—a role that requires time and experience before it becomes comfortable.

Preparing well for your first teaching position will make your entry into the profession rewarding and personally satisfying. This chapter discusses how to obtain your first teaching position, how to make the first days and weeks of teaching productive and satisfying, and how to become part of a professional, collaborative learning community.

How Will You Become Certified or Licensed to Teach?

A **teaching certificate** is actually a licence to teach. The majority of Canadian provinces and territories require completion of a professional teacher education program consisting of a minimum of 30 semester credit-hours of course work and a practicum for teacher certification.

In terms of course work, in general, provinces and territories do not prescribe content; however, course work in teaching methodology and educational psychology is common to all teacher education programs. With the exception of Ontario, approved teacher education programs in Canada contain a minimum 12-week practicum experience (Council of Ministers of Education 1999).

Provincial Certification Requirements

Although all jurisdictions, through the power of legislation, have the ultimate authority to change certification requirements in order to comply with the spirit of the Agreement on Internal Trade/Teaching Profession (AIT), some have contractual arrangements that require consultation with, or approval by, the professional teachers' union.

Most jurisdictions require that all teachers undertake post-secondary course work in the subject areas of their own K (or Primary)–12 school curriculum. This is emphasized more clearly in the preparation of secondary teachers, who are expected to have some depth of knowledge in the subjects they teach. This is normally completed during undergraduate studies.

Also in most jurisdictions, elementary teachers are expected to complete course work in the subject areas of their curricula. This varies by province or territory, from New Brunswick's requirement of course work in general subject areas to Ontario's acceptance of any bachelor's degree. In British Columbia, the course work requirement is 60 credits, including six credits of English, six credits of Canadian studies, three credits of mathematics, and three credits of lab science.

Some jurisdictions recognize subject areas not found in their own K–12 curriculum. For example, religious, heritage, international, and First Nations languages studies are specific to jurisdiction.

Teachers wishing to move between provinces and territories must have access to information on the requirements for qualification specific to each jurisdiction. All jurisdictions publish their certification requirements on an annual basis, post them online, and make them available to the Council of Ministers of Education, Canada. You may contact the teacher certification department in the province where you plan to teach.

Teacher Certification and Classification for Each Province

Mobility provisions under the AIT entitle a teacher to receive a teaching credential from the receiving province or territory under the following conditions:

All applicants must:

- hold a valid teaching credential from a Canadian province or territory
- have completed a professional teacher education program consisting of a minimum of 30 semester credit hours of course work and a practicum for teacher certification
- provide all documents required by the receiving province or territory
- satisfy any requirements of the receiving province or territory with respect to "fit and proper person," currency of practice, and language proficiency

Applicants fall into one of three (3) categories.

Category 1

Applicants who have completed a minimum of four years of post-secondary education and hold a degree completed at a university that is a member of the Association of Universities and Colleges of Canada or any other university degree(s) deemed equivalent by the receiving province or territory will be issued a teaching credential in the receiving province or territory based on the following:

An applicant who satisfies the basic requirements of the receiving province or territory will be granted a teaching credential by that receiving province or territory.

OR

An applicant who does not satisfy all requirements of the receiving province or territory will be granted a teaching credential valid for a period of time (to be determined by the receiving province or territory). Said time will be a reasonable period during which the teacher will be required to complete successfully any outstanding academic or professional preparation requirements of the receiving province or territory.

Category 2

Applicants who hold a degree or diploma in vocational, technical, or technological studies equivalent to the requirements of the receiving province or territory will be issued a teaching credential by the receiving province or territory based on the following specifications.

Applicants who satisfy the equivalent standards, including any work experience requirements, of the receiving province or territory will be granted an appropriate teaching credential by the receiving province or territory. In some instances, the teacher may be required to complete successfully any outstanding academic or professional preparation requirements of the receiving province or territory during the validity period of the teaching credential.

Category 3

Applicants who hold a teaching credential based on academic or professional preparation that does not fall into either of the above two categories will be assessed on a case-by-case basis by the receiving province or territory, and may be granted a teaching credential in the receiving province or territory if they meet the necessary equivalent academic and professional preparation requirements. In some instances, the teacher may be required to complete successfully any outstanding academic or professional preparation requirements of the receiving province or territory during the validity period of the teaching credential (Council of Ministers of Education 1999).

Will You Have Difficulty Finding a Teaching Job?

When you think ahead to a career in teaching, two questions you are likely to ask are, "How hard will it be to find a job?" and "Where will I teach?" From time to time, teacher demand and supply figures have painted a rather bleak picture for those entering the teaching profession. At other times, finding a job in a preferred location has been relatively easy.

Frequently, Canadian regions report significant difficulties in hiring substitute teachers, and the shortage of substitutes can fluctuate during the school year. Furthermore, Canadian teachers are being offered significant financial incentives to teach in parts of the United States and in other countries (Canadian Teachers' Federation 2000).

An empirical study of possible teacher shortages was conducted by the Canadian Teachers' Federation in 2000. The study was a survey of senior administrators from 272 of 490 public school boards across Canada, and the sample was stratified by size of district based on enrolments. Survey highlights include:

- Administrators reported increased difficulty in recruiting.
- The most prevalent teacher shortage exist in science subjects (science, chemistry, biology, physics)
- Varied shortages occur based on region-specific issues, such as language of instruction or rural versus non-rural. (Canadian Teachers' Federation 2000)

A Favourable Job Market

The description of the trends in demand and supply of teachers due to retirement and attrition does not lead to the firm conclusion that there will be shortages of teachers overall in future. There are differing views on this important issue, but a general consensus exists regarding expected shortages in certain subjects, such as math, science, and technology.

With very low unemployment rates for elementary and secondary teachers, the supply of new, additional workers very much depends on the output of graduates from teacher training programs. While there may be different prospects for actual employment gains based on changes in funding, policy, and limited growth in the youth population, the majority of openings are expected to occur as a result of retirement. Statistics from the period of 1998 to 2008, when compared to the 1988 to 1998 decade, suggest that the supply of new graduates should be at least the same or somewhat larger than the current number of employed teachers (Teacher Supply and Demand: Facts and Statistics on Education Funding and Teaching in Alberta n.d.).

The ease with which you will find your first teaching position is also related to your area of specialization and to the part of the country you wish to reside in. In mid-February of each year, the various school boards around the country accept applications from both experienced teachers and teacher candidates still completing their course work.

Finding a Teaching Position in Canada

Finding a teaching position in Canada requires a plan. For current employment opportunities, the following job-search resources may be helpful:

- The Education Canada Network has developed a website to assist job seekers: www.educationcanada.com. This site posts teaching positions from the individual school districts across Canada, and includes a résumé registry, My ECN Centre, where visitors can post, edit, renew, or delete their own résumé for free. Employers are provided with user IDs and passwords to search the résumé database.
- Apply to *Education* is a recruitment database for teachers, school boards, and hiring principals maintained by Industry Canada: www.attn.org. A registration fee is required.
- Jobs in Education also assists job seekers: www.jobsineducation.com.
- Assistance is provided free of charge by the Canada Employment Centres, which are located in all major provincial cities. In Quebec, inquiries should be directed to the nearest Centre Travail. However, not all teaching vacancies are listed.

- Lists of school boards may be obtained from provincial authorities, and inquiries regarding possible vacancies can be made directly to the boards: www.cdnsba.org. It is, however, considered a breach of professional ethics to apply for a position in an area where the board's relationship with the teachers has been declared unsatisfactory by the teachers' association.
- Prospective teachers seeking positions in private schools should get in touch with the Canadian Association of Independent Schools: www.cais.ca.

Most teaching positions are advertised in local newspapers between February and June, with duties commencing September of the following year. Vacancies may occur throughout the school year. Applicants must generally be present in Canada and available for interviews.

When considering demand and supply estimates, remember that jobs are still available in oversupplied areas, but job hunting will be more competitive.

Other Career Opportunities for Teachers

There are also a great many nonteaching jobs in education and education-related fields, such as principal, assistant principal, librarian, and counsellor. In addition, there are many jobs that, although removed from the world of the classroom, would nevertheless enable you to use your teaching skills.

The following outline lists several places other than schools where individuals with teaching backgrounds are often employed. The number of education-related careers is likely to increase in the coming decades.

Industry

- Publishers
- Educational materials and equipment suppliers
- Specialized educational service firms
- Communications industries
- Research and development firms
- Management consulting firms
- Education and training consultants

Government

- Jobs in provincial departments of education

Education-Related Associations

- Research centres and foundations
- Professional associations such as teachers' associations or teachers' unions

Community Organizations

- Community action programs—neighbourhood health and legal services centres
- Social service agencies—Boy Scouts, Girl Scouts, YMCAs and YWCAs, boys' and girls' clubs, women's shelters, etc.
- Adult education centres
- Museums
- Hospitals

How Will You Find Your First Teaching Job?

As indicated by the previous discussion, employment opportunities in teaching can be hard to predict and will vary according to your area of teaching specialty, to shifts in enrolment due to population dispersal, to financial well being of provinces and school boards, and to the thoroughness of your preparation and search for a position. Furthermore, many teachers begin their careers as substitutes who then might become "term contract" teachers who then become eligible for a tenure-track position. Thus two other factors in the search for a teaching job emerge: persistence and patience. In the remainder of this section, we discuss five critical steps relevant to your search: finding out about teaching vacancies, preparing a résumé, writing letters of inquiry and letters of application, being interviewed, and selecting a position.

Finding Out about Teaching Vacancies

Your college or university probably has a **placement service** designed to help graduates find jobs. On a regular basis, placement offices publish lists of vacancies, which are posted through online group mail-outs and on various bulletin boards on campus, and, in many cases, mailed to students who have registered with the office and set up a credentials file. You can use the internet to connect with other universities that have accessible online placement services.

A **credentials file** (known as placement papers at some institutions) usually includes background information on the applicant, the type of position sought, a list of courses taken, performance evaluations by the applicant's cooperative teacher, and three or more letters of recommendation. With each job application, the candidate requests that his or her credentials be sent to the appropriate person at the school district, or the school district itself may request the applicant's papers. Placement offices usually charge a small fee each time a candidate's papers are sent out.

A job announcement describes the position and its requirements and provides the name and address of the individual to contact at the school district. For each position you are interested in, send a letter of application to the appropriate person along with your résumé. In addition, you may have your placement office send your credentials file. Placement offices also frequently set up on-campus interviews between candidates and representatives of school district personnel departments.

Personal networking will play an important role in landing the right job. Let people know you are looking for a job—friends, teachers at schools you've attended, faculty at the school where you student teach, and people you meet at workshops and conferences. Also, with access to the internet, you can conduct a global job search and even make your résumé available to millions of people.

Job Fairs

Some provinces have used **job fairs** to advertise and fill teaching positions. Job fairs are designed to bring potential teachers to one location for interviews and information sessions. The procedures used for job fairs vary from province to province. There are usually a number of school boards present, and some have specific job openings, whereas others will give candidates a general idea of possible upcoming positions. A common practice is for job fair organizers to offer and require an online registration for the fair.

Job fairs for beginning teachers usually operate like a marketplace, where each school or school board has its own table or area, and candidates visit with the administrators or senior board personnel to talk about positions. Often, candidates are given a specific time to arrive at the fair location. These fairs give beginning teachers the opportunity to network, participate in interview situations, and gain an understanding of the hiring process of various school districts.

Candidates attending job fairs should take along a carefully prepared résumé and a letter of inquiry, and be prepared for an interview. Potential employers may have specific vacancies, and may be prepared to offer a contract that day, especially in specialty areas that are hard to fill such as technology, music, French, and science.

Preparing Your Résumé

A **résumé** presents a concise summary of an individual's professional experiences, education, and skills. Résumés must be typed and, preferably, no longer than one page (two pages at most). Though there is no right way to prepare a résumé, it should present—in a neat, systematic way—key information that will help an employer determine your suitability for a particular position. Because your résumé will most likely be your first contact with an employer, it must make a good impression. Avoid using heavy or significantly designed or coloured paper for your résumé as it does not photocopy well.

Ordinarily, a résumé contains the following information:

- Personal data
- Education
- Certificates held
- Experience
- Activities and interests
- Honours and offices held
- Professional memberships
- References

Figure 11.1 is a résumé prepared by Linda M. Abbott, which you can use as a model. Please note that this is only one form of a résumé; there are many other available from a variety of sources. Another sample can be found at http://resumes-for-teachers.com/samples/secondary-resume-example.aspx. It is important to realize that although a résumé is your individual reflection of your life in brief, there are formats that are more serviceable than others. Make certain your information is relevant to the job for which you are applying and that it is accessible at a glance. Remember, you want your résumé to stand out, and it should be in a format that members of a hiring committee can read quickly. Since there are many individuals, agencies, and online resources to help you with this important presentation, be sure to look for examples of how to proceed and get someone you trust to critique your documentation before you send it in.

Writing Letters of Inquiry and Application

As a job seeker, you will most likely have occasion to write two kinds of letters: letters of inquiry and letters of application. A **letter of inquiry** is used to determine if a school district has, or anticipates, any teaching vacancies. This type of letter states your general qualifications and requests procedures to be followed in making a formal

Linda M. Abbott

Personal Data

Address and Phone: 641 Montbeck Crescent

Mississauga, Ontario L5G 1P4

905-891-1248

Education

Bachelor of Arts (English), Queen's University, Kingston, Ontario, May 2007

Bachelor of Education, Faculty of Education, Queen's University, Ontario, May 2008

Certificates Held

Major Area: Elementary/Middle School Education, K-8

Minor Area: Bilingual Education

Experience

Student Teaching, Greenbank Middle School, 168 Greenbank Road, Nepean, Ontario K2H 5V2, Spring 2007 and 2008. Cooperating teacher: Mrs. Becky Jones. Observed, assisted, and taught regular and accelerated Grade 3 classes in a multilingual setting. Organized after-school tutoring program and developed a unit on using the web in the classroom. Attended site-based council meetings with Mrs. Jones and assisted in the development of community-based partnerships.

Camp counsellor and Recreation Director, YWCA Summer Camp, Nepean, Ontario. Directed summer recreation programs consisting of 10 counsellors and 140 elementary aged girls.

Volunteer Telephone Counsellor, Nepean Crisis Hotline, June 2004–June 2007

Activities and Interests

Nepean Historical Society, Secretary, 2001

Member, Queen's University Community Service Learning Centre

Hobbies: Jogging, Aerobics, Piano, Water Skiing

Honours

Bachelor of Arts with Honours, Queen's University, May 2007

Queen's University Faculty of Education Scholarship

Professional Memberships

Ontario Council of Elementary Educators

Second Language Teachers of Ontario

Instructional Technology Skills

Word processing, internet and web, optical scanner, interactive whiteboard, LCD projection panel, NovaNet (computer-based learning system, multimedia skills)

Career Objective

Seeking K-8 position in multicultural/multilingual setting

References

References and credentials file available upon request.

Figure 11.1

Résumé

Linda M. Abbott
641 Montbeck Crescent
Mississauga, Ontario L5G 1P4

April 5, 2008

Dr. Lawrence Walker
Human Resources Department
Ottawa-Carleton District School Board
133 Greenbank Road
Nepean, Ontario K2H 6L3

Dear Mr. Walker:

This letter is to express my interest in a teaching position with the Ottawa-Carleton School Board. Specifically, I would like to know if you anticipate any vacancies at the elementary level for the fall of 2008. This May I will receive my Bachelor of Education degree from Queen's University in Kingston, Ontario. My specialization area is teaching English as a second language.

As a student teacher during the past two years, I taught regular and accelerated Grade 3 classes at Greenbank Elementary/Middle School in Nepean, Ontario. One class had 25 students, three of whom were diagnosed with learning disabilities. At Greenbank School, I introduced students to science resources on the web, and each student learned to send email messages to students in other countries.

My education at Queen's University, I believe, has prepared me well to teach in today's classrooms. I have had a course that focuses on meeting the needs of at-risk learners, and my area of specialization in bilingual education has prepared me to meet the challenges of working with students from diverse linguistic backgrounds. If possible, I would like a position that would allow me to develop programs for students with non-English backgrounds.

Enclosed you will find my résumé, which provides additional information about my experience and activities. If there are any positions for which you think I might be suited, please send application materials in the enclosed, self-addressed envelope. I appreciate your consideration, and I look forward to hearing from you.

Sincerely,

Linda M. Abbott

Linda M Abbott

Figure 11.2

Letter of Inquiry

application (see Figure 11.2). A letter of inquiry should include your résumé and a self-addressed, stamped envelope for the school district's convenience. Be prepared not to receive a reply for each letter of inquiry you send out. Many school districts are unable to respond to all inquiries.

A **letter of application** (often called a cover letter) indicates your interest in a particular position and outlines your qualifications for that job. As most districts have several vacancies at any given time, it is important that the first sentence of your letter refer to the specific position for which you are applying. The body of the letter should then highlight why you would be an excellent choice to fill that position. Inform the reader that your credentials file will be sent on request or will be forwarded by your placement office. Close the letter by expressing your availability for an interview (see Figure 11.3).

Linda M. Abbott
641 Montbeck Crescent
Mississauga, Ontario L5G 1P4

May 5, 2008

Dr. Lawrence Walker
Human Resources Department
Ottawa-Carleton District School Board
133 Greenbank Road
Nepean, Ontario K2H 6L3

Dear Mr. Walker:

This letter is in support of my application for the position of Grade 4 teacher at Elgin Street Public School. This May I will receive my Bachelor of Education degree from Queen's University in Kingston, Ontario. My specialization area is teaching English as a second language.

As my enclosed resume indicates, I just completed my student teaching at Greenbank Elementary/Middle School in Nepean, Ontario. During that 20 week period, I taught regular and accelerated Grade 3 classes. One class had 25 students, 3 of whom were diagnosed with learning disabilities. I also organized an after-school tutoring program and assisted my cooperating teacher in developing community-based partnerships.

A major interest of mine is using technology in the classroom. I am familiar with various hypermedia programs and NovaNET, a computer-based learning system. At Greenbank Elementary School, I introduced students to science resources on the web, and each student learned to send email messages to students in other countries.

As a result of my rewarding experiences at Greenbank Elementary School and in light of my preparation in bilingual education, I believe I could make a significant contribution to the educational program at Elgin Street Public School.

I have arranged for my credentials to be forwarded from Queen's University's placement office. If you require additional information of any sort, please feel free to contact me. At your convenience, I am available for an interview in Nepean. I thank you in advance for your consideration.

Sincerely,

Linda M. Abbott

Linda M Abbott

Participating in a Job Interview

Figure 11.3

Letter of Application

The interview is one of the most important steps in your search for an appropriate position. As the dialogue in the scenario at the beginning of this chapter suggests, school district representatives may ask a wide range of questions, both structured and open-ended.

In some districts, you might be interviewed by the principal only; in others, the superintendent, the principal, and the department chairperson might conduct the interview, and in still others, classroom teachers might interview you. Regardless of format, the interview enables the district to obtain more specific information regarding your probable success as an employee, and it gives you an opportunity to ask questions about what it is like to teach in the district. By asking questions, you can demonstrate your interest in working in the district. Increasingly, just as is the case with model résumés, an internet search will yield suggestions for interview questions that might be asked, and even suggestions of questions you might choose to ask when

What questions might be asked in an interview for a teaching position? What questions should you prepare about the teaching position? About the school?

the lead interviewer looks at you, smiles, and says, "Your turn." At some point in the interview process, you may be given an opportunity to present brief highlights from your professional portfolio. Or, if you have created internet or electronic versions of your portfolio, you could give the hiring official(s) the URL or a copy of the CD-ROM or DVD. See the third item under the MyEducationLab heading at the end of this chapter to locate additional helpful information relating to résumés and interview preparation.

Accepting an Offer

Imagine that you are notified that a school district would like to hire you. Your job search efforts have paid off! In the competition for positions, you have been successful. However, accepting your first teaching position is a major personal and professional step. Before signing a contract with a district, you should carefully consider job-related questions such as the following:

- In regard to my abilities and education, am I suited to this position?
- Would I like to work with this school's students, administrative staff, and teachers?
- Is the salary I am being offered sufficient?
- Will this position likely be permanent?
- Would I like to live in or near this community?
- Would the cost of living in this community enable me to live comfortably?
- Are opportunities for continuing education readily available?

If you accept the offer, you will need to return a signed contract to the district, along with a short letter confirming your acceptance. As a professional courtesy, you should notify other districts to which you have applied that you have accepted a position elsewhere. The following Professional Reflection can help you identify the type of school that would be most satisfying for your first teaching position.

Job satisfaction as a teacher depends on many factors: the size and location of a school, the backgrounds of students, the surrounding community, and the climate or culture of the school itself, to name a few. The following sentence completion items can help you determine what conditions are essential for your job satisfaction. Write your responses on a separate sheet or in your teacher's journal. For each item, write at least a few additional words to elaborate on how you completed the sentence.

1. Ideally, my first position would be teaching students who had the following backgrounds and characteristics: . . .
2. For me, an ideal work setting would be a school that . . .
3. My fellow teachers would help me during my first year of teaching by . . .
4. When not in school, my colleagues and I would enjoy . . .
5. My principal and/or supervisor would appreciate the way I . . .
6. In his or her feedback on my teaching, my principal and/or supervisor would be most impressed with . . .
7. During my first year at the school, I would volunteer to . . .
8. Five years after I begin teaching at this school, I would like to be . . .

What Can You Expect as a Beginning Teacher?

Once you accept the professional challenge of teaching, it is important to prepare well in advance of the first day of school. In addition to reviewing the material you will teach, you should use this time to find out all you can about the school's students, the surrounding community, and the way the school operates. Also reflect on your expectations.

The First Day

The first day of school can be frightening, as the following beginning teacher admits:

> My first day of teaching in the classroom—alone! All of the other teachers look calm and are even smiling. I'm so nervous about fitting in at this school, making friends with my colleagues, and being respected by my students. What if the students misbehave and I don't handle it properly? Or what if the principal walks in unannounced? (Hauser & Rauch 2002, 35)

Veteran teachers can also feel anxious on the first day of school, but anxiety can be used to set a positive tone for the rest of the school year, as the following experienced teacher points out:

> The anxiety level for both teachers and students about [the] first day is high. Taking advantage of these feelings can make for a good beginning.

> Students like to have guidelines on how the class will be run as well as what is expected of them academically. I always begin by welcoming the students into my class and immediately giving them something to do. I hand them their textbook and an index card. On the card, they write their name, address, telephone number, and book number.

Finding One's Comfort Level

Trina Arsenault
Elementary Teacher, Zumikon International School, Switzerland

To a New Teacher:

Stepping into the classroom, on your own, for the first time can be very daunting and even scary. My first thoughts on my first teaching day included, "I can't believe they trust me to do this. Do I know what I am doing? How do I teach? What do I teach? Do the students know how nervous I am?"

That was 10 years ago, and, even today, I sometimes have these thoughts. I am now comfortable in the classroom and love what I do, but these concerns still surface now and again. For me, these thoughts are natural and normal and keep me striving to do better. As a new teacher, these types of thoughts are not just expected, they are part of wanting to do a good job and wanting to be successful. If you are asking these types of questions in the first place, it means you want to succeed and do well with your students.

While we cannot choose the size and space we work in, we can make it our own. My advice would be to spend time in your classroom before students begin, even if you have to start a few days early. Sit in your room, explore it, and get to know the area, the space and the conditions. Check for hazards and have them fixed, adjust climate controls to appropriate settings and then work on classroom set-up.

Experiment with your space and move furniture around until you find the best set-up that works for you.

Of course, this may change after you have students in your room for the first time, but that is okay. I usually readjust my classroom at least two to three times during the year, as concerns, problems, or even curriculum, demands.

Once your space is established, make your classroom a visually exciting environment for your students to enter. Have the walls appropriately decorated for your age group and, at the primary level, have their names on display somewhere so they know you have been waiting for them to arrive. I continue to add new names as new students enter throughout the year, being sure the names go up before they arrive, if possible. As important as decoration is, it is more important to have space for the students to show their work. During the first day of school, students should create something to be displayed, something they feel proud of on the first day. I feel this is important, as it shows students that I place the highest value on their work. Students are always excited to show parents what they have accomplished on the first day of school.

Once you have established your physical environment, it is easier to think about the what and how of teaching. Read through and get to know your documentation, curriculum, resources, and materials. While it is difficult to go through everything at the start of the year, it is important to be familiar with as much of the material as possible. Before the year begins, be sure to have all the information you need for the first month or two of teaching.

Three areas I feel are important for becoming a great teacher are subject expertise, strong personal skills, and good student interaction. The expertise aspect comes with time and experience. Often the other two are natural skills and are not so easily practised. However, it helps to be relaxed—not necessarily in your attitude, style of teaching, or discipline policies, but in your ability to show confidence and comfort in what you are doing.

Finally, I think it is important for new teachers to know that it takes time to become a good teacher, let alone a great teacher. Do not expect to do everything right the first time, and expect a lot of trial and error in the first few years of teaching. Mistakes are a normal part of any aspect of life. The best teachers learn from their mistakes, and, more importantly, they take time to learn from their students.

While the students are filling out their cards and looking at the textbook, I set up my seating chart and verify attendance. Within ten minutes of meeting the students, I begin my first lesson. By keeping clerical chores to a minimum, I try to have more time on task. After a closure activity, somewhere in the middle of the class period I take a few minutes to explain how their grade will be determined, the rules of the class, and when extra help sessions are available.

Next, we deal with some curriculum content, and then I make a homework assignment. I tell the students that any homework assignment will be written on the chalkboard every day in the same location.

Setting high standards on the first day makes the following days easier. We will always need to monitor and adjust, but this will be within the framework set on the first day. (Burden & Byrd 1999, 177)

Advice from Experienced Teachers

In working with schools and teachers, the authors have gathered recommendations on preparing for the first day from experienced K–12 teachers in urban, suburban, and rural schools. Teachers' recommendations focus on planning, establishing effective management practices, and following through on decisions.

There are little things you can do, such as having a personal note attached to a pencil welcoming each child. You may want to do a few little tricks in science class or read them your favourite children's story. But don't put all your energy into the first day and have that day be the highlight of the year. Be well prepared and have plenty of things to do. Don't worry if you don't get everything done. Remember, you have all year.

—Middle school science teacher

It is vitally important to over prepare; always be prepared for several days in advance in case "today's" lesson expires early for some reason. Students appreciate seeing that their teachers know what they are dong—that there is a long-term plan. Thorough preparation inspires confidence in your students and this, in turn, generates a feeling of respect and well-being in the classroom.

—Senior high school English teacher

It really helps on the first day to have plenty of material to cover and things to do. I'd recommend taking the material you plan to cover that day and doubling it. It's better to have too much than to run out. What you don't use the first day, you use the next. It takes a while to get a feeling for how fast the kids are going to go.

—Grade 3 teacher

The first day is a good time to go over rules and procedures for the year. But don't overdo it. Be very clear and specific about your expectations for classroom behaviour.

—Grade 6 teacher

From the beginning, it's important to do what you're there to do—that's teach. Teach the class something, maybe review material they learned last year. That lets them know that you're in charge, you expect them to learn. They'll look to you for direction—as long as you give it to them, you're fine.

—Junior high language arts teacher

How Can You Become a Part of Your Learning Community?

Your success in your first year of teaching will be determined by the relationships you develop with the pupils, their families, your colleagues, school administrators, and other members of the school community. All of these groups contribute to your effectiveness as a teacher, but the relationships you establish with students will be the most important (and complex) you will have as a teacher.

Relationships with Students

The quality of your relationships with students will depend in large measure on your knowledge of students and commitment to improving your interactions with them. As a first-year teacher put it:

> It is amazing when every student is involved and enjoying the lesson. At moments like these, I realize that I'm educating real people and making a difference in their futures.

> I really connected with my students because they saw that learning can be fun. They realized that I, too, am a person who cares about them and wants them to succeed. It makes my job feel complete and I know I'm in the right profession. (Hauser & Rauch 2002, 36)

Your relationships with students will have many dimensions. Principally, you must see that each student learns as much as possible; this is your primary responsibility as a professional teacher. You will need to establish relationships with a great diversity of students based on mutual respect, caring, and concern. Without attention to this personal realm, your effectiveness as a teacher will be limited. In addition, teachers are significant models for students' attitudes and behaviours.

Relationships with Colleagues and Staff

Each working day, you will be in close contact with other teachers and staff members. As the following experience told to the authors by a teacher suggests, it will definitely be to your advantage to establish friendly, professional relationships with them:

> I was on a staff with a group of teachers who really supported me. They made it a part of their day to come into my room and see how I was doing and to share things. They made it easy to ask questions and work with them. They started me on the track of cooperating with other teachers and sharing my successes and failures with them.

> They did such a good job of taking care of each other that my needs were always met. I had plenty of supplies, counselling help, administrative help. The school was a community. Anything I needed to be successful was provided.

During your first few months at the school, it would be wise to communicate to colleagues that you are willing to learn all you can about your new job and to be a team player. In most schools, it is common practice to give junior faculty members less desirable assignments, reserving the more desirable ones for senior teachers. By demonstrating your willingness to take on these responsibilities with good humour and to give them your best effort, you will do much to establish yourself as a valuable faculty member. Your colleagues may also appreciate learning from you about new approaches and materials—if you share in a manner that doesn't make others feel inferior. The following comments by a high school department chair, for example, illustrate a first-year French teacher's positive influence on others:

> She won the respect of all her colleagues in the school who have dealt with her almost immediately, not because she's so competent in French and not because she's so competent as a teacher, but because she handles everything with such sensitivity and sensibleness.

> Because of the way she operates—which is quietly but effectively—she has raised the whole tenor of expectations in the department. We have some very fine faculty in French, but I would speculate they don't see their group self-image as intellectuals but rather as "people people." Because of what Elizabeth has brought to the school: the knowledge about how to use computers, her knowledge of foreign language oral proficiency, her knowledge of French film and French authors, she has kind of lifted everybody up and helped her colleagues see themselves in a little bit different light and to improve professionally. (Dollase 1992, 49)

It is important that you get along with your colleagues and contribute to a spirit of professional cooperation or **collegiality** in the school. Some you will enjoy being around; others you may wish to avoid. Some will express obvious enthusiasm for teaching; others may be bitter and pessimistic about their work. Be pleasant and friendly with both types. Accept their advice with a smile, and then act on what you believe is worthwhile.

Relationships with Administrators

Pay particular attention to the relationships you develop with administrators, department heads, and supervisors. Though your contact with them will not be as frequent as that with other teachers, they can do much to ensure your initial success. They are well aware of the difficulties you might encounter as a first-year teacher, and they are there to help you succeed.

The principal or vice-principal of your new school will, most likely, be the one to introduce you to other teachers, members of the administrative team, and staff. He or she should inform you if there are other administrators who can help you obtain supplies, enforce school rules, and keep accurate records. The principal may also assign an experienced teacher to serve as a mentor during your first year. In addition, your principal or vice-principal will indicate his or her availability to discuss issues of concern, and you should not hesitate to do so, if the need arises.

Relationships with Parents

Developing positive connections with your students' parents can contribute significantly to students' success and to your success as a teacher. In reality, teachers and parents are partners—both concerned with the learning and growth of the children in their care.

It is important that you become acquainted with parents at school functions, at meetings of the parent–teacher association or organization (PTA or PTO) or school councils, at various community events, and in other social situations. To develop good communication with parents, you will need to be sensitive to their needs, such as their work schedules and the language spoken at home.

By maintaining contact with parents and encouraging them to become involved in their children's education, you can significantly enhance the achievement of your students. It is important that you be willing to take the extra time and energy to pursue strategies such as the following for involving parents:

- Ask parents to read aloud to their children, to listen to their children read, and to sign homework papers.
- Encourage parents to run math and spelling drills with their children and to help with homework lessons.
- Encourage parents to discuss school activities with their children, and suggest ways parents can help teach their children at home. For example, a simple home activity might be alphabetizing books; a more complex one would be using kitchen supplies in an elementary science experiment.
- Send home suggestions for games or group activities related to a child's schoolwork that parent and child can play together.
- Many parents have access to the internet; suggest to those who do to access the school's website on a regular basis in order to keep track of homework, test, and special event information.
- Encourage parents to participate in school activities, such as a sports booster club, a career day, and music and drama events.
- Involve parents in their children's learning by having them co-sign learning contracts and serve as guest speakers.

Family involvement and child-focused resources are available on the internet. Sites helpful for parents include:

- **Canadian Education Association** www.cea-ace.ca
- **Breakfast for Learning** www.breakfastforlearning.ca
- **Canadian Association for School Health** http://cash-aces.ca
- **Canadian Child Care Federation** www.cccf-fcsge.ca/subsites/familytp/english/resources_en.htm

The Canadian Child Care Federation (CCCF) has numerous "Resource Sheets" that help parents explore topics such as a healthy physical environment, streetproofing, and nutrition. In addition, most schools have local home and school associations or school advisory councils (sometimes called parent advisory councils) that serve in an advocacy capacity.

For parents and teachers interested in how Canadian student achievement levels stack up internationally, information is available at the Council of Ministers of Education Canada (CMEC) website, www.cmec.ca/Pages/default.aspx. Among other things, the CMEC publishes reports dealing with such matters as student literacy across the country.

Community Relations

Communities provide significant support for the education of their young people and determine the character of their schools. In addition, communities often help schools by recruiting volunteers, providing financial support for special projects, and operating homework hotline programs. For example, school–community partnerships have been formed through business and community connections in parts of Canada.

- Canadian businesses have recognized the importance of disseminating knowledge to their employees about their children's schools and programs. Businesses such as State Farm Insurance have given their employees notification that if they wish to volunteer at their children's school, they will be given a day's pay to do so. It is their belief that good corporate citizen policies make for stronger and happier parents and a more productive workforce.

- Service clubs and business associations often develop strong partnerships with the education community. Examples in New Brunswick include the Lions Quest program for self-esteem building, sponsored by the Lions Club and the Fredericton Chamber of Commerce, who published for schools a directory of businesses that want to help out by making presentations or offering job placements for students.
- Safety of school children is another concern of businesses. The New Brunswick Telephone Company has a safe blue telephone truck operating in the Perth Andover area. Whenever children feel they have a problem or need help from an adult, they simply walk up to a telephone employee. Employees have offered to help children in whatever manner is necessary (Love 1994).

How Can You Participate in Teacher Collaboration?

The relationships that build a learning community involve **collaboration**—working together, sharing decision making, and solving problems. As a member of a dynamic, changing profession, your efforts to collaborate will result in an increased understanding of the teaching–learning process and improved learning for all students.

By working with others on school governance, curriculum development, school–community partnerships, and educational reform, you will play an important role in enhancing the professional status of teachers.

The heart of collaboration is meaningful, authentic relationships among professionals. Such relationships, of course, do not occur naturally; they require commitment and hard work. Friend and Bursuck (2002, 76–77) identified seven characteristics of collaboration, which are summarized in the following:

- Collaboration is voluntary. Teachers make a personal choice to collaborate.
- Collaboration is based on parity. All individuals' contributions are valued equally.
- Collaboration requires a shared goal.
- Collaboration includes shared responsibility for key decisions.
- Collaboration includes shared accountability for outcomes.
- Collaboration is based on shared resources. Each teacher contributes something—time, expertise, space, equipment, or other resource.
- Collaboration is emergent. As teachers work together, the degree of shared decision making, trust, and respect increases.

Schools that support the essential elements of collaboration are collegial schools "characterized by purposeful adult interactions about improving school-wide teaching and learning" (Glickman, Gordon, & Ross-Gordon 2004, 6). In the following sections, we examine four expressions of teacher collaboration: peer coaching, staff development, team teaching, and co-teaching.

Peer Coaching

Experienced teachers traditionally help novice teachers, but more formal peer coaching programs extend the benefits of collaboration to more teachers. **Peer coaching** is an arrangement whereby teachers grow professionally by observing one another's teaching and providing constructive feedback. The practice encourages teachers to learn together in an emotionally safe environment. According to

What are some forms of professional collaboration in which you will participate as a teacher? What benefits might be enjoyed as a result of such collaboration?

Bruce Joyce, Marsha Weil, and Emily Calhoun (2000, 440), peer coaching is an effective way to create communities of professional educators, and all teachers should be members of coaching teams.

If the authors had their way, all school faculties would be divided into coaching teams—that is, teams who regularly observe one another's teaching and learn from watching one another and the students. In short, we recommend the development of a "coaching environment" in which all personnel see themselves as coaches (Joyce, Weil, & Calhoun 2000, 440).

Through teacher-to-teacher support and collaboration, peer coaching programs improve teacher morale and effectiveness.

Staff Development

Increasingly, teachers are contributing to the design of staff development programs that encourage collaboration, risk-taking, and experimentation. Some programs, for example, give teachers the opportunity to meet with other teachers at similar grade levels or in similar content areas for the purpose of sharing ideas, strategies, and solutions to problems. A day or part of a day may be devoted to this kind of workshop or idea exchange. Teachers are frequently given released time from regular duties to visit other schools and observe exemplary programs in action.

Team Teaching

In **team teaching** arrangements, teachers share the responsibility for two or more classes, dividing up the subject areas between them, with one preparing lessons in mathematics, science, and health, for instance, while the other plans instruction in reading, language arts, and social studies. The division of responsibility may also be made in terms of the performance levels of the children, so that, for example, one teacher may teach the lowest- and highest-ability reading groups and the middle math group, while the other teaches the middle-ability reading groups and the lowest and highest mathematics group. In many schools, team teaching arrangements are so extensive that children move from classroom to classroom for 40- to 50-minute periods just as students do at the high school level.

The practice of team teaching is often limited by student enrolments and budget constraints. As integrated curricula and the need for special knowledge and skills increase, however, the use of collegial support teams will become more common. A **collegial support team (CST)** provides teachers with a "safe zone" for professional growth. As one teacher commented:

> [The CST] allows me much discretion as to the areas I'd like to strengthen. Therefore, I am truly growing with no fear of being labelled or singled out as the "teacher who is having problems." I am aware of problem spheres and I work to correct these with the aid of my colleagues. (Johnson & Brown 1998, 89)

The members of a team make wide-ranging decisions about the instruction of students assigned to them, such as when to use large-group instruction or small-group instruction, how teaching tasks will be divided, and how time, materials, and other resources will be allocated.

Co-Teaching

In **co-teaching** arrangements, two or more teachers, such as a classroom teacher and a special education teacher or other specialist, teach together in the same classroom.

Co-teaching builds on the strengths of two teachers and provides increased learning opportunities for all students (Friend & Bursuck 2002). Typically, co-teaching arrangements occur during a set period of time each day or on certain days of the week. Among the several possible co-teaching variations, Friend and Bursuck (2002) have identified the following:

- One teach, one support—One teacher leads the lesson, the other assists.
- Station teaching—The lesson is divided into two parts: One teacher teaches one part to half of the students while the other teaches the other part to the rest. The groups then switch and the teachers repeat their part of the lesson. If students can work independently, a third group may be formed, or a volunteer may teach at a third station.
- Parallel teaching—A class is divided in half, and each teacher instructs half the class individually.
- Alternative teaching—A class is divided into one large group and one small group. For example, one teacher may provide remediation or enrichment to the small group, while the other teacher instructs the large group.

How Will Your Performance as a Teacher Be Evaluated?

Most teachers are evaluated on a regular basis to determine whether their performance measures up to acceptable standards and whether they are able to create and sustain effective learning environments for students. Performance criteria used to evaluate teachers vary and are usually determined by the school principal, the district

Beginning Teaching
Monique Martin
Georges Vanier Catholic Fine Arts School, Saskatoon
K–8 Designated Fine Arts School
Visual Art Instructor, previously taught Grades 2–7

Photo credit: Darlene Polachic

Planning is the most important part of being a teacher. Materials are prepared well in advance so that I can focus exclusively on my delivery of lessons and have that as my main focus during the school year. My year plans keep the scope and sequence of my year in order even when events and activities interrupt the flow of my teaching. I keep a log where I record strategies that worked and that didn't work, or how I might change a lesson. Planning entails having goals. Every January I write lifetime goals in a special book. Many of those goals I never thought I would achieve, but many, many of them I have. The benefit of a long career is being able to realize goals that once seemed off in the distance. I share with my students whenever I reach a lifetime goal and I explain all the little goals that had to be reached to get there.

I believe the most important thing to teach children, your own or someone else's, is that you believe in them and that dreams can be achieved with hard work and goal setting. If your belief and faith in the children is genuine, and they trust that you are interested in their growth, the possibilities are staggering.

You must have realistic yet high expectations for yourself and for your students. I provide students examples from my own life as I teach. They know that I travel the world with my art and my teaching. I set the bar higher for my students than some would, but we have been successful in a wide range of areas.

The learning community is not just the other teachers in your school or school division. Doing real life projects allows students to learn about real life challenges, deadlines, disappointments, and joys. In 2009 the students created an entire bus advertising campaign for the Rideau Canal Festival in Ottawa in partnership with Pattison Outdoor Advertising (a major Canadian Advertising firm). They created the illustrative/artwork, the research for the text, and all of the graphics. The youngest student involved was five years old. Of course at the onset of the project people told me I was crazy, but by pre-planning for the year before starting the project, and by being very clear about my expectations, it was a goal that was realized. It is important to note that large scale projects such as the Rideau Canal project were years in the building and preparation. The project was not the goal but an outcome of smaller projects and goals prior to this.

Modelling the behaviour of an artist is very important to the success of my students. I have exhibitions of my work often, and I often include my students in the exhibitions in some way. When in Vallauris, France, as Artist in Residence, I had an exhibition of my students' artwork at the University of Nice. There have been other international opportunities as well for the students in my school using my experiences outside of teaching. They know that I create work all the time and I have brought in my own work that was successful. Just as important, I have brought in to school work that was not successful so that they can see that not every piece works. We all can't be great every time we try something; we all miss the mark sometimes. The students actually think it is funny when they come across a ripped or cut-up piece of my work in the collage paper box.

Engagement of learners is easy if you love what you are doing and share energy and enthusiasm for it. It is also easy to engage learners when you have a large knowledge base or background for what you are teaching. The incidental learning that occurs when a student poses an interesting question is wonderful. If you don't have the background, the lesson can fall flat because of the stop of flow and their questioning of your knowledge on the subject. You don't need to know everything, but you do need to know more than just the direct content that you are delivering. If you don't have the answer, knowing where to find it and teaching the inquiring mind how to find it is an important life lesson.

Motivating students at this time in history is difficult. Everything in their lives is instantaneous and exciting. Text messages fly around quickly; music videos are mesmerizing. How can a teacher compete with that? Be yourself, have feelings, engage yourself in students' lives, talk to and acknowledge them. I do this by framing student art and hanging it all over the school. I also have permanent displays in many places in my city. Now this is not easy to keep going but it is incredibly motivating. Often I will hear, "I am going to make this one so great that it goes in an art show." This motivation was so significant for one boy with some learning challenges that he worked harder than ever to get his artwork selected for the ad campaign in Ottawa. It was selected and he now calls himself an "Artist." Students are motivated by the belief that they are artists because they have seen their art on display at the airport, in the galleries, at the hospital; I have also taken it to other countries with me. One student said, "You have left a fingerprint on my soul through your teaching of art."

As a beginning teacher expect to work harder than you have ever worked before. Be more organized than you think is possible. Label everything—every box, every file—keep it all together. Starting off that way will keep you sane on the days where it seems like the world is falling apart.

Decide what needs to be better in your teaching; analyze your lesson to improve on it. Continually be thinking of new ways to teach something or better ways to teach it. Figure out the best way to have the classroom organized. Evaluate each day, every day, so that you become better. Having your administrator come and watch you teach once or twice is not going to impact your teaching as much as daily evaluation of your own delivery of lessons. However, a word of caution: Be gentle with yourself, for no one is perfect.

Monique Martin teaches at a designated Fine Arts School in Saskatoon. She teaches all the art from Kindergarten to Grade 8. Monique has lectured at workshops and taught in classrooms in many countries, and is a three-time winner of a National Teaching Award (1999, 2001, 2009) for combining art into other subject areas. Exhibitions of her professional work have been held in Australia, England, France, the United States, and many galleries in Canada. She was also the World Tulip Summit Society Ambassador and Artist in Residence at the Bytown Museum in Ottawa during the summer of 2010.

office, the school board, or a provincial education department. In most schools, the principal or a member of the leadership team performs the evaluations.

Teacher evaluations serve many purposes: to determine whether teachers should be retained, should receive tenure, or should be given merit pay. Evaluations also help teachers assess their effectiveness and develop strategies for self-improvement. In fact, "teachers who receive the most classroom feedback are also most satisfied with teaching" (Glickman, Gordon, & Ross-Gordon 2004, 323).

Quantitative and Qualitative Evaluation

Typically, supervisors use quantitative or qualitative approaches (or a combination of the two) to evaluate teachers' classroom performance. **Quantitative evaluation** involves pencil-and-paper rating forms marked by the supervisor objectively record classroom events and behaviours in terms of their number or frequency. For example, a supervisor might focus on the teacher's verbal behaviours—questioning, answering, praising, giving directions, and critiquing.

Qualitative evaluation, in contrast, includes written, open-ended narrative descriptions of classroom events in terms of their nature and qualities. These more subjective measures are equally valuable in identifying teachers' weaknesses and strengths. In addition, qualitative evaluation can capture the complexities and subtleties of classroom life that might not be reflected in a quantitative approach to evaluation.

Clinical Supervision

Many supervisors follow the four-step **clinical supervision** model, in which the supervisor first holds a pre-conference with the teacher, then observes in the classroom, analyzes and interprets observation data, and finally holds a post-conference with the teacher (Acheson & Gall 1997; Glickman 2002; Goldhammer, Anderson, & Krajewski 1993; Pajak 1999; Smyth 1995; Snyder & Anderson 1996). During the pre-conference, the teacher and supervisor schedule a classroom observation and determine its purpose and focus and the method of observation to be used. At the post-conference, the teacher and supervisor discuss the analysis of observation data, and jointly develop a plan for instructional improvement.

Fulfilling the clinical supervision model is difficult and time-consuming, and time-pressed administrators must often modify the approach. For example, when Kim Marshall was principal at a Boston elementary school with 39 teachers, he made four random, unannounced five-minute visits to classrooms each day. This schedule allowed him to observe every teacher during a two-week period, and each teacher about 19 times during a year. According to Marshall,

> [A] regular cycle of five-minute classroom visits with a follow-up conversation after each one is the most efficient way for a principal to monitor classrooms and find the answers to [the following] key questions:
>
> - Are teachers on track with the curriculum?
> - Are the students learning?
> - Are teachers "happy campers" in terms of their jobs and their lives?
> - Do some teachers deserve special praise?
> - Do some teachers need redirection, emergency support, or a negative evaluation? (Marshall 2003, 703)

Regardless of the approach a school district will use to evaluate your performance as a beginning teacher, remember that evaluation will assist your professional growth and development. Experienced teachers report that periodic feedback and assistance from knowledgeable, sensitive supervisors is very beneficial; such evaluation results in "improved teacher reflection and higher-order thought, more collegiality, openness, and communication, greater teacher retention, less anxiety and burnout, greater teacher autonomy and efficacy, improved attitudes, improved teaching behaviors, and better student achievement and attitudes" (Glickman, Gordon, & Ross-Gordon, 2001, 329).

SUMMARY

First Steps Toward Becoming a Teacher

- Thinking about and preparing for your first job will boost your confidence and help you secure your first teaching position.
  - Get ready to make the transition from your well-practiced role as a student to your new role as teacher
  - Think clearly about what it is like to take on the expectations that you and other people have of a person who is a "teacher"
  - Take a comprehensive approach towards getting ready to apply for a position; try to avoid last minute preparations of portfolios, letters of application, transcripts, references, and the like
  - Plan for the first few weeks of your initial teaching assignment; this will increase your readiness and self-assurance

How Will You Become Certified or Licensed to Teach?

- Mobility provisions under the Agreement on Internal Trade/Teaching Profession entitle a teacher to receive a teaching credential from the receiving province or territory under the following conditions. All applicants must:

  - Hold a valid teaching credential from a Canadian province or territory
  - Have completed a professional teacher education program consisting of a minimum of 30 semester credit-hours of course work and a practicum for teacher certification
  - Provide all documents required by the receiving province or territory

  - Satisfy any requirements of the receiving province or territory with respect to "fit and proper person," currency of practice, and language proficiency

Will You Have Difficulty Finding a Teaching Job?

- Teacher demand and supply in content areas and geographic regions influences finding a teaching position.
- A recent empirical study of possible teaching shortages revealed the following:
  - Teacher shortages, where they exist, have been the most prevalent in science subjects for the past four years (science, chemistry, biology, physics).
  - Shortages in some areas vary by language of instruction or rural versus non-rural locations.
  - Education-related career opportunities for teachers include principal, assistant principal, librarian, counsellor, and teaching roles in government and the private sector.

How Will You Find Your First Teaching Job?

- Information about teaching vacancies may be obtained through placement services, provincial departments of education, and personal networking on the internet.
- A résumé is a concise summary of an individual's experiences, education, and skills. A letter of inquiry is used to find out if a school district has any teaching vacancies, and a letter of application (or cover letter) indicates an individual's interest in and qualifications for a teaching position.

What Can You Expect as a Beginning Teacher?

- Beginning teachers should prepare instructional strategies and materials and learn about their students and the community well in advance of the first day of school.
- Experienced teachers' recommendations for beginning teachers focus on planning, organizing, and following through.

How Can You Become a Part of Your Learning Community?

- The learning community includes students, their families, colleagues, and members of the community.
- Research indicates that parental involvement is a key factor in children's academic achievement.

- Training programs, hotlines, referral networks, school-based electronic message boards, and partnership programs are among the resources teachers can use to involve parents and members of the community.

How Can You Participate in Teacher Collaboration?

- Teachers collaborate through participation in school governance, curriculum development, school-community partnerships, and educational reform.
- Four approaches to teacher collaboration are peer coaching, staff development, team teaching, and co-teaching.

How Will Your Performance as a Teacher Be Evaluated?

- Performance criteria for evaluating teachers are developed by school principals, districts, school boards, or provinces. School district approaches to performance appraisal continually evolve.
- Quantitative approaches to teacher evaluation focus on the incidence, frequency, or amount of teacher or student behaviour in various categories.
- Qualitative approaches to teacher evaluation are usually written narratives focusing on qualities of classrooms and events such as classroom climate and teaching style.

KEY TERMS AND CONCEPTS

clinical supervision, 341
collaboration, 337
collegial support team (CST), 339
collegiality, 335
co-teaching, 339

credentials file, 325
job fairs, 325
letter of application, 328
letter of inquiry, 326
peer coaching, 337
placement service, 325

qualitative evaluation, 341
quantitative evaluation, 341
résumé, 326
teaching certificate, 320
team teaching, 338

APPLICATIONS AND ACTIVITIES

Teacher's Journal

1. Record in your journal your plan for becoming certified or licensed to teach.

2. Develop answers to possible interview questions, and brainstorm questions to ask.

3. Envision your first day as a teacher and describe what you see.

4. When you become a teacher, in what collaborations and partnerships will you participate? How might these activities contribute to your effectiveness as a teacher? How might your involvement enhance students' learning and your relationships with them?

Theory into Practice

This chapter's Theory into Practice exercise requires that you participate in a simulated job fair. As stated in the chapter, job fairs are designed to bring potential teachers to one location for interviews and information sessions. There are usually a number of school boards present, and some have specific job openings while others will give candidates a general idea of possible upcoming positions. Job fairs for beginning teachers operate much like a marketplace, where each school or school board has its own table or area and candidates visit with administrators or senior board personnel to talk about positions.

For the job fair simulation exercise, each student will have the opportunity to play the role of a prospective teacher looking for a job and an employer representing a school that is interviewing teachers to fill specific vacant teaching positions.

Directions for Preparing to be Part of a School Hiring Team

- Your class will be divided into small groups of three. Each small group will be assigned an actual school and a fictitious list of vacant positions for that school by the instructor. For example, Abbott School in Edmonton, Alberta, (http://abbott. epsb.ca) has the following vacant teaching positions: Grade 5, Grade 1, Kindergarten, French immersion, classroom music.

- The group members will go to the school's website and become familiar with its size, facilities, mission statement, school philosophy, special programs, the type of population it serves, etc.

- Each of the three-person school groups will decide on who will assume the role of principal, vice-principal, and senior school board personnel during the job fair simulation.

- Each group will formulate a list of questions and will decide who asks what questions of the prospective teachers.

- For the simulation, each "school" group will have a desk in a specific assigned area and will have a sign that indicates the school they are representing.

Directions for Preparing to be Interviewed at the Job Fair

- For this task, each student in a group will receive a list of schools and vacant positions.

- From the list, each student will choose job vacancies for at least three schools to which they wish to apply. Students need to prepare for being interviewed by these schools at the job fair.

- Students should "visit" the schools' websites and find out everything they can about them, including such things as size, facilities, mission statement, school philosophy, special programs, type of populations they serve, etc.

- Students will prepare an application package that includes:
  - A résumé
  - Practicum reports
  - Transcripts
  - Reference lists
  - Letters
  - A portfolio

- Students should bring enough copies of their résumé and a notepad to write on.

- Students need to develop and practise a "one-minute sell" stating who they are and what skill sets and experience set them apart (name, major, graduation date, career interest, relevant experience, interest in the district, etc.)

- Students need to prepare questions to ask of the schools' representatives. (See "Suggested Questions to Ask of School Hiring Team" below.)

- It is important for students to dress professionally for the job fair.

Suggested Questions to Ask of School Hiring Team

- What is the hiring and interviewing process?

- What kinds of resources are available to me (i.e., textbook series, district curriculum resources)?

- What level of technology is offered to teachers?

- What kind of mentoring or beginning teacher program is available?

The Job Fair Simulation

- During the first half of the job fair simulation, half of the class will play the role of prospective employers in their assigned groups and will conduct interviews for the vacant positions. The other half will play the role of prospective teachers and will approach and be interviewed by at least five schools each.

- During the second half of the job fair simulation, the roles will be switched.

- The instructor will determine who will assume what roles for each of the two job fair sessions.

- By the end of the simulation, all students will have had the opportunity to interview and be interviewed.

Observations and Interviews

1. If you can arrange it, observe the first day of classes at a local school. What strategies did the teachers use to begin the year on a positive, task-oriented note? What evidence did you see that the teachers followed the advice given by the experienced teachers in this chapter?

2. Survey teachers at a local school to get information about how they prepare for the first day of school.

3. Prepare a questionnaire and then survey a group of experienced teachers for their recollections about the triumphs and defeats they experienced as beginning teachers. What lessons are evident in their responses? Are there common themes that characterize the triumphs? The defeats?

4. Interview teachers and administrators about their experiences with professional collaboration and parental involvement. What examples do they provide, and how do these reflect the seven characteristics of collaboration presented in this chapter? How do students benefit from collaboration and parental involvement? What suggestions do the teachers and administrators have for improving collaboration and parental involvement?

Professional Portfolio

1. Draft a preliminary professional résumé. (Review the section in this chapter titled "Preparing Your Résumé" and the résumé prepared by Linda M. Abbott in Figure 11.2.)

In your résumé, under "Personal Data," provide a current address and a permanent address. Also, under "Education," specify an anticipated graduation date. Under "Experience," include work experience that indicates your ability to work with people. Begin with your most recent experiences and present information in reverse chronological order.

When you have finished your preliminary résumé, exchange with a classmate and critique each other's work.

2. Draft an essay describing what you will bring to your first year of teaching. It may help to review the essay you wrote for the Chapter 1 portfolio entry on what drew you to the profession.

My Education Lab

PEARSON
myeducationlab

For "Helpful Hints for New Teachers," go to Module 2 in the Managing to Teach tab at www.MyEducationLab.com. Explore this section carefully, clicking on the "I want" figures and then clicking on the blue text under "Hints." Make notes of those ideas that seem to be of major importance to you as you contemplate starting a career in teaching.

To hear experienced teachers offering some advice for new teachers, go to Module 2 in the Managing to Teach tab at www.MyEducationLab.com and click on "Advice." Ask yourself how you might benefit from this advice.

For information on "Getting the Job," go to the Career Tab on www.MyEducationLab.com. Use the material in the "Preparing for an Interview" section to inform your own preparation for the interview process.

12

Education Issues for the Twenty-First Century

At the turn of the century, more and more educators are working in a world of intensifying and rapid change. . . . New technologies, greater cultural diversity, the skills called for in a changing economy, restructured approaches to administration and management, and a more sophisticated knowledge-base about teaching and learning, are all pulling students and their teachers in new directions.

—Mission Statement excerpt, International Centre for Educational Change, Ontario Institute for Studies in Education, University of Toronto

focus
questions

1. What knowledge and skills will prepare students for a global information age?

2. How can schools and teachers provide an outstanding education for all learners?

3. How can community-based partnerships address social problems that hinder students' learning?

4. How will the fledgling charter school movement affect equity and excellence in education?

5. What can teachers and schools learn from international education?

6. What is our vision for the future of education?

How will education change during the twenty-first century? What new school–community linkages will help schools meet the needs of all learners? In what ways will teachers' professional lives become more collaborative and oriented toward system-wide reform? How likely is it that, as a teacher, you will have experiences similar to the following?

After a short drive through early-morning traffic, you arrive at school in time for a 7:30 a.m. meeting of the Teacher Leadership Team (TLT), a group that makes curricular and instructional decision for the school. The TLT works directly with the school's Site-Based Council (SBC), which makes budget, personnel, and other policy decisions. SBC members include three teachers, the principal, five community teachers, and two professors from a nearby university.

Like most schools around the country, the changing demographics of the community are reflected in an increasingly diverse student population. About 15 percent of students are from families who live below the poverty line, and one in eight students is learning with English as a second language. According to a district survey, students represent 18 different language groups, with Arabic being second to English as the most prevalent tongue. Overall, students at your school score in the top percentiles on provincial examinations. Fifty percent of students go on to college, and 15 percent enrol in other forms of post-secondary programs.

With a few minutes before the meeting begins, you head to the classroom of another TLT member. Both of you were selected to be part of a nationwide network of teachers who will field-test an interactive computer simulation developed by an instructional technology laboratory at a major university. Last week, you both received the beta-test (trial) software, field-test guidelines, and registration materials for a four-day preparatory workshop to be held at the university. The university is paying for travel plus expenses, as well as providing a stipend.

"Well, did you have a chance to try out the software?" you ask upon entering the room. "I did last night, and it looks pretty impressive. I'm anxious to see what the kids think."

"I haven't had a chance yet—I've been preparing for this morning's TLT meeting," your friend says, pausing momentarily as she staples handouts arranged in neat stacks on top of her desk. Last spring, she was elected to be one of the school's two curriculum coordinators. At today's TLT meeting, she and the other coordinator are presenting a model for school-wide curriculum integration. "What do we have to do as field testers?" she asks, continuing her stapling task. "I just glanced at the field-test guidelines."

"Well, actually quite a lot, but I think it'll be interesting," you answer. "The lab wants us to use the software every day for two weeks. We also collect student performance data on a regular basis and samples of students' work. Plus, students will complete a survey at the beginning and at the end of the field test. That's about it . . . Oh, I forgot—they want us to do some student interviews. There's a set of constructivist-oriented questions we're supposed to use. Basically, the lab wants us to develop a picture of students' problem-solving strategies as they work through the simulation."

"That does sound interesting," your colleague says.

"Right. Well, I better get out of here and let you finish getting ready for the TLT meeting," you say.

Walking to the conference room, you think about how satisfying it is to teach at your school. Teachers are hard-working and share a strong commitment to good teaching and to building a collegial professional community. Ample leadership opportunities, common planning-periods, stimulating colleagues who are professionally involved, and solid support from the district and community are just a few of the factors that make working conditions at your school very positive.

Though no one has an educational crystal ball that can give a totally accurate glimpse of how the profession of teaching will evolve during the twenty-first century, powerful forces are shaping schools and teaching. Moreover, thousands of teachers are collaborating and playing key leadership roles in shaping that future. The conditions under which teachers will work in this century will provide a dramatic contrast to those that many teachers experienced throughout much of the previous century. Isolation, lack of autonomy and self-governance, and few chances for professional growth are being replaced by collaboration, empowerment, stronger professionalism, and opportunities to provide leadership for educational change.

What Knowledge and Skills Will Prepare Students for a Global Information Age?

What knowledge and skills will students need to succeed in a global information age? Teachers in every generation have asked this question. At the beginning of this century, the answer is confounded by conflicting theories, expectations, and values. One thing everyone agrees on, however, is that increasing cultural diversity in Canada and other countries and increasing global economic interdependence will call for strong communication and cooperation skills. People will need to be able to live together well and use environmental resources wisely. To equip students to do this, teachers will need to ensure that all students develop knowledge, skills, attitudes, and values in nine key areas (see Figure 12.1). Though these nine areas of learning will not be all that students will need, learning in these areas will best enable them to meet the challenges of the future.

Literacy in Language, Mathematics, and Science

To solve the problems of the future, students will need to be able to write and speak clearly and succinctly. To access critical information from enormous data banks, they will need to be able to read complex material with a high degree of comprehension. Moreover, the continued development of "user-friendly" technologies, such as voice-activated computers and reading machines, will not reduce the need for high-level language arts literacy. In addition to strong skills in reading and writing, students will need to be able to apply mathematical and scientific concepts to solve new problems. For example, they will need to be able to analyze unfamiliar situations, pose appropriate questions, use trial-and-error methods to gather and evaluate relevant data, and summarize results.

New Technology Skills

Students of the future will also need to attain high levels of skill in computer-based technologies. To teach students skills in accessing the vast stores of information that computers routinely handle today, our nation's schools will become more technologically rich, and teachers more technologically sophisticated. No longer able to resist the "irresistible force" of Information Age

Figure 12.1

Educational priorities for the future

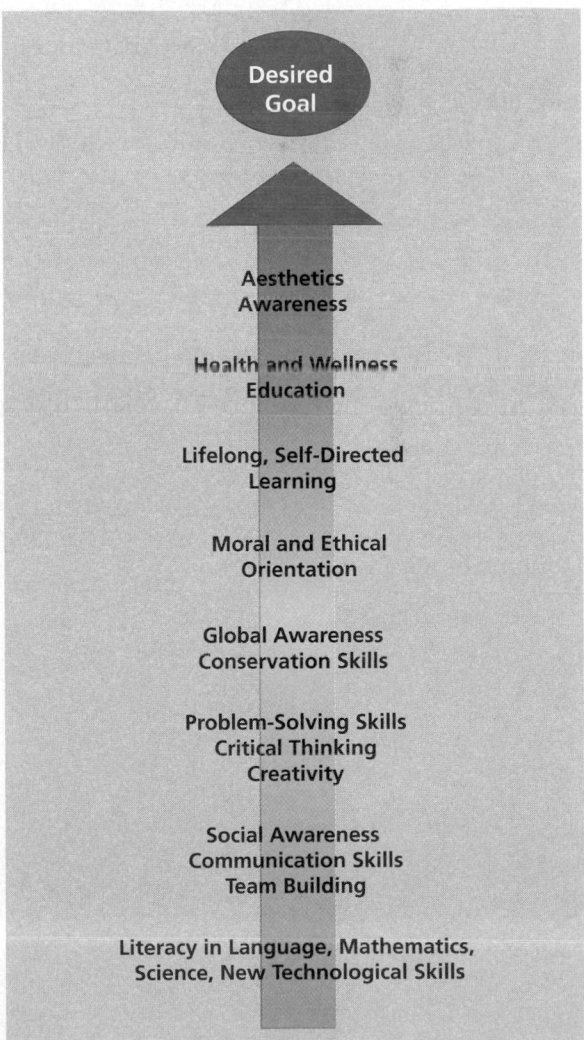

Desired Goal

Aesthetics Awareness

Health and Wellness Education

Lifelong, Self-Directed Learning

Moral and Ethical Orientation

Global Awareness Conservation Skills

Problem-Solving Skills Critical Thinking Creativity

Social Awareness Communication Skills Team Building

Literacy in Language, Mathematics, Science, New Technological Skills technology (Mehlinger 1996), schools will join the larger society where "the computer is a symbol of the future and all that is good about it" (Morton 1996, 417). In such an environment, students will not only learn to use computers as "tools" to access information, they will use them to communicate globally and to generate creative solutions to real-world problems.

Problem Solving, Critical Thinking, and Creativity

Students of the future will need to be able to think, rather than remember. Although the information that students learn in schools may become outdated, the thinking processes they acquire will not. These processes focus on the ability to find, obtain, and use information resources for solving problems or taking advantage of opportunities. Students will need to learn how to cope with change, how to anticipate alternative future developments, how to think critically, and how to analyze and synthesize large amounts of complex data.

Forecasts about the future share one common factor—they place a priority on creative thinking to solve problems. The acquisition of structured bodies of knowledge, while important, is not sufficient preparation for the future. Students must learn to think creatively. Students who are stretched to develop their creativity today will become the adults who solve tomorrow's problems.

Can creative thinking be taught? William J. J. Gordon (1968, 1971a, 1971b, 1975), who has devoted his career to the study of creativity, believes it can. Gordon developed synectics, a teaching method based on the thinking process, which is designed to "teach" creativity through the use of metaphor and analogy. **Synectics** is based on the assumptions that (1) creativity is important (2) creativity is not mysterious; (3) in all fields, creative invention draws from the same underlying intellectual

What knowledge and skills for the twenty-first century does this learning activity support? What else will students need to know and be able to do in the future?

processes; and (4) the creativity of individuals and groups is similar (Joyce, Weil, & Calhoun 2004).

Social Awareness, Communication Skills, and Team Building

Tomorrow's students must be able to communicate with people from diverse cultures. The ability to create a better world in the future, then, will surely depend on our willingness to celebrate our rich diversity through the kind of communication that leads to understanding, friendly social relations, and the building of cohesive teams. "[T]he classroom should be a laboratory for collaborative decision making and team building" (Uchida, Cetron, & McKenzie 1996, 8).

An important lesson for students is that poverty, discrimination, violence, crime, and unequal opportunities, wherever they occur, affect us all. To solve these and other social problems, students will need to become socially aware, politically active, and skilled in conflict resolution strategies.

For suggestions regarding how to make your lessons more interesting, go to Teacher's Resource 12.1, The Teacher's Scribe: "Am I boring you?" on www.MyEducationLab.com.

Global Awareness and Conservation Skills

Tomorrow's students will need to recognize the interconnectedness they share with all countries and with all people. Our survival may depend on being able to participate intelligently in a global economy and respond intelligently to global threats to security, health, environmental quality, and other factors affecting the quality of human life. The curriculum of the future must emphasize cultural diversity to honour Canada's changing population. Respect for the views and values held by others, an orientation toward international cooperation for resolving global issues, and practical knowledge and skills on, for example, the conservation of natural energy resources are issues that will challenge students in the very near future.

Health and Wellness Education

With ever-increasing health care costs, the spread of diseases such as AIDS and socially transmitted diseases (STDs), increased risks of cancer, and longer life spans, it is imperative that students acquire appropriate knowledge, skills, and attitudes in the area of health education. To live healthy lives, then, students of tomorrow will need consumer education to select from among an increasingly complex array of health care services. In addition, they will need to be able to make informed choices among alternatives for the prevention or treatment of problems relating to substance abuse, nutrition, fitness, and mental health. Sex education, still a matter for debate in some communities, seems more critical today than at any time in the past.

Moral and Ethical Orientation

The school culture and the curriculum reflect both national and community values. The traditional practice of using values-clarification activities in the classroom, however, has been criticized by some for promoting relativism at the expense of family values or religious doctrines. (See Teacher's Resource 12.1, Teacher's Scribe: "Are you trying to tell me what to think?" on www.MyEducationLab.com.) Yet as we witness the effects of violence in schools, racial intolerance, sexual exploitation of children, drunk driving, white-collar crime, false advertising, unethical business practices, excessive litigation, and so on, many citizens are calling for schools to pay more attention to issues of public morality and ethical behaviour. "[T]o survive and prosper in the twenty-first century, students will need self-discipline, which entails an ethical code and the ability to set and assess progress toward their own goals" (Uchida, Cetron, & McKenzie 1996, 17). In response to harassment and intimidation that can lead to violence in the hallways, for example, many Canadian schools have implemented anger management programs similar to the Peaceful Schools International program (see Chapter 5).

Aesthetic Awareness

Another challenge for teachers and schools is to encourage creativity and greater appreciation for the arts. Many observers of Canadian education contend that emotional, spiritual, aesthetic, and reflective, or meditative, dimensions of life receive less emphasis than analytical thinking and practical life skills. Although literature and drama are standard fare in curricula, for example, most students know little about music, painting, and sculpture. Public school students are rarely taught art history or principles of design or other criteria for evaluating creative works. As a result, students may lack the concepts and experiences that lead to an appreciation of beauty and the development of aesthetic judgment.

Lifelong Self-Directed Learning

The key educational priority that should guide teachers of the future is to cultivate within each student the ability, and the desire, to continue self-directed learning throughout his or her life.

It has often been said that one of the primary purposes of schooling is for students to learn how to learn. In a world characterized by rapid social, technological, economic, and political changes, all persons must take responsibility for their own learning. Career changes will be the norm, and continuing education over a lifetime will be necessary.

How Can Schools and Teachers Provide an Outstanding Education for All Learners?

Although we don't know exactly how teaching will change during this century, we do know that teachers will continue to have a professional and moral obligation to reach all learners, many of whom will be from environments that provide little support for education.

Although the family will continue to remain a prominent part of our culture, evidence indicates that many children live in families that are under acute stress. Soaring numbers of runaway children and cases of child abuse suggest that "the family" is in trouble. In addition, teachers will continue to find that more and more of their students are from families that are small, have working parents, have a single parent present, or have unrelated adults living in the home.

Equity for All Students

A dominant political force in the twenty-first century will be continued demands for equity in all sectors of Canadian life, particularly education. For example, the legalities of school funding laws will be challenged where inequities are perceived, and tax reform measures will be adopted to promote equitable school funding. Classroom teachers will continue to be held accountable for treating all students equitably.

In Chapter 5, you learned about the importance of preparing multicultural instructional materials and strategies to meet the learning needs of students from diverse cultural, ethnic, and linguistic backgrounds. In Chapter 6, you learned how to create an inclusive classroom to meet the needs of all students, regardless of their developmental levels, intelligences, abilities, or disabilities. In addition, you should create a learning environment in which high-achieving and low-achieving students are treated the same way. Thomas Good and Jere Brophy (2003) reviewed the research in this area and found that several teacher behaviours revealed an unequal treatment of students. The behaviours identified include waiting less time for them to answer questions, interacting with them less frequently, giving less feedback, calling on them less often, seating them farther way, failing to accept and use their ideas, smiling at them less often, making less eye contact, praising them less, demanding less, grading their tests differently, and rewarding inappropriate behaviours.

Effective teachers establish respectful relationships with *all* students; they listen to them, they give frequent feedback and opportunities to ask questions, and they demand higher-level performance. In their assessment of students' learning, they give special attention to the questions they ask of students. Research indicates that most questions teachers ask are **lower-order questions** (those that assess students' abilities to recall specific information). Effective teachers, however, also ask **higher-order questions**, which demand more critical thinking and answers to questions such as "Why?" and "What if?" (See Teacher's Resource 12.2, Teacher's Scribe: "Does anyone have a question?" on MyEducationLab.com.) In addition, to reach all learners and prepare them for the future, effective teachers provide students with active, authentic learning experiences.

myeducationlab)

Active, Authentic Learning

Since the 1970s, educational researchers have increased our understanding of the learning process. Though learning theorists and researchers disagree about a definition for *learning*, most agree that **learning** "occurs when experience causes a relatively permanent change in an individual's knowledge or behavior" (Woolfolk 1998, 204). Research into multiple intelligences and multicultural learning modes has broadened our understanding of this definition of learning. In addition, research in the fields of neurophysiology, neuropsychology, and cognitive science will continue to expand our knowledge of how people think and learn.

Our growing understanding of learning indicates that all students learn best when they are actively involved in authentic activities that connect with the "real world." Small-group activities, cooperative learning arrangements, field trips, experiments, and integrated curricula are among the instructional methods you should incorporate into your professional repertoire.

An Exemplary School

The following material, slightly edited, is taken from a taped interview conducted with Ms. Cathy Woodford, the principal of Port Williams Elementary School (PWES) in Nova Scotia's Annapolis Valley. Ms. Woodford responded to a variety of questions, the subject of which appears in italics.

Background information: Our school is 41 years old, has 240 mainly rural students placed in classes from Primary to Grade 5, has 10 classroom teachers, 6 specialists, 6 EAs [educational assistants], a lunchroom supervisor, a secretary, and a janitor. Our school is not sufficiently large for it to have a vice-principal. I am the only administrator and have had this position for the last three years.

Role of the principal: We are nothing if not a democracy, rooted in respect for all of its members. I know that I am technically the educational leader of the school, but the school is actually led by a democratic team. Staff, students, parents/guardians, and community members are all part of that team. Each of us has a different role within that team, but no one's role is more important than another's. Together, we work making all decisions based on what's best for children and their education. We routinely meet and discuss individual students and their educational progress and emotional well-being. We make formal and informal support plans in which anyone in the school may play a role. For instance, our caretaker takes care of much more than our building. He listens to a certain child read, and other children are given the privilege of working with him to collect the recyclable materials at noon.

I am the behind-the-scenes person who ensures that the stage is set based on caring and respect for all. I must remove "road blocks" and see that the curriculum is understood and being taught, that materials are available, and that all individuals in the building have a safe and caring place for learning, teaching, and working together. I am the supporter, the encourager, the consoler, and the cheerleader. My enthusiasm, optimism, determination, belief in all children and their ability to learn, and desire to help each staff member give his/her all so our students may have the best education possible—these are what I give to PWES in my role as principal.

It is a privilege to close the school at night. Walking by each classroom, I see concrete evidence of learning, and feel an immense sense of pride that I am part of such an important team. As I recently watched our school musical from the back of the gym, I saw many children on stage who have overcome personal obstacles and were successfully taking part in this production. All members of our school community have helped to make this happen. It is my role to make sure that we keep doing great things in education for our students.

School and community relationship: Several years ago, our school was recognized by *Today's Parent* magazine as one of five great Canadian schools for its strong connections to its local community. We, and the local population, have continued this tradition and are truly a school community. We are all supporting children in their education. It's not just the school personnel; it's parents, grandparents, friends, relatives, churches, and service clubs that are all helping out.

- We have a "Special Friends" program where people from the community come to the school and work with individual students.
- We recently held a birthday party for a 75-year-old grandmother who asked that any gifts she might receive be books to be placed in our school library. Celebrating things together is an important element of who we are.
- University students come by and volunteer to help teachers in any way they can.
- We have a free after-school program for students, and all teachers and support staff voluntarily drive the students home afterwards. There are no fees or transportation barriers, so that all children can participate.
- Our breakfast program is very successful, and parents often take part as well. Some of our more affluent parents make quiet donations of cash to ensure that no child is left out—as do local churches and groups such as the Lions Club.
- During our weekly Friday morning assemblies, we typically have 60 or more parents, relatives, and friends of students in attendance.
- The community makes extensive use of our facilities and, during evenings and weekends, all sorts of activities (from meetings to parties) take place in our classrooms and gymnasium.
- We take part in the Terry Fox Run, the Jump Rope for Heart program, UNICEF, and we also raise funds for various other local purposes.

I could go on, but I think you get the idea. This school is an important part of the local community, and the local community is an important part of our school. The two are actually one. We teach our students that, as members of a community, they must give back as well as receive. As simple examples, our students sing songs for the residents of a local nursing home, conduct litter pick-up drives, and a great many other things.

Major goals of the school: We have a two-pronged approach. First, the staff of our school strongly believe that children must be emotionally stable if they are to learn effectively. They must be properly fed and emotionally nurtured. Some children need additional doses of TLC and we try to provide it through various means. Children at our school, and the staff as well, get lots of hugs, and no one here—including the staff—is afraid to cry. And second, we are strongly focused upon two academic areas: literacy, which is absolutely fundamental for them to be effective learners, and math skills, which are essential for lasting success as students and adults.

Special in-school programs: Our weekly assembly is an important part of our school's life. Half of these assemblies are MC'd by the students, and the remainder by me. Student performances are a common feature of these assemblies—as are two other things. First, there is the Environmental Trophy, awarded to the individual or group that has been the most diligent in its environment practices; and second, there is the Good News award, for whoever has achieved some personal or academic success or received good news about a social situation—such as a friend or relative recovering from an illness.

Other school features/programs: By teacher request, all of our classes are based on the multi-age model. We have implemented the Positive Effective Behavior Support program (www.pbis.org) and, nine years ago, became the first school in the province to establish firm guidelines for healthy eating. Junk food, while not strictly banned, is certainly frowned upon. In addition, we do everything we possibly can to develop our students' leadership skills and pride in their school and community.

Typical length of Ms. Woodford's day as principal: 6:00 a.m. until 6:00 p.m., plus additional meetings, as necessary, during evenings and weekends.

Questions

1. What features of this school are exemplary?

2. What societal problems are addressed by the school? How?

3. Do you agree with the school's position on the importance of community involvement? Why or why not?

4. What are your views regarding Ms. Woodford's comments about her role as the principal of Port Williams Elementary School?

5. Many schools have a "no touching" policy, which prevents teachers, except under exceptional circumstances, from touching a student. Teachers at Port Williams Elementary schools are under no such restriction. What are your views regarding this topic?

6. As a school administrator, Ms. Woodford's work week of 60 plus hours is not unusual. Would you be interested in eventually applying for such a position?

7. Would you want a child of your own to attend this school? Why or why not?

How Can Community-Based Partnerships Address Social Problems That Hinder Students' Learning?

Earlier in the book, we examined social problems that affect schools and that place students at risk of dropping out: poverty, family stress, substance abuse, violence and crime, teen pregnancy, HIV and AIDS, and suicide (see Chapter 5). We also looked at intervention programs that schools have developed to ensure the optimum behavioural, social, and academic adjustment of at-risk children and adolescents to their school experiences: peer counselling, full-service schools, school-based inter-professional case management, compensatory education, and alternative schools and curricula. Here, we describe innovative, community-based partnerships that some schools have developed recently to prevent social problems from hindering students' learning.

The range of school–community partnerships found in today's schools is extensive. For example, Exeter High School in suburban Toronto has developed partnerships with 13 community organizations and more than 100 employers. Through Exeter's Partners in Learning program, business, industry, service clubs, and social service agencies make significant contributions to students' education.

The Community as a Resource for Schools

To assist schools in addressing the social problems that impact students, many communities are acting in the spirit of a recommendation made by Ernest Boyer: "Perhaps the time has come to organize, in every community, not just a *school* board, but a *children's* board. The goal would be to integrate children's services and build, in every community, a friendly, supportive environment for children" (Boyer 1995, 169). Partnerships between communities and schools form when individuals, civic organizations, or businesses select a school, or are selected by a school, to work together for the good of students. The ultimate goals of such projects are to provide students with better school experiences and to assist students at risk.

Civic Organizations

To develop additional sources of funding, many local school districts have established partnerships with community groups interested in improving educational opportunities. Some groups, such as the Lions Club, have actively supported a variety of school projects. Others adopt or sponsor schools and enrich their educational programs by providing funding, resources, or services.

Volunteer Mentor Programs

Mentorship is a trend in community-based partnerships today, especially with students at risk. Parents, business leaders, professionals, and peers volunteer to work with students in neighbourhood schools. Goals might include dropout prevention, high achievement, improved self-esteem, and healthy decision making. Troubleshooting on lifestyle issues often plays a role, especially in communities plagued by drug dealing, gang rivalry, casual violence, and crime. Mentors from organizations such as Big Brothers and Big Sisters of Canada also model success for participating children and adolescents.

Corporate-Education Partnerships

Business involvement in schools has taken many forms, including, for example, contributions of funds or materials needed by a school, release time for employees to visit classrooms, adopt-a-school programs, cash grants for pilot projects and teacher development, educational use of corporate facilities and expertise, employee participation, and student scholarship programs. Extending beyond advocacy, private sector efforts include job initiatives for disadvantaged youths, in-service programs for teachers, management training for school administrators, minority education and faculty development, and even construction of school buildings.

Involvement of the business community with education is not without its critics. Maude Barlow, in her article *The Assault on Canadian Schools* (1995, 1–8), points out, in strong language, that the effort of transnational corporations to infiltrate Canadian schools is a serious problem that must be addressed. She writes about the United States, where Burger King operates fully accredited high schools, as does its main competitor, McDonald's, and writes also of New Zealand, where "students are writing exams brought to them by Reebok and Coca Cola . . . [with] the corporate logos on each exam." (Barlow 1995, 7) Chief executive officers of 99 Canadian corporations surveyed by the *Financial Post* "said they should be, and very soon would be, in the schools (Barlow 1995, 7).

Schools as Resources for Communities

The view that schools should serve as multipurpose resources *for* the community is a shift from the more traditional perspective of schools needing community support to meet the needs of students affected by social problems. By focusing not only on the development of children and youth, but on their families as well, schools ultimately enhance the ability of students to learn. As Ernest Boyer (1995, 168) puts it, "No arbitrary line can be drawn between the school and life outside. Every [school] should take the lead in organizing a *referral service*—a community safety net for children that links students and their families to support agencies in the region—to clinics, family support and counseling centers, and religious institutions."

Beyond the School Day

Many schools and school districts are serving their communities by providing educational and recreational programs before and after the traditional school day and during the summers. Increasingly, educational policy-makers recognize that the traditional school year of approximately 190 days is not the best arrangement to meet students' learning needs. As the RCM Research Corporation, a nonprofit group that studies issues in educational change, points out: "Historically, time has been the glue that has bonded the traditions of our public school system—i.e., equal class periods, no school during summer months, 12 years of schooling, etc.,—and, as a result, the use of time has become sacrosanct, 'We have always done it this way!' How time is used by schools often has more to do with administrative convenience than it does with what is best educationally for the student" (RCM Research Corporation 1998, 1). In 2003, for example, British Columbia considered having the regular school day extended in length while reducing the actual number of school days per week to four from the more customary five. In the late 1990s, some Nova Scotia school districts also considered, but eventually rejected, a similar possibility.

Proposals for year-round schools and educationally oriented weekend and after-school programs address the educational and developmental needs of students impacted by social problems. While Canadian provinces and territories have yet to make substantive changes to the regular school year, examples of what might eventually take place can be found in the United States. There, according to the San Diego–based National Association for Year-Round Education, more than 2800 public schools now extend their calendars into the summer, and more than 2 million students go to school year-round. In Austin, Texas, for example, schools can participate in an Optional Extended Year (OEY) program that allows them to provide additional instruction in reading and mathematics to students at risk of being retained a grade. Schools participating in OEY can choose from among four school-day options: (1) extended day, (2) extended week, (3) intersession of year-round schools, and (4) summer school (Idol 1998; Washington 1998). Futurist Marvin Cetron predicts that, soon, "schools will educate and train both children and adults around the clock: the academic day will stretch to seven hours for children; adults will work a 32-hour week and prepare for their next job in the remaining time" (Uchida, Cetron, & McKenzie 1996, 35).

Programs that extend beyond the traditional school day also address the needs of parents and the requirements of the work world. Every day, thousands of elementary-age "latchkey" children arrive home to an empty house. As one elementary teacher said, "Many of my students just hang around at the end of every day. They ask what they can do to help me. Often there's no one at home, and they're afraid to go home or spend time on the streets" (Boyer 1995, 165).

After-school educational and recreational programs are designed to (1) provide children with supervision at times when they might become involved in antisocial activities, (2) provide enrichment experiences to widen children's perspectives and increase their socialization, and (3) improve the academic achievement of children not achieving at their potential during regular school hours (Fashola 1999). Ernest Boyer argues that schools should adapt their schedules to those of the workplace so that parents can become more involved in their children's education, and that businesses, too, should give parents more flexible work schedules. Drawing on the model of Japan, Boyer suggests that the beginning of the school year could be a holiday to free parents to attend opening day ceremonies and celebrate the launching and continuation of education, in the same way that we celebrate its ending.

Although some research indicates that extended school days and school calendars have a positive influence on achievement (Gandara & Fish 1994; Center for Research on Effective Schooling for Disadvantaged Students 1992), the Center for Research on the Education of Students Placed at Risk (CRESPAR) at Johns Hopkins University concluded that "there is no straightforward answer to the question of what works best in after-school programs" (Fashola 1999). According to CRESPAR, few studies of the effects of after-school programs on measures such as achievement or reduction of antisocial behaviour meet minimal standards for research design. Nevertheless, CRESPAR found that after-school programs with stronger evidence of effectiveness had four elements: training for staff, program structure, evaluation of program effectiveness, and planning that includes families and children (Fashola 1999).

Social Services

In response to the increasing number of at-risk and violence-prone children and youth, many schools are also providing an array of social services to students, their families, and their communities. The following comments by three female students highlight the acute need for support services for at-risk youth who might turn to aggression and violence in a futile attempt to bolster their fragile self-esteem and to cope with the pain in their lives. All three girls have been involved in violent altercations in and around their schools, and all three frequently use alcohol and illegal drugs.

Fifteen-year-old "Mary" has been physically abused by both her father and mother, and she was raped when she was 14. "Linda," also 15 years old, was sexually molested during a four-year period by a family acquaintance, and she endures constant physical and psychological abuse from her father. Fourteen-year-old "Jenny" is obsessed with death and suicide, and she aspires to join a gang.

> When you're smoking dope, you just break out laughing, you don't feel like punching people because it's just too hard. It takes too much. . . . You're mellow. . . . You just want to sit there and trip out on everybody. . . . It's even good for school work. When I used to get stoned all the time last year, I remember, I used to sit in class and do my work because I didn't want the teacher to catch me, and this year I'm getting failing marks 'cause I'm not doing my work 'cause I'm never stoned (Mary).

> I just know I got a lot of hatred. . . . And there's this one person [Jenny], and it just kinda happened after she mouthed me off, I was just like totally freaked with her and now I just want to slam her head into something. I wanna shoot her with a gun or something. I wanna kill her. . . . If I could get away with it I'd kill her. I wouldn't necessarily kill her, but I'd get her good. I just want to teach her a lesson. I'd beat the crap out of her. She's pissed me off so badly. I just want to give her two black eyes. Then I'd be fine. I'd have gotten the last word in (Linda).

> I like fighting. It's exciting. I like the power of being able to beat up people. Like, if I fight them, and I'm winning, I feel good about myself, and I think of myself as tough. . . . I'm not scared of anybody, so that feels good. My friends are scared of a lot of people, and I go "Oh yeah, but I'm not scared of them. . . . All these people in grade eight at that junior high are scared of me, they don't even know me, and they're scared of me. It makes me feel powerful (Jenny). (Artz 1999, 127; 136; 157)

In Chapter 5, we looked at how some schools provide educational, medical, social, and/or human services, and how the school-based inter-professional case management model uses case managers to deliver services to at-risk students and their families. Although many believe that schools should not provide such services, an increase in the number of at-risk students like Mary, Linda, and Jenny suggest that the trend is likely to continue, with more schools requiring a service agency "which brings together all of the community agencies concerned with children, coordinates the services, increases support, and prepares a report card on progress" (Boyer 1995, 169). More social initiatives, such as parent support groups, infant nurseries, and programs for students with special needs, are likely to form a more prominent part of future Canadian schooling.

How Will the Fledgling Charter School Movement Affect Equity and Excellence in Education?

One of the most interesting experiments in Canadian education during the past decade has been the development of **charter schools**. While there are only 12 such schools in Canada, all in Alberta, these schools present a new direction in educational reform. Charter schools offer a modern and flexible approach to the complex teaching environment of today. While held fully accountable to a publicly elected government body, they control their own budget, staffing, programs, and services to better meet the needs of their students.

Charter schools are independent, innovative, outcome-based public schools.

The charter school concept allows a group of teachers, parents, or others who share similar interests and views about education to organize and operate a school. Charters can be granted by a local school district or by the province. In effect, charter schools offer a model for restructuring that gives greater autonomy to individual schools and promotes school choice by increasing the range of options available to parents and students within the public schools system. (Wohlstetter & Anderson 1994, 486).

To open a charter school, an original charter (or agreement) is signed by the school's founders and a sponsor (usually the local school board). The charter specifies the learning outcomes that students will master before they continue their studies. Charter schools, which usually operate in the manner of autonomous school districts (a feature that distinguishes them from the alternative schools operated by many school districts), are public schools and must teach all students. If admission requests for a charter school exceed the number of available openings, students are selected by a draw.

Because charter schools are designed to promote the development of new teaching strategies that can be used at other public schools, they can prove to be an effective tool for promoting educational reform and the professionalization of teaching in the future. Moreover, charter schools give teachers unprecedented leadership opportunities and the ability to respond quickly to students' needs.

The United States and For-Profit Schools

Other than a short-lived experiment in Nova Scotia with Public–Private Partnership (P–3) schools, there are no **for-profit schools** in Canada. However, in the United

States—which often provides us with a hint of future educational directions—one of the most controversial educational issues for the twenty-first century is the practice of turning the operation of public schools over to private, for-profit companies. Advocates of the **privatization movement** believe privately operated schools are more efficient; they reduce costs and maximize "production"—that is, student achievement. Opponents are concerned that profit, rather than increasing student achievement, is the real driving force behind for-profit schools. Critics are also concerned that school districts may not be vigilant enough in monitoring the performance of private education companies.

Like Maude Barlow, Canadian essayist and novelist John Ralston Saul is very concerned about the possible privatization of our schools. In his article "In Defense of Public Education" (Saul 2002, 12) he states: "Our country has been built, from the very beginnings of its democratic system 150 years ago, upon a happy linkage between democracy and public education." He makes the additional comment that "if society and its leaders are not willing to fund the [educational] system, then we collectively, and they specifically, must all take responsibility for the decline of our own children and the children of our fellow citizens" (Saul 2002, 12). Whether Canadian schools will succumb to the private sector's desire to become more deeply involved in education as a business initiative is an unsettled issue.

What Can Teachers and Schools Learn from International Education?

The world has truly become smaller and more interconnected as telecommunications, cyberspace, and travel by jet bring diverse people and countries together. As we continue to move closer together, it is clear that education is crucial to the well-being of every country and to the world as a whole. "For teachers, on whom the quality of education ultimately depends, the challenges and opportunities the twenty-first century will bring are remarkably similar worldwide, and there is much [we] can learn from other countries about the conditions that promote the ability of teachers and students to deal with that future" (Parkay & Oaks 1998). For example, an observation in a *Bangkok Post* editorial on the need to prepare Thai youth for a changing world echoes calls for educational improvement in Canada. "The country's policy planners should seriously review and revamp the national education system to effectively prepare our youths [for] the next century" (Sricharatchanya 1996). Similarly, a community leader's comments about educating young substance abusers in Bangkok's Ban Don Muslim community could apply to youth in scores of Canadian communities: "We are in an age of cultural instability. Children are exposed to both good and bad things. [I]t's hard to resist the influences and attitudes from the outside world that are pulling at the children's feelings" (Rithdee 1996, 11). Lastly, the curriculum goals at Shiose Junior High School in Nishinomiya, Japan, are based on Japan's fifteenth Council for Education and would "fit" Canadian junior high schools as well; according to principal Akio Inoue (1996, 1), "Students will acquire the ability to survive in a changing society, that is, students will study, think and make judgments on their own initiative. It is also important that we provide a proper balance of knowledge, morality, and physical health, and that we nurture humanity and physical strength for that purpose." As a result of the universal challenges that confront educators, we are entering an era of increasing cross-national exchanges that focus on sharing resources, ideas, and expertise for the improvement of education worldwide.

Comparative Education

As the nations of the world continue to become more interdependent, educational policies and practices will be influenced increasingly by **comparative education**—the study of educational practices in other countries. Comparative education studies show how school systems in other countries work and how Canadian students compare with students in other countries on certain measures of schooling and achievement. In addition, research in comparative education enables professionals to share information about successful innovations internationally. Teachers can collaborate on global education projects and test change models that other countries have used to help match educational and societal needs and goals.

As an example, in a comparative study of Japanese education, Harry Wray (1999, 137) concludes that Japan's system of national examinations "reinforce[s] excessive conformity, passivity, standardization, anxiety, group consciousness, and controlled education." Wray goes on to say that, "Excessive emphasis on passing entrance examinations plays a contributing role in killing most students' interest in studying and scholarship after entering a university, especially for those outside the science, engineering, and medical areas. Students exhausted by the dehumanizing methodology lose motivation and curiosity" (1999, 138). Additionally, provincial examinations have been criticized because they encourage students to take a narrow view of learning, and tend to emphasize lower-order thinking skills that can be assessed easily by pencil-and-paper measures. As one Japanese university student confided to Wray: "In elementary school we had many occasions to give our opinions; however, after we entered junior high school, we did not get such opportunities because all the studies are for high school entrance examinations, and all the studies in high school are for university entrance examinations. One who is considered 'intelligent' is one who can get good grades, not those who have their own opinions" (1999, 137).

Lessons from Other Countries

The previous comments about Japanese education aside, Canadian educators can learn a great deal from their colleagues around the world regarding what works and what doesn't work in other countries. When considering the possibility of adopting practices from other countries, however, it is important to remember that educational practices reflect the surrounding culture. When one country tries to adopt a method used elsewhere, a lack of support from the larger society may doom the new practice to failure. In addition, it is important to recognize that the successes of another country's educational system may require sacrifices that are unacceptable to our way of life. Nevertheless, there are many practices around the world that Canadian educators and policy-makers might consider.

Support for Teachers and Teaching

In many other countries, teachers and the profession of teaching receive a level of societal support that surpasses that experienced by teachers in Canada. For example, teachers in many countries are accorded greater respect than their Canadian counterparts. In addition, most Canadian teachers have about one hour or less per day for planning, and Canadian high school teachers teach about 30 classes a week, compared with 20 hours by teachers in Germany and fewer than 20 hours by Japanese teachers. While teachers from these latter two countries have over 15 hours per week to work collaboratively on school-based endeavours, little such time is available to Canadian teachers. Among Western countries, the average number of contracted hours is 704, but varies from over 1000 in Mexico and the United Stated to 534 in Japan (OECD 2006). Other countries also invest their resources in hiring more teachers, who make up a statistically higher proportion of total staff than is the case in Canada. While exact data for the Canadian context are not available, in the United States, where teaching loads are comparable, the OECD's 1995 study noted that "too many people and resources are allocated to activities outside of classrooms, sitting on the sidelines rather than the front lines of teaching and learning" (OECD 1995). Many countries also invest more resources in beginning-teacher support programs to provide novice teachers with experiences that are more positive than those of their Canadian counterparts. In the United States, for example, the National Education Association (NEA), in its 2003 report *Meeting the Challenges of Recruitment and Retention*, highlights the following beginning-teacher support programs.

1. New teachers are viewed as professionals on a continuum, with increasing levels of experience and responsibility; novice teachers are not expected to do the same job as experienced teachers without significant support.
2. New teachers are nurtured and not left to flounder on their own; interaction with other teachers is maximized.
3. Teacher induction is a purposive and valued activity.
4. Schools possess a culture of shared responsibility and support, in which all or most of the school's staff contributes to the development and nurturing of the new teacher.
5. Assessment of new teachers is downplayed.

Parental Involvement

The powerful influence of parental involvement on students' achievement is well documented (Booth & Dunn 1996; Buzzell 1996; ERIC Clearinghouse and Eugene 1993; Epstein 1992). Japan probably leads the world when it comes to parental involvement in education. Japanese mothers frequently go to great lengths to ensure that their children get the most out of the school's curriculum. The *kyoiku mama* (literally, education mother) will tutor her child, wait for hours in lines to register her child for periodic national exams, prepare healthy snacks for the child to eat while studying, forego television so her child can study in quiet, and ensure that her child arrives on time for calligraphy, piano, swimming, or martial arts lessons. Though few Canadian parents might wish to assume the role of the *kyoiku parent*, it seems clear that Canadian students would benefit from greater parental involvement.

Pressure to Excel

There have been many calls to make Canadian schooling more rigorous; a longer school calendar, longer school days, more homework, and harder examinations, for example, have all been proposed. These changes, it is assumed, would increase student achievement and find favour with the majority of the public that wants greater academic rigour. More often than not, Japan, Korea, and other Asian countries are held up as models for the direction Canadian education might emulate. But should Canadian schools be patterned after schools in these countries? Several people who have studied and experienced Asian schools are beginning to think not. If parents want their children to achieve at the level of Asian students, which is often only a few percentage points higher on standardized examinations, they must understand the sacrifices made by Asian students and their parents and be prepared to adhere to these guidelines:

1. [W]hen their children come home from public school, they should feed them and then ship them off to a private school or tutor until 10 PM; most youngsters, both elementary and secondary, will need to go to school all day on Sunday, too.

2. [They should] spend 20 to 30 percent of their income on [a]fter-school schools.
3. [W]hen their children turn four, they should take them on their knees and tell them, "You are big boys and girls now, so you need to start practicing for college entrance examinations." (Bracey 1996, 128)

The educational culture of Canada is such that neither parents nor their children are prepared to make these types of sacrifices.

What Is Our Vision for the Future of Education?

Imagine that it is the year 2020, and we are visiting Westside Elementary School in a medium-sized city. All the teachers at Westside are fully certified and have salaries that are on par with those of other professionals with comparable education and training. About half of the 55 teachers at Westside have also earned advanced professional certification. These teachers are known as lead teachers and may earn as much as $100 000 per year. Westside has no principal; the school is run by an executive committee of five lead teachers elected by all teachers at the school. One of these lead teachers is elected to serve as committee chair for a two-year period. In addition, the school has several student interns and educational assistants who are assigned to lead teachers as part of their graduate-level teacher-preparation program. Finally, teachers are assisted by a diagnostician; a hypermedia specialist; a computer specialist; a video specialist; a social worker; a school psychologist; four counsellors; special remediation teachers in reading, writing, mathematics, and oral communication; bilingual and English as a second language teachers; and special-needs teachers.

Westside Elementary operates many programs that illustrate the close ties the school has developed with parents, community agencies, and businesses. The school houses a daycare centre that provides after-school employment for several students from the nearby high school. On weekends and on Monday, Wednesday, and Friday

What vision of the school of the future does this photograph suggest? What might you add to the image to achieve a broader perspective on tomorrow's teachers and learners?

evenings, the school is used for adult education and for various community group activities. Executives from three local businesses spend one day a month at the school visiting with classes and telling students about their work. Students from a nearby college participate in a tutoring program at Westside, and the college has several on-campus summer enrichment programs for Westside students.

Westside has a school-based health clinic that offers health care services and a counselling centre that provides individual and family counselling. In addition, from time to time, Westside teachers and students participate in service-learning activities in the community. At the present time, for example, the Grade 5 classes are helping the city develop a new recycling program.

All the facilities at Westside—classrooms, the library, the multimedia learning centre, the gymnasium, the cafeteria, and private offices for teachers—have been designed to create a teaching–learning environment free of all health and safety hazards. The cafeteria, for example, serves meals based on findings from nutrition research about the best foods and methods of cooking. The school is carpeted, and classrooms are soundproofed and well lit. Throughout, the walls are painted in soft pastels tastefully accented with potted plants, paintings, wall hangings, and large murals depicting life in different cultures.

The dress, language, and behaviours of teachers, students, and support personnel at Westside reflect a rich array of cultural backgrounds. In the cafeteria, for example, it is impossible not to hear several languages being spoken and to see at least a few students and teachers wearing non-Western clothing. From the displays of students' work on bulletin boards in hallways and in classrooms to the international menu offered in the cafeteria, there is ample evidence that Westside is truly a multicultural school and that gender, race, and class biases have been eliminated.

Each teacher at Westside is a member of a teaching team and spends at least part of his or her teaching time working with other members of the team. Furthermore, teachers determine their schedules, and every effort is made to assign teachers according to their particular teaching expertise. Students attend Westside by choice for its excellent teachers; its curricular emphasis on problem solving, human relations, creative thinking, and critical thinking; and its programs for helping at-risk students achieve academic success.

Instruction at Westside is supplemented by the latest technologies. The school subscribes to several computer databases and cable television services, which teachers and students use regularly. The hypermedia learning centre has an extensive collection of CD-ROMs and computer software, much of it written by Westside teachers. The centre also has virtual-reality interactive videodisc systems, workstations equipped with the latest robotics, and an extensive lab with voice-activated computers. The computer-supported interactive multimedia in the centre use the CD-ROM format and the more advanced Integrated Services Digital Network (ISDN) delivery system based on optical fibre.

Every classroom has a video camera, fax machine, hypermedia system, and telephone that, in addition to everyday use, are used frequently during satellite video teleconferences with business executives, artists, scientists, scholars, and students at schools in other provinces and countries. Westside Elementary's technological capabilities permit students to move their education beyond the classroom walls, as they determine much of how, when, where, and what they learn.

Tomorrow's Teacher

Teaching and the conditions under which teachers work may change in some fundamental and positive ways during the next two decades. Teaching will become increasingly professionalized, for example, through such changes as more lengthy and rigorous preservice training programs, salary increases that put teaching on par with other professions requiring similar education, greater teacher autonomy, and an expanded role for teachers in educational policy-making. There will be more male teachers who are African-Canadian, Arabic, and Asian, or members of other ethnic and racial groups. There will be greater recognition for high-performing teachers and schools through such mechanisms as merit pay plans, master teacher programs, and career ladders. Tomorrow's teachers will achieve new and higher levels of specialization. The traditional teaching job will be divided into parts. Some of the new jobs appear on the following list:

- Learning diagnostician
- Researcher for software programs
- Courseware writer
- Curriculum designer
- Mental health diagnostician
- Evaluator of learning performances
- Evaluator of social skills
- Small-group learning facilitator
- Large-group learning facilitator
- Media-instruction producer
- Home-based instruction designer
- Home-based instruction monitor

Though we cannot claim to have handed you an educational crystal ball so that you can ready yourself for the future, we hope you have gained both knowledge and inspiration from our observations in this chapter. Certainly, visions of the future, such as the one of Westside Elementary, will not become a reality without a lot of dedication and hard work. The creation of schools like Westside will require commitment and vision on the part of professional teachers like you.

Professional Reflection   What Does the Future Hold for Your Province or Territory?

Predict the future of education in your province or territory in terms of the following list of innovations and trends. Rate each development according to whether it already exists in your province or when you think it will become common practice in the schools—within the next 5 or the next 15 years. If you don't know the status of a particular development in your province, find out. Add at least one new item representing a trend in your province that does not appear on the list. When you have finished rating the items, share your results with your classmates. What reasons or evidence will you give for your predictions?

Innovation/Trend	Now	Within 5 years	Within 15 years	Not likely
1. Alternative, authentic assessment of students' learning	____	____	____	____
2. Cross-age tutoring/mentoring	____	____	____	____
3. Peer counselling/peer coaching	____	____	____	____
4. Faculty teams/team teaching	____	____	____	____

Innovation/Trend	Now	Within 5 years	Within 15 years	Not likely
5. Business–school partnerships	——	——	——	——
6. Community–school teaming	——	——	——	——
7. School-based clinics/counselling centres	——	——	——	——
8. Organized after-school programs	——	——	——	——
9. Year-round schools	——	——	——	——
10. School development	——	——	——	——
11. Equity in school funding	——	——	——	——
12. Open enrolment/school choice	——	——	——	——
13. Telephones in the classroom	——	——	——	——
14. Student computer networking	——	——	——	——
15. Video teleconferencing	——	——	——	——
16. Interactive multimedia/hypermedia	——	——	——	——
17. Multimedia distance learning	——	——	——	——
18. Sex education	——	——	——	——
19. AIDS education	——	——	——	——
20. Character education curricula	——	——	——	——
21. Globalism/multiculturalism	——	——	——	——
22. Aesthetics orientation	——	——	——	——
23. Alcohol and drug intervention	——	——	——	——
24. Reduction of gender bias	——	——	——	——
25. Reduction of racial/ethnic prejudice	——	——	——	——
26. Inclusion of students who have special needs	——	——	——	——
27. Teacher empowerment	——	——	——	——
28. Constructivist teaching approaches	——	——	——	——
29. Charter schools	——	——	——	——
30. Corporate-education partnerships	——	——	——	——
31. For-profit schools	——	——	——	——
32. _____	——	——	——	——
33. _____	——	——	——	——

SUMMARY

What Knowledge and Skills Will Prepare Students for a Global Information Age?

- Conflicting theories, expectations, and values make it difficult to answer what students need to know and be able to do in the future; however, increasing cultural diversity and global economic interdependence call for communication and cooperation skills and wise use of environmental resources.

- To meet the challenges of the future, students will need knowledge, skills, attitudes, and values in nine key areas: literacy in language, mathematics, and science; new technological skills; problem solving, critical thinking, and creativity; social awareness, communication skills, and team building; global awareness and conservation skills; health and wellness education; moral and ethical orientation; aesthetics awareness; and lifelong, self-directed learning.

How Can Schools and Teachers Provide an Outstanding Education for All Learners?

- To reach all learners, teachers must understand how some families are under acute stress, how crime and violence impact students' lives, and how to develop multicultural curricula and instructional repertoires that develop the potentials of students from varied backgrounds.

- In addition to preparing multicultural instructional materials and strategies for students from diverse cultural, ethnic, and linguistic backgrounds, teachers treat students equitably when they treat high- and low-achieving students the same way. Research has identified several teacher behaviours that reflect inequitable treatment of low-achieving students: waiting less time for them to answer questions, interacting with them less frequently, giving them less feedback, calling on them less often, seating them farther away, failing to accept and use their ideas, smiling at them less often, making less eye contact, praising them less, demanding less from them, grading their tests differently, and rewarding inappropriate behaviours.

- Effective teachers establish positive relationships with all students by listening to them, giving frequent feedback and opportunities to ask questions, and demanding higher-level performance by asking higher-order questions that require more critical thinking.

- To reach all learners, teachers should provide them with active, authentic learning experiences.

How Can Community-Based Partnerships Address Social Problems That Hinder Students' Learning?

- Communities help schools address social problems that hinder students' learning by providing various kinds of support.

- Civic organizations raise money for schools, sponsor teams, recognize student achievement, award scholarships, sponsor volunteer mentor programs, and provide other resources and services to enrich students' learning.

- Corporate–education partnerships provide schools with resources, release time for employees to visit schools, scholarships, job initiatives for disadvantaged youth, in-service programs for teachers, and management training for school administrators.

- Schools serve as resources for their communities by providing educational and recreational programs before and after the school day, and by providing health and social services.

How Will the Fledgling Charter School Movement Affect Equity and Excellence in Education?

- Charter schools and U.S. for-profit schools, both part of the privatization movement, were developed in response to perceived inadequacies in the public schools.

- Charter schools are independent, innovative, outcome-based public schools started by a group of teachers, parents, or others who obtain a charter from a local school district, a province, or the federal government.

What Can Teachers and Schools Learn from International Education?

- The challenges and opportunities for teachers in the twenty-first century are remarkably similar worldwide, and teachers in different countries can learn much from one another. Comparative education, the study of educational practices in other countries, enables educators to collaborate internationally.

- A study conducted by the Organization for Economic Cooperation and Development (OECD) indicates that Canadian schools are among the best in the world.

- Education in many other countries is centralized, and teachers follow a national curriculum. In Canada, each province and territory is responsible for the education of its children.

- Many other countries tend to provide greater support for teachers and teaching, and have greater parental involvement—two practices that would benefit Canadian education. However, pressure for students in other countries to excel is often extreme.

- Many other countries provide greater support for teachers and the teaching profession, have greater parental involvement, and take more steps to nurture beginning teachers.

What Is Our Vision for the Future of Education?

- It is not unrealistic to imagine that teachers in schools during the year 2020 will be well-paid, self-governing professionals who have developed specialized areas of expertise. This vision becomes more possible with each teacher who makes a commitment to its realization. However, the constancy of change is a reality with which all teachers must learn to contend. As recently retired teacher and educator Dr. J. R. Harris writes in the following essay, change can be a very positive thing, but the teaching profession is not without its constancies.

> Heraclitus is credited with observing approximately 2500 years ago that nothing endures but change; this remark is repeated nowadays to the point of cliché. Change being a constant is good news for educators. Why? In most North American jurisdictions, young persons surrender approximately 12 000 hours to some sort of formal schooling. Most students are conscious during these hours, and for most young people, these hours are tendered during what is arguably the most dynamic time of their lives. Consequently, it is fervently hoped that educators guide, orchestrate, and assist with enormous change during each student's time in their care. If describable (measurable) change does not occur each school year for each and every student, then student needs are not being met, which implies that schools operate in a state of educational deficiency.

> Change itself, however, can promote both advancements and a feeling that we can never catch up; the advent of information technology serves as an example of both of these conditions. It is astonishing to think that in 1970 personal computers did not exist. Computers were primitive and cumbersome, and one dared not "fold, staple, or mutilate" in any way the data cards used to feed information to computers. Less than half a century later, it is estimated that over one billion personal computers are in use, some of them so small that they require a small stylus for use, the average person's fingers being too large to be effective. As their size has decreased, computers have developed inversely and exponentially in terms of

storage capacity. Nevertheless, there are constraints to advances in the realm of information technology, including:

- the cost of staying "up to date,"
- having technology sufficient for and appropriate to the needs of all learners,
- the explosion of available information with no certain way of ensuring the quality of that information,
- time management,
- the increasing ease with which learners can plagiarize, and
- the protection of individual privacy, to name but a few.

The reality and inevitability of upheaval in curriculum for schools seems to bear out the view that the only constant is change.

- Ongoing change in the teaching of mathematics and language arts appears to be an enduring norm.
- Many jurisdictions have many more mathematics courses at the secondary level than was the case in the 1960s when students took algebra and geometry.
- The aims and methodologies of teaching language arts go through regular cycles. How many decades has it been since it was standard pedagogical practice for English teachers standing "in front" of a room full of students to refer to the "subject," "predicate," or "subordinate clause" of a sentence?
- In the 1960s and 1970s, courses with names such as (or similar to) Personal Development and Relationships, Career and Life Management, and Computer Technology *did not exist*.
- How many people in 1960 imagined that a day would come when students living in remote, rural communities could earn their high school certificate though the delivery of curriculum via technology-based virtual learning environments?

Schools continue to evolve to reflect societal pressures with respect to priorities in curriculum, equity issues, human rights, and personal safety. A few examples follow:

- second language immersion,
- lack of program availability resulting in litigation,
- the multilingual/multiethnic classroom,
- first nations curriculum,
- the inclusive classroom,
- school board positions in which someone's job description includes words such as "human rights," and/or "race relations," and/or "cross cultural understanding,"
- substance abuse education programs, and
- the school's "lockdown practice" becoming as prevalent as the fire drill.

In the twenty-first century, it is demanded that education budgets be stretched further and further. The size of most school systems administered by school boards has increased dramatically, and the busing of students to and from school now governs school daily schedules so that buses can perform more than one run for different populations. Consequently, sometimes students in one school start classes at 8:00 a.m., with students being dismissed at 2:00 p.m., while in a neighboring school, teaching starts at 9:10 with dismissal occurring at 3:30. Economy thus dictates that busing has a direct and powerful effect on most schools' scheduling, curriculum, teaching, learning, and extracurriculars.

There have always been those who enjoy portraying the teaching profession as an easy job with a short working day enjoyed by overpaid teachers with numerous holidays and long lazy summers beckoning them towards their natural state of sloth. While this stereotype has never been true, the teaching profession and teachers are adapting to reflect the times:

- In many jurisdictions, teacher education programs require prospective teachers to complete a two-year program after their first baccalaureate degree.
- Increasingly, teachers are accountable to register for, participate in, and file with their school board their completion of a certain number of in-service/professional development experiences during a stipulated timeframe.
- It is expected that teachers function adeptly in classrooms composed of increasingly diverse student populations.
- Increasingly, the idea of year-long schooling is moving from theoretical concept to legislated probability.

Having made these observations, though, it is important to note that some things really do remain the same. Students still need:

- teachers who try to understand them,
- teachers who are concerned with the entire learner (not just the course syllabus),
- teachers who strive to provide their students with a rich and meaningful delivery and mediation of curriculum,
- teachers who are concerned for the well-being, emotional health, and safety of their students,
- teachers who offer encouragement,
- teachers who provide students with appropriate curricular and co-curricular challenges,
- teachers who provide students with frequent and fair assessment and evaluation,
- teachers who teach appropriately to the assessments they set for students, and
- teachers who establish a caring and respectful learning environment for *all* students.

About 600 years after Heraclitus, Marcus Aurelius uttered a statement linking the ever-changing universe to individual thought. If teachers make available the pedagogical conditions listed above, then (to paraphrase Marcus Aurelius) there is reason to hope for our students; regardless of the persistence of change in education, the lives of learners will be what their thoughts make them.

Source: Essay by J. R. Harris, 2007; original material prepared for this text.

KEY TERMS AND CONCEPTS

charter schools, 362
comparative education, 364
for-profit schools, 362

higher-order questions, 355
learning, 355
lower-order questions, 355

privatization
    movement, 363
synectics, 352

APPLICATIONS AND ACTIVITIES

Teacher's Journal

1. Write a scenario forecasting how the teaching profession will change during the next two decades.

2. Select one of the following areas and develop several forecasts for changes that will occur during the next two decades: energy, environment, food, the economy, governance, family structure, demographics, global relations, media, and technology. On what current data are your forecasts based? How might these changes affect teaching and learning?

3. Think about two children you know and project them into the future, 20 years from now. What skills are they likely to need? Which talents should help them? How can schools better promote the development of these skills and talents?

Theory into Practice

1. Environmental Conservation: If students are to live in a world where all living things exist in a sustainable environmental balance, they must be made aware of how such a state can be achieved. In a small group, select a grade level and one of the following subject areas: English, mathematics, social studies. Determine three things that you as a teacher could do, within the grade level and subject area you selected, to encourage your students' participation in attaining such a condition. Be prepared to present your recommendations to the class.

2. Obesity: Approximately 30 percent of Canadian students are either overweight or obese. In a small-group situation, determine two means by which teachers might deal with this topic without injuring the egos of students who are either overweight or obese. Assume you are teaching a class where healthy lifestyles are the primary focus. Be prepared to present your suggestions to the class.

3. Values (Character) Education: There is a general belief among parents and other members of the public that schools should inculcate in students good moral values. Many teachers, however, are uncomfortable with the idea of teaching a values-based curriculum. Instead, they prefer to teach about values, presenting all sides of an issue, then letting students make their individual decisions as to the position they adopt. In a small-group situation, examine the values listed below. Determine which ones, if any, should be directly taught to students at the junior high level. Be prepared to make a report to the class.

   - Stealing is always wrong.

   - Democracy is the best possible system of government.

   - Except in special circumstances, abortion is always wrong.

   - Moderate drinking of alcohol is acceptable for those of legal age.

   - Prejudice against others is never acceptable.

Teacher's Database

1. Investigate the websites for the Organization for Economic Cooperation and Development (OECD) and the Canadian Teachers' Federation (CTF) and gather information on educational systems in other countries. In what areas of the curriculum, and at what levels, is the achievement of Canadian students at, or above, the international average? What conclusions about the strengths and weaknesses of Canadian schools can you draw from your analysis of these data?

2. Explore the field of international education or comparative education and talk to teaching professionals in other countries online. For example, you might ask them what they see as the greatest challenge facing educators in their respective countries. Or you might ask them about working conditions for teachers—that is, number of students taught, time for planning, professional responsibilities beyond the classroom, and so on.

Observations and Interviews

1. Interview the principal at a nearby school and ask him or her to describe what the school will be like in 10 years. Then interview several teachers at the school. Compare the forecasts of the principal with those of the teachers. What might account for any differences you find?

2. Search for examples of school–community partnership arrangements in the local school district. Find out if these partnerships are progressing and propose a new one based on your specific knowledge of the community.

Professional Portfolio

Prepare a portfolio entry of instructional resources—curriculum guides, teaching tips, assessment strategies, relevant professional associations, books and articles, software, and online resources—related to one of the nine areas of learning students will need in order to meet the challenges of the future (i.e., literacy in language, mathematics, and science; new technological skills; problem solving, critical thinking, and creativity; social awareness, communication skills, and team building; global awareness and conservation skills; health and wellness education; moral and ethical orientation; aesthetics awareness; and lifelong, self-directed learning). For each entry include a brief annotation describing the materials, how you will use them, and where they may be obtained. After you have prepared this portfolio entry, meet with your classmates and exchange information.

MyEducationLab

For suggestions regarding the teaching of values, go to Teacher's Resource 12.1, Teacher's Scribe: "Are you trying to tell me what to think?" on www.MyEducationLab.com.

Glossary

A

Academic learning time (p. 213): the amount of time students spend working on academic tasks with a high level of success (80 percent or higher).

Action research (p. 307): classroom-based study, by teachers, of how to improve their instruction.

Aesthetics (p. 65): the branch of axiology concerned with values related to beauty and art.

Aims of education (p. 134): what a society believes the broad, general purposes of education should be— for example, socialization, achievement, personal growth, and social improvement.

Allocated time (p. 213): the amount of time teachers allocate for instruction in various areas of the curriculum.

Alternative school (p. 156): a small, highly individualized school separate from a regular school; designed to meet the needs of students at risk.

American tradition (p. 73): an approach to education which the frontier experience of the United States modified to make it more practical than the British model upon which it was originally based.

Assertive discipline (p. 217): an approach to classroom discipline requiring that teachers establish firm, clear guidelines for student behaviour and follow through with consequences for misbehaviour.

Assistive technology (p. 187): technological advances (usually computer-based) that help exceptional students learn and communicate.

Attention deficit disorder (ADD) (p. 182): a learning disability characterized by difficulty in concentrating on learning.

Attention deficit hyperactivity disorder (ADHD) (p. 182): a learning disability characterized by difficulty in remaining still so that one can concentrate on learning.

Authentic learning tasks (p. 212): learning activities that enable students to see the connections between classroom learning and the world beyond the classroom.

Axiology (p. 64): the study of values, including the identification of criteria for determining what is valuable.

B

Behaviourism (p. 70): a philosophical orientation based on behaviouristic psychology that maintains that environmental factors shape people's behaviour.

Benefit packages: (p. 10): various negotiated nonsalary compensation provided to teachers in addition to their negotiated salaries

Between-class ability grouping (p. 211): the practice of grouping students at the middle and high school levels for instruction on the basis of ability or achievement; often called *tracking*.

Bioecological systems theory (p. 135): theory that children have five major ecologies (environments) with which they interact (socialize), which mould and shape their development.

Block scheduling (p. 213): a high school scheduling arrangement that provides longer blocks of time each class period, with fewer periods each day.

British North America Act (*BNA Act*) **(pp. 81, 101):** the act that established Canada as a nation and laid the framework for public institutions such as schools.

C

Canadian Charter of Rights and Freedoms (p. 185): 1982 document that enshrined rights and freedoms to serve as the guiding law of the land and that applies to all levels of government.

Canadian Parents for French (p. 108): nationwide volunteer organization to promote teaching of French in schools, especially French immersion programs.

Canadian School Boards Association (p. 104): national voice of school boards in Canada, comprised of 10 provincial school board associations.

Canadian Teachers' Federation (CTF) (p. 301): national bilingual Canadian organization with 240 000 members from all provinces and territories.

Caring classroom (p. 207): a classroom in which the teacher communi-cates clearly an attitude of caring about students' learning and their overall well-being.

CD-ROM (p. 266): a small plastic disk (usually 4.72 or 5.25 inches in diameter) that holds 600 or more megabytes of information that can be read by a computer.

CEGEP (p. 85): (collège d'enseignement général et professional) a Quebec junior college that students can attend for one or two years of study.

Character education (p. 170): an approach to education that emphasizes the teaching of values, moral reasoning, and the development of "good" character.

Charter schools (p. 362): independent schools, often founded by teachers, that are given a charter to operate by a school district, province, or national government, with the provision that students must demonstrate mastery of predetermined outcomes.

Chat rooms (p. 273): internet sites where students can participate in online discussions by typing in their comments and questions.

Child abuse (p. 121): any kind of harm that causes injury to a child, including physical, sexual, emotional abuse and neglect.

Child Abuse Registry (p. 152): record kept of individuals who have abused children.

Choice theory (p. 218): an approach to classroom management, developed by psychiatrist William Glasser, based on a belief that students will usually make good choices (i.e., behave in an acceptable manner) if they experience success in the classroom and know that teachers care about them.

Classroom climate (p. 203): the atmosphere or quality of life in a classroom, determined by how individuals interact with one another.

Classroom culture (p. 140): the "way of life" characteristic of a classroom group; determined by the social dimensions of the group and the physical characteristics of the setting.

Classroom management (p. 214): day-to-day teacher control of student behaviour and learning, including discipline.

Classroom organization (p. 211): how teachers and students in a school are grouped for instruction and how time is allocated in classrooms.

Clinical supervision (p. 342): a four-step model supervisors follow in making teacher performance evaluations.

Code of ethics (p. 112): a set of guidelines that defines appropriate behaviour for professionals.

Cognitive development (p. 166): the process of acquiring the intellectual ability to learn from interaction with one's environment.

Cognitive science (p. 71): the study of the learning process that focuses on how individuals manipulate symbols and process information.

Collaboration (p. 337): the practice of working together, sharing in decision making, and solving problems among professionals.

Collaborative consultation (p. 189): an approach in which a classroom teacher meets with one or more other professionals (such as a special educator, school psychologist, or resource teacher) to focus on the learning needs of one or more students.

Collective bargaining (p. 116): a process followed by employers and employees in negotiating salaries, hours, and working conditions; in most provinces, school boards must negotiate contracts with teacher organizations.

Collegial support team (CST) (p. 339): a team of teachers—created according to subject area, grade level, or teacher interests and expertise—who support one another's professional growth.

Collegiality (p. 335): a spirit of cooperation and mutual helpfulness among professionals.

Comparative education (p. 364): the comparative study of educational practices in different countries.

Computer-assisted instruction (CAI) (p. 268): the use of computers to provide individualized drill-and-practice exercises or tutorials to students.

Computer-enhanced instruction (CEI) (p. 269): the use of computers to provide students with inquiry-oriented learning experiences, such as simulations and problem-solving activities.

Computer-managed instruction (CMI) (p. 269): the use of computers to evaluate and diagnose students' learning needs and record students' progress for teachers to monitor.

Concrete operations stage (p. 167): the stage of cognitive development (seven to 11 years of age) proposed by Jean Piaget in which the individual develops the ability to use logical thought to solve concrete problems.

***Constitution Act, 1982* (p. 101):** historic act amending Canada's constitution, most notably by setting out the *Charter of Rights and Freedoms* and by providing methods to further amend the constitution without the British parliament.

Constructivism (p. 70): a psychological orientation that views learning as an active process in which learners *construct* understanding of the material they learn—in contrast to the view that teachers transmit academic content to students in small segments.

Constructivist teaching (p. 223): a method of teaching based on students' prior knowledge of the topic and the processes they use to *construct* meaning.

Cooperative education programs (p. 254): programs designed to develop employability skills and help students explore career options by offering both an in-school and a work experience component.

Cooperative learning (p. 212): an approach to teaching in which students work in small groups, or teams, sharing the work and helping one another complete assignments.

Core curriculum (p. 244): a set of fundamental courses or learning experiences that are part of the curriculum for all students at a school.

Core French (p. 252): second language instruction that emphasizes basic communication skills, language knowledge, and appreciation of French culture.

Corporal punishment (p. 120): physical punishment applied to a student by a school employee as a disciplinary measure.

Co-teaching (p. 339): an arrangement whereby two or more teachers teach together in the same classroom.

Council of Ministers of Education, Canada (p. 102): established in 1967, acts as a forum for provincial and territorial ministers of education to meet and discuss matters of mutual interest.

Credentials file (p. 325): a file set up for students registered in a teacher placement office at a college or university, which includes background information on the applicant, the type of position desired, transcripts, performance evaluations, and letters of recommendation.

Criminal record (p. 152): record kept of individuals convicted of criminal offences.

Critical pedagogy (p. 69): educational theory and teaching and learning practices designed to raise students' critical awareness regarding oppressive social conditions.

Critical reflective practice (p. 299): highest level of reflection in which the teacher asks: "How does my teaching positively influence students in their lives beyond the classroom?"

Cross-age tutoring (p. 226): a tutoring arrangement in which older students tutor younger students; evidence indicates that cross-age tutoring has positive effects on the attitudes and achievement of tutee and tutor.

Cultural identity (p. 142): an overall sense of oneself, derived from the extent of one's participation in various subcultures within the national macroculture.

Culture (p. 141): the way of life common to a group of people; includes knowledge deemed important, shared meanings, norms, values, attitudes, ideals, and view of the world.

Curriculum (p. 234): the school experiences, both planned and unplanned, that enhance (and sometimes impede) the education and growth of students.

Cyberbullying (p. 12): the use of digital technology devices such as cell phones and the internet to harass, threaten, or intimidate others.

D

Dame-schools (p. 73): colonial schools, usually held in the homes of widows or housewives, for teaching children basic reading, writing, and mathematical skills.

Democratic classrooms (p. 214): a classroom in which the teacher's leadership style encourages students to take more power and responsibility for their learning.

Departmentalization (p. 140): an organizational arrangement for schools in which students move from classroom to classroom for instruction in different subject areas.

Department of education (p. 103): the provincial government ministry responsible for all aspects of education.

Deputy minister of education (p. 103): appointed civil servant whose position is directly below the minister of education; responsible for the day-to-day management of the department of education.

Digital divide (p. 283): inequities in access to computer technology that are related to minority-group status, family income, and gender.

Direct instruction (p. 221): a systematic instructional method focusing on the transmission of knowledge and skills from the teacher to the students.

Discovery learning (p. 224): an approach to teaching that gives students opportunities to inquire into subjects so that they "discover" knowledge for themselves.

Distance learning networks (p. 266): two-way, interactive telecommunications systems used to deliver instruction to students at various locations.

Diversity (p. 140): differences among people in regard to gender, race, ethnicity, culture, and socio-economic status.

Due process (p. 116): a set of specific guidelines that must be followed to protect individuals from arbitrary, capricious treatment by those in authority.

Duty of care (p. 118): special obligation of teachers to prevent reasonably foreseeable harm to those under their supervision. Duties often clarified through regulations, school board bylaws, policy statements, and job descriptions.

E

E-learning (p. 267): education that is delivered via the internet, satellite broadcast, interactive television, or CD-ROM.

Education act (p. 103): provincial statute that creates an education system and provides for its management and funding.

Educational philosophy (p. 61): a set of ideas and beliefs about education that guide the professional behaviour of educators.

Educational Resources Information Center (ERIC) (p. 307): a U.S. national information system made up of 16 clearinghouses that disseminate descriptions of exemplary programs, results of research and development efforts, and related information.

Educational technology (p. 266): computers, software, multimedia systems, and advanced telecommunications systems used to enhance the teaching–learning process.

Emotional intelligence (p. 135): a level of awareness and understanding of one's emotions that allows the person to achieve personal growth and self-actualization.

English as a second language (ESL) (p. 88): English language training for individuals whose first language is not English.

English tradition (p. 72): a model of education based on church control, class, and separate schools for boys and girls.

Epistemology (p. 64): a branch of philosophy concerned with the nature of knowledge and what it means to know something.

ERIC clearinghouses (p. 307): 16 U.S. Educational Resources Information Center Clearinghouses that disseminate descriptions of exemplary educational programs, the results of research and development efforts, and related information.

Essentialism (p. 67): formulated in part as a response to progressivism, this philosophical orientation holds that a core of common knowledge about the real world should be transmitted to students in a systematic, disciplined way.

Ethical dilemmas (p. 115): problem situations in which an ethical response is difficult to determine; that is, no single response can be called "right" or "wrong."

Ethics (p. 64): a branch of philosophy concerned with principles of conduct and determining what is good and evil, and right and wrong, in human behaviour.

Ethnic group (p. 141): individuals within a larger culture who share a racial or cultural identity and a set of beliefs, values, and attitudes and who consider themselves members of a distinct group or subculture.

Exceptional learners (p. 178): students whose growth and development deviate from the norm to the extent that their educational needs can be met more effectively through a modification of regular school programs.

Existentialism (p. 68): a philosophical orientation that emphasizes the individual's experiences and maintains that each individual must determine his or her own meaning of existence.

Explicit curriculum (p. 235): the behaviour, attitudes, and knowledge that a school intends to teach students.

Extracurricular/cocurricular programs (p. 237): school-sponsored activities students may pursue outside of, or in addition to, academic study.

F

Field experiences (p. 40): opportunities for teachers-in-training to experience firsthand the world of the teacher, by observing, tutoring, and instructing small groups.

Formal operations stage (p. 167): the stage of cognitive development (11 to 15 years of age) proposed by Jean Piaget, in which cognitive abilities reach their highest level of development.

For-profit schools (p. 362): schools that are operated, for profit, by private educational corporations.

French tradition (p. 72): based on church-controlled schools with classes often taught by members of the clergy.

Full inclusion (p. 188): the policy and process of including exceptional learners in general education classrooms.

G

Gender bias (p. 148): subtle bias or discrimination on the basis of gender;

reduces the likelihood that the target of the bias will develop to the full extent of his or her capabilities.

Gender-fair classroom (p. 148): education that is free of bias or discrimination on the basis of gender.

Gentle teaching (p. 189): a philosophical stance directly based upon Maslow's hierarchy of needs.

Gifted and talented (p. 182): exceptional learners who demonstrate high intelligence, high creativity, high achievement, or special talent(s).

Grievance (p. 116): a formal complaint filed by an employee against his or her employer or supervisor.

Group investigation (p. 226): an approach to teaching in which the teacher facilitates learning by creating an environment that allows students to determine what they will study and how.

H

Hidden curriculum (p. 235): the behaviours, attitudes, and knowledge the school culture unintentionally teach students.

Hierarchy of needs (p. 170): a set of seven needs, from the basic needs for survival and safety to the need for self actualization, that motivate human behaviour.

Higher-order questions (p. 355): questions that require the ability to engage in complex modes of thought (synthesis, analysis, and evaluation, for example).

Home–school communication systems (p. 272): computer-based systems that allow schools to disseminate information to parents and, in turn, enable parents to communicate directly with school personnel.

Home-schooling (p. 90): the practice of parents taking on the role of teacher and educating their children at home.

Humanism (p. 69): a philosophy based on the belief that individuals control their own destinies through the application of their intelligence and learning.

Humanistic psychology (p. 69): an orientation to human behaviour that emphasizes personal freedom, choice, awareness, and personal responsibility.

Hypermedia (p. 271): an interactive instructional system consisting of a computer, CD-ROM drive, videodisc player, video monitor, and speakers. Hypermedia systems allow students to control and present sound, video images, text, and graphics in an almost limitless array of possibilities.

I

Inclusion (p. 187): the practice of integrating all students with disabilities into general education classes.

Independent schools (p. 89): also known as private schools, which charge a tuition fee.

Individualized education plan (IEP) (p. 186): a plan for meeting an exceptional learner's educational needs, specifying goals, objectives, services, and procedures for evaluating progress.

Information processing (p. 224): a branch of cognitive science concerned with how individuals use long- and short-term memory to acquire information and solve problems.

Inquiry learning (p. 224): an approach to teaching that gives students opportunities to explore, or *inquire* into, subjects so that they develop their own answers to problem situations.

In-service workshops (p. 50): on-site professional development programs in which teachers meet to learn new techniques, develop curricular materials, share ideas, or solve problems.

Institution (p. 137): any organization a society establishes to maintain, and improve, its way of life.

Integrated curriculum (p. 239): a school curriculum that draws from two or more subject areas and focuses on a theme or concept rather than on a single subject.

Intelligence (p. 174): the ability to learn; the cognitive capacity for thinking.

Interactive multimedia (p. 271): computer-supported media that allow the user to interact with a vast, nonlinear, multimedia database to combine textual, audio, and video information.

Interactive teaching (p. 16): teaching characterized by face-to-face interactions between teachers and students; in contrast to preactive teaching.

Inter-cultural education (p. 145): education committed to the goal of providing all students—regardless socio-economic status, gender, sexual orientation or ethnic, racial, or cultural background—with equal opportunities to learn in school.

Internet (pp. 51, 273): many interconnected computer networks created for the rapid dissemination of vast amounts of information around the world.

J

Job analysis (p. 36): a procedure for determining the knowledge and skills needed for a job.

Job fairs (p. 325): information sessions that bring teacher candidates and potential employees together to provide information about job openings.

K

Knowledge base (p. 31): the body of knowledge that represents what teachers need to know and to be able to do.

L

Latchkey children (p. 152): children who, because of family circumstances, must spend part of each day unsupervised by a parent or guardian.

Learning (p. 355): changes in behaviour the individual makes in response to environmental stimuli; the acquisition and organization of knowledge and skills.

Learning disability (LD) (p. 180): a limitation in one's ability to take in, organize, remember, and express information.

Learning styles (p. 176): cognitive, affective, and physiological behaviours through which an individual learns most effectively; determined by a combination of hereditary and environmental influences.

Least restrictive environment (p. 186): an educational program that meets a disabled student's special needs in a manner that is identical, insofar as possible, to that provided to students in general education classrooms.

Letter of application (p. 328): a letter written in application for a specific teaching vacancy in a school district.

Letter of inquiry (p. 326): a letter written to a school district inquiring about teaching vacancies.

Liability (p. 120): responsibility for damages or harm.

Logic (p. 65): a branch of philosophy concerned with the processes of reasoning and the identification of rules that will enable thinkers to reach valid conclusions.

Lower-order questions (p. 355): questions that require students to recall specific information.

M

Mainstreaming (p. 187): providing students with the least restrictive academic environment in which they may comfortably learn the curriculum.

Mastery learning (p. 222): an approach to instruction based on the assumptions that (1) virtually all students can learn material if given enough time and taught appropriately and (2) learning is enhanced if students can progress in small, sequenced steps.

Mentor (pp. 48, 300): a wise, knowledgeable individual who provides guidance and encouragement to someone.

Mentoring (p. 48): an intensive form of teaching in which a wise and experienced teacher (the mentor) inducts a student (the protegé) into a professional way of life.

Metaphysics (p. 63): a branch of philosophy concerned with the nature of reality.

Microcomputer-based laboratory (MBL) (p. 270): the use of computers to gather and then analyze data that students have collected in a school laboratory or in the field.

Microteaching (p. 41): a brief, single-concept lesson taught by a teacher education student to a small group of students; usually designed to give the education student an opportunity to practice a specific teaching skill.

Minister of education (p. 103): elected cabinet minister with the formal responsibility for the provincial department of education and its staff.

Modelling (p. 222): the process of "thinking out loud," which teachers use to make students aware of the reasoning involved in learning new material.

Modes of teaching (p. 19): different aspects of the teaching function—for example, teaching as a way of being, as a creative endeavour, as a live performance, and so on.

Montessori method (p. 89): a method of teaching, developed by Maria Montessori, based on a prescribed set of materials and physical exercises to develop children's knowledge and skills.

Moral reasoning (p. 166): the reasoning process people follow to decide what is right or wrong.

Multicultural education (p. 145): education that provides equal educational opportunities to all students—regardless of socio-economic status; gender; or ethnic, racial, or cultural backgrounds—and is dedicated to reducing prejudice and celebrating the rich diversity of multicultural life.

Multiculturalism (p. 143): a set of beliefs based on the importance of seeing the world from different cultural frames of reference and valuing the diversity of cultures in the global community.

Multiple intelligences (p. 176): a perspective on intellectual ability, proposed by Howard Gardner, suggesting that there are at least seven types of human intelligence.

N

Negligence (p. 118): failure to exercise reasonable, prudent care in providing for the safety of others.

Newsgroups (p. 273): internet sites where students can post and exchange information on electronic bulletin boards.

Normal schools (p. 72): schools that focus on the preparation of teachers.

Null curriculum (p. 236): the intellectual processes and subject content that schools do not teach.

O

Observations (p. 40): field experiences wherein a teacher education student observes a specific aspect of classroom life, such as the students, the teacher, the interactions between the two, the structure of the lesson, or the setting.

Open-space schools (p. 139): schools that have large instructional areas with movable walls and furniture that can be rearranged easily.

Opportunity to learn (OTL) (p. 213): the time during which a teacher provides students with challenging content and appropriate instructional strategies to learn that content.

Outcome-based education (pp. 35, 245): an educational reform that focuses on developing students' ability to demonstrate mastery of certain desired outcomes or performances.

Outcome-based teacher education (p. 35): an approach to teacher education emphasizing outcomes (what teachers should be able to do, think, and feel) rather than the courses they should take.

P

Pan-Canadian Education Indicators Program (PCEIP) (p. 151): a joint venture of Statistics Canada and the Council of Ministers of Education.

Parochial schools (p. 72): schools founded on religious beliefs.

Pedagogical content knowledge (p. 30): the knowledge accomplished teachers possess regarding how to present subject matter to students though the use of analogies, metaphors, experiments, demonstrations, illustrations, and other instructional strategies.

Peer coaching (p. 337): an arrangement whereby teachers grow professionally by observing one another's teaching and providing constructive feedback.

Peer counselling (p. 155): an arrangement whereby students, monitored by a school counsellor or teacher, counsel one another in such areas as low achievement, interpersonal problems, substance abuse, and career planning.

Peer-mediated instruction (p. 224): approaches to teaching, such as cooperative learning and group investigation, that utilize the social relationships among students to promote their learning.

Peer-tutoring (p. 226): an arrangement whereby students tutor other students in the same classroom or at the same grade level.

Perennialism (p. 66): a philosophical orientation that emphasizes the ideas contained in the great books and maintains that the true purpose of education is the discovery of the universal, or perennial, truths of life.

Performance-based education (p. 245): an educational reform that focuses on developing students' ability to demonstrate mastery of certain desired performances or outcomes.

Performance-based teacher education (p. 35): an approach to teacher education emphasizing performance (what teachers should be able to do, think, and feel) rather than the courses they should take.

Personal-development view (p. 35): the belief that teachers become more effective by increasing their self-knowledge and developing themselves as persons.

Petites écoles (p. 72): early schools within the French tradition that provided a rudimentary education.

Phi Delta Kappa (PDK) (p. 303): a professional and honourary fraternity of educators with 650 chapters and 130 000 members.

Placement service (p. 325): a school, government, or commercial service that matches job applicants with job openings and arranges contacts between employers and prospective employees.

Practicum (p. 42): a short field-based experience during which teacher education students spend time observing and assisting in classrooms.

Praxis (p. 69): practical application or exercise of an art, science, skill, or branch of learning.

Preoperational stage (p. 167): the stage of cognitive development (two to seven years of age), proposed by Jean Piaget, in which the individual begins to use language and symbols to think of objects and people outside of the immediate environment.

Privatization movement (p. 363): moving an organization or institution from public (government) ownership to private ownership.

Problem-centred learning (p. 250): an approach to instruction in which students work in small groups on problems that have many or open-ended solutions.

Profession (p. 294): an occupation that requires a high level of expertise, including advanced study in a specialized field, adherence to a code of ethics, and the ability to work without close supervision.

Professional portfolio (p. 46): a collection of various kinds of evidence (e.g., projects, written work, and video demonstrations of skills) documenting the achievement and performance of individuals in an area of professional practice.

Progressivism (p. 67): a philosophical orientation based on the belief that life is evolving in a positive direction, that people may be trusted to act in their own best interests, and that education should focus on the needs and interests of students.

Prosocial values (p. 135): values such as honesty, patriotism, fairness, and civility that promote the well-being of a society.

Psychosocial crisis (p. 167): a life crisis at one of eight different stages of growth and development. According to psychologist Erik Erikson, individuals must resolve each crisis to reach the next stage.

Psychosocial development (p. 166): the progression of an individual through various stages of psychological and social development.

Public–private partnerships (p. 109): partnerships, sometimes referred to as P3s, between local school districts with the private sector; includes funds or materials for a variety of school needs.

Q

Qualitative evaluation (p. 341): the appraisal of teacher performance through the use of written, open-ended descriptions of classroom events in terms of their qualities.

Quantitative evaluation (p. 341): the appraisal of teacher performance by recording classroom events in terms of their number or frequency; for example, teacher verbal behaviours such as questioning, praising, or critiquing.

R

Race (p. 141): a concept of human variation used to distinguish people on the basis of biological traits and characteristics.

Reflection (p. 49): the process of thinking carefully and deliberately about the outcomes of one's teaching.

Reflection-in-action (p. 298): the process of engaging in serious, reflective thought about improving one's professional practice while engaged in that practice.

Reflective teaching log (p. 44): a journal of classroom observations in which the teacher education student systematically analyzes specific episodes of teaching.

Research-based competencies (p. 35): specific behaviours that educational research has identified as characteristic of effective teachers.

Résumé (p. 326): a concise summary of an individual's professional experiences and education.

S

Scaffolding (p. 223): an approach to teaching based on the student's current level of understanding and ability; the teacher varies the amount of help given (e.g., clues, encouragement, or suggestions) to students based on their moment-to-moment understanding of the material being learned.

School advisory councils (p. 104): councils mandated at school levels to allow and encourage parents and community members to become involved in school-level decision making

School-based management (p. 108): various approaches to school improvement in which teachers, principals, students, parents, and community members manage individual schools and share in the decision-making processes.

School boards (p. 104): the primary governing body of a local school district.

School choice (p. 108): various proposals that would allow parents to choose the schools their children attend.

School culture (p. 139): the collective "way of life" characteristic of a school; a set of beliefs, values, traditions, and ways of thinking and behaving that distinguish it from other schools.

School-to-work programs (p. 254): educational programs, often developed collaboratively by schools and industry, that emphasize the transfer of knowledge and skills learned at school to the job setting.

School-within-a-school (p. 156): an alternative school (within a regular school) designed to meet the needs of students at risk.

School year (p. 85): the required number of days required for students to attend school.

Scottish tradition (p. 73): offered both elementary and secondary education to boys and girls in combined classes regardless of their social class.

Self-assessment (p. 49): the process of measuring one's growth in regard to the knowledge, skills, and attitudes possessed by professional teachers.

Self-contained classroom (p. 139): an organizational structure for schools in which one teacher instructs a group of students (typically, 20 to 30) in a single classroom.

Separate schools (p. 72): publicly funded schools based on religion or language.

Sex role socialization (p. 147): socially expected behaviour patterns conveyed to individuals on the basis of gender.

Sex role stereotyping (p. 147): beliefs that subtly encourage males and females to conform to certain behavioural norms regardless of abilities and interests.

Social reconstructionism (p. 68): a philosophical orientation based on the belief that social problems can be solved by changing, or *reconstructing,* society.

Special education (p. 184): a teaching specialty for meeting the special educational needs of exceptional learners.

Stages of development (p. 166): predictable stages through which individuals pass as they progress through life.

Standard of care (p. 118): level of care expected of school personnel; level of care to be that of careful or prudent parents in the care of their own children.

State agents (p. 120): teachers in the role, and carrying out the duties, as defined in education statutes, *Charter of Rights and Freedoms,* and provincial human rights codes.

Stereotyping (p. 144): the process of attributing behavioural characteristics to all members of a group; formulated on the basis of limited experiences with, and information about, the group, coupled with an unwillingness to examine prejudices.

Student-centred curriculum (p. 239): curricula that are organized around students' needs and interests.

Student diversity (p. 4): differences among students in regard to gender, race, ethnicity, culture, and socioeconomic status.

Student-mobility rates (p. 12): the proportion of students within a school or district who move during an academic year.

Student variability (p. 4): differences among students in regard to their developmental needs, interests, abilities, and disabilities.

Students at risk (p. 151): students whose living conditions and backgrounds place them at risk for dropping out of school.

Students with disabilities (p. 179): students who need special education services because they possess one or more of the following disabilities: learning disabilities, speech or language impairments, mental retardation, serious emotional disturbance, hearing impairments, orthopedic impairments, visual impairments, or other health impairments.

Subject-centred curriculum (p. 238): a curriculum that places primary emphasis on the logical order of the discipline students are to study. Teachers of such a curriculum are content area experts and concerned primarily with helping students understand facts, laws, and principles of the discipline.

Substitute teaching (p. 45): temporary teachers who replace regular teachers absent due to illness, family responsibilities, personal reasons, or professional workshops and conferences.

Successful school (p. 149): schools characterized by a high degree of student learning, results that surpass those expected from comparable schools, and steady improvement rather than decline.

Superintendent (p. 106): the chief administrator of a school district.

Supply teaching (p. 45): temporary teachers who replace regular teachers absent due to illness, family responsibilities, personal reasons, or professional workshops and conferences.

Synectics (p. 352): a method for "teaching" creativity through the use of metaphors and analogies.

T

Teacher centres (p. 50): centres where teachers provide other teachers with instructional materials and new methods, and where teachers can exchange ideas.

Teacher–leader (p. 303): a teacher who assumes a key leadership role in the improvement and/or day-to-day operation of a school.

Teacher–researcher (p. 306): a teacher who regularly conducts classroom research to improve his or her teaching.

Teacher-student ratios (p. 11): a ratio that expresses the number of students taught by a teacher.

Teachers' craft knowledge (p. 32): what teachers know about teaching; also called practitioner knowledge.

Teaching certificate (p. 320): a licence to teach issued by a province or, in a few cases, a large city.

Teaching simulations (p. 41): an activity in which teacher education students participate in role plays designed to create situations comparable to those actually encountered by teachers.

Team teaching (p. 338): an arrangement whereby a team of teachers teaches a group of students equal in number to what the teachers would have in their self-contained classrooms.

Time on task (p. 213): the amount of time students are actively and directly engaged in learning tasks.

Tort liability (p. 118): conditions that would permit the filing of legal charges against a professional for breach of duty and/or behaving in a negligent manner.

Tyler rationale (p. 238): a four-step model for curriculum development in which teachers identify purposes, select learning experiences, organize experiences, and evaluate.

V

Vicarious liability (p. 120): responsibility of an employer for damage caused by an employee, even though the employer may not have done anything wrong.

Videoconferencing (p. 274): the use of computer-mounted video cameras to conduct two-way interactive conferences over the internet.

Videodisc (p. 271): a 12-inch plastic disc, each side of which holds about 30 minutes of motion video or 54 000 frames of video; each frame can be frozen with a high degree of clarity.

Virtual schools (pp. 90, 267): public schools that offer programs over the internet.

W

World Wide Web (p. 273): the most popular connection to the internet; comprising homepages, which users access through browser programs such as Microsoft Internet Explorer, Mozilla Firefox, or Apple Safari.

Whole-language approach (p. 247): the practice of teaching language skills (listening, reading, and writing) as part of students' everyday experiences, rather than as isolated experiences.

Within-class ability grouping (p. 211): the practice of creating small, homogeneous groups of students within a single classroom for the purpose of instruction, usually in reading or mathematics, at the elementary level.

Y

Youth Criminal Justice Act **(p. 117):** act replacing the *Young Offenders' Act* to ensure criminal justice for youth; emphasizes rehabilitation and reintegration of youth.

References

Abrahamsson, B. (1971). *Military professionalization and political power.* Stockholm: Allmanna Forlagret.

Acheson, A. A., and Gall, M. D. (1997). *Techniques in the clinical supervision of teachers: Preservice and inservice applications,* 4th ed. New York: Longman.

Aristotle. (1941). Politics (Book VIII). In Richard McKoen (Ed.), *The basic works of Aristotle.* New York: Random House.

Armstrong, H. D. (Ed.). (2004). *Praxis of school administration and teacher leadership.* Calgary, AB: Detselig Enterprises.

Armstrong, A., and Casement, C. (2000). *The child and the machine: How computers put our children's education at risk.* Beltsville, MD: Robins Lane Press.

Artz, S. (1999). *Sex, power, and the violent school girl.* New York: Teachers College Press.

Ballantine, J. H. (1997). *The sociology of education: A systematic analysis,* 4th ed. Upper Saddle River, NJ: Prentice Hall.

Banks, J. A. (1997). *Teaching strategies for ethnic studies,* 6th ed. Boston: Allyn and Bacon.

Banks, J. A, (1999). *An introduction to multicultural education,* 2nd ed. Boston: Allyn and Bacon.

Barlow, M. (with Robertson, H.) (1994). *Class warfare: The assault on Canada's schools.* Toronto: Key Porter.

Barman, J., McCaskill, D., and Hebert, Y. (1986). *Indian education in Canada. Volume 1: The legacy.* Vancouver: University of British Columbia Press.

Beard, C. (1938). *The nature of the social sciences.* New York: Charles Scribner.

Becker, H. J. (1999). *Internet use by teachers: Conditions of professional use and teacher-directed student use.* The University of California, Irvine, and The University of Minnesota: Center for Research on Information Technology and Organizations.

Bennett, C. I. (1999). *Comprehensive multicultural education: Theory and practice,* 4th ed. Boston: Allyn and Bacon.

Bennett, W. J., and Gelernter, D. (2001, March 14). Improving education with technology. *Education Week* on the Web. Retrieved October 18, 2007 from www. edweek.org/ew/ewstory/cfm?slug= 16onlineh20.

Berliner, D. C., and Biddle, B. J. (1995). *The manufactured crisis: Myths, fraud, and the attack on America's public schools.* Reading, MA: Addison Wesley.

Besner, H. F., and Spungin, C. I. (1995). *Gay and lesbian students: Understanding their needs.* Washington, DC: Taylor and Francis.

Bezeau, L. M. (2007). *Educational administration for Canadian teachers.* Retrieved February, 2010, from www.unb.ca/education/bezeau/eact/ eacttoc.html.

Bitter, G. G., and Pierson, M. E. (2005). *Using technology in the classroom,* 6th ed. Boston: Allyn and Bacon.

Bloom, B. S. (1981). *All our children learning: A primer for parents, teachers, and other educators.* New York: McGraw-Hill.

Bolman, L. G., and Deal, T. E. (2002). *Reframing the path to school leadership: A guide for teachers and principals.* Thousand Oaks, CA: Corwin Press.

Booth, A., and Dunn, J. F. (Eds.), (1996). *Family–school links: How do they affect educational outcomes?* Mahwah, NJ: Lawrence Erlbaum Associates.

Borich, G. D. (2000). *Effective teaching methods,* 4th ed. Upper Saddle River, NJ: Merrill.

Borich, G. D. (2007). *Effective teaching methods: Research-based practice.* Upper Saddle River, NJ: Pearson Education.

Bowerman, M. (2005). Technology for all: Successful strategies for meeting the needs of diverse learners. *Technological Horizons in Education (T.H.E.) Journal,* 32(10), 20, 22, 24.

Boyer, E. (1995). *The basic school: A community for learning.* Princeton, NJ: The Carnegie Foundation for the Advancement of Teaching.

Bracey, G. W. (1993). "Now then, Mr. Kohlberg, about moral development in women . . ." In G. Hass, and F. W. Parkay (Eds.), *Curriculum planning: A new approach,* 6th ed. Boston: Allyn and Bacon, 165–66.

Brameld, T. (1956). *Toward a reconstructed philosophy.* New York: Holt, Rinehart and Winston.

Brameld, T. (1959). Imperatives for a reconstructed philosophy of education. *School and Society,* 87, 246–67.

Brien, K. (2002, January). School discipline and the law: Perspective of high school vice-principals. Paper presented for the University of Calgary Online Conference "Linking Educational Research and Practice." Retrieved October 24, 2003, from www.ucalgary.ca/~lrussell/brien. html.

British Columbia Teachers' Federation. (2007). Code of ethics. In Members' guide to the BCTF 2003–2004. Retrieved August 10, 2007 from http://bctf.ca/Professional Responsibility.aspx?id=4292&print Page=true.

Bronfenbrenner, U. (1979). *The ecology of human development: Experiments by nature and design.* Boston: Harvard University Press.

Brown, F. B., Kohrs, D., and Lanzarro, C. (1991). The academic costs and consequences of extracurricular participation in high school. Paper presented at the Annual Meeting of the Educational Research Association.

Bruner, J. S. (1960). *The process of education.* New York: Random House.

Bryce, P. H. (1922). *The story of a national crime: An appeal for justice to the Indians of Canada.* Ottawa: James Hope and Sons.

Bucky, P. A. (1992). *The private Albert Einstein.* Kansas City: Andrews and McMeel.

Burden, P. R., and Byrd, D. M. (1999). *Methods for effective teaching,* 2nd ed. Boston: Allyn and Bacon.

Burnaford, G., Fischer, J., and Hobson, D. (1996). *Teachers doing research: Practical possibilities.* Mahwah, NJ: Lawrence Erlbaum Associates.

Burstall, K. (1993, Spring). The quality teacher. *Aviso.* Nova Scotia Teachers Union.

Buzzell, J. B. (1996). *School and family partnerships: Case studies for regular and special educators.* Albany, NY: Delmar Publishers.

Calkins, L. (1991). *Listening between the lines.* Portsmouth, NH: Heinemann.

Campbell, D. M., Melenyzer, B., Nettles, D., and Wyman, R. (2003). *How to develop a professional portfolio: A manual for teachers*, 3rd ed. Boston: Allyn and Bacon.

Canadian Association for Health, Physical Education, Recreation and Dance (CAHPERD). (2006). Quality daily physical education. Retrieved August 20, 2007, from www.cahperd.ca/eng/physicaleducation/about_qdpe.cfm.

Canadian Association for Health, Physical Education, Recreation and Dance (CAHPERD). (August 2006). Awards news. Retrieved July 24, 2007 from www. cahperd.ca/eng/story_detail.cfm?id=225.

Canadian Association of Second Language Teachers. (2003). Beliefs. Retrieved November 3, 2003 from www.caslt.org/Info/mission.htm#beliefs.

Canadian Education Research Information System (CERIS). (n.d.) Introduction to Canadian education. Retrieved August 10, 2007 from www.cea ace.ca/res.cfm?sub-section=rep.

Canadian Institute of Child Health. (2000). *The health of Canada's children: A CICH profile*, 3rd ed. Ottawa: Canadian Institute of Child Health.

Canadian Teachers' Federation. (2000). Assessment and evaluation. Retrieved November 15, 2003, from www.ctf-fce.ca/en/issues/assessment/testing-policy.html.

Canadian Teachers' Federation. (2003). What is CTF? Retrieved November 1, 2003, from www.ctf-fce.ca/en/default.htm.

Canadian Teachers' Federation. (2006). Make a Difference: Be the Change. Retrieved 09 July, 2010 from www.ctf-fce.ca/TIC/Default.axpx?SID=625892.

Canadian Teachers' Federation. (2008). Cyberbullying in schools: national poll shows Canadians' growing awareness. Retrieved July 9, 2010 from www.ctf-fce.ca/Newsroom/news.aspx?NewsID=-873341035.

Cantor, L. (1989). Assertive discipline—more than names on the board and marbles in a jar. *Phi Delta Kappan*, 71(1), 57–61.

Carmichael, L. B. (1981). McDonogh 15: *The making of a school*. New York: Avon Books.

Cawelti, G. (1999). *Portraits of six benchmark schools: Diverse approaches to improving student achievement*. Arlington, VA: Educational Research Service.

Carroll, J. (1963). A model of school learning. *Teachers College Record*, 64, 723–33.

Center for Research on Effective Schooling for Disadvantaged Students. (1992). Helping students who fall behind, Report No. 22. Baltimore, MD: The Johns Hopkins University.

Center for the Study and Prevention of Violence, University of Colorado at Boulder. (1998). Response to the Columbine school incident. Retrieved April 21, 1999 from www.colorado.edu/cspv.

Centers for Disease Control and Prevention. (1998). Youth risk behavior surveillance—United States, 1997. Atlanta, GA: Centers for Disease Control and Prevention.

Cheeks, E. H., Flippo, R. F., and Lindsey, J. D. (1997). *Reading for success in elementary schools*. Madison, WI: Brown and Benchmark.

Coladarci, T., and Cobb, C. D. (1996). Extracurricular participation, school size, and achievement and self-esteem among high school students: A national look. *Journal of Research in Rural Education*, 12(2), 92–103.

Collins, A. and Halverson, R. (2009). *Thinking education in the age of technology* New York: Teachers College Press.

Colucci, K. (2000). Negative pedagogy. In J. L. Paul and K. Colucci (Eds.), *Stories out of school: Memories and reflections on care and cruelty in the classroom*. Stamford, CT: Ablex, 27–44.

Committee for Economic Development. (1994). *Putting learning first: Governing and managing schools for high achievement*. New York: Research and Policy Committee, Committee for Economic Development.

Council of Ministers of Education. (1995, February). Pan-Canadian protocol for collaboration on school curriculum. Retrieved November 3, 2003, from www.cmec.ca/protocol-eng.htm.

Council of Ministers of Education. (1999, September) AGREEMENT-IN-PRINCIPLE: Labour mobility chapter of the Agreement on Internal Trade/Teaching Profession. Retrieved August 27, 2007, from www.cmec.ca/else/agreement.en.stm.

Counts, G. (1932). *Dare the school build a new social order?* New York: The John Day Company.

Crowther, F., Kaagan, S. S., Ferguson, M., and Hann, L. (2002). *Developing teacher leaders: How teacher leadership enhances school success*. Thousand Oaks, CA: Corwin Press.

Curwin, R. and Mendler, A. (1988, October) Packaged discipline programs: Let the buyer beware. *Educational Leadership*, 46(6), 68–71.

Curwin, R., and Mendler, A. (1989, March). We repeat, let the buyer beware: A response to Canter. *Educational Leadership*, 46(6), 83.

Davis, G. A., and Rimm, S. B. (1998). *Education of the gifted and talented*, 4th ed. Boston: Allyn and Bacon.

Deal, T. E., and Peterson, K. D. (1999). *Shaping school culture: The heart of leadership*. San Francisco: Jossey–Bass Publishers.

Dede, C. (2005). Planning for neomillenial learning styles: Implications for investments in technology and faculty. In *Educating the net generation*. D. Oblinger and J. Oblinger (Eds.) Boulder, CO: EDUCAUSE.

Dede, C., Dieterle, E., Clarke, J., Jass Ketelhut, D. and Nelson, B. (2007). Media-based learning styles. In Michael Moore (Ed.) *Handbook of distance education*. Florence, KY: Routledge.

Dell'Olio, J. M., and Donk, T. (2007). *Models of teaching: Connecting student learning with standards*. Thousand Oaks, CA: Sage.

Department of Justice Canada. (1982). *Canadian Charter of Rights and Freedoms*. Enacted as Schedule B to the Canada Act 1982 (U.K.), 1982, c. 11, which came into force on April 17, 1982. Retrieved October 3, 2003, from http://laws.justice.gc.ca/en/Charter.

Dobbins, K. (2005). Getting ready for the net generation. *EDUCAUSE Review*, 40(5), 8–9.

Dollase, R. H. (1992). *Voices of beginning teachers: Visions and realities*. New York: Teachers College Press.

Dryfoos, J. (1998). *Safe passage: Making it through adolescence in a risky society*. New York: Oxford University Press.

Dykgraaf, C. L., and Kane, S. (1998, October). For-profit charter schools: What the public needs to know. *Educational Leadership*, 56(2), 51–53.

Eby, J. (1996). *Reflective planning, teaching, and evaluation: K–12*, 2nd ed. Upper Saddle River, NJ: Merrill, 14.

Economist. (1999 January 16). A contract on schools: Why handing education over to companies can make sense.

education@canada. (n.d.) International gateway to education in Canada. Retrieved August 10, 2007, from www.education-canada.cmec.ca/EN/home.php.

Education Week on the Web. (1999, July 29). Issue paper: Privatization of public education.

Eggen, P., and Kauchak, D. (2007). *Educational psychology: Windows on classrooms*, 7th ed. Upper Saddle River, NJ: Pearson Education.

Eisner, E. (2002). *The educational imagination: On the design and evaluation of school programs*, 3rd ed. New York: Macmillan College.

Eisner, E. (2006). The satisfactions of teaching: How we teach is ultimately a reflection of why we teach. *Educational Leadership*, 44–46.

Elam, S. M., Rose, L. C. and Gallup, A. M. (September, 1996). The 28th Annual Phi Delta Kappan Gallup Poll of the public's attitudes toward the public schools. *Phi Delta Kappan*, 41–59.

Ellis, L., Robb, B., and Burke, D. (2005) Sexual orientation in United States and Canadian college students. *Archives of Sexual Behavior*, 34(5), 569–81.

Emerson, R., Fretz, R., and Shaw, L. (Eds.). (1995). *Writing ethnographic fieldnotes*. Chicago: University of Chicago Press.

Emmer, E. T., and Evertson, C. M. (2009). *Classroom management for middle and high school teachers*. 8th ed. Boston: Pearson Education.

Epstein, J. L. (1992). School and family partnerships. In M.C. Alkin (Ed.). *Encyclopedia of Educational Research*, 6th ed., New York: MacMillan.

ERIC Clearinghouse. (1993). Value search: Parent involvement in the educational process. Eugene, OR: ERIC Clearinghouse on Educational Management.

Erickson, H. I. (2008). *Stirring the head, heart, and soul: Redefining curriculum, instruction, and concept-based learning*. Thousand Oaks, CA. Corwin Press.

Fashola, O. (1999). Review of day and after-school programs and their effectiveness. John Hopkins University: Centre for Education Study for Research on the Education of Children Placed at Risk.

Feldhusen, J. F. (1997). Educating teachers for work with talented youth. In N. Colangelo and G. A. Davis (Eds.), *Handbook of gifted education*. Boston: Allyn and Bacon.

Ferris, S. (2008). A teacher's voice: Lost and found in paradox. In *Curriculum in Context*, 35(1), 16–17.

Fleming, T. (1997, November). Provincial initiatives to restructure Canadian school governance in the 1990s. *Canadian Journal of Education Administration and Policy*, 11. Retrieved May 26, 2003, from www.umanitoba.ca/publications/cjeap/articles/thomasfleming.html.

Freedman, S., Jackson, J., and Botes, K. (1983). Teaching: An imperiled profession. In L. Shulman, and G. Sykes, (Eds.), (1983). *Handbook of teaching and policy*. New York: Longman.

Friend, M., and Bursuck, W. D. (2002). *Including students with special needs: A practical guide for classroom teachers*. Boston: Allyn and Bacon.

Fuligni, A. J., and Stevenson, H. W. (1995). Home environment and school learning. In Lorin W. Anderson (Ed.), *International encyclopedia of teaching and teacher education*, 2nd ed. Oxford: Pergamon, 378–82.

Furger, R. (1999, September). Are wired schools failing our kids? PC World. Retrieved October 18, 2007, from www.pcworld.com/printable/article/id,11950/printable.html.

Gagné, R. M. (1974). *Essentials of learning for instruction*. Hinsdale, IL: Dryden.

Gagné, R. M. (1977). *The conditions of learning*, 3rd ed. New York: Holt, Rinehart and Winston.

Gandara, P., and Fish, J. (Spring 1994). Year-round schooling as an avenue to major structural reform. *Educational Evaluation and Policy Analysis*, 16(1), 67–85.

Garbarino, J. (1999). *Lost boys: Why our sons turn violent and how we can save them*. New York: Free Press.

Gardner, H. (1983). *Frames of mind*. New York: Basic Books.

Gardner, H. (1995, November). Reflections on multiple intelligences: Myths and messages. *Phi Delta Kappan*, 200–203, 206–209.

Gardner, H. (1999). *The disciplined mind: What all students should understand*. New York: Simon and Schuster.

Gaskell, J. (1995). *Secondary schools in Canada: The national report of the Exemplary Schools Project*. Toronto: Canadian Education Association.

Gehrke, N. (1988, Summer). Toward a definition of mentoring. *Theory into Practice*, 190–194.

George Lucas Educational Foundation. (2008, February 9). Visual acuity: From consumers to critics and creators. Retrieved July 9, 2010 from www.edutopia.org/media-literacy-skills.

George, P. (1995). *The Japanese secondary school: A closer look*. Columbus, OH: National Middle School Association; and Reston, VA: National Association of Secondary School Principals.

George Lucas Educational Foundation. (2004, February 9). From hula to high tech. Retrieved from www.glef.org/php/article.php?id=Art_1126&key=137.

Gerber, S. B. (1996). Extracurricular activities and academic achievement. *Journal of Research and Development in Education*, 30(1), 42–50.

Gerstner, L. V., Semerad, R. D., Doyle, D. P., and Johnston, W. B. (1994). *Reinventing education: Entrepreneurship in America's public schools*. New York: Dutton.

Ghosh, R. (2001). *Redefining Multicultural Education*, 2nd ed. Toronto, Ontario: Nelson Thomas Learning (1996, First Edition Toronto Harcourt Brace & Co.).

Gilligan, C. (1993). *In a different voice: Psychological theory and women's development*, 2nd ed. Cambridge, MA: Harvard University Press.

Giroux, H. A. (1999). Schools for sale: Public education, corporate culture, and the citizen-consumer.

The Educational Forum, 63(2), 140–49.

Glasser, W. R. (1997, April). A new look at school failure and school success. *Phi Delta Kappan*, 596–602.

Glasser, W. R. (1998a). *Quality school*, 3rd ed. New York: Harper Perennial.

Glasser, W. R. (1998b). *The quality school teacher: Specific suggestions for teachers who are trying to implement the lead-management ideas of the quality school.* New York: Harper Perennial.

Glasser, W. R. (1998c). *Choice theory: A new psychology of personal freedom.* New York: HarperCollins.

Glasser, W. R., and Dotson, K. L. (1998). *Choice theory in the classroom.* New York: Harper Perennial.

Glickman, C., Gordon, S. P., and Ross-Gordon, J. M. (2001). *SuperVision and instructional leadership*, 5th ed. Boston: Allyn and Bacon.

Glickman, C., Gordon, S. P., and Ross-Gordon, J. M. (2004). *SuperVision and instructional leadership*, 6th ed. Boston: Allyn and Bacon.

Gmelch, W. H., and Parkay, F. W. (1995). Changing roles and occupational stress in the teaching profession. In M. J. O'Hair, and S. J. Odell (Eds.), *Educating teachers for leadership and change: Teacher education yearbook III.* Thousand Oaks, CA: Corwin Press, 46–65.

Goldhammer, R., Anderson, R. H., and Krajewski, R. J. (1993). *Clinical supervision: Special methods for the supervision of teachers*, 3rd ed. Fort Worth, TX: Harcourt Brace Jovanovich.

Goleman, D. (1997). *Emotional intelligence.* New York: Bantam Books.

Goleman, D. (1998). *Working with emotional intelligence.* New York: Bantam Books.

Gonzales, L. D. (2004). *Sustaining school leadership: Beyond the boundaries of an enabling school culture.* Landham, MD: University Press of America.

Good, T. E., and Grouws, D. (1979). The Missouri mathematics effectiveness project: An experimental study in fourth-grade classrooms. *Journal of Educational Psychology*, 71, 355–62.

Good, T. L., and Brophy, J. E. (2008). *Looking in classrooms*, 10th ed. Boston: Pearson Education.

Goodlad, J. (1990). *Teachers for our nation's schools.* San Francisco: Jossey-Bass.

Gordon, D. T. (Ed.). (2003). *Better teaching and learning in the digital classroom.* Cambridge, MA: Harvard Education Press.

Gordon, W. J. J. (1968). *Making it strange, Books 1 and 2.* Evanston, IL: Harper and Row.

Gordon, W. J. J. (1971a). *Invent-o-rama.* Cambridge, MA: Porpoise Books.

Gordon, W. J. J. (1971b). *What color is sleep?* Cambridge, MA: Porpoise Books.

Gordon, W. J. J. (1975). *Strange and familiar, Book 1.* Cambridge, MA: Porpoise Books.

Grant, G. and Murray, E. (1999). Using video cases to promote reflection among preservice teachers: qualitative inquiry. Paper presented at the annual meeting of the American Educational Research Association, New York.

Grant, P. G., Richard, K. J., and Parkay, F. W. (1996, April). Using video cases to promote reflection among preservice teachers: A qualitative inquiry. Paper presented at the Annual Meeting of the American Educational Research Association, New York.

Greene, M. (1995). What counts as philosophy of education? In Wendy Kohli (Ed.), *Critical conversations in philosophy of education.* New York: Routledge.

Hallahan, D. P., and Kauffman, J. M. (1997). *Exceptional learners: Introduction to special education*, 7th ed. Boston: Allyn and Bacon.

Hallahan, D. P., and Kauffman, J. M. (2000). *Exceptional children: Introduction to special education*, 8th ed. Boston: Allyn and Bacon.

Hanvey, L. (November 2001). Children and youth with special needs. Ottawa: Canadian Council on Social Development. Retrieved August 30, 2007, from www.ccsd.ca/pubs/2001/specialneeds/specialneeds.pdf.

Hardman, M. L., Drew, C. J., and Egan, M. W. (1999). *Human exceptionality: Society, school, and family*, 6th ed. Boston: Allyn and Bacon.

Harris, A., and Muijs, D. (2004). *Improving school through teacher leadership.* Berkshire, UK: Open University Press.

Hauser, M., and Rauch, S. (2002). *New teacher! An exciting and scary time.* 2002 job search handbook for educators. Columbus, OH: American Association for Employment in Education.

Henriques, M. E. (1997, May). Increasing literacy among kindergartners through cross-age training. *Young Children*, 42–47.

Henry, M. (1993). *School cultures: Universes of meaning in private schools.* Norwood, NJ: Ablex.

Henry, M. E. (1996). *Parent–school collaboration: Feminist organizational structures and school leadership.* Albany, NY: State University of New York Press.

Holland, A., and Andre, T. (1987, Winter). Participation in extracurricular activities in secondary schools. *Review of Educational Research*, 437–66.

Holly, M. L., and McLoughlin, C. (Eds.), (1989). *Perspectives on teacher professional development.* New York: Falmer Press.

Holt-Reynolds, D. (1999). Good readers, good teachers? Subject matter expertise as a challenge in learning to teach. *Harvard Educational Review*, 69(1), 29–50.

Howe, N. and Strauss, W. (2000). *Millennials rising—The next greatest generation.* New York: Vintage Books.

HP Home: HP Canada Awards $336,000 in Technology. Retrieved July 24, 2007, at www.hp.ca/corporate/features/featurestory.php?fileId=57420.

Hunter, M. (1994). *Enhancing teaching.* New York: Macmillan.

Hurwitz, S. (1999, April). New York, New York: Can Rudy Crew hang tough on vouchers and pull off a turnaround in the nation's biggest school system? *The American School Board Journal*, 36–40.

Idol, L. (1998). Optional extended year program, *Feedback*, Publ. No. 97.20. Austin Independent School District, TX, Office of Program Evaluation.

Igoa, C. (1995). *The inner world of the immigrant child.* New York: Lawrence Erlbaum Associates, Publishers.

Inoue, A. (1996, October 10). Creating schools with special characteristics. Paper presented at the eighth Washington State University

College of Education/Nishinomiya Education Board Education Seminar. Washington State University, Pullman.

International Reading Association. (1999, April). *Using multiple methods of beginning reading instruction.* Newark, DE: International Reading Association.

Jackson, P. (1965). The way teaching is. *NEA Journal*, 54, 10–14.

Jackson, P. (1990). *Life in classrooms.* New York: Teachers College Press.

Jeary, J. (2001). *Character education.* Calgary Board of Education.

Jonassen, D. (2000). *Computers as mindtools for schools: Engaging critical thinking*, 2nd ed. Columbus, Ohio: Merrill.

Johnson, D. W., and Johnson, R. T. (1999). *Learning together and alone: Cooperative, competitive, and individualistic learning*, 5th ed. Boston: Allyn and Bacon.

Johnson, M. J., and Brown, L. (1998). Collegial support teams. In D. J. McIntyre, and D. M. Byrd (Eds.), *Strategies for career-long teacher education: Teacher education yearbook VI.* Thousand Oaks, CA: Corwin Press.

Johnson, J., and Immerwahr, J. (1994). *First things first: What Americans expect from the public schools, a report from Public Agenda.* New York: Public Agenda.

Jonassen, D. H., Peck, K. L., and Wilson, B. G. (1999). *Learning with technology: A constructivist perspective.* Upper Saddle River, NJ: Merrill.

Jones, J. (1994). Integrated learning systems for diverse learners. *Media and Methods*, 31(3).

Jordan, W. J., and Nettles, S. M. (1999). *How students invest their time out of school: Effects on school engagement, perceptions of life chances, and achievement.* Baltimore, MD: Center for Research on the Education of Students Placed at Risk.

Joyce, B., Weil, M., and Calhoun, E. (2004). *Models of teaching*, 7th ed. Boston: Allyn and Bacon.

Joyce, B., Weil, M., and Calhoun, E. (2009). *Models of teaching*, 8th ed. Boston: Allyn & Bacon.

KIDLINK. (2002). Kidproj in Kid-Space. KIDLINK Society. Retrieved August 30, 2007, from www.kidlink.org/KIDPROJ/projects.html.

Kirkpatrick, H., and Cuban, L. (1998). Computers make kids smarter—right? *TECHNOS Quarterly*, 7(2), 26–31.

Kohlberg, L. (2000). The cognitive-developmental approach to moral education. In F. W. Parkay, and G. Hass, (Eds.), *Curriculum planning: A contemporary approach*, 7th ed. Boston: Allyn and Bacon, 136–48.

Krogh, S. L. (2000). Weaving the web. In F. W. Parkay, and G. Hass, (Eds.), *Curriculum planning: A contemporary approach*, 7th ed. Boston: Allyn and Bacon, 338–41.

Leahy, T., and Harris, R. (2001). *Learning and cognition*, 5th ed. Upper Saddle River, NJ: Merrill/Prentice Hall.

Learning Disabilities Association of Canada. (2002, January). Official definition of learning disabilities. Retrieved August 16, 2007, from www.ldac-taac.ca/Defined/defined_new-e.asp.

Levey, S. (1996). *Starting from scratch: One classroom builds its own curriculum.* Portsmouth, NH: Heinemann.

Levin, D., and Arafeh, S. (2002). *The digital disconnect: The widening gap between Internet-savvy students and their schools.* Washington, DC: The Pew Internet and American Life Project.

Lewis, A. (1992). Helping young urban parents educate themselves and their children. *ERIC/CUE Digest*, 85.

Lewis, R. B., and Doorlag, D. H. (1999). *Teaching special students in general education classrooms*, 5th ed. Upper Saddle River, NJ: Merrill.

Lieberman, A. (1990). Foreword. In S. Mei–ling Yee, (Eds.), *Careers in the classroom: When teaching is more than a job.* New York: Teachers College Press.

Lieberman, A., and Miller, L. (2004). *Teacher leadership.* San Francisco: Jossey-Bass.

Littky, D. (2004). *The big picture: Education is everyone's business.* Alexandria, VA: Association for Supervision and Curriculum Development.

Love, K. M. (1994). We've only just begun . . . in New Brunswick. *Journal of the Canadian Association of Community* (5). Retrieved November 16, 2003, from www.nald.ca/cace/journal/net3.htm.

MacKay, A. W., and Sutherland, L. I. (1992). *Teachers and the law: A practical guide for educators.* Toronto: Edmond Montgomery Publications.

MacKinnon, G. R. and Aylward, L. (2000). Coding electronic discussion groups. *International Journal of Educational Telecommunications* 6(1), 53–61.

MacKinnon, G. and Vibert, C. (2002). Judging the constructive impacts of communication technologies: A business education study, *Education & Information Technologies*, 7(2), 127–135.

MacKinnon, G. and Vibert, C. (2004). Webcasting: Modeling distance collaboration in corporate settings. *Journal of Instruction Delivery Systems*, 18(1), 19–22.

MacKinnon, G. (2006). Contentious issues in science education: Building critical thinking patterns through two-dimensional concept mapping. *Journal of Educational Multimedia and Hypermedia*, 15(4), 433–445. Chesapeake, VA: AACE.

MacNaughton, R. H., and Johns, F. A. (1991, September). Developing a successful schoolwide discipline program. *NASSP Bulletin*, 47–57.

Maddux, R., and Johnson, L. (2006). *Type II uses of technology in education: Projects, case studies and software applications.* Binghampton: Haworth.

Mahoney, J., and Cairns, R. B. (1997). Do extracurricular activities protect against early school dropout? *Developmental Psychology*, 33(2), 241–53.

Marshall, K. (2003, May). Recovering from HSPS (hyperactive superficial principal syndrome): A progress report. *Phi Delta Kappan*, 701–09.

Martinez, M. E. (2006). What is metacognition? *Phi Delta Kappan*, 87(9), 696–699.

Maslow, A. (1954). *Motivation and personality.* New York: Basic Books.

Maslow, A. (1962). *Toward a psychology of being.* New York: Basic Books.

McBeath, A. (2002, April). Untitled. *Educational Leadership*, 15.

McCain, T., and Jukes, I. (2001). *Windows on the future: Education in the age of technology.* Thousand Oaks, CA: Corwin Press.

McCoubrey, S., and Sitch, G. (2001). Instructor's guide: Teaching students' rights to pre-service and beginning teachers. *Education and Law Journal*, 11.

McCourt, F. (2005). *Teacher man: A memoir*. New York: Simon & Schuster.

McHugh, J. (2005). Synching up with the iKid: Connecting to the twenty-first-century student. *Edutopia Magazine*, October 2005.

McKenna, M. and Wilms, J.D. (1998, September). Expanding parental involvement in Canadian schools. Policy Brief, Atlantic Centre for Policy Research, University of New Brunswick, 3–4.

Mehlinger, H. D. (1996, February). School reform in the Information Age. *Phi Delta Kappan*, 400–07.

Merideth, E. M. (2000). *Leadership strategies for teachers*. Arlington Heights, IL: SkyLight Professional Development.

Miller, B., Moon, J., Elko, S., and Spencer, D. B. (2000). *Teacher leadership in mathematics and science: Casebook and facilitator's guide*. Portsmouth, NH: Heinemann.

Modi, M., Konstantopoulos, S., and Hedges, L. V. (1998). Predictors of academic giftedness among U.S. high school students: Evidence from a nationally representative multivariate analysis. Paper presented at the Annual Meeting of the American Educational Research Association, San Diego. ERIC Document No. ED422-356.

Molino, F. (1999). My students, my children. In M. K. Rand, and S. Shelton-Colangelo, (Eds.), *Voices of student teachers: Cases from the field*. Upper Saddle River: Merrill, 55–56.

Montgomerie, T., King, C., and Dropko, K. (1994). A needs assessment and a design for a distance education system: The Rural Advanced Community of Learners (RACOL). Retrieved August 21, 2007, from www.racol.ualberta.ca/documents/documents/RACOLfinal.doc.

Moore, D. R. (1992). Voice and choice in Chicago. In W. H. Clune, and J. F. Witte (Eds.), *Choice and control in American education*. Volume II: The practice of choice, decentralization and school restructuring. Philadelphia: Falmer Press.

Morris, V. C., and Pai, Y. (1994). *Philosophy and the American school: An introduction to the philosophy of education*. Lanham, MD: University Press of America.

Morton, C. (1996, February). The modern land of Laputa: Where computers are used in education. *Phi Delta Kappan*, 416–19.

Murnane, R. J., and Levy, F. (1996). *Teaching the new basic skills: Principles for educating children to thrive in a changing economy*. New York: Free Press.

Murphy, J. (1999, April). Reconnecting teaching and school administration: A call for a unified profession. Paper presented at the Annual Meeting of the American Educational Research Association, Montreal.

Murphy, J. (2005). *Connecting teacher leadership and school improvement*. Thousand Oaks, CA: Corwin Press.

National Center for Education Statistics. (2008, February 28). Fast facts. Retrieved from http://nces.ed.gov/fastfacts/display.asp?id=372.

National Council for the Social Studies. (1994). *Expectations of excellence: Curriculum standards for the social studies*. Washington, DC: National Council for the Social Studies.

National Education Association. (2003). *Meeting the Challenges of Recruitment and Retention*, 1st ed. Washington DC: NEA Press. Retrieved October 18, 2007, from www.nea.org/teachershortage/images/rrg-full.pdf.

National School Safety Center. (2007). *Working together to create safe schools*. California: Westlake Village.

Nelson, J. L., Carlson, K., and Palonsky, S. B. (2000). *Critical issues in education: A dialectic approach*, 4th ed. New York: McGraw-Hill.

Newmann, F. M., et al. (Eds.), (1996). *Authentic achievement: Restructuring schools for intellectual quality*. San Francisco: Jossey-Bass.

Newmann, F. M., and Wehlage, G. G. (1995). *Successful school restructuring: A report to the public and educators by the Center on Organization and Restructuring of Schools*. Madison, WI: University of Wisconsin, Center on Organization and Restructuring of Schools.

Nieto, S. (2003). *What keeps teachers going?* New York: Teachers College Press.

Noddings, N. (2002). *Educating moral people: A caring alternative to character education*. New York: Teachers College Press.

Noddings, N. (2007). *When school reform goes wrong*. New York: Teachers College Press.

Noll, J. W. (Ed.), (1999). *Taking sides: Clashing views on controversial educational issues*, 10th ed. Guilford, CT: McGraw–Hill.

Norris, C. (1994). Computing and the classroom: Teaching the at-risk student. *Computing Teacher*, 21(5), 12, 14.

North Central Regional Educational Laboratory. (1993). Policy briefs, report 1, 1993. Elmhurst, IL: NCREL.

Northwest Regional Educational Laboratory. (1999). *Arts education: Basic to learning*. Portland: Northwest Regional Educational Laboratory.

Nova Scotia Department of Education. (2001). *Nova Scotia teacher certification handbook*. Halifax: Nova Scotia Department of Education.

Nova Scotia Department of Education. (2007). *Nova Scotia Public Education Teacher Supply and Demand: 2007 Update Report*. Halifax: Nova Scotia Department of Education.

Nova Scotia Education and Culture. (1999). *Foundation for the Atlantic Canada social studies curriculum*. Halifax, NS: Atlantic Provinces Education Foundation.

Oakes, J. and Lipton, M. (2007). *Teaching to change the world*, 3rd ed. Boston: McGraw-Hill.

OECD Indicators. (2006). Education at a Glance. Retrieved August 30, 2007, from www.oecd.org/dataoecd/32/0/37393408.pdf.

Ontario Human Rights Commission. (December, 2001). *Report of the Ontario Human Rights Commission*. Queen's Printer for Ontario, 2006.

Oppenheimer, T. (1997, July). The computer delusion. *The Atlantic Monthly*, 45–62.

Ormrod, J. E. (2003). *Educational psychology: Developing learners*, 4th ed. Upper Saddle River, NJ: Merrill Prentice Hall.

Ormrod, J. E., and McGuire, D. J. (2007). *Case studies: Applying educational psychology.* Upper Saddle River, NJ: Pearson Education.

Ottawa-Carlton District School Board (Board Procedure PR.585.CUR), June, 2000.

Ottawa Citizen. Canada's Top 20 Jobs, 30 March 2007.

Ozmon, H. W., and Craver, S. M. (1999). *Philosophical foundations of education,* 6th ed. Upper Saddle River, NJ: Merrill.

Pajak, E. (1999). *Approaches to clinical supervision: Alternatives for improving instruction.* Norwood, MA: Christopher-Gordon.

Pansegrau, M. (1997, Fall). Public education governance undergoes facelift as change sweeps nation's school boards. *Spectrum.* Retrieved October 3, 2003, from www.cdnsba.org/energyinnovators/articles.html.

Parkay, F. W. (1988). Reflections of a protégé. *Theory into Practice,* 27, 195–200.

Parkay, F. W., Anctil, E., and Hass, G. (2006). *Curriculum planning: A contemporary approach,* 8th ed. Boston: Allyn and Bacon.

Parkay, F. W., and Oaks, M. M. (1998, April 15). Promoting the professional development of teachers: What the U.S. can learn from other countries. Paper presented at the Annual Meeting of the American Educational Research Association, San Diego.

Pashler, H., and Carrier, M. (1996). Structures, processes, and the flow of information. In E. Bjork and R. Bjork (Eds.), *Memory.* San Diego, CA: Academic Press, 3–29.

Paul, J. L., Christensen, L., and Falk, G. (2000). Accessing the intimate spaces of life in the classroom through letters to former teachers: A protocol for uncovering hidden stories. In J. L. Paul and T. J. Smith (Eds.), *Stories out of school: Memories and reflections on care and cruelty in the classroom.* Stamford, CT: Ablex, 15–26.

Piirto, J. (1999). *Talented children and adults: Their development and education.* Upper Saddle River, NJ: Merrill.

Pitton, D. E. (1998). *Stories of student teaching: A case approach to the student teaching experience.* Upper Saddle River, NJ: Merrill.

Portelli, J., and Solomon, R. P. (2001). *A wolf in sheep's clothing: The erosion of democracy in education.* Calgary, AB: Detselig Enterprises, 136.

Posner, G. J. (2003). *Field experience: A guide to reflective teaching,* 6th ed. Boston: Pearson Education.

Power, E. J. (1982). *Philosophy of education: Studies in philosophies, schooling, and educational policies.* Englewood Cliffs, NJ: Prentice Hall.

Rallis, S. F. (1990). Professional teachers and restructured schools: Leadership challenges. In B. Mitchell, and L. L. Cunningham, (Eds.), *Educational leadership and changing contexts of families, communities, and schools* (89th NSSE yearbook). Chicago: University of Chicago Press.

RCM Research Corporation. (1998). *Time: Critical issues in educational change.* Portsmouth, NH: RCM Research Corporation.

Renzulli, J. S. (1998). The three-ring conception of giftedness. In S. M. Baum, S. M. Reis, and L. R. Maxfield, (Eds.), *Nurturing the gifts and talents of primary grade students.* Mansfield Center, CT: Creative Learning Press.

Richardson, V. (ed.). (2001). *Handbook of research on teaching,* 4th ed. Washington, DC: American Educational Research Association.

Rideout, V., Roberts, D. F., and Foehr, U. G. (2005). *Generation M: Media in the lives of 8–18-year olds.* Menlo Park, CA: Kaiser Family Foundation.

Ripple, R. E., and Rockcastle, V. E. (Eds.). (1964). *Piaget rediscovered: A report of the conference on cognitive studies and curriculum development.* Ithaca, NY: Cornell University, School of Education.

Roehr Institute. (2000). *Count us in: A demographic overview of childhood and disability in Canada.* Toronto: Roehr Institute.

Rogon, K.(1993). Grouping the gifted and talented. *Roper Review,* 16, 8–12.

Rogers, B. (2002). *Teacher leadership and behaviour management.* London; Thousand Oaks, CA: Sage Publications.

Rogers, C. (1961). *On becoming a person.* Boston: Houghton Mifflin.

Rogers, C. (1982). *Freedom to learn in the eighties.* Columbus, OH: Merrill.

Rogers, K. (1991). *The relationship of grouping practices to the education of the gifted and talented learner.* Storrs, CT: University of Connecticut, National Research Center on the Gifted and Talented.

Rosenshine, B. (1988). Explicit teaching. In D. Berliner, and B. Rosenshine (Eds.). *Talks to teachers.* New York: Random House.

Rosenshine, B. (1995). Advances in research on instruction. *The Journal of Educational Research,* 88(5), 262–68.

Rosenshine, B., and Stevens, R. (1986). Teaching functions. In Merlin C. Wittrock (Ed.). *Handbook of research on teaching,* 3rd ed. New York: Macmillan.

Rosenshine, B., Meister, C., and Chapman, S. (1996). Teaching students to generate questions: A review of the intervention studies. *Review of Educational Research,* 66(2), 181–221.

Salas, K., Tenorio, R., Walters, S., and Weiss, D. (2004). *The new teacher book: Finding purpose, balance, and hope during your first years in the classroom.* Milwaukee, WI: Rethinking Schools.

Sallie Mae Corporation. (1995). *A report from the 1994 Sallie Mae symposium on quality education.* Washington, DC: Sallie Mae Corporation.

Salovey, P., and Sluyter, D. J. (Eds.). (1997). *Emotional development and emotional intelligence: Educational implications.* New York: Basic Books.

Sandholtz, J. J., Ringstaff, C., and Dwyer, D. C. (1997). *Teaching with technology: Creating student-centered classrooms.* New York: Teachers College Press.

Saskatchewan School Trustees Association. (1997). Canadian educational governance update. Retrieved June 12, 2003, from www.ssta.sk.ca/research/governance/csbacan.htm.

Scardamalia, K. and Bereiter, C. (1994). Computer support for knowledge-building communities. *Journal of Learning Sciences,* 3(3), 265–283.

Scardamalia, M., and Bereiter, C. (2003). Knowledge building environments: Extending the limits of the possible in education and knowledge work. In A. Distefano, K. E. Rudestam, and R. Silverman (Eds.), *Encyclopedia of distributed learning*. Thousand Oaks, CA: Sage, 269–272.

Saul, J. R. (2002). In defense of public education. *Horizons*, 1(1), 8–14. Ottawa: Canadian Teachers' Federation.

Schaefer, R. (1967). *The school as the center of inquiry*. New York: Harper and Row.

Schmuck, R. A., and Schmuck, P. A. (2001). *Group processes in the classroom*, 8th ed. Boston: McGraw-Hill.

Schneider, R. B., and Barone, D. (1997, Spring). Cross-age tutoring. *Childhood Education*, 136–43.

Schön, D. (1983). *The reflective practitioner: How professionals think in action*. New York: Basic Books.

Schön, D. (1987). *Educating the reflective practitioner: Toward a new design for teaching and learning in the professions*. San Francisco: Jossey-Bass.

Schön, D. (1991). *The reflective turn: Case studies in and on educational practice*. New York: Teachers College Press.

Schunk, D. (2004). *Learning theories: An educational perspective*. 4th ed. Upper Saddle River, NJ: Merrill/Prentice Hall.

Schwartz, J. E., and Beichner, R. J. (1999). *Essentials of educational technology*. Boston: Allyn and Bacon.

Schwebel, A. J., Coslett, H.B., Bradt, J., Friedman, R. (1996). *The student teacher's handbook*, 3rd ed. Mahwah, NJ: Lawrence Erlbaum Associates.

Sharan, Y., and Sharan, S. (1989/1990, December/January). Group investigation expands cooperative learning. *Educational Leadership*, 17–21.

Shenk, D. (1998). *Data smog: Surviving the information age*. New York: HarperEdge.

Sigalit, U., and Van Lehn, K. (1995). STEPS: A simulated, tutorable physics student. *Journal of Artificial Intelligence in Education*, 6(4), 405–37.

Singer, A. (1994, December). Reflections on multiculturalism. *Phi Delta Kappan*, 284–88.

Skinner, B. F. (1972). Utopia through the control of human behavior. In J. M. Rich (Ed.), *Readings in the philosophy of education*. Belmont, CA: Wadsworth.

Slavin, R. E. (2000). *Educational psychology: Theory and practice*, 6th ed. Boston: Allyn and Bacon.

Smith, D. D. (1998). *Introduction to special education: Teaching in an age of challenge*, 2nd ed. Boston: Allyn and Bacon.

Smith, K. B., and Meier, K. K. (1995). *The case against school choice: Politics, markets, and fools*. Armonk, NY: M.E. Sharpe.

Smolkin, R. (1999, February 27–28). The reading debate rages. Moscow-Pullman *Daily News*, 1A, 10A.

Smyth, W. (1995). *Clinical supervision: Collaborative learning about teaching*. New York: State Mutual Book and Periodical Service.

Snyder, K. J., and Anderson, R. H. (Eds.). (1996). *Clinical supervision: Coaching for higher performance*. Lanham, MD: Scarecrow Press.

Sowell, E. J. (1996). *Curriculum: An integrative introduction*. Boston: Allyn and Bacon.

Spring, J. (1998). *Conflict of interests: The politics of American education*, 3rd ed. Boston: McGraw-Hill.

Spring, J. (1999). *American education*, 8th ed. New York: McGraw-Hill.

Sricharatchanya, P. (1996, November 5). Education reforms are also crucial. *Bangkok Post*, 15.

Statistics Canada. (2001a). *A profile of disability in Canada*. Catalogue No. 89-577-XIE. Ottawa: Housing, Family and Social Statistics Division. Retrieved August 30, 2007, from www.statcan.ca/english/freepub/89-577-XIE/89-577-XIE2001001.pdf.

Statistics Canada. (2001b). *Canada's ethnocultural portrait: The changing mosaic*. Retrieved October 11, 2003, from www12.statcan.ca/english/census01/Products/Analytic/companion/etoimm/canada.cfm.

Statistics Canada. (2001c). Sprott, J. B., Doob, A. N., and Jenkins, J. *M. Problem behaviour and delinquency in children and youth*. Catalogue number 85-002-XPE Vol. 21, No 4. Retrieved August 18, 2007, from www.statcan.ca/english/freepub/85-002-XIE/0040185-002-XIE.pdf.

Statistics Canada, (2002a). Bushnik, T., Barr-Telford, L., and Bussière, P. *In and out of high school: Results from the first cycle of the Youth in Transition Survey*. Catalogue # 81-593-MIE_No. 014.

St. Michel, T. (1995). *Effective substitute teachers: Myth, mayhem, or magic?* Thousand Oaks, CA: Corwin Press.

Stanford, B. H. (1992). Gender equity in the classroom. In D. A. Byrnes and G. Kiger (Eds.), *Common bonds: Anti–bias teaching in a diverse society*. Wheaton, MD: Association for Childhood Education International.

Steinberg, L., Dornbusch, S., and Brown, B. (1996). *Beyond the classroom: Why school reform has failed and what parents need to do*. New York: Simon and Schuster.

Sternberg, R. J. (1996, March). Myths, countermyths, and truths about intelligence. *Educational Researcher*, 11–16.

Sternberg, L., Dornbusch, S., and Brown, B. (1996). *Beyond the classroom: Why school reform has failed and what parents need to do*. New York: Simon & Schuster.

Stoll, C. (1996). *Silicon snake oil: Second thoughts on the information highway*. New York: Anchor.

Stoll, C. (1999). *High-tech heretic: Why computers don't belong in the classroom and other reflections by a computer contrarian*. New York: Doubleday.

Stone, R., and Cuper, P.H. (2006). *Best practices for teacher leadership: What award-winning teachers do for their professional learning communities*. Thousand Oaks, CA: Corwin Press.

Tapscott, D. (1999, July 6). Kids, technology and the schools. Computerworld.

Teacher supply and demand: Facts and statistics on education funding and teaching in Alberta. (n.d.). Retrieved August 27, 2007, from www.education.gov.ab.ca/FactsStats/PWC/supply.pdf.

Terman, L. M., and Oden, M. H. (1947). The gifted child grows up. In L. M. Terman (Ed.), *Genetic studies of genius*, Vol. 4. Stanford, CA: Stanford University Press.

Terman, L. M., and Oden, M. H. (1959). The gifted group in mid-life. In L. M. Terman (Ed.), *Genetic* studies of genius, Vol. 5. Stanford, CA: Stanford University Press.

Terman, L. M., Baldwin, B. T., and Bronson, E. (1925). Mental and physical traits of a thousand gifted children. In L. M. Terman (Ed.), Genetic studies of genius, Vol. 1. Stanford, CA: Stanford University Press.

Thelen, H. A. (1960). Education and the human quest. New York: Harper and Row.

Tombari, M. L., and Borich, G. D. (1999). Authentic assessment in the classroom: Applications and practice. Upper Saddle River, NJ: Merrill.

Trotter, A. (1998, October 1). A question of effectiveness. Education Week: Technology Counts '98, 18, 6–9

Turnbull, M. (2000). Introduction: What is core French? Core French FAQ. Retrieved October 11, 2003 from www.cpfnb.com/core_FAQ/CoreFAQ.html.

Tyler, R. (1949). Basic principles of curriculum and instruction. Chicago: University of Chicago.

Uchida, D., Cetron, M., and McKenzie, F. (1996). Preparing students for the 21st century. Arlington, VA: American Association of School Administrators.

Utay, C., and Utay, J. (1997). Peer-assisted learning: The effects of cooperative learning and cross-age peer tutoring with word processing on writing skills of students with learning disabilities. Journal of Computing in Childhood Education, 8(2/3), 165–85.

Vaughn, S., Bos, C. S., and Schumm, J. S. (1997). Teaching mainstreamed, diverse, and at-risk students in the general education classroom. Boston: Allyn and Bacon.

Vygotsky, L. S. (1978). Mind in society: The development of higher mental process. Cambridge, MA: Harvard University Press.

Vygotsky, L. S. (1986). Thought and language. Cambridge, MA: MIT Press.

Wagner, K. (1998). Choice in public education. Policy Watch. Vancouver: Society for the Advancement of Excellence in Public Education. Retrieved October 24, 2002, from www.geocities.com/Athens/5909/choices.html.

Walberg, H. J., and Greenberg, R. C. (1997, May). Using the learning environment inventory. Educational Leadership, 45–47.

Wallace, R. M. (2004, Summer). A framework for understanding teaching with the internet. American Educational Research Journal, 41(2), 447–88.

Walsh, M. (1999, May). Two reports offer bright outlook for education industry. Education Week, 18(36), 5.

Walters, L. S. (1999, January/February). What makes a good school violence prevention program? Harvard Education Letter.

Washington, W. (1998). Optional extended year program feedback. Austin Independent School District, TX, Department of Accountability, Student Services, and Research.

Wasserman, S. (1994, April). Using cases to study teaching. Phi Delta Kappan, 602–11.

Webb, L. D., Metha, A., and Jordan, K. F. (1999). Foundations of American education, 3rd ed. Englewood Cliffs, NJ: Prentice Hall.

Wechsler, D. (1958). The measurement and appraisal of adult intelligence, 4th ed. Baltimore, MD: Williams and Wilkins.

Western Canadian Protocol for Collaboration in Basic Education. (2000). Retrieved October 20, 2003, from www.wcp.ca.

Williams, J. (1999, April 18). Urban schools' obstacles hindering technology. Milwaukee Journal Sentinel.

Wiske, M. S., Rennebohm Franz, K., Breit, L. (2005). Teaching for understanding with technology. San Francisco: Jossey-Bass.

Wirt, F. M., and Kirst, M. W. (1997). The political dynamics of American education. Berkeley: McCutchan.

Wohlstetter, P. (1995, September). Getting school-based management right: What works and what doesn't. Phi Delta Kappan, 22–24, 26.

Wohlstetter, P., and Anderson, L. (1994, February). What can U.S. charter schools learn from England's grant-maintained schools? Phi Delta Kappan, 486–91.

Wolfgang, C. H. (2001). Solving discipline problems: Methods and models for today's teachers, 5th ed. Boston: Allyn and Bacon.

Woolfolk, A. E. (2007). Educational psychology, 10th ed. Boston: Allyn & Bacon.

Wray, H. (1999). Japanese and American education: Attitudes and practices. Oxford, UK: Bergin and Garvey Publishers.

Yamamoto, K., Davis, O. L. Jr., Dylak, S., Whittaker, J., Marsh, C., and van der Westhuizen, P. C. (1996, Spring). Across six nations: Stressful events in the lives of children. Child Psychiatry and Human Development, 139–50.

Zepeda, R., Mayers, R. S., Benson, B. N. (2002). The call to teacher leadership. West Larchmont, NY: Eye on Education, 71–91.

Name Index

Subject Index

Photo Credits